TEXT AND RITUAL IN THE PENTATEUCH

Text and Ritual in the Pentateuch

A Systematic and Comparative Approach

EDITED BY
CHRISTOPHE NIHAN AND JULIA RHYDER

EISENBRAUNS | University Park, Pennsylvania

The publication of this book has been made possible thanks to the financial support of the Institut Romand des Sciences Bibliques (IRSB) and the Centre Interdisciplinaire d'Histoire et des Sciences des religions (CIHSR) at the University of Lausanne, Switzerland.

Library of Congress Cataloging-in-Publication Data

Names: Nihan, Christophe, 1972– editor. | Rhyder, Julia, 1987– editor.
Title: Text and ritual in the Pentateuch : a systematic and comparative approach / edited by Christophe Nihan and Julia Rhyder.
Description: University Park, Pennsylvania : Eisenbrauns, [2021] | Includes bibliographical references and index.
Summary: "A collection of essays examining the conceptual and methodological issues that currently inform the study of text and ritual in the Pentateuch"—Provided by publisher.
Identifiers: LCCN 2021016498 | ISBN 9781646021413 (hardback)
Subjects: LCSH: Bible. Pentateuch—Criticism, interpretation, etc. | Rites and ceremonies in the Bible. | Ritual—Middle East—History—To 1500. | Judaism—Liturgy. | LCGFT: Essays.
Classification: LCC BS1225.52 .T49 2021 | DDC 222/.106—dc23
LC record available at https://lccn.loc.gov/2021016498

Copyright © 2021 The Pennsylvania State University
All rights reserved
Printed in the United States of America
Published by The Pennsylvania State University Press,
University Park, PA 16802-1003

Eisenbrauns is an imprint of The Pennsylvania State University Press.

The Pennsylvania State University Press is a member of the Association of University Presses.

It is the policy of The Pennsylvania State University Press to use acid-free paper. Publications on uncoated stock satisfy the minimum requirements of American National Standard for Information Sciences—Permanence of Paper for Printed Library Material, ANSI Z39.48–1992.

CONTENTS

Preface vii
List of Abbreviations ix

Introduction 1
Christophe Nihan

CHAPTER 1. Rituals in the Spells of the *Book of the Dead*
in Ancient Egypt 30
Giuseppina Lenzo

CHAPTER 2. Between Utterance and Dedication: Some Remarks
on the Status of Textuality in Greek Ritual Practices 58
Dominique Jaillard

CHAPTER 3. Inscriptions and Ritual Practices in the Neo-Assyrian
Period: The Construction of a Building as an Example 78
Lionel Marti

CHAPTER 4. Between Text and Ritual: The Function(s) of the Ritual
Texts from Late Bronze Age Emar (Syria) 107
Patrick Michel

CHAPTER 5. The Textualization of Priestly Ritual in
Light of Hittite Sources 121
Yitzhaq Feder

CHAPTER 6. Diversity and Centralization of the Temple Cult
in the Archeological Record from the Iron II C to the Persian and
Hellenistic Periods in Judah 151
Rüdiger Schmitt

CHAPTER 7. Texts Are Not Rituals, and Rituals Are Not Texts, with an Example from Leviticus 12. 172
James W. Watts

CHAPTER 8. The Texture of Rituals in the Book of Numbers: A Fresh Approach to Ritual Density, the Role of Tradition, and the Emergence of Diversity in Early Judaism 188
Christian Frevel

CHAPTER 9. Speaking with a Divine Voice: The Rhetoric of Epistolary Performance in Numbers 6:22–27 215
Jeremy D. Smoak

CHAPTER 10. The Ritual Texts of Leviticus and the Creation of Ritualized Bodies 240
Dorothea Erbele-Küster

CHAPTER 11. The Reception of Ritual Laws in the Early Second Temple Period: Evidence from Ezra-Nehemiah and Chronicles 255
Julia Rhyder

CHAPTER 12. Text and Ritual in the Dead Sea Scrolls 280
Daniel K. Falk

CHAPTER 13. "And They Would Read Before Him the Order for the Day": The Textuality of Leviticus 16 in Mishnah Yoma, Tosefta Kippurim, and Sifra Aḥare Mot 312
William K. Gilders

List of Contributors. 327
Index of Ancient Sources. 329
Subject Index 331

PREFACE

In recent decades, scholarship on the relationship between text and ritual in the Pentateuch has been significantly enhanced, as biblical researchers have increasingly engaged with ritual studies and ethnographic descriptions of rituals and explored the construction of pentateuchal rituals in light of comparative evidence. However, so far this analysis of the ritual texts of the Pentateuch has been treated largely from distinct perspectives, with no monograph or volume yet integrating the various approaches and results that characterize the field at this time.

The present volume seeks to map the main conceptual and methodological issues that currently inform the study of text and ritual in the Pentateuch, and to gain new insights by contrasting the relationship between text and ritual in ancient Israel with that of other ancient Mediterranean and Western Asian societies. The majority of the essays in this volume originated in a conference held at the University of Lausanne in May 2016, entitled "Text and Ritual in the Pentateuch: A Systematic and Comparative Approach," although all the chapters have been updated in the light of peer commentary during and after the conference, and several additional chapters have been commissioned.

The publication of the volume could not have been achieved without the assistance of several institutions. The conference was funded by the Swiss National Science Foundation (SNF project number 160441), as well as by the Institut romand des sciences bibliques of the University of Lausanne. The Faculty of Theology and Religious Studies of the University of Lausanne also provided additional funding to assist with the publication of this volume. We are grateful to these institutions for their support. We would also like to express our thanks to Ms. Aude Lovey and Ms. Anita Dirnberger for their valuable technical assistance with the preparation of the manuscript.

—Christophe Nihan and Julia Rhyder

ABBREVIATIONS

AB	Anchor Bible
ABD	*Anchor Bible Dictionary*. Edited by David Noel Freedman. 6 vols. New York: Doubleday, 1992.
AfOB	Archiv für Orientforschung: Beiheft
AIL	Ancient Israel and Its Literature
Ant.	Josephus, *Jewish Antiquities*
AOAT	Alter Orient und Altes Testament
ATANT	*Abhandlungen zur Theologie des Alten und Neuen Testaments*
BaM	*Baghdader Mitteilungen*
BASOR	*Bulletin of the American Schools of Oriental Research*
BETL	Bibliotheca Ephemeridum theologicarum Lovaniensium
BJS	Brown Judaic Studies
BKAT	Biblischer Kommentar, Altes Testament
BN	*Biblische Notizen*
Bo	Inventory numbers of Bogazköy tablets excavated 1906–12
BZABR	Beihefte zur Zeitschrift für altorientalische und biblische Rechtsgeschichte
BZAW	Beihefte zur Zeitschrift für die alttestamentliche Wissenschaft
CBQ	*Catholic Biblical Quarterly*
CGRN	J.-M. Carbon, S. Peels, and V. Pirenne-Delforge. *A Collection of Greek Ritual Norms*. Liège: University of Liège, 2016–. http://cgrn.ulg.ac.be.
CM	Cuneiform Monographs
CTH	Emmanuel Laroche. *Catalogue des textes hittites.* Paris: Geuthner, 1963.
Descr.	Pausanias, *Description of Greece*
DJD	Discoveries in the Judaean Desert
DSD	*Dead Sea Discoveries*

EJL	Early Judaism and Its Literature
FAT	Forschungen zum Alten Testament
FIOTL	Formation and Interpretation of Old Testament Literature
HCOT	Historical Commentary on the Old Testament
HR	*History of Religions*
HTR	*Harvard Theological Review*
IBoT	Istanbul Arkeoloji Müzelerinde Bulunan Bogazköy Tabletleri(nden Seçme Metinler)—Istanbul 1944, 1947, 1954; Ankara 1988
ID	*Inscriptions de Délos*. Paris: Académie des inscriptions et belles lettres, 1926–72.
IEJ	*Israel Exploration Journal*
IG	*Inscriptiones Graecae. Editio Minor.* Berlin: de Gruyter, 1924–.
JANER	*Journal of Ancient Near Eastern Religions*
JAOS	*Journal of the American Oriental Society*
JBL	*Journal of Biblical Literature*
JCS	*Journal of Cuneiform Studies*
JDS	Judean Desert Studies
JHebS	*Journal of Hebrew Scriptures*
JNES	*Journal of Near Eastern Studies*
JSJ	*Journal for the Study of Judaism in the Persian, Hellenistic, and Roman Periods*
JSOT	*Journal for the Study of the Old Testament*
JSOTSup	Journal for the Study of the Old Testament Supplement Series
J.W.	Josephus, *Jewish War*
KBo	*Keilschrifttexte aus Boghazköi*. Leipzig: Hinrichs, 1916–23; Berlin: Gebr. Mann, 1954–.
KTU	*Die keilalphabetischen Texte aus Ugarit*. Edited by M. Dietrich, O. Loretz, and J. Sanmartín. Münster: Ugarit-Verlag, 2013. 3rd enl. ed. of *KTU: The Cuneiform Alphabetic Texts from Ugarit, Ras Ibn Hani, and Other Places*. Edited by M. Dietrich, O. Loretz, and J. Sanmartín. Münster: Ugarit-Verlag, 1995.
KUB	*Keilschrifturkunden aus Boghazköi*. Berlin: Akademie, 1921–
LAPO	Littératures anciennes du Proche-Orient
LCL	Loeb Classical Library
LHBOTS	The Library of Hebrew Bible / Old Testament Studies
LSCG	F. Sokolowski. *Lois Sacrées des Cités Grecques*. Paris: Ed. E. de Boccard, 1969.
LXX	Septuagint
m.	Mishnah
MC	Mesopotamian Civilizations
MT	Masoretic Text

NEAEHL	*The New Encyclopedia of Archaeological Excavations in the Holy Land.* Edited by Ephraim Stern. 4 vols. Jerusalem: Israel Exploration Society & Carta; New York: Simon & Schuster, 1993.
Numen	*Numen: International Review for the History of Religions*
OBO	Orbis Biblicus et Orientalis
OBOSA	Orbis Biblicus et Orientalis, Series Archaeologia
OIS	Oriental Institute Seminars
Or	*Orientalia (NS)*
ORA	Orientalische Religionen in der Antike
OTL	Old Testament Library
OtSt	*Oudtestamentische Studiën*
P. BM	Papyrus of British Museum
RBS	Resources for Biblical Study
RIMA	The Royal Inscriptions of Mesopotamia, Assyrian Periods
RINAP	Royal Inscriptions of the Neo-Assyrian Period
RlA	*Reallexikon der Assyriologie.* Edited by E. Ebeling, et al. Berlin: de Gruyter, 1928–.
RS	Ras Shamra
SAA	State Archives of Assyria
SAAS	State Archives of Assyria Studies
SEG	Supplementum epigraphicum graecum
SMEA	*Studi Micenei ed Egeo-Anatolici*
SP	Samaritan Pentateuch
StBoT	Studien zu den Boğazköy-Texten
STDJ	Studies on the Texts of the Desert of Judah
t.	Tosefta
TA	*Tel Aviv*
TAD	B. Porten and A. Yardeni. *Textbook of Aramaic Documents from Ancient Egypt: Newly Copied, Edited, and Translated into Hebrew and English.* 4 vols. Winona Lake, IN: Eisenbrauns, 1986–1999.
UF	*Ugarit-Forschungen*
VT	*Vetus Testamentum*
VTSup	Supplements to Vetus Testamentum
WAW	Writings from the Ancient World
WMANT	Wissenschaftliche Monographien zum Alten und Neuen Testament
WO	*Die Welt des Orients*
ZA	*Zeitschrift für Assyriologie*
ZAW	*Zeitschrift für die alttestamentliche Wissenschaft*

Introduction

Christophe Nihan

THE PRESENT VOLUME ORIGINATED in a conference organized at the University of Lausanne in May 2016. The main goal of the conference was to reexamine the relationship between "ritual" and "text" in the Hebrew Bible—predominantly in the Pentateuch—from various perspectives, and with a view to comparing and contrasting the situation in ancient Israel/early Judaism with other cultures of the Mediterranean and Western Asian world. The present introduction aims to (1) present the main methodological and theoretical issues involved in this collection, (2) outline the contents of its essays, and (3) identify some of the perspectives they open for future discussions on ritual texts and rituals in the Hebrew Bible from a comparative perspective. Scholarly literature on biblical rituals has grown abundantly in the last decade or so. This introduction does not claim to be comprehensive but rather focuses some of the most important discussions for the topic addressed in the present collection, namely, the relationship between text and ritual. Furthermore, because of the comparative focus of this collection, this introduction is meant to be accessible to scholars of the ancient world, and also students of rituals in general, who have little or even no familiarity with the biblical traditions; accordingly, some of the more technical discussions will only be briefly addressed or referenced here.

i.1. Text and Ritual in the Pentateuch: A Survey of Methodological and Theoretical Issues

For historians who seek to reconstruct the rituals performed in ancient societies, written evidence about rituals is often a primary source of information. Much of our knowledge of Ugaritic rituals of the Late Bronze Age, for example, is based on cuneiform alphabetic tablets discovered on the site of Ras Shamra that contain instructions for the performance of various rituals.¹ To be sure, there are other sources as well that can be used for the reconstruction of ancient rituals. Archaeology, in well-documented contexts, can provide us with substantial information regarding some key aspects of ritual performance, especially as regards their spatiality and materiality. But archaeology alone cannot reconstruct the way in which rituals were performed at a given site, and sometimes even the very nature of those rituals remains elusive. For several cultures of the ancient Mediterranean and Western Asian world, iconography can also be a valuable source for the reconstruction of rituals, giving access to important details concerning ritual performance, such as how ritual agents are positioned, how animals involved in the ritual are handled, and so on. But if the iconographic evidence does not include inscriptions detailing the nature and the contents of the ritual described, it may be quite difficult to determine the circumstances of that ritual as well as its functions and significance. In general, and without overstating the importance of written sources, it is arguably fair to say that the comprehensive reconstruction of a given ritual in its ancient context(s) remains a challenge without at least some sort of textual evidence.²

Yet if written evidence is instrumental for historians who seek to offer redescriptions of ancient rituals, such evidence raises specific issues that have not always been sufficiently considered. To begin with, the performance of a ritual and its textual representation are not one and the same thing. This distinction is documented through a number of ethnographic studies, which show that in the context of communities preserving written descriptions of their rituals, those descriptions are not necessarily regarded as normative for ritual performance and can actually be quite different from the rituals effectively practiced by these communities. For the practitioners of these rituals, what is usually decisive is the observance of customary practices, not the adherence to a written script.³ Likewise, in ancient Mediterranean societies rituals were first and foremost transmitted through a set of unwritten customs; in general, the

---

1. For the edition of these texts, see D. Pardee, *Les textes rituels*, 2 vols., Ras Shamra-Ougarit 12 (Paris: Éditions Recherche sur les Civilisations, 2000); D. Pardee, *Ritual and Cult at Ugarit*, WAW 10 (Atlanta: Society of Biblical Literature, 2002).

2. On the limitations of reconstructing ancient religions without textual evidence, see, e.g., T. J. Lewis, "Syro-Palestinian Iconography and Divine Images," in *Cult Image and Divine Representation in the Ancient Near East*, ed. N. H. Walls, American Schools of Oriental Research Book Series 10 (Boston: American Schools of Oriental Research, 200), 69–107 at 75–76, who notes that while "iconography complements texts, it cannot replace them." For a more radical position on this issue, see V. Hurowitz, "Picturing Imageless Deities: Iconography in the Ancient Near East," *Biblical Archaeology Review* 23.3 (1997): 46–69, esp. 69.

3. A textbook example of this phenomenon is provided by the ethnographic study of the Jains of Jaipur by C. Humphrey and J. Laidlaw, *The Archetypal Actions of Ritual: A Theory of Ritual Illustrated by the Jain Rite of Worship*, Oxford Studies in Social and Cultural Anthropology (Oxford: Clarendon Press, 1994), 191–210.

"textualization" of the ritual—namely, the creation of a written version of that ritual—was not a necessary condition for the success of the ritual performance. This observation, in turn, raises two related questions: first, how close are ritual texts to actual ritual performance? And second, if the success of ritual performance was defined primarily through custom rather than through textual authority, what were the functions of ritual texts in ancient Mediterranean societies?

(1) Regarding the first issue, Catherine Bell, in her 1992 monograph *Ritual Theory, Ritual Practice*, already insisted on the gap that can exist between textual descriptions of rituals and their actual performance. In particular, she noted that textual descriptions tend to promote a single, unified version of a given ritual, which does not account for the variations that can be involved in actual performances of that same ritual. As a result, Bell argues, the textualization of rituals can often result in fairly formalized and standardized descriptions that can be quite distant from actual practice. "Textual codification and standardization also open a gap between what is written and what is done by promoting an ideal of uniformity and the elimination or marginalization of alternatives. Frequently the result is a written ideal quite alienated from what is in fact being done in common practice."[4] She also notes further implications of the textualization of ritual such as especially the fact that textual codification often involves a shift in ritual expertise, conferring authority to those experts who control access to and interpretation of the texts.

Bell's remarks about the consequences of textualization on the representation of rituals are important, and they are consistent—at least to an extent—with the observations about the common gap between ritual text and ritual performance that is documented in several ethnographic studies, as mentioned above. At the same time, however, Bell can also be challenged on the grounds that—in the previous quote at least—she appears to assume a relationship between "text" and "ritual" that is perhaps too static and that does not consider the possibility of more complex and intricate interactions between these entities.[5] A good illustration of this point is provided by Christian de Pee's comprehensive study of Chinese wedding traditions from the Middle Period (eighth to fourteenth century CE).[6] In particular, de Pee observed that the diversity of local practices related to weddings appears to be partly preserved in those writings that were

---

4. C. Bell, *Ritual Theory, Ritual Practice* (Oxford: Oxford University Press, 1992), 137. See further C. Bell, "Ritualization of Texts and Textualization of Ritual in the Codification of Taoist Liturgy," *HR* 27.4 (1988): 366–92. On the gap between ritual and text, ritual practice and ritual text, see also the essay by J. W. Watts in this volume.

5. For a discussion and a critique of Bell's construal of the relationship between text and ritual, see also the essay by J. Rhyder in this volume.

6. C. de Pee, *The Writing of Weddings in Middle Period China: Text and Ritual Practice in the Eighth Through Fourteenth Centuries*, SUNY Series in Chinese Philosophy and Culture (Albany: State University of New York Press, 2007).

themselves closely related to, or even embedded in, that practice: ritual manuals, wedding correspondence, and so on. On the other hand, the imperial laws and decrees relating to weddings tend to dissolve such local complexities of wedding practices as a consequence of the hegemonic perspective imposed by the imperial administration, to the point that "the practice of the text tends to obscure the practice of the ritual."

> The practice of wedding ritual survives where writing is a ritual practice and where the text is a ritual object: in the exegetical choreographies of ritual manuals, in the cultural capital of wedding correspondence, and in the cosmological calculations of almanacs and calendars. In those archaist ceremonies, in those displays of wit and erudition, in those prognostications of cosmic danger are lastingly configured living discursive notions of time, space, bodies, and text that forever await their refiguration in ritual performance or in reading. Where writing is not part of the ritual practice of weddings, and where the text is not a ritual object intended for nuptial exchanges, *the practice of the text obscures the practice of ritual*. Laws and verdicts circulated as ritual objects in the grand ceremony of imperial government. *They translate the time, space, bodies, and texts of weddings into the transparent, universal hierarchy of that government, thereby subjecting the local practice of weddings to the universalist practice of the legal text*—just as the writing of local customs disperses both the locality and the practicality of local weddings by placing them in the centered literary landscape of a civilizing empire.[7]

These sorts of observations open the way to a more dynamic understanding of the relationship between text and ritual. Bell's point remains correct at a general level: because ritual is first and foremost a performance, and not the mere repetition of a script, there will always be a gap between ritual performance and its textual representation. As such, ritual texts can only provide us with, at best, a broad approximation of an ancient ritual performance, even when these texts claim to describe that performance in detail.[8] And yet, simultaneously, one should recognize that the relationship between text and ritual is never simple, or straightforward, but can cover in fact a wide range of possibilities depending on the degree of a text's embedding within the ritual practice that it claims to represent. Consider, for instance, ritual "checklists" or *aide-mémoires*, which are abundantly documented in the Western Asian world. The description of rituals

---

7. Ibid., 242–23, my emphasis.
8. This observation also means, conversely, that ritual texts have a performative dimension of their own, which is not merely identical with the ritual performance, and which needs to be analyzed for itself. See further on this point below.

in these texts is certainly standardized, possibly even idealized, but it is unlikely to be completely divorced from actual ritual performance.[9] This is already suggested by the nature of the details preserved in these texts, which often only make sense if they were meant to be used by ritual experts.[10] Furthermore, in a number of instances, we even have actual evidence that these texts were effectively used for ritual practice.[11] A similar point could be made with regard to the so-called Greek sacrificial calendars (although "sacrificial lists" would arguably be a better descriptor), which could be consulted when conflicts arose over the way in which a public sacrifice had been conducted.[12] The actual performance of these sacrifices may not always have been conducted according to the details preserved in these lists. But the lists nonetheless inform us about the way in which local communities would have expected these sacrifices to take place.

On the other hand, other written sources may present us with textual representations of rituals that are less directly embedded in, and therefore more distant from, actual practice. Royal inscriptions commemorating (or claiming to commemorate) rituals performed by a king can provide typical examples of this distance between text and practice, because in this case the primary function of the inscription was propagandistic—namely, to promote a certain ideal of the king as ritual agent—rather than strictly ritual (e.g., to provide a description that could serve for possible future reenactments of the ritual mentioned in the inscription). Even so, one should keep in mind that the difference between these written sources about rituals is relative rather than absolute. After all, even ritual descriptions in the context of royal inscriptions with a strong political and ideological agenda had to conform to certain social and cultural codes (or "canons" in Bourdieu's terms) in order to be relevant for the audiences of these inscriptions. Conversely, checklists and similar texts used by ritual experts may well be closely embedded in the ritual practice of those experts, but they could also

---

9. On the category of ritual "checklists" in the Western Asian world, see also the essay by P. Michel in this volume, who discusses various documents used by the main diviner of Emar.

10. While no single, rigid pattern can be observed, ritual texts from Ugarit generally include details concerning the date of a given ritual, the materials to be sacrificed, the recipient deities, possibly also the place where sacrifices are to be made. Other significant actions required for the performance of the ritual, such as the way in which the sacrificial animals are slaughtered, the distribution of sacrificial portions among divine and human participants, or even the ritual agents involved, are usually omitted from the description. Apparently, these aspects of the ritual performance were known by the practitioners and did not need to be written down.

11. For instance, in Ugarit, a list of deified kings that was circulated in Ugaritic and in Akkadian contains marks left by a scribe alongside the names of the king. These marks have been interpreted as "check marks" pointing to the effective usage of these lists in a sacrificial context. See D. Arnaud, "Prolégomènes à la rédaction d'une histoire d'Ougarit II: Les bordereaux de rois divinisés," *SMEA* 41.8 (1998): 153–73 at 168; also Pardee, *Ritual and Cult*, 200.

12. See on this now S. Georgoudi "Comment régler les *théia pragmata*: Pour une étude de ce qu'on appelle 'lois sacrées,'" *Mètis*, n.s., 8 (2010): 39–54.

serve other, additional functions as well—for instance, by conferring authority and status to their owner, or granting legitimacy in case of a dispute arising after the ritual performance.[13] It would be wrong, therefore, to oppose "practical" and "ideal" descriptions of rituals in ancient written sources. It is more helpful to think of these distinctions in terms of a *continuum*, with most ancient sources exemplifying both practical and ideal features in their representation of rituals, albeit to different degrees.[14]

(2) One of the main implications of the previous discussion is that it turns our attention to what could be called the *pragmatics* of ritual texts in the ancient Mediterranean. Because the textualization of rituals is not a necessary or logical outgrowth of ritual performance but a strategic activity, and because this strategic activity usually presupposes a larger body of customary ritual practices with which it interacts in different ways, and to various degrees, the question of the functions and the goals of ritual texts represents a key issue in the analysis of such texts.[15] In other words, historians must not merely look at *what* these texts say about rituals (as they have sometimes tended to do) but also, and perhaps even more importantly, at *how* these texts were effectively used in relation to ritual performance in the ancient Mediterranean.

The essays collected in this volume document a wide range of possibilities in this regard, each depending on the specific contexts in which these texts were practiced. A comprehensive mapping of the functions and purposes of ritual texts in the ancient Mediterranean remains a scholarly desideratum, although the present volume will hopefully represent a step in that direction. Examples already mentioned here include the use of ritual texts as *aide-mémoires* or "checklists" of sorts for the correct sequence of a ritual, as well as the creation

---

13. On this issue, see also the remarks by P. Michel, in this volume, with regard to the uses of the ritual texts for the diviner of Emar as well as the comments by D. Jaillard on the function of sacrificial lists in ancient Greek cities.

14. This approach is well illustrated, in particular, in the essay by D. K. Falk in this volume, who proposes different "maps" to construe the relationship between text and ritual in Qumran. The same approach is further reflected, to various degrees, in the essays by G. Lenzo, on Egyptian rituals, especially in the *Book of the Dead*, and D. Jaillard, on ancient Greek rituals.

15. This point is well illustrated, for instance, by the essays collected in A. Barchiesi, J. Rüpke, and S. A. Stephens, eds., *Rituals in Ink: A Conference on Religion and Literary Production in Ancient Rome Held at Stanford University in February 2002*, Potsdamer Altertumswissenschaftliche Beiträge 10 (Stuttgart: Steiner, 2004). In their short introduction, the editors aptly comment that, "Texts participate in the wider society in which they were created. In that space texts have a performative dimension regardless of the mimetic or fictitious character of their embedded rituals. Such texts were part of their contemporary religious discourse; they are part of textual communication with their ancient audience, and they are inevitably part of a specific mode of communication that we call religion" (vii–viii). (This statement holds true whether or not one considers that "religion" is best described as a "mode of communication," which I would personally question.) Further on this issue, see in the same volume especially the essay by J. Rüpke, "Acta aut agenda: Relations of Script and Performance," 23–43. See also the comments by D. Falk in his essay for the present volume.

of a (relatively) authoritative version of a ritual, to which ritual agents and participants could then turn in case of disputes over the performance of that ritual. Other documented examples include (but are by no means restricted to) the use of ritual texts to legislate exceptional situations, to introduce or legitimize innovations in the performance of a ritual,[16] or to ensure the adequate distribution of the economic resources involved in the ritual performance among the participants, and many more possible scenarios. One particularly interesting example of the pragmatics of ritual texts in antiquity is when the creation and disposal of the text forms the main part of the ritual performance itself, rather than a kind of external commentary upon that performance. This is the case, for instance, when written "spells" were buried in Egypt to accompany the deceased in his or her journey in the afterlife,[17] the deposit of ritual tablets in the foundations of royal buildings such as palaces and temples in Mesopotamia,[18] or the Jewish practice of inscribing amulets with passages from the Torah (*tefillin* and *mezzuzot*).[19] In such instances, the textualization of the ritual goes hand in hand with the ritualization of the text: the two processes belong together, so to speak, and generate new ritual dynamics. This also means that the alleged transition from "ritual" to "textual" coherence in ancient societies[20] arguably corresponds to what is, in fact, a much more complex process. In the examples mentioned here, as well as in several others discussed in the following essays, it would be more accurate to say that the texutalization of rituals—in various forms and according to various degrees—provides the basis for new forms of ritual coherence.

The examples mentioned here already raise the larger comparative issue that underlies the collection of essays gathered in the present volume. Some documented uses of ritual texts can be found across several ancient Mediterranean and Western Asian societies. This is the case, for instance, of texts used as checklists or *aide-mémoires* for ritual experts, of texts used to facilitate or even legitimize ritual innovation, of inscribed amulets used in the context of prophylactic rituals, and so on. Other textual practices, for example, the burial of written spells to accompany the deceased in the afterlife, are more distinctive of a specific culture (in this case, Egypt). Furthermore, even in the case of textual practices that are documented across several ancient Mediterranean societies,

---

16. This was arguably one of the key functions of the so-called sacred laws in ancient Greece; on which see now J.-M. Carbon and V. Pirenne-Delforge, "Codifying 'Sacred Laws' in Ancient Greece," in *Writing Laws in Antiquity / L'écriture du droit dans l'Antiquité*, ed. D. Jaillard and C. Nihan, BZABR 19 (Wiesbaden: Harrassowitz Verlag, 2017), 141–57.
17. On this, see the essay by G. Lenzo in this volume.
18. See the essay by L. Marti in this volume.
19. See the essay by D. K. Falk in this volume.
20. See especially the section titled "Von ritueller zu textueller Kohärenz" in J. Assmann, *Das kulturelle Gedächtnis. Schrift, Erinnerung und politische Identität in frühen Hochkulturen*, 3rd ed. (Munich: Beck, 2000), 87–103.

these practices frequently evince significant differences relating to the local context in which they are documented. Conversely, a textual practice more specific to a given culture can migrate (so to speak) to nearby societies and even become a "marker" of foreign cultural influence in these societies. In these respects, the relationship between "text" and "ritual" is a topic that logically invites a comparative approach, on several levels simultaneously: differential, analogical, and even genetic. The purpose of such a large comparative perspective is not only to map the rich variety of ways in which ritual texts could be used in ancient Mediterranean societies and trace specific influences from one culture to another with regard to ritual textualization; it is also to better understand the specifics of ritual textualization in these societies.

What, then, about the Pentateuch? The Pentateuch, which technically denotes the first five books of the Hebrew Bible (from Genesis to Deuteronomy), presents us with a complex but nonetheless intriguing relationship between text and ritual. Rituals comprise a substantial portion of the Pentateuch, especially (albeit not exclusively) in connection with the establishment of the cult in the wilderness, which is recounted in Exodus, Leviticus, and Numbers (approximately Exod 19 to Num 10), as well as in portions of Deuteronomy. If we consider the Pentateuch as a foundational narrative about the origins of "Israel" as an ethnic group, then it is not excessive to state that rituals form one of the most central aspects in the definition of Israel. As Julia Rhyder demonstrated in a recent book,[21] it is through rituals, in particular, that the various groups composing Israel negotiate their relationships to the central sanctuary (the Tabernacle), the patron deity (the god YHWH), and its (main) ritual agents (the Aaronite priests). But this image of the Israelite cult is a highly idealized one: it is a narrative fiction, set in a foundational time (the exodus and the march toward the promised land) and space (the wilderness) and associated with foundational figures (like Moses, Israel's lawgiver).[22] It is usually difficult to know how the institutions and the customs described in the Pentateuch were meant to translate into the practice of ancient audiences, especially for the pre-Hasmonean period (i.e., before the middle of the second century BCE), and this certainly holds true for rituals as well.

---

21. J. Rhyder, *Centralizing the Cult: The Holiness Legislation in Leviticus 17–26*, FAT 134 (Tübingen: Mohr Siebeck, 2019).

22. I would avoid the term "myth," even though it has been commonly used to describe the narrative of the Pentateuch. The use of this term certainly accounts for the fact that the events described in the Pentateuch are not historical, at least not according to the primary meaning of this term. But defining "myths" simply as the opposite of "historical" facts betrays a narrow understanding of what myths are and how they operated in ancient societies. On the role of Moses as lawgiver from a Mediterranean comparative perspective, see now G. N. Knoppers, "Moses and the Greek Lawgivers: The Triumph of the Torah in Ancient Mediterranean Perspective," in *Writing Laws in Antiquity / L'écriture du droit dans l'Antiquité*, 50–77.

Previous research generally assumed that the rituals described in the Pentateuch would represent more or less the codification of actual practice, although there was much discussion regarding whether the practice reflected in these texts would reflect the period of the First Temple, the Second Temple, or a combination of both.[23] However, as the previous discussion suggests, recent scholarship indicates that the model of a narrow relationship between the ritual texts of the Pentateuch and the ritual practice of ancient Israel is problematic, to say the least, and is unlikely to do justice to the complexity of these issues. In effect, the limited evidence we have for the pre-Hasmonean period suggests that this relationship, in the case of the rituals of the Pentateuch, is anything but straightforward. Some of the ritual texts of the Pentateuch, especially in the "Priestly" portions of Exodus, Leviticus, and Numbers, present substantial parallels, both in form and in content, with the Western Asian ritual checklists already mentioned above, and it is possible that *some* of these instructions go back to such lists.[24] Yet Priestly ritual instructions also present some significant differences with these lists. Ritual checklists, as noted above, were used primarily (if not exclusively) by ritual experts on specific ritual occasions; by contrast, Priestly ritual instructions are now part of a grand narrative of origins, in the course of which these instructions are to be disclosed to "all Israel."[25] The obvious parallel between the blessing formula prescribed in Num 6:24–26 and the text inscribed on two silver plates found in Ketef Hinnom (KH 1 and 2) confirms that *some* of the materials used in the rituals of the Pentateuch is consistent with the language used in Hebrew inscriptions from the Iron Age II or the early Persian period.[26] But the comparison between these texts also shows the degree of fluidity that the reuse of traditions (whether written or oral) in the Pentateuch could actually involve.[27] The comparison between the ritual texts of the Pentateuch and the

---

23. For a survey of this issue, see my discussion in C. Nihan, *From Priestly Torah to Pentateuch: A Study in the Composition of Leviticus*, FAT 2/25 (Tübingen: Mohr Siebeck, 2007), 1–19.

24. On this issue, see the essay by Y. Feder in this volume. For an attempt at a reconstruction, see also my previous discussion in ibid., 215–19.

25. See also on this point the discussion by Y. Feder in this volume. Although the "narrativization" of rituals (i.e., the combination of rituals with narratives), is not unattested in the Western Asian world (one may think, for instance, of the story of El's divine feast in *KTU* 1.114, which ends in the final lines with a recipe, apparently for curing the effects of a hangover), this phenomenon is not widely attested, and it is not found on the scale of what we have in the Priestly texts.

26. For the edition of these texts, see G. Barkay et al., "The Amulets from Ketef Hinnom: A New Edition and Evaluation," *BASOR* 334 (2004): 41–71. The Ketef Hinnom silver plates were initially dated to the Iron Age IIC, but this dating has been challenged in various recent publications. See, especially, A. Berlejung, "Ein Programm fürs Leben: Theologisches Wort und anthropologischer Ort der Silberamulette von Ketef Hinnom," *ZAW* 120.2 (2008): 204–30; more recently, N. Na'aman, "A New Appraisal of the Silver Amulets from Ketef Hinnom," *IEJ* 61.2 (2011): 184–95. See also the essay by C. Frevel in this volume.

27. For further discussion on this important issue, see now the two essays by C. Frevel and J. D. Smoak in this volume.

customs documented by archaeological findings points to a similarly complex and nuanced picture. For instance, recent archaeological analyses by Lidar Sapir-Hen and others suggest that the prohibition of the pig may reflect in part the situation prevailing in the territory of Judah in the Iron Age II B and C, but not in several parts of the kingdom of Samaria, especially the northern lowlands where pig consumption is still well attested at these times.[28] On the other hand, fish bones discovered in Iron Age II strata in Jerusalem, Ramat Raḥel, and other sites in Judah as well, include fish defined as unclean according to the biblical legislation.[29]

In short, comparison with the material culture—when it *is* possible—suggests that some of the rituals described in the Pentateuch may have their origins in Iron Age II customs (or possibly even earlier), while other rules may be completely invented.[30] Furthermore, even in those cases where it seems possible to relate the ritual texts of the Pentateuch with actual ritual practice in the Iron Age II or later, this practice is usually more varied and flexible than what the Pentateuch describes. Here also, therefore, it might be best to regard the relationship between the ritual texts of the Pentateuch and ritual practice as a continuum of sorts, with some texts being arguably more grounded in practice than others. Yet even in the case of ritual texts that present close ties with customs documented in the material culture of ancient Israel, the Pentateuch describes a ritual ideal that implies substantial standardization of a practice that was, in fact, much more diverse.

There is, however, a further aspect to consider. The relationship between the ritual texts of the Pentateuch and actual practice may be complex and nonlinear, for the reasons described above, but there can be no question that these texts, in turn, had a significant impact on the ritual practice of emerging Jewish and Samaritan communities. There is increasing evidence in the Hellenistic and Roman periods that these communities claimed at least some degree of conformity with the ritual norms defined in the Pentateuch and consequently sought to align their practices with these norms. Furthermore, as James W. Watts in particular has insisted, this development is prepared by the rhetorical strategies of the Pentateuch itself, which repeatedly claims maximal authority for the rituals

---

28. L. Sapir-Hen et al., "Pig Husbandry in Iron Age Israel and Judah: New Insights Regarding the Origins of the 'Taboo,'" *Zeitschrift des deutschen Palästina-Vereins* 129 (2013): 1–20. In a forthcoming publication, Sapir-Hen goes further and explains the distribution of pig remains in the southern Levant predominantly in terms of the distinction between urban and nonurban contexts.

29. See D. N. Fulton et al., "Feasting in Paradise: Feast Remains from the Iron Age Palace of Ramat Rahel and Their Implications," *BASOR* 374 (2015): 29–48.

30. On this latter aspect, see, especially, the essay by J. W. Watts in this volume. As Watts observes, several biblical texts refer to mandatory donations to the temple for the firstborn of both humans and animals, but the obligation defined in Lev 12 for the new mother to bring sacrifices to the temple for *every* newborn is never mentioned elsewhere in the biblical traditions and may well reflect, therefore, an innovation by the Priestly writers of Leviticus. See also the essay by D. Erbele-Küster in this volume, which deals with similar issues.

it describes. These strategies include, but are not restricted to, presenting these rituals as divine oracles and using formulations that insist that rituals can only be performed in the way described in the Pentateuch.[31] Furthermore, the two aspects are, in effect, closely tied, generating a mutually reinforcing dynamic: the more authoritative the Pentateuch became, the more authoritative its rituals would be, and vice versa. As such, the composition and transmission of the Pentateuch marks, in many ways, the beginning of a long and complex trajectory in which the textualization and scripturalization of rituals play an increasing role in the development of early Jewish and Samaritan communities in antiquity. But this trajectory is, again, anything but linear and straightforward.[32] For communities who claimed conformity with the Pentateuch there were many ways to relate to the rituals it describes, as is already shown by the importance of the debates and conflicts that ritual interpretation would generate among Jewish and Samaritan communities in the late Second Temple period and beyond (up to today, actually). Moreover, the authority of the ritual texts of the Pentateuch did not mean that the transmission of these texts was perfectly stable: on the contrary, they could still be transmitted in multiple versions, undergo revisions, or be amplified and expanded.[33] In several instances, differences in these versions can be linked to different views regarding the way in which a pentateuchal ritual should be performed.

For these reasons, the Pentateuch offers, in many respects, a remarkable case study of the complexities of the relationship between text and ritual in antiquity. The Pentateuch and its early Jewish reception exemplarily document a situation characterized by a growing interaction between text and ritual. In many ways, this growing interaction can be seen as one of the key components in the transition (itself complex and anything but linear) leading from ancient Israel to early

---

31. See, especially, J. W. Watts, "The Rhetoric of Ritual Instruction in Leviticus 1–7," in *The Book of Leviticus: Composition and Reception*, ed. R. Rendtorff and R. A. Kugler, VTSup 93, FIOTL 3 (Leiden: Brill, 2003), 79–100; J. W. Watts, *Ritual and Rhetoric in Leviticus: From Sacrifice to Scripture* (Cambridge: Cambridge University Press, 2007). On this issue, see also now Rhyder, *Centralizing the Cult*, as well as the essay by C. Frevel in this volume.

32. On this important issue, see the essays by D. K. Falk and W. K. Gilders in this volume.

33. Sarianna Metso and Eugene Ulrich have proposed relating the greater textual stability of Leviticus to its use in the cult of the Second Temple period. See S. Metso and E. Ulrich, "The Old Greek Translation of Leviticus," in *The Book of Leviticus: Composition and Reception*, ed. R. Rendtorff and R. A. Kugler, VTSup 93, FIOTL 3 (Leiden: Brill, 2003), 247–68, as well as S. Metso, "Evidence from the Qumran Scrolls for the Scribal Transmission of Leviticus," in *Editing the Bible: Assessing the Task Past and Present*, ed. J. S. Kloppenborg and J. H. Newman, RBS 69 (Atlanta: Society of Biblical Literature, 2012), 67–79. This may well be true in general, but even in the case of Leviticus there are some clear exceptions. One good example is the additional instruction for the wood offering in one Qumran manuscript, 4Q365 23. Apparently, this instruction was considered to be part of the text of Leviticus in Qumran, on which see my discussion in C. Nihan, "Supplementing Leviticus in the Second Temple Period: The Case of the Wood Offering in 4Q365 23," in *Supplementation and the Study of the Hebrew Bible*, ed. S. Olyan and J. Wright, BJS 361 (Princeton: Princeton University Press, 2018), 183–204. On this issue, see also the discussion by J. Rhyder in this volume.

Judaism. This growing interaction had a significant impact on ritual practice itself in the centuries before and after the turn of the era, in that the textualization of rituals generated new ritual dynamics: a number of earlier ritual practices were eliminated to the benefit of new rituals, while other practices were more closely aligned with ritual texts—or, more exactly, with the local interpretation of these texts. Finally, the texts themselves were more closely integrated into communal rituals, either as icons or as the object of ritual manipulations.[34] Each of these processes, however, has parallels in other cultures of the ancient world, as the previous discussion suggests and various essays in this volume effectively demonstrate. In this regard, the Pentateuch and its early Jewish reception point to a set of ritual dynamics that, while exemplary, are not necessarily unique and can therefore be of interest for other scholars of the ancient world.

i.2. Summary of the Essays

The first essay, by Giuseppina Lenzo, discusses Egyptian funerary texts, specifically the different versions of the *Book of the Dead* from the New Kingdom and Third Intermediate Period. Lenzo begins by surveying the variety of funerary texts found in Egypt, noting the difficulties involved in providing clear-cut typological and chronological distinctions between these texts. Evidently, there was considerable fluidity in the transmission of these texts, which did not diminish the importance and efficiency of the funerary rituals, or "spells," which they contain. Turning to the spells found in the *Book of the Dead*, Lenzo demonstrates that the relationship between the ritual text and its performance is a complex one. The writing down of the spells was considered efficient in and of itself, because it provided the deceased with the knowledge required for his or her journey in the afterlife, yet actual performance of the ritual described in these spells could also take place. Comparison with material evidence from the New Kingdom and Third Intermediate Period, especially with regard to protective bricks and amulets, shows that the ritual that was practiced was generally consistent, but not identical, with the description found in the spells. Lenzo notes a number of differences and concludes that the spell represents a "written

---

34. On the significance of the iconic dimension of the Torah for the development of Judaism in Antiquity, see already the essay by K. van der Toorn, "The Iconic Book: Analogies Between the Babylonian Cult of Images and the Veneration of the Torah," in *The Image and the Book: Iconic Cults, Aniconism, and the Rise of Book Religion in Israel and the Ancient Near East*, ed. K. van der Toorn, Contributions to Biblical Exegesis and Theology 21 (Leuven: Peeters, 1997), 229–48. On this issue in connection with the rise of Judaism, Christianity, and Islam more generally, see further the useful discussion by J. W. Watts, "The Three Dimensions of Scriptures," *Postscripts* 2.2–3 (2006/8): 135–59; reprinted in *Iconic Books and Texts*, ed. J. W. Watts (London: Equinox, 2013), 9–32. See also the essay by D. K. Falk in the present volume.

ideal": the actual practice allowed for significant adjustments and variations, especially with regard to costly materials like gold. Furthermore, the comparison between copies of the *Book of the Dead* from the New Kingdom and Third Intermediate Period also shows that the transmission of spells was independent from their actual performance. Overall, the evidence she presents suggests that the composition and transmission of ritual texts and ritual performance are parallel processes that can occasionally coincide but do not overlap: the writing down is enough to warrant the efficiency of the spell for the deceased, but the ritual performance will usually deviate—sometimes even significantly—from the written script. Lenzo concludes her essay by highlighting that modern descriptions of Egyptian evidence must be able to account for the considerable degree of fluidity that can be observed with regard to both the transmission of the spells and their relationship to actual ritual performance.

The following essay, by Dominique Jaillard, discusses various key issues regarding the role of texts, textuality, and textualization in Greek ritual practice. Jaillard begins by noting a number of methodological issues, such as the deeply local character of ritual practices and its impact on textualization, as well as the fact that texts about rituals could be publicly displayed or, on the contrary, concealed by the ritual itself. Jaillard then discusses the case of written texts about rituals that are not directly involved in the ritual performance, taking sacrificial calendars as an example. As he shows, these calendars do not represent a coherent and systematic codification of ritual practice, but rather a selection of specific aspects of the ritual performance, especially those aspects that were susceptible to become a matter of dispute—such as the distribution of the meat, the remuneration of the officiants, and so on. In specific cases, such as the laws from Kos or from Mykonos, the details of the ritual may be more comprehensive, but even then the written text is far from a complete description of the ritual; as Jaillard notes, "Most of the ritual knowledge that was needed to perform the ritual gestures remained implicit." In other contexts, especially those related to less public and more private forms of ritual practice, the written text served to confer authority to the ritual practitioners. Jaillard then turns to other contexts, in which the written text is more closely embedded into the ritual practice itself. He begins by discussing the practice of dedicating hymns and other poems as *anáthemata* in the sanctuary of a god, especially in the context of festivals. In this case, the production of the text is not oriented toward the recitation of the hymn but rather represents "another, complementary way to honor the gods, and to please them." In other contexts, such as the obligatory recitation of paeans in sanctuaries, the text can become a script for the ritual performance. In some instances, the written text can even *replace* the ritual utterance, as in the case of the *katádesmos*, or written ritual bindings that were buried in the ground. Even in this case, however, the written text requires the ritual performance in order to be efficient. Jaillard concludes by noting that it is the concept of "text" that is problematic and requires further study: in particular, the text should not be identified with the mere writing but, rather, with the actualization of the text through each performance.

Lionel Marti turns our attention to the relationship between text and ritual in Mesopotamia through the example of inscriptions relating to the construction of royal buildings (such as temples and palaces) in the Neo-Assyrian period. After discussing the interest of these inscriptions for the larger issue of the relationship between text and ritual in Mesopotamia, as well as the sources at our disposal and the nature of the corpus, Marti turns to a detailed analysis of the main stages of building construction during the Neo-Assyrian period and the role of texts and rituals in this process. Among other observations, he remarks that various sets of rituals were involved at each and every stage of the construction process, although the apparent brevity and simplicity of the formulas used in some royal inscriptions may often conceal the complexity of the ritual processes actually involved. In many cases, only a portion of these rituals may effectively be reconstructed on the basis of the available evidence. Several rituals were concerned with securing the assent of the gods for the building project, especially during the preliminary steps involved in the construction work. However, the most important part of the building or rebuilding process had to do with the foundations and the materials deposited within them. Although the role of writing in these deposits remains unclear, they were commemorated in various foundation inscriptions that often use the same materials as the deposits themselves and appear to have enjoyed a votive status of sorts. The primary function of these inscriptions appears to have been the memorialization of the king; additionally, they were also used by later kings to legitimize their own building or rebuilding projects. In the third part of his essay, Marti illustrates the complex relationship between the status conferred to royal foundation inscriptions and the possibility of adjustments in the face of new historical and political circumstances, with the example of the rebuilding of Babylon by Assarhaddon. He concludes his study by highlighting a number of methodological points, such as the basic difference between texts describing rituals and texts directly used in ritual performance, like foundation inscriptions, as well as the importance of acknowledging how the royal dimension of these documents, "written in order to exalt the ruler's achievements," significantly impacts their formulation.

The essay by Patrick Michel is devoted to the relationship between text and ritual in the Late Bronze Age city of Emar. Michel begins by situating the historical and geographical context of Emar, which was located at the juncture of the Syro-Anatolian and Assyro-Babylonian cultures. He then turns his attention to the texts preserving evidence about religion and rituals in Emar, especially three tablets that can be considered to preserve some of the most significant information about ritual practice in that city: the installation of the *entu*-priestess of Baal (Emar 369), the installation of the *maš'artu*-priestess (Emar 370), and the *zukrum* festival (Emar 373), in the course of which the statue of Dagan was brought outside of the sanctuary and carried in the countryside. Michel focuses on three key features found in these texts, which illustrate the insights that these tablets provide into ritual practice at Emar. The first feature concerns the prescriptions regarding the veiling and unveiling of the deity during the procession, as well as of the *entu*- and *maš'artu*-priestesses during their installations. Michel shows that the issue of visibility was an important one during the performance of these rituals, and this seems to be the reason why the texts provide substantial details regarding this point. The second feature concerns the role of anointing in these rituals; here also, the nature of the details provided in the texts suggests that this procedure was especially significant in the ritual performance. The third feature concerns the offering of the *kubadu*, a type of burnt sacrifice, which is specific to the *zukru* festival. Michel concludes that these tablets are not liturgical texts properly speaking but reflect practical concerns by one of the main functionaries of the city. This functionary, Michel suggests, should presumably be identified with the diviner who supervised the main ceremonies in the city, and one of the main functions of the tablets would have been to ensure his payment in the course of the rituals. Overall, the features selected in these tablets seem to correspond to aspects of the ritual that were of particular importance. However, other aspects that must have been important for ritual performance at Emar, like prayers and hymns, are simply not documented in these texts.

Yitzhaq Feder offers a detailed discussion of Hittite rituals and their contribution to interpreting the Priestly texts of the Pentateuch. In this regard, his essay provides a transition of sorts from the ancient Mediterranean and Western Asian evidence to the biblical texts more specifically. After noting the interest and significance of the Hittite ritual texts for biblical scholars, and proposing a first, general description of these texts, Feder focuses on two main issues: first, how Hittite ritual texts were composed, and the type of scribal activity they reflect, and second, the purpose and function of these texts. With regard to the first point, Feder helpfully observes that Hittite ritual texts cannot be dichotomized according to simplistic oppositions (such as innovation vs conservation) but actually exemplify a broad range of scribal activities with various degrees of intervention. These activities include (but are not necessarily restricted to) copying (with the possibility of several variants being accidental rather than deliberate), compiling (including cross-referencing two or more tablets), adjusting rituals to new situations, and introducing ritual innovations. Concerning the second point, Feder argues that the primary function of these texts appears to have been serving as *aide-mémoires* for ritual specialists, but this aspect did not prevent other additional functions, including "the long-term preservation of ritual traditions, imposition of royal authority over local cults, and regulation of legitimate practice." In the last section of his essay, Feder turns to a comparison with the biblical ritual texts, especially those preserved in the Priestly traditions of the Pentateuch. He observes that the two corpora present several formal similarities (including their casuistic structure, chronologically arranged instructions, or lists of paraphernalia), but also significant differences: Priestly rituals are part of a larger narrative; they seldom exist in multiple forms, or versions; and they present detailed instructions for ritual performance (e.g., Lev 1–7 in the case of sacrifices) that are generally unparalleled in Hittite or Ugaritic texts. Feder concludes by suggesting that the two corpora are likely to originate from similar contexts of usage, "as aids to ritual practice," but that Priestly textualization of rituals exemplifies a greater degree of control because the editors of these texts had a specific "literary, ideological, and socioreligious agenda" to which they sought to adapt their rituals.

In his contribution to this volume, Rüdiger Schmitt provides a helpful survey of the evidence regarding the archaeological evidence for cultic activity in the territory of Judah (and beyond) from the Iron Age II C (corresponding to the late monarchic period) to the Persian period. Although the essay does not address directly the issue of the relationship between text and ritual in ancient Israel, it does provide an important background for the essays that follow. Schmitt begins by observing that the longstanding view of E. Stern and others according to which cultic diversity would be a characteristic of the Iron Age II but would not be continued in the Persian period has been challenged from various sides recently and that the time is ripe for a reassessment of the evidence with regard to this issue. Using the typology for cult places that he developed with Rainer Albertz, he then offers a comprehensive summary of the evidence for each of these types, first in the Iron Age II C—and then in the Persian period. The summary includes a discussion of the cultic assemblages found on each site, along with other relevant material evidence regarding ritual performance at these sites. With regard to the archaeological evidence for the Iron Age II C, Schmitt observes that the number of cult places related to the royal administration remains limited and that there is much more diversity when we consider "carrier groups of cultic activities below the stratum of official bodies," such as households, specialized ritual sites (e.g., for the care of the dead), regional sanctuaries connected to trade routes, and so on. Furthermore, Schmitt notes, a substantial portion of this cultic and ritual diversity carried over to the Persian period, as is evinced by limestone altars, terracotta figurines, and other types of evidence. Such evidence should also be considered alongside that of various Yahwistic sanctuaries besides the temple of Jerusalem in the Persian and Hellenistic periods—the "solar shrine" in Lachish, the "house of Yahû" (*byt yhw*) mentioned in an Idumena ostracon, the temple in Yeb/Elephantine, the

Samaritan sanctuary on Mount Gerizim, and the Oniad temple in Leontopolis. Together, this evidence indicates that cultic centralization was emerging and not (yet) fully developed in these time periods. The difference with the Iron Age II C should be qualified, and the evidence for the Persian and Hellenistic periods suggests that there was still "a pluriform Yahwism with different social, local and/or regional, and political bodies as carrier groups of cultic activities."

The essay by James W. Watts consists of two main parts. The first part focuses on the distinction between ritual and text, and the impact of this distinction on ritual studies in general and the study of biblical rituals in particular. After noting that "the meaning or function of the ritual is not the same thing as the meaning of the text describing the ritual" and that the ritual itself and its "verbal reflections, oral and written," are distinct types of socially situated acts, Watts shows how this distinction has impacted research on biblical rituals in the last decades. He provides a helpful survey of biblical scholarship, identifying several significant trends. He notes, in particular, the critique of attempts to identify singular meanings in biblical descriptions of rituals and the development of alternative approaches, such as the indexical approach inspired from C. S. Peirce, as well as growing scholarly attention paid to the *rhetorical* dimension of biblical texts about rituals. On the other hand, he also remarks that more classical approaches that view biblical rituals from a symbolic or theological perspective have remained quite popular. Additionally, several new approaches have been developed that are based on the analogy between ritual and language. Against these linguistic approaches to biblical rituals, Watts notes that, while ritual and language share some general features (in particular, they are rule-bound and conventional), the status of meaning is different: while meaning is usually essential to the success of linguistic acts, "a ritual's meaning is not essential to its function and can vary with each participant." In the second part of his essay Watts turns to a case study, the ritual for the new mother in Lev 12, in order to show the difference between "textual rhetoric about ritual and ritual practice." Specifically, Watts argues that the text of Lev 12 does not provide information about rituals for new mothers in Israel but rather informs us about the distinct agenda of the Priestly writers of Leviticus. In this respect, he proposes that we understand the text of Lev 12 as being first and foremost a "payment schedule," defining which offerings need to be brought to the sanctuary by the new mother, and when. It is also possible that the request to bring offerings for each human birth is an innovation by these same authors, since this obligation is referenced nowhere else in the biblical texts. Overall, the text's function is predominantly economic, whereas the specific form of the ritual it describes depends on literary conventions.

Christian Frevel offers a comprehensive discussion of rituals in the book of Numbers, and their contribution to our understanding of the relationship between ritual, tradition, and community in the emergence of Judaism. He begins by observing that the Mosaic Torah is an example of a (more or less homogeneous) tradition shared by several communities simultaneously (namely, Jews and Samaritans inside and outside their homeland) and inquires as to the role of the rituals described in the Torah in negotiating relations between these communities. He notes that the relationship of these ritual texts to actual practice is a complex one and that simplistic alternatives should be avoided: the rituals of the Pentateuch are neither a codification of practice nor simply divorced from it; they have a symbolic, or theological, meaning, but they are not entirely consistent and do not form a closed "system" of values. The textualization of rituals in the Pentateuch, especially in its "Priestly" portions, should be viewed as a complex, multidimensional process that engages issues of "authority, regulation, homogenization, and representation" for the communities for which these texts were written. Turning to the book of Numbers, Frevel observes that the importance of rituals in this book witnesses a form of "ritual densification," to use the category introduced by Bell, which (building on Bell's insights) is likely to reflect larger formative social, economic, political, and religious processes at the time Numbers was composed. Frevel then illustrates this point by discussing key aspects of the textualization of rituals in Numbers, especially by means of a detailed case study of the so-called Priestly blessing of Num 6 and its relationship to the silver scrolls of Ketef Hinnom (KH 1 and 2). He concludes that textualization, in this instance, produces and legitimizes a new ritual practice, which does not need to correspond "in every aspect" to the written ideal but remains nevertheless bound to the latter. This relationship between ritual text and ritual practice has significant implications for the construction of communal identity in the Second Temple period. Frevel continues this argument by discussing the various dimensions of textualization, noting that the production of ritual texts not only leads to standardization and homogenization but also enables variance in the performance of rituals. Based on these observations, Frevel argues in the final part of his essay that the textualization of rituals was a central component in the creation of the Torah as an "identity reservoir" for various communities during the Second Temple period.

The essay by Jeremy D. Smoak is likewise devoted to the Priestly blessing in Num 6:22–27, although his approach differs from Frevel's in various respects. Smoak begins by presenting the text of Num 6 and its place in the scholarship on biblical rituals. He notes that much of the research conducted during the twentieth century looked at the Priestly texts primarily as a source for Israelite ritual practice in the monarchic period and often understood these texts as a mere "codification" of that practice. More recent studies, however, have shifted the focus to the performative aspect of these texts, especially their *rhetorical* dimension (Watts and others). Applying this approach to the Priestly blessing in Num 6 implies, according to Smoak, that we must consider this text not only in relation to the temple and the cult but also in relation to the authority of the priesthood (as the intended performers of the blessing) and the creation of the ritual rhetoric of the Torah in general. Smoak addresses these issues by analyzing how the wording of the Priestly blessing in Num 6 defines what he terms a "carefully crafted chain of authority that closely identifies the priestly act of blessing Israel with the divine commands of Yahweh." He notes that the syntax that is used has close parallels in scribal epistolary discourse and provides a useful comparison of this syntax with epistolary conventions used in Iron Age letters. In particular, he argues that Num 6 has adapted such epistolary conventions in order to construe the blessing as an authoritative message from Yahweh to Israel and to project the priest as the messenger tasked to read and perform this message. "Numbers 6:22–27 cast the blessing as something that should be performed before audiences as part of the ritual reading of *torah*. The blessing was a divine message given from Yahweh to Israel but delivered and performed by Yahweh's messengers—the sons of Aaron." In the final section of his essay, Smoak compares this reading of Num 6 with two other biblical texts that describe priests reading texts to an audience, Jer 29 and Neh 8. He shows that both texts document the way in which priestly reading bridged scribal authority and oral performance by locating the authority of the texts in the realm of "secondary orality," while simultaneously articulating and maintaining religious hierarchies. Additionally, in the case of Num 6 (and Torah reading in general), priestly performance also served to bridge the distance with the foundational past of the Sinai revelation, thereby conferring further authority to both the divine instructions and their priestly performers.

The topic of the performance of the ritual texts found in the Pentateuch is also addressed by Dorothea Erbele-Küster, albeit from a distinct perspective. Specifically, Erbele-Küster looks at the way in which these texts, and especially the collection preserved in Lev 12–15, project and define a specific construal of bodies. After discussing some key methodological issues involved in the study of these texts, such as the numerous "gaps" found in the description of rituals in the Pentateuch, she analyzes first the obligation to circumcise male newborns in Lev 12. She argues that while circumcision presupposes the sexual difference rather than creates it, it plays a central role nonetheless in the gendering of the child and his integration into the cultic community. At the same time, Erbele-Küster also remarks that the text contains no instruction for the performance of circumcision and that all bodily details regarding this act remain likewise unmentioned: "A tension exists between an embodied and a disembodied manner of description, between the body's visibility and invisibility in the text." She further notes that the subsequent instructions in Lev 12 for the purification of the new mother imply a similarly complex construal of her body in ritual perspective, since her impurity is defined with regard to her child (the duration of impurity being longer in the case of a girl than of a boy) as well as to the sanctuary, and not primarily with regard to her postpartum blood emissions, as it is sometimes assumed. She concludes that the text of Lev 12 mirrors "the socioreligious structure" that produced it and "is a fine example of the priestly ideology wherein ritual place and ritually defined time intersect and define the body." Turning to her second text, Lev 15, Erbele-Küster shows how the complex model of contamination, direct and indirect, articulated in this chapter further contributes to a construction of gendered bodies (with both parallels and differences between women and men), in a way that now also integrates domestic objects such as beds and seats. In the last section of her essay, she concludes that the aim of these texts is not to describe realistically physiological phenomena but to construe gendered bodies through the description of ritual performance. This construal, in turn, cannot be dissociated from the ideological perspective that informs the Priestly texts.

Julia Rhyder addresses the relationship between text and ritual in the early Second Temple period through a close reading of selected texts from Nehemiah and Chronicles. She begins by noting that the notion that the writing of ritual texts would foster ritual standardization has become axiomatic in ritual studies and that the existence of narratives recounting the celebration of festivals instructed in the Pentateuch provides us with a fine opportunity to verify this notion. While these descriptions do not reflect actual historical events, they inform us nonetheless about "the diverse ways in which [...] scribes imagined that the law might be ideally applied." Basing her analysis on three key texts (Neh 8; 2 Chr 30; 2 Chr 34), Rhyder argues that in each of these accounts the description of the festivals claims to adhere to the instructions found in earlier laws, while in fact simultaneously presenting many examples of adaptation, innovation, and revision with regard to them. The story of Neh 8 presents "a new conception" of how the feast of Sukkôt (Booths) "was to be applied to the urban context of Jerusalem specifically," which connects in particular the feast more closely to the household than the corresponding law in Lev 23. Second Chronicles 30, which recounts Hezekiah's Passover, presents substantial deviations from the pentateuchal model for this festival—such as the celebration of the feast in the second month instead of the first, or the eating of the sacrificial meat by unclean members of the community—which in turn justify the introduction not only of new ritual customs but also of new forms of ritual agency (especially, albeit not exclusively, royal agency). Similar findings apply in the case of Josiah's Passover in 2 Chr 35; additionally, the latter account introduces new references to written authorities, associated with the royal figures of David and Solomon respectively, which supplement the written authority of the pentateuchal texts. In her conclusion, Rhyder remarks that, while these texts recognize the pentateuchal rituals as normative, the relationship to the pentateuchal norm is dynamic and flexible rather than static. She also makes the important point that "the ritual law serves functions that extend beyond that of providing a ritual standard," such as introducing new ritual roles, negotiating new ritual hierarchies, or even justifying departure from the law's prescriptions. These conclusions, in turn, force us to qualify and complicate the relationship between textualization and ritual standardization.

The essay by Daniel K. Falk offers a detailed and careful discussion of the relationship between text and ritual in the Dead Sea Scrolls, focusing specifically on the prayer texts and their uses in diverse contexts. Falk highlights the interest of the Qumran evidence for the discussion of the relationship between text and ritual and remarks that "Qumran has unique data for the study of this problem in the ancient world because of the density of its ritual life and the abundance of texts dealing with rituals in various ways." He notes, furthermore, that the issue of ritual in the Scrolls requires developing models that can account for the *materiality* of texts in relation to ritual, and he emphasizes the need to maintain the distinction between text and ritual while also acknowledging that texts can be used as ritual artifacts. Based on these preliminary remarks, Falk proceeds to analyze prayer texts used in four different contexts in Qumran: (1) purification liturgies, (2) collections of liturgical prayers, (3) *tefillin*, and (4) covenant ceremony. Each of these texts provides different, but also complementary, types of evidence regarding the relationship between text and ritual in Qumran. In the case of purification liturgies, two scrolls at least (4Q414 and 4Q512) show a close connection with ritual performance itself; in this case, Falk argues, "prayer is a significant, scripted element in a complex ritual." A similar conclusion applies in the case of collections of liturgical prayers; the corresponding manuscripts contain a number of indications that they could be used as scripts in a ritual performance, which also accounts for the amount of ritual details that they preserve. The *tefillin*—small leather pouches worn on the arm and the forehead and inscribed with scriptural passages—present us with a different type of evidence because they are clear ritual artifacts, but their ritual usage is never mentioned in the texts of Qumran themselves. It is therefore difficult to map precisely their place in the ritual practice of the community. In any case, the *tefillin* present one of the clearest examples of the material, rather than merely functional, use of texts in ritual contexts. Finally, the covenant ceremony described in the Community Rule (1QS 1:18–2:18) provides yet another type of evidence, preserving the outline of what was a constitutional ceremony for the community; in this case, its relationship to ritual performance would be indirect at best. Through his analysis of these four cases, Falk delineates four corresponding "grids" that, together, provide a comprehensive framework for some of the main parameters involved in the relation between text and ritual at Qumran.

The final essay, by William K. Gilders, addresses the ways in which the ritual text of Lev 16, describing the ceremony that will become Yôm Kippur in Second Temple Judaism, is handled in various rabbinic traditions such as the Mishnaic tractate Yoma (m. Yoma), the Toseftim tractate Kippurim (t. Kippurim), and the halakhic midrash Sifra Aḥare Mot. Gilders begins by observing that the literary description of a ritual, such as Lev 16, is not the ritual performance itself; consequently, his study deals with "how a textual ritual can embody interpretations of an earlier textual ritual." The three rabbinic texts are themselves interconnected, and rather than treating them sequentially, Gilders opts for an approach comparing the way in which they handle key issues regarding the interpretation of Lev 16. A first issue concerns the authority of Lev 16. The Mishna, Gilders observes, insists that conformity with a textual norm—presumably represented by Lev 16—is instrumental for the performance of the ritual. But it nonetheless implicitly acknowledges that this textual norm may not be sufficient to cover all the aspects of the performance itself: "While of fundamental significance, the scriptural text is not the only source of relevant information." Gilders then goes on to address various prescriptive details in the text of Lev 16 that required interpretation. The rabbinic interpretation reflected in m. Yoma and t. Kippurim rejects the Boethusian interpretation according to which incense should be placed on the coals of the censer held by the high priest before entering the inner sanctum. Both m. Yoma and Sifra Aḥarei Mot interpret the reference to *kipper* in verse 6 and 11a of Lev 16 as denoting a confession spoken by the high priest, in addition to the confession already mentioned explicitly in verse 21. Finally, m. Yoma, t. Kippurim, and Sifra Aḥarei Mot disagree on the wording of the confession recited by the high priest. All these examples attest to complex and creative engagements with the text of Lev 16. Gilders remarks, for instance, that the reference to additional confessions in m. Yoma and Sifra Aḥarei Mot substantially reframes the ceremony, reinforcing the significance of the high priest but also his own need for divine forgiveness. The whole discussion has larger implications regarding the way in which textual interpretations of an earlier ritual text operate, all the more so since the rabbinic texts became themselves ritual manuals "also requiring interpretation in new contexts."

i.3. Perspectives for Future Discussion

It is not possible to discuss here all the findings brought by this rich collection of essays. However, by way of a conclusion to the present introduction, I would like to highlight some of the key perspectives that emerge from the collection and show potential for future research and discussion. Since most of the essays in this volume deal with the Pentateuch and early Jewish rituals, the following survey will focus on these topics. However, some of the points mentioned arguably remain of relevance to scholars from other fields as well.

(1) *The relevance of a comparative approach.* A first point concerns the relevance of a large comparative approach. Rituals in the Pentateuch, and in

the Hebrew Bible more generally, have been the subject of several studies in the last two decades (a helpful survey of which is provided by James W. Watts in his essay for the present volume). Many of these studies are influenced by, or conversant with, developments in theoretical and ethnographic approaches in the study of rituals. But they have tended to focus on these rituals in their ancient Israelite and early Jewish contexts predominantly, or sometimes even exclusively, without necessarily considering other questions that could arise from adopting a larger comparative perspective. Occasionally, some of these studies have addressed specific instances of comparison with selected Western Asian rituals, but even then the comparative approach has usually remained genetic or analogical.[35] However legitimate such an approach may be, it also runs the risk of circular reasoning, because the questions that are considered relevant for the study of ancient Israelite and early Jewish rituals tend to be primarily reconstructed on the basis of the biblical texts themselves (and, occasionally, similar Western Asian traditions), rather than considering the whole range of possibilities evidenced by the study of ritual texts and ritual practices in antiquity. By contrast, a comparative approach that is not merely genetic and analogical but is first and foremost *differential*[36] can provide a larger background for the study of biblical rituals and illuminate the specifics of these rituals in the context of ancient societies. This is all the more necessary in the case of biblical rituals because, as mentioned above, the rituals of the Pentateuch present a written ideal, which can at times be quite remote from (or even foreign to) actual practice. By contrast, comparing these rituals to those documented in ancient Greece, Egypt, Anatolia, Mesopotamia, and other ancient cultures as well, forces the students of biblical and postbiblical rituals to ask new questions about their own materials. For instance, such comparison highlights the degree to which the Pentateuch erases local Israelite customs in its representation of rituals, to the exclusive benefit of a centralized cult.[37] This observation, in turn, highlights the importance of centralization in the description of pentateuchal rituals; it also raises further questions regarding the extent to which local customs and traditions may nonetheless be preserved in some biblical descriptions of rituals.

35. Consider, for instance, the important study on Hittite and Israelite blood rituals by Y. Feder, *Blood Expiation in Hittite and Biblical Ritual: Origins, Context, and Meaning* (Atlanta: Society of Biblical Literature, 2011).
36. On the comparative approach in the study of antiquity, see, in particular, the essays collected in C. Calame and B. Lincoln, eds., *Comparer en Histoire des religions antiques* (Liège: Presses universitaires de Liège, 2012).
37. The deeply local nature of rituals in ancient societies, and correspondingly the importance of local and regional variations in ritual performance, are especially noted in the essay by D. Jaillard and R. Schmitt in the present volume. It is also evident, to some extent, in the essays by G. Lenzo, L. Marti, P. Michel, and C. Frevel.

(2) *The need for more complex models.* A second point concerns the need for more complex models for the relationship between text and ritual, in the Pentateuch and beyond. In the case of the Pentateuch, earlier discussions of this issue have often tended to focus on the question of whether or not these rituals were practiced at the time of their writing. Yet this may well be a false alternative in many respects. As several essays in the present volume document, the relationship between text and ritual in antiquity was never simple or straightforward. Rather, several possibilities could coexist, even at the same time and in the same place, ranging from the text as a guide to ritual practice to the text as a substitute for the practice it claims to describe.[38] The situation may not be different in the case of the Pentateuch, or other biblical rituals for that matter, and this point is corroborated, to an extent, by the limited evidence that can be gained from the comparison with the material culture of ancient Israel, as noted above. This conclusion, in turn, corroborates the point already made above, namely, that it would be helpful for biblical scholars (and for scholars of the ancient Mediterranean and Western Asian world in general) to think of the relationship between text and ritual in terms of a continuum, rather than of a rigid alternative. In some cases, the ritual described in the Pentateuch may represent the generalization of a local custom; in other cases, it may textualize a well-accepted norm; and in yet other instances, it may represent a complete innovation. It is highly unlikely, however, that the same rule should apply to all the rituals described in the Pentateuch. Furthermore, and no less importantly, highlighting the complexities involved in the relationship between text and ritual in ancient societies also raises new questions regarding the textualization of ritual in the Pentateuch. What effect, precisely, did the texts of the Pentateuch have on ritual performance in the Second Temple period, and how were they embedded in this practice? In this regard, the demonstration by Daniel K. Falk, in his essay for this volume, that the evidence from Qumran points to different degrees of involvement of texts in the ritual practice of the community is an important step forward. However, more studies will be required on this topic in the future.

(3) *The relevance of material culture.* A third point concerns the significance of analyzing and interpreting biblical rituals in closer connection with the study of the material culture of ancient Israel. This issue is addressed and developed in several essays of the present volume, especially by Rüdiger Schmitt, Christian Frevel, and Jeremy Smoak, in the case of ancient Israelite and biblical rituals, and Daniel K. Falk, in the case of Qumran rituals. It confirms a recent scholarly trend to insist on the importance of grounding more firmly the study of biblical rituals in the material culture of the society that

---

38. This point is well illustrated, in particular, in the essay by G. Lenzo with regard to funerary papyri of ancient Egypt in the New Kingdom and Third Intermediate Periods.

produced these texts.³⁹ Much more remains to be done in this regard, however. Especially in the case of the "Priestly" texts of the Pentateuch, a comprehensive analysis of the *realia* mentioned in these texts from an archaeological, historical and exegetical perspective remains largely a scholarly desideratum.⁴⁰ Other important issues that require further exploration include (but are not restricted to) economic aspects involved in the biblical rituals,⁴¹ constructions of spatiality and their relationship to actual ritual spaces in the Levant,⁴² or the relationship of biblical rituals to cultic materials documented by archaeological finds.⁴³ The discussion of epigraphic evidence for ancient Israelite rituals, and the significance of that evidence for biblical descriptions of rituals, remains an important area of research, although some substantial work has already been done on this topic.⁴⁴ On the other hand, it is important to keep in mind that biblical texts

---

39. See, e.g., B. B. Schmitt, *The Materiality of Power: Explorations in the Social History of Early Israelite Magic*, FAT 105 (Tübingen: Mohr Siebeck, 2016). See also, programmatically, F. Stavrakopoulou, "Materialist Reading: Materialism, Materiality, and Biblical Cults of Writing," in *Biblical Interpretation and Method: Essays in Honour of John Barton*, ed. K. J. Dell and P. M. Joyce (Oxford: Oxford University Press, 2013), 223–42.

40. See, for instance, my discussion of the vestments of the high priest in C. Nihan, "Le pectoral d'Aaron et la figure du grand prêtre dans les traditions sacerdotales du Pentateuque," in *Congress Volume Stellenbosch 2016*, ed. L. Jonker et al., VTSup 177 (Leiden: Brill, 2017), 23–55, as well as my discussion of the recipe for the sacred compound of incense in Exod 30 in C. Nihan, "Une recette pour l'encens," *Revue de Théologie et de Philosophie* 149 (2017): 305–22.

41. This issue remains understudied. See, however, P. Altmann, *Economics in Persian-Period Biblical Texts: Their Interactions with Economic Developments in the Persian Period and Earlier Biblical Traditions*, FAT 109 (Tübingen: Mohr Siebeck, 2016), esp. 192–96 and passim. On the relationship between the sacrificial calendar, patterns of reproduction, and seasonal availability during the year, see also N. J. Ruane, *Sacrifice and Gender in Biblical Law* (Cambridge: Cambridge University Press, 2013), 62–64.

42. See, for instance, J. D. Smoak, "From Temple to Text: Text as Ritual Space and the Composition of Numbers 6:24–26," *JHebS* 17 (2017): 1–27, doi:10.5508/jhs.2017.v17.a2. On this topic, see also the earlier study by M. K. George, *Israel's Tabernacle as Social Space* (Atlanta: SBL Press, 2009); J. Rhyder, "Space and Memory in the Book of Leviticus," in *Scripture as Social Discourse: Social-Scientific Perspectives on Early Jewish and Christian Writings*, ed. T. Klutz, C. A. Strine, and J. M. Keady (London: T&T Clark, 2018), 83–96; Rhyder, *Centralizing the Cult*.

43. On incense altars and incense burners, see, e.g., the earlier study by W. Zwickel, *Räucherkult und Räuchregeräte. Exegetische und Archäologische Studien zum Räucheropfer im Alten Testament*, OBO 97 (Fribourg: Editions universitaires; Göttingen: Vandenhoeck & Ruprecht, 1990); more recently on this topic, see C. Frevel and K. Pyschny, "Perserzeitliche Räucherkästchen. Zu einer wenig beachteten Fundgattung im Kontext der These Ephraim Sterns," in *A "Religious Revolution" in Yehûd? The Material Culture of the Persian Period as a Test Case*, ed. C. Frevel, K. Pyschny, and I. Cornelius, OBO 267 (Freiburg: Academic Press; Göttingen: Vandenhoeck & Ruprecht, 2014), 111–220.

44. See, for example, the important study on blessing rituals and practices by M. Leuenberger, *Segen und Segenstheologien im alten Israel: Untersuchungen zu ihren religions- und theologiegeschichtlichen Konstellationen und Transformationen*, ATANT 90 (Zürich: TVZ, 2008), which compares and contrasts epigraphic and literary evidence in ancient Israel. The Ketef Hinnom silver plates and their parallels with Num 6 have already been the subject of substantial research in particular; see on this the essays by C. Frevel and J. D. Smoak in this volume, with references to earlier scholarship.

tend to provide a highly idealized description of rituals—an aspect that is also highlighted in various essays in the present volume.[45] In this regard, the contextualization of biblical rituals in the material culture of ancient Israel does not only serve to re-create the material and practical background against which these ritual texts were formed and transmitted. It also serves, simultaneously, to highlight the significant differences and discontinuities that can exist between biblical descriptions and ancient Israelite or early Jewish practices—or to put it somewhat bluntly: between what people were told to do (or even were told that they were doing) and what they effectively did.[46] Much as the comparative approach highlighted above, the contextualization of biblical rituals in the material culture of ancient Israel is made possible only when scholars attend to both parallels and contrasts.[47]

(4) *Bridging the study of biblical and early Jewish rituals.* Last but not least, another point concerns the relevance of a kind of *longue durée* approach for the study of biblical rituals. Until now, the study of biblical rituals and of early Jewish rituals from the Second Temple period have largely developed independently of each other. While this is understandable, the present collection suggests that there is much to be gained in bringing these two fields of study more closely together. First, later Jewish traditions can often illuminate the gaps, ambiguities, and problems perceived by ancient interpreters in a biblical ritual. These traditions can therefore provide an important source of information regarding how these rituals were effectively read and practiced, even if we always need to take into account the specifics of these traditions, which have their own agendas.[48] Second, and even more important, later Jewish traditions can often illuminate the complex issue of the authority of biblical rituals, and the nature of that authority. In many documented cases, the authority of the biblical ritual does not translate into a kind of literal application of that ritual. In fact, as William K. Gilders aptly comments in his essay for this volume, the biblical text is usually a major source of inspiration for later tradents, but *not* necessarily the only one. In this regard, the authority of biblical rituals is *dynamic* rather

---

45. On this basic issue, see, especially, the essays by J. W. Watts and D. Erbele-Küster in this volume.
46. In this volume, see, especially, the essay by R. Schmitt, which shows that, from the Iron Age II C to the Persian or even Early Hellenistic periods there existed a degree of cultic diversity and plurality that significantly contrasts with, and even contradicts, the image of a fully centralized cult that tends to be projected in several traditions of the Pentateuch.
47. For such contextualization, the basic parameters identified by R. Grimes that define the "field" of ritual activity—ritual space, objects, time, sound, and language, etc.—can prove to be especially helpful. See R. L. Grimes, *Beginnings in Ritual Studies*, rev. ed. (Columbia: University of South Carolina Press, 1995), 24–39.
48. This approach is well illustrated, in the case of the ritual of Lev 16, in the essay by W. K. Gilders in this volume.

than static: it is by being continuously reinterpreted and recontextualized that these rituals could effectively be kept alive, even in a sense *after* the destruction of the Second Temple in 70 CE. Interpretation, in this case, is not just required by the gaps or the difficulties of the ritual text; it is first and foremost the activity through which the authority of the ritual text is reaffirmed and negotiated in new contexts.[49] The specifics of this process, by which the authority of ritual texts is shaped and transmitted, may and of course do vary from one culture to another in the ancient world. But the process itself is arguably present, in one way or another, in all ancient cultures that resort to ritual textualization. The case of the Pentateuch and its ancient Jewish reception is exemplary in this regard, because it allows us to trace the emergence and the development of the authority of ritual texts across several centuries. As such, it is of interest not only to biblical scholars and students of ancient Judaism but also to students of ritual and ancient historians in general.

BIBLIOGRAPHY

Altmann, P. *Economics in Persian-Period Biblical Texts: Their Interactions with Economic Developments in the Persian Period and Earlier Biblical Traditions.* FAT 109. Tübingen: Mohr Siebeck, 2016.
Arnaud, D. "Prolégomènes à la rédaction d'une histoire d'Ougarit II: Les bordereaux de rois divinisés." *SMEA* 41.8 (1998): 153–73.
Assmann, J. *Das kulturelle Gedächtnis: Schrift, Erinnerung und politische Identität in frühen Hochkulturen.* 3rd ed. Munich: Beck, 2000.
Barchiesi, A., J. Rüpke, and S. A. Stephens, eds. *Rituals in Ink: A Conference on Religion and Literary Production in Ancient Rome Held at Stanford University in February 2002.* Potsdamer Altertumswissenschaftliche Beiträge 10. Stuttgart: Steiner, 2004.
Barkay, G., M. J. Lundberg, A. G. Vaughn, and B. Zuckerman. "The Amulets from Ketef Hinnom: A New Edition and Evaluation." *BASOR* 334 (2004): 41–71.
Bell, C. "Ritualization of Texts and Textualization of Ritual in the Codification of Taoist Liturgy." *HR* 27.4 (1988): 366–92.
———. *Ritual Theory, Ritual Practice.* Oxford: Oxford University Press, 1992.
Berlejung, A. "Ein Programm fürs Leben: Theologisches Wort und anthropologischer Ort der Silberamulette von Ketef Hinnom." *ZAW* 120.2 (2008): 204–30.
Calame, C., and B. Lincoln, eds. *Comparer en Histoire des religions antiques.* Liège: Presses universitaires de Liège, 2012.
Carbon, J.-M., and V. Pirenne-Delforge. "Codifying 'Sacred Laws' in Ancient Greece." Pages 141–57 in *Writing Laws in Antiquity / L'écriture du droit dans l'Antiquité.* Edited by D. Jaillard and C. Nihan. BZABR 19. Wiesbaden: Harrassowitz Verlag, 2017.

---

49. On this issue, in addition to the essay by W. K. Gilders, see also the essays by C. Frevel, J. Rhyder, and D. K. Falk, all of which also deal with communal interpretive strategies as a key aspect of the negotiation of authority in relationship to ritual texts.

Feder, Y. *Blood Expiation in Hittite and Biblical Ritual: Origins, Context, and Meaning.* Atlanta: Society of Biblical Literature, 2011.

Frevel, C., and K. Pyschny. "Perserzeitliche Räucherkästchen. Zu einer wenig beachteten Fundgattung im Kontext der These Ephraim Sterns." Pages 111–220 in *A "Religious Revolution" in Yehûd? The Material Culture of the Persian Period as a Test Case.* Edited by C. Frevel, K. Pyschny, and I. Cornelius. OBO 267. Freiburg: Academic Press; Göttingen: Vandenhoeck & Ruprecht, 2014.

Fulton, D. N., Y. Gadot, A. Kleiman, L. Freud, O. Lernau, and O. Lipschits. "Feasting in Paradise: Feast Remains from the Iron Age Palace of Ramat Rahel and Their Implications." *BASOR* 374 (2015): 29–48.

Georgoudi, S. "Comment régler les *théia pragmata*: Pour une étude de ce qu'on appelle 'lois sacrées.'" *Mètis*, n.s., 8 (2010): 39–54.

Grimes, R. L. *Beginnings in Ritual Studies.* Rev. ed. Columbia: University of South Carolina Press, 1995.

Humphrey, C., and J. Laidlaw. *The Archetypal Actions of Ritual: A Theory of Ritual Illustrated by the Jain Rite of Worship.* Oxford Studies in Social and Cultural Anthropology. Oxford: Clarendon Press, 1994.

Hurowitz, V. "Picturing Imageless Deities: Iconography in the Ancient Near East." *Biblical Archaeological Review* 23.3 (1997): 46–69.

Leuenberger, M. *Segen und Segenstheologien im alten Israel: Untersuchungen zu ihren religions- und theologiegeschichtlichen Konstellationen und Transformationen.* ATANT 90. Zürich: TVZ, 2008.

Lewis, T. J. "Syro-Palestinian Iconography and Divine Images." Pages 69–107 in *Cult Image and Divine Representation in the Ancient Near East.* Edited by N. H. Walls. American Schools of Oriental Research. Book Series 10. Boston: American Schools of Oriental Research, 2005.

Metso, S. "Evidence from the Qumran Scrolls for the Scribal Transmission of Leviticus." Pages 67–79 in *Editing the Bible: Assessing the Task Past and Present.* Edited by J. S. Kloppenborg and J. H. Newman. RBS 69. Atlanta: Society of Biblical Literature, 2012.

Metso, S., and E. Ulrich. "The Old Greek Translation of Leviticus." Pages 247–68 in *The Book of Leviticus: Composition and Reception.* Edited by R. Rendtorff and R. A. Kugler. VTSup 93. Leiden: Brill, 2003.

Na'aman, N. "A New Appraisal of the Silver Amulets from Ketef Hinnom." *IEJ* 61.2 (2011): 184–95.

Nihan, C. *From Priestly Torah to Pentateuch: A Study in the Composition of Leviticus.* FAT 2/25. Tübingen: Mohr Siebeck, 2007.

———. "Le pectoral d'Aaron et la figure du grand prêtre dans les traditions sacerdotales du Pentateuque." Pages 23–55 in *Congress Volume Stellenbosch 2016.* Edited by L. Jonker et al. VTSup 177. Leiden: Brill, 2017.

———. "Une recette pour l'encens." *Revue de Théologie et de Philosophie* 149 (2017): 305–22.

———. "Supplementing Leviticus in the Second Temple Period: The Case of the Wood Offering in 4Q365 23." Pages 183–204 in *Supplementation and the Study of the Hebrew Bible.* Edited by S. Olyan and J. Wright. BJS 361. Princeton: Princeton University Press, 2018.

Pardee, D. *Les textes rituels.* 2 vols. Ras Shamra-Ougarit 12. Paris: Editions Recherche sur les civilisations, 2000.

———. *Ritual and Cult at Ugarit*. WAW 10. Atlanta: Society of Biblical Literature, 2002.
Pee, C. de. *The Writing of Weddings in Middle Period China: Text and Ritual Practice in the Eighth Through Fourteenth Centuries*. SUNY Series in Chinese Philosophy and Culture. Albany: State University of New York Press, 2007.
Rhyder, J. *Centralizing the Cult: The Holiness Legislation in Leviticus 17–26*. FAT 134. Tübingen: Mohr Siebeck, 2019.
———. "Space and Memory in the Book of Leviticus." Pages 83–96 in *Scripture as Social Discourse: Social-Scientific Perspectives on Early Jewish and Christian Writings*. Edited by T. Klutz, C. A. Strine, and J. M. Keady. London: T&T Clark, 2018.
Ruane, N. J. *Sacrifice and Gender in Biblical Law*. Cambridge: Cambridge University Press, 2013.
Rüpke, J., "Acta aut agenda: Relations of Script and Performance." Pages 23–43 in *Rituals in Ink: A Conference on Religion and Literary Production in Ancient Rome Held at Stanford University in February 2002*. Edited by A. Barchiesi, J. Rüpke, and S. A. Stephens. Potsdamer Altertumswissenschaftliche Beiträge 10. Stuttgart: Steiner, 2004.
Sapir-Hen, L., G. Bar-Oz, Y. Gadot, and I. Finkelstein. "Pig Husbandry in Iron Age Israel and Judah: New Insights Regarding the Origins of the 'Taboo.'" *Zeitschrift des deutschen Palästina-Vereins* 129 (2013): 1–20.
Schmidt, B. *The Materiality of Power: Explorations in the Social History of Early Israelite Magic*. FAT 105. Tübingen: Mohr Siebeck, 2016.
Smoak, J. D. "From Temple to Text: Text as Ritual Space and the Composition of Numbers 6:24–26." *JHebS* 17 (2017): 1–27. doi:10.5508/jhs.2017.v17.a2.
Stavrakopoulou, F. "Materialist Reading: Materialism, Materiality, and Biblical Cults of Writing." Pages 223–42 in *Biblical Interpretation and Method: Essays in Honour of John Barton*. Edited by K. J. Dell and P. M. Joyce. Oxford: Oxford University Press, 2013.
Toorn, K. van der. "The Iconic Book: Analogies Between the Babylonian Cult of Images and the Veneration of the Torah." Pages 229–48 in *The Image and the Book: Iconic Cults, Aniconism, and the Rise of Book Religion in Israel and the Ancient Near East*. Edited by K. van der Toorn. Contributions to Biblical Exegesis and Theology 21. Leuven: Peeters, 1997.
Watts, J. "The Rhetoric of Ritual Instruction in Leviticus 1–7." Pages 79–100 in *The Book of Leviticus: Composition and Reception*. Edited by R. Rendtorff and R. A. Kugler. VTSup 93. FIOTL 3. Leiden: Brill, 2003.
———. *Ritual and Rhetoric in Leviticus: From Sacrifice to Scripture*. Cambridge: Cambridge University Press, 2007.
———. "The Three Dimensions of Scriptures." *Postscripts* 2.2–3 (2006/8): 135–59. Repr. as pages 9–32 in *Iconic Books and Texts*. Edited by J. W. Watts. London: Equinox, 2013.
Zwickel, W. *Räucherkult und Räuchregeräte. Exegetische und Archäologische Studien zum Räucheropfer im Alten Testament*. OBO 97. Fribourg: Editions universitaires; Göttingen: Vandenhoeck & Ruprecht, 1990.

CHAPTER 1

Rituals in the Spells of the *Book of the Dead* in Ancient Egypt

Giuseppina Lenzo

1.1. Preliminary Remarks on the Issue

The present essay discusses the relationship between text and ritual on the basis of ancient Egyptian funerary texts, specifically the different versions of the *Book of the Dead* in the New Kingdom and the Third Intermediate Period. In particular, the essay explores the categories construed by scholars in light of the evidence we have for the composition and usage of funerary texts, it gathers evidence for the performance or nonperformance of the rituals described in these texts, and it discusses the possible significance of the various arrangements of ritual formulae, or spells (Egyptian *r:w*), for the relationship between text and ritual in ancient Egypt. Among other findings, the evidence surveyed shows that even though the written ritual was considered to have an efficacy in and of itself and could therefore be known by the deceased or simply be placed in his or her tomb, in several cases this phenomenon did not prevent the actual performance of the ritual described—an observation that raises in turn important questions regarding the actual dynamics of text and ritual in ancient Egypt.

1.1.1. Rituals in Ancient Egypt

Rituals in ancient Egypt are well attested in temples as well as in funerary contexts. In both cases, an ample number of documents have survived: there are obviously those that are preserved on the walls of the temples, but there also those that are found in tombs, coffins, stelae, statues, papyri, ostraca, and on many other objects.

In temple contexts, the daily offering ritual for the gods served as one of the most important ritual sequences.[1] The scenes carved on the walls of the temples show that the episodes were to be performed by the Pharaoh, but since

---

1. The bibliography on this topic is large. See, most recently, N. Tacke, *Das Opferritual des ägyptischen Neuen Reiches*, OLA 222 (Leuven: Peeters, 2013).

he obviously could not be present in every temple of Egypt on every day, the priests would replace him. Many excerpts of this ritual are also found on papyri that were used in temples, most likely in liturgical capacities, but that also appear in funerary papyri that were designed to benefit the deceased.[2] Indeed, texts that are usually found in the temples appear to have been reused in funerary contexts, especially during the first millennium BCE.[3] Therefore, the distinction between texts used in the temples and those used in funerary contexts is a modern one, which remains heuristically helpful but does not necessarily reflect ancient Egyptian practices.

1.1.2. Funerary Texts in Ancient Egypt

Funerary texts are attested during a long period of ancient Egyptian history (see table 1.1): they were probably transmitted in an oral form since the first dynasties[4] and were then written down from the time of the Old Kingdom (from ca. 2350 for the *Pyramid Texts*) to the Roman period, with the last funerary papyri stemming from the second century CE. This amounts to a period of almost 2,600 years.

It is important to observe that the category of "funerary texts" is also a modern construction, which denotes all the texts written to help the deceased in the Afterlife. Jan Assmann was the first scholar who attempted to provide a comprehensive classification of these texts.[5] In his view, two categories can be distinguished:

---

2. See below §1.4.2.
3. See, for example, J. F. Quack, "Redaktion und Kodifizierung im spätzeitlichen Ägypten: Der Fall des Totenbuches," in *Die Textualisierung der Religion*, ed. J. Schaper, FAT 62 (Tübingen: Mohr Siebeck, 2009), 13; S. Vuilleumier, *Un rituel osirien en faveur de particuliers à l'époque ptolémaïque: Papyrus Princeton Pharaonic Roll 10*, Studien zur spätägyptischen Religion 15 (Wiesbaden: Harrassowitz, 2016); and the many articles in B. Backes and J. Dieleman, eds., *Liturgical Texts for Osiris and the Deceased in Late Period and Greco-Roman Egypt: Proceedings of the Colloquiums at New York (ISAW), 6 May 2011, and Freudenstadt, 18–21 July 2012*, Studien zur spätägyptischen Religion 14 (Wiesbaden: Harrassowitz, 2015).
4. B. Mathieu, "La distinction entre Textes des Pyramides et Textes des Sarcophages est-elle légitime?," in *D'un monde à l'autre: Textes des Pyramides et Textes des Sarcophages, Actes de la table ronde internationale "Textes des Pyramides versus Textes des Sarcophages" IFAO, 24–26 septembre 2001*, ed. S. Bickel and B. Mathieu, Bibliothèque d'Étude 139 (Cairo: Institut français d'archéologie orientale, 2004), 247–62 at 253–54 n. 13.
5. J. Assmann, *Mort et au-delà dans l'Egypte ancienne* (Monaco: Éditions du Rocher, 2003), 359–78. Assmann wrote many articles and books about this topic; see also J. Assmann, *Images et rites de la mort dans l'Egypte ancienne: L'apport des liturgies funéraires* (Paris: Cybèle, 2000); J. Assmann, *Altägyptische Totenliturgien*, vol. 1, *Totenliturgien in den Sargtexten des Mittleren Reiches*, Supplemente zu den Schriften der Heidelberger Akademie der Wissenschaften, Philosophisch-Historische Klasse 14 (Heidelberg: Universitätsverlag C. Winter, 2002); J. Assmann, *Altägyptische Totenliturgien*, vol. 2, *Totenliturgien und Totensprüche in Grabinschriften*

- The first category includes texts that were recited during the funerary cult and that Assmann defines as the "liturgies" or "mortuary liturgies" (*Totenliturgien*) and as the "artificial voice," because they accompany a specific act to be performed during the ritual, which is then also repeated in the tomb.
- The second category includes texts that helped the deceased in the Afterlife, consisting of what Assmann describes as "funerary literature" (*Totenliteratur*): they were not recited within the cult but were only used as an "artificial memory" or "magical knowledge." This means that simply knowing a given spell was sufficient for the deceased: it was not necessary that it be performed. In this case, some "liturgies" can also be considered to fall within the category of "funerary literature." According to Assmann, the *Book of the Dead* belongs to this category because it does not contain any liturgies.[6]

However, some scholars have questioned this distinction posited by Assmann. For example, in 2009 Mark Smith questioned the use of this terminology, noting that the distinction between "liturgies" and "funerary literature" is not always clear-cut, especially because—as already acknowledged by Assmann himself—liturgies can also be used for the Afterlife and not only in the cult.[7] Smith also highlighted the fact that written texts "abolish the temporal limitations of the spoken word and extend its effectiveness to infinity."[8] In effect, the very act of writing down, or copying, the texts makes them efficient, irrespective of whether, or not, these texts are actually recited.

Various Egyptologists have made similar remarks and raised related questions concerning these distinctions in a recent publication of the proceedings of two colloquiums on *Liturgical Texts for the Osiris and the Deceased in Late Period and Greco-Roman Egypt*.[9] Again, these essays stress that the distinction between "liturgies" and "funerary literature" is often unclear. Jacco Dieleman and Burkhard Backes, for example, question the term "liturgy" since it can imply

---

des Neuen Reiches, Supplemente zu den Schriften der Heidelberger Akademie der Wissenschaften, Philosophisch-Historische Klasse 17 (Heidelberg: Universitätsverlag C. Winter, 2005).

6. Assmann, *Mort et au-delà*, 376–77.

7. M. Smith, *Traversing Eternity: Texts for the Afterlife from Ptolemaic and Roman Egypt* (Oxford: Oxford University Press, 2009), 209–14.

8. Ibid., 210.

9. For example, D. Luft, "Funerär und liturgisch. Gedanken zur Verbindung von Inhalten, Funktionen und Verwendungsbereichen altägyptischer religiöser Texte," and M. Stadler, "Prätexte funerärer Rituale: Königsliturgie, Tempelliturgie, Totenliturgie," in *Liturgical Texts for Osiris and the Deceased in Late Period and Greco-Roman Egypt: Proceedings of the Colloquiums at New York (ISAW), 6 May 2011, and Freudenstadt, 18–21 July 2012*, ed. B. Backes and J. Dieleman, Studien zur spätägyptischen Religion 14 (Wiesbaden: Harrassowitz, 2015), 37–54 and 75–90 respectively.

a codified way of performing rituals.[10] They also emphasize the role that this category has played in the way modern scholars insert the *Book of the Dead* within the category of "funerary literature" as if it contained no liturgical element. New studies have demonstrated the problematic nature of the assumptions underlying Assmann's model. For instance, Daniela Luft has shown that formulae of the *Book of the Dead*, such as spell 128, have a clear cultic origin.[11] In fact, it is generally difficult to classify texts according to such categories—a point illustrated in this essay with aide of specific examples from the *Book of the Dead*.

1.1.3. Pyramid Texts and Coffin Texts

Before focusing on the *Book of the Dead*, it is important to highlight some very general considerations about the first funerary texts—namely, the *Pyramid Texts* and the *Coffin Texts*.[12] The earliest attested spells of the *Pyramid Texts* are found in the pyramid of Unas (in Saqqara), the last Pharaoh of the 5th Dynasty (2375–2345 BCE). The goal of these texts was to help the deceased King in his travel in the Afterlife.[13] Very schematically, *Coffins Texts* came to replace *Pyramid Texts* during the First Intermediate Period (2160–2055 BCE) and were

---

10. J. Dieleman and B. Backes, "Current Trends in the Study of Liturgical Papyri," in *Liturgical Texts for Osiris and the Deceased in Late Period and Greco-Roman Egypt: Proceedings of the Colloquiums at New York (ISAW), 6 May 2011, and Freudenstadt, 18–21 July 2012*, ed. B. Backes and J. Dieleman, Studien zur spätägyptischen Religion 14 (Wiesbaden: Harrassowitz, 2015), 1–13 at 2–3.
11. Ibid., 6–7; for spell 128, see Luft, "Funerär und liturgisch," esp. 51–53.
12. These titles are modern.
13. The origins of the *Pyramid Texts* have been much discussed, but nowadays there is a consensus that these texts were not composed during the time of Unas. As shown by Mathieu ("Distinction," 253–54), the tradition probably goes back to the 2nd Dynasty (ca. 2700 BCE), with spells being added over time. It should be noted that the choice of spells differs from one pyramid to another (J. Baines, "Modelling Sources, Processes, and Locations of Early Mortuary Texts," in *D'un monde à l'autre: Textes des Pyramides et Textes des Sarcophages, Actes de la table ronde internationale "Textes des Pyramides versus Textes des Sarcophages" IFAO, 24–26 septembre 2001*, ed. S. Bickel and B. Mathieu, Bibliothèque d'Étude 139 [Cairo: Institut français d'archéologie orientale, 2004], 15). These spells were certainly recited and their origins can vary widely (B. Mathieu, "Que sont les Textes des Pyramides?," *Égypte, Afrique et Orient* 12 [1999]: 16). Egyptologists generally agree that they were liturgical texts recited by a priest for the deceased (for example, see Assmann, *Mort et au-delà*, 359–65; L. Coulon, "Rhétorique et stratégies du discours dans les formules funéraires: Les innovations des Textes des Sarcophages," in *D'un monde à l'autre: Textes des Pyramides et Textes des Sarcophages, Actes de la table ronde internationale "Textes des Pyramides versus Textes des Sarcophages" IFAO, 24–26 septembre 2001*, ed. S. Bickel and B. Mathieu, Bibliothèque d'Étude 139 [Cairo: Institut français d'archéologie orientale, 2004], 122; J. P. Allen, *The Ancient Egyptian Pyramid Texts*, WAW 23 [Atlanta: Society of Biblical Literature; Leiden: Brill, 2005], 4). The use of written rituals afforded the possibility that the deceased might benefit from the spells for eternity (Baines, "Modelling Sources," 151), with a continuous effectiveness assured by its having been put in writing; see, for example, A. J. Morales, "Text-Building and Transmission of Pyramid Texts in the Third Millennium B.C.E.: Iteration, Objectification, and Change," *JANER* 15 (2015): 169–201 at 189, who considers their "performative nature." This "magic" value is certainly valid for all the

especially used by the elite during the Middle Kingdom (2055–1773 BCE), particularly on coffins. In reality, the process was probably still more complex,[14] as *Coffin Texts* include *Pyramid Texts* spells, as well as new spells.

However, the evidence is somewhat more complex than the table below may suggest. While copies of *Pyramid Texts* and *Coffin Texts* are mostly found during the Old and Middle Kingdoms, spells from these collections are also found in writings from later periods, as well as on various mediums (namely, papyri, tomb walls, coffins, etc.).[15]

1.2. The *Book of the Dead*

1.2.1. General Presentation

As in case of the transition from *Pyramid Texts* to *Coffins Texts*, the passage from *Coffin Texts* to *Book of the Dead* is not easy to delimit. At the end of the Second Intermediate Period (ca. 1600–1550 BCE), new texts were generally added to the core of the *Coffins Texts* and some spells were simultaneously changed. As argued by Alexandra von Lieven, many *Book of the Dead* spells probably had no funerary origin.[16]

The change of medium, from coffins to other kinds of material, such as papyri or walls of the tombs, should also be considered. As illustrated in table 1.1, *Book of the Dead* spells were used for a very long period, from the end of the Second Intermediate Period and the New Kingdom (ca. 1600–1550 BCE) to the Graeco-Roman Period, hence for more than 1,500 years.[17]

Despite their many versions, Egyptologists have long classified the *Book of the Dead* according to two main traditions: the so-called Theban redaction (New Kingdom, 1550–1069 BCE) and the so-called Saite redaction (Late and Ptolemaic Periods, 664–30 BCE). However, these redactions were identified without considering the gap of 400 years between these two periods—namely, the Third Intermediate Period (1069–664 BCE), a timeframe that has only been systematically studied in the course of the past fifteen years.

---

funerary texts (see, for example, J. H. Taylor, *Death and the Afterlife in Ancient Egypt* [London: The British Museum Press, 2001], 193).

14. Mathieu, "Distinction."

15. See most recently F. Scalf, "From the Beginning to the End: How to Generate and Transmit Funerary Texts in Ancient Egypt," *JANER* 15 (2015): 202–23 at 205, who reminds us of the attestation of *Pyramid Text* spells in the Roman period.

16. A. von Lieven, "Book of the Dead, Book of the Living: BD Spells as Temple Texts," *Journal of Egyptian Archaeology* 98 (2012): 249–67 at 265; see also Luft, "Funerär und liturgisch," 37–54.

17. Only extracts are used in the Roman period, with the *Book of Breathing* being generally preferred and coming to replace the *Book of the Dead*.

TABLE 1.1. Schematic Presentation of the Main Funerary Texts in Ancient Egypt

Modern division Manetho's division (dynasties)	Dates	Main funerary texts
Early Dynastic Period 1st–2nd Dynasties	3000–2686 BCE	Oral texts?
Old Kingdom 3rd–6th Dynasties	2686–2160 BCE	Oral texts *Pyramid Texts* (5th Dynasty)
First Intermediate Period 7th–11th Dynasties	2160–2055 BCE	*Pyramid Texts* *Coffin Texts*
Middle Kingdom 11th–12th Dynasties	2055–1773 BCE	*Coffin Texts*
Second Intermediate Period 13th–17th Dynasties	1773–1550 BCE	*Coffin Texts* *Book of the Dead*
New Kingdom 18th–20th Dynasties	1550–1069 BCE	*Book of the Dead* Other funerary compositions (*Amduat, Book of the Gates, Book of Caverns, Book of the Earth* …)
Third Intermediate Period 21st–25th Dynasties	1069–664 BCE	
Late Period 26th–30th Dynasties	664–332 BCE	
Alexander the Great **Ptolemaic Period**	332–30 BCE	Many rituals for the deceased *Book of Breathing*
Roman Period	30 BCE–395 CE	*Book of the Dead* (extracts) *Book of Breathing* *Embalming Ritual* Other funerary compositions

In order to understand why scholars focused their interest for so many years on these two traditions—namely, the "Theban" and "Saite" redactions—for the *Book of the Dead* and thereby neglected traditions from other periods, it is important to return to the first edition of the *Book of the Dead* by Richard Lepsius in 1842, which included the publication of a papyrus from the Ptolemaic Period.[18] Lepsius gave the title *Todtenbuch* to his study—this is why we now call this corpus *Totenbuch* in German, *Book of the Dead* in English, and *Livre des Morts* in French. But this is not the title given to this collection of texts by the ancient Egyptians, which was in fact *Spells for Going Out in Daylight*. This

18. P. Turin 1791; R. Lepsius, *Das Todtenbuch der Ägypter nach dem hieroglyphischen Papyrus in Turin* (Leipzig: Wigand, 1842).

already suggests that the text preserves "spells" or "formulae," and also gives us a clear indication of the main goal of this collection of texts for the deceased in antiquity—namely, to go out of the tomb, mainly in order to receive the offerings and thereby "live" in the Afterlife.

Lepsius also numbered the spells from 1 to 165—a numbering system that has been subsequently adopted by modern scholars. This system is useful because it assigns the same number to each spell irrespective of the particular tradition in which it is attested. However, it represents, at best, the so-called Saite redaction that was in use in the Late and Ptolemaic Periods (664–30 BCE) but hardly corresponds to other versions or redactions. Lepsius's system has also played a key role in supporting the idea of a "standard" *Book of the Dead*—a notion that has increasingly been acknowledged to be problematic (see below point 1.5). Gradually, scholars have also turned their attention to the copies of the *Book of the Dead* from the New Kingdom, because of their good quality and number; these papyri were then grouped under the designation of "Theban" redaction, which is parallel to the "Saite" redaction from the Late and Ptolemaic Periods.

In reality, what is now called the *Book of the Dead* consisted of more than 200 spells, which are never found all together in a single version.[19] They are a miscellany of spells, gathered to help the deceased in his or her travel. They originated—as already indicated—as spells of the *Coffin Texts*, as well as new spells.

1.2.2. Structure of a Spell

Spells in the *Book of the Dead* often present the same structure. The main characteristics are:

- the title, which begins with "Spell for *(r n)* ...";
- followed by "Words spoken by (*dd mdw in*)" and the name of the deceased;
- the content of the spell; and
- at the end of the spell, a rubric (also called "postscript") sometimes gives a practical explanation about what has to be known or done. This point is very interesting, because it gives us precious information about practical aspects that could help us determine what was considered to be a ritual.[20]

---

19. Some spells have no number. For a good overview of virtually all the spells, see the recent translation of S. Quirke, *Going Out in Daylight—prt m hrw: The Ancient Egyptian Book of the Dead*, GHP Egyptology 20 (London: Golden House, 2013).

20. See also von Lieven, "Book of the Dead," 265 n. 62, concerning the use of the postscripts. As she stated, a complete study on the rubrics is missing and remains to be done. There are not only indications of practical aspects but also references to the origin of some spells; for example, the origin of spell 30B is supposed to be from the time of Pharaoh Mykerinos of the 4th Dynasty (2532–2503 BCE).

However, this structure is not attested in all instances, as a rubric has not always been written. The length can also be very different from one formula to another, extending from some lines or columns to several sheets of papyrus.

1.2.3. Spells in the Book of the Dead: *The Importance of Knowing a Spell*

The importance of knowing a spell is frequently mentioned in the rubrics of the *Book of the Dead*—for instance, in the following two examples from spells 58 and 68.[21]

> BD 58
> Title: "**Formula for breathing air and having power over water in** the god's land"
> Rubric: "**Anyone who knows this formula, can enter after going out in the god's land.**"[22]

> BD 68
> Title: "**Formula for going out in the day**"
> Rubric: "**Whoever knows this book**[23] **will go out by day, and walk on earth among the living, and has not perished forever. A matter a million times true.**"[24]

These spells were probably not recited during a ritual but were written to give power over elements or entities to the deceased, in this case to the benefit of water or air (BD 58), or more generally to go out (BD 68). Knowing a spell—or the names of frightening entities in other BD spells—was enough to assure its effectiveness. Thus, they have in common the performative aspect: being put in writing was an important mechanism for "activating" the text so that it could be used in the Afterlife by the deceased. These kinds of spells were not performed rituals but rather can be linked to the "funerary literature," as per the category set out by Assmann.

Let us now consider spell 1 of the *Book of the Dead*, which concerns the burial. The spell begins like this:

---

21. Modern conventions for the translation: bold text refers to a text written in red in the papyrus; "N." means "Name," instead of giving the name of the deceased owner of the papyrus. "BD" in English, "Tb" in German, and "LdM" in French are the common, abbreviated ways of referring to a spell.
22. P. BM EA 10470 (Ani), 19th Dynasty, ca. 1275 BCE, translation Quirke, *Going Out in Daylight*, 143.
23. Lit. "papyrus-roll" (Lenzo).
24. P. BM EA 10477 (Nu), 18th Dynasty, ca. 1400 BCE, translation Quirke, *Going Out in Daylight*, 166–67.

FIGURE 1.1. P. BM EA 10470, sheet 6. BD 1, Ani, 19th Dynasty, ca. 1275 BCE. Photo © The Trustees of the British Museum.

> [1,1] Beginning of the formulae for going out in daylight, to rise up and to glorify in the necropolis, what is said on the day of the burial. Enter after going out by the Osiris N. Words spoken ... [25]

The indication "what is said on the day of the burial" seems to mean, on the face of it, that this text should be recited during the burial. And if we consider the vignette that accompanies the text, it seems that it corresponds to a real burial ending with the lector-priest who recited the ritual and the priests who opened the mouth of the mummy (fig. 1.1).

But if we consider the end of the same spell, the rubric, we can get a different impression.

> **As for anyone who knows this papyrus-roll upon earth,[2,8] or who puts it in writing for a burial, he will go out every day he has wished and enter this place[2,9] without being detained.**
> **Bread, beer and a great portion of meat are given to him on the offerings table of Ra and his grant of land in the Marsh[2,10] of Reeds. Barley**

---

25. P. Greenfield, 21st Dynasty, ca. 950 BCE, my translation.

and emmer are given to him there, so that he will be prosperous as he is upon earth.[26]

The important aspect is found at the beginning of the part that reads, "As for anyone *who knows* this papyrus-roll upon earth, *or who puts it in writing* for a burial." The idea of knowledge and of putting in writing reveals that this was what was most important: it had to be written somewhere in order to be efficient. As indicated above, it was enough simply to know a spell in order to ensure its efficacy. The question then arises: does this mean that the ritual was performed with the burial? And if this was indeed the case, was it performed in the manner indicated in BD 1? In trying to answer these questions, let us focus on the last phase of the burial procession, namely, the opening of the mouth performed on the mummy before it entered the tomb, as we can see in the papyrus of Ani (fig. 1.1).[27]

If we compare the structure of the tomb as it appears in the papyri with the archaeological remains, we can see that the two match: the superstructure served as the chapel where the offering for the deceased was made, while the burial chamber was underground (a space that is usually not represented in the papyri). While this observation does not prove that the ritual was effectively performed as it is described in the funerary text, it may nonetheless present a first indication that there was at least some degree of continuity between the ritual performed and the ritual described, at least during the New Kingdom (1550–1069 BCE).[28] This means that the performative aspect involved in the written text did not exclude the possibility that the ritual described actually took place. Nonetheless, irrespective of whether or not the ritual described was actually performed, knowledge of the spell by the deceased was in any case sufficient for his or her travel in the Afterlife.

1.3. Evolution of the *Book of the Dead* During the New Kingdom (1550–1069 BCE) and the Third Intermediate Period (1069–664 BCE)

The New Kingdom and the Third Intermediate Period are considered first, because the evolution of the texts during this time affords us precious information

---

26. P. Greenfield, 21st Dynasty, ca. 950 BCE, my translation.
27. Another example is the papyrus of Hunefer (P. BM EA 9901, 19th Dynasty), J. H. Taylor, *Journey Through the Afterlife: Ancient Egyptian Book of the Dead* (London: The British Museum, 2010), 94–95.
28. As argued, for example, by Taylor (ibid., 191). The question is more complicated for other periods, such as the Third Intermediate Period (1069–664 BCE), for which there is no longer clear attestation of chapels where the ritual could be performed.

concerning the possible pragmatic function of these texts in ritual practice (issues concerning the "Saite" redaction are addressed below, point 1.5).[29]

1.3.1. The "Theban" Redaction (New Kingdom, 1550–1069 BCE)

The *Book of the Dead* papyri that stem from this period are in cursive hieroglyphs and are long, about 15–30 m, with an average length of 20 m. They possess many vignettes, most of the time in color, which illustrate the content of the spells. Many versions of the book are preserved from this period, as opposed to a single tradition. Spells have been gathered in groups according to one or more themes that are called "sequences." Scholars have emphasized the coexistence of different traditions in their analysis of the text during this time.[30]

1.3.2. The Book of the Dead *in the Third Intermediate Period (1069–664 BCE)*

The passage from the New Kingdom to the Third Intermediate Period is marked by a political, social, and economic crisis, which had a number of consequences for funerary beliefs.[31] In Thebes, tombs are no longer decorated, and the objects that they contain are no more those of daily life, as they had been before. But one of the most important changes is the use of collective tombs (also called "cachettes" in modern literature),[32] as well as the reuse of ancient tombs, rather than individual or family tombs as were used before. This usage continues until the Late and Ptolemaic Periods.[33]

---

29. The use of the term "Theban" is due to the fact that the capital of Egypt during the 18th Dynasty (first dynasty of the New Kingdom) was Thebes.

30. The different sequences in the papyri of the New Kingdom have been studied by I. Munro, *Untersuchungen zu den Totenbuch-Papyri der 18. Dynastie: Kriterien ihrer Datierung* (London: Kegan Paul International, 1988); G. Lapp, *The Papyrus of Nu (BM EA 10477)*, Catalogue of the Books of the Dead in the British Museum 1 (London: The British Museum Press, 1997); G. Lapp, *The Papyrus of Nebseni (BM EA 9900)*, Catalogue of the Books of the Dead in the British Museum 3 (London: The British Museum Press, 2004).

31. Concerning these changes see J.-L. De Cenival, "Hors catalogue ou, comment les objets ordinaires accumulés peu à peu dans un musée complètent le tableau qu'on déduirait des chefs-d'œuvre exposés ici," in *Tanis, l'or des pharaons* (Paris: Ministère des Affaires Étrangères / Association Française d'Action Artistique, 1987), 273–80.

32. The most famous "cachette" is the Royal Cachette of Deir el-Bahari (officially discovered in 1881), which contained the hidden mummies of the Pharaohs of the New Kingdom as well as the members of the family of the High Priest of Amun of the Karnak Temple during the 21st Dynasty. The other famous collective tomb is the Second Cachette of Deir el-Bahari, or Bab el-Gasus Cachette (discovered in 1891), with 153 priests and priestesses of Karnak having been buried there.

33. In the North, such as in Memphis or Tanis, tombs are decorated, but most of the time they are collective tombs.

The lack of decoration on the walls of the tombs is, in a certain way, replaced by new and rich compositions on coffins and papyri. Funerary papyri are very frequent and many traditions can be linked to the *Book of the Dead*. In this period hieratic is frequently used instead of hieroglyphs (hieroglyphs are attested only during the 21st Dynasty). And while long papyri of about 6–18 m are still in use during the 21st Dynasty, they are mostly replaced by very short papyri measuring between 1–3 m, probably since the time of the High Priest of Amun Pinedjem II (ca. 988–966 BCE). Vignettes are also different: there is often only one "opening" vignette with a scene of adoration of Osiris or another deity by the deceased (fig. 1.2);[34] or a papyrus can be composed of vignettes alone (what Egyptologists called "mythological" or "Amduat" papyri, see fig. 1.3). The specificity is the choice of which vignettes, spells, and rituals were to be used according to the principle of *pars pro toto* (part for the whole).[35] The choices reflected in the different traditions inform us about the most important beliefs and rituals at a given time.

1.4. Rituals in the *Book of the Dead* During the New Kingdom (1550–1069 BCE) and the Third Intermediate Period (1069–664 BCE)

Observing the changes in the funerary beliefs during these two periods can be a useful means of determining whether or not these texts were really used in ritual performance. Two examples can be highlighted to illustrate this point: first, the protection of the mummy with protective bricks (BD 151 d–g) and amulet spells (BD 155–156–157–158–159), and second, the rituals for the deceased and rituals for the gods.

---

34. See G. Lenzo, "La vignette initiale dans les papyrus funéraires de la Troisième Période intermédiaire," *Bulletin de la Société d'Égyptologie, Genève* 26 (2004): 43–62.

35. A. Niwiński (*Studies on the Illustrated Theban Funerary Papyri of the 11th and 10th Centuries B.C.*, OBO 86 [Göttingen: Vandenhoeck & Ruprecht, 1989]) was the first to present the different traditions in the funerary papyri of this period. For a recent presentation, see G. Lenzo, "The Book of the Dead in the Third Intermediate Period," in *The Oxford Handbook of the Egyptian Book of the Dead*, ed. R. Lucarelli and M. Stadler (Oxford: Oxford University Press, forthcoming). R. Lucarelli has highlighted one of the traditions of the 21st Dynasty through the study of the long papyrus of the priestess Gatseshen (P. Cairo JE 95838; R. Lucarelli, *The Book of the Dead of Gatseshen: Ancient Egyptian Funerary Religion in the 10th Century B.C.*, Egyptologische Uitgaven 21 [Leiden: Nederlands Instituut voor het Nabije Oosten, 2006]). I have discussed the abbreviated *Book of the Dead* of this period (G. Lenzo, *Manuscrits hiératiques du Livre des Morts de la Troisième Période intermédiaire [Papyrus de Turin CGT 53001–53013]*, Catalogo del Museo Egizio di Torino, Serie seconda—Collezioni 6 / Cahiers de la Société d'Égyptologie, Genève 8 [Genève: Société d'Égyptologie, 2007]). Nevertheless, many other traditions still need to be analyzed in detail.

FIGURE 1.2. P. New York MMA 25.3.32. Book of the Dead of Gatsesehn, 21st Dynasty, ca. 1000 BCE. Photo: Metropolitan Museum of Art, New York, http://www.metmuseum.com.

FIGURE 1.3. P. New York MMA 25.3.31. "Mythological" or "Amduat" papyrus of Gatsesehn, 21st Dynasty, ca. 1000 BCE. Photo: Metropolitan Museum of Art, New York, http://www.metmuseum.com.

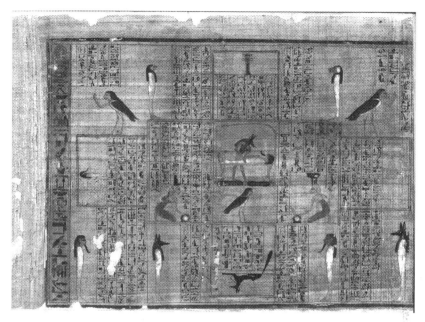

FIGURE 1.4. P. BM EA 10010, sheet 5. BD 151, Muthetepty, 21st Dynasty, ca. 1050 BCE. Photo © The Trustees of the British Museum.

1.4.1. The Protection of the Mummy: Protective Bricks (BD 151 d–g) and Amulet Spells (BD 155–156–157–158–159)

The first interesting example is found in the spells linked with the protection of the mummy: the protective bricks (BD 151 d–g) and the amulet spells (BD 155–156–157–158–159). In these cases, we have the opportunity to compare the content of the text with the archaeological context (tombs, objects, mummies), which can help us consider whether, and in what way, the written ritual corresponds to reality.

1.4.1.1. BD 151 d–g

BD 151 is about the protection of the mummy and the use of protective bricks, as is attested, for example, in a papyrus of the 21st Dynasty (fig. 1.4).[36]

---

36. B. Lüscher, *Untersuchungen zu Totenbuch Spruch 151*, Studien zum Altägyptischen Totenbuch 2 (Wiesbaden: Harrassowitz, 1998); I. Régen, "When a Book of the Dead Text Does Not Match Archaeology: The Case of the Protective Magical Bricks (BD 151)," *British Museum Studies in Ancient Egypt and Sudan* 15 (2010): 267–78, http://www.britishmuseum.org/research/online_journals/bmsaes/issue_15/regen.aspx.

FIGURE 1.5. Bricks BM EA 41544–41545–41546–41547. 19th Dynasty, ca. 1250 BCE. Photo © The Trustees of the British Museum.

In the middle of the scene, Anubis is preparing the mummy. To protect the mummy, four bricks were placed in the four cardinal points of the burial room, each brick bearing a figurine: a mummiform figurine for the North, a torch figurine for the South, a *djed*-pilar figurine for the West and an Anubis figurine for the East. Rubrics in this spell are very useful in understanding what has to be done, as, for example, the one for the mummiform figurine.

> This spell is to be said over an unbaked clay brick on which this spell has been carved. Make a niche for in the walls of the netherworld and set an image of *ima*-wood 7 digits high, whose mouth has been opened, firmly on this brick on the northern wall, its face toward the south, and cover its face.[37]

Bricks like this have been found in the tombs, which amounts to proof that the ritual was indeed performed in reality (fig. 1.5). However, the question remains as to whether the ritual was performed in exactly the same way as is indicated in the written spell. The title of Isabelle Régen's article provides a clear answer: the evidence for actual practice does not consistently match the written rituals.[38] In effect, she highlighted many differences between the two:[39]

---

37. P. Turin inv. suppl. 8438 (Kha), 18th Dynasty, ca. 1360 BCE, translation Régen, "When a Book of the Dead," 269.
38. Régen, "When a Book of the Dead." See also C. Theis, "Wenn Archäologie und Philologie nicht harmonieren: Magische Ziegel, ihre Nischen und Totenbuchspruch 151d–g," *Zeitschrift für ägyptische Sprache und Altertumskunde* 143 (2015): 85–95, who considers more attestations and has similar conclusions, and Scalf, "Beginning to the End," 208 n. 20, with a complete bibliography.
39. Régen, "When a Book of the Dead," 273.

- spells can be painted and are not always carved on the brick;
- fired bricks are sometimes used instead of unbaked clay brick;
- amulets can be drawn instead of being physically present on the brick;
- five bricks instead of four have been found in the tomb of Tutankhamun;
- two bricks with Anubis have been found in the tomb of Amenhotep II (one with the text of the torch);
- bricks have not always been found in a niche, but also on the floor; and, finally,
- the position linked with the cardinal points does not always correspond to reality.

Régen also tries to explain these differences, concluding that the written version of BD 151 is an "ideal application of the ritual."[40] Rituals were adapted with time but the written version remained unchanged.

If we compare this with the Third Intermediate Period, we find that this spell is sometimes attested.[41] In one case, we have both the vignette with the bricks and the archaeological context: in fact a papyrus from the end of the 21st Dynasty comes from the Second Cachette of Deir el-Bahari discovered in 1891, and no bricks were found in this tomb.[42]

Thus, archaeological evidence confirms that BD 151 was indeed performed during the New Kingdom,[43] but not in exactly the same way as is suggested by its written form. Moreover, during the Third Intermediate Period, the written text was in use but may not always have been performed. For example, we do not know for sure if chapels where the other rituals could be performed were still in use. Thus, its effectiveness was given through the papyrus itself, as opposed to its actual practice.

1.4.1.2. The Amulet Spells BD 155–159

The amulet spells were also used for the protection of the mummy, and a comparison between texts and objects is also possible due to the spells BD 155–159.[44] Listed in table 1.2 are the spells, the amulet to which they refer, the material with

---

40. Ibid.
41. Sixteen attestations are registered in the database of the *Totenbuch-Projekt* of the University of Bonn, http://totenbuch.awk.nrw.de.
42. P. Cairo S.R. VII 10653, unpublished, short description only in A. Niwiński, *Studies on the Illustrated Theban Funerary Papyri*, Cairo 106, 290–91. 153 priests and priestesses of Karnak were buried in the Second Cachette of Deir el-Bahari (or Bab el-Gasus Cachette) discovered in 1891. About the "cachettes," see above n. 32.
43. See the list of bricks found in Theis, "Archäologie und Philologie," 88; they all date from the New Kingdom.
44. Marie Vandenbeusch (British Museum) is currently studying the position of the amulets on the mummies; I thank her for discussions on this topic and her suggestions.

TABLE 1.2. Amulet Spells BD 155–159

Spell	Amulet	Material according to the spell	Place on the mummy according to the spell
BD 155	*Djed*-pillar	Gold	Neck
BD 156	Isis-knot	Red jasper[a]	Neck
BD 157	Vulture	Gold	Neck
BD 158	Broad-collar	Gold	Neck
BD 159	*Wadj*-pillar	Green stone[b]	Neck

[a]Jasper was used to render the blood of Isis mentioned in the spell.
[b]The *wadj*-pillar has a papyrus form, *wadj* means "papyrus" as well as "to be green, to flourish," which explains the green color of the amulet.

which the amulet should be made, and the place on the mummy's person where the amulet should be worn, all according to the spell. Most of the time, amulets are required to be made of gold and to be placed on the neck of the deceased.

1.4.1.3. Example of the Structure of a Spell: BD 155

> Formula for **a *djed*-pillar of gold.**
> Words spoken by N.:
> Raise yourself, Osiris, to set yourself on your side, as I place water under you. I have brought you a *djed*-pillar of gold, over which rejoice.
> **Words spoken over a *djed*-pillar of gold, strung on sycamore fibres, placed at the neck of a transfigured spirit, on the day of burial.
> Anyone at whose neck this amulet is placed, shall be an excellent transfigured spirit, one who is** in the god's land, **the day of the first of the year, like Those who are in the Following of** Osiris.
> **A matter a million times true.**[45]

Now, if we consider the vignettes that accompany these spells, we can indeed observe that they sometimes correspond to the text—for example, in the papyrus of Nakht, the Isis-knot is red and the *djed*-pillar is yellow for gold (fig. 1.6). But sometimes they are drawn in different colors.[46] And if we go further by looking at the physical amulets that were found on the mummies, it seems that the ones in gold are in fact rare, probably because they were expensive. While the redknot was usually in red jasper, the other amulets were often made of another, less

45. P. BM EA 10477 (Nu), ca. 1400 BCE, translation Quirke, *Going Out in Daylight*, 385.
46. For example, P. BM EA 10470 (Ani, 19th Dynasty), see Taylor, *Journey Through the Afterlife*, 128.

FIGURE 1.6. P. BM EA 10473, extract sheet 15. BD 155–156, Nakht, 18th Dynasty, ca. 1300 BCE. Photo © The Trustees of the British Museum.

expensive material, such as the *djed*-pillars that are often in faience, sometimes gilded with gold. But we also must note that the material used is also difficult to determine when scanning the mummies, and the topic needs to be studied more extensively.

Finally, what can we say if we check the position of the amulets directly on the mummies? An interesting example is the mummy of Tutankhamun. Here we find amulets on the neck of the King, some of which are made of gold, such as the *djed*-pillar for Tutankhamun;[47] however, others are made of faience or only gilded with gold.

While museums across the globe possess hundreds of amulets, the provenance of these objects is usually ignored once they have been removed from

---

47. For the amulets on the neck of Tutankhamun, see the archive of the Griffith Institute in Oxford, http://www.griffith.ox.ac.uk/gri/carter/256-p0774a.html; for the *djed*-pillar amulet in gold, compare http://www.griffith.ox.ac.uk/gri/carter/256kk-p0835.html.

their original context. Indeed, the wrappings of the first mummies were taken away without any consideration of the precise position of the amulets on the mummies' bodies. But with new technology, it is now possible to scan the mummies, without destroying them, to see where the amulets were positioned and to compare this with where the texts state that they should be worn.

New, innovative investigations of the mummies have been undertaken by the British Museum as part of the exhibition "Ancient Lives, New Discoveries: Eight Mummies, Eight Stories" in 2014. The preliminary result is very interesting: amulets were not worn where they were supposed to; this can be seen, for example, with the mummy of Tamut of the 22nd Dynasty (ca. 800 BCE), on which amulets were positioned on the abdomen and one on the neck (as opposed to all at the neck where they were all supposed to be according to the BD spells) and were not made of gold.[48]

There is even a late *Book of the Dead* with a visual representation of where the amulets were supposed to be on the mummy. Yet the evidence listed above suggests that this is an ideal positioning that does not correspond to reality.[49] We can also suggest that this practice does not always correspond to the ideal but depends rather on other considerations, such as the financial means of the family of the deceased or the techniques of the various workshops of embalmers. Moreover, the evolution of the practices was not necessarily reported in the texts. What was written was ritually efficient, not on account of its exact resemblance of what was actually performed but by its mere existence as a text. It seems that these spells with practical aspects are not to be considered as "funerary literature" but as rituals or liturgies if we return to the term used by Assmann.[50]

1.4.2. Rituals for the Deceased and Rituals for the Gods

The final examples are spells that do not come from the traditional repertoire of the *Book of the Dead* but whose origins may be found in other contexts.[51]

---

48. For the mummy of Tamut BM EA 22939, see J. H. Taylor and D. Antoine, *Ancient Lives, New Discoveries: Eight Mummies, Eight Stories* (London: The British Museum Press, 2014), 67–91; D. Antoine and M. Vandenbeusch, with J. H. Taylor, *Egyptian Mummies: Exploring Ancient Lives* (Sydney: Museum of Applied Art and Sciences, 2016), 54–81. Marie Vandenbeusch considers that the amulets were probably also placed where the embalmer wanted them to be, following other criteria than those that are in the BD spells (personal communication).

49. P. BM EA 10098, Ptolemaic Period. See C. Andrews, *Amulets of Ancient Egypt* (London: The British Museum Press, 1994), 8 fig. 2.

50. On the amulets and the rituals, see in this volume the contribution by D. K. Falk about the *tefillin* phylacteries found at Qumran, which were worn as amulets, and compare also C. Frevel's essay in the context of the *Ketef Hinnom* silver scrolls used as amulets.

51. In this part, we do not consider spells of the *Book of the Dead* that have been carved on the walls of the temple. For this topic, see the comprehensive article of von Lieven, "Book of the Dead," 249–67. She also highlighted the fact that many spells do not have a funerary origin (265).

The first example is the *Book of the Dead* of Queen Nedjmet, from the beginning of the 21st Dynasty (ca. 1050 BCE).[52] In the middle of the spells we find one that is not attested in any other papyrus. This spell clearly has a ritual origin, as can be seen in its opening statement.

Beginning of the new spell in P. Nedjmet:
IX,1 Instructions: Spell for bringing the garland of triumph during the *wag*-feast in *Upeqer*, the first month of the *akhet*-season, (day) 4.[53]

The title—with the mention of the "instructions"—indicates that the ritual was performed by a priest during the *wag*-feast in Abydos linked with Osiris. The title is then followed by the acts that the priest of Harendotes (lit. "Horus-protector-of-his-father") should perform before reciting the spell. The content informs us that the main goal of the spell was to repel the enemies of the god. Besides this document, the existence of this ritual is attested on a statue of a priest of Osiris and Harendotes Wennefer of the 19th Dynasty, which indicates that he performed the ritual.[54] Finally, garlands of flowers have been found on coffins or mummies. Taken together, this evidence suggests that the ritual mentioned in the spell of P. Nedjmet could correspond to a real practice.[55]

In the papyrus of Nedjmet, the speech as well as the acts of the priest of Harendotes (for example, purifications and offerings) serve to ensure triumph over one's enemies—namely, over the serpent Apophis for Ra, and over Seth for Osiris. At the end, the deceased is named in the ritual in order to repel her enemies in the Afterlife. This part was probably added for the specific funerary context and was certainly not performed for Nedjmet. Its presence can be explained when we examine the spells in their entirety. Their selection shows a parallel between the journey of the deceased and the travel of the sun and its meeting with Osiris, with the triumph over the enemies fitting perfectly within

---

52. P. BM EA 10490, found in the Royal Cachette of Deir el-Bahari in the 1870s, bought by the British consul in Egypt Edward Stanton, and acquired by the British Museum in 1894. About the papyrus, see Taylor, *Journey Through the Afterlife*, 234, 271; G. Lenzo, "The Two Funerary Papyri of Queen Nedjmet (P. BM EA 10490 and P. BM EA 10541 + Louvre E. 6258)," *British Museum Studies in Ancient Egypt and Sudan* 15 (2010): 63–83, http://www.britishmuseum.org/research/online_journals/bmsaes/issue_15/lenzo.asp. About the cachette, see above n. 32.

53. P. BM EA 10490, 21st Dynasty, ca. 1050 BCE, my translation.

54. Statue Louvre A 66; the links between the statue and the papyrus have been given by P. Derchain, "La couronne de justification. Essai d'analyse d'un rite ptolémaïque," *Chronique d'Egypte* 30 (1955): 235–37. For a photo of the statue, see http://cartelfr.louvre.fr/cartelfr/visite?srv=car_not_frame&idNotice=19050.

55. As, for example, on those of the Pharaohs of the New Kingdom, whose garlands have been recently rediscovered at the University of Zurich and exhibited at the Laténium of Neuchâtel in 2013; see the catalogue by C. Jacquat and I. Rogger, *Fleurs des Pharaons. Parures funéraires en Egypte antique* (Hauterive: Laténium, 2013).

the overall theme. Indeed, it is a logical step in her travel in the Hereafter and is perfectly adapted to the whole sequence of spells, as shown by Lenzo.[56] Ph. Derchain has also shown that this spell was the origin of the ritual for the offering of the crown of triumph in the temples of the Ptolemaic Period, serving in this case to repel the enemies of the temples.[57]

Another example is given by the Greenfield Papyrus. As indicated above (§1.3), during the Third Intermediate Period, papyri were mostly very short. However, the Greenfield Papyrus, from the end of the 21st Dynasty (ca. 950 BCE), presents a notable exception. At 37 meters in length and divided today into 96 sheets, it is the longest known funerary papyrus. It contains *Book of the Dead* spells as well as other original funerary compositions.[58]

Following more or less traditional *Book of the Dead* spells, 14 sheets contain several hymns and litanies for different forms of the sun (Ra, Ra-Horakhty, Ra-Atum, Atum) and for Osiris. Such kinds of texts are often attested in this context, but it is unusual to find them in such a large number.[59] Assmann suggested that it constitutes a liturgical section, in that it was probably recited during the rituals to the gods.[60] Indeed, some of these texts are also present in other contexts,[61] as is the case of an extract of the offering ritual[62] which is reused at

---

56. Hypotheses for the presence of this new spell are explained in G. Lenzo, "Two Funerary Papyri of Queen Nedjmet," 70–74; G. Lenzo, "Les papyrus funéraires des 21ème–22ème dynasties et les liens avec les textes gravés sur les parois des tombes et des temples," in *Schrift und Material: Praktische Verwendung religiöser Text- und Bildträger als Artefakte im Alten*, ed. J. F. Quack and D. C. Luft, Orientalische Religionen in der Antike 41 (Tübingen: Mohr Siebeck, 2021), 207–34.

57. Derchain, "Couronne de justification."

58. P. BM EA 10554, found in the Royal Cachette of Deir el-Bahari in the 1870s, was bought by Herbert Greenfield and then donated to the British Museum in 1910 by Edith Mary Greenfield. It was then quickly presented to modern scholars thanks to the publication of Budge in 1912. See E. A. W. Budge, *The Greenfield Papyrus in the British Museum* (London: British Museum, 1912). Since then, numerous publications have been devoted to different parts of the document. It has recently, in 2010, been exhibited in its entirety at the British Museum and then also in Japan, in 2012, during the *Book of the Dead* exhibition. See the catalogues of Taylor, *Journey Through the Afterlife*, and, for the Japanese version, which contains photos of the entire papyrus, J. H. Taylor and J. Kondo, eds., *Ancient Egyptian Book of the Dead, Journey Through the Afterlife* (Tokyo: Asahi Shimbun / NHK / NHK Promotions, 2012). I thank the colleagues of the British Museum Neal Spencer, Ilona Regulski, John Taylor, and the former curator Richard Parkinson, for their kind help and for granting me access to the papyrus. I also wish to thank Matthieu Pellet (University of Lausanne) for his help with the catalogue in Japanese.

59. P. Greenfield, sheets 64–78; see C. Zaluskowski, *Texte außerhalb der Totenbuch-Tradierung in Pap. Greenfield* (Bonn: Friedrich-Wilhelms-Universität, 1996); Quirke, *Going Out in Daylight*, 564–80.

60. J. Assmann, *Liturgische Lieder an den Sonnengott: Untersuchungen zur altägyptischen Hymnik I*, Münchner Ägyptologische Studien 19 (Berlin: Hessling, 1969), 24, 165; D. Luft, "Funerär und liturgisch," 38.

61. Details in Lenzo, "Papyrus funéraires."

62. P. Greenfield, sheet 68; for examples of the episode 28 of the offering ritual, see Tacke, *Opferritual*, 84–85.

the end of a litany for Ra-Horakhty: in this case again, the text perfectly suits the overall context of this part of the prayer.

But in this case we have strong indications that these rituals were in fact performed. Specifically, if we observe the many titles of the owner of the Greenfield Papyrus, three of them can help us understand the probable context for the usage of these texts. Nestanebetisheru—daughter of the High Priest of Amun Pinedjem II—was in fact "The first leader-in-chief of musicians of Amun-Ra, king of the gods" and "Singer of the chorus of Mut, the great, mistress of Isheru." She was therefore the superior of the musicians and singers who performed texts, hymns, and liturgies recited during the rituals in the Karnak Temple. We can wonder, as does S. Quirke, whether the texts were chosen because they were used in the rituals for which Nestanebetisheru was responsible,[63] and perhaps even personally selected by her. She was also "Servant of the inventory/lists of Amun-Ra, king of the gods," which probably means that she had access to the archives where rituals were kept.

In the case of the Greenfield Papyrus, we can therefore suggest that the personal interest of the owner influenced the choice of the texts. Furthermore, she was probably willing to include the Afterlife rituals that she performed during her life as priestess in the Karnak Temple.[64]

This use of rituals for the gods in funerary papyri became increasingly popular during the first millennium BCE and further increased during the Ptolemaic Period. This point has been a focus of recent scholarly discussion,[65] and these new studies allow us to better understand the funerary texts.

1.5. The "Saite" Redaction of the *Book of the Dead*: A Canonized Version?

While these new arrangements of texts are common in the later periods, the *Book of the Dead* spells also underwent an important change at the same time. At the end of the 25th Dynasty or the beginning of the 26th Dynasty (ca. 700–650 BCE), there was a clear willingness to put the spells in a certain order, probably according to the priests' decisions,[66] in what has been described by

---

63. Quirke, *Going Out in Daylight*, 564. Budge (*Greenfield Papyrus*, xxiv) was the first to suggest this explanation.

64. Another well-known ritual in a funerary papyrus of the 21st Dynasty, which is later attested in the Ptolemaic Temple of Edfu, is in the Papyrus of Gatseshen (P. Cairo JE 95838). See Lucarelli, *Book of the Dead of Gatseshen*, 175–81.

65. Smith, *Traversing Eternity*; more recently, the studies in Backes and Dieleman, *Liturgical Texts*; Vuilleumier, *Rituel osirien*.

66. For the "canonized" version, see Quack, "Redaktion und Kodifizierung," esp. 22–26. He shows, for example, how the spells during the "Saite" redaction have been arranged together according

Egyptologists as the "Saite" redaction.[67] In this redaction, the many traditions of the Third Intermediate Period are no longer in use. After the use of hieratic only during at least the 22nd and 23rd Dynasties, cursive hieroglyphs were adopted again, as well as long papyri and many vignettes. The order of the spell corresponds to the numbering of Lepsius 1–165. It is therefore possible that there was a kind of standardization, with the position of the spells often being the same, and displaying a certain level of organization that was not evident in the prior periods. A question remains, however, as to whether this can be properly considered a "canonized" version.

In particular, not all of the spells are always attested; editorial choices were evidently made, with the spells sometimes used in abbreviated versions.[68] Moreover, M. Mosher Jr. identifies different traditions in the Late Period—for example, the Theban and Memphite traditions, and the tradition from Akhmim.[69] M. Müller-Roth also stresses that many traditions can be identified in the vignettes, as opposed to a standardized form.[70] The question of the performance of rituals during this period is also difficult to understand, but further research on this question would be warranted.

1.6. Concluding Remarks

In conclusion, these examples are useful for discussing the theoretical aspects indicated at the beginning of this article, concerning the difference between "liturgies"—that is the texts recited by the priests during the funerary cult—and the "funerary literature" that served a "magical" purpose, as suggested by Assmann. Concerning the *Book of the Dead* specifically, Assmann states that "Le Livre

---

to those themes that are often repeated, but he also admits that the spells were already arranged in this way during the New Kingdom.

67. "Saite" because of the name of the capital of Egypt during the 26th Dynasty—namely, Sais in the Delta.

68. See, for example, Taylor, *Journey Through the Afterlife*, 76.

69. M. Mosher Jr., "Theban and Memphite Book of the Dead Traditions in the Late Period," *Journal of the American Research Center in Egypt* 29 (1992): 143–72; for the lists of the spells in different papyri of the Akhmim tradition in the Late Period, see M. Mosher Jr., *The Papyrus of Hor*, Catalogue of the Books of the Dead in the British Museum 2 (London: The British Museum Press, 2001), esp. 28–29, and recently M. Mosher Jr., *The Book of the Dead, Saite Through Ptolemaic Periods: A Study of Traditions Evident in Versions of Texts and Vignettes*, 8 vols, Saite Through Ptolemaic Book of the Dead Studies 1–10 (Charleston, SC: SPBD Studies, 2016–20), esp. 1:6–37. I thank Malcolm Mosher for a number of interesting discussions on this topic.

70. M. Müller-Roth, "From Memphis to Thebes: Local Traditions in the Late Period," *British Museum Studies in Ancient Egypt and Sudan* 15 (2010): 173–87, http://www.britishmuseum.org/pdf/Mueller_a.pdf.

des Morts fonctionne comme un équipement magique dont la part liturgique est extrêmement réduite."[71]

Based on the evidence surveyed in his essay, we can highlight the following points.

- For many of the spells, their importance is effectively related to the ability of the dead to "know" the spell—an efficacy that shows similarities to the category of funerary "literature" identified by Assmann (BD 58, BD 68).[72] This means that, at least from the perspective of their efficacy, the boundary between "funerary" and "liturgical" texts is, in fact, highly fluid.
- Some spells with practical aspects concerning the protection of the mummy, such as the protective bricks (BD 151 d–g) and the amulet spells (BD 155 to 159), can be compared with archaeological data. This suggests that these specific rituals were indeed performed, albeit not necessarily in complete agreement with the details of the descriptions provided by the text. In this case, the term "liturgy" can still be used, so long as it does not imply a codified act. The more general term "ritual" may be more appropriate.
- Some spells have a ritual background, in that they were probably performed at a certain point, most likely during the New Kingdom (BD 1, BD 151). While they were still in use during the Third Intermediate Period, this was in the form of written papyri, the creation of which did not depend on the ritual being performed in reality, or at least being performed with literal precision. Written versions represent an ideal ritual, which could substitute the real performance.
- Finally, rituals of other origins (rituals performed during the *wag*-feast for the papyrus of Nedjmet), as well as rituals most likely recited as the hymns of the Greenfield Papyrus, and more generally the texts of the Third Intermediate Period, show the diversity of the spells. It also shows that their efficacy was due to their having been put in writing, irrespective of whether they were in fact performed.

What precedes shows that many versions are attested: texts were therefore always adapted and rearranged. Moreover, spells stem from different origins: temples rituals, liturgies, protective spells, spells to avoid dangers, etc. The

---

71. Assmann, *Images et rites de la mort*, 36; see also Assmann, *Mort et au-delà*, 376, where he declares "Le Livre des Morts est un livre de magie." Quack ("Redaktion und Kodifizierung," 18) also asserts a distinction between spells to be known and those that belong to the liturgies.

72. While I have taken into account only the spells that have so far been mentioned, many other spells indicate the importance of knowledge.

function of each type of text in each specific period is difficult to determine. But it is nevertheless important to consider their probable use, as per the suggestion of Daniela Luft.[73] If making categories helps us understand the funerary texts, it seems important not to forget that such categories must be highly flexible, as opposed to measures of the single group that each text might fit within. Without such a willingness to hold these categories loosely, we are ultimately unable to understand the texts in all their complexity.

Finally, if most of the spells first had a performative value and then what could be considered a "magical" value due to their permanent effectiveness, it seems that the liturgies or rituals should not be underestimated in the *Book of the Dead*, even if the manner in which they were performed—or *not* performed—underwent change.

BIBLIOGRAPHY

Allen, J. P. *The Ancient Egyptian Pyramid Texts*. WAW 23. Atlanta: Society of Biblical Literature; Leiden: Brill, 2005.

Andrews, C. *Amulets of Ancient Egypt*. London: The British Museum Press, 1994.

Antoine, D., and M. Vandenbeusch, with J. H. Taylor. *Egyptian Mummies: Exploring Ancient Lives*. Sydney: Museum of Applied Art and Sciences, 2016.

Assmann, J. *Altägyptische Totenliturgien*. Vol. 1, *Totenliturgien in den Sargtexten des Mittleren Reiches*. Supplemente zu den Schriften der Heidelberger Akademie der Wissenschaften, Philosophisch-Historische Klasse 14. Heidelberg: Universitätsverlag C. Winter, 2002.

———. *Altägyptische Totenliturgien*. Vol. 2, *Totenliturgien und Totensprüche in Grabinschriften des Neuen Reiches*. Supplemente zu den Schriften der Heidelberger Akademie der Wissenschaften, Philosophisch-Historische Klasse 17. Heidelberg: Universitätsverlag C. Winter, 2005.

———. *Death and Salvation in Ancient Egypt*. Ithaca: Cornell University Press, 2005.

———. *Images et rites de la mort dans l'Egypte ancienne: L'apport des liturgies funéraires*. Paris: Cybèle, 2000.

———. *Liturgische Lieder an den Sonnengott: Untersuchungen zur altägyptischen Hymnik I*. Münchner Ägyptologische Studien 19. Berlin: Hessling, 1969.

———. *Mort et au-delà dans l'Egypte ancienne*. Monaco: Éditions du Rocher, 2003.

———. *Tod und Jenseits im alten Ägypten*. München: C. H. Beck, 2001.

Backes, B., and J. Dieleman, eds. *Liturgical Texts for Osiris and the Deceased in Late Period and Greco-Roman Egypt: Proceedings of the Colloquiums at New York (ISAW), 6 May 2011, and Freudenstadt, 18–21 July 2012*. Studien zur spätägyptischen Religion 14. Wiesbaden: Harrassowitz, 2015.

Baines, J. "Modelling Sources, Processes, and Locations of Early Mortuary Texts." Pages 15–41, in *D'un monde à l'autre: Textes des Pyramides et Textes des Sarcophages, Actes de la table ronde internationale "Textes des Pyramides versus Textes*

---

73. Luft, "Funerär und liturgisch," 65–73.

des Sarcophages" IFAO, 24–26 septembre 2001. Edited by S. Bickel and B. Mathieu. Bibliothèque d'Étude 139. Cairo: Institut français d'archéologie orientale, 2004.

Budge, E. A. W. *The Greenfield Papyrus in the British Museum.* London: British Museum, 1912.

Coulon, L. "Rhétorique et stratégies du discours dans les formules funéraires: Les innovations des Textes des Sarcophages." Pages 119–42 in *D'un monde à l'autre: Textes des Pyramides et Textes des Sarcophages, Actes de la table ronde internationale "Textes des Pyramides versus Textes des Sarcophages" IFAO, 24–26 septembre 2001.* Edited by S. Bickel and B. Mathieu. Bibliothèque d'Étude 139. Cairo: Institut français d'archéologie orientale, 2004.

De Cenival, J.-L. "Hors catalogue ou, comment les objets ordinaires accumulés peu à peu dans un musée complètent le tableau qu'on déduirait des chefs-d'œuvre exposés ici." Pages 273–80 in *Tanis, l'or des pharaons.* Paris: Ministère des Affaires Étrangères / Association Française d'Action Artistique, 1987.

Derchain, P. "La couronne de justification. Essai d'analyse d'un rite ptolémaïque." *Chronique d'Egypte* 30 (1955): 225–87.

Dieleman, J., and B. Backes. "Current Trends in the Study of Liturgical Papyri." Pages 1–13 in *Liturgical Texts for Osiris and the Deceased in Late Period and Greco-Roman Egypt: Proceedings of the Colloquiums at New York (ISAW), 6 May 2011, and Freudenstadt, 18–21 July 2012.* Edited by B. Backes and J. Dieleman. Studien zur spätägyptischen Religion 14. Wiesbaden: Harrassowitz, 2015.

Jacquat, C., and I. Rogger. *Fleurs des Pharaons. Parures funéraires en Egypte antique.* Hauterive: Laténium, 2013.

Lapp, G. *The Papyrus of Nebseni (BM EA 9900).* Catalogue of the Books of the Dead in the British Museum 3. London: The British Museum Press, 2004.

———. *The Papyrus of Nu (BM EA 10477).* Catalogue of the Books of the Dead in the British Museum 1. London: The British Museum Press, 1997.

Lenzo, G. "The Book of the Dead in the Third Intermediate Period." In *The Oxford Handbook of the Egyptian Book of the Dead.* Edited by R. Lucarelli and M. Stadler. Oxford: Oxford University Press (forthcoming).

———. *Manuscrits hiératiques du Livre des Morts de la Troisième Période intermédiaire (Papyrus de Turin CGT 53001–53013).* Catalogo del Museo Egizio di Torino, Serie seconda—Collezioni 6 / Cahiers de la Société d'Égyptologie, Genève 8. Genève: Société d'Égyptologie, 2007.

———. "Les papyrus funéraires des 21ème–22ème dynasties et les liens avec les textes gravés sur les parois des tombes et des temples." Pages 207–34 in *Schrift und Material: Praktische Verwendung religiöser Text- und Bildträger als Artefakte im Alten.* Edited by J. F. Quack and D. C. Luft. Orientalische Religionen in der Antike 41. Tübingen: Mohr Siebeck, 2021.

———. "The Two Funerary Papyri of Queen Nedjmet (P. BM EA 10490 and P. BM EA 10541 + Louvre E. 6258)." *British Museum Studies in Ancient Egypt and Sudan* 15 (2010): 63–83. http://www.britishmuseum.org/research/online_journals/bmsaes/issue_15/lenzo.aspx.

———. "La vignette initiale dans les papyrus funéraires de la Troisième Période intermédiaire." *Bulletin de la Société d'Égyptologie, Genève* 26 (2004): 43–62.

Lepsius, R. *Das Todtenbuch der Ägypter nach dem hieroglyphischen Papyrus in Turin.* Leipzig: Wigand, 1842.

Lieven, A. von. "Book of the Dead, Book of the Living: BD Spells as Temple Texts." *Journal of Egyptian Archaeology* 98 (2012): 249–67.

Lucarelli, R. *The Book of the Dead of Gatseshen: Ancient Egyptian Funerary Religion in the 10th Century B.C.* Egyptologische Uitgaven 21. Leiden: Nederlands Instituut voor het Nabije Oosten, 2006.

Luft, D. "Funerär und liturgisch. Gedanken zur Verbindung von Inhalten, Funktionen und Verwendungsbereichen altägptischer religiöser Texte." Pages 37–54 in *Liturgical Texts for Osiris and the Deceased in Late Period and Greco-Roman Egypt: Proceedings of the Colloquiums at New York (ISAW), 6 May 2011, and Freudenstadt, 18–21 July 2012*. Edited by B. Backes and J. Dieleman. Studien zur spätägyptischen Religion 14. Wiesbaden: Harrassowitz, 2015.

Lüscher, B. *Untersuchungen zu Totenbuch Spruch 151*. Studien zum Altägyptischen Totenbuch 2. Wiesbaden: Harrassowitz, 1998.

Mathieu, B. "La distinction entre Textes des Pyramides et Textes des Sarcophages est-elle légitime?" Pages 247–62 in *D'un monde à l'autre: Textes des Pyramides et Textes des Sarcophages, Actes de la table ronde internationale "Textes des Pyramides versus Textes des Sarcophages" IFAO, 24–26 septembre 2001*. Edited by S. Bickel and B. Mathieu. Bibliothèque d'Étude 139. Cairo: Institut français d'archéologie orientale, 2004.

———. "Que sont les *Textes des Pyramides*?" *Égypte, Afrique et Orient* 12 (1999): 13–22.

Morales, A. J. "Text-Building and Transmission of Pyramid Texts in the Third Millennium B.C.E.: Iteration, Objectification, and Change." *JANER* 15 (2015): 169–201.

Mosher, M., Jr. *The Book of the Dead, Saite Through Ptolemaic Periods: A Study of Traditions Evident in Versions of Texts and Vignettes*. 8 vols. Saite Through Ptolemaic Book of the Dead Studies 1–10. Charleston, SC: SPBD Studies, 2016–20.

———. *The Papyrus of Hor*. Catalogue of the Books of the Dead in the British Museum 2. London: The British Museum Press, 2001.

———. "Theban and Memphite Book of the Dead Traditions in the Late Period." *Journal of the American Research Center in Egypt* 29 (1992): 143–72.

Müller-Roth, M. "From Memphis to Thebes: Local Traditions in the Late Period." *British Museum Studies in Ancient Egypt and Sudan* 15 (2010): 173–87. http://www.britishmuseum.org/pdf/Mueller_a.pdf.

Munro, I. *Untersuchungen zu den Totenbuch-Papyri der 18. Dynastie: Kriterien ihrer Datierung*. London: Kegan Paul International, 1988.

Niwiński, A. *Studies on the Illustrated Theban Funerary Papyri of the 11th and 10th Centuries B.C.* OBO 86. Göttingen: Vandenhoeck & Ruprecht, 1989.

Quack, J. F. "Redaktion und Kodifizierung im spätzeitlichen Ägypten: Der Fall des Totenbuches." Pages 11–34 in *Die Textualisierung der Religion*. Edited by J. Schaper. FAT 62. Tübingen: Mohr Siebeck, 2009.

Quirke, S. *Going Out in Daylight—prt m hrw: The Ancient Egyptian Book of the Dead*. GHP Egyptology 20. London: Golden House, 2013.

Régen, I. "When a Book of the Dead Text Does Not Match Archaeology: The Case of the Protective Magical Bricks (BD 151)." *British Museum Studies in Ancient Egypt and Sudan* 15 (2010): 267–78. http://www.britishmuseum.org/research/online_journals/bmsaes/issue_15/regen.aspx.

Scalf, F. "From the Beginning to the End: How to Generate and Transmit Funerary Texts in Ancient Egypt." *JANER* 15 (2015): 202–23.

Smith, M. *Traversing Eternity: Texts for the Afterlife from Ptolemaic and Roman Egypt*. Oxford: Oxford University Press, 2009.

Stadler, M. "Prätexte funerärer Rituale: Königsliturgie, Tempelliturgie, Totenliturgie." Pages 75–90 in *Liturgical Texts for Osiris and the Deceased in Late Period and Greco-Roman Egypt: Proceedings of the Colloquiums at New York (ISAW), 6 May 2011, and Freudenstadt, 18–21 July 2012*. Edited by B. Backes and J. Dieleman. Studien zur spätägyptischen Religion 14. Wiesbaden: Harrassowitz, 2015.

Tacke, N. *Das Opferritual des ägyptischen Neuen Reiches*. OLA 222. Leuven: Peeters, 2013.

Taylor, J. H. *Death and the Afterlife in Ancient Egypt*. London: The British Museum Press, 2001.

———. *Journey Through the Afterlife: Ancient Egyptian Book of the Dead*. London: The British Museum Press, 2010.

Taylor, J. H., and J. Kondo, eds. *Ancient Egyptian Book of the Dead, Journey Through the Afterlife*, Tokyo: Asahi Shimbun / NHK / NHK Promotions, 2012.

Taylor, J. H., and D. Antoine. *Ancient Lives, New Discoveries: Eight Mummies, Eight Stories*. London: The British Museum Press, 2014.

Theis, C. "Wenn Archäologie und Philologie nicht harmonieren: Magische Ziegel, ihre Nischen und Totenbuchspruch 151d–g." *Zeitschrift für ägyptische Sprache und Altertumskunde* 143 (2015): 85–95.

Vuilleumier, S. *Un rituel osirien en faveur de particuliers à l'époque ptolémaïque: Papyrus Princeton Pharaonic Roll 10*. Studien zur spätägyptischen Religion 15. Wiesbaden: Harrassowitz, 2016.

Zaluskowski, C. *Texte außerhalb der Totenbuch-Tradierung in Pap. Greenfield*. Bonn: Friedrich-Wilhelms-Universität, 1996.

CHAPTER 2

Between Utterance and Dedication: Some Remarks on the Status of Textuality in Greek Ritual Practices

Dominique Jaillard

TO THE HISTORIAN AND ANTHROPOLOGIST of Greek religion, "texts" present themselves first and foremost as written documents, on the basis of which the religious practices of the ancient world, as well as the systems of categories and representations that underpinned them, might be reconstructed and understood. As witnesses to the diversity of practices that characterized Greek polytheism, "religious" texts comprise a highly heterogeneous assemblage, consisting of cultic regulations, sacrificial calendars, accounts and inventories of temples and sanctuaries, oracular responses, or narratives of divine epiphanies and "miraculous" healings. In the main, these texts are epigraphic documents; "texts" that were written on more ephemeral supports have almost entirely disappeared. On a *prima facie* understanding—which, as will be shown below, is in fact largely misleading for the Greek world—the textualization of rituals seems to blend with more general processes of writing.

Yet some of these texts were an integral part of ritual performance itself. They could, for instance, serve as instruments for ritual performance, as per the lead tablets in the oracle of Dodone, on which a person consulting the oracle could write his or her question before the tablets were folded up and made unreadable.[1] They could also be uttered during the performance of the ritual, as per the hymn inscribed at the end of a sacred law regulating the sacrifices to Asclepios and Apollon in Erythrea in the fourth century BCE.[2] In such instances, the written document constitutes a text *in an entirely different sense*—namely, the text is part of the ritual, for example, because it is included as an object to manipulate, or by virtue of the instructions it contains for the ritual's correct performance, or because the text forms the "booklet" or the "score" of the ritual (at least for some of its parts). Such texts can be defined as "ritual texts" in a narrower sense since they are more directly involved in the performance of the ritual. However, we must immediately clarify that the contents of these texts are

1. E. Lhôte, *Les lamelles oraculaires de Dodone* (Geneva: Droz, 2006).
2. D.-L. Page, ed., *Poetae Melici Graeci* (Oxford: Clarendon Press, 1962), 933–34.

almost entirely lost to us, even though many of the texts are mentioned in other sources (mostly literary sources). Those texts that existed in only one exemplar, or in few copies, and that were written on materials that did not withstand the passage of time, have disappeared. Pausanias's *Description of Greece*, with its distinctive focus on local particularisms, provides us with an invaluable source of information in this regard. For example, for the rites (*teleté*) of Dionysos and Demeter in Lerna, in Argolide,[3] the "things done" (*ta drómena*), that is to say the rite proper, were accompanied by the "things spoken" (*ta legómena*), which were inscribed in a Dorian dialect consisting of a mixture of prose and poetry onto a piece of copper shaped in the form of a heart. We may also mention in this context the passage concerning the rites belonging to Demeter Eleusinia in the small town of Phenea in the mountains of Arcadia.

> Beside the sanctuary of the Eleusinian has been set up what they name the Petroma, consisting of two large stones fitted one to the other. When every other year they celebrate what they call the "Greater rites" (*teletèn meízona*), they open these stones. They take from out them the writings that refer to the rites (*teleté*), read them in the hearing of the initiated, and return them on the same night.[4]

As far as Greece is concerned, the contents of these and other ritual texts were almost always inaccessible to us.

Which ritual strategies dictated these processes of textualization, understood this time as the usage of a written document in the performance of the ritual? The diversity of contexts does not permit a single answer. Instead the place and the use of the written text must be considered according to the specific strategies that were operative in each setting. All the more so since many contexts that might at first sight seem quite similar do not have the same approach to writing. In a significant number of cases, the need for secrecy favors recourse to a written text in order to ensure exactness in the performance of the ritual, while also restricting access to a small number of authorized persons in the relevant context. In such cases, the rite must not be revealed: it is *apórretos*, inexpressible, as Pausanias reminds us; on occasion a dream warns Pausanias against disclosing what must remain unspoken,[5] be it the name of a deity (for instance the *despoina* of Lykosoura[6]) or the rites themselves, "performed" and/or "uttered."[7]

---

3. Pausanias, *Descr.*, trans. W. H. S. Jones, LCL 188 (Cambridge: Harvard University Press, 1938), 2.37.3.
4. Pausanias, *Descr.* 8.15.1–2.
5. Pausanias, *Descr.* 1.14.3, 1.38.7.
6. Pausanias, *Descr.* 8.37.9.
7. Pausanias, *Descr.* 2.37.6.

Yet in many other cases, the secret nature of the rite is perfectly consistent with oral transmission. A *hieros logos* is not necessarily written.

One of the paradoxes of textualization in Greek polytheistic practices is that the texts that *are meant to be seen* do not necessarily have a "ritual" usage. (While these texts are meant to be seen, they are not necessarily meant to be read; this category refers to those texts whose main *raison d'être* is their public display.) It was not necessary for ancient Greeks to have a "sacred law" or a festal calendar with them in order to perform a sacrifice. Yet at times it was imperative that the corresponding texts be publicly displayed and accessible, so that anyone concerned might refer to them.[8] It also ensured that when a given rite—which was to be performed according to the customary usage (*nomos* or *patria*)—was not performed correctly, it was possible to turn to the written text. Conversely, the text that was manipulated in a ritual sequence could serve to *conceal* what had been written. This was the case in some oracular practices in which the written text containing the oracular question and/or the reply of the god was sealed. It was, for instance, the case for the oracle of Apollo *Koropaîos*, where the issue at hand was ensuring the faithful, and indisputable, transmission of the answer of the god.[9]

At this point, we also need to stress a key aspect of ancient polytheistic practices. These practices were predominantly *local*. To be sure, broader common patterns existed, and a shared sacrificial pattern meant that the majority of the great sacrificial feasts had a marked alimentary character in the Greek cities. Yet the details of those practices were always particular, made up of innumerable and significant variants. Such variants may be connected to some specific traits of the relevant deities, to the traditions of a certain sanctuary or city, to the distinctive aims pursued by the performed rite, or to the explicit connection to a given myth of origins.[10] As a matter of fact, it made little sense in ancient Greece to circulate texts outside the sanctuary or the community in which their usage was required. We must exclude here specific cases, such as those cults that considered themselves to have a "foreign," or transregional

---

8. M. Detienne, "L'espace de la publicité: Ses opérateurs intellectuels dans la cité," in *Les savoirs de l'écriture en Grèce ancienne*, ed. M. Detienne (Lille: Presses universitaires de Lille, 1992), 29–81.

9. L. Robert, "Sur l'oracle d'Apollon *Koropaios*," *Hellenica* 5 (1948): 16–28; S. Georgoudi, "Le porte-parole des dieux: Réflexions sur le personnel des oracles grecs," in *Sibille e linguaggi oracolari: Mito Storia Tradizione; Atti del convegno Macerata-Norcia Settembre 1994*, ed. I. Chirasi Colombo and T. Seppili (Pise: Istituti editoriali e poligrafici internazionali, 1998), 315–65 at 363–64; D. Jaillard, "Memory, Writing, Authority: The Place of the Scribe in Greek Polytheistic Practice," in *Writing the Bible: Scribes, Scribalism and Script*, ed. P. R. Davies and T. Römer (Durham: Acumen Publishing, 2013), 23–34 at 27–28.

10. M. Detienne, "A Polytheistic Garden," in *The Daily Life of the Greek Gods*, ed. M. Detienne and G. Sissa, trans. J. Lloyd (Stanford: Stanford University Press, 2000), 150–65.

dimension (such as the cult of Isis), or cults associated with marginal groups, like the enigmatic Orphics. Such cults are precisely less firmly anchored in a given territory because they are far less connected to a political community, a city.[11]

This "local" character applies first and foremost to those ritual "texts" that have a prescriptive dimension—those that state how a rite is to be accomplished—namely, the so-called sacred laws and regulations.[12] There is no panhellenic prescriptive text. If in the sacrifices described in the Homeric poetry the Greeks could recognize a *nomos hellenikos*—that is, a distinctively Greek way of sacrificing to distinguish them from the barbarians[13]—Homer would still be of little value for understanding how a Greek ritual was effectively performed, since the Homeric sacrifice does not exactly reflect what we know about how sacrifices were effectively offered in the cities of archaic and classical Greece.

But does it follow from this that the sacred laws inscribed on stone transcribe the local ritual custom? Do they represent something like the *text* of the rite? As fascinating and instructive as these documents may be in terms of what they tell us about the way(s) in which Greek polytheisms worked, to what extent can they be regarded as ritual codes, which comprise the systematic writing down of the customary rules governing local practice? Let us consider, for instance, the sacrificial calendars, such as the so-called calendar of Nikomachos in Athens (end of the fifth century BCE), or the calendar of the deme of Thorikos in Attic (fourth century BCE). The Athenian calendar edited by Nikomachos (as *anagrapheús*) is the work of a committee tasked with the collection, clarification, and revision of the list of sacrifices and "offerings" owed by the city.[14] The calendar recalls throughout the year the names of the deities, feasts, relevant sacrificial

---

11. A. Heinrichs, "Writing Religion: Inscribed Texts, Ritual Authority, and the Religious Discourse of the Polis," in *Written Texts and the Rise of Literate Culture in Ancient Greece*, ed. H. Yunis (Cambridge: Cambridge University Press, 2003), 15–58 at 54; A. Heinrichs, "*Hieroi logoi* and *hierai biblioi*: The (Un)written Margins of the Sacred in Ancient Greece," *Harvard Studies in Classical Philology* 101 (2003): 207–66.

12. R. Parker, "What Is Sacred Law?," in *The Law and the Courts in Ancient Greece*, ed. E. M. Harris and L. Rubinstein (London: Duckworth, 2004), 57–70; S. Georgoudi "Comment régler les *théia pragmata*: Pour une étude de ce qu'on appelle 'lois sacrées,'" *Mètis* 8 (2010): 39–54; M. Carbon and V. Pirenne-Delforge, "Beyond Greek 'Sacred Laws,'" *Kernos* 25 (2012): 163–82; M. Carbon and V. Pirenne-Delforge, "Codifying 'Sacred Laws' in Ancient Greece," in *Writing Laws in Antiquity—L'écriture du droit dans l'Antiquité*, ed. D. Jaillard and C. Nihan, BZABR 19 (Wiesbaden: Harrassowitz, 2017), 141–57.

13. Pausanias, *Descr.* 1.24.2; V. Pirenne-Delforge, *Retour à la source: Pausanias et la religion grecque*, Kernos Supplément 20 (Liège: Centre international d'étude de la religion grecque antique, 2008), 179–83.

14. S.-D. Lambert, "The Sacrificial Calendar of Athens," *The Annual of the British School at Athens* 97 (2002): 353–99.

victims or "offerings," prices to be paid for each one, and occasional details regarding their age, color, and other particularities, as well as the place of the celebration or the portion due to the priest and other officiants. By way of an example, let us consider the entry of the calendar corresponding to the fourteenth of Skirophorion, the day of the feast for Zeus *Polieús*, namely, the *Dipóleia*.

> [...?] [the bovines] from the driving round, the first six [*price*];
> for the priestess, *apometra* [*amount*];
> the piglets [*price*];
> for the heralds who [*verb*] at the Dipólieia [*perquisites*][15]

Or let us consider, for the same month, the calendar of the deme of Thorikos. It combines feasts that are specific to the deme with others that parallel the rites that were celebrated for the entire city on the same date.

> In Skirophorion, an oath victim shall be provided; at the Plynteria, for Athena, a choice sheep; for Aglauros, a sheep; for Athena a choice lamb; for Cephalus a bovine worth not less than forty up to fifty drachmas; for Procris a sheep worth 20 drachmas (?).[16]

The document contains precise calendric prescriptions, yet none of its entries allows us to form a *clear and comprehensive view* of the ceremonies mentioned; the most relevant details for the performance of the sacrifices are not included. Most of the time, we have no idea of the sequence of gestures and words, or the various objects involved in the sacrificial procedure. Additionally, there are reasons to suspect that a significant portion of the sacrifices performed by the city or by the demes is not included in the calendar.

In other words, the ritual "code" here is nothing more than an incomplete calendrical *scheme*. It adds some specific ritual prescriptions that, we may presume, would have resulted in grave consequences if they were forgotten or that may have had an emblematic value. But most of the knowledge required for the performance of these rites was *not* written down. Rather, it rested upon traditional knowledge, the *nomos*, the *patria*, of which the written and published rule only selects a minimal portion. Similar calendrical outlines can be found in the ritual texts found at Ugarit in the late second millennium BCE, which mention day by day the deities and the sacrificial victims for various festivals during the

---

15. Translation from ibid., 394.
16. SEG 32.147; edition, translation, and commentary in E. Lupu, *Greek Sacrificial Law: A Collection of New Documents*, 2nd ed., Religions in the Graeco-Roman World 152 (Leiden: Brill, 2009), 115–49.

year.¹⁷ Yet such documents are by no means comparable to the detailed descriptions found in a book like Leviticus or certain writings from Qumran.

Therefore, the textual status of these inscriptions, which were published by and for the city itself, does not exactly amount to a "textualization" of the ritual procedure; the latter continues to be ruled and informed by a strictly customary *nomos*, whose knowledge is required for ritual performance given that such limited information is provided by the inscriptions themselves. These laws are mnemonic and clearly manifest the concern of the city for the affairs of the gods, but as written ritual prescriptions, they are irremediably deficient, insufficient. Or to put it differently: the contents of the "sacred law," when the latter is effectively put into practice, are always much more substantial than the written sketch itself. At times, the law might even be silent about what can be considered the most striking aspect of the rite, mentioning instead only very prosaic detail. This is the case, for instance, in the *Dipóleia* for the trial of the sacrificial knife (*machaira*) and the motif of putting the ox back on its feet. Neither of these is mentioned in the calendars. We only know about them because they caught the attention of antiquarians and philosophers.¹⁸

Is it possible to form a more precise idea of the criteria of selection that led to the writing down of specific portions, or aspects, of some rituals? There is an entire complex of myths about how a forgotten sacrifice was a major cause of disturbance in the relationship of a human community and its gods. The need for scrupulous and regular performance might explain why the calendric prescriptions showed such a concern for detail. Failure to respect the ritual specifics that were connected to a given power or cult would have likely invalidated or perverted the presumed effects of the rite. As such, the inscription provided an additional guarantee that could supplement the "shared knowledge" or specific competences of the officiants. Yet most of the time, the pragmatic dimension of the written text seems to have primarily concerned the management of possible conflicts between humans, rather than their relations with the gods. A significant portion of the instructions found in the sacred laws address matters related to *conflicts of rights or potential abuses to be feared*. Questions pertaining to the distribution of meat, especially the attribution of the *geraa* (the privileged parts of the animal), the remuneration of the officiants, and, more generally, various financial aspects (for instance, the cost of the sacrificial victims and the presentation of accounts), are given considerable attention in this corpus.¹⁹ Issues

---

17. See, for example, RS 1.009; 24.253; 24.284. For the edition and translation of these texts, compare D. Pardee, *Ritual and Cult in Ugarit* (Atlanta: Society of Biblical Literature, 2002), ad loc., and his comments on p. 25.

18. J.-L. Durand, *Sacrifice et labour en Grèce ancienne* (Paris: La Découverte; Rome: Ecole française de Rome, 1986), 43–86.

19. Georgoudi, "Comment régler les *théia pragmata*," 50–51.

concerning ritual exactness, by contrast, *frequently appear as a minor, subordinated topic in the written rules*. We may also recall in this context the requirement for public diffusion, already mentioned above, which was fundamental in a city like Athens, but largely absent (at least in this form) in an "oligarchic" city like Sparta.[20]

There are, however, some sacred laws that are more detailed when it comes to ritual procedure—for instance, those from Kos in the fourth century BCE,[21] or from Mykonos around 200 BCE.[22] Indeed, various details of the ritual were meticulously specified. Consider the following example:

> On the 11th: an ox is selected for Zeus *Machaneús* every other year, the one during which the *Karneia*-days take place, just as during Batromios the ox is selected for Zeus *Polieús*, and a piglet is preliminarily burned (whole), and a preliminary proclamation is made just as for (Zeus) *Polieus*. On the 12th: to Zeus *Machaneús*, three adult male sheep and the ox that has been selected (15) every other year, the one during which the *Karneia*-days take place; every other year, three adult male sheep. The priest of the Twelve Gods sacrifices these and provides the (supplementary) sacred offerings (*hierá*). He offers as a preliminary sacrifice for these (gods) at their common (altar), the things which the Phyleomachidai bring, a half-hekteus of barley-groats, a *tetarteus* of wine. From the ox, perquisites (*geré*) are given to the Phyleomachidai: the horns (or hooves), the shanks; from the sheep, the shoulder, (20) from which the divine portion (*theomoiría*) is cut [...]. On the same day: to Athena *Machanís* a selected heifer every other year, the one during which the *Karneia*-days take place; on the other year, (only) an adult ewe. The priestess sacrifices and is sprinkled about with sea water. No take-away from these (animals). As (supplementary) sacred offerings are given to the goddess: (25) four *kotylai* of olive oil, a *tetarteus* of wine, two new ewers and three new drinking-cups.[23]

Why such a luxury of details? This calendar was redacted after the synoikism of 366 BCE that merged all the communities of the island into a single city. This resulted in a fusion and reorganization of the cults, which up until then had been administered by the various cities that comprised Kos.[24] It also

---

20. Detienne, "Espace de la publicité."
21. *IG* 12.4, 274–78; *CGRN* 86 (*LSCG* 151); S. Paul, *Cultes et sanctuaires de l'île de Cos*, Kernos Supplément 28 (Liège: Centre international d'étude de la religion grecque antique, 2013).
22. *CGRN* 156 (*LSCG* 96).
23. *CGRN* 86 (*LSCG* 151) D. 10–24; translation of M. Carbon and S. Peels in *Collection*, http://cgrn.ulg.ac.be/file/86/.
24. Georgoudi, "Comment régler les *théia pragmata*," 51; Paul, *Cultes et sanctuaires*, 19–23, 149–50, 285–89.

meant that common cults had to be established for the new civic community. While it is difficult to assess the modifications and changes that were introduced, the general concern would have been to address the needs of a now unified city, and also to ensure the continuity, at the cost of some adaptations, of cults that belonged to the traditional prerogatives of the gods. This was a difficult operation. It created a complex situation that had the potential to disturb the proper functioning of traditional memory—a situation in which there was considerable risk of error or oversight, and a temptation to ignore the new rule, especially when the latter contradicted previous local practices. The detailed writing down of the rite would thus have seemed the most fitting or efficient instrument to ensure the effective performance of the ritual *nomos*. One century later, a similar context of synoikism gave rise to a detailed redaction of the Hellenistic calendar of Mykonos.[25] In the case of Kos, it is interesting to note that the usage of a greater specification of the written rules had a lasting impact on local practice. And yet, most of the ritual knowledge that was needed to perform the ritual gestures remained implicit. One cannot but ask to what extent the process by which the written rule was produced—the only one still accessible to us—does not actually conceal the processes of formalizing and transmitting the ritual through custom. It was, after all, the relationship with custom that gave the written rules their meanings and their pragmatic value.[26]

One should also note that the ritual exactness of the text is often a function of the *private* character of the ritual knowledge concerned, or its connection with groups that were more or less marginal in comparison to the official or dominant practices of the cities. The great "cathartic" law from Selinous (end of the fifth century BCE),[27] which is characterized by its precision in pronouncing the ritual, leaves the prescribing authority anonymous, yet the high degree of ritual expertise that it involved points to ritual specialists comparable to those mentioned in the *Derveni Papyrus*,[28] whose knowledge was, however, transmitted first and foremost orally. Could it be, then, that a certain degree of (written)

---

25. Reger, "The Mykonian Synoikismos," *Revue des études anciennes* 103 (2001): 157–81; for the cultic and pantheonic reconfigurations related to the 408/407 synoikism in Rhodes, compare Paul, *Cultes et sanctuaires*, 270–71.

26. For a complementary proposition on the "stratigraphy" of norms, compare A. Chaniotis, "The Dynamics of Ritual Norms in Greek Cult," in *La norme en matière religieuse en Grèce ancienne*, ed. P. Brulé, Kernos Supplément 21 (Liège: Presses universitaires de Liège, 2009), 91–105.

27. For the puzzling hybrid ritual prescriptions, possibly influenced by the Near East, compare M. H. Jameson, D. R Jordan, and R. D. Kotansky, *A Lex Sacra from Selinous* (Durham: Duke University, 1993); on the new Thessalian inscription from Marmatini, compare J.-C. Decourt and A. Tziaphalias, "Un règlement religieux de la région de Larissa: Cultes grecs et 'orientaux,'" *Kernos* 28 (2015): 13–51; R. Parker and S. Scullion, "The Mysteries of the Goddess of Marmarini," *Kernos* 29 (2016): 209–66.

28. Col. 20 ll. 3–4: *hósoi dè parà toû téchnem poiouménou tà hierá*.

textualization should be explained by other parameters, such as the relationship to the "client," specific functions, and other constructions of authority, as well as the specifics of the rite, or the distance from common (ritual) knowledge? For private mantic specialists like the Athenian chresmologues,[29] the resort to written oracles attributed to such-and-such god or such-and-such prophetic figure of acknowledged authority, like Bakis, conferred to these specialists the authority of divine sanction.[30] So, in many cases, the tendency to rely on the authority of writing must be understood in relation to the private or at least less official status of the ritualist, and, in such contexts, a more detailed written account of ritual specifics is related to very specific practices involving specialists with their own "private" knowledge.

Greek cities document the existence of specialists in exegeting rites. These specialists could either officiate privately or be officially commissioned by the city, as we see in Athens with the three exegetes designated by the *pólis* after the end of the Peloponnesian war.[31] They were consulted by individuals, as well as by magistrates, to illuminate difficult ritual issues;[32] a portion of their knowledge was transmitted in treaties of *Exegetics*, of which only a few rare fragments have survived.[33] Such writing down of ritual usages appears to have often been related to an "antiquarian" activity: the formatting of local traditions. The Athenian authors of *Exegetics* were also "Atthidographers" who wrote the ancient history of Attica and its myths.[34] It was a private scriptural activity, even though it could be linked to public functions (in the case of Athens's three public exegetes), or more traditional ones (the chresmologues). A fragment from Anticleides pertaining to the installation in the storerooms for house supplies of Zeus *Ktesios*—that is the Zeus of the acquisition, custody, and consumption of riches—attests to a distinctive prescriptive style that parallels the style of Hippocratic doctors.

> The *semeîa* of Zeus *Ktésios* should be established as follows. Place a lid on a new two-handled *kadískos*; wrap the handles with white wool, and from the right shoulder and the front ... of the piece of wool; put whatever

---

29. See J. Dillery, "Chresmologues and *Manteis*: Independent Diviners and the Problem of Authority," in *Mantikê: Studies in Ancient Divination*, ed. S. Iles Johnston and P. T. Struck (Leiden: Brill, 2005), 169–220, whose arguments I do not follow; R. Parker, *Polytheism and Society at Athens* (Oxford: Oxford University Press, 2005), 111–15.

30. Aristophanes, *Birds* 971–72; on prophetical chains, compare A. Motte, "Qu'entendait-on par *prophètès* dans la Grèce ancienne?," *Kernos* 26 (2013): 9–23.

31. J. H. Oliver, *The Athenian Expounders of the Sacred and Ancestral Law* (Baltimore: Johns Hopkins University Press, 1950).

32. Theophrastus, *Characters* 16; see the reference to "the superstitious man."

33. A. Tresp, *Die Fragmente der griechischen Kultschriftsteller* (Giessen: A. Töppelmann, 1914).

34. J. Dillery, "Greek Sacred History," *American Journal of Philology* 126 (2005): 505–26 at 508.

you find into it; and pour in ambrosia. Ambrosia is clean water, olive oil, and fruit of all sorts; place these items inside it.[35]

For the modern historian, it is very difficult to interpret the various details in this text.[36] For the Athenian who enjoyed a ritual competence of cultural relevance, as well as shared knowledge on the god, the indications provided in this text were apparently enough to avoid serious mistakes and oversights. For instance, the instruction *kaì estheînai hó ti àn heúres* "put whatever you find into it," cannot be understood without prior knowledge, independent of the letter of the text. But who was *reading* and *using* such a text? The Athenian who had to perform this rite and could orally consult the exegete (as is attested by Theophrastus in his *Characters*)? The specialist whose advice was sought? Or the historian and the erudite who collected and rewrote the local specifics of a given cult? If the users of this and similar texts were predominantly to be found among ritual specialists, what was the role of this type of writing in the transmission of their knowledge? Only a complex, pluralist approach—one that acknowledges the presence of *different types* of memory operating together and that conceives writing and orality not in opposition but rather as complementing each other according to modalities that differed from one context to another—can allow us to formulate plausible hypotheses.[37]

However, it is among the groups and practices that were located in the margins of the "public" religion—and often difficult to define socially—that we see the largest flourishing of ritual texts: the *hieroi logoi* of the dionysiac associations in Ptolemaic Egypt; the so-called Orphic funerary plates (although their Orphic affiliation is questionable in my view); the papyri from Gumol, as well as various "magical" papyri (cases in which Egypt, the land of writing, plays a significant role);[38] or earlier on, the tablets from the *orphikoi* of Olbia.[39] An important part of this corpus of texts, the contents of which may in fact be "mythical" as much as ritual, is placed under the protean authority of

---

35. Anticleides, in Athenaeus, *Deipnosophistae* 473b–c, trans. from Athenaeus, *The Learned Banqueters*, vol. 5, *Books 10.420e–11*, trans. S. Douglas Olson, LCL 274 (Cambridge: Harvard University Press, 2009).

36. D. Jaillard, "'Images' des dieux et pratiques rituelles dans les maisons grecques: L'exemple de Zeus Ktésios," *Mélanges de l'École française de Rome* 116.2 (2004): 871–93.

37. On the respective place of writing and orality in Athenian memory in the fifth century BCE, see R. Thomas, *Oral Tradition and Written Record in Classical Athens* (Cambridge: Cambridge University Press, 1989), esp. 100–31.

38. For further discussion of these texts, and various other issues, see Heinrichs, "*Hieroi logoi* and *hierai biblioi*"; F. Graf and S. I. Johnston, *Ritual Texts for the Afterlife: Orpheus and the Bacchic Gold Tablets* (London: Routledge, 2007); C. Calame, "Les lamelles funéraires d'or: Textes pseudo-orphiques et pratiques rituelles," *Kernos* 21 (2008): 299–311.

39. Chapter 1, "L'Orphée de la mer noire," in M. Detienne, *Les dieux d'Orphée* (Paris: Gallimard, 2007), 22–25.

Orpheus.[40] However, the "marginal" position of these texts, especially in the Classical Period, is apparent in the case of the curses of Theseus against his son Hippolytus in the homonymous tragedy by Euripides (952–54).

> Will you puff yourself up, boast about these vegetarian meals (*apsúchon*) and, taking Orpheus as your master, act as a bacchant by honoring (*timôn*) the smoke (*kapnoús*) of innumerable books/writings (*pollôn grammáton*): you are uncovered.

The reference to the smoke—that is, the smoke of sacrifices—is a clear indication of the ritual dimension of these writings.

Even in the public space of the city, where writing of the ritual was subjected to specialized and sophisticated techniques, it remained—in certain contexts—a potentially *suspect* activity.[41] As was already highlighted, the writing of the ritual was often either unnecessary or secondary to the performance of the rite itself (this was a difference with the situation in Rome[42]), at least when the inscribed object was not integral to the ritual manipulations.[43]

This survey may either disappoint us or suggest that we have directed our attention primarily toward the more marginal areas of ritual practice. But it should in fact press us to reconsider our initial question: what is meant by the notion of "text" in the ritual practices of Greek polytheisms? Besides the diversity of definitions that the modern historian may provide, we also need to look at what the Greeks themselves included under the label of what we call "text." It is only by starting from the Greek practices themselves that we may be able to enter into a more "autochthonous" relationship to textuality, as well as to the connection between "text" and "rite."

I will begin here with an anecdote, which may be more invented than historical, but which is in any case meaningful to a system of representation and its corresponding ritual logic, and which, in a sense, better accounts for the status of the text than the mere inventory of Greek writings and their usages. The *Homeric Hymn to Apollo*, which was (in at least one of its versions) the object of a performance in a Delian festival, was kept as an *anáthema*, an "offering" deposited in the sanctuary of Artemis in Delos. In the mythical account found in the *Certamen*, it is Homer himself who would have recited the hymn beside

---

40. M. Detienne, *L'écriture d'Orphée* (Paris: Gallimard, 1989).
41. Detienne, "Espace de la publicité"; Jaillard, "Memory, Writing, Authority," 24, 29, 32.
42. J. Scheid, *La religion des Romains* (Paris: A. Colin / Masson, 1998), 85.
43. On this last case, compare M. Carastro, "Les liens de l'écriture: *Katadesmoi* et instances de l'enchaînement," in *Architecturer l'invisible: Autels, ligatures, écritures*, ed. M. Cartry, J.-L. Durand and R. Koch-Piettre, Bibliothèque de l'Ecole des Hautes Etudes, Sciences religieuses 138 (Turnhout: Brepols, 2009), 263–91.

the horned altar dedicated to Apollo; the Delians, having conferred citizenship on Homer, transcribed the Hymn on wooden tablets in order to consecrate (*anéthekan*) it in the sanctuary of Artemis, which belonged to the then sanctuary of Apollo in Delos.[44] We also know from the Delian inventories that a "book" by the lyrical poet Alcaeus, of Lesbos, was among the *anathémata* deposited in the sanctuary.[45]

The parallel with other cases of dedicated archaic poems, such as the *Works and Days* by Hesiod, of which Pausanias was able to see an old "manuscript" made of skin in a sanctuary on the Helicon,[46] suggests—as Claude Calame has shown—that "the consecration of poems intended for oral performance in a sanctuary may well have been, especially on the occasion of the heroisation of their author, one of the triggers for their transcription."[47] I will not develop this aspect here, as interesting as it may be, but focus instead on the status of the writing that forms its corollary. To produce a written text does not serve to ensure its memorization or its transmission, or to provide a support for its oral enunciation, as we would spontaneously tend to assume. For that, *aoidoi* and rhapsodes, in particular, have quite efficient techniques at their disposal. Rather, the production of the text participates in a ritual practice both distinct from and complementary with the oral performance that took place in the context of a competition or a religious festival—the *anathéma*. The associated value of dedication and consecration has to do with the gesture of depositing the object, in this case the *inscribed* object, which, in the process, gains a new quality—it is *hieros*—and becomes the property of the god, under whose watch it is placed.[48] As such, it is another, complementary way to honor the gods, and to please them. The status of the deposited text is analogous to that of an "image" or a material "offering," such as a statue or a vase, presented to a divine power,[49] or to that of

---

44. *The Contest of Homer and Hesiod* 18, in *Homeric Hymns; Homeric Apocrypha; Lives of Homer*, trans. M. L. West, LCL 496 (Cambridge: Harvard University Press, 2003), 350.

45. *ID* 1400, 7; *ID* 1409. Heraclitus the philosopher would have dedicated his book in the Delian sanctuary of Artemis (Diogenes Laertius, *Lives* 9.6), Pindar's seventh Olympics in the sanctuary of Athena in Lindos (in golden letters, Scolia I, 195 Drachmann). See J. Herington, *Poetry into Drama: Early Tragedy and the Greek Poetic Tradition* (Berkeley: University of California Press, 1985), 201–3.

46. Pausanias, *Descr.* 9.31.4.

47. C. Calame, "Montagne des Muses et Mouséia: La consécration des *Travaux* et l'héroïsation d'Hésiode," in *La montagne des Muses*, ed. A. Hurst and A. Schachter (Genève: Droz, 1996), 43–56 at 56: "la consécration de poèmes destinés à la communication orale dans un sanctuaire, pourrait bien avoir été, à l'occasion (notamment) de l'héroïsation de leur auteur, un des moteurs de leur transcription"; see also C. Calame, *Sentiers transversaux: Entre poétiques grecques et politiques contemporaines* (Grenoble: Millon, 2008), 133–43.

48. J. Rudhardt, *Notions fondamentales de la pensée religieuse et actes constitutifs du culte dans la Grèce classique* (Picard: Paris, 1992), 22–30.

49. D. Jaillard, "L'image dans la stratégie du rituel," in *Image et religion dans l'Antiquité gréco-romaine: Actes du colloque de l'École française de Rome, 11–13 décembre 2003*, ed. S. Estienne

the pieces of meat deposited on tables (*trapezómata*)—an important and often neglected constituent of the gods' portion in Greek sacrificial practices.[50]

The practice of inscribing poems that were orally performed during a feast or a ceremony is well documented. In the case of Delphi, it is enough to mention here the paean to Dionysos by Philodamos of Skarpheia (around 340–339 BCE), the hymn to Hestia and the paean to Apollo of Aristonoos (third quarter of the fourth century BCE), or the two paeans to Apollo that contain a musical notation and that were offered on the occasion of the Pythais festivals in 138–128 BCE.[51] For Crete, we may mention the hymn to Zeus *Diktaios* that was discovered in Palaikastro, nearby Mount Dikta, where an inscription from the third century CE transcribes an older inscription from the fourth or third century BCE.[52] In this case, the ritual orientation of the hymn is clearly shown by the *self-referential* nature of the utterances that were placed in the mouth of the choir of young people: they performed them in a declarative context in which their proclamations referred, among others things, to the altar around which the choir moved.

The production of the written text as *anáthema*, the object of a dedication, *duplicates* the cultic act. To the song uttered during the musical performance to confer honor (*géras*) to the god, whose *timé* is increased by the ritual,[53] is added the lasting deposition of the inscription inside the sanctuary. The writing here functions as a memory of the performance, but it is also an integral part of a specific, complementary religious act: the ritual deposit of an inscribed object for the god. The text may be related to a specific circumstance and not intended for other, later performances, or it can—on the contrary—comprise the very text of the cultic hymn that is uttered every year during the festival, as in the case of the Cretan inscription of Palaikastro.

But in this case, we need to ask what constitutes the ritual text proper? It is doubtful that the inscription was used to repeat and renew the performance, even in those cases where the text corresponded to a regular performance (rather

---

et al. (Naples: Centre Jean Bérard, 2008), 97–99; I. Patera, *Offrir en Grèce ancienne: Gestes et contextes*, Postdamer Altertumswissenschaftliche Beiträge 41 (Stuttgart: F. Steiner, 2012).

50. D. Gill, "*Trapezomata*: A Neglected Aspect of Greek Sacrifice," *HTR* 67.2 (1974): 117–37; M. H. Jameson, "Theoxenia," in *Ancient Greek Cult Practice from the Epigraphical Evidence*, ed. R. Hägg, Kernos Supplément 26 (Stockholm: P. Åströms, 1994), 35–57; G. Ekroth, "Meat for the Gods," in *"Nourrir les dieux?" Sacrifice et representation du divin*, ed. V. Pirenne-Delforge and F. Prescendi, Kernos Supplément 26 (Liège: Centre international d'étude de la religion grecque antique, 2011), 15–41.

51. W. D. Furley and J. M. Bremer, eds., *Greek Hymns* (Tübingen: Mohr Siebeck, 2001), respectively 2.5, 2.3, 2.4, 2.6.1, 2.6.2.

52. Ibid., 1.1.

53. D. Jaillard, "'Il réalisa les dieux immortels et la terre ténébreuse' (Hymne homérique à Hermès 427)," in *Linguaggi del potere, poteri del linguaggio: Atti del Colloquio internazionale del PARSA, 6–8 novembre 2008*, ed. E. Bono and M. Curnis, Culture antiche, studi e testi (Alessandria: Edizioni dell'Orso, 2010), 51–66.

than a unique one). At most, the inscription ensured public diffusion, as per the inscribed law. As a ritual "text," the hymn is the "text" sung and danced by the choir, *not* the text inscribed. To be sure, it is possible that *another* written support, easier to handle and more ephemeral, was also used either for the composition of the hymn or for the training of the choir every year. But even so, it is only *from within the immanent logic of the ritual* that the process of textualization, as fixation of the authoritative version of the traditional hymn, may be properly understood. This means, among other things, that in Greece the relations between *text* and *ritual* cannot be understood primarily on the basis of the writing practice.

In the rite of the *anáthema* ("dedication/consecration"), the writing may form an integral part of the ritual handling itself. The deposited object may contain an inscription that describes the purpose of the ritual; it is, in fact, one of the oldest attested ways of using writing in Ancient Greece. On a statue from the end of the eighth or the beginning of the seventh century BCE we read, "Mantiklos dedicated me to the Far-Shooter, silver-bowed god, as a tithe; Phoibos, provide *charis* in return."[54] As is customary with the earliest dedications (mainly before 550 BCE), it is the object itself that speaks here.[55] When reading the inscription, a visitor to the sanctuary lent his voice to the object and reactivated the inscribed utterance; the practice of reading aloud was standard in Greece. In the process, the writing *does not duplicate* the words with which the dedicator consecrated the statue when he deposited it. Rather, the writing is part of a distinct declarative strategy, distinct from the speech uttered by the dedicator when he accomplished his dedication (which was, in this case, dedicated to the god in his own name).[56]

The transcription of a hymn, since I have chosen here to focus on this type of text, can also be included with the utterance of a "sacred law." The same paean, related to the cult of Asclepios, can be found in inscriptions from Erythrea in Asia Minor, Dion in Macedonia, and Ptolemais in Egypt, as well as in Athens. Here we are dealing with a distinct phenomenon, connected to cults whose transregional interests predominate over their local anchoring. In one of these instances, however, the text of the hymn not only is inscribed but also contains the *obligation* to sing the hymn in accompaniment to the sacrifice. The text of the paean is thus made available to those persons consulting Asclepios, who

---

54. M. L. Lazzarini, *Le formule delle dediche votive nella Grecia arcaica* (Rome: Accad. nazionale dei Lincei, 1976), 795.

55. J. Svenbro, *Phrasikleia: An Anthropology of Reading in Ancient Greece*, trans. J. Lloyd (Ithaca: Cornell University Press, 1993), 26–43; P. Pucci, "Inscriptions archaïques sur les statues des dieux," in *Les savoirs de l'écriture en Grèce ancienne*, ed. M. Detienne (Lille: Presses universitaires de Lille, 1992), 480–97.

56. Svenbro, *Phrasikleia*, 44–63.

must have at their disposal not only the sacrificial rule but also the hymn to be uttered to the god.

> If anyone, after sleeping in the temple or making a vow is offering due sacrifice to Asclepius and Apollo, when he puts on the altar the sacred portion (*hierà moîra*), he must first sing this paean three times around Apollo's altar.[57]

After this follows the text of the paean. Here the written text no longer serves as a dedication, as per the *anáthema* discussed above, but serve as a *script* for the person consulting the god[58] and as a support for the *textualization* of the rule. The written text, however, acquired a function and status that are properly ritualized only if, and when, it was *uttered* by the visitor in the relevant ritual context, *in relation to the altar*, when the sacrificial offering was deposited in the sanctuary. The paean, which must be repeated three times, comprised part of the sacrificial speech. As a *ritual text*, it exists only *in* and *through* the ritual, as an element of the sacrifice by which humans and gods are brought together around the altar.

But when the possibility of utterance was suspended by the ritual procedure itself, the act of writing could be invested with a "religious" efficiency, in that the efficiency of the ritual act was concentrated within it. The Classical Greek world abundantly attests to the practice of ritual binding, the *katádesmos*.[59] These *defixiones* of lead, inscribed with signs, names, and malevolent formulas, which were then rolled up or folded and sometimes pierced with nails, were then buried in the ground, especially in graves or under sanctuaries. Formulas such as "I am writing (*katagrápho*) NP toward," followed by the invocation of various powers capable of binding and chaining (such as Hermes *Chtónios*, Gê *Chtónia*, Hecate, Kore, and others), appear to be strictly equivalent to formulas such as "I am binding" or "I am retaining NP toward." In such cases the graphic apparatus (that is, the written lead plates) is not meant to be read by humans, even less in a public space; it was deposited in the earth, "written downward" so that the bearer of the inscribed name would be possessed—that his tongue, some corporal functions, his various skills, or his renown would be bound. The linguistic dimension of the writing, in relation with the figurative handling and—occasionally—the piercing of the plates, mimics and performs the action of the divine powers that are summoned. The very act of inscribing the name

---

57. Page, *Poetae Melici Graeci*, 933–34.
58. "As for script, I mean a narrower category, where the written text is a prerequisite for performance"; G. Nagy, *Poetry as Performance: Homer and Beyond* (Cambridge: Cambridge University Press, 1996), 112.
59. M. Carastro, *La cité des mages: Penser la magie en Grèce ancienne* (Grenoble: J. Millon, 2006), 163–88.

activates the binding, under the condition that the latter is buried—*tháptein*, the same verb used in funerary rites—and, by this gesture, entrusted to the action of the relevant powers. It is by being articulated with the ritual sequence, with the required gestures, that the written text receives its own efficacy.

As these examples suggest, it remains highly difficult to define in Greek, and according to Greek categories, the notion of "text." Such an approach would require us to analyze, in the wake of the seminal work by Jesper Svenbro,[60] the metaphors of weaving (*huphaínein*) that were used in the choral lyric of the fifth and fourth centuries to describe the processes involved in the composition of songs—"Weave (*exúphaine*), sweet Lyre, weave without further ado, on the Lydian mode, this song (*mélos*) loved by Oenone and Cyprus"[61]—or to describe the activity of the rhapsode as the one who "sews back up" the song (*ráphtein aoidén*).[62] There is also, from the late Hellenistic period onward, the complex interplay with the Latin *textus*, translated in Greek by *húphos*, fabric or web.[63] Plato speaks thus of the interlacing (*sumploké*) of the letters that "weave" the syllables,[64] or of the nouns and verbs that comprise the *lógos*.[65] This Greek concept of the "weaving" of the text does not exclude writing (as is already shown by the image of the *sumploké* formed by letters), but it is not based on it. The text exists not as a written form but as "spoken writing" (*une écriture parlée*), so to speak: that is, an audible utterance for which the writer uses the reader "as the instrument indispensable for the full realization of his written word"[66]—not unlike the *erastes* uses the *eromenes*. In Plato's *Phaedrus*, the writing is a "booklet" through which the absent writer is present (*parôn*), so long as, like the warp interweaving with the woof, he is able to unite himself with the reader who realizes the "text" through his voice.[67] The text, then, is not the writing itself but the weaving between writing and utterance, the actualization through the performance of the writing each and every reading. The studies on the genesis of epic traditions, especially those by Gregory Nagy on the Homeric traditions, have developed the notion of an *oral* textuality, the implications of which have not yet been sufficiently considered in the field of ritual studies.[68]

---

60. J. Svenbro, "The Cloak of Phaedrus: The Prehistory of the 'Text' in Greece," in *The Craft of Zeus: Myths of Weaving and Fabric*, ed. J. Scheid and J. Svenbro (Cambridge: Harvard University Press, 1996), 111–30.
61. Pindar, *Nemean* 4, 44–46.
62. Hesiod, frag. 357; compare J. Svenbro, *La parole et le marbre* (Lund: Klassiska Institutionen, 1976), 201–2.
63. Svenbro, "Cloak of Phaedrus," 128.
64. Plato, *Politicus* 277d.
65. Plato, *Sophista* 259e, 262b–e.
66. Svenbro, "Cloak of Phaedrus," 125.
67. Plato, *Phaedrus* 228e.
68. G. Nagy, *Homeric Questions* (Austin: University of Texas Press, 1996), 69–70.

By way of conclusion, I would like to offer one final comment on the ritual text in Greece, which involves a portion of the systems of categories and representations underlying Greek ritual practice and, as such, raises valid questions for the historian and anthropologist. Under certain conditions—depending on the ritual context—the ritual utterance can produce effects that are themselves described in the very terms of sacrificial practice, as we can read, for instance, in the following statement attributed to Pindar by Philodemus of Gadara: "By means of the poems, the honor (*timé*) [of the gods] grows [...]. Pindar was of the same opinion, when he was saying that he was going to sacrifice a dithyramb."[69] This power to augment the divine *timaí*, the prerogatives of the gods, the Greeks attributed it to the sacrifices by which men honor (*timân*) the divine powers, and it is in reference to this power of sacrifices that Philodemus introduces Pindar's image of the dithyramb sacrificed to the gods (*thúson dithúrambon*)—an image that emerges elsewhere when Pindar mentions, in the context of a poem sung on the occasion of the *theoxénia* of Delphi, a "meal of paeans" (*paieónon ádorpon euáxomen*).[70] We therefore also need to understand this sacrificial context for the hymnic utterance—namely, its capacity to increase the *timai* of the gods and to delight them—when we try to understand the status of the text in the ritual, as well as the various configurations of orality and writing that were present in the complex world of Greek polytheism. Even in the margins of the city, the writings of Orpheus that are said by Euripides's Theseus to have perverted his son, are still a form of sacrificial smoke "honored" (*timôn*) by Hippolytes—even if only the smoke of letters (*kapnous grammatôn*).

BIBLIOGRAPHY

Athenaeus. *The Learned Banqueters*. Vol. 5, *Books 10.420e–11*. Translated by S. Douglas Olson. LCL 274. Cambridge: Harvard University Press, 2009.

Calame, C. "Les lamelles funéraires d'or: Textes pseudo-orphiques et pratiques rituelles." *Kernos* 21 (2008): 299–311.

———. "Montagne des Muses et Mouséia: La consécration des *Travaux* et l'héroïsation d'Hésiode." Pages 43–56 in *La montagne des Muses*. Edited by A. Hurst and A. Schachter. Genève: Droz, 1996.

———. *Sentiers transversaux: Entre poétiques grecques et politiques contemporaines*. Grenoble: Millon, 2008.

Carastro, M. *La cité des mages: Penser la magie en Grèce ancienne*. Grenoble: J. Millon, 2006.

---

69. Philodemus of Gadara, *De musica* 4, col. 21.6–13 = Pindar, frag. 86; see Jaillard, "Dieux immortels," 51–54.

70. Pindar, *Hymns* 6.127–28.

———. "Les liens de l'écriture: *Katadesmoi* et instances de l'enchaînement." Pages 263–91 in *Architecturer l'invisible: Autels, ligatures, écritures*. Edited by M. Cartry, J.-L. Durand, and R. Koch-Piettre. Bibliothèque de l'Ecole des Hautes Etudes. Sciences religieuses 138. Turnhout: Brepols, 2009.

Carbon, M., and V. Pirenne-Delforge. "Beyond Greek 'Sacred Laws.'" *Kernos* 25 (2012): 163–82.

———. "Codifying 'Sacred Laws' in Ancient Greece." Pages 141–57 in *Writing Laws in Antiquity—L'écriture du droit dans l'Antiquité*. Edited by D. Jaillard and C. Nihan. BZABR 19. Wiesbaden: Harrassowitz, 2017.

Chaniotis, A. "The Dynamics of Ritual Norms in Greek Cult." Pages 91–105 in *La norme en matière religieuse en Grèce ancienne*. Edited by P. Brulé. Kernos Supplément 21. Liège: Presses universitaires de Liège, 2009.

Decourt, J.-C., and A. Tziaphalias. "Un règlement religieux de la région de Larissa: Cultes grecs et 'orientaux.'" *Kernos* 28 (2015): 13–51.

Detienne, M. *Les dieux d'Orphée*. Paris: Gallimard, 2007.

———. *L'écriture d'Orphée*. Paris: Gallimard, 1989.

———. "L'espace de la publicité: Ses opérateurs intellectuels dans la cité." Pages 29–81 in *Les savoirs de l'écriture en Grèce ancienne*. Edited by M. Detienne. Lille: Presses universitaires de Lille, 1992.

———. "A Polytheistic Garden." Pages 150–65 in *The Daily Life of the Greek Gods*. Edited by M. Detienne and G. Sissa. Translated by J. Lloyd. Stanford: Stanford University Press, 2000.

Dillery, J. "Chresmologues and *Manteis*: Independent Diviners and the Problem of Authority." Pages 169–220 in *Mantikê: Studies in Ancient Divination*. Edited by S. Iles Johnston and P. T. Struck. Leiden: Brill, 2005.

———. "Greek Sacred History." *American Journal of Philology* 126 (2005): 505–26.

Durand, J.-L. *Sacrifice et labour en Grèce ancienne*. Paris: La Découverte; Rome: Ecole française de Rome, 1986.

Ekroth, G. "Meat for the Gods." Pages 15–41 in *"Nourrir les dieux?" Sacrifice et representation du divin*. Edited by V. Pirenne-Delforge and F. Prescendi. Kernos Supplément 26. Liège: Centre international d'étude de la religion grecque antique, 2011.

Furley, W. D., and J. M. Bremer, eds. *Greek Hymns*. Tübingen: Mohr Siebeck, 2001.

Georgoudi, S. "Comment régler les *théia pragmata*: Pour une étude de ce qu'on appelle 'lois sacrées.'" *Mètis* 8 (2010): 39–54.

———. "Le porte-parole des dieux: Réflexions sur le personnel des oracles grecs." Pages 315–65 in *Sibille e linguaggi oracolari: Mito Storia Tradizione; Atti del convegno Macerata-Norcia Settembre 1994*. Edited by I. Chirasi Colombo and T. Seppili. Pise: Istituti editoriali e poligrafici internazionali, 1998.

Gill, D. "*Trapezomata*. A Neglected Aspect of Greek Sacrifice." *HTR* 67.2 (1974): 117–37.

Graf, F., and S. I. Johnston. *Ritual Texts for the Afterlife: Orpheus and the Bacchic Gold Tablets*. London: Routledge 2007.

Heinrichs, A. "*Hieroi logoi* and *hierai biblioi*: The (Un)written Margins of the Sacred in Ancient Greece." *Harvard Studies in Classical Philology* 101 (2003): 207–66.

———. "Writing Religion: Inscribed Texts, Ritual Authority, and the Religious Discourse of the Polis." Pages 15–58 in *Written Texts and the Rise of Literate Culture in Ancient Greece*. Edited by H. Yunis. Cambridge: Cambridge University Press, 2003.

Herington, J. *Poetry into Drama: Early Tragedy and the Greek Poetic Tradition.* Berkeley: University of California Press, 1985.
Homeric Hymns; Homeric Apocrypha; Lives of Homer. Translated by M. L. West. LCL 496. Cambridge: Harvard University Press, 2003.
Jaillard, D. "L'image dans la stratégie du rituel." Pages 97–99 in *Image et religion dans l'Antiquité gréco-romaine: Actes du colloque de l'École française de Rome, 11–13 décembre 2003.* Edited by S. Estienne, D. Jaillard, N. Lubtchansky, and C. Pouzadoux. Naples: Centre Jean Bérard, 2008.
———. "'Images' des dieux et pratiques rituelles dans les maisons grecques: L'exemple de Zeus *Ktésios.*" *Mélanges de l'École française de Rome* 116.2 (2004): 871–93.
———. "Memory, Writing, Authority: The Place of the Scribe in Greek Polytheistic Practice." Pages 23–34 in *Writing the Bible: Scribes, Scribalism and Script.* Edited by P. R. Davies and T. Römer. Durham: Acumen Publishing, 2013.
———. "'Il réalisa les dieux immortels et la terre ténébreuse' (Hymne homérique à Hermès 427)." Pages 51–66 in *Linguaggi del potere, poteri del linguaggio: Atti del Colloquio internazionale del PARSA, 6–8 novembre 2008.* Edited by E. Bono and M. Curnis. Culture antiche, studi e testi. Alessandria: Edizioni dell'Orso, 2010.
Jameson, M. H. "Theoxenia." Pages 35–57 in *Ancient Greek Cult Practice from the Epigraphical Evidence.* Edited by R. Hägg. Kernos Supplément 26. Stockholm: P. Åströms, 1994.
Jameson, M. H., D. R. Jordan, and R. D. Kotansky. *A Lex Sacra from Selinous.* Durham: Duke University, 1993.
Lambert, S.-D. "The Sacrificial Calendar of Athens." *Bulletin of Sumerian Agriculture* 97 (2002): 353–99.
Lazzarini, M. L. *Le formule delle dediche votive nella Grecia arcaica.* Rome: Accad. nazionale dei Lincei, 1976.
Lhôte, E. *Les lamelles oraculaires de Dodone.* Geneva: Droz, 2006.
Lupu, E. *Greek Sacrificial Law: A Collection of New Documents.* 2nd ed. Religions in the Graeco-Roman World 152. Leiden: Brill, 2009.
Motte, A. "Qu'entendait-on par *prophètès* dans la Grèce ancienne?" *Kernos* 26 (2013): 9–23.
Oliver, J. H. *The Athenian Expounders of the Sacred and Ancestral Law.* Baltimore: Johns Hopkins University Press, 1950.
Nagy, G. *Homeric Questions.* Austin: University of Texas Press, 1996.
———. *Poetry as Performance: Homer and Beyond.* Cambridge: Cambridge University Press, 1996.
Page, D.-L., ed. *Poetae Melici Graeci.* Oxford: Clarendon Press, 1962.
Pardee, D. *Ritual and Cult in Ugarit.* Atlanta: Society of Biblical Literature, 2002.
Parker, R. *Polytheism and Society at Athens.* Oxford: Oxford University Press, 2005.
———. "What is Sacred Law?" Pages 57–70 in *The Law and the Courts in Ancient Greece.* Edited by E. M. Harris and L. Rubinstein. London: Duckworth, 2004.
Parker, R., and S. Scullion. "The Mysteries of the Goddess of Marmarini." *Kernos* 29 (2016): 209–66.
Patera, I. *Offrir en Grèce ancienne: Gestes et contextes.* Postdamer Altertumswissenschaftliche Beiträge 41. Stuttgart: F. Steiner, 2012.
Paul, S. *Cultes et sanctuaires de l'île de Cos.* Kernos Supplément 28. Liège: Centre international d'étude de la religion grecque antique, 2013.

Pausanias. *Description of Greece.* Vol. 2, *Books 3–5*. Translated by W. H. S. Jones. LCL 188. Cambridge: Harvard University Press, 1938.

Pirenne-Delforge, V. *Retour à la source: Pausanias et la religion grecque.* Kernos Supplément 20. Liège: Centre international d'étude de la religion grecque antique, 2008.

Pucci, P. "Inscriptions archaïques sur les statues des dieux." Pages 480–97 in *Les savoirs de l'écriture en Grèce ancienne.* Edited by M. Detienne. Lille: Presses universitaires de Lille, 1992.

Reger, G. "The Mykonian Synoikismos." *Revue des études anciennes* 103 (2001): 157–81.

Robert, L. "Sur l'oracle d'Apollon *Koropaios*." *Hellenica* 5 (1948): 16–28.

Rudhardt, R. *Notions fondamentales de la pensée religieuse et actes constitutifs du culte dans la Grèce classique.* Paris: Picard, 1992.

Scheid, J. *La religion des Romains.* Paris: A. Colin / Masson, 1998.

Svenbro, J. *La parole et le marbre.* Lund: n.p., 1976.

———. *Phrasikleia: An Anthropology of Reading in Ancient Greece.* Translated by J. Lloyd. Ithaca: Cornell University Press, 1993.

———. "The Cloak of Phaedrus: The Prehistory of the 'Text' in Greece." Pages 111–30 in *The Craft of Zeus: Myths of Weaving and Fabric.* Edited by J. Scheid and J. Svenbro. Cambridge: Harvard University Press, 1996.

Thomas, R. *Oral Tradition and Written Record in Classical Athens.* Cambridge: Cambridge University Press, 1989.

Tresp, A. *Die Fragmente der griechischen Kultschriftsteller.* Giessen: A. Töppelmann, 1914.

CHAPTER 3

Inscriptions and Ritual Practices in the Neo-Assyrian Period: The Construction of a Building as an Example

Lionel Marti

MESOPOTAMIA IS OFTEN CONSIDERED the land of writing, not the least because of the very high number of texts that were found there. The place of the text in these societies is a topic that has generated considerable interest but that confronts us with a diversity of corpuses and a variety of contexts.[1] To what extent was writing, as a gift from the gods, sacred in Mesopotamia? How did a letter written by a god to a merchant differ from a letter written by one merchant to another?

The case of building construction is interesting in this regard. It is situated at the intersection of several corpuses: ritual texts, letters, and royal inscriptions ceremoniously deposited in building foundations. In order to analyze this case, we need to inquire about the status of each of these texts and the nature of the written evidence.

The following study will focus on the Neo-Assyrian period. Traditionally, this period has been thought to extend from the tenth and ninth centuries to the end of the seventh century BCE, with the fall of the Assyrian urban centers: the sack of Aššur in 614; the fall of Nineveh in 612; and the defeat of the last Assyrian king, Aššur-uballiṭ II, in 610 in Harran.

During this period, the time of the Sargonids—from Tiglath-phalazar III (744–727 BCE) to the sons of Aššurbanipal—deserves particular attention, since it corresponds to the apogee of the empire: it is a period of prosperity, when many victorious campaigns provided the Assyrian kings with the resources to undertake extensive building works.

These building works are a blessing for the historian: they led to the writing of abundant documents, several of which were later found in the course of archaeological excavations. The writing of commemorative inscriptions by the Mesopotamian kings goes back to an earlier period—namely, the middle

---

1. For a good discussion of this issue, see D. Charpin, *Reading and Writing in Babylon* (Cambridge: Harvard University Press, 2010).

of the third millennium BCE. Assyrian kings soon modified this genre by adding the narrative intercalation of royal feats to its classical form, which had consisted of the royal titles and the description of the event being commemorated.[2] Hence, it is not unusual for these documents to exceed 400 lines in the Neo-Assyrian period—for instance, a prism of Assarhaddon consists of 494 lines,[3] among which 367 are devoted to the campaigns of the king. Documents from this period also witness the amplification of the royal titles, as per those found in the "Annals" of Aššurnaṣirpal II (883–859 BCE), which comprise no less than 43 lines.[4] Another significant development during this period concerns the building narratives, placed toward the end of these texts, which grow longer and begin to include the description of ritual procedures.

During the same period, the Assyrian kings established a "library," which was discovered during the excavations in Nineveh and formed the basis for Assyriological studies. It is known as "Aššurbanipal's library"[5] and was presumably a site for gathering the scientific knowledge of that time in order to assist scholars, diviners, physicians, and exorcists, and others as well, perform their roles. It is important to recall that the Nineveh archives were discovered during earlier excavations[6] and that scholars have often found it difficult to

---

2. The bibliography on Assyrian royal inscriptions is vast. See, in particular, the seminal studies by M. Liverani, "Memorandum on the Approach to Historiographical Texts," *Or* 42 (1973): 178–94; A. K. Grayson, "Assyria and Babylonia," *Or* 49 (1980): 140–94; and the essays collected in F. M. Fales, ed., *Assyrian Royal Inscriptions: New Horizons in Literary, Ideological and Historical Analysis* (Rome: Istituto per l'Oriente, 1981). More recently, see also F. M. Fales, "Assyrian Royal Inscriptions: Newer Horizons," *State Archives of Assyria Bulletin* 13 (1999–2001), 115–44.

3. R. C. Thompson, *Prisms of Esarhaddon and of Ashurbanipal Found at Nineveh, 1927–1928* (Oxford: Oxford University Press, 1931), 7–28; republished in E. Leichty, *The Royal Inscriptions of Esarhaddon, King of Assyria (680–669 BC)*, RINAP 4 (Winona Lake, IN: Eisenbrauns, 2011), 9–26, text 1.

4. A. K. Grayson, *Assyrian Rulers of the Early First Millennium BC I (1114–859 BC)*, RIMA 2 (Toronto: University of Toronto Press, 1991), 193–97, (A.0.101.1). See also the comments by B. Cifola, *Analysis of Variants in the Assyrian Royal Titulary from the Origins to Tiglath-Pileser III* (Napels: Istituto Universitario Orientale, 1995), 92–100.

5. On the Nineveh libraries, see O. Pedersén, *Archives and Libraries in the Ancient Near East, 1500–300 B.C.* (Bethesda, MD: CDL Press, 1998), 158–65; Charpin, *Reading and Writing*, 186–200. Compare also S. Parpola, "Assyrian Library Records," *JNES* 42.1 (1983): 1–29.

6. For a recent synthesis of the Nineveh excavations and the archives that were found there, see J. E. Reade, "Ninive (Nineveh)," *RlA* 9 (2000): 388–433. For further information, see S. Parpola, "The Royal Archives of Nineveh," in *Cuneiform Archives and Libraries: Papers Read at the 30e Rencontre Assyriologique Internationale, Leiden, 4–8 July 1983*, ed. K. R. Veenhof (Istanbul: Nederlands Historisch-Archaeologisch Instituut, 1986), 223–36; J. E. Reade, "Archaeology and the Kuyunjik Archives," in *Cuneiform Archives and Libraries: Papers Read at the 30e Rencontre Assyriologique Internationale, Leiden, 4–8 July 1983*, ed. K. R. Veenhof (Istanbul: Nederlands Historisch-Archaeologisch Instituut, 1986), 213–22; J. C. Fincke, "The British Museum's Ashurbanipal Library Project," *Iraq* 66 (2004): 55–60; G. Frame and A. George, "The Royal Libraries of Nineveh: New Evidence for King Ashurbanipal's Tablet Collecting," *Iraq* 67.1 (2005): 265–84;

understand how they were organized: what we have is a vast corpus including epistolary and administrative documents,[7] and a great number of scientific works. Yet despite these difficulties, it remains possible in several cases to match the practices described in the letters with what we know from learned texts, especially the numerous ritual texts.

A significant number of these learned documents only survive in the form of titles preserved in the catalogues of the series that were included in the libraries.[8] Others can be identified by means of the colophons found on certain tablets, which specify the title of the series, the rank of the document in that series, and sometimes the number of lines that it contains. To take but one example:

> 58th tablet of the series "When Anum and Enlil," (containing) 115 lines, copied on the original and collated. Tablet of PN, etc. [...].[9]

Beside the library of the palace there was another library, located inside the temple of Nabû, the god of writing and knowledge: it served symbolically as an offering to that god who, in return, ensured the protection of the king.[10] One colophon of a tablet found in that library, for instance, reads:

> I (Aššurbanipal) wrote on tablets, verified and collated the wisdom of Ea (god of wisdom, magic and incantations), the science of the exorcist, the secret of the sages [...] based on exemplars from Assyria and Babylonia, and I placed them in the library (*girginakku*) of Ezida (True House), temple of the god Nabu, my lord, in Nineveh. O Nabu, king of the whole heaven and earth, look favorably therefore on this library and give your blessing every day to Aššurbanipal, your servant who reveres your divinity, so that I may ceaselessly praise your divinity.[11]

This duality of palace/temple shows that written texts served the purposes of conservation and consultation, but also another significant role: written texts

---

J. C. Fincke, "The Babylonian Texts of Nineveh: Report on the British Museum's *Ashurbanipal Library Project*," *Archiv für Orientforschung* 50 (2003/4): 111–32.

7. The Nineveh archives are currently being reedited in SAA.

8. See, especially, the examples of catalogues in F. M. Fales and J. N. Postgate, *Imperial Administrative Records*, part 1, *Palace and Temple Administration*, SAA 7 (Helsinki: Helsinki University Press, 1992), 62–69.

9. H. Hunger, *Babylonische und assyrische Kolophone*, AOAT 2 (Vluyn: Verlag Butzon & Bercker Kevelaer, 1968), 138 n. 512.

10. See Pedersén, *Archives and Libraries*, 163; Reade, "Ninive," 423.

11. Charpin, *Reading and Writing*, 198.

did not merely allow communication among humans, but also with the gods. Indeed, letters could be sent to the gods,[12] and the gods themselves sent letters to the king.[13] The gods also communicated with humans through multiple signs (the so-called unprovoked omens),[14] which could also be "written" on various supports, the most common being the liver of a lamb.[15]

In the first millennium BCE, rituals of a certain importance would take the following form. A text describes the sequence of events: it includes the incantations to recite through the utterance of their incipit, specifies the gestures to perform, and so on. The document would then be associated with others that provided the same text of the incantations.[16]

Ritual practices, codified actions, and the like were constantly present in everyday life. The construction of a building by the Assyrian king was no exception. It followed strict rules, requiring the intervention of several specialists as well as the performance of several rituals. The whole procedure was commemorated by inscriptions placed outside the building, or at the level of its

---

12. See, for example, the case of the campaign reports written by the kings to the god Aššur, such as the famous eighth campaign of Sargon II: F. Thureau-Dangin, *Une relation de la huitième campagne de Sargon*, Textes cunéiformes, Musée du Louvre 3 (Paris: Geuthner, 1912); W. Mayer, "Sargons Feldzug gegen Urartu 714 v. Chr. Text und Übersetzung," *Mitteilungen der Deutschen Orient-Gesellschaft* 115 (1983): 65–132; W. Mayer, *Assyrien und Urarṭu I. Der Achte Feldzug Sargons II. im Jahr 714 v. Chr.*, AOAT 395/1 (Münster: Ugarit Verlag, 2013). Compare also the letter to Aššur by Assarhaddon in Leichty, *Royal Inscriptions*, 79–86.

13. See the examples collected in A. Livingstone, *Court Poetry and Literary Miscellanea*, SAA 3 (Helsinki: Helsinki University Press, 1989), 108–15, texts 41–47.

14. S. Maul, "How the Babylonians Protected Themselves against Calamities Announced by Omens," in *Mesopotamian Magic: Textual, Historical, and Interpretative Perspectives*, ed. T. Abusch and K. van der Toorn, Ancient Magic and Divination 1 (Groningen: Styx, 1999), 123–29; S. B. Noegel, "'Sign, Sign, Everywhere a Sign': Script, Power and Interpretation in the Ancient Near East," in *Divination and Interpretation of Signs in the Ancient World*, ed. A. Annus, OIS 6 (Chicago: Oriental Institute of University of Chicago, 2010), 143–62.

15. Compare I. Starr, *Queries to the Sungod: Divination and Politics in Sargonid Assyria*, SAA 4 (Helsinki: Helsinki University Press, 1990), xxxvi–lv; and U. Koch-Westenholz, *Babylonian Liver Omens: The Chapters manzâzu, padânu and pân tâkalti of the Babylonian Extispicy Series Mainly from Aššurbanipal's Library*, The Carsten Niebuhr Institute Publications 25 (Copenhagen: Museum Tusculanum Press, 2000).

16. One very clear example is provided by the *šurpu* ("cremation") ritual, which was used to remove the stain of a sin: E. Reiner, *Šurpu: A Collection of Sumerian and Akkadian Incantations*, AfOB 11 (Graz: Im Selbstverlage des Herausgebers, 1958); R. Borger, "Shurpu II, III, IV und VIII in 'Partitur,'" in *Wisdom, Gods and Literature: Studies in Assyriology in Honour of W. G. Lambert*, ed. A. R. George and I. L. Finkel (Winona Lake, IN: Eisenbrauns, 2000), 15–90; J. Bottéro, *Mythes et rites de Babylone* (Geneva: Slatkine / Honoré Champion, 1985), 163–219; M. J. H. Linssen, "Unpublished Fragments from the Burning Ritual Series (Šurpu) from the British Museum," in *Studies in Ancient Near Eastern World View and Society Presented to Marten Stol on the Occasion of His 65th Birthday*, ed. R. J. van der Spek (Bethesda, MD: CDL Press, 2008), 47–52.

foundations. The inscription itself was considered an integral part of the offerings that were to be presented in the course of the ceremony.

This essay will survey and analyze the rituals performed in the context of the construction of a building and, above all, the role of the texts in these rituals. To that effect, it will begin (1) by considering the conditions required for the construction and then (2) looking at the rituals used in the case when a building is restored; finally, (3) special attention will be given to a famous rebuilding, which was the subject of unprecedented propaganda, namely, the rebuilding of Babylon by Assarhaddon.

3.1. The Conditions of Building and Rebuilding

In the Mesopotamian mentality, the relations between divine and nondivine agents were manifold, and the communication between gods and humans constant.

First, the concept of "destiny" was mitigated by fortuitous signs that informed humans of the circumstances that awaited them and allowed them to adjust to these circumstances. Several divinatory series offer an interpretation of these divine signs: anomalous births (*šumma izbu*);[17] events happening in a town or a city (*šumma âlu*);[18] celestial phenomena (*enûma Anu Enlil*);[19] and so on. Second,

---

17. E. Leichty, *The Omen Series* Šumma Izbu, Texts from Cuneiform Sources 4 (New York: J. J. Augustin, 1970); N. de Zorzi, *La serie teratomantica* šumma izbu: *Testo, tradizione, orizzonti culturali*, History of the Ancient Near East / Monographs 15/1–2 (Padova: Sargon, 2014).

18. A portion of the tablets in this series (tablets 1–21) was edited by S. M. Freedman, *If a City Is Set on a Height: The Akkadian Omen Series Šumma Alu ina Mēlê Šakin*, vol. 1, *Tablets 1–21*, Occasional Publications of the Samuel Noah Kramer Fund 17 (Philadelphia: The University of Pennsylvania Museum, 1998), 119 l. 99. Tablets 22–40 are published in S. M. Freedman, *If a City Is Set on a Height: The Akkadian Omen Series Šumma Alu ina Mēlê Šakin*, vol. 2, *Tablets 22–40*, Occasional Publications of the Samuel Noah Kramer Fund 19 (Philadelphia: The University of Pennsylvania Museum, 2006).

19. This series has not yet been fully edited. See, provisionally, U. Koch-Westenholz, *Mesopotamian Astrology: An Introduction to Babylonian and Assyrian Celestial Divination*, The Carsten Niehbuhr Institute Publications 19 (Copenhagen: The Carsten Niebuhr Institute of Near Eastern Studies, 1995), 54–73; E. Gehlken, "Die Adad-Tafeln der Omen serie Enūma Anu Enlil Teil 1: Einführung," *BaM* 36 (2005): 235–73. The series comprises a compilation of celestial omens that, in its canonical form in the first millennium BCE, comprised around seventy tablets for a total of about 6,500 to 7,000 omens. These omens were classified by theme: thus, tablets 15–23 deal with moon eclipses, tablets 24–40 deal with omens linked to the sun, and so on. For the version from Aššur, see especially J. C. Fincke, "Der Assur-Katalog der Serie enūma anu enlil (EAE)," *Or* 70 (2001): 19–39. For astral divination in general, see especially H. Hunger and D. Pingree, *Astral Sciences in Mesopotamia*, Handbuch der Orientalistik 44 (Leiden: Brill, 1999); D. Brown, *Mesopotamian Planetary Astronomy-Astrology*, CM 18 (Groningen: Styx, 2000); N. Veldhuis, "The Theory of Knowledge and the Practice of Celestial Divination," in *Divination and Interpretation of Signs in the Ancient World*, ed. A. Annus, OIS 6 (Chicago: Oriental Institute of the University of Chicago, 2010), 77–91.

direct communication from the gods to humans was mediated by prophecies.[20] Third, humans could obtain answers to specific questions by means of divination, which consisted mainly in the study of lamb livers.[21]

From a methodological perspective, finally, it is important to note that kings in their accounts do not distinguish between "building" and "rebuilding," even though archaeological evidence demonstrates that buildings being "rebuilt" did not always remain at the exact same location.

3.1.1. The Initiative

The royal inscriptions suggest that the initiative for the construction could originate with the gods or the king. In the case of the building or rebuilding of a temple, the gods were most often the instigators.

In earlier royal inscriptions, the reasons for the construction of a building are often not given. We merely find a general formula, by which the king states that "such and such building was in ruin, I rebuilt it from its foundations to its top." Below is an example, found on a foundation brick in the temple of Ištar in Nineveh.

> Aššurnaṣirpal, appointed of the god Enlil, vice-regent of Aššur, son of Tukultī-Ninurta (II), appointed of the god Enlil, vice-regent of Aššur, son of Adad-nārārī (II), appointed of the god Enlil, vice-regent of Aššur: I completely rebuilt the temple of the goddess Ištar of Nineveh, my mistress, from top to bottom.[22]

The simplicity and brevity of this formula should not blind us to the significant number of rituals and oracular inquiries that this construction involved, since no construction could take place without the gods being consulted. The inscription

---

20. The scholarship on ancient Near Eastern prophecies is vast. For the Old Babylonian period, see especially J.-M. Durand, *Archives épistolaires de Mari I/1*, Archives royales de Mari, transcrite et traduite 26/1 (Paris: ERC, 1988), 377–452; D. Charpin, "Prophètes et rois dans le Proche-Orient amorrite: Nouvelles données, nouvelles perspectives," in *Florilegium marianum VI: Recueil d'études à la mémoire d'André Parrot*, Mémoires de N.A.B.U. 7, ed. J. M. Durand and D. Charpin (Paris: SEPOA, 2002), 7–38. For the Neo-Assyrian period, see the reedition of these prophecies in S. Parpola, *Assyrian Prophecies*, SAA 9 (Helsinki: University of Helsinki Press, 1997); see also M. Nissinen, *Prophets and Prophecy in the Ancient Near East*, WAW 12 (Atlanta: Society of Biblical Literature, 2003); M. Nissinen, "Prophecy and Omen Divination: Two Sides of the Same Coin," in *Divination and Interpretation of Signs in the Ancient World*, ed. A. Annus, OIS 6 (Chicago: Oriental Institute of the University of Chicago, 2010), 341–51; M. J. de Jong, *Isaiah Among the Ancient Near Eastern Prophets: A Comparative Study of the Earliest Stages of the Isaiah Tradition and the Neo-Assyrian Prophecies*, VTSup 117 (Leiden: Brill, 2007).
21. See, for instance, the texts edited by Starr, *Queries to the Sungod*.
22. Grayson, *Assyrian Rulers of the Early First Millennium BC I*, text A. 0.101.133.

is short because the king did not take the trouble to reference these procedures, which were taken to be self-evident.

Variations emerge clearly from the inscriptions commemorating the rebuilding of the temple of Ištar of Aššur by Tukultî-Ninurta I (1233–1197). All ten copies of this text that have come down to us include a description of the rebuilding.

> At that time the temple of the Assyrian Ištar, my mistress, which Ilu-šumma (king of the beginning of the 2nd millennium BCE), my forefather, a king who preceded me, had previously built—720 years had passed (and) that temple had become dilapidated and old. At that time (I rebuilt it).[23]

Yet only one of these copies mentions, toward the end of the text, that the rebuilding goes back to a divine intervention.

> At that time, at the beginning of my sovereignty, the goddess Ištar, my mistress, requested of me another temple which would be holier than her (present) shrine [...].[24]

By which medium did the goddess address her request to the king? It could have been through prophecies, dreams, or presages. We simply do not know.

We must wait until the time of the Sargonids to witness detailed explanations for the reasons underlying the construction of a building.

3.1.2. The Beginnings of the Construction

Once the decision was made to build or rebuild, several precautions were in order. The king had his diviners verify that the project enjoys the agreement of the gods, and inquired about the right time to perform the various tasks involved.

Thus Sennacherib, when he undertook the rebuilding of the temple of the Akîtu in Aššur, stated:

> [...] I made up my mind to (re)build th(at) akītu-house, and (then) I found out the will of the gods Šamaš (and) Adad, and they answered me with a firm "yes" and commanded me to (re)build (it).[25]

---

23. A. K. Grayson, *Assyrian Rulers of the Third and Second Millennium BC (to 1115 BC)*, RIMA 1 (Toronto: University of Toronto Press, 1987), 254 text A.0.78.11 ll. 15–33.

24. Ibid., 255–56 text A.0.78.11 exemplar 1 ll. 82–86; compare also the commentary by R. Pruzsinszky, *Mesopotamian Chronology of the 2nd Millennium B.C.: An Introduction to the Textual Evidence and Related Chronological Issues* (Vienna: Verlag der Österreichischen Akademie der Wissenschaften, 2009), 144–46.

25. D. D. Luckenbill, *The Annals of Sennacherib*, Oriental Institute Publications 2 (Chicago: University of Chicago Press, 1924), 137 ll. 28–30; the edition of the passage should be corrected

The formulation may seem redundant at first sight. Yet the apparent banality of this statement involves three distinct stages:

the king presumably wished to rebuild the temple;
the gods sent him signs encouraging him in his project;
a third stage involves verification through hepatoscopy, thereby procuring the divine approval that was necessary for the enterprise to be undertaken.

Once divine assent had been secured, it was still necessary to follow various steps when building.

The first step was to act on an auspicious day.[26] In Sennacherib's inscription mentioned above, the king continues thus:

> In a favorable month, on a propitious day through the craft of the purification priest (and) the wisdom of the exorcist, I laid its foundation [...].[27]

All the rituals involved in building or rebuilding activities use that expression: a diviner could only act on an auspicious day. In the royal correspondence, Issaršumu-ereš (a chief astrologer) thus responds to king Assarhaddon:

> Concerning the cella of (the temple) of (the god) Nusku, about which the king, my lord, wrote to me: "Look up a favourable day, and also write down and send me how it should be *erected*." Sivan (iii) would have been a good month and the 17th a good day. (However) now the month is completely gone, (so) when can they do it? Elul (vi) is a good month: it is (really) the month for it. During it they should make it, and also during it they should *erect* it.[28]

---

with E. Frahm, *Einleitung in die Sanherib-Inschriften*, AfOB 2 (Vienna: Selbstverlag des Instituts für Orientalistik der Universität Wien, 1997), 173–74; see also A. K. Grayson and J. Novotny, *The Royal Inscriptions of Sennacherib, King of Assyria (704–681 BC), Part 2*, RINAP 3/2 (Winona Lake, IN: Eisenbrauns, 2014), 248 text 168.

26. For the Assyrian hemerologies, see L. Marti, "Les hémérologies néo-assyriennes," in *Divination et magie dans les cultures de l'Orient: Actes du Colloque organisé par le Collège de France, le CNRS et la Société Asiatique, Paris 19–20 juin 2008*, ed. J.-M. Durand and A. Jacquet, Cahiers de l'Institut du Proche-Orient ancien du Collège de France 3 (Paris: Maisonneuve, 2010), 41–60; L. Marti, "Chroniques bibliographiques 16: Les hémérologies mésopotamiennes," *Revue d'assyriologie et d'archéologie orientale* 108 (2014): 161–99; A. Livingstone, *Hemerologies of Assyrian and Babylonian Scholars*, Cornell University Studies in Assyriology and Sumerology 25 (Bethesda, MD: CDL Press, 2013); E. Jiménez and S. F. Adali, "The 'Prostration Hemerology' Revisited: An Everyman's Manual at the King's Court," *ZA* 105 (2015): 154–91; E. Jiménez, "Loose Threads of Tradition: Two Late Hemerological Compilations," *JCS* 68 (2016): 197–227.

27. Luckenbill, *Annals of Sennacherib*, 137 l. 30; Grayson and Novotny, *Royal Inscriptions of Sennacherib*, 248 text 168.

28. S. Parpola, *Letters from Assyrian and Babylonian Scholars*, SAA 10 (Helsinki: University of Helsinki Press, 1993), text 14.

Issar-šumu-ereš's reply comes from the consultation of collections of hemerologies, which, in the collection *iqqur îpuš* ("he destroyed, he rebuilt"), state that:

If, in month iii (*simânu*) (the king of the country builds a temple,
   or restores a sanctuary): the god will listen to the prayers of that man.
If, in month iv (*dûzu*): *idem*, his days will be short.
If, in month v (*abu*): *idem*, the gods [...].
If, in month vi (*ulûlu*): *idem*, the god will listen to the prayers of that man.[29]

This series, *iqqur îpuš*, consisting of at least ten tablets, consists in particular of a compilation of auspicious and inauspicious works, of all sorts, performed in a house, from its rebuilding to the opening of a well etc., according to the days and months in the year.

Additionally, the "Aššur hemerologies" indicate that the seventeenth day in month iii (*simânu*) is an auspicious day.[30]

Changes in the layout of a building also need to be approved by the gods. A rather dramatic case is the restoration of Aššur's temple in the city of Aššur.

At that time, with regard to "House, Mountain of the Lands" (é-hur-sag-gal-kur-kur-ra), which is within "House of the Universe" (é-šár-ra), the sanctuary of (the god) Aššur—the great lord, my lord—(and) whose *proper orientation* fell by the wayside in distant days: Its gate openend toward the south. With the extensive wisdom that the god Ea had given me, with the perspicacity that (the god) Aššur had granted to me, I took counsel with myself and made up my mind to open the gate of "House, Mountain of the Lands" toward the rising sun, facing east.[31]

All these justifications are written on supports placed inside the foundations of the new building; they explain to the gods, but also to later restorers, what the king did.

3.1.3. Making a Clean Sweep

Clearing the site was a key stage in the course of rebuilding. It was needed for several reasons: *material reasons*, to begin with, since in the case of buildings

---

29. R. Labat, *Un calendrier babylonien des travaux des signes et des mois (séries* iqqur îpuš*)* (Paris: Honoré Champion, 1965), 94–95 §32.

30. R. Labat, *Hémérologies et ménologies d'Assur* (Paris: Adrien Maisonneuve, 1939), 87 l. 47; see also C. M. Casaburi, *ūmē ṭābūti "I Giorni Favorevoli,"* Studies in the History of the Ancient Near East 8 (Padoue: S.A.R.G.O.N., 2003), 59 §109.

31. Luckenbill, *Annals of Sennacherib*, 144–45 ll. 8–15; Frahm, *Einleitung*, 163–64; Grayson and Novotny, *Royal Inscriptions*, 243 text 166.

built with raw bricks it is necessary to begin by clearing the zone to rebuild, and *ritual reasons*, since clearing the site made it possible not only to purify the site but also to rediscover the original layout of the former building. In the case of temples, the original layout should not be altered, except in very rare circumstances; additionally, it was also necessary to find the foundation inscriptions left by the previous builders, in order to avoid their curses.

3.2. The Beginning of the Building Works

3.2.1. Building: A Matter for Specialists

There were at least four specialists implicated in the foundation rituals: the exorcist (*āšipu*), who was responsible for the various purifications of the site; the lamenter (*kalû*), whose task was to appease the gods by his songs; the musician (*nâru*); and the diviner (*bârû*), who was in charge of asking the gods for the smooth running of the construction and for finding the plans of the former building.[32] Most of the texts we have deal with the knowledge of the first two categories of experts, the exorcist and the lamenter.

Thanks to the "manual of the exorcist,"[33] we know at least the full name of a series of tablets describing a ritual of foundation: "$^{d}SIG_{4}$," in Sumerian, meaning the god Kulla, god of the raw brick. In the manual of the exorcist, the title for this series is glossed as: "(ritual to) lay the foundations for the house of a god" (suhuš é dingir [šub[34]]).[35]

---

32. C. Ambos, "Building Rituals from the First Millennium BC," in *From the Foundation to the Crenellations: Essays on Temple Building in the Ancient Near East and Hebrew Bible*, ed. M. J. Boda and J. Novotny, AOAT 366 (Münster: Ugarit Verlag, 2010), 221–38 at 222.

33. This so-called manual actually comprises a repertory that provides the names of all the writings an exorcist was required to know in order to perform his office. It consists of several main rubrics and appears to have grown over time to include new knowledge. In its final form it covers a significant portion of the learned texts that are otherwise known from Mesopotamia, including many texts related to purification and the struggle against evil forces and that make the exorcist an expert in the elimination of impurity in all its forms and aspects. See C. Jean, *La magie néo-assyrienne en contexte: Recherches sur le métier d'exorciste et le concept d'āšipūtu*, SAAS 17 (Helsinki: Helsinki University Press, 2006), 62–82. For a study of the titles found in the "manual" and their classification, see M. J. Geller, "Incipits and Rubrics," in *Wisdom, Gods and Literature: Studies in Assyriology in Honour of W. G. Lambert*, ed. A. R. George and I. L. Finkel (Winona Lake, IN: Eisenbrauns, 2000), 225–58; and the comments by A. Lenzi, *Secrecy and the Gods: Secret Knowledge in Ancient Mesopotamia and Biblical Israel*, SAAS 19 (Helsinki: Helsinki University Press, 2008), 85–95; P. Clancier, "Le manuel de l'exorcise d'Uruk," in *Et il y eut un esprit dans l'Homme: Jean Bottéro et la Mésopotamie*, ed. X. Faivre, B. Lion, and C. Michel (Paris: De Boccard, 2009), 105–17.

34. For the collation of the passage, see C. Ambos, *Mesopotamische Baurituale aus dem 1. Jahrtausend v. Chr.* (Dresde: Islet, 2004), 7.

35. Jean, *Magie néo-assyrienne*, 63–64.

The first lines of some of the tablets in that series show that these tablets serve to describe rituals to perform during the construction, such as:[36]

"When one opens the gate of the river"
"When the wall of the temple of Anu falls"
"When the wall of the house of the god falls"
"When you build an earthen wall"
"When the (gate) supports are fixed"
"When you set the foundations of the house of a man"
"Tablet of what is needed for making the foundations of the house of a god"[37]

The titles of these tablets thus indicate that there must have been a specific ritual for each type of construction work, depending on the specialists involved. These rituals appear to have had similar contents; below is an excerpt from the ritual named "When opening the foundations of the house of a man . . ."

> When you open the foundations of the house of a man, in a favorable month and on a good day, as soon as you open the foundations (and) lay the brick, you install three altars to Ea, Šamaš, and Asalluhi, two altars to Kûbu. You place a censer with juniper; you make libations: you pour the beer and the wine; you pour for Kûbu beer, wine, oil, honey, and milk.
> You prepare the ritual for Kulla, the lord of foundations and of bricks. You place a censer with juniper. You pour the beer of highest quality. You pour into the middle of the river filtered oil, cedar oil, cypress, oil, honey, milk, precious stones of all sorts, silver, gold, aromatic plants of all sorts; you slaughter a lamb and pour its blood inside the foundations; you recite three times the incantation "O, Ea, Šamaš, Asalluhi, great gods!"[38]

After a stroke for separation, the tablet contains an incantation addressed to the following gods: "O Ea, Šamaš, Asalluhi, great gods . . ."

3.2.2. The Foundation Deposit

The most important part of the (re)building process was the making of the building foundations and the deposits that relate to them. It is consecration par

---

36. Compare Ambos, *Mesopotamische Baurituale*, 156 l. 1.
37. See the list provided by ibid., 273.
38. Ibid., 132–33 II.A.3.

excellence and instrumental to the (re)building process, since it ensures that the foundations will be stable.³⁹

The description of these deposits may occasionally differ slightly between the rituals and the building accounts, even though the two types of documents are complementary. It is interesting to note that the section about deposits is the only section of the foundation rituals to be reproduced in the Assyrian royal inscriptions found within the foundations.

In addition to various substances that must be deposited inside the foundations of the building and that are described in the rituals, the procedure also involves the placement of the first brick. In Akkadian, this component is termed *libittu mahrîtu*, an expression that can be rendered in two different ways: "first brick" or "ancient brick." Royal inscriptions sometimes describe the nature of the brick, which is the equivalent to our "first stone," the very basis of an edifice. It is a raw brick (SIG_4 = *libittu*), specially modeled with clay mixed with various fragrant products.

One of the surprising aspects of this *libittu mahrîtu* is that when a ruler rebuilds a building, his first task is to clear out its dilapidated structures in order to find this brick. This raises the issue of how this brick was identified, since a raw brick in a wall is rather hard to isolate.

A ritual from Seleucid times, which the *kalû*- (lamenter) priests had to perform, states:

When the walls of a temple fall into ruins, in order to demolish, and to found (again) this temple [*there follows the description of the first rituals*].⁴⁰

The builder of that house puts on a pure garment (and) he puts a ring of tin on his hand. He takes an axe of lead and removes a "former brick" (libittu maḫrītu) (from the debris/the collapsed wall) and places it in a restricted room. You place an offering table in front of the brick for the god of the foundations (var.: the goddess Bēlet-ilī). You perform an offering, scatter (aromatic) seed(s) of all kind [...]. They offer honey, ghee, milk, beer, wine and fine oil on (the brick) and the lamentation singer (*kalû*) recites the incantation "When Anu created the heaven" before the brick.⁴¹

---

39. On this issue, see the excellent remarks by S. Lackenbacher, *Le roi bâtisseur: Les récits de construction assyriens des origines à Teglatphalasar III* (Paris: ERC, 1982), 140–44.
40. F. Thureau-Dangin, *Rituels accadiens* (Paris: E. Leroux, 1921), 40–47.
41. New translation by Ambos, "Building Rituals," 227. For a full transcription and translation, see Ambos, *Mesopotamische Baurituale*, 178–81.

As this example shows, the "first" or "ancient" brick was apparently associated with the symbolism of birth.[42]

A further question, for which we currently have no answer, is whether or not this brick was inscribed.[43] It seems difficult to inscribe a raw brick in a durable way. Yet the building contexts do not permit us to disregard the possibility that this raw brick, after it was shaped with the various ingredients listed above, was then baked in order to reinforce it and ensure its inscription remained durable, as is the case with some baked bricks discovered in the foundations of buildings. This conclusion is further supported by the observation that the ritual that was performed on the first brick when it was discovered was very similar to those that were performed by kings when they found the inscriptions commemorating the building foundation of a previous king. Observe, for example, the conclusion preserved on the stone foundation tablets of Aššurnaṣirpal II that were found inside a stone box on the site of Balawat.

> He who will see these foundation inscriptions, will read them, anoint them with oil, perform a sacrifice, and put them back in place; Aššur, the great god, will listen to his prayers [...].[44]

Royal inscriptions only detail a portion of the ritual procedures otherwise known from learned texts, yet they preserve a stage that is never mentioned in the rituals themselves, namely, the placing of a commemorative inscription.

3.2.3. The Foundation Inscription

The only case where an inscription is mentioned in a ritual concerns the placing of figurines inside the foundations of a temple; in this case, the end of a ritual text states:[45]

> After you have done this, you will go on the third day to the clay pit that you consecrated. With a spade, you will cut the clay that you consecrated and make the figurine of Ninšubur. [...] You will make him (Ninšubur)

---

42. Ambos, "Building Rituals," 227; W. G. Lambert and A. R. Millard, *Atra-ḫasīs: The Babylonian Story of the Flood* (Oxford: Clarendon Press, 1969), 60–65; for the deities present during birth, see M. Stol, *Birth in Babylonia and the Bible: Its Mediterranean Setting*, CM 14 (Groningen: Styx, 2000), 74–83, 112–22.

43. Compare the initial comments on this issue by R. S. Ellis, *Foundation Deposits in Ancient Mesopotamia*, Yale Near Eastern Researches 2 (New Haven: Yale University Press, 1968), 26–29, and, more recently, the comments by Ambos, "Building Rituals," 228.

44. Grayson, *Assyrian Rulers of the Early First Millennium BC I*, 321, text A.0.101.50 ll. 44–47.

45. Ambos, "Building Rituals," 233; Ambos, *Mesopotamische Baurituale*, 158–59.

carry a scepter of gold in his hand. On him (Ninšubur) you will write as follows: "Vizier of the gods, the commander, who gathers all the storms!"

It is very likely that the text, placed on the statuette,[46] corresponds to the beginning of an incantation. Taking into account the function of Nin-šubur (Illabrat) as vizir of the gods, the statuette must have served to ensure the good relationship between the king and his gods.[47] Still, the text itself does not have a commemorative function.

Assyrian buildings, especially palaces, were full of inscribed materials.[48] These include the bas-reliefs describing the royal campaigns, or the commemorative steles that every visitor could read (or, at least, contemplate), but these inscribed materials also comprised various documents hidden from human sight.[49] For this latter category, different supports could be used, but especially tablets made of various materials.[50] One example is provided by Sargon II in his inscriptions commemorating the building of Dûr-Šarrukin, his new capital.[51]

> I wrote my name upon tablets of gold, silver, bronze, tin, lead, lapis lazuli and alabaster, and placed them inside their foundations.

As a matter of fact, a portion of them was found on the site during the excavations. The materials used for these tablets match the requirements of texts and rituals for foundation deposits. Thus, the inscriptions commemorating the restoration of Aššur's temple by Shalmanazar I state: "I placed in its foundations stones, silver, gold, iron, copper, tin, and aromatic plants."[52]

---

46. On the placement of figurines inside foundations, see A. Schmitt, "Deponierungen von Figuren bei der Fundamentlegung assyrischer und babylonischer Tempel," in *Mesopotamische Baurituale aus dem 1. Jahrtausend v. Chr.*, ed. C. Ambos (Dresde: Islet, 2004), 229–34.

47. F. A. M. Wiggermann, *Mesopotamian Protective Spirits: The Ritual Texts*, CM 1 (Groningen: Styx, 1992), 127.

48. See on this topic the excellent study by J. M. Russell, *The Writing on the Wall: Studies in the Architectural Context of Late Assyrian Palace Inscriptions*, MC 9 (Winona Lake, IN: Eisenbrauns, 1999).

49. This is the case, for instance, with the inscriptions written on the back of the bas-reliefs of Khorsabad. For the texts, see A. Fuchs, *Die Inschriften Sargons II aus Khorsabad* (Göttingen: Cuvillier Verlag, 1993), 54–59 and 300–302, and the comments by B. André-Salvini, "Remarques sur les inscriptions des reliefs du palais de Khorsabad," in *Khorsabad, le palais de Sargon II, roi d'Assyrie: Actes du colloque organisé au musée du Louvre par le Service culturel les 21 et 22 janvier 1994*, ed. A. Caubet (Paris: La documentation française, 1995), 15–45.

50. See, especially, Ellis, *Foundation Deposits*, 94–107.

51. These mentions occur in several of the Khorsabad inscriptions. For the edition of these texts, see Fuchs, *Inschriften Sargons*; for the text written on foundation tablets made of metals, see pp. 45–53.

52. Grayson, *Assyrian Rulers of the Third and Second Millennium BC*, 185 text A.0.77.1 ll. 141–43.

Shalmanazar III, commemorating the restoration of the city wall of Aššur, also states:

> I mixed its clay with honey, fine oil, cedar resin, beer and wine; I made its bricks with trowels and cedar molds. At the heart of her foundations I laid silver, gold, lapis lazuli, alabaster (*pappardillû*), cornelian, shells, and all sorts of spices.[53]

This is reminiscent of the ritual of the *kalû*, which required the ritual actor to "pour honey, butter, milk, good quality beer, wine, and fine oil";[54] it also brings to mind the ritual that was to be performed on the foundations of a house.

> You (sing.) pour filtered oil, cedar oil, cypress oil, honey, and milk; stones of all sorts, silver, gold, spices of all sorts, you pour in the middle of the river ...[55]

We are also fortunate to have a letter, most likely from Assarhaddon's time, that concerns the rebuilding of Marduk's temple in Babylon, the Esaggil (or "tall-headed house"),[56] which ends by stating:

> Concerning the perfumes, sweet-scented oil, red earth paste and precious stones [which] we are to lay [in] the foundations, let [the king] my [lo]rd, issue an order for them to give (them) to us.[57]

Tablets of precious metals matched the ritual practice of depositing precious matters inside the foundations; in addition, by their inscribed nature they also served to preserve the memory of the ruler. These inscriptions, of varying length, had several functions, and the written text itself (besides its interest for future historians!) was as much a ritual object on which rites had to be performed as a source of divine power, owing to the blessing and curse formulae that were inscribed upon it.

For other types of support, besides the tablets, writing seems to have been more important than the materials themselves; this is especially the case for

---

53. Grayson, *Assyrian Rulers of the Early First Millennium BC II*, 56 text A.0.102.10 col. iv l. 52–lower edge, l. 1.

54. Ambos, *Mesopotamische Baurituale*, 180–81 ll. 21–22.

55. Ibid., 132–33 II.A.3.

56. On Esarhaddon's policy of reintegrating Babylonia into the Assyrian empire, in opposition to the policy of his father Sennacherib, see especially B. N. Porter, *Images, Power, Politics: Figurative Aspects of Esarhaddon's Babylonian Policy* (Philadelphia: American Philosophical Society, 1993).

57. S. W. Cole and P. Machinist, *Letters from Priests to the Kings Esarhaddon and Assurbanipal*, SAA 13 (Helsinki: Helsinki University Press, 1998), 134 text 161 ll. r. 7–11.

terracotta prisms. This material, strikingly absent from those mentioned in the rituals, allows for more important narrative developments, since it allows for a greater number of signs. The offering, then, was no longer the material itself but rather the text that was written upon it.

The first function of these materials was the memorialization of the king, as a prism of Tiglath-phalazar I shows.

> I wrote on my monumental and clay inscriptions my heroic victories, my successful battles, (and) the suppression of the enemies (and) foes of the god Aššur, which the gods Anu and Adad granted me. I deposited (them) in the temple of the gods Anu and Adadn the great gods, my lords forever. In addition, the monumental inscriptions of Šamšī-Adad (III) my forefather I anointed with oil, made sacrifices, (and) returned them to their places.[58]

Some documents include explicit rationales for the composition of these texts, as per the below passage of Sennacherib's inscriptions that describes the restoration of the *Bît Akîti*.

> O you, foundation inscriptions (*temennu*), speak favorable things to (the god) Aššur about Sennacherib, king of the land of Aššur, the one who loves justice, the one who fashioned the image of (the god) Aššur, (and) the one who built the temple [...].[59]

The term "foundations" (*temmenu*) is ambiguous, since it may refer to the foundation document, to the inscription, and to the foundation itself. Since the inscription mentions "speaking" to Aššur, the referent here is presumably the inscription. This example therefore provides a clear illustration of the function of inscriptions—namely, to communicate with the divine.

Another function of these inscriptions was to be read by the king's successors,[60] as the following text by Aššurnaṣirpal II illustrates.

> O later prince among the kings my sons whom Aššur will name: (when) this temple becomes dilapidated (and) you see and read my foundation documents, restore its weakened (portions); write your name with mine (and) return (it) to its place [...].[61]

---

58. Grayson, *Assyrian Rulers of the Early First Millennium BC I*, 30 text A.0.87.1 col. viii 39–46.

59. Luckenbill, *Annals of Sennacherib*, 138–39 ll. 55–57; Ambos, "Building Rituals," 230; Grayson and Novotny, *Royal Inscriptions*, 249 text 168.

60. Regarding the injunctions to the "future prince," see especially Lackenbacher, *Roi bâtisseur*, 145–47.

61. Grayson, *Assyrian Rulers of the Early First Millennium BC I*, 320 text A.0.101.50 ll. 34–38.

This is why pious rulers, when restoring old buildings, took considerable care to retrieve the inscriptions of their predecessors in order to replace them with their own inscriptions, in keeping with divine injunctions.

Such descriptions are particularly abundant in the Neo-Babylonian period,[62] especially under Nebuchanedzar II and Nabonid.[63] Below is Nebuchanedzar II's report about the renovation of the temple of Ninurta of Merad.

> I praised Lugal-Marada, my lord, and I searched carefully for the ancient foundation-(document) of "House, Eye of the Land" (é-igi-kalam-ma), his temple in Marad whose old foundation-(document) no earlier king had seen since the old days [...] I found the foundation-(document) of Naram-Sin, king of Babylon, my distant ancestor. I did not alter his inscription, but deposited my inscription together with his [...][64]

Some Assyrian rulers likewise mention the care with which they handled the documents deposited by their predecessors inside the buildings. Note, for example, the following report by Assarhaddon concerning the restoration of his palace in Nineveh.

> In the future, may one of the kings, my descendants, whom the god Aššur and the goddess Ištar name to rule the land and people, renovate the dilapidated section(s) of that palace when it becomes old and dilapidated. Just as I placed an inscription written in the name of the king, (my) father, who engendered me, beside an inscription written in my name, so you (too) should be like me (and) read an inscription written in my name, anoint (it) with oil, make an offering, and place (it) beside an inscription written in your name. The god Aššur and the goddess Ištar will (then) hear your prayers.[65]

Assyrian inscriptions occasionally mention inscriptions that were placed by an earlier king inside a building, rediscovered and then put back in place by a later

---

62. See on this H. Schaudig, "The Restoration of Temples in the Neo- and Late Babylonian Periods," in *From the Foundation to the Crenellations: Essays on Temple Building in the Ancient Near East and Hebrew Bible*, ed. M. J. Boda and J. Novotny, AOAT 366 (Münster: Ugarit Verlag, 2010), 141–64.

63. The latter is sometimes designated the "archaeologist" king; see A. Schnapp, *La conquête du passé: Aux origines de l'archéologie* (Paris: Éditions Carré, 1993), 17–23; H. Schaudig, "Nabonid, der 'Archäologe auf dem Königsthron' Erwägungen zum Geschichtbild des ausgehenden neubabylonischen Reiches," in *Festschrift für Burkhart Kienast zu seinem 70. Geburstage dargebracht von Freunden, Schülern und Kollegen*, ed. G. J. Selz (AOAT 274; Münster: Ugarit Verlag, 2003), 447–97.

64. Ellis, *Foundation Deposits*, 180–81.

65. Leichty, *Royal Inscriptions*, 231–36 text 1 col. vi ll. 65–74.

king. For instance, in the case of the rebuilding of the temple of Anu and Adad, Tiglath-phalazar I states, after having deposited his own foundation inscriptions,

> In addition, the foundation inscriptions of Samsi-Adad,[66] my ancestor, I anointed with oil, made sacrifices, and return them to their place.[67]

Some archaeological discoveries confirm that the injunctions left by earlier kings in these inscriptions were effectively observed by their successors. One spectacular case is provided by a foundation deposit found in the northeastern corner of the wall surrounding the new palace of Aššur built by Salmanazar III (858–824). The deposit consists of three tablets carefully preserved inside a vase.[68] Two of these tablets, one made of gold and the other of silver, describe the work of Tukultî-Ninurta I (1233–1197) in building a temple that had already been rebuilt once by his father Salmanazar I (1263–1234).

> At that time, the temple of the goddess Nunaittu, my mistress, which the kings who preceded me had previously built—that temple had become dilapidated and old. Salmaneser (I), my father [...] had cleared away its debris down to the bottom of its foundation pit. He had laid its foundation (and) rebuilt that temple making it seventy-two layers of brick high. Then (I), Tukultī-Ninurta, [...] added to the twenty layers of brick (and) installed the beams and the doors. I finished the construction of the temple [...].[69]

The third tablet, made of gold, dates precisely to the reign of Salmanazar I. It states:

> at that time the ancient temple of the goddess Ninuaittu, my mistress, which the kings who preceded me had previously built, had become dilapidated and I rebuilt (it) from the top to bottom. I restored it and deposited my monumental inscription.[70]

---

66. The case of these inscriptions is quite interesting; presumably, their discovery by Tiglath-phalazar I accounts for the mention (earlier in the text) of this ruler—otherwise almost unknown to us—as builder; see further Grayson, *Assyrian Rulers of the Early First Millennium BC I*, 28 col. vii ll. 62 and 29 col. viii l. 2. On the identity of this ruler, see Pruzsinszky, *Mesopotamian Chronology*, 138–39.
67. Grayson, *Assyrian Rulers of the Early First Millennium BC I*, 30 text A.0.87.1 col viii ll. 47–49.
68. On the archaeological context of this discovery, see W. Andrae, *Die Jüngeren Ischtar-Tempel in Assur*, Wissenschaftliche Veröffentlichung der deutschen Orient-Gesellschaft 58 (Leipzig: J. C. Hinrichs, 1935), 51–55 plate 24.
69. Grayson, *Assyrian Rulers of the Third and Second Millennium BC*, 264–65 text A.0.78.17 ll. 5–23.
70. Ibid., 196 text A.0.77.7 ll. 6–20.

The story of these three texts, and of the temple, presumably goes like this: Salmanazar I wished to rebuild the temple. While clearing out the rubble, he was unable to find the inscriptions of previous rulers, which is why they are not named in the tablets. Salmanazar's death then interrupted the rebuilding works. By then, the tablet dating to his reign was probably already placed inside the foundations. His son resumed the work and placed his inscription alongside one of the inscriptions of his father. Four centuries later, Salmanazar III discovered these foundation inscriptions while he was building a wall on the site of the temple. Keeping with the instructions that were written on these tablets—namely, that they should not be moved elsewhere—he placed them inside the new structure, alongside his own inscriptions.

The use of precious metals for the foundation tablets of royal buildings, as in the example discussed here, was common: in the omen literature, this type of material was considered to present a real danger to the future restorer of the building who was to find them.[71] In effect, the *iqqur îpuš* series mentions[72] various bad omens[73] for a man who would find such metals inside the foundations of a building, as is the case in the below example.[74]

> If (when building his house, in the ancient foundations) he finds gold, the building of this house is not approved by the god, the owner of this house will die.

It seems unlikely, however, that rulers intentionally placed objects in the foundations that might harm their successors.[75]

3.3. A Dramatic Case: The Rebuilding of Babylon by Assarhaddon

So far, this essay has surveyed the general principles underlying building or rebuilding activities, the role played by rituals in such activities, the various agents involved, and the place of texts. The case of the rebuilding of Babylon by Assarhaddon is especially interesting for two reasons: first, it takes up all these

---

71. See on this the relevant comments by Ambos, "Building Rituals," 232.
72. Labat, *Calendrier babylonien*, 62–65 §6. Possibly similar omens are mentioned in the third tablet of the *šumma âlu* series; see Freedman, *If a City*, 1:78–81.
73. We may also mention here one letter from Mari, in which the deity forbids in a dream the rebuilding of a house: Durand, *Archives épistolaires de Mari I/1*, 476 text 234. See also J.-M. Durand, *Documents épistolaires du palais de Mari*, vol. 3, LAPO 18 (Paris: Le Cerf, 2000), 85 text 935, and Nissinen, *Prophets and Prophecy*, 65 text 39.
74. Labat, *Calendrier babylonien*, 62–63 §6 l. 5.
75. Ellis, *Foundation Deposits*, 103.

principles, and second, it demonstrates the room for manipulating the texts and construing a certain account of past events.

From a broader historical perspective, the control of Babylonia by the Assyrians was always problematic. The Sargonids appear to have been torn between admiration and exasperation when it came to Babylonia, and their political fumbles manifest the difficulties they had in controlling this kingdom. Sennacherib in particular took an extreme stance toward Babylon. After the unexpected death of his father Sargon II on the battlefield, his son Sennacherib, like many of his predecessors, had to face various rebellions in the empire, among which was the uprising of "Babylonia." After defeating the Babylonian coalition for the first time, he sought to stabilize the country through various means. The first was to install on the throne a Babylonian named Bêl-Ibni who had been educated in Assyria. It resulted in failure. After a new campaign to reestablish order in the country, Sennacherib installed his elder son, Aššur-nâdin-šumi, on the throne of Babylon. Six years later, the Babylonians revolted again and delivered Aššur-nâdin-šumi into the hands of the Elamites. The military campaign that followed was very long and quite harsh; Sennacherib gave his vengeance free rein. He himself declares, in his inscriptions, that he left the city to be sacked, with no respect for cultic places; among other things, the statue of the city god Marduk was deported to Assyria. After it was methodically destroyed, the city was flooded. The importance of the destruction seems nonetheless to be less great than what Sennacherib affirms, but his action against Babylon was still deemed sacrilegious and may have been one of the causes leading to his assassination several years later. As a result of Sennacherib's last campaign, the throne of Babylon was left unoccupied and Babylonia was reduced to the rank of a mere province of the Assyrian empire.[76]

Following Sennacherib's assassination in 681, his son Assarhaddon took the throne and decided very early on in his reign that his policy toward Babylonia would be the opposite to that of his father.[77] To that end, the priority was to rebuild the capital, Babylon—a highly complex enterprise! Assarhaddon could not go against his father's policy, since in the Assyrian imperial logic the acts of the kings were dictated by the gods, even if they were to instigate an opposing policy. The solution he opted for illustrates, among other things, the considerable importance of both the written text and ritual in the Mesopotamian world. A significant portion of our information concerning that case comes from the foundation inscriptions that were found in Babylon.[78]

---

76. On Sennacherib's reign, and his Babylonian "problem," see E. Frahm, "Sīn-aḫḫē-erība," in *The Prosopography of the Neo-Assyrian Empire*, vol. 3, part 1, *P–S*, ed. H. D. Baker (Helsinki: Helsinki University Press, 2002), 1113–27.

77. On Esarhaddon's new policy toward Babylonia, see the study by Porter, *Images*.

78. The destruction and rebuilding of Babylon are mentioned, with varying detail, in several of Esarhaddon's inscriptions coming from Babylon. For Esarhaddon's inscriptions coming from Babylon, see Leichty, *Royal Inscriptions*, 193–258. The present translation is from text 114, pp. 231–37.

In order to avoid acting against his father's will, Assarhaddon had to invent a cause for Babylon's destruction. He therefore presented the following account:

> Before my time, in the reign of a previous king, bad omens occurred in Sumer and Akkad. The people living there were answering each other yes (for) no (and) were telling lies. They put the[ir] hands on the possessions of Esagil, the palace of the gods, and they sold the gold, sil[ver], (and) precious stones at market value to the land of Elam. The Enlil of the gods, the god Marduk, became angry and plotted evilly to level the land (and) to destroy [its] people ... [79]

Thus Assarhaddon explained Babylon's destruction by reference to the wrath of the city god, Marduk, who unleashed the flood upon the Babylonians because the latter continued their impious behaviors despite the god's warnings. Sennacherib, unnamed in this account, became here a mere executant of the god's will.

What remained to be explained was Marduk's decision to destroy Babylon, which the Assyrian king could not openly oppose, but which he could mitigate.

> The merciful god Marduk wrote that the calculated time of its abandonment (should last) 70 years, (but) his heart was quickly soothed, and he reversed the numbers and (thus) ordered its (re)occupation to be (after) 11 years. You [truly] selected me, Esarhaddon, in the assembly of my older brothers, to put these matters right, and you (are the one) who placed your sweet [protec]tion over me, swept away all of my enemies like [a flood], killed all of my [foes] and [made] me attain my wish, (and), to appease the heart of your great divinity (and) to please your spirit, you entrusted (me) with shepherding Assyria.[80]

This passage demonstrates that, while it was not possible to reverse a decision written by the gods, it was always possible to manipulate it. Marduk's decision was that Babylon would be abandoned for "seventy" years. Marduk himself could not reverse his own decision, but he could turn the tablet upside-down and, through this manipulation, shorten the length of Babylon's punishment to "eleven" years.[81] The fact that Marduk, Babylon's highest ranking god, and not Aššur, was the one who chose Assarhaddon as king of Assyria evidently reflects the context that gave rise to this text, as well the intention behind it.

---

79. Ibid., 231–36 text 114 col. i l. 7–col. ii l. 11.
80. Ibid., 236 text 114 col. ii l. 1–col. iii l. 8.
81. On this manipulation, see ibid., 196, with the note for col. ii ll. 6–7; P. A. Beaulieu, "An Excerpt from a Menology with Reverse Writing," *Acta Sumerologica* 17 (1995): 1–14.

Following this preamble, and having obtained Marduk's agreement, Assarhaddon must take several precautions.

> At the beginning of my kingship, in my first year, when I sat in greatness on (my) royal throne, [good] signs were [est]ablished for me; in heaven (and) on earth, [he (the god Marduk) constantly se]nt me his omen(s). [...][82]

Similar passages are found in the majority of Assarhaddon's inscriptions. Nonetheless, Babylon is mentioned only in the Babylonian versions of these inscriptions. Another text provides additional details on the "signs" mentioned by Assarhaddon.

> The angry [gods] were reconciled (and) [they repeatedly] disclosed [fav]orable [signs] concerning the (re)building of Babylon (and) [the renovation of] Esagil. [Br]ight [Jupiter, the giver of decisions on Akkad, came near in Simānu (iii) and stood in the place where the sun shines. It was shining brightly (and) its appearance] was red. It reached (its) hypsoma for a second [time] in the month "Opening of the Door" and stayed in its place.[83]

The ruler reports here the omens that his astrologers were able to observe. After the first "fortuitous" good omens, further investigation was required.

> [I was afraid] (and) worried [to] preform that work (and) I knelt before the gods Šamaš, [Adad], (and) Marduk, the great judge(s), the god[s], my lords. In the diviner's bowl, trustworthy oracles were established for me, and they had (their response) concerning the (re)building of Babylon (and) the renovation of Esagil written on a liver. I trusted in their fi[rm] "yes" and I mustered all of my craftsmen and the people of Karduniaš (Babylonia) to its full extent. I had them wield hoes and I imposed baskets (on them). I mixed (the mud for) its revetment with fine oil, honey, ghee, kurunnu-wine, (and) pure mountain beer. I raised a basket onto my head and carried (it) myself. I had its bricks made for one year in brickmolds of ivory, ebony, boxwood, (and) musukkannu-wood.[84]

In this text, the ruler presents the various steps involved in the oracular consultation. He therefore begins by the prayers toward various deities. Then,

---

82. Leichty, *Royal Inscriptions*, 237 text 114 col. iii ll. 9–14.
83. Ibid., 245 text 105 rev. col. iii 5–18.
84. Ibid., 237 text 114 col. iii l. 16–col. iv l. 15.

he requires additional confirmation from his diviners, first by means of lecanomancy, second by means of hepatoscopy, thus finally obtaining a firm "yes."[85]

After this, the rebuilding works may begin, and the procedure described in Assarhaddon's inscriptions matches the rituals that serve to prepare the foundations.[86] The text ends, unsurprisingly, with the description of the foundation ritual.

> I had foundation inscriptions made of silver, gold, bronze, lapis lazuli, alabaster, basalt, pendû-stone, alallu-stone (and) white limestone, (as well as) inscribed objects of baked clay, and (then) I depicted on them hieroglyphs representing the writing of my name.[87] I wrote on them the might of the great hero, the god Marduk, (and) the deeds that I had done, my pious work, (and) I placed (these inscriptions) in the foundations (and) left (them) for far-off days.[88]

There follow blessings and curses, and finally the date of the document—namely, the "first year of Assarhaddon, king of the land of Aššur."

3.4. Conclusions

The previous analysis allows for some general conclusions on the relationship between "text" and "ritual" in the case of Akkadian building and rebuilding projects.

In very general terms, the written text can be divided into two main categories: "practical" text and "symbolic" text, the latter of which carries a supernatural force.

Ritual texts and letters belong to the first category. The rituals themselves are not thought to be endowed with supernatural strength; they are mere "recipes" of sorts to ensure that a given action will be successful. As such, the rituals performed in the course of building activities serve to make the building durable by protecting it against supernatural attacks. Such a result is achieved not through the intrinsic power of the text itself but through the performance of the actions described in it, especially the recitation of incantations. This is why

---

85. On this divinatory practice, see J. Novotny, "Temple Building in Assyria: Evidence from Royal Inscriptions," in *From the Foundation to the Crenellations: Essays on Temple Building in the Ancient Near East and Hebrew Bible*, ed. M. J. Boda and J. Novotny, AOAT 366 (Münster: Ugarit Verlag, 2010), 114–15.

86. See on this aspect the comments by Novotny in ibid., 119–20.

87. See Leichty, *Royal Inscriptions*, 238–43, especially p. 243 for a survey of the various interpretations proposed. Compare also the remarks by Brown, *Mesopotamian*, 112.

88. Leichty, *Royal Inscriptions*, 209–10 text 105 col. ix ll. 21–36.

we never find ritual texts among the texts placed as votive offerings inside the foundations; it is rather the royal inscriptions that describe how the process was accomplished. The titles of the incantations could, however, be mentioned in the ritual texts; this shows that the power of the verb (reciting the incantation) can also be activated simply through the writings, under certain specific conditions.

The foundation inscriptions, for their part, belong to the second category. The fact that they are not mentioned in the rituals indicates either that they are not compulsory or that we have not found the ritual texts in which they are mentioned. Nevertheless, their omnipresence in all types of construction achieved by the Mesopotamian rulers highlights their key role.

The fact that the materials used for these inscriptions can be similar to those used for the deposits shows that the written text has a votive status. The rituals used by the kings to (re)discover the inscriptions of their predecessors also suggest that they somehow had the status of sacred objects. The ambiguity of some Akkadian terms assimilating foundations, foundation deposits, and foundation inscriptions (see above) points in the same direction. The powerful curses, found in these texts, against persons who would alter or erase them underline their unchanging character. Nevertheless, the case of Babylon analyzed here also demonstrates that manipulations were always possible.

An important point to keep in mind is that commemorative inscriptions were written in order to exalt the ruler's achievements; that is why rituals, when they are described, are usually incomplete and exclude nonroyal agents specifically.

Commemorative inscriptions somehow serve to materialize the king's achievements, even when the latter have disappeared. This point is well illustrated by the case of the inscriptions of Shalmanazar I and Tukulti-Ninurta I: their distant successor carefully put into place their inscriptions commemorating the building of a temple that, by then, no longer existed because it had been replaced by a wall.

The foundations of buildings often comprised several foundation deposits. Thus, for instance, no less than four different texts, attested by nineteen documents, come from the temple of Anu-and-Adad in the city of Aššur, which was rebuilt by Shalmanazar III.

The function of these texts was twofold, since it simultaneously presented the gods and humans with the achievements of a ruler, and the changes he had made to a building. Indeed, from early times onward, the Mesopotamian rulers were aware that the written text was the solution most appropriate to the problem caused by the ephemeral nature of their buildings, made of raw bricks. The point was already illustrated by the ending of the Gilgamesh poem, which was for these rulers one of their main sources of inspiration.

Thus the purpose of the written text to immortalize royal achievements somehow succeeded beyond all the hopes that these rulers could possibly entertain.

Which of them could have imagined that, more than 2,500 years after the disappearance of their empire, and the almost complete erasure of their civilization, that these inscriptions would provide the very basis for the rediscovery of that empire? Indeed, the birth of Assyriology as an academic discipline was officially declared in 1857 following the joint decipherment by several scholars of one of the foundation prisms of Tiglath-phalazar I recounting the building of the temple of Anu-and-Adad in the city of Aššur.

BIBLIOGRAPHY

Ambos, C. "Building Rituals from the First Millennium BC." Pages 221–38 in *From the Foundation to the Crenellations: Essays on Temple Building in the Ancient Near East and Hebrew Bible*. Edited by M. J. Boda and J. Novotny. AOAT 366. Münster: Ugarit Verlag, 2010.

———. *Mesopotamische Baurituale aus dem 1. Jahrtausend v. Chr*. Dresden: Islet, 2004.

Andrae, W. *Die Jüngeren Ischtar-Tempel in Assur*. Wissenschaftliche Veröffentlichungen der deutschen Orient-Gesellschaft 58. Leipzig: J. C. Hinrichs, 1935.

André-Salvini, B. "Remarques sur les inscriptions des reliefs du palais de Khorsabad." Pages 15–45 in *Khorsabad, le palais de Sargon II, roi d'Assyrie: Actes du colloque organisé au musée du Louvre par le Service culturel les 21 et 22 janvier 1994*. Edited by A. Caubet. Paris: La documentation française, 1995.

Beaulieu, P. A. "An Excerpt from a Menology with Reverse Writing." *Acta Sumerologica* 17 (1995): 1–14.

Borger, R. "Shurpu II, III, IV und VIII in 'Partitur.'" Pages 15–90 in *Wisdom, Gods and Literature: Studies in Assyriology in Honour of W. G. Lambert*. Edited by A. R. George and I. L. Finkel. Winona Lake, IN: Eisenbrauns, 2000.

Bottéro, J. *Mythes et rites de Babylone*. Geneva: Slatkine / Honoré Champion, 1985.

Brown, D. *Mesopotamian Planetary Astronomy-Astrology*. CM 18. Groningen: Styx, 2000.

Casaburi, C. M. *ūmē ṭābūti "I Giorni Favorevoli."* Studies in the History of the Ancient Near East 8. Padoue: S.A.R.G.O.N., 2003.

Charpin, D. "Prophètes et rois dans le Proche-Orient amorrite: Nouvelles données, nouvelles perspectives." Pages 7–38 in *Florilegium marianum VI: Recueil d'études à la mémoire d'André Parrot*, Mémoires de N.A.B.U. 7. Edited by J. M. Durand and D. Charpin. Paris: SEPOA, 2002.

———. *Reading and Writing in Babylon*. Cambridge: Harvard University Press, 2010.

Cifola, B. *Analysis of Variants in the Assyrian Royal Titulary from the Origins to Tiglath-Pileser III*. Napels: Istituto Universitario Orientale, 1995.

Clancier, P. "Le manuel de l'exorcise d'Uruk." Pages 105–17 in *Et il y eut un esprit dans l'Homme: Jean Bottéro et la Mésopotamie*. Edited by X. Faivre, B. Lion, and C. Michel. Paris: De Boccard, 2009.

Cole, S. W., and P. Machinist. *Letters from Priests to the Kings Esarhaddon and Assurbanipal*. SAA 13. Helsinki: Helsinki University Press, 1998.

Durand, J.-M. *Archives épistolaires de Mari I/1*. Archives royales de Mari, transcrite et traduite 26/1. Paris: ERC, 1988.

———. *Documents épistolaires du palais de Mari*, vol. 3. LAPO 18. Paris: Le Cerf, 2000.

Ellis, R. S. *Foundation Deposits in Ancient Mesopotamia*. Yale Near Eastern Researches 2. New Haven: Yale University Press, 1968.

Fales, F. M., ed. "Assyrian Royal Inscriptions: Newer Horizons." *State Archives of Assyria Bulletin* 13 (1999–2001): 115–44.

———. *Assyrian Royal Inscriptions: New Horizons in Literary, Ideological and Historical Analysis*. Rome: Istituto per l'Oriente, 1981.

Fales, F. M., and J. N. Postgate, *Imperial Administrative Records*. Part 1, *Palace and Temple Administration*. SAA 7. Helsinki: Helsinki University Press, 1992.

Fincke, J. C. "Der Assur-Katalog der Serie enūma anu enlil (EAE)." *Or* 70 (2001): 19–39.

———. "The Babylonian Texts of Nineveh: Report on the British Museum's *Ashurbanipal Library Project*." *Archiv für Orientforschung* 50 (2003/4): 111–32.

———. "The British Museum's Ashurbanipal Library Project." *Iraq* 66 (2004): 55–60.

Frahm, E. *Einleitung in die Sanherib-Inschriften*. AfOB 2. Vienna: Selbstverlag des Instituts für Orientalistik der Universität Wien, 1997.

———. "Sīn-aḫḫē-erība." Pages 1113–27 in *The Prosopography of the Neo-Assyrian Empire*, vol. 3, part 1, *P–S*. Edited by H. D. Baker. Helsinki: Helsinki University Press, 2002.

Frame, G., and A. George. "The Royal Libraries of Nineveh: New Evidence for King Ashurbanipal's Tablet Collecting." *Iraq* 67.1 (2005): 265–84.

Freedman, S. M. *If a City Is Set on a Height: The Akkadian Omen Series Šumma Alu ina Mēlê Šakin*. Vol. 1, *Tablets 1–21*. Occasional Publications of the Samuel Noah Kramer Fund 17. Philadelphia: The University of Pennsylvania Museum, 1998.

———. *If a City Is Set on a Height: The Akkadian Omen Series Šumma Alu ina Mēlê Šakin*. Vol. 2, *Tablets 22–40*. Occasional Publications of the Samuel Noah Kramer Fund 19. Philadelphia: The University of Pennsylvania Museum, 2006.

Fuchs, A. *Die Inschriften Sargons II aus Khorsabad*. Göttingen: Cuvillier Verlag, 1993.

Gehlken, E. "Die Adad-Tafeln der Omen serie Enūma Anu Enlil Teil 1: Einführung." *BaM* 36 (2005): 235–73.

Geller, M. J. "Incipits and Rubrics." Pages 225–58 in *Wisdom, Gods and Literature: Studies in Assyriology in Honour of W. G. Lambert*. Edited by A. R. George and I. L. Finkel. Winona Lake, IN: Eisenbrauns, 2000.

Grayson, A. K. "Assyria and Babylonia." *Or* 49 (1980): 140–94.

———. *Assyrian Rulers of the Early First Millennium BC I (1114–859 BC)*. RIMA 2. Toronto: University of Toronto Press, 1991.

———. *Assyrian Rulers of the Third and Second Millennium BC (to 1115 BC)*. RIMA 1. Toronto: University of Toronto Press, 1987.

Grayson, A. K., and J. Novotny, *The Royal Inscriptions of Sennacherib, King of Assyria (704–681 BC), Part 2*. RINAP 3/2. Winona Lake, IN: Eisenbrauns, 2014.

Hunger, H. *Babylonische und assyrische Kolophone*. AOAT 2. Vluyn: Verlag Butzon & Bercker Kevelaer, 1968.

Hunger, H., and D. Pingree. *Astral Sciences in Mesopotamia*. Handbuch der Orientalistik 44. Leiden: Brill, 1999.

Jean, C. *La magie néo-assyrienne en contexte: Recherches sur le métier d'exorciste et le concept d'āšipūtu.* SAAS 17. Helsinki: Helsinki University Press, 2006.
Jiménez, E. "Loose Threads of Tradition: Two Late Hemerological Compilations." *JCS* 68 (2016): 197–227.
Jiménez, E., and S. F. Adali. "The 'Prostration Hemerology' Revisited: An Everyman's Manual at the King's Court." *ZA* 105 (2015): 154–91.
Jong, M. J. de. *Isaiah Among the Ancient Near Eastern Prophets: A Comparative Study of the Earliest Stages of the Isaiah Tradition and the Neo-Assyrian Prophecies.* VTSup 117. Leiden: Brill, 2007.
Koch-Westenholz, U. *Babylonian Liver Omens: The Chapters manzâzu, padânu and pân tâkalti of the Babylonian Extispicy Series Mainly from Aššurbanipal's Library.* The Carsten Niehbuhr Institute Publications 25. Copenhagen: Museum Tusculanum Press, 2000.
———. *Mesopotamian Astrology: An Introduction to Babylonian and Assyrian Celestial Divination.* The Carsten Niehbuhr Institute Publications 19. Copenhagen: The Carsten Niebuhr Institute of Near Eastern Studies, 1995.
Labat, R. *Un calendrier babylonien des travaux des signes et des mois (séries iqqur îpuš).* Paris: Honoré Champion, 1965.
———. *Hémérologies et ménologies d'Assur.* Paris: Adrien Maisonneuve, 1939.
Lackenbacher, S. *Le roi bâtisseur: Les récits de construction assyriens des origines à Teglatphalasar III.* Paris: ERC, 1982.
Lambert, W. G., and A. R. Millard. *Atra-ḥasīs: The Babylonian Story of the Flood.* Oxford: Clarendon Press, 1969.
Leichty, E. *The Omen Series* Šumma Izbu. Texts from Cuneiform Sources 4. New York: J. J. Augustin, 1970.
———. *The Royal Inscriptions of Esarhaddon, King of Assyria (680–669 BC).* RINAP 4. Winona Lake, IN: Eisenbrauns, 2011.
Lenzi, A. *Secrecy and the Gods: Secret Knowledge in Ancient Mesopotamia and Biblical Israel.* SAAS 19. Helsinki: Helsinki University Press, 2008.
Linssen, M. J. H. "Unpublished Fragments from the Burning Ritual Series (Šurpu) from the British Museum." Pages 47–52 in *Studies in Ancient Near Eastern World View and Society Presented to Marten Stol on the Occasion of His 65th Birthday.* Edited by R. J. van der Spek. Bethesda, MD: CDL Press, 2008.
Liverani, M. "Memorandum on the Approach to Historiographical Texts." *Or* 42 (1973): 178–94.
Livingstone, A. *Court Poetry and Literary Miscellanea.* SAA 3. Helsinki: Helsinki University Press, 1989.
———. *Hemerologies of Assyrian and Babylonian Scholars.* Cornell University Studies in Assyriology and Sumerology 25. Bethesda, MD: CDL Press, 2013.
Luckenbill, D. D. *The Annals of Sennacherib.* Oriental Institute Publications 2. Chicago: University of Chicago Press, 1924.
Marti, L. "Chroniques bibliographiques 16: Les hémérologies mésopotamiennes." *Revue d'assyriologie et d'archéologie orientale* 108 (2014): 161–99.
———. "Les hémérologies néo-assyriennes." Pages 41–60 in *Divination et magie dans les cultures de l'Orient: Actes du Colloque organisé par le Collège de France, le CNRS et la Société Asiatique, Paris 19–20 juin 2008.* Edited by J.-M. Durand and A. Jacquet. Cahiers de l'Institut du Proche-Orient ancien du Collège de France 3. Paris: Maisonneuve, 2010.

Maul, S. "How the Babylonians Protected Themselves against Calamities Announced by Omens." Pages 123–29 in *Mesopotamian Magic: Textual, Historical, and Interpretative Perspectives*. Edited by T. Abusch and K. van der Toorn. Ancient Magic and Divination 1. Groningen: Styx, 1999.
Mayer, W. *Assyrien und Urarṭu I. Der Achte Feldzug Sargons II. im Jahr 714 v. Chr.* AOAT 395/1. Münster: Ugarit Verlag, 2013.
———. "Sargons Feldzug gegen Urartu 714 v. Chr. Text und Ubersetzung." *Mitteilungen der Deutschen Orient-Gesellschaft* 115 (1983): 65–132.
Nissinen, N. "Prophecy and Omen Divination: Two Sides of the Same Coin." Pages 341–51 in *Divination and Interpretation of Signs in the Ancient World*. Edited by A. Annus. OIS 6. Chicago: Oriental Institute of the University of Chicago, 2010.
———. *Prophets and Prophecy in the Ancient Near East*. WAW 12. Atlanta: Society of Biblical Literature, 2003.
Noegel, S. B. "'Sign, Sign, Everywhere a Sign': Script, Power and Interpretation in the Ancient Near East." Pages 143–62 in *Divination and Interpretation of Signs in the Ancient World*. Edited by A. Annus. OIS 6. Chicago: Oriental Institute of University of Chicago, 2010.
Novotny, J. "Temple Building in Assyria: Evidence from Royal Inscriptions." Pages 114–15 in *From the Foundation to the Crenellations: Essays on Temple Building in the Ancient Near East and Hebrew Bible*. Edited by M. J. Boda and J. Novotny. AOAT 366. Münster: Ugarit Verlag, 2010.
Parpola, S. "Assyrian Library Records." *JNES* 42.1 (1983): 1–29.
———. *Assyrian Prophecies*. SAA 9. Helsinki: University of Helsinki Press, 1997.
———. *Letters from Assyrian and Babylonian Scholars*. SAA 10. Helsinki: University of Helsinki Press, 1993.
———. "The Royal Archives of Nineveh." Pages 223–36 in *Cuneiform Archives and Libraries: Papers Read at the 30ᵉ Rencontre Assyriologique Internationale, Leiden, 4–8 July 1983*. Edited by K. R. Veenhof. Istanbul: Nederlands Historisch-Archaeologisch Instituut, 1986.
Pedersén, O. *Archives and Libraries in the Ancient Near East, 1500–300 B.C.* Bethesda, MD: CDL Press 1998.
Porter, B. N. *Images, Power, Politics: Figurative Aspects of Esarhaddon's Babylonian Policy*. Philadelphia: American Philosophical Society, 1993.
Pruzsinszky, R. *Mesopotamian Chronology of the 2nd Millennium B.C.: An Introduction to the Textual Evidence and Related Chronological Issues*. Vienna: Verlag der Österreichischen Akademie der Wissenschaften, 2009.
Reade, J. E. "Archaeology and the Kuyunjik Archives." Pages 213–22 in *Cuneiform Archives and Libraries: Papers Read at the 30e Rencontre Assyriologique Internationale, Leiden, 4–8 July 1983*. Edited by K. R. Veenhof. Istanbul: Nederlands Historisch-Archaeologisch Instituut, 1986.
———. "Ninive (Nineveh)." *RlA* 9 (2000): 388–433.
Reiner, E. *Šurpu: A Collection of Sumerian and Akkadian Incantations*. AfOB 11. Graz: Im Selbstverlage des Herausgebers, 1958.
Russell, J. M. *The Writing on the Wall: Studies in the Architectural Context of Late Assyrian Palace Inscriptions*. MC 9. Winona Lake, IN: Eisenbrauns, 1999.
Schaudig, H. "Nabonid, der 'Archäologe auf dem Königsthron' Erwägungen zum Geschichtbild des ausgehenden neubabylonischen Reiches." Pages 447–97 in *Festschrift für Burkhart Kienast zu seinem 70. Geburtstage dargebracht von Freunden,*

Schülern und Kollegen. Edited by G. J. Selz. AOAT 274. Münster: Ugarit Verlag, 2003.

———. "The Restoration of Temples in the Neo- and Late Babylonian Periods." Pages 141–64 in *From the Foundation to the Crenellations: Essays on Temple Building in the Ancient Near East and Hebrew Bible*. Edited by M. J. Boda and J. Novotny. AOAT 366. Münster: Ugarit Verlag, 2010.

Schmitt, A. "Deponierungen von Figuren bei der Fundamentlegung assyrischer und babylonischer Tempel." Pages 229–34 in *Mesopotamische Baurituale aus dem 1. Jahrtausend v. Chr.* Edited by C. Ambos. Dresde: Islet, 2004.

Schnapp, A. *La conquête du passé: Aux origines de l'archéologie*. Paris: Éditions Carré, 1993.

Starr, I. *Queries to the Sungod: Divination and Politics in Sargonid Assyria*. SAA 4. Helsinki: Helsinki University Press, 1990.

Stol, M. *Birth in Babylonia and the Bible: Its Mediterranean Setting*. CM 14. Groningen: Styx, 2000.

Thompson, R. C. *Prisms of Esarhaddon and of Ashurbanipal Found at Nineveh, 1927–1928*. Oxford: Oxford University Press, 1931.

Thureau-Dangin, F. *Une relation de la huitième campagne de Sargon*. Textes cunéiformes, Musée du Louvre 3. Paris: Geuthner, 1912.

———. *Rituels accadiens*. Paris: E. Leroux, 1921.

Veldhuis, N. "The Theory of Knowledge and the Practice of Celestial Divination." Pages 77–91 in *Divination and Interpretation of Signs in the Ancient World*. Edited by A. Annus. OIS 6. Chicago: Oriental Institute of the University of Chicago, 2010.

Wiggermann, F. A. M. *Mesopotamian Protective Spirits: The Ritual Texts*. CM 1. Groningen: Styx, 1992.

Zorzi, D. de. *La serie teratomantica* šumma izbu*: Testo, tradizione, orizzonti culturali*. History of the Ancient Near East / Monographs 15/1–2. Padova: Sargon, 2014.

CHAPTER 4

Between Text and Ritual: The Function(s) of the Ritual Texts from Late Bronze Age Emar (Syria)

Patrick Michel

4.1. Historical Context: Aštata and the Hittite Empire

Emar was important as a traffic junction, occupying a liminal position between Upper Mesopotamia (Assyro-Babylonia) and the Syro-Anatolian cultural sphere. From the fourteenth century, Hittite power controlled Aštata, in which Emar was one of the most important cities,[1] on account of the kings in Karkemiš.[2] It is worth noting that king Muršili II (1321–1295) had carried out a vast campaign of reconquest of the south of the Empire to counter the revolt of the Syrian subjects.

As winters were long and hard in Anatolia, there was no possibility to campaign abroad. As a result, the Hittite empire preferred to annex and associate vassal states rather than integrate them on economic and political levels. The Hittites therefore left the administration of these states to the local elites,[3] or to princes from the Hittite court. Vassals had to pay tribute to the Empire, to supply soldiers, and to forego relations with foreign empires or kingdoms. Hittite garrisons were placed in the vassal kingdoms in order to ensure better control, which

---

1. See Y. Cohen, "The Administration of Cult in Hittite Emar," *AFo* 38 (2009): 145–57, who defines Emar as the "capital" (154 n. 57). It is sometimes possible that the geographical words "Emar" and "Land of Aštata" are commutable.
2. Šuppiluliuma I conquered Karkemiš, reorganized northern Syria, and put the king of Mitanni under his guardianship. He used two different vassal states—Karkemiš in the East and Aleppo in the center—in order to control the whole of Aštata. Šuppiluliuma gave power to his son Piyaššili (Šarri-Kušuḫ) to control the area. He was king of Karkemiš and viceroy of Ḫatti in Syria. For a full bibliography, see P. M. Michel, *Le culte des pierres à Emar à l'époque hittite* (Fribourg: Academic Press; Göttingen: Vandenhoeck & Ruprecht, 2014), 41–49.
3. G. M. Beckman, "Hittite Administration in Syria in the Light of the Texts from Hattusa, Ugarit and Emar," in *New Horizons in the Study of Ancient Syria*, ed. M. W. Chavalas and J. L. Hayes, Bibliotheca Mesopotamica 25 (Malibu: Undena, 1992), 41–49 at 45; G. Kestemont, *Diplomatie et droit international en Asie occidentale (1600–1200 av. J.C.)*, Publications de l'Institut orientaliste de Louvain 9 (Louvain-la-Neuve: Université catholique de Louvain Institut orientaliste, 1974).

was also the case with regard to Emar.[4] Indeed, the Hittite viceroy in Syria was usually involved in the administration of Emar.[5] The *Bēl Madgalti*, "margrave, district governor" in Hittite Anatolia, was an officer involved in military affairs but also in the general administration of the province. Therefore, he was also present during the registration of legal documents and is cited among the legal witnesses. As is attested in Emar 460, the *Bēl Madgalti* also took part in the local religious life. In this text, he participates in the cult of Ištar taḫazi (^{d}INANNA MÈ) and consumes beer together with the diviner, the Lady of the Palace, and the blacksmith of the city.[6]

Arguably the most important discovery on the site was that of a religious area, which included several temples exhibiting Syro-Hittite architectural features. A double sanctuary was dedicated to Baal and perhaps also to his Syrian consort. The building M_1 was also found at the same time in the lower city. This building is important because of the numerous texts that were found in its archive. A letter dating back to the reign of the Babylonian king Melisi-ḪU allows us, according to Daniel Arnaud,[7] to assign the destruction of the city to the year 1187 BCE.[8]

Since this document is the latest known, it binds the dramatic events of the end of the Late Bronze Age—namely, the destruction of empires and kingdoms around the Mediterranean—to an absolute chronology. The city could not have been destroyed before this date.[9]

Documents from Emar provide a very valuable source of information concerning the organization of the Hittite administration in Syria. In particular, they help us to understand the interaction between the two cultures—those of Syria and Anatolia—in Emar, which lay on the border of two different worlds.[10]

---

4. Two Hittite letters attest to the presence of Alziyamuwa (the commander of the garrison) in Emar. The first is written by the king of Ḫatti; see E. Laroche, "Documents hittites et hourrites," in *Meskéné Emar: Dix ans de travaux 1972–1982*, ed. Dominique Beyer (Paris: Editions Recherche sur les civilisations, 1982), 53–60 at 54. The other is written by the king of Karkemiš; see I. Singer, "A New Hittite Letter from Emar," in *Landscapes: Territories, Frontiers and Horizons in the Ancient Near East; Papers Presented to the XLIV Rencontre Assyriologique Internationale, Venezia, 7–11 July 1997*, part 2, *Geography and Cultural Landscapes*, ed. L. Milano et al. (Padua: Sargon, 2000), 65–72; M. Salvini and M.-C. Trémouille, "Les textes hittites de Meskéné/Emar," *SMEA* 45.2 (2003): 225–71.

5. Several private documents were written in the presence of king Ini-Tešup; e.g., Emar 18, 177, and 202.

6. [x DUG KA]Š ŠE.MEŠ *a-na* ^{lú}UGULA.KALAM.MA.

7. D. Arnaud, "Les textes d'Emar et la chronologie de la fin du Bronze récent," *Syria* 52 (1975): 87–92.

8. I. Singer ("Dating the End of the Hittite Empire," *Hethitica* 8 [1987]: 413–22) proposed 1180 as a date.

9. See, e.g., J. D. Hawkins, "Karkamish and Karatepe: Neo-Hittite City-States in North Syria," in *Civilizations of the Ancient Near East*, ed. J. M. Sasson (New York: Scribner, 1995), 2:1301.

10. On the interaction between Emar and the Hittite culture, see Michel, *Culte des pierres*.

The international nature of this area can be seen in the variety of languages attested in the Emar documents: Babylonian and Assyrian Akkadian, Hittite or Hurrian.[11]

Governed by a local vassal dynasty, under the narrow control of Hittite officers, Emar existed for approximately 130 years as a provincial city, whose only goal was to close the passage from West to East to the Assyrians; the city disappeared shortly after the end of the Hittite Empire.

4.2. The Site of Emar

The site of Tell Meskéné lies in the Middle Euphrates valley, which is today partially covered by the Assad Lake (*buḥayrat al-'Assad*). The first cuneiform tablet was discovered on this site in 1971; after that, the Syrian government planned the construction of the Tabqa dam. This discovery prompted the need for an important archaeological exploration. French excavations took place between 1970 and 1976.

Because of the lack of vestiges of the older city, Jean Margueron assumed that the Hittite king undertook the construction of a new city outside the easily flooded zone. This would likely have been due to the development of a meander of the Euphrates by 1320 BCE. In this interpretation, the site would have undergone two distinct phases: the city of the Middle Bronze, on the one hand, and the city of the Late Bronze Age, on the other.[12] However, German excavations allow us today to discuss this theory further. From 1996 to 2004, the site was excavated anew by the German University of Tübingen, in collaboration with Princeton University and the Syrian Antiquities Department. This project—the most recent of the excavations of Emar—has allowed us to better understand the history of the site. In particular, it is clear that the ancient city of Emar has always been situated at the same place. Whereas the French excavations only found Late Bronze Age remains, the University of Tübingen excavated eighteenth-century walls. They therefore concluded that Emar was not a new town established only during the period of the Late Bronze Age period.[13] Emar

---

11. Beckman, "Hittite Administration."
12. J. C. Margueron, "Quatre campagnes de fouilles à Emar (1972–1974): Un bilan provisoire," *Syria* 52 (1975): 53–85; J. C. Margueron, "Rapport préliminaire sur les 3e, 4e, 5e et 6e campagnes de fouilles à Meskéné-Emar," *Les annales archéologiques arabes syriennes: Revue d'archéologie et d'histoire* 32 (1982): 233–49.
13. U. Finkbeiner, "Emar 1999: Bericht über die 3. Kampagne des syrisch-deutschen Ausgrabungen," *BaM* 32 (2001): 41–120; U. Finkbeiner, "Emar 2001: Bericht über die 4. Kampagne des syrisch-deutschen Ausgrabungen," *BaM* 33 (2002): 106–46; U. Finkbeiner and U. Sakal, "Emar 2003: Bericht über die 5. Kampagne des syrisch-deutschen Ausgrabungen," *BaM* 34 (2003): 9–117.

was then part of the Hittite Empire. Indeed, by the end of the fourteenth century BCE, Aštata and Emar had entered the Hittite sphere of influence.

4.3. The Emar Texts

More than 1170 cuneiform tablets were found on the site and offer a prosopography of more than three and a half generations.[14]

About 800 texts come from the French excavations, while the rest turned up on the art market. The majority of the texts are written in Akkadian, but about 100 texts are in Hurrian and a few are in Hittite.[15]

Most of the excavated religious documents for local cults were discovered in building M_I, called "Temple of the diviner," together with lexical texts in the Mesopotamian tradition and legal records (dealings in real estate, marriages, or adoptions). This house was the archive, library, and school of a family of diviners, the Zū-Ba'la family. The texts can be divided into three main categories: ephemeral documents, cultic documents, and scholarly texts.[16] It is important to underline the fact that the religious texts that we deal with in this article were discovered in this very house.

Thanks to the Mari archives, one can appreciate the commercial power of the city at the time of Hammurabi of Babylon. For the later Mitanni period, it is the Ugaritic archives that provide particular insight.

4.4. Religion and Rituals

Turning now to some ritual texts, such evidence allows us to gain a better understanding of the textualization of rituals practiced in Emar. Which rituals are described in the Emar texts? Why are some aspects of the cult described in detail while others seem to be totally lost?

Three main rituals texts from the end of the Late Bronze Age have been preserved, two of which shed light on the ritual practices associated with the installation of priestesses and one of which concerns the religious life of the whole city.

---

14. D. E. Fleming, *Time at Emar* (Winona Lake, IN: Eisenbrauns, 2000), 26–29; Cohen, "Administration of Cult in Hittite Emar," 145–47.

15. M. Salvini, *Les textes hourrites de Meskéné/Emar*, 2 vols., Analecta Orientalia 57/1–2 (Rome: Pontifical Biblical Institute / GBPress, 2015).

16. There are two different Tablet types in Emar (S = Syrian; SH = Syro-Hittite), recently labeled "conventional" and "free format" by D. E. Fleming and S. Démare-Lafont, "Tablet Terminology at Emar: Conventional and Free Format," *Aula Orientalis* 27 (2009): 19–26.

The first ritual pertains to the *entu*-priestess of Baal (Emar 369); the second is an installation ritual for the *maš'artu* (Emar 370), apparently consecrated to Ištar in her military guise; the third is the great *zukrum* festival text (Emar 373).

4.4.1. Religious Practices, Rituals Described or Mentioned in Texts

In this essay, I will focus on select examples, such as procession and veiling, anointing, and burnt offerings.

During the *zukrum* (which happened every seven years), the most noteworthy element is the bringing out of the anthropomorphic statue of the god from his temple, and also out of the city to reach an open-air sanctuary in the countryside. This open-air sanctuary contains the different elements necessary for the rituals, the first of which are the standing stones of the gods. These stones also give their name to the sacred place: "Gate of the *sikkānu*."[17]

It is worth noting that the *zukrum* text (by which we mean the tablet) is divided by a double horizontal line, which is inscribed on the tablet. The text therefore forms two parts, each of which contains the same schedule but underlines different elements, even for the same day of the festival or for the same rite during the festival.[18] Indeed, line 38 states, after having given all the information needed for the preparation, "During the next year, they perform the *zukrum* festival. During the month of SAG.MU ... ," and in line 169 (the second part of the text) the text begins again by the introductory sentence, "When the sons of Emar give the *zukrum* festival to Dagan Lord of the Offspring during the seventh year...."

The first example illustrating the function of the ritual texts concerns the procession and the visual access to the divine statue. The second part of the *zukrum* text insists on the visibility of the statue of Dagan. The deity is unveiled only in front of the sacred stones, which underlines the importance of this ritual moment. However, on 15 SAG.MU of the sixth year, Dagan goes out of the city without a veil. No explanation is given for this. When we review the available information about Dagan's appearance, we observe the following.

15 SAG.MU of the 6th year:
the statue of Dagan EN *buqari* is unveiled when he goes out in procession (l. 172);
the statue of Dagan is veiled after the sacrifice (l. 173); and
statues of Dagan and NIN.URTA are veiled during the procession (l. 176).

---

17. Michel, *Culte des pierres*, 225–26.
18. See Fleming's edition in Fleming, *Time at Emar*, Part I: 1–168; Part II: 169–205.

25 Niqali of the 6th year, all the gods are brought to the standing stones:
the statue of Dagan EN *buqari* is veiled when the god goes in procession (l. 180); and
the statue of Dagan is veiled for going out and returning (l. 181).

15 SAG.MU of the 7th year:
the statue of Dagan is veiled for going out (l. 189);
the statue of Dagan passes unveiled between the stones (ll. 163–64); and
the statue of Dagan is veiled for the return from the open-air sanctuary of standing stones (l. 192).

The 7th day of the 7th year:
the statue of Dagan is veiled to go to the standing stones (l. 198); and
the statue of Dagan is unveiled after a fire is set, in order to pass between the stones (l. 202).

4.4.1.1. Procession and Veiling

The second part of the *zukrum* text (373: 169–206) mentions a procession for the "going out" and one for the "returning" of Dagan.[19] The first procession takes place between the temple in the center of the city and the open-air sanctuary outside. The "returning" procession takes place during the return journey at night. Dagan's passing between the stones (373: 163, 174, 183–84, 191–92, 202–3) was a very important moment of the celebration during the *zukrum* since the meeting of Dagan with the standing stones was the main purpose of the festival, and it allowed the god to meet the divine assembly. This is the reason why the text insists precisely on the visibility and the aspect of Dagan. After passing between the stones, Dagan goes to the statue of NIN.URTA,[20] the tutelary deity of the city, who climbs into the chariot and joins Dagan (*ittīšu ušrakkabū*).[21] This is the last step of the lithic ritual before the celebrants turn back to the city.

This section of the ritual text thus clearly insists on the visibility of the statue of Dagan. The deity could be unveiled only in front of the sacred stones (the sacred assembly), which underlines the importance of this ritual moment.[22] This

---

19. For the text, see ibid., 248–57.
20. He is his son, as well as the city's deity; cf. 373: 164, 175, 184, *ana lū* ᵈNIN.URTA *illak*, 373: 203 *ana muhhi* ᵈNIN.URTA *illak*. This detail is omitted in line 192 of the description of the fifteenth SAG.MU of the seventh year.
21. This detail is omitted in lines 184, 192. Nevertheless, one could imagine that the same procedure took place at every procession.
22. This is despite the fact that Dagan goes out the city without a veil on 15 SAG.MU of the sixth year, as noted above.

practice would avoid any bad omen during the procession of the deity. The celebrants do not want Dagan to look favorably upon the enemy's side, and there was also a desire to control the people's access to Dagan through the vehicle of his statue. It is rare to have such attention to veiling the god in an ancient ritual text.

Veiling was also used during the installation of the *entu*-priestess. At the moment she leaves her father's house, the EREŠ.DINGIR priestess of Baal is veiled. This occurs on the last day of the ritual (Emar 369: 60–64). Upon leaving, her face was covered with a red fabric that belongs to the temple of ^{d}NIN.KUR. On the first day of the ritual, ^{d}NIN.KUR herself was covered with a veil when she appeared in the home of the priestess's father. It is likely that this was the same veil that was used by the priestess during her final procession to the temple of Baal.

During the *maš'artu* installation (Emar 370), at the moment of the consecration of the priestess, a bed was set up with a chair, so as to signify the furnishing of the room, and the text mentions the bearing of a red cloth, possibly a fabric similar to the one attested in the ritual for Baal's *entu*. Acting by night or using a veil, the visibility of cult functionaries and deities was always controlled, with access to the divine sphere being rarely opened to everyone.

From this first point, one could offer the preliminary conclusion that visibility was an issue during the performance of rituals at Emar, and that the ritual texts needed to provide clear information about this issue. Furthermore, the fact that the *zukrum* text repeats the schedule twice, insisting on different aspects, could indicate that the tablet had a practical function—namely, to give a precise schedule first, and then to deal with the visibility of the divine statue of Dagan.

4.4.1.2. Anointing

During the ritual for the installation of Baal's *entu*,[23] Ḫebat's standing stone is anointed with oil by the priestess (Emar 369: 34–35). Then the priestess herself is anointed in a similar fashion by the great diviner of the city.

This occurs on the *qaddušu* day, which the text also mentions is when the diviner is to be paid. As the new priestess is chosen by the casting of lots, one can understand that the diviner is paid for his job. After that, the ritual text mentions the *gallubu*, which is the shaving of the priestess's head. Her head will then be immediately anointed.

---

23. D. E. Fleming, *The Installation of Baal's High Priestess at Emar*, Harvard Semitic Studies 42 (Cambridge: Harvard Semitic Museum, 1992); see also P. M. Michel, "Syrian Priestess in the Late Bronze Age," in *Women in Antiquity: Real Women Across the Ancient World*, ed. S. Budin (London: Routledge, 2016), 441–52.

Emar 369: 3–5
[...] Ì.DU$_{10}$.GA *iš-tu* É.GAL-*lì*
ù iš-tu É ^{d}NIN.KUR *i-laq-qu-mi a-na* SAG-DU-*ši i-šak-kán-nu* [...]
1 GÍN KÙ.BABBAR *a-na* ^{lú}ḪAL SÌ

Fine oil from the Palace and from the temple of NIN.KUR they will take, and on her head they put (it). [...] one shekel of silver is given to the diviner.[24]

The unction establishes a strong link between the heavenly spouse of the god and her earthly cognate.

In the *zukrum*, anointing the stones takes place after the deities feast with the blood of the sacrificed animals,[25] and Dagan passes between the stones before the offering ritual (SISKUR) *kubadu*. But the unction that is described is made of a mix of blood and oil.

373: 34 (consecration) *ki-i-me-e* KÚ NAG ^{na4meš} *gáb-bá iš-tu* Ì^{meš} *ù* UŠ^{meš} *i-ṭa-ru-u*

373: 60 (celebration) [*ki-i*]*-me-e* KÚ NAG $^{na4.meš}$*si-ka-na-ti iš-tu* Ì^{meš} UŠ^{meš} [*i/ú-pá-š*]*a-šu*

The anointing of stones with blood is a way to make the stones participate in feasting on the blood of the sacrificed animals. Note that despite the name of the sacred open-air sanctuary the standing stones are worshipped only after the feasting: it is only after "eating and drinking" that the stones are anointed (Emar 373: 34, 60, 68?). After the anointing, the procession goes back to town. As it took place at the end of the whole ritual, the unction cannot then be considered a consecration rite.[26] Furthermore, as we understand the standing stone of the god, it is not a "house" for the deity but a way to materialize and embody the divine power.[27]

During the consecration, on the twenty-fifth of Niqali of the sixth year (part I of the text, Emar 373: 34), the verb *tarā'u* is used to describe the anointing of stones, which is normally expressed by *pašāšu* (Emar 373: 60). This special verb may indicate that oil and blood were mixed together. Such a special unction would have required contact with hands.[28] Here the ritual text distinguishes

---

24. Text edited by Fleming, *Installation*, 49–59.
25. Following the text of the first of the seventh day feast, which provides the most complete version.
26. Fleming, *Time at Emar*, 87.
27. Michel, *Culte des pierres*, 11–17.
28. Fleming, *Time at Emar*, 86.

two different ways of anointing at two different moments of the ritual. The use of different verbs to describe the same action should be interpreted as a practical indication. The first one seems to be more "tactile" than the latter. It is then interesting to note this difference, which could have been the reason why a written version of the ritual was needed. Regarding the *entu*'s installation, the written version was clearly important for the diviner who was responsible for the different actions (shaving, anointing) during the ritual.

4.4.1.3. Kubadu and Burnt Offerings

The particular *kubadu* offering ritual appears at several moments of the *zukrum* celebration and is here deeply linked to the burnt offering *ambaššu/i*.[29] The *kubadu* is not specific to the *zukrum*; we find it in several festivals of Emar. But the *kubadu* of a burnt animal is specific to the *zukrum*.[30] We find it nowhere in Syria or in Mesopotamia. However, examples of burnt animal offerings are attested in Hittite Anatolia and in the Bible.[31]

When the celebrants return to town, a goat is burnt for Dagan and NIN. URTA at the Great Central Gate[32] (Emar 373: 36–37, same rite mentioned in lines 62–63).

I UDU.U$_8$ *ša-a-ši a-na gáb-bi* DINGIR^{meš} *i-qa-al-lu-ú*
They burn this goat for all the gods.

The use of the Akkadian verb *qalû* is unique in the *zukrum* text. It may mean that the goat is completely burnt, as is also the case during the *ambaššu/i* offering. The use of this specific verb is important and significant and could indicate as

---

29. *ambaššu* is an Akkadien spelling of Hittite/Hurrian *ambašši*.
30. *qalû* "to burn" in Emar 373:36–37; see Michel, *Culte des pierres*, 231–40; contra Y. Feder, "A Levantine Tradition: The Kizzuwatnean Blood Rite and the Biblical Sin Offering," in *Pax Hethitica: Studies on the Hittites and Their Neighbours in Honour of Itamar Singer*, ed. Y. Cohen, A. Gilan, and J. L. Miller (Wiesbaden: Harrassowitz Verlag, 2010), 110–11.
31. Exodus 29:18 mentions this noble sacrifice: "and burn the whole ram upon the altar; it is a burnt offering to the Lord; it is a pleasing odor, an offering by fire to the Lord" (Revised Standard Version). Among Hittite texts, for example, *CTH* 486 (*KUB* 43.50 + *KUB* 15.36 + IBoT 4.26 + *KUB* 12.27 + Bo 4373 + Bo 6523 + IBoT 2.112 + *KUB* 48.100 + *KUB* 12.31 + *KUB* 43.51 + Bo 6967 + Bo 10023 + *KBo* 4.2 + Bo 8293 + Bo 8032), §3 and §5.
32. See Emar 373: 62, [*i-na pa-n*]*i* KÁ.GAL *ša* [*qa-a*]*b-li ku-ba-da*, or Emar 373: 166–67; Fleming, *Time at Emar*, 247–49. "When they reach [the great gate of] battle [a different possible translation of *qablu/qablû* would be 'central/middle'], they perform the lesser sacrificial homage (*kubadu*). They burn for all the gods [one ewe, two] pair of thick loaves, and [one] jar from the King. They anoint [the stones with oil and blood]." It is possible to imagine that during this *kubadu* the divine statues are anointed rather than the stones, see Michel, *Culte des pierres*, 70 and n. 317; P. M. Michel, "Ritual at Emar," in *Approaching Rituals in Ancient Cultures*, ed. C. Ambos and L. Verderame (Pisa: Fabrizio Serra Editore, 2013), 187–96.

well that it was necessary to practice the ritual with reference to written prescriptions, in order to completely burn the goat to the gods.

Finally, the *kubadu* ritual at Emar could take different forms, as can be seen in its determination: the big one (GAL hitt. *šalli*) *kubadu* mentioned in Emar 373: 33′–35′, and the small one (TUR hitt. *tepu*) mentioned in Emar 373: 177′. For A. Mouton, burning birds as *ambašši* is an expiatory sacrifice, sometimes also cathartic.[33]

Furthermore, it is interesting to note that this practice is also attested during the Hittite New Kingdom period outside Syria and outside Kizzuwatna: during the AN.TAḪ.ŠUM[sar] (*CTH* 594), the combination of *ambašši* and *keldi* (well-being) appears on the twenty-fifth day, worshipping the Hurrian goddess Šawoška[34] of Ḫattarina, and at Zippalanda (*KUB* 20.96, rev. iv 15).

am-ba-aš-ši a-ra-aḫ-za-an-da KAŠ.GEŠTIN š[i-pa-an-ti
They make a libation in *ambašši* form with wine-beer.

An *ambaššu* with liquids is attested at Emar as well, in the so-called *Anatolian ritual* (Emar 471: 30–33).

DUG ḫu-ur-ti-ia-lu KAŠ GEŠTIN.MEŠ
DUG ḫu-ur-ti-ia-lu KAŠ ŠE.MEŠ
a-na am-ba-aš-ši ú-šar-ra-pu
A vase *ḫurtialu* of wine, a vase *ḫurtialu* of barley beer, they burn for the *ambašši*.

Anatolian rituals are recorded in Akkadian in the corpus of Emar texts. These texts (Emar 471–91 + CM 13:31) attest that rites for the gods of Hatti were actually performed at Emar. And this can also be deduced from the next document to which we will now turn.[35]

4.4.2. The Practice of Rites

Outside ritual texts, Emar letter 271 could inform us of an actual aspect of the cult—that is, the feeding of gods. It also proves that rites for Hittite deities in Emar were performed not by Hittite officials but rather by local people.

---

33. A. Mouton, *Rêves hittites* (Leiden: Brill, 2007), 65. See also H. Otten, "Eine Beschwörung der Unterirdischen aus Boghazköy," *ZA* 54 (1961): 114–57 at 116–17. For a general discussion on the burnt offering, see D. Schwemer "Das alttestamentliche Doppelritual ʿlwt wšlmym im Horizont der hurritischen Opfertermini ambašši und keldi," *Studies on the Civilization and Culture of Nuzi and the Hurrians* 7 (1995): 81–116.

34. For an etymology, see I. Wegner, "Der Name der So(w)uska," *Studies on the Civilizations and Culture of Nuzi and the Hurrians* 7 (1995): 117–20.

35. J. T. Thames, *The Politics of Ritual Change: The* Zukru *Festival in the Political History of Late Bronze Age Emar* (Leiden: Brill 2020).

In the morning, send your son to feed the Hittite deities. Do not make him late: the beer should not go stale. Concerning the carpenter about whom you wrote me, I sent him to you [...].[36]

Hittite deities were fed in Emar and formed part of the local pantheon. This young boy, a local inhabitant, shows us how divinities of Hatti were worshipped: at least with the mention of "feeding" and the use of beer.[37] This suggests to me that Anatolian rituals were translated from Hittite into Akkadian for local purposes. In Emar, Hittite deities such as IŠKUR *piḫaimmi* in Msk 74176, *ḫabaimmi*, and *putalim(m)i* or Mt. Ḫarḫarwa (Emar 472: 44′) and Mt. Zaliyanu (ʰᵘʳ·ˢᵃᵍ*da-li-ia-nu*, Emar 472: 44′)—both important in the cult of the storm god of Nerik—are attested in Anatolian rituals and are all to be worshipped in the Hittite manner. Furthermore, both Daḫagu and Daḫagunanu—personifications of *daḫanga* known only from the cult of the storm god of Nerik—are also attested.[38]

This letter gives us a very rare example of the private practice of the cult. Unlike the official cults attested in the ritual texts, this document indicates that a child was able to feed and to offer beer to the gods, small offerings being the most popular way for people to worship deities.

4.4.3. Prayers

Direct speech is quoted only once in the ritual texts from Emar. It appears in the installation ceremony of the *maš'artu* (Emar 370), on the seventh day.

> A.MEŠ *a-na ra-ma-ki* ᵈ*Išₐ-tár* GAŠAN-*ia lu-uḫ-bi-mì*[
> (Indeed), I drew water for the bath of my Lady Astarte.

Here one could imagine that the text was necessary as a *memento* for the priestess to ensure that she did not forget the precise word to pronounce, even if the sentence was very short. Indeed, Hittite ritual texts attest several prayers, as stated by Itamar Singer, "only rarely is the ritual part recorded or preserved . . . and conversely, almost every ritual contains some short invocation or praise to the god."[39]

As several *maš'artu* are attested in the administrative texts where the relevant witnesses sign as "son or brother of the *maš'artu*,"[40] we can deduce that

---

36. Michel, *Culte des pierres*, 70 with n. 317; Michel, "Ritual at Emar."
37. For a different point of view, see A. Archi, "Astata: A Case of Hittite Imperial Religious Policy," *JANER* 14 (2014): 141–63 at 155–56.
38. This specific occurrence clearly links the cults of Emar with Hittite Anatolia of Hattušili III and his son Tudhaliya IV.
39. I. Singer, *Hittite Prayers* (Leiden: Brill, 2002), 4.
40. See Emar 124 or Emar 209.

this ritual tablet was used on a practical level by different women. However, since we only have one unique version, we cannot detect possible variants. The general view is that writing down the rituals was meant to give a standard, or unique, version and to permit a common practice among the Zū-Ba'la family of diviners (of structure M_1). In that way, the Emar corpus seems to indicate a tendency toward standardization.

4.5. Conclusion

These ritual texts were not liturgical texts *per se* but more likely texts redacted by one of the functionaries as a response to organizational matters. This figure was most likely the diviner (^{lú}HAL). He lived in the structure M_1, discovered in the lower city of Emar containing numerous religious texts, including the three discussed here. The diviner was one of the most important functionaries in these rituals and was paid repeatedly during their performance. This is especially the case in the ritual for the *entu* where the diviner is mentioned almost every day: "They will place 10 shekels into the hand of the diviner in the form of a roll of silver" (Emar 369: 43).

The diviner was likewise present at numerous religious enactments at Emar, and several prescriptions indicated in the above ritual suggest that he redacted such a text, at least in part in order to assure his own interests.[41] It was upon him to anoint the priestess (twice) but also to choose her through divination. He was compensated for each of his actions.

The author of the text influences the content of the text. I tried to show here that, since the author was the diviner, the text most likely served a practical purpose of ensuring that he was paid.

We also saw how the same text could provide different information even for the same day. The visibility of the statue of Dagan was of particular importance, and the second part of the ritual text of the *zukrum* seems to deal especially with this issue. Furthermore, the fact that different verbs can be used in the same ritual context may indicate that there was a need to distinguish different ways of accomplishing the ritual.

We also noticed that prayers are hardly ever provided in the tablets. However, this observation does not mean that such prayers would not have been written elsewhere. We just simply do not know. Thus, for the case of Emar, we have to admit that we are dependent on archaeology and the findings made on site.

Finally, it was possible to add an administrative document (namely, a letter) to the discussion, thereby providing further information on how the rituals

---

41. Michel, *Culte des pierres*, 134–41.

described in the ritual texts may have actually been practiced. In the end, the view concerning Emar is that it was necessary for the great diviner to write and use the ritual texts in light of his roles as the one who was responsible for the religious *affaires* in the city. He also was responsible vis à vis the Hittite power. Last but not least, he was the only one able to install priests and priestesses and was capable to ensure his own "salary."

BIBLIOGRAPHY

Archi, A. "Astata: A Case of Hittite Imperial Religious Policy." *JANER* 14 (2014): 141–63.
Arnaud, D. "Les textes d'Emar et la chronologie de la fin du Bronze Récent." *Syria* 52 (1975): 87–92.
Beckman, G. M. "Hittite Administration in Syria in the Light of the Texts from Hattusa, Ugarit and Emar." Pages 41–49 in *New Horizons in the Study of Ancient Syria*. Edited by M. W. Chavalas and J. L. Hayes. Bibliotheca Mesopotamica 25. Malibu: Undena, 1992.
Cohen, Y. "The Administration of Cult in Hittite Emar." *AFo* 38 (2009): 145–57.
Feder, Y. "A Levantine Tradition: The Kizzuwatnean Blood Rite and the Biblical Sin Offering." Pages 101–14 in *Pax Hethitica: Studies on the Hittites and Their Neighbours in Honour of Itamar Singer*. Edited by Y. Cohen, A. Gilan, and J. L. Miller. Wiesbaden: Harrassowitz Verlag, 2010.
Finkbeiner, U. "Emar 1999: Bericht über die 3. Kampagne des syrisch-deutschen Ausgrabungen." *BaM* 32 (2001): 41–120.
———. "Emar 2001: Bericht über die 4. Kampagne des syrisch-deutschen Ausgrabungen." *BaM* 33 (2002): 106–46.
Finkbeiner, U., and U. Sakal. "Emar 2003: Bericht über die 5. Kampagne des syrisch-deutschen Ausgrabungen." *BaM* 34 (2003): 9–117.
Fleming, D. E. *The Installation of Baal's High Priestess at Ema*. Harvard Semitic Studies 42. Cambridge: Harvard Semitic Museum, 1992.
———. *Time at Emar*. Winona Lake, IN: Eisenbrauns, 2000.
Fleming, D. E., and S. Démare-Lafont. "Tablet Terminology at Emar: Conventional and Free Format." *Aula Orientalis* 27 (2009): 19–26.
Hawkins, J. D. "Karkamish and Karatepe: Neo-Hittite City-States in North Syria." Pages 1295–307 in vol. 2 of *Civilizations of the Ancient Near East*. Edited by J. M. Sasson. New York: Scribner, 1995.
Kestemont, G. *Diplomatie et droit international en Asie occidentale (1600–1200 av. J.C.)*. Publications de l'Institut orientaliste de Louvain 9. Louvain-la-Neuve: Université catholique de Louvain Institut orientaliste, 1974.
Laroche, E. "Documents hittites et hourrites." Pages 53–60 in *Meskéné Emar: Dix ans de travaux 1972–1982*. Edited by D. Beyer. Paris: Recherche sur les civilisations, 1982.
Margueron, J.-C. "Quatre campagnes de fouilles à Emar (1972–1974): Un bilan provisoire." *Syria* 52 (1975): 53–85.
———. "Rapport préliminaire sur les 3e, 4e, 5e et 6e campagnes de fouilles à Meskéné-Emar." *Les annales archéologiques arabes syriennes: Revue d'archéologie et d'histoire* 32 (1982): 233–49.

Michel, P. M. *Le culte des pierres à Emar à l'époque hittite*. Fribourg: Academic Press; Göttingen: Vandenhoeck & Ruprecht, 2014.
———. "Ritual at Emar." Pages 187–96 in *Approaching Rituals in Ancient Cultures*. Edited by C. Ambos and L. Verderame. Pisa: Fabrizio Serra Editore, 2013.
———. "Syrian Priestess in the Late Bronze Age." Pages 441–52 in *Women in Antiquity: Real Women Across the Ancient World*. Edited by S. Budin. London: Routledge, 2016.
Mouton, A. *Rêves hittites*. Leiden: Brill, 2007.
Otten, H. "Eine Beschwörung der Unterirdischen aus Boghazköy." *ZA* 54 (1961): 114–57.
Salvini, S. *Les textes hourrites de Meskéné/Emar*. 2 vols. Analecta Orientalia 57/1–2. Rome: Pontifical Biblical Institute / GBPress, 2015.
Salvini, M., and M. C. Trémouille, "Les textes hittites de Meskéné/Emar." *SMEA* 45.2 (2003): 225–71.
Schwemer, D. "Das alttestamentliche Doppelritual 'lwt wšlmym im Horizont der hurritischen Opfertermini ambašši und keldi." *Studies on the Civilization and Culture of Nuzi and the Hurrians* 7 (1995): 81–116.
Singer, I. "Dating the End of the Hittite Empire." *Hethitica* 8 (1987): 413–21.
———. *Hittite Prayers*. Leiden: Brill, 2002.
———. "A New Hittite Letter from Emar." Pages 65–72 in *Landscapes: Territories, Frontiers and Horizons in the Ancient Near East; Papers Presented to the XLIV Rencontre Assyriologique Internationale, Venezia, 7–11 July 1997*, part 2, *Geography and Cultural Landscapes*. Edited by L. Milano et al. Padua: Sargon 2000.
Thames, J. T. *The Politics of Ritual Change: The* Zukru *Festival in the Political History of Late Bronze Age Emar*. Harvard Semitic Monographs 65. Leiden: Brill, 2020.
Wegner, I. "Der Name der So(w)uska." *Studies on the Civilizations and Culture of Nuzi and the Hurrians* 7 (1995): 117–20.

CHAPTER 5

The Textualization of Priestly Ritual in Light of Hittite Sources

Yitzhaq Feder

IMAGINE THE COVER-UP OF THE CENTURY. What if yet another cave had been discovered in Qumran, but its contents were so startling that they were never revealed to the public? What if in this cave was found the *genizah* of the Priestly school, containing the discarded rough drafts of ritual texts that ultimately were included—in a much more polished form—in the Priestly materials of the Pentateuch? What would be the implications of such a discovery?

While this scenario is a mere fantasy of a biblical scholar, we do have some very real evidence that *might* shed light on the formative phases of the Priestly source (P).[1] The aim of this essay is to offer a preliminary assessment of how the study of Hittite ritual traditions can contribute to the study of the formation of Priestly ritual texts. Research into the formation and transmission of the Hittite ritual texts has made remarkable progress in the past fifteen years and is blessed with both a rich body of primary data and a growing scholarly interest in the relationship between ritualistic and scribal activity.

Before presenting this evidence in more detail, it may be helpful to compare the much more meager evidence with which biblical scholars have accustomed themselves. The textual variants from the Masoretic Text of P (Samaritan, LXX, Qumran) are from the late Second Temple period at the earliest and, aside from a few notable exceptions, offer little direct insight into the formative period of the Priestly text. As such, the primary source of information regarding the prehistory of P is the existence of inconsistencies within and between different Priestly texts. How these inconsistencies are assessed varies on a spectrum from more harmonistic approaches, such as that of David Zvi Hoffmann, to the detailed stratification of layers of Karl Elliger. While one may highly value (as I do) the ingenuity involved in critical methods and accept the plausibility of their

---

I thank Amir Gilan and Shai Gordin for sharing their extensive knowledge and insight during the preparation of this paper.
  1. In this essay, I will use Priestly writings or P to include also the Holiness Source (H) and possibly later layers. In the final section, a more differentiated view will be presented, as will be clear from the context.

conclusions, the fact remains that without an external frame of reference it is difficult to know what is the real significance of these inconsistencies.

Here lies the key interest of the Hittite ritual texts. Not only do individual "manuscripts" (cuneiform tablets) attest to the types of inconsistencies identified by biblical scholars, but, more importantly, the Hittite archives have yielded multiple parallel copies to particular ritual compositions with very significant variants. These variants can even be dated to specific stages in the development of the Hittite cuneiform script.

The archives of the Hittite capital Hattuša (modern Boğazköy) have yielded hundreds of ritual compositions written on cuneiform tablets, supplying modern scholarship with the largest corpus of ritual texts known from the ancient Near East. This corpus spans from the sixteenth century BCE to the collapse of the Hittite empire around 1200, with most of the surviving texts pertaining to the latter phase. A given ritual composition may be attested on one tablet or on over a dozen roughly parallel copies, reflecting often minor but sometimes major variations. The implications of these variants for the study of the transmission and scribal activity responsible for these texts has been subjected to several important studies in recent years, as will be discussed in some detail below.

At this point, it will be useful to offer a general categorization of the textual materials at our disposal. The Hittite scribes distinguished between "festivals" (EZEN$_4$) and "ritual" (SISKUR/SÍSKUR) texts. Gary Beckman elucidates this difference as follows:

> Modern scholars have observed that, with rare exceptions, *festivals* are ceremonies of the state cult, to be performed periodically—monthly, yearly, or on the occasion of particular recurrent natural events ... or agricultural activities. In contrast, *rituals* are to be carried out only in response to special crises affecting an individual or group—impotence, miscarriage, strife within a family, a lost battle, and so on.[2]

Both of these subgenres find parallels in P. Regarding the latter, I would suggest substituting the designation "cultic" for "festival," to designate both the instructions for regular offerings of the official cult (e.g., Lev 1–3) and festival instructions, strictly defined (Lev 23; Num 28–29). The designation "ritual" can be applied to irregular offerings such as those for expiation (e.g., Lev 4–5) and purification rites (Lev 12–15), including those for unique circumstances, such as those for the suspected adulteress (Num 5:11–31) or the nazirite (Num 6:1–21).

These terminological parallels are not mere exercises in classification for its own sake but rather invite more sustained cross-cultural comparisons with

---

2. G. Beckman, *The* babilili-*Ritual from Hattusa* (Winona Lake, IN: Eisenbrauns, 2014), 1.

important implications for the meaning and historical background of P's ritual practices and their textualization. Whereas *cultic* practices focus on paying homage to a given deity and ensuring the continuance of divine favor, *rituals* usually attend to emergent situations that are of dire concern to the patron(s). These distinct functions find expression in formal differences between these genres. For example, while the ritual texts are usually introduced with casuistic formulas, cultic texts are generally introduced by reference to the calendric date(s) or season(s) of their performance.[3] While this distinction between festivals and rituals is crucial for understanding the ancient evidence, the present essay will employ the term "ritual" as an inclusive analytic category that encompasses these two types, consistent with its use in modern academic discourse ("ritual" studies). When necessary to distinguish subgenres, the designation "therapeutic rituals" will be used.

Before presenting current research on Hittite ritual texts, it may be useful to raise some fundamental questions that a biblical scholar may want to ask regarding this evidence.

Who produced these ritual texts, and why?
What type of authority (if any) was ascribed to these texts?
What can the variation between exemplars teach us regarding the roles of oral and written transmission of these traditions?

These topics have been addressed by the current wave of Hittitological research, yet the richness of the textual data has enabled Hittitologists to formulate even more focused questions. Some of these studies have dealt with the origins of these texts, specifically the role of ritualists and scribes in producing them. A key question is whether these rituals originated as descriptions of rituals, produced either by observation of their performance or by interviewing the practitioner, or as a prescriptive ritual in which the scribes took more liberty in their formulation. A related question that has been asked regarding particular rituals, such as the royal funerary ritual (*šalliš waštaiš*), is whether these texts originated in reference to a particular performance involving a named monarch, only later to be transformed into a generic text, or vice versa: the name of a specific

---

3. More precisely, several different types of texts related to festivals can be identified, including outline tablets for multiple festivals, outline tablets for a single complex festival, detailed descriptions of particular days within a festival, ration tablets, and other administrative and oracle documents. See D. Schwemer, "Quality Assurance Managers at Work: The Hittite Festival Tradition," in *Liturgie oder Literatur: Die Kultrituale der Hethiter im transkulturellen Vergleich*, ed. G. G. W. Müller, StBoT 60 (Wiesbaden: Harrasowitz, 2016), 1–29 at 7–12. My reference here to "cultic" texts (as contrasted with therapeutic rituals) refers specifically to the detailed daily descriptions, which comprise the bulk of the Hittite festival corpus.

monarch was later added to an originally generic ritual tradition.[4] Other studies have focused on the question of the transmission of these rituals, specifically on the role of visual copying, dictation, and memorization in the production of multiple versions of a single textual tradition. To make life more interesting, the conclusions reached by scholars to these questions have not always been the same, requiring that each ritual tradition be evaluated on a case-by-case basis. At any rate, before drawing analogies to Priestly ritual, it is necessary to review this research in more detail.

The review of research on Hittite rituals is divided into two sections. The following section attempts to characterize the role of scribes in the production of ritual texts and deals with the vexed question of the authorship of these rituals. The subsequent section focuses on the function of ritual texts, specifically their relationship to ritual practice. Put differently, these two lines of inquiry can be framed as questions. First, how were the Hittite ritual texts composed? Second, why were they composed? As will be seen, these topics can be dealt with largely independently of one another.

5.1. Scribal Activity in the Production of Ritual Texts

Probably the most fundamental question that needs to be addressed pertains to the relative contributions of the ritualists and scribes in the formation of these texts. Were the scribes merely responsible for transcribing the dictated words of ritualists and for the mechanical process of duplicating texts, or did they take a more creative role in the production of these texts? Put in extreme terms, we may ask whether the ritual texts are the *ipsissima verba* of the ritualists, written and duplicated faithfully by scribal secretaries, or, to take the more skeptical stance, were these rituals scribal inventions, such that the ritualist "authors" were mere literary fictions?[5]

While there may be heuristic value in drawing a strict dichotomy between viewing the textualization of ritual traditions as a mechanical versus creative process, it is obvious that reality was much more complicated. Between the two

---

4. For the royal funerary ritual, see T. van den Hout, "Death as a Privilege," in *Hidden Futures: Death and Immortality in Ancient Egypt, Anatolia, the Classical, Biblical and Arabic-Islamic World*, ed. J. M. Bremmer, T. van den Hout, and R. Peters (Amsterdam: Amsterdam University Press, 1994), 37–75; T. van den Hout, "Zu einer Stratigraphie der hethitischen Totenrituale," in *Saeculum: Gedenkschrift für Heinrich Otten anlässlich seines 100. Geburtstags*, ed. A. Müller-Karpe, E. Rieken, and W. Sommerfeld, StBoT 58 (Wiesbaden: Harrassowitz, 2015), 301–6; A. Kassian, A. Korolëv, and A. Sidel'tsev, *Hittite Funerary Ritual: šalliš waštaiš*, AOAT 288 (Münster: Ugarit-Verlag, 2002).

5. So K. Hecker, "Tradition und Originalität in der altorientalischen Literatur," *Archív orientální* 45 (1977): 245–58 at 248–49.

extremes, there was a wide spectrum of scribal functions. A helpful framework for surveying the relevant data can be taken from Karel van der Toorn's study of scribal culture, which can be reorganized to depict escalating degrees of scribal intervention as follows:

1. transcription of oral lore (dictation);
2. production of duplicates;
3. compilation of existing lore, either oral or written;
4. integration of individual documents into more comprehensive compositions;
5. expansion of an inherited text;
6. adaptation of an existing text for a new audience/situation; and
7. invention of a new text.[6]

5.1.1. The Scribes as Secretaries and Copyists

A major breakthrough in the study of Hittite rituals was Jared Miller's 2004 monograph *Studies in the Origin, Development and Interpretation of the Kizzuwatna Rituals*, focusing on the Hittite rituals that originated in the area of Kizzuwatna (classical Cilicia) in southeastern Anatolia.[7] As implied by the title, Miller devotes considerable attention to the problem of origins, specifically whether these rituals originated as strict records of the words of ritual practitioners (conveyed by interviews or dictation) or as more freely composed scribal constructs. Miller conducts this inquiry by means of a two-pronged approach: first, by means of detailed examinations of specific textual compositions as represented in parallel versions; second, by a broad survey of formal and grammatical characteristics represented in the Kizzuwatna texts.

Starting with the first type of evidence, what can be observed by the comparison of textual variants? In comparing variants of the Maštigga Ritual Against Domestic Quarrel (*KBo* 39.8++), Miller finds both minor (orthographic and linguistic) and major variants. The latter category includes:

differences in the number of ritual patrons (one or two);
the absence in a group of copies of numerous sections at the beginning of the text (§§2–11), containing the list of paraphernalia and the beginning of the ritual;

---

6. K. van der Toorn, *Scribal Culture and the Making of the Hebrew Bible* (Cambridge: Harvard University Press, 2007), 110–41. The fifth of these ("expansion") will not be thematized below, since it is discussed in reference to several of the other functions.
7. J. L. Miller, *Studies in the Origins, Development and Interpretation of the Kizzuwatna Rituals*, StBoT 46 (Wiesbaden: Harrassowitz, 2004).

changes in sequence of sections in the ritual;[8] and

lack of full correspondence between the list of paraphernalia and the materials used in the ritual sections of the text.

Though Miller seeks to mine this data for its implications regarding the origins of the ritual texts,[9] it is not clear that the textual variants analyzed in this section of his work are reflective of the *origins* of this textual tradition. As pointed out by Miller himself, many of the major variants (e.g., the discrepancy between one or two ritual patrons) are attested already in the earliest manuscript evidence (from the Middle Hittite period; ca. the fourteenth century BCE), such that the formative phase of this textual tradition remains obscure. In other words, these manuscripts are at least a few generations removed from their original composition.

More fundamentally, as pointed out by Hannah Marcuson and Theo van den Hout in their reevaluation of this data, these textual variants are much more informative of the process of transmission of these textual traditions.[10] Building on an earlier study of Sumerian textual criticism by Paul Delnero,[11] Marcuson and van den Hout argue that the differences between duplicates of ritual texts are best understood as memory variants.[12] However, despite their careful analysis, it is often difficult to isolate memory variants from other forms of copying "errors."[13] Furthermore, the existence of additions and corrections to these manuscripts indicates that they have been (visually) proofread in comparison with their *Vorlagen*.[14] More generally, we should be wary of exaggerating the distinction between visual copying and memorization, since these complementary processes often took place in tandem, as has been repeatedly stressed by David Carr.[15] Nonetheless, the important point for our purposes is that many differences between

---

8. See especially the comparisons of Text 1 and Text 2 (ibid., 244–51).

9. See, e.g., ibid., 253.

10. H. Marcuson and T. van den Hout, "Memorization and Hittite Ritual: New Perspectives on the Transmission of Hittite Ritual Texts," *JANER* 15 (2015): 143–68.

11. P. Delnero, "Memorization and the Transmission of Sumerian Literary Compositions," *JNES* 71 (2012): 198–208.

12. For a similar view regarding the relationship of *KBo* 13.145 to the Hantitaššu ritual tradition, see B. J. Collins, "The Place of *KBo* 13.145 in the Hantitaššu Text Tradition," in *Beyond Hatti: A Tribute to Gary Beckman*, ed. B. J. Collins and P. Michalowski (Atlanta: Lockwood Press, 2013), 63–74.

13. M. Worthington, *Principles of Akkadian Textual Criticism* (Berlin: de Gruyter, 2012), 13–16.

14. Note, for example, the omission of the conjunctive *–ia* in MS II.B i 2 (*KUB* 12.34) of the Maštigga ritual (Marcuson and van den Hout, "Memorization," 151), which was then added above the line (Miller, *Studies in the Origins*, 61 n. 94). For further discussion of proofreading, see S. Gordin, *Hittite Scribal Circles: Scholarly Tradition and Writing Habits*, StBoT 59 (Wiesbaden: Harrassowitz, 2015), 33–34.

15. D. Carr, *Writing on the Tablet of the Heart: Origins of Scripture and Literature* (Oxford: Oxford University Press, 2005); D. Carr, *The Formation of the Hebrew Bible: A New Reconstruction* (Oxford: Oxford University Press, 2011).

duplicates and even internal inconsistencies (e.g., between paraphernalia lists and their corresponding ritual descriptions) could be explained as mere accidents of the copying process, not as deliberate editorial changes made by scribes.

5.1.2. Scribes as Compilers

On the other hand, there are numerous points of evidence—both explicit and implicit—for more active participation of scribes in the production of these texts. For example, there is ample evidence for the role of scribes as compilers, integrating originally independent rituals. In particular, such a process of compilation might account for internal inconsistencies found in texts, such as the alternation between single and multiple ritual patrons and the vacillation between first-, second-, and third-person grammatical forms. While some cases may be best explained as deliberate scribal adaptations of an existing ritual (see below), at least some of the inconsistencies appear to reflect the attempt of scribes to integrate distinct documents into a single ritual text.[16] For example, while discrepancies between paraphernalia lists and the corresponding ritual instructions might be explained ostensibly as lapses of memory on the part of the scribes, it is worth noting that the colophon of one ritual (*KUB* 41.21 iv 16′–18′) explicitly notes that the utensil list was written on a separate tablet: "Words of Allaiturahhi. The ritual paraphernalia (are on) another tablet."[17] Likewise, some texts appear to be combinations of separate rituals for distinct deities (e.g., *CTH* 391).[18]

The explicit references to the consultation of tablets provide incontrovertible evidence to the scribal function as compilers.[19] These references break the continuity of a ritual text to note that certain information—the instructions for a specific rite or a list of paraphernalia—are recorded on a separate tablet. For example, the Hittite birth ritual *KBo* 17.65 + makes several references to additional tablets. Most interestingly, the ritual concludes with the requirement to celebrate the "Fertility Festival" but notes that the precise instructions are found in the archives of Kizzuwatna.

> But when (they celebrate) the Fertility Festival, when she [gi]ves birth, how they celebrate the festival is recorded on a writing-board (*kurta-*),

---

16. B. Christiansen, *Die Ritualtradition der Ambazzi: Eine philologische Bearbeitung und entstehungsgeschichtliche Analyse der Ritualtexte CTH 391, CTH 429 und CTH 463*, StBoT 48 (Wiesbaden: Harrassowitz, 2006), 122.

17. See Miller, *Studies in the Origins*, 512.

18. See J. L. Miller, review of *Die Ritualtradition der Ambazzi: Eine philologische Bearbeitung und entstehungsgeschichtliche Analyse der Ritualtexte CTH 391, CTH 429 und CTH 463*, by B. Christiansen, *ZA* 99 (2009): 155–56.

19. See Miller, *Studies in the Origins*, 511–23.

and it is (in) Kizzuwatna. I am unable to recite it by heart, so they will bring it from there.[20]

This use of cross-referencing can be illuminated further by comparison with the ritual texts found in neighboring cultures—for example, the deity lists from Ugarit,[21] which will be discussed later. These systems of intertextual cross-referencing suggest a scholarly milieu in which the production of texts involved collation of discrete documents, even those from distant archives, and the practice of ritual could involve the synthesis of information garnered from the simultaneous comparison of these texts.

5.1.3. Adapting a Ritual to a New Situation

Furthermore, the Hittite scribes did not shy away from adapting an existing tradition to a new situation. This role is demonstrated clearly by cases of discrepancies between parallel copies of a particular ritual, where one version refers to the ritual patron generically and another refers to a specific king, queen, or member of the royal family. In these cases, it is typically assumed that one of the versions is the more original, leaving the question whether a historical event has been reformulated as a generic ritual or whether a generic ritual has been reformulated in reference to specific historical figures. Interestingly, studies of these cases have led to contradictory conclusions. For example, Billie Jean Collins's study of the Hantitaššu ritual identifies it as an example of "royal co-option of a popular ritual."[22] On the other hand, Stefano de Martino and Aygül Süel's edition of the third tablet of the Itkalzi Ritual distinguishes between (a) a long and presumably original series of twenty-two tablets taken to Hattuša from Šapinuwa written only in Hurrian and (b) a shortened series of ten tablets with

---

20. *KBo* 17.65 + obv. 37–39/rev. 45–46. Text edition: G. Beckman, *Hittite Birth Rituals*, StBoT 29 (Wiesbaden: Harrassowitz, 1983), 136, 144; translation adapted from Miller, *Studies in the Origins*, 518, based on the composite text.

21. D. Pardee, *Ritual and Cult at Ugarit*, WAW 10 (Atlanta: Society of Biblical Literature, 2002), 11–24.

22. B. J. Collins, "Royal Co-option of a Popular Ritual: The Case of Hantitaššu," in *Proceedings of the Eighth International Congress of Hittitology, Warsaw, 5–9 September 2011*, ed. P. Taracha and M. Kapełus (Warsaw: Agade, 2014), 185–201. See also B. Christiansen, "Ein Ensuhnungsritual fur Tuthaliya und Nikalmati? Betrachrungen zur Entstehungsgeschichte von KBo 15.10+," *SMEA* 49 (2007): 93–107. For the apparent adaptation of a ritual of Allaiturahhi dedicated to Šuppiluliumma II (*CTH* 781), see V. Haas, "Die hurritisch-hethitischen Rituale der Beschwörerin Allaiturah(h)i und ihr literarhistorischer Hintergrund," in *Hurriter und Hurritisch*, ed. V. Haas, Konstanzer Althistroische Vorträge und Forschungen 21 (Konstanz: Xenia, 1988), 120; G. Torri, "Subject Shifting in Hittite Magical Rituals," in *Tabularia Hethaeorum: Hethitologische Beiträge; Silvin Košak zum 65 Geburtstag*, ed. D. Groddek and M. Zorman, Dresdner Beiträge zur Hethitologie 25 (Wiesbaden: Harrassowitz, 2007), 672.

prescriptive portions written in Hittite and incantations in Hurrian.[23] The main difference between the two series is that the longer Hurrian version frequently mentions the ritual patrons, Queen Tadu-Ḫeba and King Tašmi-šarri, whereas the shorter bilingual version employs the generic fill-in-the-blank designation "ritual patron." De Martino and Süel draw the likely conclusion that the bilingual is an adaptation of the original that focused on the specific royal couple.[24] Accordingly, it seems necessary to consider the possibility that such processes of textual adaptation could be carried out in both directions. More fundamentally, these processes indicated the active role of scribes in revising ritual texts.

5.1.4. Scribes as Ritual Inventors?

But the role of scribes may have been even more extensive than transcription, compilation, and adaptation. Put differently, despite the formulas employed in the incipits and colophons attributing the text to specific ritual experts, scholars have begun to cast doubt on the assumption that these ritualists were the actual authors of the words attributed to them.

In twentieth-century research, the issue of the formation of ritual texts was often conceptualized in light of Baruch Levine's distinction between descriptive and prescriptive texts. Based on comparative evidence from Ugarit, Hatti, and Mesopotamia, Levine claimed that the descriptive rituals in the Bible were based on archival documents.[25] However, after several decades of further research, it would appear that the corpus of descriptive rituals is exceedingly slim (if it exists at all). As for the Ugaritic evidence, Dennis Pardee, representative of the general tendency in Ugaritic scholarship, classifies "the vast majority of these texts as prescriptive in nature."[26] Indeed, in his own more recent discussion of the topic, Levine subtly backtracks from his earlier distinction, referring to the "process by which descriptive rituals gradually appropriate prescriptive formulations as their functional role comes to determine their formal structure to an ever greater extent."[27] David Clemens unpacks this dense restatement

---

23. S. de Martino and A. Süel, *The Third Tablet of the itkalzi Ritual* (LoGisma: Torino, 2015), 15–17.

24. Ibid., 17.

25. B. A. Levine, "Ugaritic Descriptive Rituals," *JCS* 17 (1963): 105–11; B. A. Levine, "The Descriptive Tabernacle Texts of the Pentateuch," *JAOS* 85 (1965): 307–18.

26. Pardee, *Ritual and Cult*, 25; see also D. M. Clemens, *Sources for Ugaritic Ritual and Sacrifice*, vol. 1, *Ugaritic and Ugarit Akkadian Texts*, AOAT 284/1 (Münster: Ugarit-Verlag, 2001), 105 n. 506.

27. B. A. Levine, "The Descriptive Ritual Texts from Ugarit: Some Formal and Functional Features of the Genre," in *The Word of the Lord Shall Go Forth: Essays in Honor of David Noel Freedman in Celebration of His Sixtieth Birthday*, ed. C. L. Meyers and M. O'Connor (Winona Lake, IN: Eisenbrauns, 1983), 469.

as follows: "A more fundamental modulation of [Levine's] previous position concerns his understanding of the term 'descriptive' itself, acknowledged to have been 'problematic since the outset.' Apparently the adjective was used to describe the form rather than the function of the texts, and he concedes that they are prescriptive in function, which is evidenced formally by the occurrence of jussive forms. This being the case, it is difficult to see why the distinction between descriptive and prescriptive is belabored at all."[28]

As far as the Hittite texts are concerned, Miller devotes considerable attention to debunking the descriptive paradigm, whether based on eyewitness "ethnographic" records or a strict transcription of the ritualist's words. Here Miller's detailed survey of formal and grammatical aspects of the Kizzuwatna rituals is particularly illuminating.[29] For example, the Hittite rituals are usually attributed to a particular ritualist or group of ritualists. The typical incipit begins by attributing the ritual to a named ritualist (*UMMA* PN), followed by a protasis stating the purpose of the ritual and a brief apodosis introducing the ritual instructions, usually phrased in the first person. For example, the Ritual of Maštigga for Domestic Quarrel opens as follows:

> Thus (speaks) Maštigga, woman of Kizzuwatna: "When a father and a son, or a man and his wife, or a brother and sister quarrel: when I reconcile them, I treat them thus. I take the following."[30]

The colophon is closely modeled after the incipit. It typically states the sequence number of the tablet and whether or not this tablet constitutes the end of the ritual. This information is followed by the "name" of the ritual, attributing it to the ritualist (*AWAT/* INIM [*ša*] PN) and restating the protasis from the incipit. The colophon concludes by identifying the scribe responsible for the tablet.[31] Here is the colophon of the same manuscript:

> First tablet: the word of Maštigga, woman of Kummanni (entitled): "If a father and son, or a husband and his wife or a brother and sister quarrel, when I bring them together, and I treat them as such. Finished: Hand of Ḫan[ikkuili, the Scribe], son of NU.[^{GIŠ}SAR]."[32]

---

28. Clemens, *Sources*, 105.
29. Miller, *Studies in the Origins*, 469–532.
30. According to MS II.B, based on the edition and translation of Miller (ibid., 61–62), with minor adaptations.
31. For a typical structure of Hittite ritual colophons and incipits, see W. Waal, "The Source as Object: Studies in Hittite Diplomatics" (PhD diss., Leiden University, 2010), 236–50; Gordin, *Hittite Scribal Circles*, 39–50.
32. According to MS II.B, with minor reconstructions (unmarked) based on parallel manuscripts (see Miller, *Studies in the Origins*, 107–8).

As will be seen, these ascriptions of authorship and function are often at least partially incongruent with the contents of the ritual texts.

Despite the close correspondence between the incipits and colophons, usually formulated in the first person, the bodies of ritual texts do not generally follow the first-person format but rather discuss the ritual activities in the third person, though there are exceptions. Moreover, in many cases, the ritual activities are performed by a different type of officiant than that of the "speaker." For example, a ritual attributed to an "old woman" (ŠU.GI) may be carried out by male priests. However, several texts revert (temporarily) to the first person in presenting the list of paraphernalia to be used in the ritual ("then I bring ..."). Some texts change unexpectedly to the second person. Since the second person is more common in Mesopotamian rituals, scholars have wondered if these texts may be betraying an Akkadian (or Hurrian) *Vorlage* or whether perhaps the scribes are imitating a Mesopotamian style.[33]

In evaluating the attributions to named ritualists, a range of plausible positions can be offered, ranging from total skepticism regarding the authenticity of the attributions to lesser or greater confidence that the main body of the ritual text was dictated by the ritualist, though perhaps reworked or reformulated by a scribe.[34] Late twentieth-century Hittitological research tended toward a more maximal assessment, based on the assumption that the ritual text was based on dictation or an interview with the ritualist. For example, Pierre Cornil suggested that the third-person formulas reflect a scribal tampering with the first-person accounts upon which the texts were based, transforming these interviews into ritual prescriptions.[35]

Recently, however, more attention has been given to the possibility that much of the materials ascribed to named ritualists was composed by the scribes themselves. Possible support for this more skeptical position can be found in the fact that, in at least six cases, it appears that the scribes were confused regarding the gender of the ritualist.[36] That is to say, ritualists such as Ammihatna and Ḫantitaššu appear sometimes with both male and female determinatives in different text copies. Yet the ignorance of later scribes regarding the gender of earlier ritualists could be taken as evidence for the contrary position—namely, that these ritual traditions have a long transmission history, resulting in inevitable distortions ("noise") in the transmission of certain details.

---

33. For the former possibility, see ibid., 507–8; for the latter, see Torri, "Subject Shifting."

34. For a detailed discussion of this problem with references to earlier literature, see Miller, *Studies in the Origins*, 469–532.

35. P. Cornil, "La tradition écrite des textes magiques hittites," *Ktèma: Civilisations de l'Orient, de la Grèce et de Rome antiques* 24 (1999): 7–16.

36. For this argument, see Miller, *Studies in the Origins*, 478, based on the data listed on 488–92. While acknowledging that some instances may simply be scribal errors, Miller contends that the number of incidents is too high to be explained as copying errors.

A more substantial argument may be raised based on the form of the attribution formulas. Recognizing the conventional nature of the first-person forms in the incipits, colophons, and often recurring at fixed points in the body of the ritual texts—specifically in the introduction of paraphernalia lists and incantation formulas, these appear to be scribal conventions that cannot automatically be assumed to be based on actual dictation from the ritual expert.[37] Furthermore, the name attributions of the various compositions served as the key datum in the composition of shelve lists by which the textual inventory of the Hittite archives was recorded.[38] The recognition of the scribal character of these conventions raises the possibility (at least) that the scribes may have added them to anonymous prescriptive texts formulated in the third person.

Moreover, as noted, Miller has found inconsistencies between the lists of paraphernalia and the ritual instructions. Many of these inconsistencies may be attributable to copying mistakes or—seemingly more likely—errors in recall, as when the materials associated with a *keldi* ritual (A ii 58) seem to be better suited to a *zurki* ritual, and in fact appear earlier in the text in that context (A ii 7).[39] Yet the curious fact remains, mentioned earlier, that on multiple occasions the paraphernalia lists continue the first person employed in the incipits and colophons.[40] Does this point indicate that the paraphernalia lists were originally independent texts (written/dictated by the ritualists themselves), or are these attributions merely scribal conventions, reverting in these sections to the first-person forms employed in the incipits and colophons?

Miller also calls attention to two Syrian ritualists, Allaiturahhi of Mukiš and Giziya of Alalah.[41] Casting doubt on the "observe and record" hypothesis, Miller argues that the Hittite versions of these rituals from the Hattuša archives may have been based on earlier (Hurrian?)[42] compositions in the Kizzuwatna archives. "In any case, that it is unlikely that any Hittite scribe ever 'interviewed' Allaiturahhi, as suggested above, might also support the proposition that Hittite scribes felt little remorse in ascribing various rituals and incantations to a ritualist of some fame in order to lend their compositions legitimacy."[43] Further evidence for questioning some ritual ascriptions has been amassed by Birgit Christiansen in her study of the Ambazzi rituals. In particular, the situations to be addressed in *CTH* 463 appear to be taken from oracular texts that

---

37. Ibid., 493–96.
38. Gordin, *Hittite Scribal Circles*, 115.
39. Miller, *Studies in the Origins*, 404–5.
40. Ibid., 493–96.
41. Ibid., 506–11.
42. See KUB 45.21, written almost exclusively in Hurrian, and attributed to Allaiturahhi (Haas, "Die hurritisch-hethitischen Rituale," 126; Torri, "Subject Shifting," 677).
43. Miller, *Studies in the Origins*, 509.

are similar to the Mesopotamian *šumma ālu* oracle series. As such, it seems more likely that this ritual is a product of scribal circles than originating from the ritual practitioner herself.[44] Indeed, it is far from clear that the female Hittite ritualists (ŠU.GI; "old woman") were literate in Hittite cuneiform, not to mention Akkadian, given that all of the known Hittite scribes were male.[45]

Yet it would appear that some of this skepticism is exaggerated. None of the evidence cited leads to the conclusion that the ritualists were mere literary inventions of the scribes (pseudonyms), employed to assert the effectiveness of the ritual.[46] For example, Miller's emphatic denial that Allaiturahhi was a ŠU.GI, used to deny her authorship of the rituals in her name, is contradicted by an explicit statement in *KUB* 24.13 III 18' (ChS I/5 text 15).[47] More generally, it is noteworthy that rituals attributed to a single "author" reflect common characteristics, which suggests at the very least that they originated in a single stream of tradition, if not derived from a common author.[48] Moreover, as Miller himself points out in an important caveat, some genealogical information is given for at least two ritualists, suggesting that these figures were not literary inventions *ex nihilo*.[49] Hence, there are grounds to adopt a more balanced view, such as that recently voiced by Gordin.

> Even if ... some "authors" were legendary pseudonyms, many others are known from a variety of sources outside ritual traditions, like the late 13th-century scribe Armaziti, the 14th-century hierodule Kuwatalla, and so on. Without questioning the author's role in producing the original composition (through dictation or otherwise), it is clear that some ritual and magical traditions existed at a remove in time or space from the producers of the late 13th-century copies and editions. This situation increased exponentially the position of the scribes in the collection, study, edition, and creation of these texts based on previous sources.[50]

In other words, the recognition of a high level of scribal involvement does not contradict the assumption that these traditions originated with earlier ritual

---

44. Christiansen, *Die Ritualtradition*, 303–4, 316–17.
45. Miller, *Studies in the Origins*, 479. It should be noted, however, that other scholars have assumed that the ŠU.GIs were both literate and multilingual (e.g., T. Bryce, *Life and Society in the Hittite World* [Oxford: Oxford University Press, 2002], 201–2).
46. As suggested by Hecker, "Tradition und Originalität," 248–49.
47. See V. Haas, review of *Studies in the Origins, Development and Interpretation of the Kizzuwatna Rituals*, by J. L. Miller, *Wiener Zeitschrift für die Kunde des Morgenlandes* 95 (2005): 441.
48. Christiansen, *Die Ritualtradition*, 317.
49. Miller, *Studies in the Origins*, 478 n. 803.
50. Gordin, *Hittite Scribal Circles*, 115. It should be kept in mind nevertheless that these examples (Armaziti, Kuwatalla) are rather exceptional.

experts. On the contrary, it is to be expected that the evidence for scribal activity will increase in correlation to the length of transmission history of a particular ritual tradition.

Further evidence supporting such an approach can be adduced from several recent studies that identify language interference stemming from difficulties in translating Hurrian and Luwian terms and grammatical forms into Hittite.[51] These studies suggest that the Hittite ritual texts from the Ḫattuša archives were based on earlier traditions (whether oral or written) in Hurrian and Luwian. Such evidence corroborates Miller's more moderate suggestion "that the earliest Allaiturahhi composition(s) may have been derived from texts composed already in northern Syria" and later appropriated by Kizzuwatnean scribes."[52]

5.1.5. Summary: Scribal Activity and the Hittite Rituals

In sum, the problem of the authorship of the Hittite rituals is far from settled, and progress will only be made by further detailed research on particular ritual compositions and the relationship between them. In the meantime, an intermediate position between blind credulity and categorical skepticism seems warranted. More fundamentally, it is necessary to recognize that *conservatism* aiming at preserving efficacious ritual traditions and *innovation* motivated by formal, literary, religious, or ideological purposes of the scribes are not mutually exclusive tendencies.

5.2. The Purpose of the Hittite Ritual Texts

It has come time to address the second line of inquiry: what were the functions of the Hittite ritual texts? To answer this question, it will be necessary to characterize the interaction between ritual text and practice. The following possibilities (not mutually exclusive) warrant consideration:

1. Memorization to facilitate ritual performance;
2. Preservation of traditions;

---

51. P. Taracha, "Hittite Rituals as Literary Texts: What Do We Know About Their Original Editions?," in *Hethitische Literatur: Überlieferungsprozesse, Textstrukturen, Ausdrucksformen und Nachwirken; Akten des Symposiums vom 18. bis 20. Februar 2010 in Bonn*, ed. M. Hutter and S. Hutter-Braunsar, AOAT 391 (Munster: Ugarit-Verlag, 2011), 275–83; E. Rieken, "Sprachliche Merkmale religiöser Textsorten im Hethitischen," *WO* 44 (2014): 162–73. For a sophisticated use of linguistic criteria applied to the tradition history of Hittite rituals reflecting Luwian influence, see H. C. Melchert, "Luvian Language in 'Luvian' Rituals from Ḫattuša," in *Beyond Hatti: A Tribute to Gary Beckman*, ed. B. J. Collins and P. Michalowski (Atlanta: Lockwood Press, 2013), 159–72.

52. Miller, *Studies in the Origins*, 507.

3. Enactments of authority;
4. Production of "new" rituals;
5. Regulation of "legitimate" practice.

5.2.1. Rituals Texts as Short-Term Memory Aids

Despite the growing emphasis in recent research on the scribal character of the Hittite ritual texts,[53] one must not assume that they were divorced from practical use in ritual performance. Indeed, numerous characteristics of the texts themselves support the assumption that they were used as *aide-mémoires* for officiants. On this point, there is a basic similarity to the function of ritual texts elsewhere in the Levant, as can be seen from the Ugaritic evidence.[54] For example, the deity list from Ugarit RS 24.264 + (*KTU* 1.118) corresponds to the sacrificial text RS 24.643 (*KTU* 1.148). This correspondence shows that the function of the deity lists was to ensure that each deity received his due, as indicated by the check marks on the left margins of RS 24.264+.[55] Hence, despite claims these deity lists served a "theological" purpose, there is little doubt that they served a practical function. A similar function is filled by the *kaluti*-lists in Hittite rituals,[56] as noted in the publication of one of these texts from Šapinuwa: "Unlike most of the cult texts that indicate the quantities and types of offerings dedicated to the gods, these tablets, at least in the preserved parts, do not contain such information, but only the long lists of deities, mountains, rivers and 'Opfertermini' and some sections in Hurrian of unknown meaning. . . . Nevertheless the presence of some brief ritual instructions in Hittite demonstrates that these texts are not pure and simple lists of deities, rivers, mountains, and 'Opfertermini,' but in all likelihood a cult *memorandum*."[57]

Furthermore, as noted by Pardee in reference to the Ugaritic corpus, the laconic nature of ritual texts, especially regarding the precise procedures implied by a particular technical term, is based on the presumption that the priests needed no instructions for such routines.[58] Miller makes a similar observation regarding the Ritual for Expanding the Night Goddess's Cult (*CTH* 481): "Indeed, it is striking that hardly any description of the ritual performances is to be found in the entire composition, in stark contrast to the sometimes

---

53. Summarized by Christiansen, *Die Ritualtradition*, 1–30.
54. Pardee, *Ritual and Cult*, 2.
55. M. C. A. Korpel, "Unit Delimitation in Ugaritic Cultic Texts and Some Babylonian and Hebrew Parallels," in *Layout Markers in Biblical Manuscripts and Ugaritic Tablets*, ed. M. C. A. Korpel and J. M. Oesch (Assen: Koninklijke Van Gorcum, 2005), 141–60.
56. See R. Strauß, *Reinigungsrituale aus Kizzuwatna* (Berlin: de Gruyter, 2006), 159–65.
57. M. Giorgieri, L. Murat, and A. Süel, "The *Kaluti*-List of the Storm-God of Šapinuwa from Ortaköy (Or. 90/175) and Its Parallels from Boğazköy," *Kaskal* 10 (2013): 160–83 at 174.
58. Pardee, *Ritual and Cult*, 26.

voluminous lists."⁵⁹ His cogent suggestions regarding the *Sitz im Leben* of this text can illuminate our understanding of this textual genre as a whole.

> These ... phenomena reinforce the hypothesis that this composition could hardly have served as the "script" according to which such a ritual was carried out, for which it would be seriously insufficient. Neither does it seem to constitute the work of a scribe or scribes assigned to observe and describe in writing ceremonies as they took place, as such a composition would surely show more consistency in its attempts to list the materials collected for the rites and then their use in those rites. Rather, as mentioned, the composition seems to constitute the "notes" jotted down and/ or copied from other sources ... in preparation for the execution of the expansion that they planned. In it they noted the primary events that were to take place, and in many cases, the items needed for them. Completeness and full consistency was not attempted, as the rites themselves were likely carried out not by reading from a "script," but from memory, the present composition serving as a memory aid before the execution of the rites.⁶⁰

In sum, the literary characteristics of the Hittite ritual texts, like those from Ugarit, suggest their use as guides to correct performance.⁶¹

5.2.2. Long-Term Preservation of Tradition

The conservatism of cultic practice is widely acknowledged, so it is hardly surprising that ritual texts were used to preserve traditions for later generations. Several colophons of festival texts offer salient expression of this dimension of textualization. For example, the colophon of *CTH* 628 reads: "When queen Puduḫepa commanded Walwaziti, the chief of scribes, to seek in Ḫattuša for tablets of Kizzuwatna, on that day he copied these tablets of the Festival of *ḫišuwa*."⁶² The need for a textual record of ritual practice became especially urgent when the stability of cultic practice was disrupted by warfare and/or foreign conquest. Such a situation is expressed clearly in the colophon of *KUB* 28.80: "Tablet of the recitation of the regular festival of Nerik. (This is) now a new tablet. When in the years of w[a]r they started to perform the festival of Nerik in Ḫakmiš, the man of the Stormgod (and) the GUDU-priest ... came from Nerik and they took this re[cit]ation from those (refugee priests)"

---

59. Miller, *Studies in the Origins*, 402.
60. Ibid.
61. See further Schwemer, "Quality Assurance Managers," 19–20; J. W. Watts, "Ritual Legitimacy and Scriptural Authority," *JBL* 124 (2005): 401–41 at 404–12.
62. Gordin, *Hittite Scribal Circles*, 41, 153; compare also Waal, *Source as Object*, 286.

(rev. IV 1′–9′).⁶³ Following an invasion by the Kaška tribes, this text records the traditions as dictated by the refugee priests of Nerik with the goal of reproducing the cultic practices in Ḫakmiš.

5.2.3. Ritual Texts and Authority

At this point, it is important to clarify the relationship between textualization of rituals and authority. The reproduction of ritual texts in duplicate copies would seem to imply a certain significance to the verbal formulation of the ritual *text*, yet it remains necessary to determine: what was the motivating force for this scribal activity?

In this discussion, it seems appropriate to distinguish between therapeutic rituals and festival (cultic) texts. Regarding the former, as is clear from the numerous variations between parallel manuscripts, these texts were not treated with scriptural sanctity,⁶⁴ nor were they ascribed directly to divine revelation like Mesopotamian incantations.⁶⁵ Rather, the *raison d'être* of therapeutic ritual texts and their source of authority was their pretense to efficacy in achieving their aims.

In comparison, festival texts would seem to be governed by the concern for meticulous fulfillment of the kingdom's obligations vis-à-vis the gods and avoiding the potentially catastrophic neglect of these obligations. Nevertheless, the concern for detail in these texts regarding the correct procedure and sequence as determined by legitimate traditions, involving consultation of "ancient" (*annala-/karuili-*) tablets, and modified by consultation with the gods via divination show that the ultimate function of the text was realizing the ideal of proper observance. In order to realize their purpose of paying homage to the gods, it was sometimes necessary—especially when changes were made—to seek divine approval by means of oracle inquiries.⁶⁶ Hence, festival texts like other ritual texts were subordinate to practice, though the textualization of ritual could have additional functions and implications, as will be discussed below.

5.2.4. Production of "New" Rituals

This focus on efficacy should also illuminate our consideration of ritual texts as scholarly literature. Obviously, the term "literature" does not imply an interest in

---

63. Waal, *Source as Object*, 293; compare also Schwemer, "Quality Assurance Managers," 13.
64. See G. Beckman, review of *Die Ritualtradition der Ambazzi: Eine philologische Bearbeitung und entstehungsgeschichtliche Analyse der Ritualtexte CTH 391, CTH 429 und CTH 463*, by B. Christiansen, *JAOS* 127.3 (2007): 375–76 at 375.
65. O. R. Gurney, *Some Aspects of Hittite Religion* (Oxford: Oxford University Press, 1977), 44; R. Schmitt, *Magie im Alten Testament*, AOAT 313 (Münster: Ugarit Verlag, 2004), 67–106.
66. Schwemer, "Quality Assurance Managers."

the aesthetic value or the "drama of reading" ritual texts, but simply their role in promulgating tradition.[67] Specifically, the intense scribal activity involved in producing these texts was motivated first and foremost by the belief in the efficacy of the rituals themselves, which invited the scribes to expand the texts by contributing their own knowledge of ritual and divinatory corpora. It also encouraged consultation with Babylonian scribes and scribal works pertaining to the fields of ritual medicine, and this veneration is amply attested in the Ḫattuša archives.[68]

As noted above, Christiansen has suggested that *CTH* 463 appears to make use of oracular texts that are similar to the Mesopotamian *šumma ālu* oracle series.[69] A similar phenomenon can be found in Mesopotamian Namburbi rituals that often refer directly to specific omens known from divinatory texts.[70] In short, it would appear that scribes could draw on multiple sources of authority in composing ritual texts, with the primary concern being the efficacy of the final result.

5.2.5. Regulation of Legitimate Practice

Yet aside from the efficacy of the ritual performance, it need not be denied that the textualization of ritual had important secondary implications. In particular, the ritual text served as an expression and enactment of the Hittite sovereign's authority, especially as represented by the hierarchy of court scribes. A vivid picture of these cult politics in action can be seen in the text *KUB* 32.133. This unique document deals with the aftermath of a cult reform by King Tudḫaliya, who made a new temple for the Night Goddess in Šamuḫa modeled after her cult in Kizzuwatna.[71] This text records Tudḫaliya's descendent, Muršili II, complaining that the local scribes of Šamuḫa have corrupted the practice of the Night Goddess's cult.

> Thus (says) His Majesty, Muršili, Great King, son of Šuppiluliuma, Great King, Hero: When my forefather, Tudḫaliya, the Great King, split the

---

67. Taracha, "Hittite Rituals," 275–83; see also Gordin, *Hittite Scribal Circles*, 73–80.
68. See Strauß, *Reinigungsrituale*, 208–15; D. Schwemer, "Gauging the Influence of Mesopotamian Magic: The Reception of Babylonian Ritual Traditions in Hittite Practice," in *Diversity and Standardization: Perspectives on Ancient Near Eastern Cultural History*, ed. E. C. Cancik-Kirschbaum, J. W. Klinger, and G. G. W. Müller (Berlin: de Gruyter, 2013), 145–72.
69. Christiansen, *Die Ritualtradition*, 303–4, 316–17.
70. See S. M. Maul, *Zukunftsbewältigung*, Baghdader Forschungen 18 (Mainz: Zabern, 1994).
71. For the historical background of this text, see Miller, *Studies in the Origins*, 350–62. For an edition of the related ritual text KUB 29.4, see ibid., 259–440. An insightful analysis of the religious background of these texts can be found in R. Beal, "Dividing a God," in *Magic and Ritual in the Ancient World*, ed. P. Mirecki and M. Meyer (Leiden: Brill, 2002), 197–208.

Night Goddess from the temple of the Night Goddess in Kizzuwatna and worshipped her separately in a temple in Šamuha, those rituals and obligations that he ordained for the temple of the Night Goddess, the *scribes-on-wood* and the temple personnel came and began to incessantly alter them. I, Muršili, Great King, have reedited (EGIR-*pa aniyanun*) them from the tablets. Whenever in the future, in the temple of the Night Goddess of Šamuha, either the king, the queen, prince, or princess come to the temple of the Night Goddess of Šamuha, these shall be the rituals.[72]

This text relates that Tudḫaliya had "ordained" (*ḫamankatta*) the rituals for the Night Goddess, implying the royal authorization for the new cult in Šamuḫa, though it seems reasonable to assume that the rites were based for the most part on the earlier rites as practiced in Kizzuwatna. Apparently, the local priests and scribes of Šamuḫa did not wholeheartedly embrace Tudḫaliya's cultic reform and made numerous changes in the (written) ritual. Alternatively, it is possible that the text implies that the Šamuḫa scribes lacked access to the original written ritual text, so that they proceeded to produce their own. In response, Muršili here claims to restore his forefather's ordinance on the basis of the original tablets.

According to the former interpretation, involving a deliberate modification of written ritual instructions, it may be significant that the king singles out for rebuke the "scribes-on-wood" (DUB.SAR.GIŠ). These scribes can be distinguished from "cuneiform scribes" (DUB.SAR) in that the former's function was "of a more clerical or secretarial nature."[73] In other words, the fact that these secretaries were meddling with the content of the ritual texts was a violation of the scribal hierarchy and ultimately of royal authority. Accordingly, this passage may offer evidence for the competition between different loci of authority in the determination of "legitimate" cult practice, with the Hittite monarch struggling to establish his authority over the conservatism of local cult officiants.[74] Importantly, the arena for this battle is the ritual text, with scribes acting as the mediators in attempts to "fix" ritual tradition in an authoritative form.

72. Adapted from Miller, *Studies in the Origins*, 312–13.
73. Gordin, *Hittite Scribal Circles*, 140. For further discussion of the use of wooden tablets and related terminology, see ibid., 17–21, 140–45 (on the scribal hierarchy); Schwemer, "Quality Assurance Managers," 11–12, 21–22. Regarding the debate concerning the designation DUB.SAR. GIŠ, see also T. P. J. van den Hout, "lúDUB.SAR.GIŠ = 'Clerk'?," *Or* 79 (2010): 255–67; W. Waal, "They Wrote on Wood: The Case for a Hieroglyphic Scribal Tradition on Wooden Writing Boards in Hittite Anatolia," *Anatolian Studies* 61 (2011): 21–34.
74. Another example of the exercise of royal authority over the cult is Tudḫaliya IV's edict regarding the cult of Nerik, which includes detailed instructions for ritual performance. See J. Součková, "Edikt von Tutḫaliia IV. zugunsten des Kults des Wettergottes von Nerik," in *Investigationes Anatolicae. Gedenkschrift für E. Neu*, ed. J. Klinger, E. Rieken, and C. Ruster, StBoT 52 (Wiesbaden: Harrasowitz, 2010), 279–300.

The legitimizing function of ritual texts raises an additional question pertaining to the relationship between ritual text and practice. Here the question "which came first" has interesting implications. For example, according to the view that takes the ritual text to be the progenitor of ritual practice, one might understand the above cited evidence for the use of ritual texts as imposing royal authority over the cult as implying that the monarch has "authored" the ritual, or at least that the ritual derives its initial authority from the royal enactment. However, in most cases, as argued above, ritual texts were ancillaries to already existing ritual practice. Hence, one may contrast two schemes for reconstructing the source of authority of ritual texts:

Royal/priestly authority > text > practice
Practice > text > royal/priestly authorization

A recognition of the greater appropriateness of the second model (in most cases) enables a refined appreciation for the functions of ritual texts *as texts*. Specifically, an important role is the function of the text as a "filter" by which authoritative practice is distinguished from "illegitimate" variations, as can be seen from Muršili II's enactment. While the king was the highest mortal authority in the regulation of cultic practice, often he was required to defer to the gods for the final authorization of any changes by means of oracular inquiry.[75]

An even more heavy-handed use of ritual texts as expressions of royal authority can be found in the "Anatolian" rituals from Emar that were copied in the period of Hittite hegemony (the thirteenth century BCE). Significantly, the "diviner" (LÚ ḪAL) Zū-Baʿla, whose subordination to Hittite authorities is well documented, was the key scribe in whose personal archive were found most of the important ritual and festival texts from Emar.[76] These texts sought to ensure the worship of the Hittite deities in Emar, as explicitly stated in the opening lines of one text: "The ritual tablet (*ṭuppu parṣi*) for the gods of the land of Ḫatti, the lower and upper cities."[77] Further evidence for the role of Zū-Baʿla's family in the administration of the Emar cult makes clear that these ritual texts were intended to be implemented in actual practice. In other words, these ritual texts served as a medium of long-distance control for implementing Hittite authority in Emar.[78]

---

75. Schwemer, "Quality Assurance Managers," 17–18.
76. D. E. Fleming, *Time at Emar: The Cultic Calendar and the Rituals from the Diviner's House* (Winona Lake, IN: Eisenbrauns, 2000), 13–47; Y. Cohen, "The Administration of Cult in Hittite Emar," *Altorientalische Forschungen* 38 (2011): 145–57.
77. Cohen, "Administration of Cult," 146.
78. Ibid., 150; P. M. Michel, *Le culte des pierres à Emar à l'époque hittite*, OBO 266 (Fribourg: Academic Press; Göttingen: Vandenhoeck & Ruprecht, 2014).

5.2.6. Summary: Functions of Hittite Ritual Texts

In sum, it seems that the primary function of the Hittite ritual texts was to serve as aids to ritual performance—namely, as short-term memory aids to officiants. At the same time, this practical motive for textualization did not preclude additional functions, including the long-term preservation of ritual traditions, imposition of royal authority over local cults, and regulation of legitimate practice.

These conclusions, drawing on a broad survey of ritual and cultic materials, dovetail with two recent studies focusing specifically on the festival traditions. In his recent analysis of the function of festival texts, Daniel Schwemer concludes that "the various activities that were immediately connected with the practice of the cult provide a sufficient and plausible explanation for the large number of festival texts and texts of related genres that have been found at Hittite sites; there is no reason to postulate any other rationale for the writing of these cuneiform texts."[79] Nevertheless, this functional perspective of ritual texts does not preclude the recognition that the textualization of ritual practice caused these written documents to take on a life of their own. Based on formal characteristics of Hittite festival texts and modern parallels, Christiansen has shown how that they could serve as a means for the preservation and regulation of traditions, while enabling "legitimate" adaptations under the strict control of cultic and royal authorities.[80] As texts, these documents became subject to intensive scribal activity, involving both conservational processes to preserve ritual traditions as well as innovations that drew upon the scholarly milieu.

5.3. The Textualization of Priestly Ritual in Light of Hittite Rituals

It has now come time to explore how this body of research on Hittite ritual can shed light on the biblical Priestly source. As a first step, it seems useful to catalog some of the fundamental similarities and differences between these two corpora. On one hand, when comparing the Hittite rituals with biblical rituals for defined situations such as Lev 13–14 (for leprosy), Lev 16 (for defilement of the temple/national catastrophe), or Num 5:11–31 for a suspected adulteress, one finds numerous formal similarities, including:

---

79. Schwemer, " Quality Assurance Managers," 23.
80. B. Christiansen, "Liturgische Agenda, Unterweisungsmaterial und rituelles Traditionsgut: Die hethitischen Festritualtexte in kulturvergleichender Perspektive," in *Liturgie oder Literatur: Die Kultrituale der Hethiter im transkulturellen Vergleich*, ed. G. G. W. Müller, StBoT 60 (Wiesbaden: Harrasowitz, 2016), 31–66. This point is also recognized by Schwemer, "Quality Assurance Managers," 16–19.

casuistic structure,
chronologically arranged instructions,
lists of paraphernalia, and
sometimes laconic references to the component rites of the ritual.

Taken together with the similarities in content with extrabiblical rituals, these characteristics would support the form-critical hypothesis that the biblical texts originated as individual ritual instructions for specific circumstances, comparable to the Hittite prescriptive rituals.

On the other hand, one must not ignore the significant differences. The most outstanding difference is the fact that Priestly ritual is inextricably integrated into the Priestly narrative. This "narrativization" of ritual is not merely a superficial framework into which ritual instructions have been clumsily added. Rather, the ritual instructions are permeated by the narrative setting of the wilderness tabernacle, including of course the key role of Aaron as high priest. Much to the dismay of historically minded scholars, and despite their sharpened scalpels ready to dissect the text into its composite layers, the degree to which this narrative framework is consistently maintained is striking, leaving few traces that can be identified as betraying the historical setting of the author(s).

A related point pertains to the nature of the textual evidence from the two corpora. The Priestly source as transmitted in the Pentateuchal text has not left us with duplicates of a particular text. The closest analogs would be the comparison of ritual laws in Ezek 44 and Lev 22, the parallel accounts (command/implementation) of the inauguration of the Tabernacle (Exod 29/Lev 8), or the sin-offering laws of Lev 4 and Num 15. The epigraphic evidence from Ketef Hinnom has provided us with amulets paralleling the Priestly blessing of Num 6:22–27. One may add the significantly divergent text of the tabernacle-building narratives of Exodus in the Septuagint. Ultimately, however widely we delineate our data set, these isolated cases offer limited insight into the prehistory of the Priestly texts. This state of affairs is in stark contrast to the existence of multiple duplicates of particular Hittite rituals, which exhibit the minor and major variations discussed above. While we might at first glance attribute this disparity between the biblical and Hittite corpora to the difference in perishability of the material employed by Israelite and Hittite scribes (parchment or papyrus versus clay tablets), the material factor is probably not the most significant. Rather, it should be recognized that the absence (or near absence) of divergent ritual traditions in ancient Israel is not accidental. Like the ubiquity of the narrative framework in the ritual materials, so too does the near absence of divergent Priestly traditions bespeak a high level of control and authority governing the perpetuation of the Priestly source.

One may even wonder if this control finds expression in the relatively high uniformity of the Second Temple manuscripts of Leviticus, as suggested by

Sarianna Metso: "It is plausible that the Jerusalem priesthood had carefully guarded the transmission of the text of Leviticus."[81] While some scholars, such as Russell Hobson with reference to the *mīs pî* manuscripts from Aššurbanipal's library, have suggested that textual control is a function of genre,[82] the Hittite evidence shows that the veneration of ritual traditions is not inevitably expressed in textual uniformity.

Turning to an additional illuminating difference between Hittite and Priestly rituals, it was noted regarding the Hittite texts that references to particular rites are usually laconic, presupposing the prior knowledge of the officiating priest. This point is valid generally for Ugaritic and Mesopotamian rituals. From this perspective, the detailed instructions for carrying out different offerings in Lev 1–7 are anomalies. How can they be explained? Taking a more historicist perspective, we may surmise that these instructions were written down during the exilic period (or soon thereafter) when the rituals were no longer practiced to ensure the preservation of these traditions. Along a similar vein, perhaps these ritual texts were somehow expected to serve as a substitute for the actual practice (analogous to how the later rabbis interpreted institutionalized prayers as substitutes for the sacrifices)?[83] While such historical explanations are almost irresistibly tempting, one cannot rule out a more ideological motivation, whereby the detailed instructions of Lev 1–7 were intended to stress that the ritual procedures must conform to the divinely revealed instructions. The centrality of this view is represented not only in the repeated formula that the tabernacle was made "as YHWH commanded Moses" (Exod 29; Lev 8) but also in the assertion that the tabernacle was created according to the "model" (*tbnyt*) shown to Moses (Exod 25:9, 40; 26:30).[84]

---

81. S. Metso, "Evidence from the Qumran Scrolls for the Scribal Transmission of Leviticus," in *Editing the Bible: Assessing the Task Past and Present*, ed. J. S. Kloppenborg and J. H. Newman (Atlanta: Society of Biblical Literature, 2012), 69. See also J. Rhyder's contribution to this volume.

82. See R. Hobson, *Transforming Literature into Scripture: Texts as Cult Objects in Nineveh and Qumran* (Sheffield: Equinox, 2012). Similarly, but with different reasoning, Kenneth Mathews writes regarding the uniformity of the textual traditions of Leviticus: "Narrative literature (e.g., Samuel), in which a smooth reading for storytelling is desired, will undergo textual activity to meet that goal. A different kind of textual activity occurs for descriptive or legal material, in which rigid formulaic patterns are more important and thus textual activity aims at textual uniformity" (K. A. Mathews, "The Leviticus Scrolls [11QpaleoLev] and the Text of the Hebrew Bible," *CBQ* 48 [1986]: 199).

83. For example, *Num. Rab.* 18:21.

84. Of course, this attitude is not exclusive to the Hebrew Bible. Divine revelation of a temple plan is an ancient Near Eastern motif that can be traced back to the third-millennium Gudea inscriptions and continued until the Neo-Babylonian period; see V. Hurowitz, *I Have Built You an Exalted House: Temple Building in the Bible in Light of Mesopotamian and Northwest Semitic Writings*, JSOTSup 115 (Sheffield: JSOT Press, 1992), 168–70 and passim. One may also compare Šamaš's revelation of the proper form of his image (*uṣurti ṣalmīšu*) in the Nabû-apla-idinna Inscription; see C. E. Woods, "The Sun-God Tablet of Nabû-apla-idinna Revisited," *JCS* 56 (2004): 23–103 at 85.

A further dimension of comparison is the role of scribal intervention in the editing of the Priestly ritual texts. Biblical scholarship has adduced numerous fairly clear cases in which an earlier form of the text has been supplemented by *Fortschreibung*. Confining myself to some relatively uncontroversial cases, it is instructive to categorize the various motives that can be deduced from these additions.

5.3.1. Lev 8:10–12

As has been recognized, the reference to the anointment of the cultic paraphernalia is absent from the parallel account in Exod 29 and has been interpolated from Exod 40:9–13. From a purely literary standpoint, this interpolation could be characterized as a harmonization between the two texts. More fundamentally, however, it resolves a contradiction pertaining to their ritual ideology. Specifically, whereas Exod 29:36–37 mentions the anointment of the altar only as the final sanctifying phase of the ritual process, Exod 40:9–13 and the dependent interpolation in Lev 8:10–12 presume that appurtenances must be "ritualized" before they can be used in the cult.[85]

5.3.2. Lev 5:7–13; 12:8; Probably Also Lev 1:14–17

In these passages, an editor has made special provisions for poor Israelites who could not afford the regular prescribed offerings. Clearly, these clauses are governed by a desire to expand the inclusiveness of the cultic institution, so that every member of the community can bring his or her offering.[86]

5.3.3. Lev 16:29–34

In contrast with the opening verses of the chapter that warn Aaron from entering the sacred precinct "at any time" (v. 2), implying that the following ritual addresses an emergency situation,[87] the summary at the end of the chapter in verses 29–34a fixes the date at the tenth day of the seventh month. This textual addition serves to systematize the Israelite cult on two levels, routinizing the purification of the sanctuary on an annual basis and integrating this day into the festival calendar.

---

85. Y. Feder, *Blood Expiation in Hittite and Biblical Ritual: Origins, Context and Meaning* (Atlanta: Society of Biblical Literature, 2011), 46–48.

86. See C. Nihan, *From Priestly Torah to Pentateuch*, FAT 2/25 (Tübingen: Mohr Siebeck, 2007), 244.

87. J. Milgrom, *Leviticus 1–16: A New Translation with Introduction and Commentary*, AB 3A (New York: Doubleday, 1991), 1012–13.

These examples allow a glimpse (albeit incomplete) into the types of concerns that prompted later editors to supplement earlier Priestly instructions. Importantly, these appear to be dominated by notions of propriety related to the cult itself and an attempt to adapt earlier instructions to a broader socioreligious framework. When evaluating the rhetorical thrust of these Priestly texts, it is important to weigh these institutionalized cultic concerns alongside any ulterior political or economic motives.[88]

A slightly different picture is achieved by considering the Holiness Source as a large-scale *Fortschreibung* of P. Alongside the additions noted above (many of which can be attributed to H), one may detect an attempt to complement P's limited focus on the cult with a comprehensive scheme for the entire nation, apparently in dialogue with other law codes of the Pentateuch.[89]

Even here a certain similarity can be found with the Hittite ritual texts. As noted, the first-person attributions to ritual experts tend to appear in the incipits and colophons of the text, though the body of the rituals tend to be more heterogeneous in content. So too, one finds an intensity of scribal activity specifically in the margins of the Priestly source, not only in the incipits and colophons of particular ritual instructions[90] but also in the references to the literary framework "at Mt. Sinai" (*bhr syny*) at the end of the Holiness Code (Lev 25:1; 26:46) to include this body of laws as the conclusion of the Sinai revelation.[91]

5.4. Conclusion

In summary, the recent explosion of research into the textualization of Hittite ritual offers fascinating prospects for understanding the formation of the Priestly source. Though these are only some first impressions on a topic that demands much more sustained research, I will venture a few observations. The similarity in form, content, and function between the two corpora suggest to me that they derive from a similar *Sitz im Leben*, as aids to ritual practice. Likewise, there is substantial evidence that these corpora were shaped by complementary processes of conserving ritual traditions while enabling necessary adaptations.

---

88. Compare J. W. Watts, *Ritual and Rhetoric in Leviticus* (Cambridge: Cambridge University, 2007); J. W. Watts, *Leviticus 1–10*, HCOT (Leuven: Peeters, 2013).
89. Nihan, *From Priestly Torah*, 548–59; J. Stackert, "The Holiness Legislation and its Pentateuchal Sources: Revision, Supplementation, and Replacement," in *The Strata of the Priestly Writings: Contemporary Debate and Future Directions*, ed. S. Shectman and J. S. Baden (Zürich: Theologischer Verlag, 2009), 187–204.
90. See M. Fishbane, "Biblical Colophons, Textual Criticism, and Legal Analogies," *CBQ* 42 (1980): 438–49.
91. See Nihan, *From Priestly Torah*, 551; Metso, "Evidence," 71.

These similarities have important ramifications for understanding the origins of the Israelite ritual traditions. Too frequently, the discussion of extrabiblical parallels to biblical rituals is entangled with the question of dating P. That is to say, the identification of precursors to biblical rituals from the Late Bronze Age Levant (e.g., Emar, Ḫatti, Ugarit) is taken to contradict the dating of P to the Persian period common among biblical scholars.[92] The recognition that the perpetuation of ritual traditions mediated by text and actual practice was a *longue durée* process shows that these positions need not be contradictory.

At the same time, the differences between the processes of transmission of Hittite and Israelite ritual traditions may be just as illuminating as their similarities. Indeed, the comparison of the evidence in our possession indicates that these two bodies of tradition went through very different processes of development. Whereas the Hittite archives have left us with abundant evidence of the messy process of promulgating ritual texts—characterized by both accidents of the duplication process stemming from mechanical errors and deliberate changes made by the scribes—the Priestly text in our possession is much more homogeneous and coherent, particularly in adherence to its literary framework. While this characteristic of P warrants further investigation, it may be postulated provisionally that the strict control reflected in P's textualization of Israelite ritual traditions was motivated not only as a reference guide for priests, since this consideration governed also the Hittite ritual literature. Rather, P's textualization of ritual traditions seeks to legitimate these practices as rooted in divine revelation,[93] but, no less importantly, serving thereby to reject alternative "illegitimate" traditions.[94]

In other words, the evidence for scribal intervention in revising the early Priestly materials reflects a concerted effort to adapt them to the literary, ideological, and socioreligious agenda of their editors. As compared with Christian Frevel's proposal that Leviticus represents a compromise document between rival Persian-period sects,[95] the state of evidence reviewed here appears to be

---

92. The same can be said about attempts to claim the antiquity of P based on these parallels, as boldly argued by M. Weinfeld, "Social and Cultic Institutions in the Priestly Source Against Their Ancient Near Eastern Background," *Proceedings of the Eighth World Congress of Jewish Studies* (1983): 95–129. For a broader discussion of this issue, see my forthcoming essay, Y. Feder, "Pentateuchal and Ancient Near Eastern Rituals," in *The Oxford Handbook of the Pentateuch*, ed. J. Baden and J. Stackert (Oxford: Oxford University Press, 2021). For a survey of some of these parallels, see Feder, *Blood Expiation*, 115–43.

93. For a discussion of revelation as a scribal strategy of legitimation, see Watts, "Ritual Legitimacy"; van der Toorn, *Scribal Culture*, 205–32.

94. For an example of the role of Priestly instructions as a filter against illegitimate traditions, see Y. Feder, "Behind the Scenes of a Priestly Polemic: Leviticus 14 and Its Extra-Biblical Parallels," *JHebS* 15.4 (2015): 1–26, doi:10.5508/jhs.2015.v15.a4.

95. See C. Frevel's essay in this volume.

more consistent with the more conventional "schism" account. In other words, the relatively "immaculate" form of the Leviticus tradition would indicate that an already authoritative form of Leviticus was accepted by different sects, either because the groups shared a common historical background or because they simply acknowledged the authority of the Jerusalem priesthood's text. On the other hand, if Leviticus was edited to serve as a compromise document, one would expect to find more evidence of a messy process of formation, reflecting the rival groups' participation in this process. So until missing Priestly scrolls are discovered in Qumran or elsewhere, we must assume that the Jerusalem priesthood's hegemony over Israelite ritual traditions was already established in the early Persian period.

BIBLIOGRAPHY

Beal, R. "Dividing a God." Pages 197–208 in *Magic and Ritual in the Ancient World*. Edited by P. Mirecki and M. Meyer. Leiden: Brill, 2002.
Beckman, G. *The* babilili-*Ritual from Hattusa*. Winona Lake, IN: Eisenbrauns, 2014.
———. *Hittite Birth Rituals*. StBoT 29. Wiesbaden: Harrassowitz, 1983.
———. Review of *Die Ritualtradition der Ambazzi: Eine philologische Bearbeitung und entstehungsgeschichtliche Analyse der Ritualtexte CTH 391, CTH 429 und CTH 463*, by B. Christiansen. *JAOS* 127.3 (2007): 375–76.
Bryce, T. *Life and Society in the Hittite World*. Oxford: Oxford University Press, 2002.
Carr, D. M. *The Formation of the Hebrew Bible: A New Reconstruction*. Oxford: Oxford University Press, 2011.
———. *Writing on the Tablet of the Heart: Origins of Scripture and Literature*. Oxford: Oxford University Press, 2005.
Christiansen, B. "Ein Ensuhnungsritual fur Tuthaliya und Nikalmati? Betrachrungen zur Entstehungsgeschichte von KBo 15.10+." *SMEA* 49 (2007): 93–107.
———. "Liturgische Agenda, Unterweisungsmaterial und rituelles Traditionsgut: Die hethitischen Festritualtexte in kulturvergleichender Perspektive." Pages 31–66 in *Liturgie oder Literature: Die Kultrituale der Hethiter im transkulturellen Vergleich*. Edited by G. G. W. Müller. StBoT 60. Wiesbaden: Harrasowitz, 2016.
———. *Die Ritualtradition der Ambazzi: Eine philologische Bearbeitung und entstehungsgeschichtliche Analyse der Ritualtexte CTH 391, CTH 429 und CTH 463*. StBoT 48. Wiesbaden: Harrassowitz, 2006.
Clemens, D. M. *Sources for Ugaritic Ritual and Sacrifice*. Vol. 1, *Ugaritic and Ugarit Akkadian Texts*. AOAT 284/1. Münster: Ugarit-Verlag, 2001.
Cohen, Y. "The Administration of Cult in Hittite Emar." *Altorientalische Forschungen* 38 (2011): 145–57.
Collins, B. J. "The Place of *KBo* 13.145 in the Hantitaššu Text Tradition." Pages 63–74 in *Beyond Hatti: A Tribute to Gary Beckman*. Edited by B. J. Collins and P. Michalowski. Atlanta: Lockwood Press, 2013.
———. "Royal Co-option of a Popular Ritual: The Case of Hantitaššu." Pages 185–201 in *Proceedings of the Eighth International Congress of Hittitology, Warsaw, 5–9 September 2011*. Edited by P. Taracha and M. Kapełuś. Warsaw: Agade, 2014.

Cornil, P. "La tradition écrite des textes magiques hittites." *Ktèma: Civilisations de l'Orient, de la Grèce et de Rome antiques* 24 (1999): 7–16.

Dardano, P. *Die hethitischen Tontafelkataloge aus Ḫattuša (CTH 276–282)*. StBoT 47. Wiesbaden: Harrassowitz, 2006.

Delnero, P. "Memorization and the Transmission of Sumerian Literary Compositions." *JNES* 71 (2012): 198–208.

De Martino, S., and A. Süel. *The Third Tablet of the itkalzi Ritual*. LoGisma: Torino, 2015.

Feder, Y. "Behind the Scenes of a Priestly Polemic: Leviticus 14 and its Extra-Biblical Parallels." *JHebS* 15.4 (2015): 1–26. doi:10.5508/jhs.2015.v15.a4.

———. *Blood Expiation in Hittite and Biblical Ritual: Origins, Context and Meaning*. Atlanta: Society of Biblical Literature, 2011.

———. "Pentateuchal and Ancient Near Eastern Rituals." Pages 421–42 in *The Oxford Handbook of the Pentateuch*. Edited by J. Baden and J. Stackert. Oxford: Oxford University Press, 2021.

Fishbane, M. "Biblical Colophons, Textual Criticism, and Legal Analogies." *CBQ* 42 (1980): 438–49.

Fleming, D. E. *Time at Emar: The Cultic Calendar and the Rituals from the Diviner's House*. Winona Lake, IN: Eisenbrauns, 2000.

Giorgieri, M., L. Murat, and A. Süel. "The *Kaluti*-List of the Storm-God of Šapinuwa from Ortaköy (Or. 90/175) and Its Parallels from Boğazköy." *Kaskal* 10 (2013): 169–83.

Gordin, S. *Hittite Scribal Circles: Scholarly Tradition and Writing Habits*. StBoT 59. Wiesbaden: Harrassowitz, 2015.

Gurney, O. R. *Some Aspects of Hittite Religion*. Oxford: Oxford University Press, 1977.

Haas, V. "Die hurritisch-hethitischen Rituale der Beschwörerin Allaituraḫ(ḫ)i und ihr literarhistorischer Hintergrund." Pages 117–44 in *Hurriter und Hurritisch*. Edited by V. Haas. Konstanzer Althistroische Vorträge und Forschungen 21. Konstanz: Xenia, 1988.

———. Review of *Studies in the Origins, Development and Interpretation of the Kizzuwatna Rituals*, by J. L. Miller. *Wiener Zeitschrift für die Kunde des Morgenlandes* 95 (2005): 435–41.

Hecker, K. "Tradition und Originalität in der altorientalischen Literatur." *Archív orientální* 45 (1977): 245–58.

Hobson, R. *Transforming Literature into Scripture: Texts as Cult Objects in Nineveh and Qumran*. Sheffield: Equinox, 2012.

Hout, T. P. J. van den. "Death as a Privilege." Pages 37–75 in *Hidden Futures: Death and Immortality in Ancient Egypt, Anatolia, the Classical, Biblical and Arabic-Islamic World*. Edited by J. M. Bremmer, T. van den Hout, and R. Peters. Amsterdam: Amsterdam University Press, 1994.

———. "^{lú}DUB.SAR.GIŠ = 'Clerk'?" *Or* 79 (2010): 255–67.

———. "Zu einer Stratigraphie der hethitischen Totenrituale." Pages 301–6 in *Saeculum: Gedenkschrift für Heinrich Otten anlässlich seines 100. Geburtstags*. Edited by A. Müller-Karpe, E. Rieken, and W. Sommerfeld. StBoT 58. Wiesbaden: Harrassowitz, 2015.

Hurowitz, V. *I Have Built You an Exalted House: Temple Building in the Bible in Light of Mesopotamian and Northwest Semitic Writings*. JSOTSup 115. Sheffield: JSOT Press, 1992.

Kassian, A., A. Korolëv, and A. Sidel'tsev. *Hittite Funerary Ritual: šalliš waštaiš*. AOAT 288. Münster: Ugarit-Verlag, 2002.

Korpel, M. C. A. "Unit Delimitation in Ugaritic Cultic Texts and Some Babylonian and Hebrew Parallels." Pages 141–60 in *Layout Markers in Biblical Manuscripts and Ugaritic Tablets*. Edited by M. C. A. Korpel and J. M. Oesch. Assen: Koninklijke Van Gorcum, 2005.

Levine, B. A. "The Descriptive Ritual Texts from Ugarit: Some Formal and Functional Features of the *Genre*." Pages 467–75 in *The Word of the Lord Shall Go Forth: Essays in Honor of David Noel Freedman in Celebration of His Sixtieth Birthday*. Edited by C. L. Meyers and M. O'Connor. Winona Lake, IN: Eisenbrauns, 1983.

———. "The Descriptive Tabernacle Texts of the Pentateuch." *JAOS* 85 (1965): 307–18.

———. "Ugaritic Descriptive Rituals." *JCS* 17 (1963): 105–11.

Marcuson, H., and T. van den Hout. "Memorization and Hittite Ritual: New Perspectives on the Transmission of Hittite Ritual Texts." *JANER* 15 (2015): 143–68.

Mathews, K. A. "The Leviticus Scrolls (11QpaleoLev) and the Text of the Hebrew Bible." *CBQ* 48 (1986): 171–207.

Maul, S. M. *Zukunftsbewältigung*. Baghdader Forschungen 18. Mainz: Zabern, 1994.

Melchert, H. C. "Luvian Language in 'Luvian' Rituals from Ḫattuša." Pages 159–72 in *Beyond Hatti: A Tribute to Gary Beckman*. Edited by B. J. Collins and P. Michalowski. Atlanta: Lockwood Press, 2013.

Metso, S. "Evidence from the Qumran Scrolls for the Scribal Transmission of Leviticus." Pages 67–79 in *Editing the Bible: Assessing the Task Past and Present*. Edited by J. S. Kloppenborg and J. H. Newman. Atlanta: Society of Biblical Literature, 2012.

Michel, P. M. *Le culte des pierres à Emar à l'époque hittite*. OBO 266. Fribourg: Academic Press; Göttingen: Vandenhoeck & Ruprecht, 2014.

Milgrom, J. *Leviticus 1–16: A New Translation with Introduction and Commentary*. AB 3A. New York: Doubleday, 1991.

Miller, J. L. *Studies in the Origins, Development and Interpretation of the Kizzuwatna Rituals*. StBoT 46. Wiesbaden: Harrassowitz, 2004.

———. Review of *Die Ritualtradition der Ambazzi: Eine philologische Bearbeitung und entstehungsgeschichtliche Analyse der Ritualtexte CTH 391, CTH 429 und CTH 463*, by B. Christiansen. *ZA* 99 (2009): 153–57.

Nihan, C. *From Priestly Torah to Pentateuch*. FAT 2/25. Tübingen: Mohr Siebeck, 2007.

Pardee, D. *Ritual and Cult at Ugarit*. WAW 10. Atlanta: Society of Biblical Literature, 2002.

———. *Les textes rituels*. 2 vols. Ras Shamra-Ougarit 12. Paris: Editions Recherche sur les civilisations, 2000.

Rieken, E. "Sprachliche Merkmale religiöser Textsorten im Hethitischen." *WO* 44 (2014): 162–73.

Schmitt, R. *Magie im Alten Testament*. AOAT 313. Münster: Ugarit Verlag, 2004.

Schwemer, D. "Gauging the Influence of Mesopotamian Magic: The Reception of Babylonian Ritual Traditions in Hittite Practice." Pages 145–72 in *Diversity and Standardization: Perspectives on Ancient Near Eastern Cultural History*. Edited by E. C. Cancik-Kirschbaum, J. W. Klinger, and G. G. W. Müller. Berlin: de Gruyter, 2013.

———. "Quality Assurance Managers at Work: The Hittite Festival Tradition." Pages 1–29 in *Liturgie oder Literature: Die Kultrituale der Hethiter im transkulturellen Vergleich*. Edited by G. G. W. Müller. StBoT 60. Wiesbaden: Harrasowitz, 2016.
Součková, J. "Edikt von Tutḫaliija IV. zugunsten des Kults des Wettergottes von Nerik." Pages 279–300 in *Investigationes Anatolicae. Gedenkschrift für E. Neu*. Edited by J. Klinger, E. Rieken, and C. Ruster. StBoT 52. Wiesbaden: Harrasowitz, 2010.
Stackert, J. "The Holiness Legislation and its Pentateuchal Sources: Revision, Supplementation, and Replacement." Pages 187–204 in *The Strata of the Priestly Writings: Contemporary Debate and Future Directions*. Edited by S. Shectman and J. S. Baden. Zürich: Theologischer Verlag, 2009.
Strauß, R. *Reinigungsrituale aus Kizzuwatna*. Berlin: de Gruyter, 2006.
Taracha, P. "Hittite Rituals as Literary Texts: What Do We Know About Their Original Editions?" Pages 275–83 in *Hethitische Literatur: Überlieferungsprozesse, Textstrukturen, Ausdrucksformen und Nachwirken; Akten des Symposiums vom 18. bis 20. Februar 2010 in Bonn*. Edited by M. Hutter and S. Hutter-Braunsar. AOAT 391. Munster: Ugarit-Verlag.
Toorn, K. van der. *Scribal Culture and the Making of the Hebrew Bible*. Cambridge: Harvard University Press, 2007.
Torri, G. "Subject Shifting in Hittite Magical Rituals." Pages 671–80 in *Tabularia Hethaeorum: Hethitologische Beiträge; Silvin Košak zum 65 Geburtstag*. Edited by D. Groddek and M. Zorman. Dresdner Beiträge zur Hethitologie 25. Wiesbaden: Harrassowitz, 2007.
Waal, W. "The Source as Object: Studies in Hittite Diplomatics." PhD diss. Leiden University, 2010.
———. "They Wrote on Wood: The Case for a Hieroglyphic Scribal Tradition on Wooden Writing Boards in Hittite Anatolia." *Anatolian Studies* 61 (2011): 21–34.
Watts, J. W. *Leviticus 1–10*. HCOT. Leuven: Peeters, 2013.
———. *Ritual and Rhetoric in Leviticus*. Cambridge: Cambridge University, 2007.
———. "Ritual Legitimacy and Scriptural Authority." *JBL* 124 (2005): 401–41.
Weinfeld, M. "Social and Cultic Institutions in the Priestly Source Against Their Ancient Near Eastern Background." *Proceedings of the Eighth World Congress of Jewish Studies* (1983): 95–129.
Woods, C. E. "The Sun-God Tablet of Nabû-apla-idinna Revisited." *JCS* 56 (2004): 23–103.
Worthington, M. *Principles of Akkadian Textual Criticism*. Berlin: de Gruyter, 2012.

CHAPTER 6

Diversity and Centralization of the Temple Cult in the Archeological Record from the Iron II C to the Persian and Hellenistic Periods in Judah

Rüdiger Schmitt

IT HAS LONG BEEN A POINT of consensus among biblical scholars, as well as among scholars of archaeology, that postexilic Judean religion underwent a transformation from heterogenity to a uniform, monopolized, centralized cult, sometimes described as a radical change or a more processional development, beginning with the so called "reform" of King Josiah, or even earlier in the times of Hezekiah.[1] I just cite here Ephraim Stern's conclusion that "since the beginning of the Persian period, in all the territories of Judah and Samaria, there is no single piece of evidence for any pagan cults! There are no sanctuaries (except, of course, for the Jewish one in Jerusalem and Samaritan one on Mount Gerizim), no figurines, and no remains of any other pagan cultic objects. This is in sharp contrast to the late Judean monarchic Period."[2] Many scholars have followed Stern, or tried to refine his thesis, like Melody Knowles in her 2006 book *Centrality Practiced*, in which she basically confirmed Stern's thesis but nevertheless tried to show that there was a geographic nuancing of religious practice concerning the use of incense.[3] However, Stern's assessment of a "religious revolution" in Yehud with a purified cult driven by the forced establishment of exclusive monotheism has been challenged in recent studies—for example, *A "Religious Revolution" in Yehûd?*, edited by Christian Frevel,

---

1. Compare (among others) the now classic book of R. Albertz, *A History of Israelite Religion in the Old Testament Period*, vol. 1, *From the Beginning to the End of the Monarchy* (London: SCM Press, 1994), 157–242.
2. E. Stern, *Archaeology of the Land of the Bible*, vol. 2, *The Assyrian, Babylonian, and Persian Periods (782–332 B.C.E.)* (Garden City, NY: Doubleday, 2001), 479; compare E. Stern, *The Material Culture of Palestine in the Persian Period* (Warminster: Aris and Phillips; Jerusalem: Israel Exploration Society, 1982), 158; E. Stern, "The Religious Revolution in Persian-Period Judah," in *Judah and the Judeans in the Persian Period*, ed. O. Lipschits and M. Oeming (Winona Lake, IN: Eisenbrauns, 2006), 199–205.
3. M. Knowles, *Centrality Practiced: Jerusalem in the Religious Practice of Yehud and the Diaspora in the Persian Period*, Archaeology and Biblical Studies 16 (Atlanta: Society of Biblical Literature, 2006).

Katharina Pyschny, and Izak Cornelius,[4] and Izaak de Hulster's monograph on Achaemenid-period figurines from Jerusalem, *Figurines in Achaemenid Period Yehud*, criticizing the "revolution narrative" in detail.[5]

Contrasting evidence, like the Yahwistic cult at Elephantine, was often exoticized and marginalized as a "heterodox" form of Yahwism at the very periphery. This also has been challenged, for instance, by Angela Rohrmoser,[6] and, most recently and much more explicitly, by Gard Granerød.[7] Recent scholarship has pointed out that the idea of a religious revolution is heavily biased by the picture of the highly edited and theologically streamlined biblical texts, mainly in the deuteronomistic and priestly line of tradition, and that a fresh look on the material culture without a viewpoint from top down, but from bottom up is in need. Frevel and Pyschny have summarized that the "religious revolution" hypothesis has to be questioned in terms of methodology; that much broader cultural approaches, including material culture, *longue durée* processes, local and regional developments, etc., have to be involved; and that the biblical evidence could not be the starting point, especially given the lack of consensus among biblical scholars about the dating, literary history, and historical reliability of the biblical sources.[8]

In this essay I will apply such a kind of "bottom up" approach, or in fact, a more "bottom only" approach: I will not address the question of the biblical texts and instead will concentrate on the archaeological evidence for cultic activities only. I will first examine the archaeological evidence for such activities and their patterns in late monarchic Judah and, second, evaluate the Persian-period material to try to offer a comparison of cultic patterns in pre- and postexilic Judah. To be clear right from the beginning: the term "cult" as used in this essay denotes any kind of ritual activity, private (or better, domestic) or public, including offerings, sacrifices, and votive and apotropaic practices, as well as the usage of different ritual media (amulets, terracotta figurines, and the like) in different spatial and societal contexts.

---

4. C. Frevel, K. Pyschny, and I. Cornelius, eds., *A "Religious Revolution" in Yehûd? The Material Culture of the Persian Period as a Test Case*, OBO 267 (Fribourg: Academic Press; Göttingen: Vandenhoeck & Ruprecht, 2014).

5. I. de Hulster, *Figurines in Achaemenid Period Yehud: Jerusalem's History of Religion and Coroplastics in the Monotheism Debate*, ORA 26 (Tübingen: Mohr Siebeck, 2017).

6. A. Rohrmoser, *Götter, Tempel und Kult der Judäo-Aramäer von Elephantine*, AOAT 396 (Münster: Ugarit-Verlag, 2014).

7. G. Granerød, *Dimensions of Yahwism in the Persian Period: Studies in the Religion and Society of the Judaean Community at Elephantine*, BZAW 488 (Berlin: de Gruyter, 2016), 324–27.

8. C. Frevel and K. Pyschny, "A 'Religious Revolution' in Yehûd? The Material Culture of the Persian Period as a Test Case: Introduction," in *A "Religious Revolution" in Yehûd? The Material Culture of the Persian Period as a Test Case*, ed. C. Frevel, K. Pyschny, and Izak Cornelius, OBO 267 (Fribourg: Academic Press Fribourg; Göttingen: Vandenhoeck & Ruprecht, 2014), 1–22 at 17–19.

Considering the aspects of location, evidence of centralized planning, architectural features, potential social carriers (which has been neglected in previous research), cult participants, cult functionaries, and assemblages of ritual or cult paraphernalia, Rainer Albertz and I have distinguished in our book *Family and Household Religion in Ancient Israel and the Levant* from 2012 eight types of cult places, with different carrier groups in the vertical social structure, from families to official social or political bodies:[9] Type I A describes common domestic cult places, with a nuclear or extended family presumed to have been the carrier group. Type I B describes larger-scale domestic cult places or shrines, for which again a nuclear or extended family is presumed to have been the carrier group also assigned to an inner circle of ritual activities. Type II describes cult places associated with work environments, within which a distinction is made between two different sizes of carrier groups, namely, (A) those of a small scale, incorporating an inner circle or nuclear family, and (B) those of a larger scale, incorporating inner and middle circles, nuclear and joint families, and their wider kin. The Type III cult place describes neighborhood installations or shrines, for which the carrier is presumed to have been a medium circle ranging from a nuclear or extended family to a coresidential lineage or neighborhood. Type IV describes those places associated with cults of the dead, with carriers also presumed to have belonged to this same medium circle. Type V describes village sanctuaries, further subdivided into (A) shrines, (B) open-air places, and (C) gate sanctuaries. Social carriers for these locations are presumed to have belonged to an outer circle incorporating members of a coresidential lineage or the local community. Type VI presumes palace shrines to have been a distinct group, representing an official variant of large-scale domestic practices performed and socially carried out by local military or elite administrative personnel. Type VII describes regional sanctuaries, subdivided into (A) shrines or temples and (B) open-air places. Carriers for these sites are presumed to have been regional tribes, inhabitants of regional communities, or perhaps official bodies. Finally, Type VIII describes supraregional sanctuaries of the official cult, whose social carriers are royal personage or associated officials. There is, of course, a degree of artificiality to these classifications, and there is some degree of flux between the different categories—for example, those of Types III (neighborhood shrines), V A (village shrines), and VII B (regional sanctuaries). Also, this classification reflects evidence drawn across a wide period of time, ranging from Iron Age I to Iron Age II C, and is intended primarily for heuristic purposes.

9. R. Albertz and R. Schmitt, *Family and Household Religion in Ancient Israel and the Levant* (Winona Lake, IN: Eisenbrauns, 2016), 220–40.

6.1. Cult Places in the Late Monarchic (Iron II C) Period

Our Type I, the domestic cultic space, is the most common in Iron Age II C Judah. Since I have dealt at length with the evidence in the 2012 monograph mentioned above, I will only offer a short summary here:[10] ovens, *tabuns*, and cooking pits would have been the most important household installations, along with things such as basins and associated tools. In most cases such facilities were installed in central courtyards, on ground floors, although they have also been found within rear rooms and longitudinal rooms. Assemblages of ritual objects, like anthro- and theriomorphic figurines, model furniture, fenestrated stands (some of which show decorations with religious content), model shrines, small altars, and incense burners, as well as nonutilitarian vessels,[11] were often assembled and arranged together with utilitarian ceramics near fire places or other facilities associated with the processing and consumption of food, like at the Lachish lower house.[12] It can therefore be concluded that ritual activities would very generally have been performed on ground stories near or in the vicinity of fireplaces.

Such patterns of association have been observed in excavations spanning the entire Iron Age up until the end of Judah in 586 BCE. Permanent installations dedicated to ritual objects and actions, such as platforms and benches, seem to have been rare. In only one case was a small domestic platform found within

---

10. For further assessment of the material, see ibid., 57–219.
11. For the criteria used for identifying possible ritual objects, see P. M. M. Daviau, *Houses and Their Furnishings in Bronze Age Palestine: Domestic Activity Areas and Artefact Distribution in the Middle and Late Bronze Ages*, JSOT and ASOR Monograph Series 8 (Sheffield: Sheffield Academic Press, 1993); P. M. M. Daviau, "Family Religion: Evidence for the Paraphernalia of the Domestic Cult," in *The World of the Aramaeans II: Studies in History and Archaeology in Honour of P. E. Dion*, ed. J. W. Wevers and M. Weigl, JSOTSup 325 (Sheffield: Sheffield Academic Press, 2001), 199–229; P. M. M. Daviau, "Anomalies in the Archaeological Record: Evidence for Domestic and Industrial Cults in Central Jordan," in *Family and Household Religion*, ed. R. Albertz et al. (Winona Lake, IN: Eisenbrauns, 2014), 103–27; Albertz and Schmitt, *Family and Household Religion*, 57–74, R. Schmitt, *Die Religionen Israels/Palästinas in der Eisenzeit, 12.–6. Jh. v. Chr.*, ÄAT 94 (Münster: Zaphon, 2020), 5–9. The present author is very well aware that identifying ritual places by means of ritual objects identified as such by their use in more or less distinct ritual places is a kind of circular reasoning, from which there is no escape. There is, however, good reason to argue that certain specialized objects were used at specialized places and *do* allow some evidence-based considerations about ritual usage patterns. Further, I believe that the deconstructivist "we cannot know anything" approach is futile for any attempt to reconstruct religious belief systems and patterns of ritual practice by means of analyzing material culture.
12. Compare Albertz and Schmitt, *Family and Household Religion*, 117–21. This observation was also made in the unpublished PhD thesis of E. A. R. Willett, "Women and Household Shrines in Ancient Israel" (PhD diss., University of Arizona, 1999), 157–65. There is nevertheless only inconclusive evidence supporting her assumption that certain domestic installations such as the alcoves at Tell el-Farʿa and the bench structure Locus 36 at Beersheba represent household shrines; these structures were in fact predominantly used for domestic activities.

a niche (at Tell Batash Locus 914);[13] while a second platform-like installation found at Tell el Sayiddiye (House 64)[14] would most likely have been a kitchen installation. Ritual objects used in domestic contexts were generally light and readily portable and may have been arranged in various ways to suit a variety of needs throughout the house. The same ritual objects appear to have often been used in different rooms, sometimes individually or in association with a group of other objects, as illustrated by the assemblages from the Lachish lower house.[15] There is strong evidence that cult objects, or even entire cult assemblages, were stored away within separate storage rooms when not in use, as seems to have been the case at Tel Halif Locus G 8005.[16] The kind of standardized "holy corner" or domestic shrine that has been found in Late Bronze Age Tall Bazi in Syria[17] does not appear to have existed in Iron Age Israel or Judah. Rather, early Iron Age assemblages appear to closely reflect local traditions that have been found in Late Bronze Age domestic cult assemblages,[18] like at "neo-Canaanite" Megiddo. There seems to be little evidence that religious activities were conducted regularly in the upper stories of houses, but this may reflect the fact that older excavation reports often did not sufficiently detail material from second stories. Two hoards from Beersheba containing ritual objects and "collectibles,"[19] as well as several finds from Tel Halif[20] and Tell Jawa,[21] certainly provide evidence of ritual objects that had been located on upper stories, and the possibility that ritual activities were performed on upper stories certainly cannot be excluded. It indeed seems that the rooms of a second story would occasionally have been used for ritual purposes, as is known to have occurred throughout many other areas within domestic structures.

Type II, the work-related cult, is a subtype of the domestic cult[22] that is sometimes difficult to distinguish. A possible example could be the vine processing

---

13. See Albertz and Schmitt, *Family and Household Religion*, 165–67.
14. Ibid.
15. Compare ibid., 117–24.
16. Compare ibid., 89–102.
17. A. Otto, *Alltag und Gesellschaft zur Spätbronzezeit: Eine Fallstudie aus Tell Bazi (Syrien)*, Subartu 19 (Bruxelles: Brepols, 2006).
18. See Daviau, *Houses and Their Furnishings*, 218–448; R. Schmitt, "Household Religion: Bronze and Iron Ages," in *The Oxford Encyclopedia of the Bible and Archaeology*, ed. D. M. Master (Oxford: Oxford University Press, 2013), 519–26.
19. Albertz and Schmitt, *Family and Household Religion*, 80–82.
20. Ibid., 102.
21. P. M. M. Daviau et al., *Excavations at Tell Jawa, Jordan*, vol. 1, *The Iron Age Town*, Culture and History of the Ancient Near East 11/1 (Leiden: Brill, 2001), 54.
22. Daviau, "Anomalies in the Archaeological Record"; R. Schmitt, "Material Remains of Family and Guild Cults in Iron Age Philistia," in *Household and Family Religion in Antiquity*, ed. J. Bodel and S. M. Olyan (Oxford: Oxford University Press, 2008), 159–70. See also R. Schmitt, "Philistäische Terrakottafiguinen," *UF* 31 (1999): 282–83.

and storage installation in the Lachish Level II cellar house, which also contained a figurine fragment. A clearly larger scale work-related cult is the olive-industry complex at Tel Miqne with its limestone altars.[23]

Type III small neighborhood or village shrines (Type V), like the examples found at Tel Reḥov[24] and Tel Motza[25] of the Iron II A period, are absent in Iron II C; they are well attested in Iron I B–II A and, less frequently, in Iron II B.[26] On the local level there is, however, a ritual installation attested inside the Lachish Stratum III gate (Type V).[27]

Type IV installations used for the ritual communication with the dead are possibly represented in Iron Age II C by the Jerusalem Caves I–III and Cave 6015.[28] It has already been proposed that the Jerusalem Caves I–III, excavated by Kathleen Kenyon, the Jerusalem Cave 6015, and Samaria Locus 207 are best understood as subterranean locations for the cult of the dead, or better, the ritual care for the deceased.[29] The caves yielded no traces of burials and were therefore likely never to have been used as tombs, but they nevertheless contained great amounts of utilitarian pottery, as well as ritual objects, like stands, terracotta figurines, etc. It therefore seems plausible to interpret the Jerusalem Caves I–III, Locus 6015 (which was located near a cemetery), and Samaria Locus E 207 as having been places of rituals intended for communicating with the dead, especially through commemorative meals wherein the living shared community with the dead. As in domestic ritual assemblages, the presence of a deity was not represented by permanent features but was evoked through ritual acts. One can therefore conclude that these caves served the families of the deceased, who met to commemorate their ancestors with meals that included the giving of portions for relatives abiding in the netherworld. Although Jerusalem Cave I could have accommodated quite a large group, it is nevertheless plausible that the cave served only nuclear or joint families, with the large amount of vessels gradually accumulating as the cave was used over an extended period of time.

23. Albertz and Schmitt, *Family and Household Religion*, 205–6. For further evidence from Judah, Israel, and Transjordan, see Schmitt, *Die Religionen Israels/Palästinas*, 109–10, 150, 180.
24. I. Ziffer, ed., *It Is the Land of Honey: Discoveries at Tel Reḥov, the Early Days of the Israelite Monarchy* (Tel Aviv: Eretz Israel Museum, 2016), 37–38.
25. S. Kisilevitz et al., "Tel Motza—Preliminary Report," *Excavations and Surveys in Israel* 126 (2014), http:// http://www.hadashot-esi.org.il/report_detail_eng.aspx?id=10582.
26. Albertz and Schmitt, *Family and Household Religion*, 229–32.
27. S. Ganor und I. Kreimerman, "Tel Lakhish (Tel Lachish)—Primary Report," *Excavations and Surveys in Israel* 136 (2018), http://www.hadashot-esi.org.il/report_detail_eng.aspx?id=25415.
28. Ibid., 462–69.
29. O. Keel and C. Uehlinger, *Götter, Göttinnen und Gottessymbole*, 6th ed. (Fribourg: Fribourg University Press, 2010), 399–401 §201; Albertz and Schmitt, *Family and Household Religion*, 462–69; see also Z. Zevit, *The Religions of Ancient Israel: A Synthesis of Parallactic Approaches* (London: Continuum, 2001), 206–9.

The fortress temple at Arad[30] was centrally located on the road to the Arabah and dominated the plain of the Eastern Negev, suggesting that it functioned as both a local and a regional sanctuary (Type VII). The temple was built inside— and protected by—the fortress and is thus likely to have been an official sanctuary that served both the military and the administrative staff of the fortress, the inhabitants of the Negev region, and traders who traveled the road. As the Arad fortress temple is the only excavated Iron II C temple building in Judah, its dating and the interpretation of its features have been crucial in the reconstruction of Iron II C cultic practices associated with temples of a larger scale than a mere shrine, in our typology Type VII; that is, temples of regional importance maintained by an official body. This is evident from an inscription of an offering dish with the letters *qof-kap* (*qadoš kohanim*) "*holy, of the priests.*"[31] Traditionally, the cult installations of the temple have been dated between the ninth and eighth centuries BCE and consisted of *maṣṣebot* and two incense altars in a niche that marked the cultic focus (orientated to the west) and an altar (most likely a platform for presenting offerings, as no traces of burning have been discovered) in the courtyard, which went out of use in Stratum VIII (late eighth century). The reassessment of the archaeological data by David Ussishkin[32] has shown however that the temple was erected in later Iron II C Stratum VII/VI (according to more recent research a single stratum), which is parallel to Lachish II (seventh and early sixth centuries BCE), and thus was in use to the very end of the Judean monarchy.

At Beersheba Stratum II, which most likely saw destruction due to Sennacherib's campaign in 701, elements of a dissembled altar, which is believed to belong to Stratum III, were incorporated into the walls of one of the large pillared buildings. Beersheba II and III have been well-planned administrative centers, serving, according to Ze'ev Herzog,[33] the region's administrative needs and housed by the civil service and military elite (the question of why Beersheba was not included into the *lmlk*-administrative system—only one early specimen of *lmlk*-stamps was found—has to remain open). As an administrative center it is likely that Beersheba III has also had a temple like Arad. It is quite clear that the dissembled altar from Tel Beersheba must have belonged to a sanctuary that—given the size of the altar of 1.6 meters—may have resembled the Arad fortress temple in size. That the temple has not been rebuilt after the destruction

---

30. See M. Aharoni, "Arad: The Israelite Citadels," NEAEHL 1:82–87; Zevit, *Religions*, 156–71; A. Jericke, *Regionaler Kult und lokaler Kult: Studien zur Kult- und Religionsgeschichte Israels und Judas im 9. und 8. Jahrhundert v. Chr.*, Abhandlungen des Deutschen Palästina-Vereins 39 (Wiesbaden: Harrassowitz, 2010), 65–67.

31. Z. Herzog et al., "The Israelite Fortress at Arad," *BASOR* 254 (1984): 12, fig. 14a–b.

32. D. Ussishkin, "The Date of the Judean Shrine at Arad," *IEJ* 38 (1988): 142–58.

33. Z. Herzog, *Archaeology of the City: Urban Planning in Ancient Israel and Its Social Implications* (Jerusalem: Emery and Claire Yass Archaeological Press, 1997), 246–47.

of Stratum II has been interpreted by Yohanan Aharoni[34] and others as a deliberate act motivated by the so-called cultic reforms of Josiah. It has to be assumed that the temple was not rebuilt after the destruction or was rebuilt at the very center of the city, which has been destroyed by later building activities.

A matter of discussion is the cultic character of Kuntillet ʿAjrud (Ḥorvat Teman), as supposed by the excavator and most recently by Brian Schmidt:[35] the bench room A contained no clear ritual objects and the painted and inscribed pithos is hardly an item representing a cultic focus—this would be without any parallel from ritual or cultic structures from Iron Age II Israel, Judah, and their Philistine and Transjordanian neighbors.

Iron II regional sanctuaries are, without much doubt, represented by the Ḥorvat Qitmit Sanctuaries A and B in the Negev[36] and ʿEn Ḥaseva. Sanctuary A at Ḥorvat Qitmit was a three-room shrine (oriented to the northeast, albeit without any apparent cult focus) with benches and an open-air cult place with a *bamah* and stone basin oriented to the south west. Ritual vessels and figurines were found at the latter spot. The second complex, Sanctuary B, was a structure of several rooms with a courtyard and *maṣṣebah* (oriented to the west) that lay in front of the main building. This sanctuary hosted an abundant ritual assemblage consisting of incense altars, perforated tripod cups, cylindrical stands, anthropoid stands, composite vessels, chalices, human and animal figurines, collectibles (especially mollusk shells), and figurines of Edomite types, together with large amounts of pottery for the storage, preparation, and consumption of food, mostly in the form of bowls.[37] Objects excavated from a favissa at the Edomite fortress at ʿEn Ḥaseva included seven stone miniature altars, three anthropomorphic stands, thirty-one stands of various shapes, eleven chalices, four perforated tripod cups, and four incense shovels.[38] The material had originally belonged to a U-shaped open-air cultic structure at the northern front of the fortress that had had a bench, an altar, and a hearth. Two *maṣṣebot* marked

---

34. Y. Aharoni, *Beer-Sheba I. Excavations at Tell Beer-Sheba 1969–1971 Seasons*, Publications of the Institute of Archaeology 2 (Tel Aviv: Institute of Archaeology, 1973).

35. Z. Meshel, *Kuntillet ʿAjrud (Ḥorvat Teman): An Iron Age II Religious Site on the Judah-Sinai Border* (Jerusalem: Israel Exploration Society, 2012); B. Schmidt, *The Materiality of Power: Explorations in the Social History of Early Israelite Magic*, FAT 105 (Tübingen: Mohr Siebeck, 2016), 17–21.

36. I. Beit-Arieh, *Horvat Uza and Horvat Radum: Two Fortresses in the Biblical Negev*, Monograph Series of the Sonia and Marco Nadler Institute of Archaeology 25 (Tel Aviv: Institute of Archaeology, 2007), 303–10, fig. 9.1–2.

37. From Complex A came 1534 bowls, 73 kraters, 15 clay basins, 39 cooking pots, 93 jars; from Complex B 605 bowls, 5 kraters, 17 clay basins, 23 cooking pots, 50 jars (Beit-Arieh, *Horvat Uza*, 209–19).

38. R. Cohen and Y. Yisrael, "Iron Age Fortresses at ʿEn Hazeva," *Biblical Archaeologist* 58 (1995): 223–35; R. Cohen and Y. Yisrael, "'En Hazeva—1990–1994," *Excavations and Surveys in Israel* 15 (1996): 110–16.

cultic foci, both directed to the southeast. One of these showed signs of having been decorated with a crescent.

While the material culture of both sanctuaries points to the Edomites, it has to be taken into consideration that Ḥorvat Qitmit and ʿEn Ḥaṣeva have been route sanctuaries that may have served a much broader group of traders on their way south, including Judeans.

Open-air cultic installations have also been assumed at Vered Jericho, Ḥorvat Radum, and Ḥorvat Uza. Stern has made the assumption that the Judean fortress at Vered Jericho had been a regional cult place:[39] a flight of steps in the courtyard behind a tabun and an *l*-shaped stone installation in the courtyard dated to the late monarchic period were interpreted as a *bamah* with adjacent ritual installations.[40] Moreover, similar steps leading to a platform near the gate at the fortresses of Ḥorvat Radum and Ḥorvat Uza have been interpreted as *bamot*.[41] At Ḥorvat Uza a thick layer of ash mixed with animal bones was found on a street between the suspected *bamah* a and building 1323, which has been related to the *bamah* and the oven uncovered next to a building by the excavator. However, the evidence from the three fortresses is more than inconclusive: there are no ritual objects at all associated with those structures and a mere flight of steps does not make a *bamah*, especially if we have two of them in the same courtyard, as at Vered Jericho. More likely, these are just simple steps.

We can conclude for the Iron Age II C evidence that there is not diversity at large in the horizontal perspective of the official cult realm by the number of cult places. Nevertheless, it seems obvious that important regional military and administrative centers like Arad and Beersheba had their own temples. In the vertical perspective of social strata, when we consider carrier groups of cultic activities below the stratum of official bodies, the diversity is much more obvious, with almost every household maintaining a family cult and its prolongation at burial sites, as well as specialized places for the ritual care of the dead; these may have had carrier groups above the family level, as well as regional sanctuaries at the southern trade routes, used—and perhaps maintained—by the traders.

6.2. Judean Cult Places in the Persian Period

Evidence for ritual activities in Persian-period households is not abundant by the matter of the fact that there are nearly no large residential quarters of the period excavated, except Tell en-Naṣbeh Stratum II, which is, however, somewhat

---

39. Stern, *Archaeology*, 201.
40. A. Sussmann, ed., "Vered Yeriḥo," *Excavations and Surveys in Israel* 1 (1982): 106–7.
41. I. Beit-Arieh, "Radum, Ḥorvat," *NEAEHL* 4:1254–55; I. Beit-Arieh, "'Uza, Ḥorvat," *NEAEHL* 4:1495–97 at 1496.

ambigous in its dating (late Babylonian–early Persian).[42] This scarce evidence could be expected, as the population has dropped to half in comparison with late monarchic Judah, with many settlements being abandoned.[43] Moreover, Persian-period settlements have been heavily destroyed by later building activities. Also, there is no archaeological evidence for a large-scale repatriation, despite what the biblical texts suggest.[44] Thus, for the reconstruction of family and household religion we are dependent on the findings from Tell en-Naṣbeh, the only city where an Iron III/Persian-period Stratum (II) has been excavated, and burials, which are an extension of the household. The material evidence from Tell en-Naṣbeh witnesses strong continuity in ritual activities in households utilizing figurines and other ritual artifacts.[45]

Although the Persian period saw the introduction of new burial types, there are some persistent patterns concerning the grave goods, in particular the ritual objects: for the Gezer tombs, the cist burials Nos. 4 and 5 and the shaft tomb 153 contained scarabs and other seal-amulets, Egyptian type object-amulets, like the *udjat*-eye, and incense boxes.[46] Outside the city of Lachish proper, the "500" cemetery contained some caves (Locus 515 and 534, Deposits 506 and 522) that were not used for burials.[47] These caves contained about 200 small limestone altars as well as other ritual objects like horse and rider figurines, among them an incense box with the Yahwistic name of Maḥalyah. Cave 515 contained a horse and rider figurine, a scarab, an ear ring, and 30 small limestone altars, cave 534 a fibula and over 150 altars. Additional altars have been found in a deposit, Locus 506, with 13 altars,[48] and Locus 522 contained approximately 42 terracotta figurines.[49] Olga Tufnell interpreted the caves as cultic depositories of some sort and Nicole Straßburger as the remains of an extramural suburban sanctuary,[50]

---

42. J. E. Balcells Gallarreta, *Household and Family Religion in Persian-Period Judah: An Archaeological Approach*, ANEM 18 (Atlanta: SBL, 2018), 134.

43. O. Lipschits and O. Tal, "The Settlement Archaeology of the Province of Judah: A Case Study," in *Judah and the Judeans in the Fourth Century BCE*, ed. O. Lipschitz, G. N. Knoppers, and R. Albertz (Winona Lake, IN: Eisenbrauns, 2007), 33–52 at 47.

44. B. Becking, "'We All Returned as One!' Critical Notes on the Myth of the Mass Return," in *Judah and the Judeans in the Persian Period*, ed. O. Lipschits and M. Oeming (Winona Lake, IN: Eisenbrauns, 2006), 213–14; O. Lipschits, "Achaemenid Imperial Policy, Settlement Process in Palestine, and the Status of Jerusalem in the Middle of the Fifth Century BCE," in *Judah and the Judeans in the Persian Period*, ed. O. Lipschits and M. Oeming (Winona Lake, IN: Eisenbrauns, 2006), 19–52 at 32–33.

45. Balcells Gallarreta, *Household and Family Religion*, 143.

46. R. A. S. Macalister, *The Excavations at Gezer, 1902–1905 and 1907–1909* (London: Murray, 1912), 289–99, figs. 151–57; Stern, *Material Culture*, 73–75.

47. For a summary, see N. Straßburger, *Heilige Abfallgruben: Favissae und Kultdeposite in Israel/Palästina von der Spätbronzezeit bis zur Perserzeit*, ÄAT 92 (Münster: Zaphon, 2018), 268–74.

48. O. Tufnell, *Lachish III: The Iron Age* (Oxford: Oxford University Press, 1958), 219–20.

49. Ibid., 224–25, plate. 33.

50. Straßburger, *Heilige Abfallgruben*, 287.

but the Iron Age parallels of the Jerusalem caves may hint to a continuation of a ritual practice associated with the care for the dead. Moreover, it is unlikely that a sanctuary was built amidst a graveyard. The fact that the altars showed no traces of soot may be interpreted as evidence that they have been used either as votives for the deceased or as gifts to be "used" by the dead. Interestingly, the small limestone altars (and fragments of such) are of the same type as that which was found at the Iron II C "lower house."

Although it is difficult to allocate a Judean sanctuary, strong Iron Age II cult traditions are also attested by the archaeological record of the Persian period: in Persian-period Palestine, in particular in the coastal plain culturally dominated by the Phoenicians, but also in the North, deposits of terracotta figurines of eastern and western types[51] and other types of votive objects like bronzes from favissae have been found[52] (among others) at Beersheba,[53] Dor,[54] Tell Sippor,[55] and Maresha.[56] Votives directly associated with sanctuaries came from Dan,[57] Makmish,[58] and Mizpe Yammim.[59] Most likely the other favissae were also related to sanctuaries, where they had been offered as votives, and have been cleared away after a certain time to make room for new votives. In contrast, these objects and the practices associated with them seem to be—as strongly emphasized by Stern—absent in contemporary Yehud. In an article published in 2003 and a more recent follow-up I have already challenged the *communis opinio*:[60] while not quite as numerous, Persian-period terracotta

51. Compare Stern, *Material Culture*, 165–82; A. Nunn, *Der figürliche Motivschatz Phöniziens, Syriens und Transjordaniens vom 6. Bis zu 4. Jh. V. Chr.*, OBOSA 18 (Fribourg: Academic Press; Göttingen: Vandenhoeck & Ruprecht, 2000), 35–81.

52. A summary of the Persian-period favissae is given by Straßburger, *Heilige Abfallgruben*, 229–87 with extensive discussion.

53. E. Stern, "Votive Figurines from the Beersheba Area," in *Bilder als Quellen / Images as Sources: Studies on Ancient Near Eastern Artifacts and the Bible Inspired by the Work of Othmar Keel*, ed. S. Bickel et al., OBO (Fribourg: Academic Press Fribourg; Göttingen: Vandenhoeck & Ruprecht, 2007), 321–27.

54. E. Stern, "Two Favissae from Tel Dor," in *Religio Phoenicia: Acta colloquii Namurcensis habiti diebus 14 et 15 mensis Decembris anni 1984*, ed. C. Bonnet, E. Lipinski, and P. Marchetti (Namur: Societé des études classiques, 1986), 277–87.

55. O. Negbi, *A Deposit of Terracottas and Statuettes from Tel Sippor*, Atiqot 6 (Jerusalem: Israel Exploration Society, 1966).

56. A. Erlich, "The Persian Period Terracotta Figurines from Maresha in Idumea: Local and Regional Aspects," *Transeuphratene* 32 (2006): 45–59; A. Erlich and A. Kloner, *Maresha Excavations Final Report II: Hellenistic Terracotta Figurines from the 1989–1996 Seasons*, IAA Reports 35 (Jerusalem: Israel Antiquities Authority), 2008.

57. A. Biran, *Biblical Dan* (Jerusalem: Israel Exploration Society, 1994), 214–15.

58. N. Avigad, "Makmish," *NEAEHL* 3:933–34.

59. R. Frankel, "Mizpe Yammim," *NEAEHL* 3:1061–63.

60. R. Schmitt, "Gab es einen Bildersturm nach dem Exil? Einige Bemerkungen zur Verwendung von Terrakottafigurinen im nachexilischen Israel," in *Yahwism After the Exile: Perspectives on Israelite Religion in the Persian Era*, ed. R. Albertz and B. Becking, Studies in Theology and Religion 5 (Assen: Van Gorkum, 2003), 186–98; R. Schmitt, "Continuity and Change in Post-Exilic

figurines (predominantly horse-and-riders or fragments of such) have been found in between the borders of Yehud, determined by the Yehud stamps, at Gezer, Ramat Raḥel, En-Gedi, Tell en-Naṣbe, and Jericho. In Gibeon there were coincidences with the lion stamps. Among the finds from the City of David excavations was a unique two-faced figurine fragment, the closest parallels of which can be dated to the Persian-Hellenistic periods.[61] In more recent and elaborate studies, de Hulster has proposed that around 49 figurines and fragments of figurines from Shiloh's Stratum 9 should be attributed to the Persian period.[62] Thus, according to de Hulster, the figurines give evidence for the persistence of late Iron II religious practices during the Persian period. This has also been observed by José E. Balcells Gallarreta for Tell en-Naṣbeh.[63] Moreover it has to be considered that also figurines found outside the borders of Yehud could have been used by Judeans, or Yahwists respectively. As Adi Erlich has demonstrated, there were strong local coroplastic traditions reaching back into Iron Age II in particular with regard to the horse-and-rider-figurines in Maresha.[64] It cannot be excluded that also the Persian-period figurines from Lachish[65] were used by Yahwists, even if they were not settling in between the borders of Yehud. Therefore, it should be considered with Erlich that it was the very same population using the figurines in the Persian period as in Iron Age II. Moreover, Egyptian type figurative amulets are also present in Iron III/Persian-period Yehud.[66] Cultic diversity on the level of family religion seems therefore quite well established in the Persian period, as far as we can see.

Concerning the horizontal diversity of sanctuaries maintained by official bodies, the most important ritual structure in Judah seems to be the so-called solar

---

Votive Practices," in *A "Religious Revolution" in Yehûd? The Material Culture of the Persian Period as a Test Case*, ed. C. Frevel, K. Pyschny, and I. Cornelius, OBO 267 (Fribourg: Academic Press; Göttingen: Vandenhoeck & Ruprecht, 2014), 95–109.

61. D. T. Ariel, "Appendix F: A Ceramic Two-Faced Figurine," in *Excavations at the City of David 1978–1985*, ed. D. T. Ariel and A. de Groot, Qedem 35 (Jerusalem: Hebrew University, 1996), 4:109–11 fig. 20.

62. I. de Hulster, "Figurines from Persian Period Jerusalem?," *ZAW* 124 (2015): 73–88; I. de Hulster, *Figurines in Achaemenid Period Yehud*, 239–41.

63. Balcells Gallarreta, *Household and Family Religion*, 136–44.

64. Erlich, "Persian Period Terracotta Figurines," 58.

65. Tufnell, *Lachish III*, 142–44; Stern, *Material Culture*, fig. 285.3 (Persian-type horse and rider), fig. 288.4 (pillar figurine head in Iron II tradition).

66. Compare C. Herrmann, *Ägyptische Amulette aus Palästina/Israel: Mit einem Ausblick auf ihre Rezeption durch das Alte Testament*, OBO 138 (Fribourg: Academic Press; Göttingen: Vandenhoeck & Ruprecht, 1994), cat. nos. 145, 283, 773, 1056; C. Herrmann, *Ägyptische Amulette aus Palästina/Israel III*, OBO 24 (Fribourg: Academic Press; Göttingen: Vandenhoeck & Ruprecht, 2003), cat. no. 318 (Jerusalem); C. Herrmann, *Ägyptische Amulette aus Palästina/Israel IV*, OBOSA 38 (Fribourg: Academic Press; Göttingen: Vandenhoeck & Ruprecht, 2016), 486, with an overview counting 211 EZ III/Persian-period amulets from the south. Nevertheless, they are massively present on the coast.

shrine at Lachish[67] (in my typology Type V: local shrine), dated by Ussishkin into the Persian period,[68] and by Alexander Fantalkin and Oren Tal[69] to the late Persian–early Hellenistic period. The building measures 27 × 17 m with courtyard and steps leading to the central square room, from which steps lead to a niche. The installations of the building comprise two floor drains. The small finds contained ten small limestone altars as well as several fragments of horse and rider figurines. The building most likely had a predecessor in building 10 measuring 25 × 16 m with a similar layout.[70] Here also a limestone altar was found, as well as other small objects that can be interpreted as votives, like a scarab and beads.[71] The similarities to the Arad sanctuary are evident and it seems that both the "solar shrine" and building 10 stand in continuity with late monarchic temple architecture. As there is no large altar for burnt offerings, it is likely that only food and incense were offered, and figurines were used for votive purposes. The drainage could point to libations and not necessarily to animal offerings.

According to an Idumean ostracon datable to the third century BCE (perhaps originated from Ḥirbet el-Kom/Makkedah) mentioning a *byt yhw* (house of Yahweh) alongside a *byt 'z'* (house of ʿUzzah), and, perhaps, also a house of Nabu,[72] there must have been a sanctuary of Yahweh of local or regional importance, which can be attributed to an Judean substratum on Idumean territory.

Regional and supraregional sanctuaries are represented by the temple at Jeb/Elephantine (local and/or regional) and the Samaritan temple on mount Gerizim (supraregional), the first being a sanctuary of a local social body, the members of the Judean military unit and their families, also used by Judeans living across the river in Syene (Assuan), maintained by a board of priests and elders of the garrison, the latter the main sanctuary of a religious-political body.

Concerning the temple at Jeb and its cultic practices, there is the problem that only traces of walls have been preserved and that there are also no traces of ritual installations from the temple. However, we know from the texts that animal sacrifice took place here, as had been the case at Arad. I cannot go deeper into the well-known controversy about the meaning of the documents *TAD* A4.9 and A4.10 dealing with the reinstallation of the offerings after the temple was

---

67. Tufnell, *Lachish III*, 141–45.
68. D. Ussishkin, *The Renewed Archaeological Excavations at Lachish (1973–1994)*, vol. 1, Monographs of the Institute of Archaeology 22 (Tel Aviv: Yass Publications, 2004), 96–97.
69. A. Fantalkin and O. Tal, "Redating Lachish Level I: Identifying Achaemenid Imperial Policy at the Southern Frontier of the Fifth Satrapy," in *Judah and the Judeans in the Persian Period*, ed. O. Lipschits and M. Oeming (Winona Lake, IN: Eisenbrauns, 2006), 167–97.
70. Tufnell, *Lachish III*, 146–49.
71. Ibid.
72. A. Lemaire, "New Aramaic Ostraca from Idumea and Their Historical Interpretation," in *Judah and the Judeans in the Persian Period*, ed. O. Lipschits and M. Oeming (Winona Lake, IN: Eisenbrauns, 2006), 413–56 at 417.

destroyed in 410 BCE, of which burnt offerings were excluded, which has been interpreted by many scholars as evidence that there has been a verdict from the authorities in Jerusalem to prevent further burnt offerings at Jeb (but not meal offerings and incense burning), because of the claim that burnt offerings only can be—according to the *torah*—performed rightfully at the central sanctuary in Jerusalem. That the permission was omitted—a formal verdict is not included in the texts—by the Persian authorities, may have had other reasons, like an interest of the Persian authorities to appease the Egyptians by not permitting offerings of sheep and goats, which may have embarrassed the locals because of Chnum's appearance as a ram, or—with Porten—a more general policy to avoid conflicts among the locals and the foreign military in Persian service. Ingo Kottsieper supposed that the Persians omitted the permission because the burnt offering would be a pollution of the fire in the eye of Zorostratians.[73] Whether such an intervention into religious issues is likely is also a matter of discussion. However, it has to be acknowledged that the argument of cult centralization is not the only argument and not the most likely, since the question if the temple of Jeb is legitimate has not been raised during the efforts of its reconstruction.

Another issue, which also can be addressed briefly, is the alleged "heterodox" character for the Yahweh cult at Jeb, as can be seen from the epigraphic evidence mentioning other deities venerated at the sanctuary, as evinced from *TAD* C3:15, a list of offerings for the Temple of Yahu at Jeb, which mentions three deities receiving gifts: Yahu, Eshembethel, and Anatbethel.

TAD C3:15: 126–128
126 *bgw lyhw k 12 š 6*
127 *lʾšmbyṭʾl kršn 7*
128 *lʿntbyṭʾl ksp kršn 7*

126 Herein: for Yahu 12 k 6 Sh
127 for Eshembethel 7 karsh
128 for Anatbethel silver, 7 karsh

I agree with Granerød that the evidence from Elephantine reveals more about the actual religious practice of the Elephantine Judaeans than what the highly edited and canonized texts of the Bible reveal about the religious practice of the contemporary Yahwistic coreligionists in Judah, and that the religion of the

---

73. I. Kottsieper, "Die Religionspolitik der Achaimeniden und die Juden von Elephantine," in *Religion und Religionskontakte im Zeitalter der Achaimeniden*, ed. R. G. Kratz, Veröffentlichungen der Wissenschaftlichen Gesellschaft für Theologie 22 (Gütersloh: Gütersloher Verlagshaus, 2002), 150–78.

Judeans at Jeb is a "snapshot" of what living religion of the period looked like.[74] I cannot go deeper into this subject, but it seems that the monotheism versus polytheism paradigm does not meet with the ambiguities of postexilic Yahwism, which escapes such assessments.[75]

The temple at Jeb may not have been the only Yahweh temple maintained by Jewish military or civil bodies in Egypt, but these are only known through literature. According to Josephus (*Ant.* 13.65–71) the Jews in Leontopolis in the district of Heliopolis operated their own temples, which were replaced by an "official"—priestly legitimized—temple by Onias IV in the middle of the second century BCE during the reign of Ptolemaios VI Philomator (180–145) that operated until 71 CE and was then closed down by the order of Vespasian (*J.W.* 7.421–436). The founding of the Leontopolis temple is the outcome of inner-dynastic struggles about the office of the high priest, in which Onias's father was beaten and expelled from office.

The Samaritan sacred precinct on Mount Gerizim was, according to the typology used here, a Type VIII supraregional cult center of the official cult circle. According to Josephus it was founded in the times of Alexander, but as recent excavations have shown the Hellenistic temple had a mid-fifth-century BCE predecessor,[76] which was (also contrary to Josephus) in operation until circa 110 BCE.[77] The founding of the Samaritan temple should not be seen as an outcome of the so-called Samaritan schism—which was a process of differentiation and not one historical "event" or a struggle between two religious parties—but rather an expression of the strong local religious traditions. That Gerizim became a rival to its Jerusalem counterpart with its own claim for centrality seems to be the result of this longer process of differentiation, but its founding cannot be related to competing religious or political bodies. In the fifth-century BCE Gerizim was—due to its size and the importance of Samaria as a provincial administrative center—of greater importance than the sanctuary at Jerusalem. The dedicatory inscriptions from the temple precinct show an extreme standardization and a strong impact on the system of family religion, thus claiming control over ritual activities that were practiced not necessarily at a sanctuary but in the household.[78] Thus, there is a certain tendency of central-

---

74. Granerød, *Dimensions of Yahwism*, 324–27.

75. R. Schmitt, "Das Monotheismus/Polytheismus-Paradigma in der religionswissenschaftlichen Forschung des 19. und 20. Jh. und sein Einfluß auf die Theoriebildung der Gegenwart," in *Die dunklen Seiten Gottes*, ed. M. L. G. Dietrich et al., Mitteilungen aus Anthropologie und Religionsgeschichte 21 (Münster: Ugarit-Verlag, 2013), 331–32.

76. Y. Magen, "The Dating of the First Phase of the Samaritan Temple on Mt Gerizim in Light of Archaeological Evidence," in *Judah and the Judeans in the Fourth Century BCE*, ed. O. Lipschitz, G. N. Knoppers, and R. Albertz (Winona Lake, IN: Eisenbrauns, 2007), 157–211 at 176.

77. Magen, "Dating of the First Phase," 193.

78. Albertz and Schmitt, *Family and Household Religion*, 406–9.

ization of ritual activities at least in Samaria—but the whole picture escapes us due to the lack of further archaeological evidence, in particular with relation to the domestic cult.

6.3. Conclusions

Table 6.1 gives an overview about the cultic or ritual structures discussed above. To sum up, we have a diversity of cult places in both periods, and there is—from the archaeological point of view—little or at least scarce evidence for the establishment of a strongly centralized cult—in the meaning of one exclusive cult center—in the Persian period.

In the Iron Age we can allocate different cultic activities to several societal levels: the domestic and work-related cult, as well as special installations serving the ritual care for the dead as in the case of the Jerusalem caves, belonging to the realm of household and family religion. Concerning the type of regional cultic centers, the Iron Age II Temple at Arad and most likely at Beersheba were official temples, maintained by official priests for and thereby perhaps (but not necessarily) filial cults of the temple in the capital. Nevertheless, there is good reason to believe that the different temples were part of a cultic network. The regional small sanctuaries at Ḥorvat Qitmit and ʿEn Ḥaṣeva most likely served the traders en route to Arabia on their journey, thus being a mixture of regional and work-related cult. Thus, we have both a social and a spatial diversity in a quite small geographical region.

The picture of the Persian- to Hellenistic-period diversity is a bit different, nevertheless somehow comparable: the evidence for ritual activities in the households is less numerous as in the Iron II C period but shows strong continuities in practices and objects, and the burial goods show that there was a strong factor of continuity. There are different sanctuaries, but they did not initially form a cultic network, and all of them were founded for different religious-political reasons

TABLE 6.1. Overview of Cultic and Ritual Structures

Type		Iron II C	Persian
I	Domestic	X	X
II	Work related	X	—
III	Neighborhood shrine	—	—
IV	Places for the care for the dead	X	X
V	Village/local shrine	—	X
VII	Regional sanctuaries	X	X
VIII	Superregional sanctuaries	X	X

and had a different spatial setting: the Gerizim temple became a superregional sanctuary during the process of differentiation of Samaritans and Judeans, serving the population of the province of Samaria and expressing a strong local and regional identity. The "solar shrine" at Lachish and its possible predecessor as a local or regional shrine maintained by the locals of Lachish, a southern sanctuary on Idumean territory, perhaps to be located at Ḥirbet el-Qom/Makkedah, served a local Jewish community; the Elephantine sanctuary was a local sanctuary serving a military body in the diaspora both locally and regionally, other local sanctuaries of the Jews in the Egyptian diaspora mentioned by Josephus and finally the temple of Onias in Leontopolis as a sanctuary founded due to religious-political struggle. It can be assumed that Judeans also participated at other local cult places or even at their own sanctuaries (like at Makkedah), but here we do not have firm archaeological evidence. The examples show that in late monarchic Judah an unquestioned cultic diversity—or with Rainer Albertz an internal religious pluralism—was at play. As said above, in the Persian period we have a different spatial diversity than in the Iron Age due to political reasons and the diaspora situation. Nevertheless we can conclude that there has been a pluriform Yahwism with different social, local and/or regional, and political bodies as carrier groups of cultic activities both in the late monarchic and in the Persian to Hellenistic periods. At least, Elephantine, Samaria, and Jerusalem show—as became evident from the written correspondence from Elephantine—some aspects of a cultic network, with a certain influence of the main sanctuaries on the local temple at Jeb, but no direct control. A wholesale theory about cult centralization thus does not fit into the archaeological picture of the Persian period. On the contrary, both the written and the archaeological evidence suggests cultic diversity on all social levels, in continuity with the late Iron Age.

BIBLIOGRAPHY

Aharoni, M. "Arad: The Israelite Citadels." *NEAEHL* 1:82–87.
Aharoni, Y. *Beer-Sheba I. Excavations at Tell Beer-Sheba 1969–1971 Seasons*. Publications of the Institute of Archaeology 2. Tel Aviv: Institute of Archaeology, 1973.
———. *Investigations at Lachish: The Sanctuary and the Residency (Lachish V)*. Publications of the Institute of Archaeology 4. Tel Aviv: Gateway, 1975.
Albertz, R. *A History of Israelite Religion in the Old Testament Period*. Vol. 1, *From the Beginning to the End of the Monarchy*. London: SCM Press, 1994.
Albertz, R., and R. Schmitt. *Family and Household Religion in Ancient Israel and the Levant*. Winona Lake, IN: Eisenbrauns, 2012.
Ariel, D. T. "Appendix F: A Ceramic Two-Faced Figurine." Pages 109–11 in vol. 4 of *Excavations at the City of David 1978–1985*. Edited by D. T. Ariel and A. de Groot. Qedem 35. Jerusalem: Hebrew University, 1996.
Avigad, N. "Makmish." *NEAEHL* 3:932–34.

Balcells Gallarreta, J. E. *Household and Family Religion in Persian-Period Judah: An Archaeological Approach*. ANEM 18. Atlanta: SBL, 2018.
Becking, B. "'We All Returned as One!' Critical Notes on the Myth of the Mass Return." Pages 3–18 in *Judah and the Judeans in the Persian Period*. Edited by O. Lipschits and M. Oeming. Winona Lake, IN: Eisenbrauns, 2006.
Beit-Arieh, I. *Ḥorvat Qitmit: An Edomite Shrine in the Negev*. Monograph Series of the Institute of Archaeology Tel Aviv University 11. Tel Aviv: Institute of Archaeology, 1995.
———. *Horvat Uza and Horvat Radum: Two Fortresses in the Biblical Negev*. Monograph Series of the Sonia and Marco Nadler Institute of Archaeology 25. Tel Aviv: Institute of Archaeology, 2007.
———. "Radum, Ḥorvat." *NEAEHL* 4:1254–55.
———. "'Uza, Ḥorvat." *NEAEHL* 4:1495–97.
Biran, A. *Biblical Dan*. Jerusalem: Israel Exploration Society, 1994.
Cohen, R., and Y. Yisrael. "'En Ḥazeva—1990–1994." *Excavations and Surveys in Israel* 15 (1996): 110–16.
———. "Iron Age Fortresses at 'En Ḥazeva." *Biblical Archaeologist* 58 (1995): 223–35.
Daviau, P. M. M. "Anomalies in the Archaeological Record: Evidence for Domestic and Industrial Cults in Central Jordan." Pages 103–27 in *Family and Household Religion*. Edited by R. Albertz, B. Alpert-Nakhai, S. Olyan, and R. Schmitt. Winona Lake, IN: Eisenbrauns, 2014.
———. "Family Religion: Evidence for the Paraphernalia of the Domestic Cult." Pages 199–229 in *The World of the Aramaeans II: Studies in History and Archaeology in Honour of P. E. Dion*. Edited by J. W. Wevers and M. Weigl. JSOTSup 325. Sheffield: Sheffield Academic Press, 2001.
———. *Houses and Their Furnishings in Bronze Age Palestine: Domestic Activity Areas and Artefact Distribution in the Middle and Late Bronze Ages*. JSOT and ASOR Monograph Series 8. Sheffield: Sheffield Academic Press, 1993.
Daviau, P. M. M., et al. *Excavations at Tell Jawa, Jordan*. Vol. 1, *The Iron Age Town*. Culture and History of the Ancient Near East 11/1. Leiden: Brill, 2001.
Erlich, A. "The Persian Period Terracotta Figurines from Maresha in Idumea: Local and Regional Aspects." *Transeuphratene* 32 (2006): 45–59.
Erlich A., and A. Kloner. *Maresha Excavations Final Report II: Hellenistic Terracotta Figurines from the 1989–1996 Seasons*. IAA Reports 35. Jerusalem: Israel Antiquities Authority, 2008.
Fantalkin A., and O. Tal. "Redating Lachish Level I: Identifying Achaemenid Imperial Policy at the Southern Frontier of the Fifth Satrapy." Pages 167–97 in *Judah and the Judeans in the Persian Period*. Edited by O. Lipschits and M. Oeming. Winona Lake, IN: Eisenbrauns, 2006.
Frankel, R. "Mizpe Yammin." *NEAEHL* 3:1061–63.
Frevel, C., and K. Pyschny. "A 'Religious Revolution' in Yehûd? The Material Culture of the Persian Period as a Test Case: Introduction." Pages 1–22 in *A "Religious Revolution" in Yehûd? The Material Culture of the Persian Period as a Test Case*. Edited by C. Frevel, K. Pyschny, and I. Cornelius. OBO 267. Fribourg: Academic Press Fribourg; Göttingen: Vandenhoeck & Ruprecht, 2014.
Frevel, C., K. Pyschny, and I. Cornelius, eds. *A "Religious Revolution" in Yehûd? The Material Culture of the Persian Period as a Test Case*. OBO 267. Fribourg: Academic Press Fribourg; Göttingen: Vandenhoeck & Ruprecht, 2014.

Ganor, S., and Kreimerman, I. "Tel Lakhish (Tel Lachish)—Priminary Report." *Excavations and Surveys in Israel* 136 (2018). http://www.hadashot-esi.org.il/report_detail_eng.aspx?id=25415.

Granerød, G. *Dimensions of Yahwism in the Persian Period: Studies in the Religion and Society of the Judaean Community at Elephantine*. BZAW 488. Berlin: de Gruyter, 2016.

Herrmann, C. *Ägyptische Amulette aus Palästina/Israel: Mit einem Ausblick auf ihre Rezeption durch das Alte Testament*. OBO 138. Fribourg: Academic Press Fribourg; Göttingen: Vandenhoeck & Ruprecht, 1994.

———. *Ägyptische Amulette aus Palästina/Israel III*. OBO 24. Fribourg: Academic Press; Göttingen: Vandenhoeck & Ruprecht, 2003.

———. *Ägyptische Amulette aus Palästina/Israel IV*. OBOSA 38. Fribourg: Academic Press; Göttingen: Vandenhoeck & Ruprecht, 2016.

Herzog, Z. *Archaeology of the City: Urban Planning in Ancient Israel and Its Social Implications*. Jerusalem: Emery and Claire Yass Archaeological Press, 1997.

Herzog, Z., M. Aharoni, A. F. Rainey, and S. Moshkovitz. "The Israelite Fortress at Arad." *BASOR* 254 (1984): 1–34.

Hulster, I. de. "Figurines from Persian Period Jerusalem?" *ZAW* 124 (2015): 73–88.

———. *Figurines in Achaemenid Period Yehud: Jerusalem's History of Religion and Coroplastics in the Monotheism Debate*. ORA 26. Tübingen: Mohr Siebeck, 2017.

Jericke, D. *Regionaler Kult und lokaler Kult: Studien zur Kult- und Religionsgeschichte Israels und Judas im 9. und 8. Jahrhundert v. Chr*. Abhandlungen des Deutschen Palästina-Vereins 39. Wiesbaden: Harrassowitz, 2010.

Keel, O., and C. Uehlinger. *Götter, Göttinnen und Gottessymbole*. 6th ed. Fribourg: Fribourg University Press, 2010.

Kisilevitz, S., et al. "Tel Motza—Preliminary Report." *Excavations and Surveys in Israel* 126 (2014). http://www.hadashot-esi.org.il/report_detail_eng.aspx?id=10582.

Knowles, M. *Centrality Practiced: Jerusalem in the Religious Practice of Yehud and the Diaspora in the Persian Period*. Archaeology and Biblical Studies 16. Atlanta: Society of Biblical Literature, 2006.

Kottsieper, I. "Die Religionspolitik der Achaimeniden und die Juden von Elephantine." Pages 150–78 in *Religion und Religionskontakte im Zeitalter der Achaimeniden*. Edited by R. G. Kratz. Veröffentlichungen der Wissenschaftlichen Gesellschaft für Theologie 22. Gütersloh: Gütersloher Verlagshaus, 2002.

Lemaire, A. "New Aramaic Ostraca from Idumea and Their Historical Interpretation." Pages 413–56 in *Judah and the Judeans in the Persian Period*. Edited by O. Lipschits and M. Oeming. Winona Lake, IN: Eisenbrauns, 2006.

Lipschits, O. "Achaemenid Imperial Policy, Settlement Process in Palestine, and the Status of Jerusalem in the Middle of the Fifth Century BCE." Pages 19–52 in *Judah and the Judeans in the Persian Period*. Edited by O. Lipschits and M. Oeming. Winona Lake, IN: Eisenbrauns 2006.

Lipschits O., and O. Tal. "The Settlement Archaeology of the Province of Judah: A Case Study." Pages 33–52 in *Judah and the Judeans in the Fourth Century BCE*. Edited by O. Lipschitz, G. N. Knoppers, and R. Albertz. Winona Lake, IN: Eisenbrauns, 2007.

Macalister R. A. S. *The Excavations at Gezer, 1902–1905 and 1907–1909*. London: Murray, 1912.

Magen, Y. "The Dating of the First Phase of the Samaritan Temple on Mt Gerizim in Light of Archaeological Evidence." Pages 157–211 in *Judah and the Judeans in the Fourth Century BCE*. Edited by O. Lipschitz, G. N. Knoppers, and R. Albertz. Winona Lake, IN: Eisenbrauns, 2007.

Meshel, Z. *Kuntillet ʿAjrud (Ḥorvat Temen): An Iron Age II Religious Site on the Judah-Sinai Border*. Jerusalem: Israel Exploration Society, 2012.

Negbi, O. *A Deposit of Terracottas and Statuettes from Tel Sippor*. Atiqot 6. Jerusalem: Israel Exploration Society, 1966.

Nunn, A. *Der figürliche Motivschatz Phöniziens, Syriens und Transjordaniens vom 6. Bis zu 4. Jh. V. Chr*. OBOSA 18. Fribourg: Academic Press; Göttingen: Vandenhoeck & Ruprecht, 2000.

Otto, A. *Alltag und Gesellschaft zur Spätbronzezeit: Eine Fallstudie aus Tell Bazi (Syrien)*. Subartu 19. Bruxelles: Brepols, 2006.

Rohrmoser, A. *Götter, Tempel und Kult der Judäo-Aramäer von Elephantine*. AOAT 396. Münster: Ugarit-Verlag, 2014.

Schmidt, B. B. *The Materiality of Power: Explorations in the Social History of Early Israelite Magic*. FAT 105. Tübingen: Mohr Siebeck, 2016.

Schmitt, R. "Continuity and Change in Post-Exilic Votive Practices." Pages 95–109 in *A "Religious Revolution" in Yehûd? The Material Culture of the Persian Period as a Test Case*. Edited by C. Frevel, K. Pyschny, and I. Cornelius. OBO 267. Fribourg: Academic Press Fribourg; Göttingen: Vandenhoeck & Ruprecht, 2014.

———. "Gab es einen Bildersturm nach dem Exil? Einige Bemerkungen zur Verwendung von Terrakottafigurinen im nachexilischen Israel." Pages 186–98 in *Yahwism After the Exile: Perspectives on Israelite Religion in the Persian Era*. Edited by R. Albertz and B. Becking. Studies in Theology and Religion 5. Assen: Van Gorkum, 2003.

———. "Household Religion: Bronze and Iron Ages." Pages 519–26 in *The Oxford Encyclopedia of the Bible and Archaeology*. Edited by D. Master. Oxford: Oxford University Press, 2013.

———. "Material Remains of Family and Guild Cults in Iron Age Philistia." Pages 159–70 in *Household and Family Religion in Antiquity*. Edited by J. Bodel and S. M. Olyan. Oxford: Oxford University Press, 2008.

———. "Das Monotheismus/Polytheismus-Paradigma in der religionswissenschaftlichen Forschung des 19. und 20. Jh. und sein Einfluß auf die Theoriebildung der Gegenwart." Pages 323–35 in *Die dunklen Seiten Gottes*. Edited by M. L. G. Dietrich, W. Dupré, A. Häußling, and R. Schmitt. Mitteilungen aus Anthropologie und Religionsgeschichte 21. Münster: Ugarit-Verlag, 2013.

———. "Philistäische Terrakottafiguinen." *UF* 31 (1999): 282–83.

———. *Die Religionen Israels/Palästinas in der Eisenzeit, 12.–6. Jh.* ÄAT 94. Münster: Zaphon, 2020.

———. "A Typology of Iron Age Cult Places." Pages 265–86 in *Family and Household Religion*. Edited by R. Albertz, B. Alpert-Nakhai, S. Olyan, and R. Schmitt. Winona Lake, IN: Eisenbrauns, 2014.

Stern, E. *Archaeology of the Land of the Bible*. Vol. 2, *The Assyrian, Babylonian, and Persian Periods (782–332 B.C.E.)*. Garden City, NY: Doubleday, 2001.

———. *The Material Culture of Palestine in the Persian Period*. Warminster: Aris and Philips; Jerusalem: Israel Exploration Society, 1982.

———. "The Religious Revolution in Persian-Period Judah." Pages 199–205 in *Judah and the Judeans in the Persian Period*. Edited by O. Lipschits and M. Oeming. Winona Lake, IN: Eisenbrauns, 2006.

———. "Two Favissae from Tel Dor." Pages 277–87 in *Religio Phoenicia: Acta colloquii Namurcensis habiti diebus 14 et 15 mensis Decembris anni 1984*. Edited by C. Bonnet, E. Lipinski, and P. Marchetti. Namur: Societé des études classiques, 1986.

———. "Votive Figurines from the Beersheba Area." Pages 321–27 in *Bilder als Quellen / Images as Sources: Studies on Ancient Near Eastern Artifacts and the Bible Inspired by the Work of Othmar Keel*. Edited by S. Bickel et al. OBO. Fribourg: Academic Press; Göttingen: Vandenhoeck & Ruprecht, 2007.

Straßburger, N. *Heilige Abfallgruben: Favissae und Kultdeposite in Israel/Palästina von der Spätbronzezeit bis zur Perserzeit*. ÄAT 92. Münster: Zaphon, 2018.

Sussmann, A., ed. "Vered Yeriḥo." *Excavations and Surveys in Israel* 1 (1982): 106–7.

Tufnell, O. *Lachish III: The Iron Age*. Oxford: Oxford University Press, 1953.

Ussishkin, D. "The Date of the Judean Shrine at Arad." *IEJ* 38 (1988): 142–58.

———. *The Renewed Archaeological Excavations at Lachish (1973–1994)*. Vol. 1. Monographs of the Institute of Archaeology 22. Tel Aviv: Yass Publications, 2004.

Willet, E. A. R. "Women and Household Shrines in Ancient Israel." PhD diss., University of Arizona, 1999.

Zevit, Z. *The Religions of Ancient Israel: A Synthesis of Parallactic Approaches*. London: Continuum, 2001.

Ziffer, I., ed. *It Is the Land of Honey: Discoveries at Tel Reḥov, the Early Days of the Israelite Monarchy*. Tel Aviv: Eretz Israel Museum, 2016.

Zwickel, W. *Der Tempelkult in Kanaan und Israel: Ein Beitrag zur Kulturgeschichte Palästinas von der Mittelbronzezeit bis zum Untergang Judas*. FAT 10. Tübingen: Mohr Siebeck, 1994.

CHAPTER 7

Texts Are Not Rituals, and Rituals Are Not Texts, with an Example from Leviticus 12

James W. Watts

THE CLAIM THAT "texts are not rituals and rituals are not texts" is an observation, first of all, about modern texts and rituals. It reflects the experience of participating in many kinds of rituals, something we all do, and reading texts about those rituals. It also reflects the twentieth-century field studies of ethnographers working in a wide variety of contemporary cultures, as well as historians writing about societies better documented than ancient Israel.

Examination of our own ritual experiences and ritual texts reveals the differences between them. It also shows that both are far removed from the traditional concerns of biblical interpreters and historians of ancient history. On the one hand, ritual experience is little concerned with the question of meaning, focusing instead on right practice and on the people participating. While many, though not all, rituals have clearly stated social functions (e.g., to marry, bury, inaugurate, etc.), participants usually have different social, professional, and personal motives for participating in the same ritual and they differ in how they interpret the ritual's importance. But these different points of view do not affect the performance of the ritual, which accommodates them all. On the other hand, ritual texts that instruct, commemorate, or encourage ritual practices are more likely to describe and commend a ritual than to explain it. Even in our highly literate cultures, texts are used to guide and authorize ritual performances more than to interpret their meaning and significance. When narrative texts describe rituals, they do so in order to advance their rhetorical agendas. Descriptions of proper ritual performances enhance the legitimacy of the people and institutions they support, while descriptions of improper ritual performances undermine them.[1]

So the meaning or function of the ritual is not the same thing as the meaning of the text describing the ritual. Conversely, interpreting a text about a ritual does not interpret the meaning or function of the ritual, except sometimes—but

---

1. P. Buc, *The Dangers of Ritual: Between Early Medieval Texts and Social Scientific Theory* (Princeton: Princeton University Press, 2001).

not usually—its meaning for the author of the text. This conclusion was generalized concisely by Nancy Jay about all forms of interpretation: "The meaning of any action not only varies with the way in which it is interpreted, it is the way in which it is interpreted.... For meaning is not a simple and direct product of action itself, but of reflection upon it. And the act of reflection is always another act, socially situated in its own way."[2] The ritual, then, is one socially situated act. All its verbal reflections, oral and written, are different acts situated in particular social relationships. As a result, texts are inevitably quite different from the rituals they mention.

Ritual studies emerged as a separate research field in the 1970–1980s through attempts to summarize and systematize the observations of anthropologists and participant observers.[3] It corrected the tendency in older twentieth-century sociologies of ritual to regard rituals as always socially conservative. Instead, ritual studies emphasized the mutability and creativity of ritualizing that can both fuel social conflicts and maintain the status quo. Ritual studies also undermined the claims of functionalist anthropologists that a culture's rituals convey a rational and consistent world view. It replaced such static conceptions of rituals with a recognition that humans regularly ritualize both in traditional and creative ways and for a wide variety of purposes.

7.1. Ritual Text and Ritual Meaning in Contemporary Biblical Research

These ideas have been seeping into biblical studies for more than two decades now. In 1993, Erhard Gerstenberger was the first person to write a commentary on Leviticus that emphasized the text's persuasive rhetoric.[4] He criticized symbolic interpretations of rituals for confusing rituals with texts. He maintained, however, an absolute distinction between didactic instruction, on the one hand, and hortatory address, on the other, so he could not take ritual rhetoric seriously as instructions for ritual performances. He concluded, therefore, that Leviticus's

---

2. N. Jay, *Throughout Your Generations Forever: Sacrifice, Religion and Paternity* (Chicago: University of Chicago Press, 1992), 8.
3. R. Grimes, *Ritual Criticism: Case Studies in Its Practice, Essays on Its Theory* (Columbia: University of South Carolina Press, 1990); C. Bell, *Ritual: Perspectives and Dimensions* (Oxford: Oxford University Press, 1997); R. Rappaport, *Ritual and Religion in the Making of Humanity* (Cambridge: Cambridge University Press, 1999). See also the review and constructive critique by J. Kreinath, "Semiotics," in *Theorizing Rituals*, ed. J. Kreinath, J. Snoek, and M. Stausberg (Leiden: Brill, 2006), 429–70 at 467–70.
4. E. S. Gerstenberger, *Leviticus: A Commentary*, trans. D. W. Stott, OTL (Louisville, KY: Westminster John Knox, 1996), esp. 25.

rhetoric must have been aimed at diasporic Jews who could not worship in the Jerusalem Temple.

In 1998, Stanley Stowers, a scholar of Hellenism and early Christianity at Brown University, observed that "practices cannot be reduced to ideas."[5] His colleague in Hebrew Bible and Jewish studies, Saul Olyan, meditated further on this distinction,[6] and Olyan's student, William K. Gilders, expounded on it. Gilders emphasized the multivocality of symbols and rituals, the rarity of symbolic interpretation in biblical texts, and ritual's performative role in creating social realities as well as reflecting them.[7] He criticized the attempts by Jacob Milgrom and many others to find singular meanings of rituals in biblical texts. Following Roy Rappaport, Gilders noted that "the written account of a ritual is not itself a ritual.... Interpreting a textually represented ritual requires attention to the text as well as to the ritual. Both must be interpreted." Ancient Israel's rituals are "not immediately accessible to the reader of the Bible."[8] Gilders demonstrated how Israel's rituals map hierarchy onto people and space by indexing persons, places, and things relative to the ritual. That does not mean, however, that this indexing ever connoted just one specific "meaning" because the rituals would have been multivalent to individuals within the groups that originally performed them and in every performance since.

Apart from this Brown school and in a self-consciously postmodern mode, Wesley Bergen argued that the meaning of a ritual can only be found by participating in it. But because Israel's temples ceased to exist long ago, he regarded Leviticus as a product of the "absence of ritual."[9] The textualization of ritual in Leviticus resulted in ritualized readings taking the place of ritual offerings both in rabbinic Judaism and in Christian interpretation.

Around the same time, Martin Modéus argued that certain life situations carry the weight of meaning while rituals call attention to these activities and define their nature to clarify situations of transition, ambiguity, or conflict.[10] Choice of ritual form is usually dictated by cultural convention and is therefore largely arbitrary—that is, unrelated to its function. Though his application of this

---

5. S. K. Stowers, "On the Comparison of Blood in Greek and Israelite Ritual," in *Hesed ve-Emet: Studies in Honor of Ernest S. Frerichs*, ed. J. Magness and S. Gitin, BJS 320 (Atlanta: Scholars Press, 1998), 179–94 at 189.

6. S. M. Olyan, *Rites and Rank: Hierarchy in Biblical Representations of Cult* (Princeton: Princeton University Press, 2000), 13–14.

7. W. K. Gilders, *Blood Ritual in the Hebrew Bible: Meaning and Power* (Baltimore: Johns Hopkins University Press, 2004), 1–11, 141.

8. Ibid., 9, 11.

9. W. J. Bergen, *Reading Ritual: Leviticus in Postmodern Culture*, JSOTSup 417 (London: T&T Clark, 2005), 1–12.

10. M. Modéus, *Sacrifice and Symbol: Biblical* Šelāmîm *in a Ritual Perspective*, Coniectanea Biblica: Old Testament Series 52 (Stockholm: Almqvist & Wiksell, 2005), 35.

theoretical model to the details of the amity slaughter offering (*zbḥ šlmym*) in the Hebrew Bible proved problematic, Modéus developed an explanatory system for ritual that can be applied with illuminating results to all kinds of ritual texts.

I built on these works to write a concise description of the differences between rituals and ritual texts and the possible relationships between them.[11] My goal was to lay the basis for a new interpretation of Leviticus that would distinguish its rhetoric from the social functions of the rituals it describes. Doing so has made it difficult to provide a ritual analysis of ancient Israel's practices because the text's rhetorical agenda interferes. However, this conflict drew my attention to the ritual functions of the text itself. Ritual theory proves less useful for describing ancient Israel's ritual practices than for explaining Leviticus's function as part of the Torah and of later scriptural collections that get ritualized through iconic display, oral and visual expression, and semantic interpretation in preaching, teaching, and commentary.[12]

During the past decade, many more scholars have subscribed to the view that the meaning of texts must be distinguished from the meaning of the rituals they describe. One or more of the works summarized above was cited approvingly by Michael Hundley, Nicole Ruane, and Thomas Hieke.[13] Most scholars currently writing commentaries on Leviticus have also subscribed to some version of this distinction. Christophe Nihan, for example, followed Gilders in adopting the philosopher C. S. Pierce's distinction between index and symbol. He argued, however, that Gilders view of the text as indexing the priests is "too restrictive ... the function of such blood rites is to index the various aspects that constitute the relation between *community* and *sanctuary*.... Although the textual representation of a ritual is quite distinct from actual ritual performance, as various authors have rightly emphasized, a text ... can nevertheless teach us something about the ritual *imaginaire* of the social group in which Leviticus was composed and transmitted."[14]

Nihan tied the textualization of ritual in Leviticus tightly to its progressive ritualization as performed and authoritative text in the Second Temple and later periods. Similarly, David P. Wright, a leading student of Jacob Milgrom, wrote

---

11. J. W. Watts, *Ritual and Rhetoric in Leviticus: From Sacrifice to Scripture* (Cambridge: Cambridge University Press, 2007), 29.

12. J. W. Watts, "The Three Dimensions of Scriptures," in *Iconic Books and Texts*, ed. J. W. Watts (London: Equinox, 2013), 8–30, revised in *How and Why Books Matter* (Sheffield: Equinox, 2019), 7–29.

13. M. B. Hundley, *Keeping Heaven on Earth: Safeguarding the Divine Presence in the Priestly Tabernacle*, FAT 2/50 (Tübingen: Mohr Siebeck, 2011), 202; N. J. Ruane, *Sacrifice and Gender in Biblical Law* (Cambridge: Cambridge University Press, 2013), 15; T. Hieke, *Levitikus*, Herders Theologischer Kommentar zum Alten Testament (Freiburg im Breisgau: Herder, 2014), 155.

14. C. Nihan, "The Templization of Israel in Leviticus: Some Remarks on Blood Disposal and Kipper in Leviticus 4," in *Text, Time and Temple: Literary, Historical and Ritual Studies in Leviticus*, ed. F. Landy, L. M. Trevaskis, and B. D. Bibb (Sheffield: Sheffield Phoenix, 2015), 94–130 at 96.

in 2012 of the need to distinguish carefully between the social practice of ritual and biblical reflections on rituals, though he did not refer to previous advocates of this position.[15]

The view that ritual texts should be analyzed as persuasive rhetoric has also gained increasing support. Eve Levavi Feinstein's discussion of *Sexual Pollution in the Hebrew Bible* focuses "on the rhetorical function of pollution language—that is, its capacity to shape a reader or listener's perspective on a person, act, or situation by eliciting feelings of disgust."[16] According to Feinstein, pollution language in the Bible does not derive so much from some kind of intellectual system as it does from feelings of disgust shaped by cultural socialization and by the rhetorical goals of biblical authors. She argued that technical or dispassionate uses of pollution language are neither logically nor chronologically prior to its emotional applications.[17] Gören Eidevall and Dorothea Erbele-Küster also employed rhetorical theories in analyzing sacrificial and purity rhetoric in pentateuchal and prophetic books.[18]

However, resistance has been voiced against the distinction between ritual process and textual meaning. Yitzhaq Feder used Pierce's theory of signs to counter criticisms of the search for meaning in rituals and to explain the arbitrariness of ritual symbols. He reemphasized a view that was traditional among earlier interpreters that the meaning of rituals was clear at their creation and became ambiguous through their fossilized repetition in changing cultural contexts.[19] Several other scholars have challenged rhetorical characterizations of priestly texts as reductionistic. Francis Landy argued for the logical priority of theology over rhetoric,[20] while Roy Gane insisted on the didactic rather than rhetorical nature of priestly texts in Leviticus.[21]

---

15. D. P. Wright, "Ritual Theory, Ritual Texts, and the Priestly-Holiness Writings of the Pentateuch," in *Social Theory and the Study of Israelite Religion*, ed. S. M. Olyan (Atlanta: Society of Biblical Literature, 2012), 195–216.

16. E. Levavi Feinstein, *Sexual Pollution in the Hebrew Bible* (Oxford: Oxford University Press, 2014), 40.

17. Ibid., 177.

18. G. Eidevall, "The Role of Sacrificial Language in Prophetic Rhetoric," in *Ritual and Metaphor: Sacrifice in the Hebrew Bible*, ed. C. A. Eberhart (Atlanta: Society of Biblical Literature, 2011), 49–61; D. Erbele-Küster, *Body, Gender, and Purity in Leviticus 12 and 15*, LHBOTS 539 (London: T&T Clark, 2017).

19. Y. Feder, *Blood Expiation in Hittite and Biblical Ritual* (Atlanta: Society of Biblical Literature, 2011), 162, 164.

20. F. Landy, "For Whom God's Name is Blotted Out," in *Text, Time and Temple: Literary, Historical and Ritual Studies in Leviticus* (Sheffield: Sheffield Phoenix, 2015), 170–95: "I assume that the text is a product of thought, that through it the author(s) sought to understand, imagine and create their world. It is not in the first instance a work of rhetoric, which attempts to persuade the audience of its truth and authority. The rhetorical function, wherewith it conveys its importance an emotional urgency through an array of poetic devices, is dependent on, and one aspect of, the intellectual effort that has gone into its composition" (172).

21. R. E. Gane, "Didactic Logic and the Authorship of Leviticus," in *Current Issues in Priestly and Related Literature: The Legacy of Jacob Milgrom and Beyond*, ed. R. E. Gane and A. Taggar-Cohen (Atlanta: Society of Biblical Literature, 2015), 197–222.

During the last three decades of the twentieth century, symbolic and theological approaches dominated interpretations of Leviticus's rituals. They were championed and exemplified especially by Jacob Milgrom and Baruch Levine in the United States; by Rolf Rendtorff, Bernd Janowski, and Adrianne Schenker in Germany; by Alfred Marx in France; and by Israel Knohl and Baruch Schwartz in Israel and used by many other scholars around the world.[22] In Great Britain, Mary Douglas made a distinctive contribution in her later work on Leviticus and Numbers.[23] Her suggestions have not gained widespread support, however, unlike her earlier work on pollution and purity, which remains central to discussions of the topic.[24] In the twenty-first century, Jonathan Klawans achieved wider recognition for his attempt to systematize the relationship between purity, ethics, and holiness in P.[25] All of these works are vulnerable to criticisms based in late twentieth-century ritual theories.[26] They do not distinguish sharply enough between ritual behavior and the verbal interpretations of rituals found in texts.

Some biblical scholars have tried to buttress symbolic interpretation of rituals by drawing an analogy between rituals and language. These linguistic

---

22. J. Milgrom, *Leviticus 1–16: A New Translation with Introduction and Commentary*, AB 3A (New York: Doubleday, 1991); J. Milgrom, *Leviticus 17–22: A New Translation with Introduction and Commentary*, AB 3B (New York: Doubleday, 2000); J. Milgrom, *Leviticus 23–27: A New Translation with Introduction and Commentary*, AB 3C (New York: Doubleday, 2001); B. A. Levine, *Leviticus*, JPS Torah Commentary (Philadelphia: Jewish Publication Society, 1989); R. Rendtorff, *Leviticus 1,1–10,20*, BKAT 3 (Neukirchen-Vluyn: Neukirchener, 1985); B. Janowski, *Sühne als Heilsgeschehen: Studien zur Sühnetheologie der Priesterschrift und zur Wurzel KPR im Alten Orient und im Alten Testament*, WMANT 55 (Neukirchen-Vluyn: Neukirchener Verlag, 1982); A. Schenker, *Studien zu Opfer und Kult im Alten Testament* (Tübingen: Mohr Siebeck, 1992); A. Marx, *Les systèmes sacrificiels de l'Ancien Testament: Formes et fonctions du culte sacrificial à Yhwh*, VTSup 105 (Leiden: Brill, 2005); I. Knohl, *The Sanctuary of Silence: The Priestly Torah and the Holiness School* (Minneapolis: Fortress, 1995); B. J. Schwartz, *The Holiness Legislation: Studies in the Priestly Code* (Hebrew) (Jerusalem: Magnes, 1999); B. J. Schwartz, "The Bearing of Sin in the Priestly Literature," in *Pomegranates and Golden Bells: Studies in Biblical, Jewish, and Near Eastern Ritual, Law, and Literature in Honor of Jacob Milgrom*, ed. D. P. Wright, D. N. Freedman, and A. Hurwitz (Winona Lake, IN: Eisenbrauns, 1995), 3–21.

23. M. Douglas, *In the Wilderness: The Doctrine of Defilement in the Book of Numbers*, JSOTSup 158 (Sheffield: Sheffield Academic Press, 1993); M. Douglas, *Leviticus as Literature* (Oxford: Oxford University Press, 1999).

24. M. Douglas, *Purity and Danger: An Analysis of Concepts of Pollution and Taboo* (London: Routledge and Kegan Paul, 1966). But see now Y. Yoo and J. W. Watts, *Cosmologies of Pure Realms and the Rhetoric of Pollution* (New York: Routledge, 2021).

25. J. Klawans, *Impurity and Sin in Ancient Judaism* (Oxford: Oxford University Press, 2000); J. Klawans, *Purity, Sacrifice, and the Temple: Symbolism and Supersessionism in the Study of Ancient Judaism* (New York: Oxford, 2006).

26. And in cognitive science, as was observed especially by T. Kazen, "Levels of Explanation for Ideas of Impurity: Why Structuralist and Symbolic Models Often Fail While Evolutionary and Cognitive Models Succeed," *Journal of Ancient Judaism* 9 (2018): 75–100. See also T. M. Lemos, "Where There Is Dirt, Is There System? Revisiting Biblical Purity Constructions," *JSOT* 37 (2013): 265–94; Yoo and Watts, *Cosmologies*, 132–40.

approaches draw their inspiration from the indologist Fritz Staal, who argued in the 1970s that ritual rules follow their own intrinsic logic, like the rules of grammar.[27] Staal therefore began to describe a ritual syntax. Roy Gane followed Staal's lead by trying to analyze biblical rituals on analogy with the self-contained rules of linguistic grammar, but he simultaneously argued that rituals refer symbolically beyond themselves.[28] Gerald Klingbeil distinguished ritual morphology (individual elements), syntax (their interaction), semantics (their cumulative meaning), and pragmatics (their effects in cultural context). He also argued that the fact that ancient rituals were written down shows that they possessed a "determinate meaning" for their writers.[29] Leigh Trevaskis adopted from cognitive linguistics the distinction between meanings that words always imply and meanings that listeners or readers access from their varied linguistic experiences. He suggested that the symbolic meanings of rituals occupy such secondary domains.[30] Naphtali Meshel was inspired by Staal to write a "grammar" of Israelite sacrifice. He found that changes in rule-bound forms of rituals accompany changes in their function or meaning. Meshel carefully hedged his analogy between language and ritual with qualifications and questions about the nature of both. He did not, however, engage the methodological issues raised by ritual studies in the last decades of the twentieth century, by biblical scholars distinguishing between texts and rituals, or by his predecessors who applied linguistics to the study of biblical ritual texts.[31]

Language and ritual do resemble each other by being rule-bound and by the fact that their functions do not dictate their forms, which are arbitrary, conventional, and culturally contingent. Meaning, however, occupies a different place in ritual than in language. While a ritual's function is often explicit and noncontroversial, a ritual's meaning is not essential to its function and can vary with every participant.[32] In language, only performative speech-acts are analogous, and they usually take ritual form.[33] Most other kinds of sentences function by communicating meaning in verbal or written form. Rhetoric depends on shared meaning to influence people's thoughts and behavior. Ritual, on the other hand,

27. F. Staal, "The Meaninglessness of Ritual," *Numen* 26.1 (1979): 2–22; F. Staal, *The Science of Ritual* (Poona: Bhandarkar Oriental Research Institute, 1982).
28. R. Gane, *Ritual Dynamic Structure* (Piscataway, NJ: Gorgias, 2004).
29. G. A. Klingbeil, *Bridging the Gap: Ritual and Ritual Texts in the Bible* (Winona Lake, IN: Eisenbrauns, 2007), 69, 127.
30. L. M. Trevaskis, *Holiness, Ethics and Ritual in Leviticus*, Hebrew Bible Monographs 29 (Sheffield: Sheffield Phoenix, 2011), 9.
31. N. S. Meshel, *The "Grammar" of Sacrifice: A Generativist Study of the Israelite Sacrificial System in the Priestly Writings with a "Grammar" of Σ* (Oxford: Oxford University Press, 2014).
32. A. Michaels, "Ritual and Meaning," in *Theorizing Rituals*, ed. J. Kreinath, J. Snoek, and M. Stausberg (Leiden: Brill, 2006), 147–61.
33. J. L. Austin, *How to Do Things with Words: The William James Lectures Delivered at Harvard University in 1955*, ed. J. O. Urmson and Marina Sbisà (Oxford: Clarendon Press, 1962).

influences people by indexing social relationships and not through rhetorical persuasion, except in so far as it includes verbal preaching and liturgies.[34]

7.2. A Case Study in Text Versus Ritual: Leviticus 12

Let me use Lev 12 as an example of the difference between textual rhetoric about ritual and ritual practice. I choose this text because the distinction appears rather obvious in the text itself. Its example therefore has implications for other ancient ritual texts whose distance from ritual practice may not be so obvious.

The eight verses of Lev 12 focus entirely on the timing of two kinds of rituals: circumcision and offerings. Verse 2 specifies that a new mother remains polluted (*ṭm'*) from bleeding during childbirth for seven days after the birth of a boy, on explicit analogy with her period of menstrual pollution (15:19). Verse 3 requires that the boy be circumcised on the eighth day after his birth. Verse 4 specifies that his mother remains in blood purification (*dmy ṭhrh*) for thirty-three more days during which she is not allowed to touch anything sacred or enter the sanctuary. Verse 5 specifies a two-week period of pollution after giving birth to a girl, followed by sixty-six days of blood purification. Verse 6 requires the mother to offer a sheep rising offering (*'lh*) and bird sin offering (*ḥṭ't*) after her period of blood purification is over. Verse 8 allows poor mothers to offer a bird rising offering instead of a sheep. Verses 7 and 8 contain the standard concluding refrain to such an offering instruction, which promises a state of purification after the offerings are complete (cf. 14:18–20, 21, 31, 53; 15:15, 30).

Interpreters of Lev 12 have focused on the rule of circumcision on the eighth day (v. 3),[35] and on the longer time that a new mother remains isolated for a girl's birth than for a boy's (vv. 4–5),[36] issues already discussed by the ancient

---

34. So Kreinath, "Semiotics," 467–70, but contra David Janzen who described a "rhetorics of ritual," by which he meant the persuasive effects of ritual performances. Janzen argued that participants in rituals do have a common understanding of its meaning that is generated by its social context and cannot be determined apart from it (D. Janzen, *The Social Meanings of Sacrifice in the Hebrew Bible: A Study of Four Writings*, BZAW 344 [Berlin: de Gruyter, 2004], 4–5, 9–35).

35. Shaye Cohen, for example, while admitting that the link between purification and circumcision in Lev 12 is only implicit, insisted: "Surely it is no coincidence that the eighth day after birth, the first day of diminished impurity for the mother, is also the day of circumcisions for the infant. Before that point, the text suggests, the mother's impurity would have made the boy too impure for the ritual; after that point the mother's own purification is accomplished through waiting and through a sacrifice, while the boy's purification is accomplished through circumcision" (S. J. D. Cohen, *Why Aren't Jewish Women Circumcised? Gender and Covenant in Judaism* [Berkeley: University of California, 2005], 19). The link has been rightly challenged by other interpreters, including D. A. Bernat (*Sign of the Covenant: Circumcision in the Priestly Tradition* [Atlanta: Society of Biblical Literature, 2009], 64–65) and Feinstein (*Sexual Pollution*, 85, 229).

36. The new mother's avoidance of the sanctuary for forty or eighty days is obviously a ritual absence. Temporarily, she no longer takes part in religious affairs of which she was, perhaps, normally

rabbis. Contemporary scholarship also tries to reconstruct the history of the text and to describe its ancient context in a patriarchal society. Historical critics have frequently judged the circumcision rule to be a secondary intrusion in a pericope otherwise concerned with the mother's purification.[37] Feminists have cited Lev 12 as a leading example of the tendency to exclude mothers and motherhood from the sacrificial cult.[38]

Almost every interpreter tries to explain how giving birth fits with the other impurities addressed in Lev 11–15—unclean animals (Lev 11), *tsaraʿat* disease (Lev 13–14), and genital emissions, both regular and irregular (Lev 15). Jacob Milgrom thought all the impurities in Lev 12–15 symbolize death. By avoiding them, Israel imitates God's holiness.[39] Others add sex to death.[40] Nihan suggested instead that Lev 12–15 is primarily about "these discharges which are either abnormal (gonorrheic issues ...) or the symptom of provisional disfunctioning of the reproductive system, such as menstrual ... and puerperal blood."[41] Erbele-Küster finds even less negative evaluation of genitical emissions in Lev 12 and 15, which instead focus on events that seem to endanger the boundaries of human bodies.[42]

Leviticus 12, however, does not mention death or sex or abnormal bleeding, unless one thinks that the (male) authors really regarded bleeding in childbirth as abnormal. Much less does it talk about a new mother's isolation or whether infant girls received a different social reception than infant boys. As Erbele-Küster observed, "It is noticeable that, in the context of the Leviticus prescriptions for the woman in childbed, the process of birth and its entire social reality,

---

a part. Leviticus 12 does not mention whether she is also isolated within her family and society, though most interpreters have assumed as much based on practices of "churching" and purification in other and later societies. Interpretation of the chapter certainly supported such later institutions.

37. See the review and critical evaluation by C. Nihan, *From Priestly Torah to Pentateuch: A Study in the Composition of the Book of Leviticus*, FAT 2/25 (Tübingen: Mohr Siebeck, 2007), 281 n. 46.

38. This argument was first voiced by Jay (*Throughout Your Generations*) and has now been demonstrated much more thoroughly for biblical literature by Ruane (*Sacrifice and Gender*).

39. Milgrom, *Leviticus 1–16*, 766–68, 1000–1004.

40. E.g., D. P. Wright, "Unclean and Clean," *ABD* 6:729–741, 739; A. Marx, "L'impureté selon P: Une lecture théologique," *Biblica* 82 (2001): 363–84.

41. Nihan, *From Priestly Torah*, 310. His discussion (pp. 306–10) follows R. Parker (*Miasma: Pollution and Purification in Early Greek Religion* [Oxford: Oxford University Press, 1983], 66) on Greek religion and the discussion of Lev 12 by H. Eilberg-Schwartz (*The Savage in Judaism: An Anthropology of Israelite and Ancient Judaism* [Bloomington: Indiana University Press, 1990]) and especially R. Whitekettle ("Leviticus 12 and the Israelite Woman: Ritual Process, Liminality and the Womb," *ZAW* 107 [1995]: 393–408).

42. Erbele-Küster, *Body, Gender, and Purity*, 152: "In Leviticus 12 and 15 these terms express no aversion to the menstruating woman. Rather, in those chapters *niddah* connotes the setting of a boundary in response to her menstruation. Only when other discourses were superimposed did a devaluation arise, with the result that *niddah* became a synonym for repulsiveness beyond Leviticus 12 and 15. The uncovering of the reception history of the term deconstructs the misogynistic body images that are bound up with it."

determined by miscarriage, stillbirth, and the risk to the mother's life, is not considered."[43]

The lesson about the difference between texts and rituals is that this text will not tell us anything more about social rituals for new mothers in ancient Israel. All it can do is tell us about the priestly writers' agenda. So how do these offering regulations for new mothers fit into P's rhetorical agenda?

From that perspective, it is clear that Lev 12 is a payment schedule: it lists how much is owed to the sanctuary for the birth of a child and when it must be paid. The text's interests lie in the timing of the rising and sin offerings that end the mother's "blood purification." The prohibition on her entering the sanctuary during her blood purification period explains why the offerings must wait until it is over. Since the text mentions no other ramifications from the new mother's period of blood purification, the enumeration of forty or eighty days serves here only to specify the timing of the offerings.

Leviticus 12, then, is *about* a payment schedule for offerings.[44] With the exception of the rule for circumcision in verse 3, the text's rhetoric is all about how much to pay and when.[45] The writers expected these questions to be uppermost in the minds of listening and reading audiences, just as they are in the minds of taxpayers today. Then as now, the urgency of the individual's economic obligation overshadows other issues. Only interpreters relieved of this obligation have the luxury of contemplating the symbolic meaning of the regulation and of the purification periods and ritual offerings that it mentions. Of course, since 70 CE, Jewish and Christian interpreters have all been relieved of the anxiety of how to afford a sheep or at least two birds in the next forty or eighty days, which has freed their minds to consider the other implications of these regulations.

Can we at least make something from the fact that these are the only offerings in P's legislation that women are required to bring to the sanctuary? The text makes no reference to male assistance, except the priest's mitigation. However, that fact serves the interests of a universal payment schedule: the omission of any information about the mother's social situation emphasizes that a rising and sin offering must be paid for every newborn child. Despite doubling the purification period for girls, the text's valuation of the sexes is economically equal: mothers incur the same costs for girl babies as for boys, and the priests gain the same income (the meat of the sin offering) from the birth of one as from the

---

43. D. Erbele-Küster, "Gender and Cult: 'Pure' and 'Impure' as Gender-Relevant Categories," in *Torah*, ed. I. Fischer and M. Navarro Puerto, with A. Taschl-Erber (Atlanta: Society of Biblical Literature, 2012), 375–405 at 375.

44. Like the surrounding chapters, it expresses a thematic concern for purification that reflects its cultural context. Every other theme that interpreters expound on this text involves speculations about institutions and ideologies that the text at most implies, but does not describe.

45. The author or a later supplementor may have included the circumcision law here simply for the sake of calendrical completeness.

other. That income is low—pigeons and landfowl were relatively cheap—but at the rate of one for every birth, they could have provided a noticeable supplement to the priests' diet (Lev 6:19, 22; 7:6–7).[46]

It is quite possible that P innovated here by expanding the number of occasions on which offerings are required. No other biblical text refers to all human births requiring offerings. The old institution of redeeming the firstborn with a rising offering is required only after the birth of a mother's first son.[47] By focusing on the mother's purification, Lev 12 can require a purifying sin offering that provides a little income to the priests after every birth along with a rising offering that does not.[48]

---

46. By comparison with the redemption of first-born sons, this represents a radical expansion of the temple's taxation system to every human birth. In its scope, it is comparable to the Second Temple's third- or half-shekel poll tax. The latter was supposed to be paid annually according to Neh 10:33 (Eng. 10:32) and may have been assessed per household. The half-shekel tax in Exod 30:11–16 is based on a census, which in ancient times counted only males and was certainly not conducted annually. By the late Second Temple period, the temple tax had been standardized at a half-shekel annually for males thirteen years and older (see M. Broshi, "The Role of the Temple in the Herodian Economy," *Journal of Jewish Studies* 38 [1987]: 35). In contrast to the temple tax (cf. Exod 30:15 with Lev 12:8), the rising offering for a birth is graduated by ability to pay, while the sin offering remains one bird. Lev 12 makes no provision for reducing the sin offering to grain, as Lev 5:11–12 does. However, the required offerings for all children's births, though assessed only once in a life-time, reach further than the temple tax by applying to female as well as male births at the same rate of payment. The gender egalitarianism of this taxation scheme has gone generally unnoticed in the shadow of the gender differentiation of the length of the purification period. The analogy with menstruation probably interfered with any thought of requiring offerings after seven days, since purification from menstrual blood required only the passage of time (15:19–24; Second Temple and later Judaisms added washing; see Erbele-Küster, "Gender and Cult," 404).

47. Exod 13:2, 12, 15; 22:30; 34:19; Num 18:15–16; Deut 15:19–22; in Neh 10:36 the fifth-century Jerusalem community promises fulfillment. Leviticus 12 extends the offering requirements to all births. Perhaps it requires less expensive offerings: neither P nor any other biblical text specifies the animal or type of offering required to redeem a firstborn son, but Num 3:47 sets its price at five shekels. The story of the Aqedah indicates that a ram rising offering would be appropriate (Gen 22:13), but rising offerings provided no income to the priests. Hannah offers a bull, flour and wine, but 1 Sam 1:24 does not specify the type of offerings.

48. There is reason to think that the sin offering was an innovation at some point in Israel's history. P or its priestly predecessors added the sin and guilt offerings to Israel's older ritual traditions of rising, commodity and amity slaughter offerings. The sin and guilt offerings earned priests higher income—all of the animal but for a token portion burned on the altar—than did the older offerings. Their introduction was therefore likely intended to increase temple revenues, either during the violent disruptions of the seventh century or in the absence of a royal patron in the Second Temple period. For further discussion, see J. W. Watts, *Leviticus 1–10*, HCOT (Leuven: Peeters, 2013), 308–14. In that case, requiring a sin offering after the birth of a child was another way of extending this ritual innovation. In place of or in addition to redeeming the oldest son with an unspecified offering, P requires that the birth of every child be marked by rising and sin offerings. P may have built the payment schedule on the preexisting custom of mothers' social isolation after giving birth, which finds parallels in many cultures (Milgrom, *Leviticus 1–16*, 750, 763–65; Nihan, *From Priestly Torah*, 319), though the ancient evidence is actually scanty (Yoo and Watts, *Cosmologies*, 56). Leviticus 12 thus represents an early step in universalizing offering/tax systems'

What is explicitly clear in Lev 12 is that the rising and sin offerings simply serve to mark the occasion of the child's birth.[49] Their ritual form has nothing to do with the nature of that occasion, either childbirth or the end of blood purification for a new mother, but is rather dictated by the standard form of these kinds of offerings (Lev 1; 4–5). Furthermore, the thematic grouping of purification rituals together in Lev 11–15 is purely literary. Neither the polluting situations nor their ritual rectification were connected in social life or by ritual performance. The internal and contextual rhetoric of Lev 12 depends on its literary form and position alone.

7.3. Meaning in Ritual Texts

The fact that the disjunction between textual rhetoric and ritual performance is so obvious in this case should caution us against drawing connections between ritual form and social significance in the case of more unusual rituals, such as the purification of those suffering from *tsara'at* disease in Lev 14 or the rite of the red heifer in Num 19. These rituals take unusual or even unique forms, at least in our textual corpus. Actually, we have no idea how typical or unusual they may have been in ancient Israel's ritual repertoire. The methodological consequence of this observation is that the form of every ritual should be regarded as arbitrary and its details as unsymbolic unless we have access to an explicit commentary tradition that interprets them. Even when we do, that tradition has no claim to being ritually authoritative. It only reflects a particular stage of interpretation.[50]

It is possible that the question of "the meaning" of a ritual is generated by its textual presentation. Participants in a ritual may ask why it is performed at this time or in this particular way as opposed to another that they may be more familiar with, but they rarely ask why one performs a ritual: its function is usually explicitly obvious. But as we have seen in Lev 12, ritual function does not dictate ritual form, which is arbitrary, conventional, and culturally contingent. The question of the meaning of the ritual's form arises from reading a ritual like a text, usually in a text, and presupposes the textualization of the

---

relationship to every individual (every mother, every child) rather than to families, villages, clans, and tribes. The fact that its rationale, purification, produces or reproduces the stigmatizing fear of women's vaginal blood is of a piece with the individualizing effects of increasing division of labor in ancient economies that weakened women's economic solidarity with each other by individualizing their roles in the households of wage-earning men—the most prominent examples of whom in the Pentateuch are priests.

49. This provides another illustration of Modéus's thesis regarding the marking function of offerings.

50. Pentateuchal studies has long recognized this in the case of Unleavened Bread and Passover legislation that seems to reinterpret older rituals within the template of the exodus from Egypt.

ritual or imagines its future textualization (such as an ethnographer who writes field notes for the purpose of eventually publishing her analysis). In that case, we should wonder to what degree questions about the meaning of the form of biblical rituals are produced by the rituals' textualization and, especially, by their scripturalization.[51]

Texts and rituals are usually the products of different social and political processes and serve different purposes. This is not a necessary difference: texts and rituals could be produced by the same political process (for example, modern revisions to a prayer book) and can serve the same purpose. But rituals usually evolve through one set of social dynamics, while their textual reflections come about for other reasons and purposes.

Abstracting formal systems from rituals, whether theological, symbolic or linguistic systems, serves the needs of readers for whom textual meaning is paramount. The anachronism of these systems prevents them from reaching the reality of ancient ritual practices as surely as the rhetorical screen of the texts themselves.

BIBLIOGRAPHY

Austin, J. L. *How to Do Things with Words: The William James Lectures Delivered at Harvard University in 1955*. Edited by J. O. Urmson and M. Sbisà. Oxford: Clarendon Press, 1962.

Bell, C. *Ritual: Perspectives and Dimensions*. Oxford: Oxford University Press, 1997.

Bergen, W. J. *Reading Ritual: Leviticus in Postmodern Culture*. JSOTSup 417. London: T&T Clark, 2005.

Bernat D. A. *Sign of the Covenant: Circumcision in the Priestly Tradition*. Atlanta: Society of Biblical Literature, 2009.

Buc, P. *The Dangers of Ritual: Between Early Medieval Texts and Social Scientific Theory*. Princeton: Princeton University Press, 2001.

Broshi, M. "The Role of the Temple in the Herodian Economy." *Journal of Jewish Studies* 38 (1987): 31–37.

Cohen, S. J. D. *Why Aren't Jewish Women Circumcised? Gender and Covenant in Judaism*. Berkeley: University of California, 2005.

Douglas, M. *In the Wilderness: The Doctrine of Defilement in the Book of Numbers*. JSOTSup 158. Sheffield: Sheffield Academic Press, 1993.

———. *Leviticus as Literature*. Oxford: Oxford University Press, 1999.

———. *Purity and Danger: An Analysis of Concepts of Pollution and Taboo*. New York: Routledge and Kegan Paul, 1966.

Eidevall, G. "The Role of Sacrificial Language in Prophetic Rhetoric." Pages 49–61 in *Ritual and Metaphor: Sacrifice in the Hebrew Bible*. Edited by C. A. Eberhart. Atlanta: Society of Biblical Literature, 2011.

---

51. Besides generating concern for textual meaning, textualizing and scripturalizing the Torah may also have generated greater diversity in ritual practice; see the essays in this volume by C. Frevel and J. Rhyder.

Eilberg-Schwartz, H. *The Savage in Judaism: An Anthropology of Israelite and Ancient Judaism*. Bloomington: Indiana University Press, 1990.

Erbele-Küster, D. "Gender and Cult: 'Pure' and 'Impure' as Gender-Relevant Categories." Pages 375–405 in *Torah*. Edited by I. Fischer and M. N. Puerto, with A. Taschl-Erber. Atlanta: Society of Biblical Literature, 2012.

———. *Body, Gender, and Purity in Leviticus 12 and 15*. LHBOTS 539. London: T&T Clark, 2017.

Feder, Y. *Blood Expiation in Hittite and Biblical Ritual*. Atlanta: Society of Biblical Literature, 2011.

Feinstein, E. L. *Sexual Pollution in the Hebrew Bible*. Oxford: Oxford University Press, 2014.

Gane, R. E. "Didactic Logic and the Authorship of Leviticus." Pages 197–222 in *Current Issues in Priestly and Related Literature: The Legacy of Jacob Milgrom and Beyond*. Edited by R. E. Gane and A. Taggar-Cohen. Atlanta: Society of Biblical Literature, 2015.

———. *Ritual Dynamic Structure*. Piscataway, NJ: Gorgias, 2004.

Gerstenberger, E. S. *Leviticus: A Commentary*. Translated by D. W. Stott. Old Testament Library. Louisville, KY: Westminster John Knox, 1996.

Gilders, W. K. *Blood Ritual in the Hebrew Bible: Meaning and Power*. Baltimore: Johns Hopkins University Press, 2004.

Grimes, R. *Ritual Criticism: Case Studies in Its Practice, Essays on Its Theory*. Columbia: University of South Carolina Press, 1990.

Hieke, T. *Levitikus*. Herders Theologischer Kommentar zum Alten Testament. Freiburg im Breisgau: Herder, 2014.

Hundley, M. B. *Keeping Heaven on Earth: Safeguarding the Divine Presence in the Priestly Tabernacle*. FAT 2/50. Tübingen: Mohr Siebeck, 2011.

Janowski, B. *Sühne als Heilsgeschehen: Studien zur Sühnetheologie der Priesterschrift und zur Wurzel KPR im Alten Orient und im Alten Testament*. WMANT 55. Neukirchen-Vluyn: Neukirchener Verlag, 1982.

Janzen, D. *The Social Meanings of Sacrifice in the Hebrew Bible: A Study of Four Writings*. BZAW 344. Berlin: de Gruyter, 2004.

Jay, N. *Throughout Your Generations Forever: Sacrifice, Religion and Paternity*. Chicago: University of Chicago Press, 1992.

Kazen, Thomas. "Levels of Explanation for Ideas of Impurity: Why Structuralist and Symbolic Models Often Fail While Evolutionary and Cognitive Models Succeed." *Journal of Ancient Judaism* 9 (2018): 75–100.

Klawans, J. *Impurity and Sin in Ancient Judaism*. Oxford: Oxford University Press, 2000.

———. *Purity, Sacrifice, and the Temple: Symbolism and Supersessionism in the Study of Ancient Judaism*. New York: Oxford, 2006.

Klingbeil, G. A. *Bridging the Gap: Ritual and Ritual Texts in the Bible*. Winona Lake, IN: Eisenbrauns, 2007.

Knohl, I. *The Sanctuary of Silence: The Priestly Torah and the Holiness School*. Minneapolis: Fortress, 1995.

Kreinath, J. "Semiotics." Pages 429–70 in *Theorizing Rituals*. Edited by J. Kreinath, J. Snoek, and M. Stausberg. Leiden: Brill, 2006.

Landy, F. "For Whom God's Name is Blotted Out." Pages 170–95 in *Text, Time and Temple: Literary, Historical and Ritual Studies in Leviticus*. Sheffield: Sheffield Phoenix, 2015.

Lemos, T. M. "Where There Is Dirt, Is There System? Revisiting Biblical Purity Constructions." *JSOT* 37 (2013): 265–94.

Levine, B. A. *Leviticus*. JPS Torah Commentary. Philadelphia: Jewish Publication Society, 1989.

Marx, A. "L'impureté selon P: Une lecture théologique." *Biblica* 82 (2001): 363–84.

———. *Les systèmes sacrificiels de l'Ancien Testament: Formes et functions du culte sacrificial à Yhwh*. VTSup 105. Leiden: Brill, 2005.

Meshel, N. S. *The "Grammar" of Sacrifice: A Generativist Study of the Israelite Sacrificial System in the Priestly Writings with a "Grammar" of Σ*. Oxford: Oxford University Press, 2014.

Michaels, A. "Ritual and Meaning." Pages 147–61 in *Theorizing Rituals*. Edited by J. Kreinath, J. Snoek, and M. Stausberg. Leiden: Brill, 2006.

Milgrom, J. *Leviticus 1–16: A New Translation with Introduction and Commentary*. AB 3A. New York: Doubleday, 1991.

———. *Leviticus 17–22: A New Translation with Introduction and Commentary*. AB 3B. New York: Doubleday, 2000.

———. *Leviticus 23–27: A New Translation with Introduction and Commentary*. AB 3C. New York: Doubleday, 2001.

Modéus, M. *Sacrifice and Symbol: Biblical Šelāmîm in a Ritual Perspective*. Coniectanea Biblica: Old Testament Series 52. Stockholm: Almqvist & Wiksell, 2005.

Nihan, C. *From Priestly Torah to Pentateuch: A Study in the Composition of the Book of Leviticus*. FAT 2/25. Tübingen: Mohr Siebeck, 2007.

———. "The Templization of Israel in Leviticus: Some Remarks on Blood Disposal and Kipper in Leviticus 4." Pages 94–130 in *Text, Time and Temple: Literary, Historical and Ritual Studies in Leviticus*. Edited by F. Landy, L. M. Trevaskis, and B. D. Bibb. Sheffield: Sheffield Phoenix, 2015.

Olyan, S. M. *Rites and Rank: Hierarchy in Biblical Representations of Cult*. Princeton: Princeton University Press, 2000.

Parker, R. *Miasma: Pollution and Purification in Early Greek Religion*. Oxford: Oxford University Press, 1983.

Rappaport, R. *Ritual and Religion in the Making of Humanity*. Cambridge: Cambridge University Press, 1999.

Rendtorff, R. *Leviticus 1,1–10,20*. BKAT 3. Neukirchen-Vluyn: Neukirchener, 1985.

Ruane, N. J. *Sacrifice and Gender in Biblical Law*. Cambridge: Cambridge University Press, 2013.

Schenker, A. *Studien zu Opfer und Kult im Alten Testament*. Tübingen: Mohr Siebeck, 1992.

Schwartz, B. J. "The Bearing of Sin in the Priestly Literature." Pages 3–21 in *Pomegranates and Golden Bells: Studies in Biblical, Jewish, and Near Eastern Ritual, Law, and Literature in Honor of Jacob Milgrom*. Edited by D. P. Wright, D. N. Freedman, and A. Hurwitz. Winona Lake, IN: Eisenbrauns, 1995.

———. *The Holiness Legislation: Studies in the Priestly Code* (Hebrew). Jerusalem: Magnes, 1999.

Staal, F. "The Meaninglessness of Ritual." *Numen* 26.1 (1979): 2–22.

———. *The Science of Ritual*. Poona: Bhandarkar Oriental Research Institute, 1982.

Stowers, S. K. "On the Comparison of Blood in Greek and Israelite Ritual." Pages 179–94 in *Hesed ve-Emet: Studies in Honor of Ernest S. Frerichs*. Edited by J. Magness and S. Gitin. BJS 320. Atlanta: Scholars Press, 1998.

Trevaskis, L. M. *Holiness, Ethics and Ritual in Leviticus.* Hebrew Bible Monographs 29. Sheffield: Sheffield Phoenix, 2011.
Watts, J. W. *Leviticus 1–10.* HCOT. Leuven: Peeters, 2013.
———. *Ritual and Rhetoric in Leviticus: From Sacrifice to Scripture.* Cambridge: Cambridge University Press, 2007.
———. "The Three Dimensions of Scriptures." Pages 8–30 in *Iconic Books and Texts.* Edited by J. W. Watts. London: Equinox, 2013, revised in *How and Why Books Matter* (Sheffield: Equinox, 2019), 7–29.
Whitekettle, R. "Leviticus 12 and the Israelite Woman: Ritual Process, Liminality and the Womb." *ZAW* 107 (1995): 393–408.
Wright, D. P. "Ritual Theory, Ritual Texts, and the Priestly-Holiness Writings of the Pentateuch." Pages 195–216 in *Social Theory and the Study of Israelite Religion.* Edited by S. M. Olyan. Atlanta: Society of Biblical Literature, 2012.
———. "Unclean and Clean." *ABD* 6:729–741.
Yoo, Y. and J. W. Watts. *Cosmologies of Pure Realms and the Rhetoric of Pollution.* New York: Routledge, 2021.

CHAPTER 8

The Texture of Rituals in the Book of Numbers: A Fresh Approach to Ritual Density, the Role of Tradition, and the Emergence of Diversity in Early Judaism

Christian Frevel

8.1. Rituals as Common Denominator

Writing an essay on the function of rituals on the hundredth anniversary of the death of Émile Durkheim (1858–1917) may be seen as bringing coals to Newcastle. In his book *The Elementary Forms of the Religious Life*, Durkheim sought to uncover the universality of religious characteristics: "How is it possible to find, underneath the disputes of theology, the variations of ritual, the multiplicity of groups and the diversity of individuals, the fundamental states characteristic of religious mentality in general?"[1] It is not about sharing the interest in the universality of religious characteristics or Durkheim's evolutionary idea of religion but rather about strengthening the implicit presuppositions of his idea that religion is related to social reality and—with the words of Catherine Bell—"religion functions to ensure the unconscious priority of communal identification."[2] The interesting point in the quote above is not the idea of the "general" but rather the elements he mentions on the secondary level—namely, theological discourse and ritual, or to put it differently, "tradition." They form the social cohesion and communal identity, or they function as an expression and denominator of identity. By relating to a common practice or a common set of ideas, community is built up beyond genealogy or cohabitation. With this we have described one of the two major and basic functions of scriptural tradition. However, there is never a total congruence between a society and its tradition. The boundaries of both are rather open and permeable. As society covers a variety of aspects that are not represented in tradition, tradition covers

---

1. É. Durkheim, *The Elementary Forms of the Religious Life* (London: George Allen & Unwin, 1915), 143.
2. C. Bell, *Ritual: Perspectives and Dimensions*, 2nd ed. (Oxford: Oxford University Press, 2009), 24.

aspects that do not represent or relate to society. In between there is plenty of room left for interpretation. Traditions contain a very high potential for variability, which implies from the very beginning the relation of text and variability, text and interpretation, text and commentary, etc.

Usually, a particular tradition is allocated to a particular community. The interesting issue now is the striking fact that several communities share the same written tradition. The situation becomes more complex if we assume that a tradition is explicitly built to match the interest of various communities. This is true for the Samaritans and the postexilic Judaic community centered in Jerusalem, who both share almost the same Torah (textual variants and slight changes admitted).[3] Probably we have to broaden this horizon to other denominations within the plurality of the formative phase of Judaism—for example, the diaspora in Egypt and Babylon, as well as "noncentralized" communities outside of Yehûd in the Negev, the Galilee, or in Transjordan.[4] All these communities committed themselves to the Torah but at the same time interpreted it differently in practice. The development was characterized by fluid boundaries and regional differentiation rather than by schisms from an orthodox and normative origin. What were the common denominators in this very tradition? In this essay, I will put forward the idea that the set of rituals in the Torah is not meant to cover the de facto ritual-household,[5] either of the cult in the desert or of the cult in the First or Second Temple period, but rather forms a framework in which the interpretative understanding of various Judaisms was possible.[6] Together

---

3. For the Samaritan question and the sharing of common traditions, see G. Knoppers, "Parallel Torahs and Inner-Scriptural Interpretation: The Jewish and Samaritan Pentateuchs in Historical Perspective," in *The Pentateuch: International Perspectives on Current Research*, ed. T. B. Dozeman, K. Schmid, and B. J. Schwartz, FAT 78 (Tübingen: Mohr Siebeck, 2011), 507–31; C. Nihan, "The Torah Between Samaria and Judah: Shechem and Gerizim in Deuteronomy and Joshua," in *The Pentateuch as Torah: New Models of Understanding Its Promulgation and Acceptance*, ed. G. Knoppers and B. L. Levinson (Winona Lake, IN: Eisenbrauns, 2007), 187–223; B. Hensel, *Juda und Samaria: Zum Verhältnis zweier nach-exilischer Jahwismen*, FAT 110 (Tübingen: Mohr Siebeck, 2016), 173–94.

4. For this religious plurality in the fifth and fourth centuries BCE, see C. Frevel, *Geschichte Israels*, Kohlhammer Studienbücher Theologie 2 (Stuttgart: Kohlhammer, 2016), 323.

5. The term "ritual-household" ("Ritualhaushalt") is used in this essay to denote the (complete) *set of rituals* performed within a community. It has nothing to do with domestic rituals.

6. For the term "Judaisms," its history, the shift from essentialist understanding to the de facto diversity and the blurred borders of this plurality, as well as for the criticism of the concept, see, e.g., the introductory chapter of M. L. Satlow, *Creating Judaism: History, Tradition, Practice* (New York: Columbia University Press, 2006), 1–21. Accordingly, in this essay I prefer to use the plural just to avoid the misunderstanding of an orthodox Judaism as normative origin. For a recent discussion, see also D. Boyarin, "Beyond Judaisms: Meṭaṭron and the Divine Polymorphy of Ancient Judaism," *JSJ* 41 (2010): 323–65 at 327, who thinks that it is now "time to move beyond it, seeing Judaism as the sum of the religious expressions of the Jews." For our purpose this does not make much sense, since "Judaism" then becomes a constructive term without any possibility to identify and get a grip on various denominations.

with the common construction of the twelve-tribe system, the formative early history of Israel outside of the land, the fictive sanctuary at Mount Sinai, the Aaronide priesthood and other aspects, the rituals in their present form are part of the reservoir of identity of Second Temple Judaism. They constitute and at the same time preserve a common and idealized past within the context of a foundational narrative. The foundational myth of the exodus was already part of the identity construction of the former *tradition*,[7] so that—as can be said to be a general rule—tradition is built on tradition, and tradition is formed by reception. However, compared to the former tradition of the prepriestly Hexateuch, which was built to include northern and southern tradition in the Judean perspective,[8] the perspective of the late-Persian Pentateuch is much more open to various groups even outside of Yehûd. Every group that wanted to have a share in these ideas could relate itself to this "Torah" without being too much restricted in its own practice. Although the Torah can be attributed more or less to the dominant priestly groups in Jerusalem, it was not totally congruent even to the practice of this particular denomination. In contrast it functioned like a common denominator that could be adapted to other communal identity concepts within Yahwism.

Michael L. Satlow has employed the concept of a "family of tradition" to avoid normativity and to denote the plurality within Judaism.[9] In my understanding the Torah *is* a "family of tradition" and the "*pater familias*" at the same time. Using the polythetic metaphor of Jonathan Z. Smith,[10] the Torah is (in pre-Hellenistic antiquity, most importantly) the "map" in which identity is plotted; it is normative in a relational rather than in an essential way. Thus, the rituals are part of this textual strategy in enabling diversity and forming the plurality of Judaisms.

To argue in this direction, I first have to answer the question of the text-practice relationship, second to elaborate on the role and function of ritual textualization. After this, I will unfold the rituals in the book of Numbers as a test case, on the one hand, to demonstrate the "late" representation of rituals in the alleged latest book of the Torah and, on the other hand, to indicate that the ritual-household of the Torah is eclectically sophisticated and related to ritual

---

7. In the context of the present argument, it is irrelevant whether the narrative bridge between the exodus narrative and the ancestors' narrative was existent before the priestly layer—a view for which I still see compelling reasons.

8. C. Frevel, "'Esau, der Vater Edoms' (Gen 36,9.43): Ein Vergleich der Edom-Überlieferungen in Genesis und Numeri vor dem Hintergrund der historischen Entwicklung," in *The Politics of the Ancestors: Exegetical and Historical Perspectives on Genesis 12–36*, ed. J. Wöhrle and M. G. Brett, FAT 124 (Tübingen: Mohr Siebeck, 2018), 329–64.

9. Satlow, *Creating Judaism*, 6.

10. J. Z. Smith, *Map Is Not Territory: Studies in the History of Religions* (Leiden: Brill, 1975), 308–9; J. Z. Smith, *Imagining Religion: From Babylon to Jonestown* (Chicago: University of Chicago Press, 1982), 18.

discussions within formative Judaism. This finally brings me to the question of the integrative function of rituals and the interpretation of the composition of rituals within the Torah as enabling plurality.

8.2. Getting Lost in Practice or in Texts? Some Introductory Remarks of False Oppositions

If the description of rituals in the Torah does not primarily function as a ritual script, and if the set of rituals represented in the composition of the Torah in its final form does not intend to cover the ritual-household of the Second Temple in Jerusalem, the issue of scripturalization with regard to rituals, or in other words the relation of text and ritual, has to be discussed. Hence, we may start with some preliminary remarks on ritual in general, ritual and practice, and ritual in the book of Numbers in particular. In contrast to older studies on the priestly source in the Pentateuch, the understanding of ritual has dramatically changed in recent times. For Julius Wellhausen and others the ritual parts of Leviticus and Numbers were the codification of actual ritual, what Christophe Nihan characterizes as a "'realistic' reading."[11] The turnaround of research has been captured by Lester L. Grabbe: "Leviticus is not primarily a book for priests. It is not a priestly manual."[12] Together with many commentaries on Leviticus and Numbers or introductory books on biblical rituals and Second Temple cult, I assume that the Bible is *not* a ritual book in the sense that it contains ritual scripts to be performed in the cult—may it be inside or outside of the temple cult. Neither do biblical rituals mirror practice as straightforward descriptions of practiced rituals, nor do they prescribe a fixed and invariant ritual practice. Although it is by no means the most interesting point in ritual studies, the textuality of ritual and its relation to performance/action is still a much-debated issue.[13] This discussion forms the background for my essay, but it is not my primary focus.

First and foremost, we have to assume a certain disparity between ritual texts and ritual practices, not only in terms of ritual experts, agency, sequence, accurateness, etc. but also in terms of rituals as such: not all the rituals stated

---

11. C. Nihan, *From Priestly Torah to Pentateuch: A Study in the Composition of the Book of Leviticus*, FAT 2/25 (Tübingen: Mohr Siebeck, 2007), 17.
12. L. L. Grabbe, "The Priests in Leviticus: Is the Medium the Message?," in *The Book of Leviticus: Composition and Reception*, ed. R. Rendtorff and R. A. Kugler, VTSup 93 (Leiden: Brill, 2003), 207–24 at 221.
13. See, for instance, A. Barchiesi, J. Rüpke, and S. Stephens, eds., *Rituals in Ink: A Conference on Religion and Literary Production in Ancient Rome*, Potsdamer Altertumswissenschaftliche Beiträge 10 (Munich: Franz Steiner Verlag, 2004); V. Nünning, J. Rupp, and G. Ahn, eds., *Ritual and Narrative: Theoretical Explorations and Historical Case Studies* (Bielefeld: Transcript, 2013); and the works of J. W. Watts and B. D. Bibb mentioned below.

were actually performed, and—I guess at least more importantly—not all rituals performed were stated. The ritual-household of a certain religious community was different and allegedly much greater than their textualized set of rituals. But we do not know very much concerning the relation of biblical rituals to the set of rituals performed in Jerusalem, on Gerizim, or in Elephantine. Tradition, innovation, orality, textuality and practice, ideal shape and everyday routine, religious practice and theological doctrine, sociological function and reflection of structure, institution and individuality, principle and application, private and public, logic and irrational, natural and supernatural, etc. form a mixture, of which the components cannot easily be kept apart. They overlap, influence each other, and vary from case to case. The meaning and function of ritual elude us as etic observers and will remain elusive even for the emic perspective. That this is one of the most puzzling obstacles of ritual studies seems to be a commonplace. On the one hand, no one proceeds on the assumption that the biblical text is a manual of ritual. On the other hand, stating the biblical text to be pure theology runs the risk of being disconnected from ritual practice and is misleading because it tends to place text and ritual in a diametrically opposed relation. For Jacob Milgrom the Priestly Code was "a self-contained system—logical, coherent and whole,"[14] realistic and strongly related to society in providing "a window to the life of Ancient Israel."[15] Rituals have a symbolic significance in communicating ethical values. But this rational system risks placing rituals too much into a theological system. However, stating that "in principle, rituals function beyond and apart from theology and other ideational components and, at times, in spite of them"[16] is even worse, because rituals are then reduced to "autonomous extensions of the human mind,"[17] whose theological indexicality is neglected.

In sum: the biblical rituals are neither a portrayal of practice nor solely informed by practice; neither do they create or sketch practice, nor do they function as a theological template of ritual practice. Current research cannot rate the

---

14. J. Milgrom, *Cult and Conscience: The Asham and the Priestly Doctrine of Repentance* (Leiden: Brill, 1976), 2; J. Milgrom, *Leviticus 1–16: A New Translation with Introduction and Commentary*, AB 3A (New York: Doubleday, 1991), 42–51. For the discussion, see M. A. Daise, "Ritual Density in Qumran Practice: Ablutions in the Serekh Ha-Yahad," in *New Perspectives on Old Texts: Proceedings of the Tenth International Symposium of the Orion Center for the Study of the Dead Sea Scrolls and Associated Literature, 9–11 January, 2005*, ed. E. G. Chazon and Betsy Halpern-Amaru, STDJ 88 (Leiden: Brill, 2010), 54, who challenges the "system" beyond the ritual.

15. J. Milgrom, *Numbers: The Traditional Hebrew Text with the New JPS Translation*, JPS Torah Commentary (Philadelphia: Jewish Publication Society, 1990), xxxvi.

16. I. Gruenwald, *Rituals and Ritual Theory in Ancient Israel* (Leiden: Brill, 2003), 143.

17. Ibid. However, Gruenwald more often uses "autonomous expressions of the human mind" (ibid., 2, 13, 55, 143) as the shortest definition of ritual. He also speaks explicitly of a "de-theologisation" of rituals (ibid., 191).

ratio between meaning and practice. Said that, the function of rituals within texts fades; it is neither documenting nor preserving nor theorizing nor reading practice. The question is not whether the textual representation may form a system or not; the question is about the expectation of consistency and sophistication toward this "system." To be clear, ritual texts in the Pentateuch are related to each other and have to be read complementarily, but ritual texts are neither completely consistent nor capable of each and every aspect being related to the system of priestly thought. This opens the argument for the issue of textualization and its function.

8.3. Textualization of Ritual Forms a Complex and an Ideal World

Ritual performance and ritual text are related to each other and they are not identical: this insight gives way to the dynamics of rituals in general and also to the dynamics of performance and textualization. Ritual practice and text are entangled in various ways—they correspond, interact, and interfere—but the relation remains asymmetrical. While ritual practice can be conceptualized or even developed completely disengaged from the textuality of ritual in terms of written traditions, ritual texts or textual rituals are related to performance, even if only theoretically or in mind. Although I tend to the broad conjecture that there *may* be *virtual rituals* in textual traditions, which have to be seen detached from ritual practice as being merely sophisticated textual constructions, I agree that rituality has *almost always* something to do with practice—if not in a world outside of the text than at least *within* the textual world. Rituals always have performative aspects and this has to be kept in mind, although practicability may not be proof for the authenticity of rituals. Given that the ritual is related to a textual ritual, the performance can be remarkably different, including variance, additional sequence of actions, distinguished roles, etc.

Beyond the general assumption that ritual script and practice cannot be considered totally independent from each other, the complex relation between text and ritual cannot be answered satisfactory. To put it more generally: whether the texture of rituals forms practice or the other way around is an interesting—but mostly unanswerable and, for the understanding of the texture of rituals, irrelevant—question. It was Brian D. Bibb, in his book *Ritual Words and Narrative Worlds in the Book of Leviticus*, who emphasized the blending of descriptive narrative and prescriptive ritual and how it "ritualizes narrative" and "narrativizes ritual."[18] Nevertheless, the concrete textual shape of rituals is much more

---

18. B. D. Bibb, *Ritual Words and Narrative Worlds in the Book of Leviticus*, LHBOTS 480 (New York: T&T Clark, 2009).

important for understanding the function of rituals within a certain cultic setting. Particularly, the textual context of the rituals in the Pentateuch shapes and transforms them in terms of their indexicality, meaning, and performance. Whether we call this aspect the "rhetoric" of ritual,[19] or emphasize that rituals are "literature,"[20] or part of—as I would put it—a complex textual world is insignificant in a way. By relating to Wolfgang Iser's concept of fiction, Hanna Liss has pointed to the transformation of legal tradition into text and I would like to expand this view on biblical rituals.

> Die Konsequenz, mit der *P* ihm vorgängige Rechtstexte in einem "Akt des Fingierens" zur Literatur umgestaltet, lässt sich gerade anhand der Abschnitte über die Kultgesetzgebung . . . sehr gut zeigen. Das Fiktive an *P*s Darstellung besteht eben darin, dass *P* weder ein Abbild bestehender Zustände noch einen idealen Entwurf, eine Utopie, zeichnen wollte. Mit dem Rückgriff auf bereits vergangene oder noch bestehende kultische Institutionen und ihrer Ausstattung sowie ihrer gleichzeitigen konsequenten Verfremdung etabliert *P* einen *Kultus im Text*. Kultische Einrichtungen und darin die Begegnung mit YHWH werden so gleichsam aus ihrem Geschichtsraum hinaus in einen "Text-Raum" hinein transponiert.[21]

P did not aim at serving as a portrayed or as an ideal utopia but rather employs a cult within the text or a fictive *textual world* that is related to history as well as to the present, to reality as well as to utopia. The text becomes an ideal world to which the real world can be related.

If "ritual is no less textual than literature, it becomes possible even to wonder whether ritual and literature are separate domains at all, however impractical a notion this might be."[22] This gives way to interesting questions regarding rituals as part of literature: how do they contribute to the construction of "identity" or how do they indicate social developments in terms of societal organization, integration, institution, hierarchy; how do they safeguard the dynamic of tradition, etc.? These are interesting questions of textualization that lay beyond the question of the documenting or preserving function of scripturalization. It is rather about issues of authority, regulation, homogenization, and representation that come into focus.

---

19. J. W. Watts, *Ritual and Rhetoric in Leviticus: From Sacrifice to Scripture* (Cambridge: Cambridge University Press, 2007).

20. M. Douglas, *Leviticus as Literature* (Oxford: Oxford University Press, 1999).

21. H. Liss, "Kanon und Fiktion. Zur literarischen Funktion biblischer Rechtstexte," *BN* 121 (2004): 7–38 at 32.

22. D. D. Leitao, "Ritual? What Ritual?," in *Rituals in Ink: A Conference on Religion and Literary Production in Ancient Rome*, ed. A. Barchiesi (Munich: Franz Steiner Verlag, 2004), 149–53 at 149.

This essay will address some aspects of this broader understanding, taking the rituals of the book of Numbers and particularly the priestly blessing as an example. Building on Bell, I will now look at the "ritual density" in the book of Numbers, then I will put forward the idea that textualization of rituals gives way to variance instead of fixation. This brings me to the function of rituals, and I will argue that rituals form a reservoir of identity that allows practical diversity within the broader framework of biblical rituals.

8.4. The Ritual Density of the Book of Numbers

Except for the offering rituals in the book of Leviticus there are—strictly speaking—not very many rituals in the Pentateuch if we accept (as a sort of definition) confining rituals in the broadest sense to actions of a mostly sequential and complex nature that are recurring, or rather laid out for repetition.[23] Beside the Pesach ritual in Exod 12, some healing and purifying rituals in Lev 11–15, and naturally the atonement ritual of Lev 16, there are not very many rituals in Exodus and Leviticus. In contrast there are several, mostly *occasional*, rituals in the book of Numbers that are often underappreciated or even neglected in scholarly literature. Ithamar Gruenwald's book *Rituals and Ritual Theory in Ancient Israel* offers a glaring example in which the author broadly elaborates on rituals in the book of Leviticus but disregards Numbers completely.[24] The pure number of rituals in the book of Numbers is (depending on the definition of ritual) striking, however:

- the Sotah ritual regarding the jealous husband and his suspicion of his wife's adultery (Num 5:11–21);
- the ritual of the Nazirite vow (Num 6:13–20) as a renewal of the Nazirite vow after its break (Num 6:9–12);
- the ritual of the priestly blessing (Num 6:23–27);
- the ritual of the postponed Pesach (Num 9:9–14);
- additional aspects of ritual offering (Num 15:1–21);
- the offering rituals of atonement of unwilling sins (Num 15:22–29);

---

23. A. Bendlin, "Ritual. I. Term," in *Brill's New Pauly: Antiquity Volumes*, ed. H. Cancik and H. Schneider (Brill Online, 2016), http://referenceworks.brillonline.com/entries/brill-s-new-pauly/ritual-e1023450: "Ritual refers to an elaborate sequence of individual rites which, following an established ritual syntax, are logically connected within a certain functional context."

24. Gruenwald, *Rituals*. The same holds true, for instance, for the article by M. Görg, "Rituale," in *Neues Bibellexikon*, ed. M. Görg and B. Lang (Zürich: Benzinger, 2001), 366. Strikingly enough, there is not even an article on "ritual" in the *ABD*.

the ordeal in Num 16:17–19 or the stopping of the plague in Num 16:46–48 may also be understood as rituals;

the ritual of the red cow, handling impurity caused by corpses (Num 19);

the situational rituals of atonement in Num 16:36–50 and Num 25:7–8;

the festival calendar in Num 28–29 is full of offering rituals accompanying the feasts; and

the practice of vows in Num 30 may also be read with respect to ritual.

Since Sinai is the preferred place of revelation with a particular emphasis on normativity, we may wonder why so many rituals can be found in the book of Numbers even beyond the departure from Sinai in Num 10:10. Before we discuss some of the various explanations for this peculiarity, it may be helpful to stick to the term "ritual density," which was introduced by Bell. What she meant was the obvious fact that "some societies or historical periods have more ritual than others."[25] Regarding the representation of rituals in textual traditions, the book of Numbers is crucially relevant in terms of "ritual density." Linked to the time period when the books of Leviticus and Numbers were formed as late parts of the priestly literature, the formative phase of the Pentateuch is a time of "ritual density." Why? The question of ritual density is one of the most intriguing ones, or, as Bell puts it, it is "arguably among the most interesting in the study of religion today."[26] However, there are "only small islands of scholarly consensus on the factors affecting density,"[27] says Bell, and thus we are encouraged to discuss the matter from the angle of biblical tradition. We have to address questions of composition, authority, and literary development as well as aspects of content and finally the role of rituals as part of the identity building processes that built on the Pentateuch as a formative record in the fifth and fourth centuries BCE.

Within the scholarly discussion, various explanations of the ritual density in the book of Numbers have been given. I confine myself to a rough overview.

1. Rituals were always important in Israel's religious practice but they were increasingly collected in the late Second Temple period. There was a growing need to textualize rituals because of the dissolution of the cult of the Second Temple. Fixation of age-old rituals took place in processes of successive addition, even and particularly in the book of Numbers as the latest book of the Pentateuch. Because the book of Leviticus was almost finalized, the rituals were attached to the book of Numbers.

---

25. Bell, *Ritual*, 173.
26. Ibid.
27. Ibid.

2. Various forms of rituals were circulating in the Second Temple period and thus biblical authors saw the necessity to preserve and homogenize ritual practice in the processes of finalizing the Pentateuch. Variance should be limited to a minimum. The rituals recorded in Numbers were more open in practice and were fixed by embedding them into the narrative.
3. Rituals became more important in the Second Temple period especially in the late Persian period of the fifth and fourth centuries BCE, and this development is the background of the quantity of rituals in the book of Numbers. The density of rituals in Numbers mirrors the density of ritual practice in the late Second Temple period. The rituals in Numbers are not a collection of age-old, traditional stuff but a form of innovative ritual practice that emerged in a timeframe informed by ritual density.
4. The ritual density has nothing to do with practice or tradition; rather, it has to do with composition. The rituals are situational and thus deliberately placed in the book of Numbers. Situational, contextual, and narrative aspects determine the density of rituals in Numbers.
5. None of the abovementioned theories is ready to explain the density of rituals in Numbers because the density is due to the function of rituals in a particular society.

Different clues inform the different options: contestation, homogenization, cultic practice, social function, textual composition, etc. Not all of the explanations provide a rationale for the bifurcation between Sinai and Wilderness. Mary Douglas has put forward aspects of societal organization: that societies with more intensive group and grid organization have a certain density of rituals. She argues in general that "the most important determinant of ritualism is the experience of closed social groups."[28] Thus, there is a connection between social grids and ritual density: "When the social group grips its members in tight communal bonds, the religion is ritualist; when the grip is relaxed, ritualism declines."[29] In this way she sees the postexilic Second Temple period or the time of Nehemiah and Ezra, when the importance of group and grid are expanding, as a ritual productive time. Because the same holds true for the importance on body and bodily purity, the ritual density is accompanied by an emphasis on purity as well. The model of Douglas, which was developed as a form of resistance against evolutionary concepts, has a heuristic value in explaining ritual density. Bell recast the Douglas model in terms of style and suggested at least four styles of ritual action: appeasement and appeal, cosmic ordering, moral redemption, and

---

28. M. Douglas, *Natural Symbols: Explorations in Cosmology*, Mary Douglas Collected Works 3 (London: Routledge, 2002), 14.
29. Ibid., 13–14.

finally personal spirituality. Bell concludes that "the degree and style of ritual density can be correlated with different types of worldviews, forms of social organization, and notions of the self."[30] In congruence with Douglas she argues that "if a society passes through social and historical changes affecting its worldview, organization, economic activities, and exposure to competing ideas, for example, it will probably witness concomitant changes in its ritual system—even though ritual systems can be particularly resistant to change."[31] This again is an argument in favor of ritual density in terms of tradition building since tradition-building processes are related to social and historical changes as well. Bell addresses ritual practices as "a type of sociocultural medium"[32] and the category of medium is in my view illuminating. She sees rituals as "ways of acting that ground a complex set of social and personal values within a person's conscious convictions and unconscious assumptions about how the universe is structured."[33] It is a question not only of the general worldview and conceptual universe but also of the level of social structure and values. Rituals are related to social order, politics, and economy—not only by generating money, structuring hierarchy, etc. but also as a part of a communal understanding and collective identity. Following Bell, rituals are a means of affiliation and bonding. With regard to rites and rituals in Jewish orthodoxy she considers "such stringent ritualization has the powerful effect of tightly binding one to a small community of like-minded people. Indeed, one of the salient features of extreme ritualization appears to be a high-profile identity as a tight-knit group of *true* followers, a position that heightens the contrast and [w]ill fit with other groups."[34]

This idea can be applied to the period of formative "densification" or traditions in the Second Temple period as well. The relation between social structure and ritual is obvious, but in the case of the biblical ritual density I would like to emphasize another aspect with regard to group building and identification processes below. But before, I want to deepen the perspective of textualization by hinting at different aspects of textualization in the set of rituals within the book of Numbers.

8.5. Aspects of Innovation in Textualization

I will not go into detail here, but the ritual composition of Num 5:5–6:21 reveals crucial aspects of innovation. In an essay for a volume edited by Nathan

30. Bell, *Ritual*, 190.
31. Ibid.
32. Ibid.
33. Ibid.
34. Ibid., 193.

MacDonald on *Ritual Innovation*,[35] I discussed the interrelation between "new" rituals and innovative aspects. It was striking that not only is the formulation of Num 5:5–8 closely related to Lev 5:20–26, but, in contrast, the whole ritual composition also comprises the Sotah in Num 5:11–31 and the Nazirite Law in Num 6:1–21. All three cases showed a specific relation to Lev 5 and differed with regard to the matter of *ritual innovation*. Numbers 5:5–10 was only comprehensible as an amendment of Lev 5:20–26. Novel aspects were generalization, public confession, and the absence of a succeeding heir. Each of these was added by drawing on the phraseology of Lev 5 in particular. The Sotah drew on Lev 5 in terms of sacrificial systematics and the related ritual practices. This also holds true for the law of the Nazirite in Num 6. In addition, the consequences of the unwittingly broken vow were developed by analogy with Lev 5. While Num 5:5–10 was obviously formulated for the present context, this solution is not compelling for the Sotah (Num 5:11–31) or the law of the Nazirite (Num 6:1–21). There are good reasons to assume that neither ritual was entirely a ritual innovation minted completely for the context of Num 5–6, but rather both were—at least in part—older "traditional" rituals.

What we can learn from the composition of rituals is that existing rituals and parts of rituals were taken up and integrated within a composition that is part of the textual world, related intensely to the sanctuary to which all three rituals have a special connection. Aspects of innovation were developed by the *réécriture* of the ritual text of Lev 5. These innovations are developed seemingly regardless of a matching practice; also, the practice may have matched the ritual script in Num 5–6. It was obvious that the general demand for purity in Num 5:1–4 as well as the priestly blessing in Num 6:22–27 were related to the concept of the composition that was spatially well organized. Aspects of ritual preservation by textualization interact with aspects of ritual amendment and innovation. Thus again, the question of textualization is much more complex than just description or prescription of practice.

8.6. Textualized Rituals and Ritualized Texts

The complexity of the text-ritual relation may be further elaborated by levels of textuality and questions of context. The priestly benediction in Num 6:22–26 can serve as a brief example. The short text (which cannot be treated here sufficiently) is a speech of God to Moses, who is commanded to direct the contents

---

35. C. Frevel, "Practicing Rituals in a Textual World: Ritual *and* Innovation in the Book of Numbers," in *Ritual Innovation in the Hebrew Bible and Early Judaism*, ed. N. MacDonald, BZAW 468 (Berlin: de Gruyter, 2016), 129–50.

to Aaron and his sons. The contents are an instruction for Aaron and his sons to perform a/the priestly benediction. Thus, it is not a ritual in itself but *contains* a ritual. It is not said where and when this ritual has to take place, only that the sons of Aaron shall perform the blessing. The demand of Moses directs the following speech act[36] by *lhm* explicitly to a plural addressee that is *bny yśr'l* "the sons of Israel." However, the blessing itself is a speech act spoken toward an *individual* (*ybrkk yhwh*). But it is not said whether this individual is the sole addressee (every single Israelite gets the blessing—partitive function of *lhm*) or whether all individuals are meant (collective function of the enclitic personal pronoun), when the priest utters the benediction toward the community as addressee. The openness is taken up in verse 27 where again a plural subject (Aaron and his sons) shall act toward a plural addressee (*'l-bny yśr'l*). Strictly spoken, the blessing can be applied in various situations and be performed in public with a singular or collective as ritual recipient. Textualization is not clear in this aspect.

The text is segmented in three parts; each begins with a *yiqtol* verbal form (jussive, optative), followed by the Tetragrammaton as subject and a second sentence introduced by another *wayyiqtol* verbal form that again has God as subject. Numbers 6:27 closes the short unit by referring back to verse 23b and an explanatory addition, stating that the speaker will bless the Israelites himself. Although it is not explicitly said in verse 27, the performative act of blessing by the priests is realized by God simultaneously rather than forming a separate act of blessing in addition to the priestly benediction. The biblical text contains a ritual that is obviously (in the given literary context) performed *in the temple* by the Aaronide priests. However, occasion, context, and frequency are not mentioned. It remains quite possible that the act of blessing is performed ritually outside of the temple cult. Jeremy D. Smoak has shown the legitimizing aspect of the fact that the written blessing is connected to the priestly class. By that a certain authorization takes place: this blessing as the performative assurance of the blessing by God is part of the priestly authority and ministry. By writing the blessing in the literacy space of Numbers, the authors of the book, most likely priests, found a new way to provide a concrete perpetual expression to their ritual authority in giving the blessing to Israel. As a result, the authority of giving the blessing was kept in the control of those who wrote, copied, and recited the text.[37]

---

36. I will not go into the text-critical argument of the infinitive absolute in v. 23bß, which functions as an imperative; see H. Seebass, *Numeri 1,1–10,10* (Neukirchen-Vluyn: Neukirchener Verlag, 2012), 168.

37. J. D. Smoak, *The Priestly Blessing in Inscription and Scripture: The Early History of Numbers 6:24–26* (Oxford: Oxford University Press, 2015), 129.

Does this exclude that blessing exists outside of the temple cult? The *Ketef Hinnom* silver scrolls seem to reveal: no! As is widely known, two badly preserved tiny silver scrolls were found in 1979 by Gabriel Barkay in a repository of a rock-cut burial chamber at *Ketef Hinnom* in the vicinity of St. Andrews southwest of the Old City overlooking the Hinnom Valley.[38] The portions of paleo-Hebrew text are often said to be the oldest quotation of a biblical text, insinuating that the priestly blessing in Num 6:22–26 is the pre-text even in an oral state of tradition.[39] The usage in a graveyard was connected with an apotropaic use and a belief of afterlife in preexilic Judahite religion, due to the fact that the burial chamber can be attributed by the pottery assemblage to a use context mainly in the seventh century BCE.[40] However, the stratigraphical context of the finds including the pottery is not indicative for the dating and opens a range from the Iron Age to the Hellenistic period. Particularly the discussion on dating the unstratified silver scrolls in *Ketef Hinnom* has challenged the assumption that the priestly benediction was "quoted" on these sheets of silver. Angelika Berlejung has argued, persuasively, in favor of a usage in the lifetime of the bearers and dated the amulets by comparison of parallels in the object class and by orthographical reasons to the Persian period.[41] Johannes Renz was the first to challenge the early date of the amulets by attributing the script paleographically to the Hellenistic period.[42] In a recent article, and building on the reading *bytw* "his house" in reference to the temple in Jerusalem, Nadav Na'aman dated the amulets to the early postexilic period "not many years after the construction of the second temple."[43] This was recently challenged by Shmuel Aḥituv who argued in favor of the "traditional" date in the late preexilic period.[44] Finally, Brian B. Schmidt has argued that the issue cannot be decided: "As matters

38. See G. Barkay, "The Priestly Benediction on Silver Plaques from Ketef Hinnom in Jerusalem," *TA* 19 (1992): 138–92. For the text, see the new edition by G. Barkay et al., "The Amulets from Ketef Hinnom: A New Edition and Evaluation," *BASOR* 334 (2004): 41–71.
39. See G. Barkay et al., "The Challenges of Ketef Hinnom: Using Advanced Technologies to Reclaim the Earliest Biblical Texts and Their Context," *Near Eastern Archaeology* 66.4 (2003): 162–71.
40. Barkay, "Priestly Benediction," 147.
41. See A. Berlejung, "Der gesegnete Mensch: Text und Kontext von Num 6,22–27 und den Silberamuletten von Ketef Hinnom," in *Mensch und König: Studien zur Anthropologie des Alten Testaments; Rüdiger Lux zum 60. Geburtstag*, ed. A. Berlejung and R. Heckl, Herders Biblische Studien 53 (Freiburg im Breisgau: Herder, 2008), 37–62; A. Berlejung, "Ein Programm fürs Leben: Theologisches Wort und anthropologischer Ort der Silberamulette von Ketef Hinnom," *ZAW* 120.2 (2008): 204–30.
42. J. Renz, *Die althebräischen Inschriften*, 2 vols. (Darmstadt: Wissenschaftliche Buchgesellschaft, 1995), 1:449–52.
43. N. Na'aman, "A New Appraisal of the Silver Amulets from Ketef Hinnom," *IEJ* 61.2 (2011): 184–95 at 192.
44. S. Aḥituv, "A Rejoinder to Nadav Na'aman's 'A New Appraisal of the Silver Amulets from Ketef Hinnom,'" *IEJ* 62.2 (2012): 223–32.

presently stand, the archaeological and paleographic data remain indecisive."[45] Although it may be true that the matter cannot be settled with confidence, the most plausible date of these objects in my understanding is the early Persian period, if they are compared with the amulet practice in the Southern Levant.[46] But for the sake of the argument here, it is important to stress that the Persian and early Hellenistic period is more or less the latest date in the debate, while the Hasmonean date can be regarded as quite unconvincing. The use of the blessing formula in amulets[47] presumes most probably that the text is *not* created for a topical purpose but rather mirrors a *tradition*. Finally, the amulets in the burial contexts primarily do not aim at the afterlife of the deceased or at the descent to the netherworld but rather witness religious practice within the life of the deceased. Thus, it is misguided to attribute the function and use of these amulets to funerary rituals. They are rather signals of a practice in the life of the deceased.[48] There are several differences in form and function of these texts if they are compared to a ritual script and the biblical text. The most important aspect is the permanent or durable character of the blessing. Blessing is not restricted to the performative act of benediction but is rather made permanent by the precious material that is carried around the neck or attached to the body as an amulet. In contrast to textual amulets on tablets or other material, the script is not visible and effective by its reading. The script is effective as such, or to put it more precisely: the implication of writing is blessing. By the process of scripting the blessing is, on the one hand, stabilized and, on the other hand, made permanently effective (by reading or representation).[49]

Although it is more or less a point of consensus that the text of the amulets is the earliest quotation of a biblical text (or even its oral or written precursor),[50] in my understanding this is by no means clear. This assumption needs to explain

---

45. B. B. Schmidt, "The Social Matrix of Early Judean Magic and Divination: From 'Top Down' or 'Bottom Up'?," in *Beyond Hatti*, ed. B. J. Collins and P. Michalowski (Atlanta: Lockwood Press, 2013), 279–93 at 286. See in addition the most recent treatment by Smoak, *Priestly Blessing*; B. B. Schmidt, *The Materiality of Power: Explorations in the Social History of Early Israelite Magic*, FAT 105 (Tübingen: Mohr Siebeck, 2016), 129–30.

46. See for this argument Na'aman, *New Appraisal*, 188 with references.

47. See for the discussion of genre M. Leuenberger, *Segen und Segenstheologien im alten Israel: Untersuchungen zu ihren religions- und theologiegeschichtlichen Konstellationen und Transformationen*, ATANT 90 (Zürich: Theologischer Verlag Zürich, 2008), 155–78.

48. Compare Smoak, *Priestly Blessing*, 52–60, 142–43, who seeks to corroborate the apotropaic function by hinting at *Khirbet el-Qôm*, where the inscription is placed *in* a burial chamber, despite *not* being a funeral inscription.

49. See N. P. Heeßel, "Amulette und 'Amulettform': Zum Zusammenhang von Form, Funktion und Text von Amuletten im Alten Mesopotamien," in *Erscheinungsformen und Handhabungen Heiliger Schriften*, ed. J. F. Quack and D. C. Luft (Berlin: de Gruyter, 2014), 53–77 at 70, 73.

50. See, for instance, W. Schniedewind, "Scripturalization in Ancient Judah," in *Contextualizing Israel's Sacred Writings: Ancient Literacy, Orality, and Literary Production*, ed. B. B. Schmidt (Atlanta: Society of Biblical Literature, 2015), 305–23 at 308.

the *differences* between the biblical text (in all available witnesses) and the text of the amulets, which becomes even greater the more we stand back from the "quotation" idea. The relation between Num 6:24–26 and the text on the silver scrolls is not that of the often-suggested "text-quotation" or "text-allusion" kind; all the more if we take into account that much of the reading of the *Ketef Hinnom* text is guided by the assumption of a quotation. Even if the *Ketef Hinnom* silver tablets are dated to the Persian period, we have to take into account that the biblical text of Num 6:22–27 in its present form *postdates* the amulets and the text represented on them (at least in the form we face in the biblical text today).[51] This is obvious if we accept a position of the text within the composition of Num 5–6 which is dependent on Lev 5.[52] In sum, the blessing in *Ketef Hinnom* is not a biblical quote! It is also not necessarily priestly, as will be shown below.

Usually it is argued that the middle part of the blessing in verses 24–26 is a more traditional text, taken up by the authors of the framework.[53] Older commentaries used this as a vehicle to date the blessing to very old times, even to Mosaic contemporaneity,[54] while recent studies treat the priestly blessing in its present context as a "recontextualization" from the preexilic period.[55] The tradition-historical separation remains possible because of the lack of priestly language and because of the change in number from the third person plural "them" to the second person singular "you," but it is by no means compelling. Often the arguments are circular, since they point to the allegedly pre- or postexilic evidence from *Ketef Hinnom*. Taking nothing else besides the text, there is not very much in these three verses that gives reliable or even decisive clues for dating the tradition (symbolism of the sun god, name theology, etc.).

The existence of even parts of the blessing in the amulets from *Ketef Hinnom* corroborates the evaluation of the textual tradition in Numbers as a representative of an older, but not necessarily cultic (in terms of a priestly temple cult), practice. Nothing indicates that the silver scrolls are a "priestly" blessing, even if we assume that priests were commissioned to bless the people. Said that, the textual composition of Num 6:24–26 may then be a ritual innovation with roots in an existing ritual practice. This (perhaps common ritual-like traditional) amulet practice was ritually coined within the process of textualization. The question is raised clearly by Brian B. Schmidt: "Was this an ancient apotropaic formula

---

51. So, correctly, Smoak, *Priestly Blessing*, 143; Leuenberger, *Segen und Segenstheologien*, 169–70.
52. See Frevel, "Practicing Rituals."
53. See D. Kellermann, *Die Priesterschrift von Numeri 1,1 bis 10,10: Literarkritisch und traditionsgeschichtlich untersucht*, BZAW 120 (Berlin: de Gruyter, 1970); Seebass, *Numeri 1,1–10,10*, 170.
54. D. N. Freedman, *Pottery, Poetry, and Prophecy* (Winona Lake, IN: Eisenbrauns, 1980), 234–35.
55. Smoak, *Priestly Blessing*, 81–83.

that originated in older family or domestic religious traditions, perhaps specifically from within the mortuary cult of family and kin, that over time spread in its usage, application, and popularity to the point that a much later reconstituted priesthood in an emerging centralized form of government co-opted the blessing and employed it not only for its traditional function in mortuary ritual, but also as the preferred rubric for a new national public community consecration (Num 6)?"[56] The evidence of *Ketef Hinnom* points to a religious practice that was settled *later* in the biblical text as a "displaced" ritual practice and that was then explicitly attributed to the priestly Aaronides. Whether the former place of the ritual was the family, funerary contexts, local sanctuaries, or any other context (blessings have presumably not merely a single context) is not decisive here. Even if it was the context of the sanctuary, the new (con)textualization and ritualization is part of a "displacement."

By bringing it into the text of the Torah, it is authorized as part of the legitimized priestly tradition. In the end, the biblical text does not represent a ritual script at all but forges a ritual practice as part of priestly action in the temple cult. It conceptually emphasizes the blessing power of the cult and the life-giving power of God in *his* blessing, which he promises at Sinai. By this, the blessing is in a way historicized. It is established as an age-old tradition from the wilderness. Thinking about this authorizing setting, the term "invention of tradition," introduced so strongly by Eric Hobsbawm,[57] comes immediately into one's mind.

Although the rhythm of verses 24–26 is sophisticated with its increasing length of lines (colometry: 15/20/25 consonants), its threefold Tetragrammaton in the first part of the lines, the sixfold enclitic personal pronoun of the second person singular, etc., it remains principally possible to unchain the components to several blessing formulas.

ybrkk yhwh   *wyšmrk:*
y'r yhwh pnyw 'lyk   *wyḥnk:*
yś' yhwh pnyw 'lyk   *wyśm lk šlwm:*

In this case verses 24–26 would compile existing formulae of blessings into a neat composition of blessing, but even this is mere speculation. If we accept the new readings of Barkay, Vaughn, Lundberg, and Zuckerman, in *Ketef Hinnom* I, 14–18 *ybrk yhwh [wy]śmrk [y] [']r yhwh pn[yw]* "may YHWH bless you and keep you, may YHWH make his face shine," and in *Ketef Hinnom* II, 5–12

---

56. Schmidt, *Social Matrix*, 293.
57. E. Hobsbawm, "Introduction: Invention of Tradition," in *The Invention of Tradition*, ed. E. Hobsbawm and T. Ranger (Cambridge: Cambridge University Press, 1983), 1–14 at 12–14.

ybrk yhwh yšmrk y'r yh [w]h pnyw ['l]yk wyśm lk š[l]m "may YHWH bless you, keep you, and may YHWH make his face shine on you and may he lay peace on you,"[58] then at least the combination of blessing, keeping, and the face of YHWH is attested beneath the biblical text. Hence, it may be the rhythmic pattern of augmentation that was formed by the biblical authors.

Most of the studies emphasize the connection of authorization and textualization. The lack of any linkage to priestly practice is striking compared to the biblical text, particularly if we accept that the blessing is not a quote from the biblical text. By framing the traditional blessing within the narrative through the role of Moses and Aaron and his sons, the act of blessing becomes the privilege of the Aaronide priests. "The citation of the blessing in Numbers not only involved a re-contextualization of its use in oral performance by the priests to the realm of a text, but also an important step in solidifying its connection to the sons of Aaron and the religious rituals that they carried out at the temple in Jerusalem."[59] This is an important aspect of textualization, but I wonder whether the function is to restrict the powers of blessing to the Aaronide priesthood (in contrast to the provision and assignment of the Levites in Deut 10:8). This becomes clear if we ask: who are these Aaronides? Priestly duties and office in the Pentateuch are assigned to the very small company "Aaron and Sons Ltd.," consisting (after the death of Nadab and Abihu, Lev 10) of Aaron, his son Eleazar, his brother Ithamar, and Aaron's grandson Phinehas. This small circle of the Aaron-Eleazar-Phinehas-line provides the candidate for the high priestly office (khn gdwl), which is a lifetime ministry (Num 35:25, 28, 32). The Pentateuch has no succession law that reaches beyond the Aaronides for this office.[60] The Aaronides are not a real existing group in Second Temple Judaism. They are rather a fictive genealogical construct to integrate *various lines* of priestly ancestry, notwithstanding the fact that there may be historical roots of the Aaronide priesthood in Bethel or wherever.[61] To make a long story short, the construct of Aaronides enables various groups to claim legitimacy in priesthood.

Following the line of interpretation above, the textualization of the priestly benediction would signify not only that the priests are authorized to use the blessing formula or formulae mentioned in the text but also that these formulae are authorized as the legitimate form of the blessing. The construction in

58. See Barkay, *Amulets*, 41–71.
59. Smoak, *Priestly Blessing*, 87–88.
60. See C. Frevel, "Ending with the High Priest: The Hierarchy of Priests and Levites in the Book of Numbers," in *Torah and the Book of Numbers*, ed. C. Frevel, T. Pola, and A. Schart, FAT 2/62 (Tübingen: Mohr Siebeck, 2013), 138–63 at 145–47.
61. See E. Otto, "Gab es 'historische' und 'fiktive' Aaroniden im Alten Testament?," *Zeitschrift für altorientalische und biblische Rechtsgeschichte* 7 (2001): 403–13; J. W. Watts, "Scripturalization and the Aaronide Dynasties," *JHebS* 13 (2013): 1–15; K. Koenen, "Aaron/Aaroniden," *Das Wissenschaftliche Bibellexikon im Internet*, http://www.bibelwissenschaft.de/stichwort/11012.

Numbers allocates a blessing at the sanctuary performed by priests, no more but also no less.[62] The textualization allegedly formed a new ritual with the Aaronide priests as ritual agents and the tent of meeting as the site where the ritual takes place. By relating to this ritual, actual practice can be legitimized and authorized. Whether the actual practice corresponded in every aspect and exact wording is not decisive. Much more important is to relate to this authoritative practice of blessing. By designating the variable practice as application of the authoritative blessing in the text, identity is construed. This brings us back to the function of the textualization of biblical rituals that we will discuss further in the section below.

8.7. Ritual and Orthodoxy and the Integrative Function of Rituals

While in earlier discussions Judaism was conceptualized from a single orthodox standpoint and schismatic secessions—be it the community attested in Elephantine, the Babylonian Jews, the Nabu-YHW-group of Makkeda, the Transjordanian "Jews," the Samaritans, or later on the Qumran community and other groups—recent discussion on plurality and diversity in early Judaism has evinced a different picture. I coined the term "interfering formation" ("*interferente Formation*"[63]) to express the discourse and variety of Judaism(s) in the Second Temple period. There is no orthodoxy even if we tend to see it in the dominant tradition of the Jerusalemites. We can assume that the Samaritan Torah did not descend out of a schism but rather existed side by side already in the Persian period. Although we cannot yet reify the process of negotiating Torah(s), from Qumran it is more or less plausible that there was not a single Torah but rather pre-Samaritan, Samarian, Judean, etc. versions. These were interdependent on various levels and in various ways. There is not a single *Torah* and not a single *Judaism* either. Even if they only differ in minor details, these various forms of the same Torah are the "overlay" of diversity. What then is the

---

62. The role of the priestly benediction in the Samaritan tradition can be seen in the Aramaic Midrash Memar Marqa MM III 59:22–23: "The High Priest has ten prerogatives by which he is distinguished above his brethren—he is pure, free of defilement, anointed, (specially) vested, gives the great Blessing (וירבך ברכתה רברבתה), begins and ends (in worship), gives judgement, and dwells in the holy place." Translation: J. MacDonald, *Mamar Marqah: The Teaching of Marqah*, 2 vols. (Berlin: Verlag Alfred Töpelmann, 1963), 2:93. H. G. Kippenberg (*Garizim und Synagoge: Traditionsgeschichtliche Untersuchungen zur samaritanischen Religion der aramäischen Periode*, Religionsgeschichtliche Versuche und Vorarbeiten 30 [Berlin: de Gruyter, 1971], 224) argued that this is the Aaronide blessing because of MM VI 137.31.

63. C. Frevel, "Alte Stücke—späte Brücke? Zur Rolle des Buches Numeri in der jüngeren Pentateuchdiskussion," in *Congress Volume Munich 2013*, ed. C. M. Maier, VTSup 163 (Leiden: Brill, 2014), 255–99 at 269.

function of rituals within the Torah, if this holds true? To answer this question I want to stick to Bell once again.

Ritual practice is a means of social differentiation *and* unification. Regardless of the level of orthopraxy *all different groups* (e.g., Judahites, Samarians, Aramaeans of Elephantine) relate to a common set of ritual. Bell considers the structuring power of rituals as "a strength in that the relative flexibility of the ritual tradition allows it to travel, adapt, and speak to other cultural groups."[64]

To put it differently: rituals have an integrating, homogenizing function, and this may be *one* function of rituals in biblical literature, especially if there is a set of rituals on which different groups in general agree: the Torah. They do not cover the entire ritual practice of the "official" cult and they do not record the ritual practice in an invariable rigid and fixed way but rather allow variance and diversity in actual practice. All ritual practitioners relate each other to this "tradition" as a sort of minimal consensus. The principle can be demonstrated with another example: all Christian communities practice the communion in one way or the other based on the words of the institutions and witnesses of early Christianity, but the theological understanding of the ritual practice between Catholics, Reformed, Lutherans, Orthodox, Calvinists, etc. varies a lot. As the Eucharist is a homogenizing factor of all Christian communities despite ritual differences and theological understanding in particular, it is the rituals prescribed and described in the Torah that unify all postexilic denominations such as Judahites, Samarians, or Aramaeans of Elephantine, etc. Sectarianism is not only a phenomenon that is due to schismatic developments beyond the fourth century BCE in pre-Hellenistic Judaism. It is rather present in the earliest stages of formation of Judaism in the sixth/fifth century BCE. It is variance and diversity that forms Judaism from the first phase on, and this is the dynamic of emergence of what we may call "early Judaisms."

Rituals take part in the dynamics of tradition. Textualized tradition is not identical with ritual practice but has ramifications for ritual practice. One of the most obvious aspects is a controlling function of textualization: "Ritual practice is deemed most correct and effective if it conforms to these normative guidelines."[65] Having said that, the contrary has to be taken into account simultaneously: on the one hand, tradition authorizes ritual practice; on the other hand, it enables a mental reference to tradition that unchains the ritual practice from its literal prescription. Bell states, "[a]s writing redefines a tradition's locus of socioreligious authority, ritual is no longer a matter of doing what it seems people have always done; it becomes the correct performance or enactment

64. Bell, *Ritual*, 194.
65. Ibid., 204.

of the textual script."⁶⁶ This understanding confines rituals to be performed without variance, but one may wonder whether the essential function of scripturalization is paradoxically different: contrary to the common understanding, the "ritual script" can become part of a common denominator of behavior that opens up ample scope of variance instead of restricting it to strict observance. This (the written ritual) is the ritual we perform (common denominator), but in fact we perform it differently (actual practice). Usually all considerations take their starting point in the relation of the biblical text to *one* ritual practice. This assumption may be challenged by the fact that the same ritual text may relate to various ritual practices. The rituals performed in the Qumran community were not congruent with the Jerusalemite temple cult, but they both relate to the *same* text. The outcome of the text is not invariance but diversity. All the more one has to admit that Elephantine or Samaritan practice relates to the Torah in the same manner than the Jerusalemite priesthood does. To put it differently, the variety of practice is confined only in a minor degree by the biblical text. The biblical text forms, if at all, the framework of ritual practice.⁶⁷ In contrast to former models that explained the ritual density as either a sequentially grown collection of traditional rituals or as a collection emanating from a documentary interest—that is, to *fix* the wording *and* to standardize the ritual performance—the model suggested in this essay employs the integrating function of selected rituals as background of the set of rituals in the book of Numbers. To put it straight and pointed, the concern of textualization of rituals is to *enable variance* rather than to confine it. The paradox facilitation of variance by scripturalization gives way to an explanation why textual rituals in the Bible are never complete and provide no ritual scripts. There is no biblical ritual that is completely reported or without possible vacancies in ritual agency, ritual media, ritual action, or intention. Some are more and some are less concrete, some cannot be performed on the basis of the OT information either. The fact that biblical rituals are mostly incomplete and that they are *no* ritual scripts to be performed step by step may corroborate this idea, which seems sophisticated only at first sight.

In my view, the embodiment of ritual practice in tradition opens room for innovation and alteration. Bell emphasizes the homogenizing or centralizing role of textualization: "The textualization of ritual, that is, the emergence of authoritative textual guidelines, can be linked to a number of other developments as well, such as the ascendancy of increasingly universal formulations of values over more local and particularistic formulations; the organization of larger,

---

66. Ibid.
67. Qumran can be used as a comparative example, although we do not know very much about ritual practice in Qumran apart from the textual tradition. At the very most we can press the water installations to purity rituals, but we have no information whether other rituals, which were not tied to the temple cult, were performed in Qumran.

more centralized, and bureaucratic institutions; and the formation of notions of orthodoxy versus heterodoxy in tandem."[68] I agree, but I confine orthodoxy not to a single concrete Jerusalemite Second Temple Judaism, to which all other forms can only be compared and evaluated as heterodox. The scriptualized Torah is the real orthodoxy by the codification of dogma. "Textually based ritual can more readily forestall and control change because of the power of the authoritative text to act as a measure of deviance."[69] Hence, the textualization of ritual "can lead to tensions between a centralized liturgical tradition that abides by written norms and local ritual life that maintains continuity with oral customs."[70] It may also be possible that there is no real center or centralized practice that forms orthodoxy against local heterodoxy. The tradition is the lay-out of orthodoxy that is not embodied in the Jerusalemite practice either. In this understanding the situation of Samarians/Samaritans and Judahites/Yehûdites relying more or less on the same set of traditions becomes obvious. Within this process the vague biblical ritual is part of the process. Rituals have an integrating, homogenizing function.

8.8. The Torah Enables Community and Diversity as an Identity Reservoir

This essay has put forward the idea that textualization of rituals is not only a means of preservation and demarcation by setting the limits of variance. I have shown that scripturalization of rituals in biblical texts does not transform variable practice into invariant and fixed actions that must be repeated without any change. On the contrary, they allow diversity and variance precisely because they are incomplete, dependent on narrative contexts, and often vague in details. Particular practice can refer to the biblical rituals by arguing "we do as prescribed in the Torah" although in the individual case the concrete practice may vary.

I have identified the field of rituals to be part of the formation of the Torah as an identity reservoir for different groups in the nascent phase of early Judaisms. I would like to emphasize again that this is not meant as attributing a sort of neutral agency to the Torah. In contrast, the Judean or Jerusalem bias is obvious, but rather not exclusive. As it is usually assumed that there was a discussion and reflection upon tradition in various groups in Jerusalem, one may assume discussions on various issues between the "Jews" outside of Yehûd and the Jerusalemite groups. We can only take a guess on the various negotiations, but at least there

68. Bell, *Ritual*, 204.
69. Ibid.
70. Ibid.

is a growing consensus that there were negotiations between groups.[71] Torah is a "map" and "'map is not territory'—but maps are all we possess."[72]

By accepting the new paradigm unfolded in this essay, the processes of formation and densification are much broader and encompass various fields. Let me shortly address three of them: the biblical organization of priesthood, the biblical organization of society, and the biblical organization of authority.

As was already indicated, the biblical organization of priesthood uses the Aaronides *in the Torah* to construe a fictive genealogy of priesthood, to which various lines of priests can be correlated by updating the genealogy. This can be observed for the Jerusalemite Zadokide priesthood, for instance, in 1 Chr 5:29–41 or 1 Chr 24. While the family of the Aaronides in the Torah is very small and strictly hierarchically organized, their genealogy beyond the narrative of the Pentateuch is much broader and can encompass all existing cultic office holders in Yehûd. They can all relate themselves to the eponymous biblical Aaron. The same holds true with the organization of society in the twelve-tribe system. While Judah like Jerusalem has a primacy within this system, it allows various groups to be related to the overarching quantity "Israel" that carries promises and blessing. Since there was never a territory of the "twelve tribes" and no tribal Israel as a political unit, this model becomes very compelling to understand the ideal system of a twelve-tribe unity from the fifth century BCE onward. The third aspect is the organization of authority. While Moses is stylized as distinct receiver of the revelation, the reference to Moses becomes authorizing. Since Moses is not only the individual and mediator but also implicitly a figurative substitute for the whole Torah, the reference becomes a homogenizing factor for the various communities that recognize his authority. All three examples point in the same direction, the building of a unifying *tradition*. They all have roots within the pre-Persian textual tradition but were employed deliberately in the late Persian period to function as what I have called "identity reservoir." This model has certain advantages compared to the model of the Torah as a "compromise."[73] It needs neither promulgation nor an extraneous influence nor

---

71. G. N. Knoppers (*Jews and Samaritans: The Origins and History of their Early Relations* [Oxford: Oxford University Press, 2013], 177) speaks of "a history of intermittent cooperation between Judean and Samarian and Samarian scribes over a considerable period of time prior to the Maccabean expansion"; compare Hensel, *Juda und Samaria*, 163–94, and, for later Hellenistic times, A. Shemesh, *Halakhah in the Making: The Development of Jewish Law from Qumran to the Rabbis* (Berkeley: University of California Press, 2009), 72–106; and many others.

72. Smith, *Map Is Not Territory*, 309.

73. See for the introduction of this term the overview in Hensel, *Juda und Samaria*, 187–93. Hensel accurately criticizes most of the former approaches as being intra-Judean oriented (different positions within Yehûd) rather than inter-Judaic (different positions of variating Judaism inside and outside of Yehûd). For former criticism of the compromise model, see C. Frevel, *Im Lesen verstehen*, BZAW 482 (Berlin: de Gruyter, 2016), 27–28, 93–95. Not *the single* Torah *as result* is a compromise, but the multiple Torahs enable various forms of Yahwism by taking the shared communalities as identity reservoir.

even impulse by the Persian authority; it is not tied to the fifth century BCE, and it is not focused on Yehûd but on the broader network of traditions within Judaisms. On the one hand, the Torah homogenizes various existing traditions by preservation, definition, and fixation. On the other hand, the same Torah enables diversity and variance. This function includes the performative dimension, which is represented in the set of rituals. Strikingly enough, all of the mentioned aspects (priesthood, leadership, society, unity, Mosaic Torah) crystallize in a specific manner in the book of Numbers. From this angle it is no surprise that ritual plays a major role in the book of Numbers. The ritual density in the book of Numbers is part of the interfering formation of various groups that all relate themselves to the Torah as foundational document.

BIBLIOGRAPHY

Aḥituv, S. "A Rejoinder to Nadav Na'aman's 'A New Appraisal of the Silver Amulets from Ketef Hinnom.'" *IEJ* 62.2 (2012): 223–32.
Barchiesi, A., J. Rüpke, and S. Stephens, eds. *Rituals in Ink: A Conference on Religion and Literary Production in Ancient Rome.* Potsdamer Altertumswissenschaftliche Beiträge 10. Munich: Franz Steiner Verlag, 2004.
Barkay, G. "The Priestly Benediction on Silver Plaques from Ketef Hinnom in Jerusalem." *TA* 19 (1992): 139–92.
Barkay, G., M. J. Lundberg, A. G. Vaughn, and B. Zuckerman. "The Amulets from Ketef Hinnom: A New Edition and Evaluation." *BASOR* 334 (2004): 41–71.
Barkay, G., M. J. Lundberg, A. G. Vaughn, B. Zuckerman, and K. Zuckerman. "The Challenges of Ketef Hinnom: Using Advanced Technologies to Reclaim the Earliest Biblical Texts and Their Context." *Near Eastern Archaeology* 66.4 (2003): 162–71.
Bell, C. *Ritual: Perspectives and Dimensions.* 2nd ed. Oxford: Oxford University Press, 2009.
Bendlin, A. "Ritual. I. Term." In *Brill's New Pauly: Antiquity Volumes.* Edited by H. Cancik and H. Schneider. Brill Online, 2016. http://referenceworks.brillonline.com/entries/brill-s-new-pauly/ritual-e1023450.
Berlejung, A. "Der gesegnete Mensch: Text und Kontext von Num 6,22–27 und den Silberamuletten von Ketef Hinnom." Pages 37–62 in *Mensch und König: Studien zur Anthropologie des Alten Testaments; Rüdiger Lux zum 60. Geburtstag.* Edited by A. Berlejung and R. Heckl. Herders Biblische Studien 53. Freiburg im Breisgau: Herder, 2008.
———. "Ein Programm fürs Leben: Theologisches Wort und anthropologischer Ort der Silberamulette von Ketef Hinnom." *ZAW* 120.2 (2008): 204–30.
Bibb, B. D. *Ritual Words and Narrative Worlds in the Book of Leviticus.* LHBOTS 480. New York: T&T Clark, 2009.
Boyarin, D. "Beyond Judaisms: Meṭaṭron and the Divine Polymorphy of Ancient Judaism." *JSJ* 41 (2010): 323–65.
Daise, M. A. "Ritual Density in Qumran Practice: Ablutions in the Serekh Ha-Yahad." Pages 51–66 in *New Perspectives on Old Texts: Proceedings of the Tenth International Symposium of the Orion Center for the Study of the Dead Sea Scrolls and*

Associated Literature, 9–11 January, 2005. Edited by E. G. Chazon and B. Halpern-Amaru. STDJ 88. Leiden: Brill, 2010.

Douglas, M. *Leviticus as Literature*. Oxford: Oxford University Press, 1999.

———. *Natural Symbols: Explorations in Cosmology*. Mary Douglas Collected Works 3. London: Taylor & Francis, 2002.

Durkheim, É. *The Elementary Forms of the Religious Life*. London: George Allen & Unwin, 1915.

Freedman, D. N. *Pottery, Poetry, and Prophecy*. Winona Lake, IN: Eisenbrauns, 1980.

Frevel, C. "Alte Stücke—späte Brücke? Zur Rolle des Buches Numeri in der jüngeren Pentateuchdiskussion." Pages 255–99 in *Congress Volume Munich 2013*. Edited by C. M. Maier. VTSup 163. Leiden: Brill, 2014.

———. *Desert Transformations: Studies in the Book of Numbers*. FAT 137. Tübingen: Mohr Siebeck, 2020.

———. "Ending with the High Priest: The Hierarchy of Priests and Levites in the Book of Numbers." Pages 138–63 in *Torah and the Book of Numbers*. Edited by C. Frevel, T. Pola, and A. Schart. FAT 2/62. Tübingen: Mohr Siebeck, 2013.

———. "'Esau, der Vater Edoms' (Gen 36,9.43): Ein Vergleich der Edom-Überlieferungen in Genesis und Numeri vor dem Hintergrund der historischen Entwicklung." Pages 329–64 in *The Politics of the Ancestors: Exegetical and Historical Perspectives on Genesis 12–36*. Edited by J. Wöhrle and M. G. Brett. FAT 126. Tübingen: Mohr Siebeck, 2018.

———. *Geschichte Israels*. Kohlhammer Studienbücher Theologie 2. Stuttgart: Kohlhammer, 2016.

———. *Im Lesen verstehen. Studien zu Theologie und Exegese*. BZAW 482. Berlin: de Gruyter, 2017.

———. "Practicing Rituals in a Textual World: Ritual *and* Innovation in the Book of Numbers." Pages 129–50 in *Ritual Innovation in the Hebrew Bible and Early Judaism*. Edited by N. MacDonald. BZAW 468. Berlin: de Gruyter, 2016.

Görg, M. "Rituale." Page 366 in *Neues Bibellexikon*. Edited by M. Görg and L. Bernhard. Zürich: Benzinger, 2001.

Grabbe, L. L. "The Priests in Leviticus: Is the Medium the Message?" Pages 207–24 in *The Book of Leviticus: Composition and Reception*. Edited by R. Rendtorff and R. A. Kugler. VTSup 93. Leiden: Brill, 2003.

Gruenwald, I. *Rituals and Ritual Theory in Ancient Israel*. Leiden: Brill, 2003.

Heeßel, N. P. "Amulette und 'Amulettform': Zum Zusammenhang von Form, Funktion und Text von Amuletten im Alten Mesopotamien." Pages 53–77 in *Erscheinungsformen und Handhabungen Heiliger Schriften*. Edited by J. F. Quack and D. C. Luft. Berlin: de Gruyter, 2014.

Hensel, B. *Juda und Samaria: Zum Verhältnis zweier nach-exilischer Jahwismen*. FAT 110. Tübingen: Mohr Siebeck, 2016.

Hobsbawm, E. "Introduction: Invention of Tradition." Pages 1–14 in *The Invention of Tradition*. Edited by E. Hobsbawm and T. Ranger. Cambridge: Cambridge University Press, 1983.

Kellermann, D. *Die Priesterschrift von Numeri 1,1 bis 10,10: Literarkritisch und traditionsgeschichtlich untersucht*. BZAW 120. Berlin: de Gruyter, 1970.

Kippenberg, H. G. *Garizim und Synagoge: Traditionsgeschichtliche Untersuchungen zur samaritanischen Religion der aramäischen Periode*. Religionsgeschichtliche Versuche und Vorarbeiten 30. Berlin: de Gruyter, 1971.

Koenen, K. "Aaron/Aaroniden. " *Das Wissenschaftliche Bibellexikon im Internet.* http://www.bibelwissenschaft.de/stichwort/11012.

Knoppers, G. *Jews and Samaritans: The Origins and History of Their Early Relations.* Oxford: Oxford University Press, 2013.

———. "Parallel Torahs and Inner-Scriptural Interpretation: The Jewish and Samaritan Pentateuchs in Historical Perspective." Pages 507–31 in *The Pentateuch: International Perspectives on Current Research.* Edited by T. B. Dozeman, K. Schmid, and B. J. Schwartz. FAT 78. Tübingen: Mohr Siebeck, 2011.

Leitao, D. D. "Ritual? What Ritual?" Pages 149–53 in *Rituals in Ink: A Conference on Religion and Literary Production in Ancient Rome.* Edited by A. Barchiesi. Munich: Franz Steiner Verlag, 2004.

Leuenberger, M. *Segen und Segenstheologien im alten Israel: Untersuchungen zu ihren religions- und theologiegeschichtlichen Konstellationen und Transformationen.* ATANT 90. Zürich: Theologischer Verlag Zürich, 2008.

Liss, H. "Kanon und Fiktion. Zur literarischen Funktion biblischer Rechtstexte." *BN* 121 (2004): 7–38.

Macdonald, J. *Memar Marqah: The Teaching of Marqah.* 2 vols. Alfred Töpelmann: Berlin, 1963.

Milgrom, J. *Cult and Conscience: The Asham and the Priestly Doctrine of Repentance.* Brill: Leiden, 1976.

———. *Leviticus 1–16: A New Translation with Introduction and Commentary.* AB 3A. New York: Doubleday, 1991.

———. *Numbers: The Traditional Hebrew Text with the New JPS Translation.* JPS Torah Commentary. Philadelphia: Jewish Publication Society, 1990.

Na'aman, N. "A New Appraisal of the Silver Amulets from Ketef Hinnom." *IEJ* 61.2 (2011): 184–95.

Nihan, C. *From Priestly Torah to Pentateuch: A Study in the Composition of the Book of Leviticus.* FAT 2/25. Tübingen: Mohr Siebeck, 2007.

———. "The Torah Between Samaria and Judah: Shechem and Gerizim in Deuteronomy and Joshua." Pages 187–223 in *The Pentateuch as Torah: New Models of Understanding Its Promulgation and Acceptance.* Edited by G. Knoppers and B. L. Levinson. Winona Lake, IN: Eisenbrauns, 2007.

Nünning, V., J. Rupp, and G. Ahn, eds. *Ritual and Narrative: Theoretical Explorations and Historical Case Studies.* Bielefeld: Transcript, 2013.

Otto, E. "Gab es 'historische' und 'fiktive' Aaroniden im Alten Testament?" *Zeitschrift für altorientalische und biblische Rechtsgeschichte* 7 (2001): 403–14.

Renz, J. *Die althebräischen Inschriften.* 2 vols. Darmstadt: Wissenschaftliche Buchgesellschaft, 1995.

Satlow, M. L. *Creating Judaism: History, Tradition, Practice.* New York: Columbia University Press, 2006.

Schmidt, B. B. *The Materiality of Power: Explorations in the Social History of Early Israelite Magic.* FAT 105. Tübingen: Mohr Siebeck, 2016.

———. "The Social Matrix of Early Judean Magic and Divination: From 'Top Down' or 'Bottom Up'?" Pages 179–93 in *Beyond Hatti.* Edited by B. J. Collins and P. Michalowski. Atlanta: Lockwood Press, 2013.

Schniedewind, W. "Scripturalization in Ancient Judah." Pages 305–23 in *Contextualizing Israel's Sacred Writings: Ancient Literacy, Orality, and Literary Production.* Edited by B. B. Schmidt. Atlanta: Society of Biblical Literature, 2015.

Seebass, H. *Numeri 1,1–10,10*. BKAT 4/1. Neukirchen-Vluyn: Neukirchener Verlag, 2012.
Shemesh, A. *Halakhah in the Making: The Development of Jewish Law from Qumran to the Rabbis*. Berkeley: University of California Press, 2009.
Smith, J. Z. *Imagining Religion: From Babylon to Jonestown*. Chicago: University of Chicago Press, 1982.
———. *Map Is Not Territory: Studies in the History of Religions*. Leiden: Brill, 1975.
Smoak, J. D. *The Priestly Blessing in Inscription and Scripture: The Early History of Numbers 6:24–26*. Oxford: Oxford University Press, 2015.
Watts, J. W. *Ritual and Rhetoric in Leviticus: From Sacrifice to Scripture*. Cambridge: Cambridge University Press, 2007.
———. "Scripturalization and the Aaronide Dynasties." *JHebS* 13 (2013): 1–15.

CHAPTER 9

Speaking with a Divine Voice: The Rhetoric of Epistolary Performance in Numbers 6:22–27

Jeremy D. Smoak

IN THE PRESENT ESSAY, I FOCUS upon the literary coherence of Num 6:22–27 by comparing its vocabulary and syntax to the messenger formula in several Iron Age Hebrew letters. I argue that the priestly blessing is ritual instruction that served to persuade and affect audiences who would have experienced it as part of the larger ritual rhetoric of Torah. The use of the epistolary formula in the instructions for the priestly blessing marked it as a divine speech from Yahweh to Israel, which was performed by a priestly messenger. The use of the letter genre *Vorlage* also enacted a chain of authority that established a connection between this blessing, the priesthood, and the revelation of Yahweh at Sinai. I show that the use of epistolary metalanguage marked the instructions that accompany the blessing as a scribal-textual work and reified the authority of the blessing in the realm of secondary orality. By formulating the instructions as a messenger performance speech, Num 6:22–27 located scribalism within the chain of authority. The instructions index the priestly scribe's silent presence and performance within the chain of revelatory authority. Where, formerly, Yahweh spoke to Moses who spoke to Aaron who spoke to Israel, the letterform implicitly included the authority of the priest-scribe within this chain.

9.1. The Priestly Blessing and the Search for the Rituals Behind the Torah

The most well-known blessing in biblical tradition is the so-called priestly blessing of Num 6:22–27.[1] The first part of the literary unit identifies the blessing

---

I would like to thank William Schniedewind and Alice Mandell for their comments on this piece. Any remaining errors are solely mine.

1. The literature on Num 6:22–27 is voluminous; for the most recent discussions, see especially J. D. Smoak, *The Priestly Blessing in Inscription and Scripture: The Early History of Numbers 6:22–27* (Oxford: Oxford University Press, 2015); J. D. Smoak, "From Temple to Text: Text as Ritual

as part of the revelation that Yahweh spoke to Moses at Sinai. Verses 23b–27 describe the instructions given to Aaron and future priestly generations for blessing the Israelites. This context defines the blessing as an utterance that the sons of Aaron shall "say" to the Israelites.[2] However, it also creates a chain of authority that traces its authoritative power from Yahweh's revelation at Sinai to the priesthood.

The instructions that cite the blessing include formal markers that differentiate divine, prophetic, and priestly speech: Yahweh speaks to Moses, Moses speaks to Aaron, and Aaron and his sons speak to the Israelites.[3] This literary "chain of command" frames the blessing and situates its authority as part of the ritual instructions of Sinai. There are three frames or levels of discourse in the verses: metalanguage about talking, instructions, and the actual blessing:

v. 22 Yahweh *spoke to* Moses, *saying*:
v. 23 *Speak to* Aaron and to his sons, *saying*, "Thus you shall bless the Israelites: You *shall say* to them,
v. 24 May Yahweh bless you and keep you;
v. 25 May Yahweh make his face to shine upon you, and be gracious to you;
v. 26 May Yahweh lift up his countenance upon you, and give you peace.
v. 27 So they shall put my name on the Israelites, and I will bless them

The lead up to the actual blessing in verses 22–23 emphasizes that the blessing was part of the oral instructions that Yahweh gave to Moses. There is an implicit distancing framework as this text presents itself as a completed unit that is meant as a model for future generations after Aaron and his sons. Yahweh then

---

Space and the Composition of Numbers 6:24–26," *JHebS* 17 (2017): 1–27, doi:10.5508/jhs.2017.v17.a2; H. Seebass, "YHWH's Name in the Aaronic Blessing (Num 6:22–27)," in *The Revelation of the Name YHWH to Moses: Perspectives from Judaism, the Pagan, Graeco-Roman World, and Early Christianity*, ed. G. H. van Kooten, Themes in Biblical Narrative 9 (Leiden: Brill, 2006), 37–54; S. Chavel, "The Face of God and the Etiquette of Eye-Contact: Visitation, Pilgrimage, and Prophetic Vision in Ancient Israelite and Early Jewish Imagination," *Jewish Studies Quarterly* 19 (2012): 1–55; J. Milgrom, *Numbers: The Traditional Hebrew Text with the New JPS Translation*, JPS Torah Commentary (Philadelphia: Jewish Publication Society, 1990), 362–67; K. Seybold, *Der aaronitische Segen* (Neukirchen: Neukirchen-Vluyn, 1977); M. C. A. Korpel, "The Poetic Structure of the Priestly Blessing," *JSOT* 45 (1989): 3–13; D. N. Freedman, "The Aaronic Benediction (Numbers 6.24–26)," in *No Famine in the Land: Studies in Honor of J. L McKenzie*, ed. J. L. Flanagan (Atlanta: Scholars Press, 1975), 35–48; M. Fishbane, "Form and Reformulation of the Biblical Priestly Blessing," *JAOS* 103 (1983): 115–21; C. Cohen, "The Biblical Priestly Blessing (Num. 6:24–26) in the Light of Akkadian Parallels," *TA* 20 (1993): 228–38; O. Loretz, "Altorientalischer Hintergrund sowie inner- und nachbiblische Entwicklung des aaronitischen Segens (Num 6.24–26)," *UF* 10 (1978): 115–19.

2. B. A. Levine, *Numbers 1–20: A New Translation with Introduction and Commentary*, AB 4A (New York: Doubleday, 1993), 227.

3. R. P. Knierim and G. W. Coats, *Numbers* (Grand Rapids, MI: Eerdmans, 2005), 94.

addresses Moses, who speaks to the sons of Aaron in the second person: Yahweh spoke to Moses, saying: "*Speak* to Aaron and his sons, saying, Thus *you shall bless* the Israelites: *You shall say* to them . . ."[4] The second part of the instructions details how the priests are to bless Israel: "So they shall put my name on the Israelites, and I will bless them" (v. 27).[5] In contrast to verses 22–23, the sons of Aaron are referred to in the third person, "Aaron and his sons." This ends with a first-person declaration by Yahweh, who resumes speech, "and *I will bless* them."[6] In this unit, then, there is an omniscient narrative frame that cues the stage directions (v. 22), the present narrative (Yahweh and Moses [23a; 27]), and a future frame (Aaron and his sons [23b–26]).

The interest of many studies on these verses lies in the origins of the blessing as an oral, performative statement that was spoken by priests.[7] Most studies analyze the instructions with the assumption that the blessing in verses 24–26 preserves a strand or tradition that dates earlier than the P material into which it has been placed. Such form critical approaches argue that the blessing represents a relic or echo of priestly ritual from the preexilic temple. While there is no substantial reason to doubt this, such a perspective typifies much of the past century's approach to the priestly material of the Torah. Many studies in the past century viewed the ritual texts of the Torah as a window into ancient Israel's cult.[8] That is, they saw much of the P material as a collection and codification of ancient Israel's ritual practice.[9]

---

4. Ibid., 93.

5. For a discussion of the meaning of this verse, see P. A. H. de Boer, "Numbers vi.27," *VT* 32 (1982): 3–13; M. Bar-Ilan, "So Shall They Put My Name Upon the People of Israel" (Hebrew), *Hebrew Union College Annual* 60 (1989): 19–31; M. Bar-Ilan, "Jewish Magical Body-Inscriptions in the First and Second Centuries" (Hebrew), *Tarbiz* 57 (1988): 37–50; S. Jacobs, "The Body Inscribed: A Priestly Initiative?," in *The Body in Biblical, Christian, and Jewish Texts*, ed. J. E. Taylor, Library of Second Temple Studies (London: T&T Clark, 2014), 1–16; Milgrom, *Numbers*, 52; Levine, *Numbers 1–20*, 228; M. Noth, *Numbers*, OTL (Philadelphia: Westminster, 1968), 57–59.

6. For discussion of the first-person form in v. 27, see Seebass, "YHWH's Name," 38; Smoak, *Priestly Blessing*, 87; Knierim and Coats, *Numbers*, 94; de Boer, "Numbers vi.27," 3–13.

7. See the many statements in the commentaries that the text of Num 6:22–27 preserves an earlier strand of Israelite ritual. The view of G. B. Gray typifies this approach: "While it formed part of P, there neither has been nor can be much doubt felt that it was not composed by P, and that it is, consequently, of earlier origin than the date of its incorporation in P" (*A Critical and Exegetical Commentary on Numbers*, ICC [New York: Scribner's Sons, 1920], 71). See also the remarks by Knierim and Coats: "Several factors . . . indicate that it is older than the priestly work and was adopted by the priestly writers as an existing and probably already paradigmatic liturgical formula, integrated into their work at its present place in the Sinai pericope" (*Numbers*, 96). For similar sentiments, see Milgrom, *Numbers*, 367, and Seebass, "YHWH's Name," 361.

8. J. Milgrom, *Leviticus 1–16: A Translation with Introduction and Commentary*, AB 3A (New York: Doubleday, 1991); J. Milgrom, *Leviticus 17–22: A New Translation with Introduction and Commentary*, AB 3B (New York: Doubleday, 2000).

9. For discussion, see C. Frevel, "The Book of Numbers: Formation, Composition, and Interpretation of a Late Part of the Torah: Some Introductory Remarks," in *Torah and the Book*

As a result, a considerable amount of effort was devoted to discussing the date, social location, and meaning of the rituals described in P.[10] In turn, P material was mined for what it might reveal about priestly cultic traditions during the period of the monarchy.[11] Studies saw P as an anthology of the various duties that priests carried out in temple worship at Jerusalem or at local shrines in ancient Israel and Judah.[12] Most notably, the ritual texts in Leviticus became an opportunity to uncover the "meaning" of sacrifice in ancient Israel.[13] A further goal of studying the priestly texts was to understand the "logic" of Israelite ritual against the background of Mesopotamian, Hittite, and Syrian ritual practice.[14] The difference between ritual "meaning" and ritual "text" was blurred as

---

of Numbers, ed. C. Frevel, T. Pola, and A. Schart, FAT 2/62 (Tübingen: Mohr Siebeck, 2013), 1–38; B. J. Schwartz, "Introduction: The Strata of the Priestly Writings and the Revised Relative Dating of P and H," in *The Strata of the Priestly Writings: Contemporary Debate and Future Directions*, ed. S. Shectman and J. S. Baden, ATANT 95 (Zürich: Theologischer Verlag, 2009), 1–12; M. Weinfeld, "Sabbatical Year and Jubilee in the Pentateuchal Laws and Their Ancient Near Eastern Background," in *The Law in the Bible and its Environment*, ed. T. Veijola, Publications of the Finnish Exegetical Society 51 (Göttingen: Vandenhoeck & Ruprecht, 1990), 39–62; A. Leveen, *Memory and Tradition in the Book of Numbers* (Cambridge: Cambridge University Press, 2008), 28–32.

10. For recent discussion of the dating of P and its relationship to the other strata of material in the Torah, see C. Nihan, *From Priestly Torah to Pentateuch: A Study in the Composition of the Book of Leviticus*, FAT 2/25 (Tübingen: Mohr Siebeck, 2007), 4–11; J. Stackert, *Rewriting the Torah: Literary Revision in Deuteronomy and the Holiness Legislation*, FAT 52 (Tübingen: Mohr Siebeck, 2007); E. Blum, "Issues and Problems in the Contemporary Debate Regarding the Priestly Writings," in *The Strata of the Priestly Writings: Contemporary Debate and Future Directions*, ed. S. Shectman and J. Baden, ATANT 95 (Zürich: TVZ, 2009), 31–44; D. Carr, *The Formation of the Hebrew Bible: A New Reconstruction* (Oxford: Oxford University Press, 2011), 298–303.

11. It is beyond the scope of the present study to cite all of the relevant literature; for discussion of this issue, see J. W. Watts, *Ritual and Rhetoric: From Sacrifice to Scripture* (Cambridge: Cambridge University Press, 2012), 39–46.

12. M. Haran, *Temples and Temple-Service in Ancient Israel: An Inquiry into Biblical Cult Phenomena and the Historical Setting of the Priestly School* (Winona Lake, IN: Eisenbrauns, 1985); M. Haran, "Shiloh and Jerusalem: The Origin of the Priestly Tradition in the Pentateuch," *JBL* 81.1 (1962): 14–24.

13. For discussion, see B. Bibb, *Ritual Words and Narrative Worlds in the Book of Leviticus* (London: T&T Clark, 2008), 7–9; see also D. Damrosch, *The Narrative Covenant: Transformations of Genre in the Growth of Biblical Literature* (San Francisco: Harper & Row, 1987), 5–9.

14. See J. Milgrom, *Cult and Conscience: The Asham and the Priestly Doctrine of Repentance* (Leiden: Brill, 1976); J. Milgrom, "Rationale for Cultic Law: The Case of Impurity," *Semeia* 45 (1989): 103–10; J. Milgrom, "The Changing Concept of Holiness in the Pentateuchal Codes with Emphasis on Leviticus 19," in *Reading Leviticus: A Conversation with Mary Douglas*, ed. J. F. A. Sawyer, JSOTSup 227 (Sheffield: Sheffield Academic Press, 1996), 65–75; B. A. Levine, "The Descriptive Tabernacle Texts of the Pentateuch," *JAOS* 85 (1965): 307–18; B. A. Levine, "The Descriptive Ritual Texts from Ugarit: Some Formal and Functional Features of the Genre," in *The Word of the Lord Shall Go Forth: Essays in Honor of David Noel Freedman*, ed. C. L. Meyers and M. O'Connor (Winona Lake, IN: Eisenbrauns, 1983), 17–58. For a recent critique of these approaches, see J. Klawans, "Pure Violence: Sacrifice and Defilement in Ancient Israel," *HTR* 94.2 (2001): 133–55; J. Klawans, *Purity, Sacrifice, and the Temple: Symbolism and Supersessionism in the Study of Ancient Judaism* (Oxford: Oxford University Press, 2006).

scholars saw the texts of the priestly literature as dim windows into the ancient temple. In sum, the function of the priestly ritual texts was assumed to be the codification of Israelite temple ritual.

Some scholars saw the language of the priestly blessing, however, to shine through the pale shadow of the priestly texts to provide a portal to the priestly rituals of the preexilic temple. Few studies bothered to ask how the literary shape of the ritual instructions for the blessing—*or even the blessing itself*— might have found its significance in relation to the ritual function of the Torah. This tendency has exerted an especially important influence upon the study of the priestly blessing in Num 6:22–27. Most notably, there is an effort to separate the blessing from its "priestly" frame by connecting the blessing's language to the temple and describing the instructions as part of the priestly editing of the Torah.[15] The blessing is isolated from the instructions that frame it and connected to a particular phase of the Israelite priesthood operant in the First Temple period.[16] Priority is placed upon using the text to uncover the oral background and meaning of the blessing in the First Temple period. Implicitly, then, such ritual blessings are viewed as a part of the rituals of the temple priesthood.

The discovery of two blessings inscribed on silver amulets in a Judean tomb at Ketef Hinnom heightened the search for the elusive background of the blessing.[17] These amulets are seen by many scholars as the earliest exemplars of the priestly blessing in Num 6:22–27.[18] The form-critical approach to the study of the priestly blessing and the language of these amulets reflects an attempt to conduct textual archaeology, again with the aim of unearthing vestiges of the First Temple priestly institutions.[19] Very few studies stop to consider how

---

15. See Smoak, *Priestly Blessing*, 89–110.
16. See I. Knohl, *The Sanctuary of Silence: The Priestly Torah and the Holiness School* (Minneapolis: Fortress, 1995), 85; Haran, *Temples and Temple-Service*, 84–89.
17. See G. Barkay, "The Priestly Benediction on Silver Plaques from Ketef Hinnom in Jerusalem," *TA* 19 (1992): 139–92; A. Yardeni, "Remarks on the Priestly Blessing on Two Amulets from Jerusalem," *VT* 41 (1991): 176–85; J. Renz, *Handbuch der althebräischen Epigraphik*, vol. 1, fasc. 1, *Die althebräischen Inschriften, Text und Kommentar* (Darmstadt: Wissenschaftliche Buchgesellschaft, 1995), 447–56; G. Barkay et al., "The Amulets from Ketef Hinnom: A New Edition and Evaluation," *BASOR* 334 (2004): 41–71; N. Na'aman, "A New Appraisal of the Silver Amulets from Ketef Hinnom," *IEJ* 61.2 (2011): 184–95.
18. For further discussion on the dating of the amulets and their relationship to Num 6:22–27, see S. Aḥituv, "A Rejoinder to Nadav Na'aman's 'A New Appraisal of the Silver Amulets from Ketef Hinnom'," *IEJ* 62.2 (2012): 225; A. Berlejung, "Der gesegnete Mensch: Text und Kontext von Num 6,22–27 und den Silberamuletten von Ketef Hinnom," in *Mensch und König: Studien zur Anthropologie des Alten Testaments; Rüdiger Lux zum 60. Geburtstag*, ed. A. Berlejung and R. Heckl, Herders biblische Studien 53 (Freiburg: Herder, 2008), 37–62; F. W. Dobbs-Allsopp et al., *Hebrew Inscriptions: From the Biblical Period of the Monarchy, with Concordance* (Princeton: Princeton University, 2005), 217–20.
19. See especially Na'aman, "New Appraisal," 184–95.

the characterization of the blessing *as* ritual instruction at Sinai in these verses served to bring its authority and function into the orbit of Torah.[20]

More recent studies on the ritual texts of the Torah emphasize the need to give greater attention to the ritual rhetoric of these texts and how their rhetoric related to the function of the Torah. Most notably, James W. Watts has drawn attention to the relationship between the rhetoric of the ritual texts from Leviticus and their function in secondary orality.[21] His approach starts with the observation that the texts of the Torah themselves point to their role in oral reading.[22] Several other recent studies have begun to approach the ritual texts of the Torah along similar lines, asking how the text's ritualization might have contributed to its rhetorical shaping and eventual "scripturalization.[23]

Returning to Num 6:22–27, the following contends that Watts's approach forms a heuristic tool for understanding the function that the instructions for

---

20. On the tendency to associate the ritual texts of the Torah with the temple rather than the priesthood, see the remarks by J. W. Watts, "The Torah as the Rhetoric of Priesthood," in *The Pentateuch as Torah: New Models for Understanding Its Promulgation and Acceptance*, ed. G. N. Knoppers and B. M. Levinson (Winona Lake, IN: Eisenbrauns, 2007), 320–22.

21. Watts, *Ritual and Rhetoric*; J. W. Watts, "Ritual Rhetoric in the Pentateuch: The Case of Leviticus 1–16," in *The Books of Leviticus and Numbers*, ed. T. Römer, BETL 215 (Leuven: Peeters, 2008), 305–18; J. W. Watts, "Ritual Legitimacy and Scriptural Authority," *JBL* 124 (2005): 401–17.

22. J. W. Watts, *Reading Law: The Rhetorical Shape of the Pentateuch*, The Biblical Seminar 59 (Sheffield: Sheffield Academic, 1999); J. W. Watts, "Using Ezra's Time as a Methodological Pivot for Understanding the Rhetoric and Functions of the Pentateuch," *The Pentateuch: International Perspectives on Current Research*, ed. T. B. Dozeman, K. Schmid, and B. J. Schwartz, FAT 78 (Tübingen: Mohr Siebeck, 2011), 489–506. See also J. W. Watts, *Understanding the Pentateuch as Scripture* (London: Wiley Blackwell, 2017).

23. See especially W. Bergen, *Reading Ritual: Leviticus in Postmodern Culture*, JSOTSup 417 (London: T&T Clark, 2005); W. K. Gilders, *Blood Ritual in the Hebrew Bible: Meaning and Power* (Baltimore: Johns Hopkins University Press, 2004); M. Leuchter, "The Politics of Ritual Rhetoric: A Proposed Sociopolitical Context for the Redaction of Leviticus 16," *VT* 60 (2010): 345–65; J. Newman, *Praying by the Book: The Scripturalization of Prayer in Second Temple Judaism*, EJL 14 (Atlanta: Scholars Press, 1999); B. J. Schwartz, "Prohibitions Concerning the 'Eating' of Blood in Leviticus 17," in *Priesthood and Cult in Ancient Israel*, ed. G. A. Anderson and S. M. Olyan, JSOTSup 125 (Sheffield: JSOT, 1991), 34–66; W. M. Schniedewind, "Scripturalization in Ancient Judah," in *Contextualizing Israel's Sacred Writings: Ancient Literacy, Orality, and Literary Production*, ed. B. Schmidt (Atlanta: Society of Biblical Literature, 2015), 305–21; D. Erbele-Küster, "Reading as an Act of Offering: Reconsidering the Genre of Leviticus 1," in *The Actuality of Sacrifice: Past and Present*, ed. A. Houtman et al., Jewish and Christian Perspectives 28 (Leiden: Brill, 2014), 34–46. See also the recent discussion of the rhetoric of Num 5–6 by C. Frevel, "Practicing Rituals in a Textual World: Ritual *and* Innovation in the Book of Numbers," in *Ritual Innovation in the Hebrew Bible and Early Judaism*, ed. N. MacDonald (Berlin: de Gruyter, 2016), 129–50; C. Frevel, "On Instant Scripture and Proximal Texts: Some Insights into the Sensual Materiality of Texts and their Ritual Roles in the Hebrew Bible and Beyond," *Postscripts* 8.1–2 (2012): 57–79; F. H. Gorman, *The Ideology of Ritual: Space, Time and Status in the Priestly Theology*, JSOTSup 91 (Sheffield: JSOT Press, 1990).

the blessing held as part of the ritual rhetoric of Torah. It considers how the instructions for the blessing located its authority within the rhetoric and performance of the priesthood. The instructions in these verses present the blessing as a divine speech of Yahweh to Moses at Mount Sinai. This means that our study of the blessing should begin with an emphasis upon its character as part of the divine speeches in the Sinai pericope rather than a search for a kernel of priestly ritual embedded into the text. As Watts reminds us, "*Texts are not rituals and rituals are not texts.*"[24] We might consider that the textualization of the blessing was motivated by the desire not only to preserve its cultic importance but also to locate its authority and function as part of the ritual rhetoric of the Torah. As Bergen observes, "The textualization of the ritual is balanced by the ritualization of the text.... So there is no loss of ritual, only its transformation."[25] Accordingly, in what follows I argue that we begin to study the blessing as part of the ritual instructions and performance of Torah in addition to a maker of temple ritual.

9.2. The Priestly Blessing as a Priestly Messenger Performance

The instructions for the priestly blessing are presented to the reader as a tightly crafted ritual instruction that elevates the blessing to the realm of divine speech. They are cast as oral revelation, but also as part of the authoritative written copy of that revelation. In this way, the blessing's authority derives both from the oral stream of tradition and also from its textuality as a scribal-textual product. In order to produce this tension, the instructions for the blessing blended the language of the blessing with the language of the instructions.[26] The interplay between the instructions and the blessing was structured as a series of instructions (Speak to X to Speak to Y: "Direct Quote") in order to harmonize their authority. For example, the instructions repeat specific verbs found in the blessing in verses 24–26.[27] The first verb *tbrkw* in verse 23 parallels the first verb *ybrkk* in the blessing in verse 24. The first verb in verse 27 *wśmw* parallels the last verb in the blessing in verse 26 *wyśm*. Moreover, the second clause in verse 27 repeats the language of the first clause in verse 23, thus producing a tension between the blessing as a blessing of the priests and the blessing as divine revelation. The last clause in the instructions resolves the tension with the

---

24. Watts, *Ritual and Rhetoric*, 29, emphasis original.
25. Bergen, *Reading Ritual*, 8.
26. See Fishbane, "Form and Reformulation," 118–21.
27. Knierim and Coats, *Numbers*, 93; Milgrom, *Numbers*, 51; G. B. Gray, *A Critical and Exegetical Commentary on Numbers* (Edinburgh: T&T Clark, 1956), 71–74.

first-person statement by Yahweh. Aaron and his sons say or recite the blessing and put the divine name on the sons of Israel, but it is Yahweh who blesses.[28]

By doing this, Num 6:22–27 fashioned a chain of authority for the blessing: it was *first* a divine messenger speech and *secondarily* a blessing of the priests. The first part of the instructions for the blessing in verses 22–23a forms a carefully crafted literary chain of authority that closely identifies the priestly act of blessing Israel with the divine commands of Yahweh. The verbal and syntactic rhetoric of the instructions frame the blessing as a model of both divine instruction and prophetic speech:

v. 22   PN *spoke* to PN, *saying*:
v. 23a *speak* to PN and his sons, *saying*:
v. 23b *you* shall bless the Israelites, *you* shall *say* to them:

Studies readily observe that the rhetoric of verse 22 forms a way to connect the instructions for the blessing to the wider network of divine instructions at Sinai.[29] The expression "Yahweh spoke to Moses" introduces many of the legal instructions in the Sinai pericope. The formula frames the instructions for the tabernacle in Exod 25:1–31:18 and the sacrificial legislation in Leviticus. The formula is also used throughout Num 1:1–10:10 to bind together the various strands of legislation found in these chapters (1:1; 2:1; 3:5, 11, 14, 44; 4:1, 17, 21; 5:1, 5, 11; 6:1; 6:22; 8:1; 8:23; 9:1, 9; 10:1).[30] These literary interplays and metapragmatic language suggest that the function of the instructions was not merely to frame the blessing as part of the Priestly code. Rather, this framework also served to harmonize the very linguistic fabric of the blessing with the language of divine speech at Sinai.

But the formula "*PN spoke to PN, saying*" also functions to locate the verse in the letter genre *Vorlage*. That is, while the verb "saying" in these contexts does introduce "direct speech" it denotes a speech act that has its context in the reading or performance of a letter. As William Schniedewind observes, "Although *l'mr* 'saying' often seems to just repeat the speech act already expressed in

---

28. Fishbane observes, concerning the language of v. 27, "It serves to emphasize that while the Aaronids articulate the Priestly Blessing (PB), it is YHWH alone who blesses; and second, it serves to emphasize that the core of the blessing is not simply the specification of the blessings—central as that is—but rather the ritual use of the sacred divine Name, thrice repeated. The PB is thus realized to be a series of optative expressions (e.g., 'May YHWH bless...; May YHWH brighten His countenance...; May YHWH raise His countenance...') referring to actions which YHWH, alone, will perform" ("Form and Reformulation," 115).

29. Knierim and Coats, *Numbers*, 93.

30. For a discussion of the literary organization of these chapters and the role that the formula plays as a structuring device in them, see W. Lee, "The Conceptual Coherence of Numbers 5,1–10,10," in *The Books of Leviticus and Numbers*, ed. T. Römer, BETL 215 (Leuven: Peeters, 2008), 473–90; J. C. Condren, "Is the Account of the Organization of the Camp Devoid of Organization? A Proposal for the Literary Structure of Numbers 1:1–10:10," *JSOT* 37.4 (2013): 423–52.

the narrative framing, it is actually the formal introduction to direct speech drawn out of the *Sitz im Leben* of messenger formulas and the letter genre."[31] In sum, the syntax *'l PN l'mr* in verse 22 resembles and indexes scribal epistolary discourse.[32]

9.3. The Chain of Authority in Epistolary Discourse

One of the main functions of the introduction of Iron Age letters was the indexing of social hierarchies, as Ben Thomas has observed.[33] The descriptions of addressees in the letters served to demarcate social status and chains of authority. As Thomas explains, "It was the frequent custom of ancient Israelite society to acknowledge the social status of the addressee, whether explicitly or implicitly, a feature also known in the Bible and probably in spoken language, too."[34] By including the addressees (*'l + PN*), the instructions for the blessing located the authority of the blessing within the realm of priestly ritual. The instructions are presented as a message from Yahweh to Aaron and his sons. Aaron and his sons were the recipients of divine revelation. Hence, by using the opening part of the letter genre in these verses the scribe found a way to present the blessing as a *priestly blessing*.

The patterning of the verbs in verses 22–23 constitutes an important element in the creation of a chain of authority in the rhetoric of the instructions. Verse 22 narrates Yahweh's instruction to Moses and introduces Yahweh's instruction as direct speech using the verbs "spoke" + "saying." Verse 23a describes the contents of the direct speech by Yahweh. Yahweh's direct speech repeats the pattern of "speak" + "saying." So, Yahweh's direct speech repeats the narrative introduction. Hence it is more correct to speak of the oral instruction repeating the scribal formula. A scribal formula introduces and describes the divine speech and then the divine speech is modeled after the scribal formula. Yahweh's direct speech also introduces a second instance of direct speech, in this

---

31. See W. M. Schniedewind, *The Finger of the Scribe: How Scribes Learned to Write the Bible* (Oxford: Oxford University Press, 2019).

32. For further on the background of the epistolary form in the ancient Near East, see D. Schwiderski, *Handbuch des nordwestsemitischen Briefformulars: Ein Betrag zur Echtheitsfrage des aramäischen Briefe des Esrabuches*, BZAW 295 (Berlin: De Gruyer, 2000); R. Hawley, "Studies in Ugaritic Epistolography" (PhD diss., University of Chicago, 2003); J. Fitzmyer, "Some Notes on Aramaic Epistolography," *JBL* 93.2 (1974): 201–25.

33. B. Thomas, "The Language of Politeness in Ancient Hebrew Letters," *Hebrew Studies* 50 (2009): 17–39. For further information on the introduction to letters, see also B. Estelle, "The Use of Deferential Language in the Arsames Correspondence and Biblical Aramaic Compared," *Maarav* 13.1 (2006): 67–81; I. Beit-Arieh and B. Cresson, "An Edomite Ostracon from Horvat 'Uza," *TA* 12 (1985): 96–101; Fitzmyer, "Some Notes," 201–25.

34. Thomas, "Language of Politeness," 20.

case a command directed to Aaron and his sons. According to verse 23, Moses represents the link in authority between Yahweh and the priesthood.

Verse 23b alters the verbal patterning slightly from "speak" + "saying" to "bless" + "say." This shift in the pattern of the verbs serves to create a disjuncture that draws attention to the relationship between the blessing ("bless") and divine speech ("speak"). Yahweh and Moses "speak" and "say"; Aaron and his sons "bless" and "say." The movement from "speak" to "bless" in the pattern identifies the priestly action of blessing as the extension of divine speech. The blessing coordinates the relationship between divine speech and priestly speech. Blessing becomes the conduit through which divine revelation travels from Sinai to Israel and from the wilderness generation to all the sons of Israel. Yahweh *spoke* to Moses who *shall speak* to Aaron and his sons who *shall bless* the sons of Israel. In this way, the reference to blessing in the instructions in verse 23b does not merely introduce the blessing that follows in verses 24–26. It defines the blessing as the priestly extension of the revelation at Sinai.

Yahweh——Moses——Aaron and his sons——sons of Israel

The emphasis that the instructions place upon the role of the priesthood in the chain of authority is all the more noticeable when compared to the narrative frames that introduce the surrounding laws. For instance, the law of the Nazarite is introduced by the following formula: "Yahweh spoke to Moses, saying: Speak to the Israelites and say to them ..." (6:1). A similar formula introduces the laws in chapter 5: "Yahweh spoke to Moses, saying: Command the Israelites ..." (5:1–2a); "Yahweh spoke to Moses, saying: Speak to the Israelites ..." (5:5–6a); "Yahweh spoke to Moses, saying: Speak to the Israelites and say to them ..." (5:11–12). The significance of the command for Moses to speak to Aaron and his sons comes into sharper focus against the formulation of the divine commands in these verses. Only in the instructions for the priestly blessing does Moses speak *to Aaron and his sons* and not directly to the Israelites. The addition of the command for Moses to speak to Aaron and his sons places the priesthood within the chain of revelation at Sinai and authorizes the priesthood as the messengers of divine speech.

At the same time, the repeated use of imperatives draws attention to the fact that verses 23–27 are all *divine speech*. While the instructions created a ritual chain of authority for the *future* ("you shall") giving of the blessing, both the instructions *and* the blessing are described here as divine speech. Verse 22 narrates Yahweh's speaking to Moses and verse 27 ends with a first-person statement by Yahweh. In the context of the Sinai revelation the priestly blessing is first a divine blessing. This fact locates the authority of *priestly* blessing in the realm of *divine* speech. The priestly *saying* of the blessing performs the divine *speaking* of the blessing. It is a saying of the blessing, but more importantly a divine reenactment of it. The significance of this rhetoric in legitimating the ritual authority of the sons of Aaron is hard to overstate. As Horst Seebass emphasizes, "The importance of vv. 23–27 is shown by the fact that they are an express revelation of YHWH to Moses.... This is all the more astonishing as we find no prayers and only few words of God in the rituals of Lev 1–9 and 16 up to Num 6 as if the Aaronites had to watch over a 'sanctuary of silence.'"[35]

9.4. A Closer Look at Speech Inscriptions in Iron Age Letters

Some of the more common elements in the openings or introductions to Iron Age Hebrew letters include the formula *PN 'l* ("PN to"), *'mr* ("say"), *'mr 'l* ("say to"), and *l'mr* ("saying").[36] This syntax is particularly evident in the extant letter exercises from Kuntillet ʿAjrud.[37]

KAjr 18:1
'mr ' šyw hmlk 'mr lyhl[l'l] wlyw'šh w[...] brkt 'tkm lyhwh šmrn wl'šrth
Thus says Ashyah, the king, "Say to Yehal[lelel] and to Yaw'sah, [...]
    I bless you by YHWH, of Samaria, and by his Asherah."

KAjr 19:1
[']*mr 'mryhw 'mr l'dny*
(Thus) [sa]ys Amariah, "Say to my lord:"

---

35. Seebass, "YHWH's Name," 38.
36. For an overview of the syntax of the epistolary genre, see especially D. Pardee, J. D. Whitehead, and P. E. Dion, "An Overview of Ancient Hebrew Epistolography," *JBL* 97.3 (1978): 321–46; D. Pardee and R. M. Whiting, "Aspects of Epistolary Verbal Usage in Ugaritic and Akkadian," *BSOAS* 50 (1987): 1–31; F. M. Cross, "Epigraphic Notes on Hebrew Documents of the Eighth-Sixth Centuries B.C.: II. The Murabbaʿat Papyrus and the Letter Found Near Yabneh-Yam," *BASOR* 165 (1962): 36–42; J. Mynářová, *Language of Amarna—Language of Diplomacy: Perspectives on the Amarna Letters* (Prague: Czech Institute of Egyptology, 2007); J. M. Lindenberger, *Ancient Aramaic and Hebrew Letters*, 2nd ed., WAW 14 (Atlanta: Society of Biblical Literature, 2003). For a description of the form of Aramaic letters, see P. S. Alexander, "Remarks on Aramaic Epistolography in the Persian Period," *Journal of Semitic Studies* 23.2 (1978): 155–70; J. A. Fitzmyer, *A Manual of Palestinian Aramaic Texts (Second Century B.C.–Second Century A.D.)* (Rome: Biblical Institute Press, 1978).
37. Z. Meshel, *Kuntillet ʿAjrud: An Iron Age II Religious Site on the Judah-Sinai Border* (Jerusalem: Israel Exploration Society, 2012); Dobbs-Allsopp et al., *Hebrew Inscriptions*, 277–98. For further discussion of the verb or noun *'mr* in the inscriptions at Kuntillet ʿAjrud, see S. Ahituv, *Echoes from the Past: Hebrew and Cognate Inscriptions from the Biblical Period*, trans. and ed. A. F. Rainey (Jerusalem: Carta, 2008), 316–26.

The use of the verb *'mr* in these two examples locates the inscriptions within the *Sitz im Leben* of epistolary performance.[38] That is, the command to "say" in the opening of the inscriptions indexes the act of reading or performing a letter to an audience. The verb *'mr* connects the content of the message from the sender to the recipient and draws attention to the performance of the messenger as the "words" or "commands" of the sender.[39]

The syntax of the Lachish letters stands even closer to the instructions for the blessing in Num 6:22–23.[40] These letters employ the syntax *'l PN + l'mr* ("to PN, saying . . .") to introduce the contents of the message of a letter.[41] The following examples illustrate the formula:

Lachish 3:20
'l šlm bn yd' m't hnb' l'mr
To Shallum, son of Yada, from the prophet saying:

Lachish 6:4
r hmlk [w't] spry hšr[m l'm]r
King's [let]ter and the officials' letter[s, saying,]

Especially relevant here is the syntax of Lachish letter 3, which opens with the formula *'l PN* and then introduces the contents of the message from the sender with the verbal expression *l'mr* "saying."[42] The significance of this formula lies in the way that it indexes the participants in the messenger performance speech. The introduction to the letter connects the sender, the recipient, and the content of the message. The introduction of the message with the verb *l'mr* marks the message as the actual spoken words of the sender; the performance of reading

---

38. See Thomas, "Language of Politeness," 21–22.

39. For earlier examples of this syntax, see *KTU* 2.10:1–3: "Message of Iwridharri to Pilsiya say" (*thm iwrdr l plsy rgm*) (J.-L. Cunchillos, "The Ugaritic Letters," in *Handbook of Ugaritic Studies*, ed. W. G. E. Watson and N. Wyatt [Leiden: Brill, 1999], 359–74; J. Huehnergard, "The Akkadian Letters," in *Handbook of Ugaritic Studies*, ed. W. G. E. Watson and N. Wyatt [Leiden: Brill, 1999], 375–89).

40. See N. H. Torczyner, *Lachish 1: The Lachish Letters* (Oxford: Oxford University Press, 1938); H. Michaud, "Les ostraca de Lakiš conserves à Londres," *Syria* 34 (1957): 39–60; D. Pardee, *Handbook of Ancient Hebrew Letters: A Study Edition*, Sources for Biblical Studies 15 (Atlanta: Scholars Press, 1982).

41. For further on the syntax of *'l PN*, see especially M. Weippert, "Zum Präskript der hebräischen Briefe von Arad," *VT* 25 (1975): 202–12, at 206.

42. On Lachish letter 3, see W. M. Schniedewind, "Sociolinguistic Reflections on the Letter of a 'Literate' Soldier (Lachish 3)," *Zeitschrift für Althebräistik* 13 (2000): 157–66; W. Richter, "Lakiš 3—Vorschlag zur Konstituieren eines Textes," *BN* 37 (1987): 73–103; F. M. Cross, "A Literate Soldier: Lachish Letter III," in *Biblical and Related Studies Presented to Samuel Iwry*, ed. A. Kort and S. Morschauser (Winona Lake, IN: Eisenbrauns), 41–47.

the letter to the recipient is the work of an unnamed party. For this reason, this messenger formula creates a textual illusion—namely, that the sender was speaking to the recipient rather than a nameless messenger.[43]

9.5. Salutations and Blessings in Letters and in the Priestly Blessing

The use of epistolary terms in the instructions brings the significance of the request for "blessing" and "peace" in the blessing in verses 24–26 into sharper focus. Two of the more common elements in letters are an opening greeting that includes expressions of wellbeing and a blessing. Arad 16 illustrates this feature of the opening greetings of letters.[44]

> Your brother, Hananiah sends for the peace (*šlm*) of Elyashib and for the peace (*šlm*) of your house. I bless you (*brktk*) to Yahweh ...

Significantly, the opening greeting in this letter includes a reference to *šlm* "wellbeing, peace." A similar opening is found in Arad 21.

> Your son Yehokal sends for the peace (*šlm*) to Gedalyahu son of Elyair and for the peace (*šlm*) of your house, I have blessed you (*brktk*) to Yahweh, and now ...

As these examples show, the words *šlm* and *brktk* form some of the core elements of introductions in Iron Age letters.[45] This introduction to the speaker is

---

43. For further discussion of the relationship between written and oral performance in epistolary discourse, see S. Niditch, *Oral World and Written Word: Ancient Israelite Literature* (Louisville, KY: Westminster John Knox, 1996), 90–91.

44. On the Arad letters, see Weippert, "Zum Präskript"; Y. Aharoni, "Hebrew Ostraca from Tel Arad," *IEJ* 16 (1966): 1–17; Y. Aharoni, "Three Hebrew Ostraca from Arad," *BASOR* 197 (1970): 16–42; Y. Aharoni, *Arad Inscriptions*, Judean Desert Studies (Jerusalem: Israel Exploration Society, 1981); A. Lemaire, *Inscriptions hébraïques 1. Les ostraca*, LAPO 9 (Paris: Cerf, 1977), 231–35.

45. For further discussion of these terms in epistolary contexts, see especially Schwiderski, *Handbuch*, 249–50; S. Aḥituv, E. Eshel, and Z. Meshel, "The Inscriptions," in *Kuntillet 'Ajrud (Ḥorvat Teman): An Iron II Age Religious Site on the Judah-Sinai Border*, ed. Z. Meshel (Jerusalem: Israel Exploration Society, 2012), 128; A. Mandell, "'I Bless You to YHWH and His Asherah'—Writing and Performativity at Kuntillet 'Ajrud," *Maarav* 19.1–2 (2012): 131–62; Beit-Arieh and Cresson, "Edomite Ostracon," 97; Alexander, "Remarks on Aramaic Epistolography," 162. For earlier examples, see D. Owen, "An Akkadian Letter from Ugarit at Tel Aphek," *TA* 8 (1981): 1–19.

usually followed by a request for a blessing and either a wish for or a question about the wellbeing of the recipient.[46]

The examples of epistolary discourse cited above suggest that Num 6:22–27 has adapted the language of the introduction, or *praescriptio*, found in letters and reformulated it as ritual instructions for the blessing. The instructions for the blessing have been described as an epistolary correspondence between Yahweh and Israel and the priests have been identified as the messengers who will "say" the message to Israel. To be clear, the instructions are not formulated as a letter from Yahweh to Aaron and his sons. *Instead, they serve to mark the blessing as something that was read and performed before an audience.* They generate the image of a messenger standing before a person or audience reading/speaking an authoritative message. This is why the epistolary genre would have been relevant for the ritual instructions for the blessing. The instructions mark the performative authority of the blessing by describing it as a messenger performance speech that was carried out by the priesthood.[47] The instructions have projected the image of the priest-scribe as the performer of a message from Yahweh to Israel. They characterize Aaron and his sons as priest-scribes and the messengers of Yahweh who will deliver the blessing of Yahweh to the Israelites.

Also important is the way in which the epistolary form with its messenger formula indexes the dynamic relationship between scribalism and oral performance. The epistolary features index the performance of the scribe as the act of textualizing the oral message of Yahweh. The authority of the instructions derives from the scribe's act of hearing the blessing recited by Yahweh and transmitting that message in writing for another audience. This implicitly sets the unnamed scribe in the story at the moment and site of revelation. The epistolary form conveyed the idea that the deity spoke to the scribe who wrote the message so that it could be "said" (*'mr*) by the priesthood. Scribes read aloud to audiences or perhaps better they recited texts from memory.[48] The use of the

---

46. Thomas, "Language of Politeness," 24–25.

47. For more on the background of the messenger speech, see S. R. Keller, "Written Communication Between the Human and Divine Spheres in Mesopotamia and Israel," in *The Biblical Canon in Comparative Perspective: Scripture in Context IV*, ed. B. F. Batto, W. W. Hallo, and K. Lawson Younger Jr., Ancient Near Eastern Texts and Studies 11 (Lewiston, ME: Edwin Mellen, 1991), 299–313; W. L. Moran, "An Ancient Prophetic Oracle," in *Biblische Theologie und gesellschaftlicher Wandel*, ed. G. Braulik, W. Groß, and S. McEvenue (Freiburg: Herder, 1993), 252–59; J. Ross, "The Prophet as Yahweh's Messenger," in *Israel's Prophetic Heritage: Essays in Honor of James Muilenberg*, ed. B. Anderson and W. Harrelson (New York: Harper, 1962), 98–107; S. Mowinckel, "'The Spirit' and the 'Word' in the Pre-Exilic Reforming Prophets," *JBL* 53 (1934): 199–227; J. Holladay, "Assyrian Statecraft and the Prophets of Israel," in *Prophecy in Israel: Search for Identity*, ed. D. Petersen (Philadelphia: Fortress; London: SPCK, 1987), 122–43.

48. On the interplay between textuality and oral performance, see D. Carr, *Writing on the Tablet of the Heart: Origins of Scripture and Literature* (Oxford: Oxford University Press, 2005), 3–14; D. Carr, "Orality, Textuality *and* Memory," in *Contextualizing Israel's Sacred Writings: Ancient*

epistolary form marked this passage as a text that was to be read to audiences as part of the performance of *torah*. By employing scribal cues that marked the instructions as epistolary discourse, the textualization of the blessing paved the way for its authority to be located in both its orality and its textuality.[49] That is, the text was written as part of Torah in order to be read aloud before an audience.[50]

9.6. Conclusion: Performing the Priestly Blessing as Torah

In the present essay, I have drawn attention to certain literary features of the priestly blessing in order to show how its rhetoric indexed priestly performance. I have argued that the instructions marked the blessing as a priestly performance

---

Literacy, Orality, and Literary Production, ed. B. B. Schmidt (Atlanta: Society of Biblical Literature, 2015), 161–74; D. Carr, "Torah on the Heart: Literary Jewish Textuality Within Its Ancient Near Eastern Context," in *Oral-Scribal Dimensions of Scripture, Piety, and Practice: Judaism, Christianity, Islam*, ed. W. H. Kelber and P. A. Sanders (Eugene: Cascade Books, 2016), 21–48; R. F. Person Jr., "The Ancient Israelite Scribe as Performer," *JBL* 117.4 (1998): 601–9; B. Pomgratz-Leisten, "Öffne den Tafelbehälter und lies . . .': Neue Ansätze zum Verständnis des Lietratur Konzeptes in Mesopotamie," *WO* 27 (1996): 67–90; A. N. Doane, "The Ethnography of Scribal Writing and Anglo-Saxon Poetry: Scribe as Performer," *Oral Tradition* 9 (1994): 420–39.

49. See the comments on epistolary performance by K. van der Toorn in *Scribal Culture and the Making of the Hebrew Bible* (Cambridge: Harvard University Press, 2007), 91:

> The transformation of speech into scripture was not a mechanical recording in writing of the oral performance. As the scribe committed the spoken word into writing, he adapted it to meet the conventions of the written genre. In the ancient Near East the most common genre for which scribes acted as transcribers was the letter . . . Trained as they were in the niceties of the epistolary genre, the terminology and phraseology the scribes used were proper to the art of their profession as well as their person talent; their style was hardly a reflection of the rhetorical gifts of their patrons. . . . Scribes, even in their most instrumental roles, impose their style, language, and ideas on the text.

See further his citation in B. D. Sommer, *Revelation and Authority: Sinai in Jewish Scripture and Tradition*, Anchor Yale Bible Reference Library (New Haven: Yale University Press, 2015), 116–17.

50. It is beyond the scope of the present study to cite all of the relevant literature on the relationship between orality and textuality in the biblical texts. For recent discussion and summary, see especially A. Schellenberg, "A 'Lying Pen of the Scribes' (Jer 8:8)? Orality and Writing in the Formation of Prophetic Books," in *The Interface of Orality and Writing: Speaking, Seeing, Writing in the Shaping of New Genres*, ed. A. Weissenrieder and R. B. Coote, Biblical Performance Criticism 11 (Tübingen: Mohr Siebeck, 2015), 285–309; J. Schaper, "Exilic and Postexilic Prophecy and the Orality/Literacy Problem," *VT* 55 (2005): 324–42; K. van der Toorn, "From the Mouth of the Prophet: The Literary Fixation of Jeremiah's Prophecies in the Context of the Ancient Near East," in *Inspired Speech: Prophecy in the Ancient Near East; Essays in Honor of H. B. Huffmon*, ed. J. Kaltner and L. Stulman (Edinburgh: T&T Clark, 2004), 191–202; W. M. Schniedewind, *How the Bible Became a Book: The Textualization of Ancient Israel* (Cambridge: Cambridge University Press, 2004), 110–17; S. Talmon, "Oral Tradition and Written Transmission, or the Heard and the Seen Word in Judaism of the Second Temple Period," in *Jesus and the Oral Gospel Tradition*, ed. H. Wansbrough, JSOTSup 64 (Sheffield: Sheffield Academic Press, 1991), 121–58.

through the use of epistolary conventions. The use of epistolary markers in the instructions conveyed the image of the priest as the messenger of Yahweh who performed the deity's blessing before an audience. By marking the blessing as a messenger formula speech, the instructions defined the blessing's authority within the ritual parameters of priestly-scribal performance. Numbers 6:22–27 casts the blessing as something that should be performed before audiences as part of the ritual reading of *torah*. The blessing was a divine message given from Yahweh to Israel but delivered and performed by Yahweh's messengers—the sons of Aaron. The use of epistolary markers in the instructions generated an important tension between the blessing as both an oral and a written authoritative "saying." The blessing was part of the textual fabric of *torah*, but its description as a performance of the priesthood ensured that it was experienced as a reenactment of Yahweh's oral revelation to Israel at Sinai.

We might use two biblical texts that contain descriptions of priests reading texts to an audience to illustrate the points made here. The description of Jeremiah's letter to the exiles in Babylon in Jer 29 provides a helpful window into some of the conventions associated with epistolary performance. In particular, the description of the instructions to write a second letter concerning Shemaiah in verses 24–32 illustrates some of the more common features found in the letter genre.[51] Verse 24 very likely contains the actual introduction to a letter built into the narrative of this chapter:

To Shemaiah (*w'l šm'yhw*) the Nehelamite you shall say (*t'mr*), saying (*l'mr*)

As several studies have noted, this address formula closely resembles the syntax of the introductions to letters seen in the epigraphic texts from the Iron Age. Most notably, this verse contains the syntax typical of the introductions to letters: *'l PN + l'mr*.

Most studies focus upon form-critical issues in this chapter of Jeremiah. The syntax of certain parts of the chapter is compared to the syntax of Iron Age letters. But it is also significant that the chapter contains a description of the priest Zephaniah performing the letter to the Jeremiah the prophet. The relevant verses (Jer 29:29–30) read:

Zephaniah the priest read (*wyqr'*) this letter to Jeremiah the prophet, and the word of YHWH came to Jeremiah, "Send to all the exiles, saying (*l'mr*) . . ."

---

51. M. Dijkstra, "Prophecy by Letter (Jeremiah xxix 24–32)," *VT* 33 (1983): 319–22; see also W. L. Holladay, *Jeremiah 2: A Commentary on the Prophet Jeremiah Chapters 26–52* (Minneapolis: Fortress, 1989), 145–47.

The description of Zephaniah reading the letter before Jeremiah illustrates the argument that stands at the core of the present study. To be sure, there is no direct relationship between this text and the instructions for the priestly blessing. However, the description of Zephaniah's performance provides a window into the way that epistolary discourse connected the authority of orality and textuality in priestly performance. Zephaniah's "reading" bridged scribal authority and oral performance.

The description of Ezra reading the book of the law of Moses in Neh 8:3–13 also sheds light on the ritual rhetoric of Num 6:22–27.[52] The passage begins by locating the performance of reading in a specific place: "all the people gathered together into the square before the Water Gate" (v. 1). The text emphasizes that Ezra brought the text "before the assembly" and that he "read it facing the square before the Water Gate" (vv. 2–3). Verse 4 describes Ezra standing on a "wooden platform that had been made for the purpose." The following verse states that Ezra "opened the book in the sight of all the people" while he stood above them. According to verse 6, after Ezra blesses Yahweh, the people bowed their heads with their faces to the ground. In this way, the text emphasizes that the priest Ezra stood elevated above and before the people and the Levites. The text describes the locations and ritual gestures that accompanied Ezra's reading performance and establishes their relationship to religious hierarchies. Bodily movement and spatial coordination index the hierarchies involved in the performance. The people lower themselves in obeisance. They are subject to the Torah's authority because Ezra is the priestly messenger of this Torah.

Significantly, verse 7 states that the Levites "helped the people to understand the law, while the people remained in their places." The emphasis that the verse places upon "while the people remained in their places" differentiates the location of the Levites and the priests in the performance. The text generates a picture of Ezra and the priests standing above the people holding and reading the Torah, but the Levites and the people hearing it from below. In other words, the text of Neh 8 has been formulated to resemble a reenactment of the giving

---

52. It is beyond the scope of the present study to cite all of the relevant literature on this passage of Nehemiah. For recent discussion with an emphasis upon the description of the Torah therein, see especially S. Japhet, "Law and 'the Law' in Ezra-Nehemiah," in *Proceedings of the Ninth World Congress of Jewish Studies*, ed. M. Goshen-Gottstein (Jerusalem: Magnes, 1988), 99–115; G. J. Venema, *Reading Scripture in the Old Testament: Deuteronomy 9–10; 31—2 Kings 22–23—Jeremiah 36—Nehemiah 8*, trans. C. E. Smit, OtSt 48 (Leiden: Brill, 2004); T. Reinmuth, "Nehemiah 8 and the Authority of Torah in Ezra-Nehemiah," in *Unity and Disunity in Ezra-Nehemiah: Redaction, Rhetoric, Reader*, ed. M. J. Boda and P. L. Reddit (Sheffield: Sheffield Phoenix Press, 2008), 241–62; J. L. Wright, "Writing the Restoration: Compositional Agenda and the Role of Ezra in Nehemiah 8," *JHebS* 7 (2007): 19–29 at 28, doi:10.5508/jhs.2007.v7.a10.8; J. L. Wright, "Seeking, Finding and Writing in Ezra-Nehemiah," in *Unity and Disunity in Ezra-Nehemiah: Redaction, Rhetoric, Reader*, ed. M. J. Boda and P. L. Reddit (Sheffield: Sheffield Phoenix Press, 2008), 294–304. See also the essay by J. Rhyder in this volume.

of divine law at Sinai where the priest-scribe enacts this chain of authority by mediating between Yahweh's speech and the people.[53]

This passage provides a window into the ways in which the instructions for the priestly blessing worked to persuade and affect audiences who would have experienced it as part of priestly performance. According to this text, priestly performance located the authority of texts in the realm of secondary orality. Moreover, the passage emphasizes the role that such performances held in articulating and maintaining religious hierarchies. Numbers 6:22–27 achieves a similar effect but with greater brevity. The instructions locate Aaron and his sons above and before Israel as the messengers of Yahweh's revelation. The references to the face of Yahweh in the blessing orchestrate the relationship between ritual and religious hierarchy. Such verbal expressions locate the performance in the realm of the interaction between the people and the priest as they face each other. As the ones who "say" the blessing, however, the instructions locate the priests as the messengers who would stand above and face the people and deliver divine revelation from Sinai. In this way, the use of the epistolary genre allowed the instructions to create a stairway of authority that descends from Yahweh to Moses to Aaron to Aaron's sons and finally to the sons of Israel. Or, to put it another way, the chain of authority in the ritual instructions for the blessing formed a microcosm of the Sinai revelation.

As a result, the ritual rhetoric of the instructions located the authority of the blessing not only in the interaction between priest and laity but also in the translocative experience of hearing it as part of the Sinai revelation. A number of biblical texts connect the identity of the postexilic community with the description of Israel during the period of the wilderness (Exod 12:14–27; 13:3–16; Lev 19:34; Deut 29:14–16). *Torah* was framed for the postexilic community as the experience of hearing divine speeches from Sinai. The use of epistolary discourse in the instructions for the priestly blessing heightened this experience. Just as the performance of a letter bridged large spatial and temporal distances, so the performance of the blessing bridged Israel's distance from Sinai.

BIBLIOGRAPHY

Ahituv, S. *Echoes from the Past: Hebrew and Cognate Inscriptions from the Biblical Period*. Translated and edited by A. F. Rainey. Jerusalem: Carta, 2008.
———. "A Rejoinder to Nadav Na'aman's 'A New Appraisal of the Silver Amulets from Ketef Hinnom.'" *IEJ* 62.2 (2012): 223–32.

---

53. On the subject of the wilderness in postexilic discourse, see most recently P. Y. Yoo, *Ezra and the Second Wilderness* (Oxford: Oxford University Press, 2017).

Aḥituv, S., E. Eshel, and Z. Meshel. "The Inscriptions." Pages 73–142 in *Kuntillet 'Ajrud (Ḥorvat Teman): An Iron II Age Religious Site on the Judah-Sinai Border*. Edited by Z. Meshel. Jerusalem: Israel Exploration Society, 2012.

Aharoni, Y. *Arad Inscriptions*. Judean Desert Studies. Jerusalem: Israel Exploration Society, 1981.

———. "Hebrew Ostraca from Tel Arad." *IEJ* 16 (1966): 1–17.

———. "Three Hebrew Ostraca from Arad." *BASOR* 197 (1970): 16–42.

Alexander, P. S. "Remarks on Aramaic Epistolography in the Persian Period." *Journal of Semitic Studies* 23.2 (1978): 155–70.

Bar-Ilan, M. "Jewish Magical Body-Inscriptions in the First and Second Centuries" (Hebrew). *Tarbiz* 57 (1988): 37–50.

———. "So Shall They Put My Name Upon the People of Israel" (Hebrew). *Hebrew Union College Annual* 60 (1989): 19–31.

Barkay, G. "The Priestly Benediction on Silver Plaques from Ketef Hinnom in Jerusalem." *TA* 19 (1992): 139–92.

Barkay, G., A. G. Vaughn, M. J. Lundberg, and B. Zuckerman. "The Amulets from Ketef Hinnom: A New Edition and Evaluation." *BASOR* 334 (2004): 41–71.

Beit-Arieh, I., and B. Cresson. "An Edomite Ostracon from Horvat 'Uza." *TA* 12 (1985): 96–101.

Bergen, W. *Reading Ritual: Leviticus in Postmodern Culture*. JSOTSup 417. London: T&T Clark, 2005.

Berlejung, A. "Der gesegnete Mensch: Text und Kontext von Num 6,22–27 und den Silberamuletten von Ketef Hinnom." Pages 37–62 in *Mensch und König: Studien zur Anthropologie des Alten Testaments; Rüdiger Lux zum 60. Geburtstag*. Edited by A. Berlejung and R. Heckl. Herders biblische Studien 53. Freiburg: Herder, 2008.

Bibb, B. *Ritual Words and Narrative Worlds in the Book of Leviticus*. London: T&T Clark, 2008.

Blum, E. "Issues and Problems in the Contemporary Debate Regarding the Priestly Writings." Pages 31–44 in *The Strata of the Priestly Writings: Contemporary Debate and Future Directions*. Edited by S. Shectman and J. Baden. ATANT 95. Zurich: TVZ, 2009.

Boer, P. A. H. de. "Numbers vi.27." *VT* 32 (1982): 3–13.

Carr, D. *The Formation of the Hebrew Bible: A New Reconstruction*. Oxford: Oxford University Press, 2011.

———. "Orality, Textuality *and* Memory." Pages 161–74 in *Contextualizing Israel's Sacred Writings: Ancient Literacy, Orality, and Literary Production*. Edited by B. B. Schmidt. Atlanta: Society of Biblical Literature, 2015.

———. "Torah on the Heart: Literary Jewish Textuality Within Its Ancient Near Eastern Context." Pages 21–48 in *Oral-Scribal Dimensions of Scripture, Piety, and Practice: Judaism, Christianity, Islam*. Edited by W. H. Kelber and P. A. Sanders. Eugene: Cascade Books, 2016.

———. *Writing on the Tablet of the Heart: Origins of Scripture and Literature*. Oxford: Oxford University Press, 2005.

Chavel, S. "The Face of God and the Etiquette of Eye-Contact: Visitation, Pilgrimage, and Prophetic Vision in Ancient Israelite and Early Jewish Imagination." *Jewish Studies Quarterly* 19 (2012): 1–55.

Cohen, C. "The Biblical Priestly Blessing (Num. 6:24–26) in the Light of Akkadian Parallels." *TA* 20 (1993): 228–38.

Condren, J. C. "Is the Account of the Organization of the Camp Devoid of Organization? A Proposal for the Literary Structure of Numbers 1:1–10:10." *JSOT* 37.4 (2013): 423–52.

Cross, F. M. "Epigraphic Notes on Hebrew Documents of the Eighth-Sixth Centuries B.C.: II. The Murabbaʿat Papyrus and the Letter Found Near Yabneh-Yam." *BASOR* 165 (1962): 36–42.

———. "A Literate Soldier: Lachish Letter III." Pages 41–47 in *Biblical and Related Studies Presented to Samuel Iwry*. Edited by A. Kort and S. Morschauser. Winona Lake, IN: Eisenbrauns, 1985.

Cuncillos, J. L. "The Ugaritic Letters." Pages 359–74 in *Handbook of Ugaritic Studies*. Edited by W. G. E. Watson and N. Wyatt. Leiden: Brill, 1999.

Damrosch, D. *The Narrative Covenant: Transformations of Genre in the Growth of Biblical Literature*. San Francisco: Harper & Row, 1987.

Doane, A. N. "The Ethnography of Scribal Writing and Anglo-Saxon Poetry: Scribe as Performer." *Oral Tradition* 9 (1994): 420–39.

Dobbs-Allsopp, F. W., J. J. M. Roberts, C. L. Seow, and R. E. Whitaker. *Hebrew Inscriptions: From the Biblical Period of the Monarchy, with Concordance*. Princeton: Princeton University, 2005.

Dijkstra, M. "Prophecy by Letter (Jeremiah xxix 24–32)." *VT* 33 (1983): 319–22.

Erbele-Küster, D. "Reading as an Act of Offering: Reconsidering the Genre of Leviticus 1." Pages 34–66 in *The Actuality of Sacrifice: Past and Present*. Edited by A. Houtman, M. Poorthuis, J. J. Schwartz, and J. Turner. Jewish and Christian Perspectives 28. Leiden: Brill, 2014.

Estelle, B. "The Use of Deferential Language in the Arsames Correspondence and Biblical Aramaic Compared." *Maarav* 13.1 (2006): 67–81.

Fishbane, M. "Form and Reformulation of the Biblical Priestly Blessing." *JAOS* 103 (1983): 115–21.

Fitzmyer, J. *A Manual of Palestinian Aramaic Texts (Second Century B.C.–Second Century A.D.)*. Rome: Biblical Institute Press, 1978.

———. "Some Notes on Aramaic Epistolography." *JBL* 93.2 (1974): 201–55.

Freedman, D. N. "The Aaronic Benediction (Numbers 6:24–26)." Pages 35–48 in *No Famine in the Land: Studies in Honor of J. L. McKenzie*. Edited by J. L. Flanagan. Atlanta: Scholars Press, 1975.

Frevel, C. "The Book of Numbers: Formation, Composition, and Interpretation of a Late Part of the Torah: Some Introductory Remarks." Pages 1–38 in *Torah and the Book of Numbers*. FAT 2/62. Edited by C. Frevel, T. Pola, and A. Schart. Tübingen: Mohr Siebeck, 2013.

———. "On Instant Scripture and Proximal Texts: Some Insights into the Sensual Materiality of Texts and their Ritual Roles in the Hebrew Bible and Beyond." *Postscripts* 8.1–2 (2012): 57–79.

———. "Practicing Rituals in a Textual World: Ritual *and* Innovation in the Book of Numbers." Pages 129–50 in *Ritual Innovation in the Hebrew Bible and Early Judaism*. Edited by N. MacDonald. Berlin: de Gruyter, 2016.

Gilders, W. K. *Blood Ritual in the Hebrew Bible: Meaning and Power*. Baltimore: Johns Hopkins University Press, 2004.

Gorman, F. H. *The Ideology of Ritual: Space, Time and Status in the Priestly Theology.* JSOTSup 91. Sheffield: JSOT Press, 1990.

Gray, G. B. *A Critical and Exegetical Commentary on Numbers.* ICC. New York: Scribner's Sons, 1920.

Haran, M. "Shiloh and Jerusalem: The Origin of the Priestly Tradition in the Pentateuch." *JBL* 81.1 (1962): 14–24.

———. *Temples and Temple-Service in Ancient Israel: An Inquiry into Biblical Cult Phenomena and the Historical Setting of the Priestly School.* Winona Lake, IN: Eisenbrauns, 1977.

Hawley, R. "Studies in Ugaritic Epistolography." PhD. diss., University of Chicago, 2003.

Holladay, J. "Assyrian Statecraft and the Prophets of Israel." Pages 122–43 in *Prophecy in Israel: Search for Identity.* Edited by D. Petersen. Philadelphia: Fortress; London: SPCK, 1987.

Holladay, W. L. *Jeremiah 2: A Commentary on the Prophet Jeremiah Chapters 26–52.* Minneapolis: Fortress, 1989.

Huehnergard, J. "The Akkadian Letters." Pages 375–89 in *Handbook of Ugaritic Studies.* Edited by W. G. E. Watson and N. Wyatt. Leiden: Brill, 1999.

Jacobs, S. "The Body Inscribed: A Priestly Initiative?" Pages 1–16 in *The Body in Biblical, Christian, and Jewish Texts.* Edited by J. E. Taylor. Library of Second Temple Studies. London: T&T Clark, 2014.

Japhet, S. "Law and 'the Law' in Ezra-Nehemiah." Pages 99–115 in *Proceedings of the Ninth World Congress of Jewish Studies.* Edited by M. Goshen-Gottstein. Jerusalem: Magnes, 1988.

Keller, S. R. "Written Communication Between the Human and Divine Spheres in Mesopotamia and Israel." Pages 299–313 in *The Biblical Canon in Comparative Perspective: Scripture in Context IV.* Edited by B. F. Batto, W. W. Hallo, and K. Lawson Younger Jr. Ancient Near Eastern Texts and Studies 11. Lewiston: Edwin Mellen, 1991.

Klawans, J. "Pure Violence: Sacrifice and Defilement in Ancient Israel." *HTR* 94.2 (2001): 133–55.

———. *Purity, Sacrifice, and the Temple: Symbolism and Supersessionism in the Study of Ancient Judaism.* Oxford: Oxford University Press, 2006.

Knierim, R. P., and G. W. Coats. *Numbers.* Grand Rapids, MI: Eerdmans, 2005.

Knohl, I. *The Sanctuary of Silence: The Priestly Torah and the Holiness School.* Minneapolis: Fortress, 1995.

Korpel, M. C. A. "The Poetic Structure of the Priestly Blessing." *JSOT* 45 (1989): 3–13.

Lee, W. "The Conceptual Coherence of Numbers 5,1–10,10." Pages 473–90 in *The Books of Leviticus and Numbers.* Edited by T. Römer. BETL 215. Leuven: Peeters, 2008.

Leeven, A. *Memory and Tradition in the Book of Numbers.* Cambridge: Cambridge University Press, 2008.

Lemaire, A. *Inscriptions hébraïques 1. Les ostraca.* LAPO 9. Paris: Cerf, 1977.

Leuchter, M. "The Politics of Ritual Rhetoric: A Proposed Sociopolitical Context for the Redaction of Leviticus 16." *VT* 60 (2010): 345–65.

Levine, B. A. "The Descriptive Ritual Texts from Ugarit: Some Formal and Functional Features of the Genre." Pages 17–58 in *The Word of the Lord Shall Go Forth:*

Essays in Honor of David Noel Freedman. Edited by C. L. Meyers and M. O'Connor. Winona Lake, IN: Eisenbrauns, 1983.

———. "The Descriptive Tabernacle Texts of the Pentateuch." *JAOS* 85 (1965): 307–18.

———. *Numbers 1–20: A New Translation with Introduction and Commentary.* AB 4A. New York: Doubleday, 1993.

Lindenberger, J. M. *Ancient Aramaic and Hebrew Letters.* 2nd ed. WAW 14. Atlanta: Society of Biblical Literature, 2003.

Loretz, O. "Altorientalischer Hintergrund sowie inner- und nachbiblische Entwicklung des aaronitischen Segens (Num 6.24–26)." *UF* 10 (1978): 115–19.

Mandell, A. "'I Bless You to YHWH and His Asherah'—Writing and Performativity at Kuntillet 'Ajrud." *Maarav* 19.1–2 (2012): 131–62.

Meshel, Z. *Kuntillet 'Ajrud: An Iron Age II Religious Site on the Judah-Sinai Border.* Jerusalem: Israel Exploration Society, 2012.

Michaud, H. "Les ostraca de Lakiš conserves à Londres." *Syria* 34 (1957): 39–60.

Milgrom, J. "The Changing Concept of Holiness in the Pentateuchal Codes with Emphasis on Leviticus 19." Pages 65–75 in *Reading Leviticus: A Conversation with Mary Douglas.* Edited by J. F. A. Sawyer. JSOTSup 227. Sheffield: Sheffield Academic Press, 1996.

———. *Cult and Conscience: The Asham and the Priestly Doctrine of Repentance.* Leiden: Brill, 1976.

———. *Leviticus 1–16: A New Translation with Introduction and Commentary.* AB 3A. New York: Doubleday, 1991.

———. *Leviticus 17–22: A New Translation with Introduction and Commentary.* AB 3B. New York: Doubleday, 2000.

———. *Numbers: The Traditional Hebrew Text with the New JPS Translation.* JPS Torah Commentary. Philadelphia: Jewish Publication Society, 1990.

———. "Rationale for Cultic Law: The Case of Impurity." *Semeia* 45 (1989): 103–10.

Moran, W. L. "An Ancient Prophetic Oracle." Pages 252–59 in *Biblische Theologie und gesellschaftlicher Wandel.* Edited by G. Braulik, W. Groß, and S. McEvenue. Freiburg: Herder, 1993.

Mowinckel, S. "'The Spirit' and the 'Word' in the Pre-Exilic Reforming Prophets." *JBL* 53 (1934): 199–227.

Mynářová, J. *Language of Amarna—Language of Diplomacy: Perspective on the Amarna Letters.* Prague: Czech Institute of Egyptology, 2007.

Na'aman, N. "A New Appraisal of the Silver Amulets from Ketef Hinnom." *IEJ* 61.2 (2011): 184–95.

Newman, J. *Praying by the Book: The Scripturalization of Prayer in Second Temple Judaism.* EJL 14. Atlanta: Scholars Press, 1999.

Niditch, S. *Oral World and Written Word: Ancient Israelite Literature.* Louisville, KY: Westminster John Knox, 1996.

Nihan, C. *From Priestly Torah to Pentateuch: A Study in the Composition of the Book of Leviticus.* FAT 2/25. Tübingen: Mohr Siebeck, 2007.

Noth, M. *Numbers.* OTL. Philadelphia: Westminster, 1968.

Owen, D. "An Akkadian Letter from Ugarit at Tel Aphek." *TA* 8 (1981): 1–19.

Pardee, D. *Handbook of Ancient Hebrew Letters: A Study Edition.* Sources for Biblical Studies 15. Atlanta: Scholars Press, 1982.

Pardee, D., J. D. Whitehead, and P. E. Dion. "An Overview of Ancient Hebrew Epistolography." *JBL* 97.3 (1978): 321–46.
Pardee, D., and R. M. Whiting. "Aspects of Epistolary Verbal Usage in Ugaritic and Akkadian." *Bulletin of the School of Oriental and African Studies* 50 (1987): 1–31.
Person, R. F. "The Ancient Israelite Scribe as Performer." *JBL* 117.4 (1998): 601–9.
Pomgratz-Leisten, B. "'Öffne den Tafelbehälter und lies ...': Neue Ansätze zum Verständnis des Lietratur Konzeptes in Mesopotamie." *WO* 27 (1996): 67–90.
Reinmuth, T. "Nehemiah 8 and the Authority of Torah in Ezra-Nehemiah." Pages 241–62 in *Unity and Disunity in Ezra-Nehemiah: Redaction, Rhetoric, Reader*. Edited by M. J. Boda and P. L. Reddit. Sheffield: Sheffield Phoenix Press, 2008.
Renz, J. *Handbuch der althebräischen Epigraphik*. Vol. 1, fasc. 1, *Die altehebräischen Inschriften, Text und Kommentar*. Darmstadt: Wissenschaftliche Buchgesellschaft, 1995.
Richter, W. "Lakiš 3—Vorschlag zur Konstituion eines Textes." *BN* 37 (1987): 73–103.
Ross, J. "The Prophet as Yahweh's Messenger." Pages 98–107 in *Israel's Prophetic Heritage: Essays in Honor of James Muilenberg*. Edited by B. Anderson and W. Harrelson. New York: Harper, 1962.
Schaper, J. "Exilic and Postexilic Prophecy and the Orality/Literacy Problem." *VT* 55 (2005): 324–42.
Schellenberg, A. "A 'Lying Pen of the Scribes' (Jer 8:8)? Orality and Writing in the Formation of Prophetic Books." Pages 285–309 in *The Interface of Orality and Writing: Speaking, Seeing, Writing in the Shaping of New Genres*. Edited by A. Weissenrieder and R. B. Coote. Biblical Performance Criticism 11. Tübingen: Mohr Siebeck, 2015.
Schniedewind, W. M. *The Finger of the Scribe: How Scribes Learned to Write the Bible*. Oxford: Oxford University Press, 2019.
———. *How the Bible Became a Book: The Textualization of Ancient Israel*. Cambridge: Cambridge University Press, 2004.
———. "Scripturalization in Ancient Judah." Pages 305–21 in *Contextualizing Israel's Sacred Writings: Ancient Literacy, Orality, and Literary Production*. Edited by B. Schmidt. Atlanta: Society of Biblical Literature, 2015.
———. "Sociolinguistic Reflections on the Letter of a 'Literate' Soldier (Lachish 3)." *Zeitschrift für Althebräistik* 13 (2000): 157–66.
Schwartz, B. J. "Introduction: The Strata of the Priestly Writings and the Revised Relative Dating of P and H." Pages 1–12 in *The Strata of the Priestly Writings: Contemporary Debate and Future Directions*. Edited by S. Shectman and J. S. Baden. ATANT 95. Zürich: Theologischer Verlag, 2009.
———. "Prohibitions Concerning the 'Eating' of Blood in Leviticus 17." Pages 34–66 in *Priesthood and Cult in Ancient Israel*. Edited by G. A. Anderson and S. M. Olyan. JSOTSup 125. Sheffield: JSOT, 1991.
Schwiderski, D. *Handbuch des nordwestsemitischen Briefformulars: Ein Betrag zur Echtheitsfrage des aramäischen Briefe des Esrabuches*. BZAW 295. Berlin: de Gruyter, 2000.
Seebass, H. "YHWH's Name in the Aaronic Blessing (Num 6:22–27)." Pages 37–54 in *The Revelation of the Name YHWH to Moses: Perspectives from Judaism, the Pagan, Graeco-Roman World, and Early Christianity*. Edited by G. H. van Kooten. Leiden: Brill, 2006.

Seybold, K. *Der aaronitische Segen*. Neukirchen: Neukirchen-Vluyn, 1989.
Smoak, J. D. "From Temple to Text: Text as Ritual Space and the Composition of Numbers 6:24–26." *JHebS* 17 (2017): 1–27. doi:10.5508/jhs.2017.v17.a2.
———. *The Priestly Blessing in Inscription and Scripture: The Early History of Numbers 6:22–27*. Oxford: Oxford University Press, 2015.
Sommer, B. D. *Revelation and Authority: Sinai in Jewish Scripture and Tradition*. Anchor Yale Bible Reference Library. New Haven: Yale University Press, 2015.
Stackert, J. *Rewriting the Torah: Literary Revision in Deuteronomy and the Holiness Legislation*. FAT 52. Tübingen: Mohr Siebeck, 2007.
Talmon, S. "Oral Tradition and Written Transmission, or the Heard and the Seen Word in Judaism of the Second Temple Period." Pages 121–58 in *Jesus and the Oral Gospel Tradition*. Edited by H. Wansbrough. JSOTSup 64. Sheffield: Sheffield Academic Press, 1991.
Thomas, B. "The Language of Politeness in Ancient Hebrew Letters." *Hebrew Studies* 50 (2009): 17–39.
Torczyner, N. H. *Lachish 1: The Lachish Letters*. Oxford: Oxford University Press, 1938.
Toorn, K. van der. "From the Mouth of the Prophet: The Literary Fixation of Jeremiah's Prophecies in the Context of the Ancient Near East." Pages 191–202 in *Inspired Speech: Prophecy in the Ancient Near East; Essays in Honor of H. B. Huffmon*. Edited by J. Kaltner and L. Stulman. Edinburgh: T&T Clark, 2004.
———. *Scribal Culture and the Making of the Hebrew Bible*. Cambridge: Harvard University Press, 2007.
Venema, G. J. *Reading Scripture in the Old Testament: Deuteronomy 9–10; 31—2 Kings 22–23—Jeremiah 36—Nehemiah 8*. Translated by C. E. Smit. OtSt 48. Leiden: Brill, 2004.
Watts, J. W. *Reading Law: The Rhetorical Shape of the Pentateuch*. The Biblical Seminar 59. Sheffield: Sheffield Academic, 1999.
———. *Ritual and Rhetoric: From Sacrifice to Scripture*. Cambridge: Cambridge University Press, 2012.
———. "Ritual Legitimacy and Scriptural Authority." *JBL* 124 (2005): 401–17.
———. "Ritual Rhetoric in the Pentateuch: The Case of Leviticus 1–16." Pages 305–18 in *The Books of Leviticus and Numbers*. Edited by T. Römer. BETL 215. Leuven: Peeters, 2008.
———. "The Torah as the Rhetoric of the Priesthood." Pages 319–31 in *The Pentateuch as Torah: New Models for Understanding Its Promulgation and Acceptance*. Edited by G. N. Knoppers and B. M. Levinson. Winona Lake, IN: Eisenbrauns, 2007.
———. *Understanding the Pentateuch as Scripture*. London: Wiley Blackwell, 2017.
———. "Using Ezra's Time as a Methodological Pivot for Understanding the Rhetoric and Functions of the Pentateuch." Pages 489–506 in *The Pentateuch: International Perspectives on Current Research*. FAT 78. Edited by T. B. Dozeman, K. Schmid, and B. J. Schwartz. Tübingen: Mohr Siebeck, 2011.
Weinfeld, M. "Sabbatical Year and Jubilee in the Pentateuchal Laws and Their Ancient Near Eastern Background." Pages 39–62 in *The Law in the Bible and Its Environment*. Edited by T. Veijola. Publications of the Finnish Exegetical Society 51. Göttingen: Vandenhoeck & Ruprecht, 1990.
Weippert, M. "Zum Präskript der hebräischen Briefe von Arad." *VT* 25 (1975): 202–12.

Wright, J. L. "Seeking, Finding and Writing in Ezra-Nehemiah." Pages 294–304 in *Unity and Disunity in Ezra-Nehemiah: Redaction, Rhetoric, Reader*. Edited by M. J. Boda and P. L. Reddit. Sheffield: Sheffield Phoenix Press, 2008.

———. "Writing the Restoration: Compositional Agenda and the Role of Ezra in Nehemiah 8." *JHebS* 7 (2007): 19–29. doi:10.5508/jhs.2007.v7.a10.

Yardeni, A. "Remarks on the Priestly Blessing on Two Amulets from Jerusalem." *VT* 41 (1991): 176–85.

Yoo, P. Y. *Ezra and the Second Wilderness*. Oxford: Oxford University Press, 2017.

CHAPTER 10

The Ritual Texts of Leviticus and the Creation of Ritualized Bodies

Dorothea Erbele-Küster

10.1. Ritual Texts and Ritualized Bodies in Leviticus

When studying, as in my case, rituals in the biblical book of Leviticus, specifically the purity regulations in chaps. 11–15, the object of study involves textually represented rituals dealing mainly with bodies and bodily issues.[1] Recent scholarship on these texts that draws on ritual studies has argued for a distinction between text and ritual, noting the difficulties created by the intertwined nature of the written text and its performance: "In other words, *texts are not rituals and rituals are not texts.*"[2] This distinction lies at the root of James W. Watts's analysis of the offering *torot* in Lev 1–7 in *Ritual and Rhetoric in Leviticus* and implies a further distinction between the way we interpret texts about rituals and how we interpret actual ritual practice. At this point, the crucial question becomes how to understand the genre of Leviticus. I argue with other scholars that attempts to understand Leviticus as a ritual agenda run up against its peculiar literary structure characterized by the absence of details concerning ritual practice and the abundance of interpretive categories such as cultic purity and gender.[3] This makes it difficult to describe actual ritual performance in ancient Israel using these texts. However, what we do have, and thus what we can describe, is the actual textual discourse that concerns the ritual—a discourse that serves ideological purposes.

---

1. See W. K. Gilders, *Blood Ritual in the Hebrew Bible: Meaning and Power* (Baltimore: Johns Hopkins University Press, 2004); J. W. Watts, *Ritual and Rhetoric in Leviticus: From Sacrifice to Scripture* (Cambridge: Cambridge University Press, 2007); H. Liss, "Ritual Purity and the Construction of Identity," in *The Books of Leviticus and Numbers*, ed. T. Römer, BETL 215 (Leuven: Peeters, 2008), 329–54; B. D. Bibb, *Ritual Words and Narrative Worlds in Leviticus* (New York: T&T Clark, 2009); W. J. Bergen, *Reading Ritual: Leviticus in Postmodern Culture*, JSOTSup 417 (London: T&T Clark, 2010).

2. Watts, *Ritual and Rhetoric*, 29.

3. Compare R. Knierim, *Text and Concept in Leviticus 1:1–9: A Case in Exegetical Method*, FAT 2/1 (Tübingen: Mohr Siebeck, 1992), 17–18, 98–106.

The title of this article combines the two concepts under discussion, text and ritual, with a third one: the body. As my analysis will show, the body is not a given but is rather constructed through the text and the rituals; in order to express this, I speak of "ritualized bodies." "Ritualized bodies" refers in principle to bodies involved in a ritual process. Thus, it can refer to bodies actually undergoing rituals, as, for example, in the case of circumcision, but it can also be used to denote the embodied knowledge of the ritual agents that enables them to fill in the gaps missing in the textual description of ritual actions.

Referring to the classic definition of Lev 11–15 as "purity regulations"[4]— since the regulations simultaneously define and create the body through their normative discourse—I have labeled these chapters "body regulations."[5] The term "body regulations" tries to capture complex relationship between body and text in Leviticus: the ritual regulations define the body and the body is the defining concept of the regulations. "Body" thus serves as a heuristic category, which can arguably shed further light on the relationship between text and ritual, especially by showing their interdependence. My aim is therefore to address this process of constructing ritualized bodies in Lev 11–15.

This textual practice (discourse) in Leviticus manifests a symbolic system with the help of the body. Body and, along with it, gender emerge in these texts from and within the ongoing process of socioreligious norming through ritualized processes, which are themselves mediated by texts and practices.[6] My concern is therefore to show how power relations and rituals, as they are described in textual discourse, work to form the body. Hence, the body and its gender are to be understood as historically shaped by performative acts without neglecting their materiality.[7]

---

4. Indeed, the common topic of Lev 11–15 is that the body must be pure—that is, compliant with the cult. To this aim the regulations construe boundaries between pure and impure, and designate persons, animals, or things as im/pure; compare C. Nihan, "Forms and Functions of Purity in Leviticus," in *Purity and the Forming of Religious Traditions in the Ancient Mediterranean World and Ancient Judaism*, ed. C. Frevel and C. Nihan, Dynamics in the History of Religion 3 (Leiden: Brill, 2013), 311–68 at 351–52, 362.

5. I coined this term in German so as to amend the traditional name *Reinheitsbestimmungen* with *Körperbestimmungen*. This definition plays on the word *bestimmen* (to define/regulate); compare D. Erbele-Küster, "Die Körperbestimmungen in Lev 11–15," in *Menschenbilder und Körperkonzepte im Alten Israel, in Ägypten und im Alten Orient*, ed. A. Berlejung, J. Dietrich, and J. F. Quack, ORA 9 (Tübingen: Mohr Siebeck, 2012), 209–24.

6. Compare M. Mauss, "Les techniques du corps," *Journal de Psychologie* 32 (1934): 271–93; M. Douglas, *Purity and Danger: An Analysis of the Concepts of Pollution and Taboo* (London: Routledge and Kegan Paul, 1966); J. Butler, *Bodies That Matter: On the Discursive Limits of "Sex"* (London: Routledge, 1993).

7. Compare Butler, *Bodies That Matter*, taking up ideas of Maurice Merleau-Ponty, Simone de Beauvoir, Mary Douglas, and Michel Foucault, among others. She states: "gender is not to culture as sex is to nature; gender is also the discursive/cultural means by which 'sexed nature' or 'a natural sex' is produced and established as 'prediscursive'" (7).

Despite the growing attention that gender issues have gained in recent scholarship on the regulations in Lev 11–15,[8] the gender category continues to be neglected in scholarly debates on the understanding of purity. This dismissal of the role gender plays in the regulations arguably reveals certain scholarly understandings of the body—namely, that the body is a given physical phenomenon. According to my reading of Lev 12, by contrast, the body and its so-called biological sex are rather defined and created by the ritual description—for example, the sex of the child is not ascribed by its body but reflected by the length of the cultic impurity of the mother, as we shall see in what follows.

10.2. Body Regulations in Lev 11–15 and Ritualized Bodies[9]

The cluster of texts under discussion circles around a variety of bodies: animals whose bodies are unclean (chap. 11), bodies that have given birth (chap. 12), bodies with skin diseases (chaps. 13–14) and genital discharges, as well as bodies that have come into contact with these sources of pollution (chap. 15).[10] Indeed, the body is of such significance to these chapters that I have labeled them "body regulations," as explained above. However, the body plays an ambiguous role in Lev 11–15: the regulations circle around bodily issues, but at the same time, the reader is confronted with the paucity of concrete depictions of bodily processes. For example, the regulations for the woman giving birth do not refer to the actual birth as a social reality characterized by several dangers: miscarriage, stillbirth, and infant mortality, not to mention the possible death of the mother.

This hints at the way the regulations in Leviticus shape bodies through discourse. I highlight three different ways in which the regulations create the body and its gender through the rituals and the various sets of actions they comprise.[11] First, I explore a ritual action that is itself performed on the body: the

---

8. To cite just a few examples, see H. Eilberg-Schwartz, *The Savage in Judaism: An Anthropology of Israelite and Ancient Judaism* (Bloomington: Indiana University Press, 1990); D. Ellens, *Women in the Sex Texts in Leviticus and Deuteronomy: A Comparative Conceptual Analysis*, LHBOTS 458 (London: T&T Clark, 2008); D. Erbele-Küster, *Körper und Geschlecht: Studien zur Anthropologie von Lev 12 und 15*, WMANT 121 (Neukirchen-Vluyn: Neukirchner Verlag, 2008); D. Erbele-Küster, *Body, Gender and Purity in Leviticus 12 and 15*, LHBOTS 539 (London: T&T Clark, 2017); N. J. Ruane, *Sacrifice and Gender in Biblical Law* (Cambridge: Cambridge University Press, 2013).

9. A comparison with Num 5 and 19 would be of interest; see C. Frevel, "Purity Conceptions in the Book of Numbers in Context," in *Purity and the Forming of Religious Traditions in the Ancient Mediterranean World and Ancient Judaism*, ed. C. Frevel and C. Nihan, Dynamics in the History of Religion 3 (Leiden: Brill, 2013), 369–411.

10. See Erbele-Küster, "Die Körperbestimmungen"; C. Nihan, *From Priestly Torah to Pentateuch: A Study in the Composition of the Book of Leviticus*, FAT 2/25 (Tübingen: Mohr Siebeck, 2007), 269–339.

11. Compare with Bibb, *Ritual Words*, 58–62.

circumcision of the male newborn body as referred to in Lev 12. Second, I turn to the process by which the new mother is purified according to that same chapter. This process involves temporary separation from the cult and concludes with a ritual action undertaken by the woman—namely, a sacrifice. In both cases, it is the performance of the ritual, or conversely its nonperformance, which defines the body, hence making it a "ritualized body." Third, and last, I shall turn to the issue of genital discharges in Lev 15 and the way in which the ritual and other performative acts laid out in this chapter (such as counting a certain time period) define men and women who are affected by such discharges. I shall focus on the ambiguous character of the description of the actions that have to be performed by those contaminated with the sort of ritual impurity that is associated with genital discharges, arguing that this description alternates between detailed prescriptions and a lack of information—what is called gaps in reception aesthetics. The gaps have been productive in creating new rituals in the course of the reception of the texts. Watts comments on the gaps in ritual texts as follows: "Rather than complaining about what is missing, we should ask why the text includes what it does."[12] Indeed, the gaps are defined by their literary context and the information this provides. Therefore, because Leviticus is fundamentally shaped by its specific rhetoric, I investigate the rhetorical structure of the text with its gaps, which are crucial to my understanding of the ritual performativity of the text.[13]

10.2.1. Circumcision

Leviticus 12:3 prescribes the circumcision of male newborns seven days after birth. Investigating this ritual act as prescribed in this verse raises a number of questions concerning the ritual agent and the ritual act: who is performing the ritual? How should the circumcision of the male body be performed, precisely? Can we deduce ritual accuracy from the texts in light of the gaps? There seems to be a disjunction between the ritual performance as it would have been practiced and the ritual performance as it is described in the textual prescriptions with its gaps. The earliest textual evidence for a detailed rite of circumcision dates from postbiblical times.[14] In the regulations for the woman after childbirth

---

12. Watts, *Ritual and Rhetoric*, 29–30.
13. F. Gorman, "Pagans and Priests: Critical Reflections on Method," in *Perspectives in Purity and Purification in the Bible*, ed. B. Schwartz et al., LHBOTS 474 (London: T&T Clark, 2008), 108: "The informational gaps in the texts might be an indication that the texts were written for writing and hearing, not for enactment."
14. The ritual itself underwent continuous change; for the development of ritual forms, see S. Cohen, *The Beginnings of Jewishness: Boundaries, Varieties, Uncertainties* (Berkeley: University of California Press, 1999).

in Lev 12, the commandment to circumcise in verse 3 is brief and does not supply specific instructions: "On the eighth day the foreskin of his member shall be circumcised."[15]

What is prescribed—the circumcision—is a performative act that unequivocally determines the infant's male gender identity.[16] As a birth rite, it anticipates the initiation rite, and as a distinctive mark of identity this ritual act is reserved for male bodies. There is some evidence that this ritual act could function as a life-cycle rite that marked the transition from boyhood to manhood (as it does in the case of Ishmael, who was circumcised at the age of thirteen in Gen 17:25). However, the timing that both Gen 17 and Lev 12 prescribe for the rite—namely, a few days after birth—pushes this potentially sexual aspect into the background.

Focusing on bodies in the described rituals leads one to ask about a number of omissions from the text—for example, the fact that we see no knife and no blood, or that the ritual agency is not clearly defined in the text. Is the supposed ritual agent of the circumcision the woman?[17] The verbal root *mwl* that is used in Lev 12:3 is unique to circumcision. Because the Niphal conjugation is used, the subject of the verb is concealed. No ceremony is described, nor is the act explained. The circumcision occurs only after the mother's seven-day period of impurity has passed.[18]

The commandment interrupts the purity rules for the parturient, shifting the reader's attention from the mother to her male offspring. Hence, we have to ask, what is the place of circumcision in the purity regulations addressing the woman after she has given birth? Circumcision here obviously does not signal the transition from childhood to manhood. Nevertheless, it is a performative act that unequivocally determines the infant's male gender identity. Circumcision thus becomes a token of male identity. The purity regulations in Lev 12 codify sexual difference at childbirth even without circumcision, but circumcision heightens this difference by emphasizing the male sex.

The body of the child is integrated into the cultic community by the ritual act and no longer belongs to the woman and her impure body. The child likewise becomes gendered, since in what follows the newborn is spoken of as son. Furthermore, it seems that the circumcision affects the body of the woman, as the

---

15. Unless otherwise stated, all biblical translations are my own.
16. Compare Erbele-Küster, *Körper und Geschlecht*, 93–94.
17. On the question of female agency in general in this chapter, compare Erbele-Küster, "'She Shall Remain in (Accordance to) Her-Blood-of-Purification': Ritual Dynamics of Defilement and Purification in Leviticus 12," in *Sacrifice, Cult, and Atonement in Early Judaism and Christianity: Constituents and Critique*, ed. H. L. Wiley and C. A. Eberhart (Atlanta: Society of Biblical Literature, 2017), 59–70.
18. The pattern of seven days plus the eighth day occupies an important place within the rituals of Leviticus (cf. Lev 9:1; 14:9–10, 23; 15:13–14, 28–29; 22:27; 23:36, 39; 25:22; Num 6:9–10).

period of her cultic disability is shorter with a boy than after having given birth to a female child. Hence, the male body is the object of the circumcision ritual and the subject of the purification ritual of the women, since he determines the period of her impurity.

We may conclude that Lev 12 does not contain any details about how the act of circumcision is to be performed. The commandment in Lev 12:3 offers no formula for a ritual, even though circumcision is clearly a rite. And it is striking that, in contrast to the Hebrew Bible's treatment of menstruation, Lev 12 says nothing about the blood that flows during circumcision. A tension exists between an embodied and a disembodied manner of description, between the body's visibility and invisibility in the text.

10.2.2. The Purification of the Mother

The regulations of Lev 12 inscribe two differently qualified postpartum periods upon the female body. While the first period of seven or fourteen days (depending on the sex of the child) can be seen to inscribe a fixed or static condition of impurity (vv. 2, 5a), the second period of thirty-three or sixty-six days may be understood as a process of purification, as it is further characterized by the phrases "blood of purification" (vv. 4, 5) and "the time of her purification" (vv. 5, 6).[19] In order to understand this expression, we should recall that blood is regarded in Leviticus as a sign of the life force, and nowhere in the Hebrew Bible is it declared impure.[20] Against this background, the nominal formation "blood of purification"/"blood purity" in verses 4 and 5 is crucial. It is paradoxical that the parturient "continues [to be] impure during her 'purity.'"[21] In the history of interpretation, this idea seems to have been repudiated not least because it is difficult to understand. The first case of such a reading may be the translation into Greek of "impure blood"; however, we should note that the uncial G and numerous minuscule still speak of pure blood. The Hebrew text suggests that the postpartum loss of blood is considered to be a purifying process—an idea that is common in antiquity.[22] Hence, the differentiation into two periods of seven plus thirty-three days (or fourteen plus sixty-six days) is based less on the bodily

---

19. For the arguments in favor of understanding *ṭhrh* as process, see Milgrom, *Leviticus 1–16*, 755; Erbele-Küster, *Body, Gender, and Purity*, 37–38.
20. Differently, Ruane, *Sacrifice and Gender in Biblical Law*, 143. According to her, female blood is for the priestly writers a substance that defiles.
21. J. Milgrom, *Leviticus 1–16: A New Translation with Introduction and Commentary*, AB 3A (New York: Doubleday, 1991), 749.
22. In classical antiquity as well in ancient Egypt, the idea prevails that menstruation is a process of purification. Soranus, *Gynecology* 16–17, calls it catharsis. H. Marsman states, "Already in Ancient Egypt menstruation was called a time of purification" (*Women in Ugarit and Israel: Their Social and Religious Position in the Context of the Ancient Near East*, OtSt 49 [Leiden: Brill, 2003], 488).

secretions of the woman who has given birth than on the desire to distinguish between two phases of the ritual: the first serves the purpose of separation and the second aims at reintegration. Therefore, the purifying process concludes with an offering at the end of the required period (vv. 6–7).[23] This offering marks the transition from the state of cultic impurity, which is a time of separation from the sanctuary, to the condition of complete cultic purity.

The regulations of Lev 12 define the body of the woman giving birth. The cult-related state of the woman's body is interwoven with that of her child and its sex, and vice versa. The body of the mother is defined by the body of the male child. Moreover, her body is seen in relation to the cult. In the description, in this chapter, of a woman's condition after childbirth, it cannot be the blood itself or the physical bleeding that functions as the point of reference for the impurity, since the duration of the postpartum bleeding varies from one instance to another and is not conditioned by the sex of the newborn child. However, the text clearly defines the length of impurity seven days after giving birth to a boy, fourteen days with a girl.[24] In the doubled length of the woman's cultic disablement after the birth of a daughter, one can see a mirroring of the socioreligious structure of the society that produced these texts. The purity regulations operate according to spatial and temporal categories: a person or object is impure if it must be kept at a distance from the cult for a specified length of time, depending on the threat it poses to the sacred order.[25] The priest's declaration seals the reintegration of that person or object into the cult. Hence, Lev 12 is a fine example of the priestly ideology wherein ritual place and ritually defined time intersect and define the body.[26] The body is shaped not so much along the physical but by social and ritual acts.

In Lev 12, impurity seems to be constructed in reference to the woman's body, but without direct consideration of the physiological processes she undergoes. Thus, rather than labeling the pollution as physical, which holds true to a certain degree, it is a cultic religious construction. The concept of impurity is therefore reflected in the body. The regulations define the body of the woman as impure, and likewise the gendered body of the child defines her cultic impurity.

---

23. In a similar vein, the summary formula "and she is cultically pure as a result of the source of her blood" (v. 7) cannot be taken to mean that the woman has been purified of her (impure) issue of blood, since earlier blood of purification was mentioned.

24. See R. Whitekettle, "Leviticus 12 and the Israelite Women: Ritual Process, Liminality and the Womb," *ZAW* 107 (1995): 393–408 at 397–99.

25. See D. Wright, *The Disposal of Impurity: Elimination Rites in the Bible and in Hittite and Mesopotamian Literature*, SBLDS 101 (Atlanta: Scholars Press, 1987), 164, 273; M. Douglas, *Leviticus as Literature* (Oxford: Oxford University Press, 1999), 150.

26. For the rituals in the so-called priestly work, see the methodological framework introduced by F. H. Gorman, *The Ideology of Ritual: Space, Time and Status in the Priestly Theology*, JSOTSup 91 (Sheffield: JSOT Press, 1990).

10.2.3. Textual Regulations and Rituals in Lev 15

Concerning Lev 15, I shall further expound on the issue of how the construction of ritual purity and body intersect. In addition, I shall illuminate how the reading of the textual regulations leads to the implementation of (new) ritual practices. The regulations concerning genital discharge in Lev 15 distinguish between the genders, starting with the male. The man with the discharge is viewed as a temporarily disabled participant in the cult. He is asked to perform a twofold purifying ritual at the end of this period: bathing in water and bringing a sacrifice. The symbolic character of the time that must pass before a man can be declared ritually pure is reflected in the number of days of his impurity: after seven days a cleansing ritual is requested and, on the eighth day, a sacrifice.

> 13 And when the man who has the discharge is ritually pure from his discharge, he shall count seven days for himself for his cleansing, wash his clothes, bathe his body in living water, and he is ritually pure. 14 On the eighth day he shall bring two turtle doves or two doves and come into YHWH's presence, at the entrance of the tent of meeting and give them to the priest. 15 The priest shall prepare one as a purification offering and one as a burnt offering. The priest completes the purification ritual for him before YHWH because of his discharge.

In the regulations for a woman with a discharge (vv. 19–24 for menstruation, and verses 25–30 for prolonged uterine bleeding), the provisions that apply to a man with a discharge (vv. 3–15 and v. 16) are not simply repeated. If the text had wanted to state it clearly, it could have used the expression $k^{\circ}\check{s}r$, which can be found in other ritual texts (e.g., Lev 4:9; cf. Deut 22:26) as shorthand for "as was explained above, so too should be done here." Hence, interpretation is necessary to determine whether and how the regulations for the discharging male are also relevant for the woman.

In the regulations concerning the menstruating woman in Lev 15, the text directs attention to the effect that such a woman has on others: "And a woman, when she has a discharge, her discharge being blood in her body, for seven days she is in her menstrual state. Whoever touches her becomes ritually impure" (v. 19b). The subsequent verses (vv. 20–22) express how impurity can be communicated by contact with a menstruating woman or with objects upon which she has sat.

The way that the text describes the communication of impurity is peculiar: the condition of impurity can be transmitted to others not just through touching the menstruating woman's bed (v. 21) but also through coming into contact with an object that is lying on that bed (v. 23: "if something[27] is on the bed or the object upon which she sits, the person who touches it shall be ritually impure until evening"). "The transmission can only occur when all of the objects and persons form a chain and are in simultaneous contact."[28] This is made clear by the construction with the feminine participle (*yōšebet*): the menstruating woman must be sitting on the bed at the same time that the other person touches the object. The chain of transmission thus has an intermediate link: the bed and/or the object that lies upon it. The direct contact between the bed and the source of the impurity—the menstruating woman—effects a union between her and the bed for as long as she stays on it, so that the object on the bed can itself communicate impurity. This is a case of tertiary contamination; both (the bed and the object) constitute a field of impurity in that moment. This shows that impurity is construed through the help of material objects (both human bodies and inanimate objects); however it goes beyond pure physical contact. Hence, it is the ritual regulation on intermediacy that creates bodily impurity, not the direct physical touch of impure objects/bodies.

The case of verse 24 introduces a further elaboration: sexual intercourse with a menstruating woman causes a man to be impure not just until the evening—that is a given for intercourse outside the woman's period (v. 18). Rather, like the woman in *ndh*, the man becomes impure for seven days, since, as the peculiar formulation states, "her *ndh* shall come upon him" (v. 24). The logic of verse 23 suggests that the man himself can also communicate impurity. He becomes a primary source of impurity, and we can assume that the same rules apply to him as to the menstruating woman. As an example of this phenomenon, verse 24b stipulates that "every bed upon which he lies shall be ritually impure." A man upon whom the cultic condition that results from menstruation (*niddâ*) has come can himself be a source of contamination (v. 24), although the text leaves open how far the chain of contamination can extend and whether he must undergo (the same) purification procedures as the menstruating woman.

At first sight, one might think that these specifications aided the practical application of the regulations. Presupposing that they were in fact practiced, they bring sexuality as a domestic practice into the communal sphere of the cult: "If the purity laws were to be followed perfectly, most sexual activity would be made known to society at large."[29] However, if one takes the gaps seriously, they favor a different direction of interpretation—one in which the text is seen

---

27. The pronoun *hû'* (masculine singular) probably refers to objects, although some scholars interpret is as designating the male person who comes in contact with the woman; see for the discussion Milgrom, *Leviticus 1–16*, 903, 938–39, and his argument for referring back to the objects mentioned in v. 22.

28. Ibid., 938.

29. Ruane, *Sacrifice and Gender*, 159.

to be programmatic, in that it serves a certain logic: the logic of communicating physical impurity without physical contact with blood, and thus the logic of the priestly system of im/purity.

Leviticus, as well as other priestly texts and narrative texts in general, reports neither this logic nor the manner in which the purity regulations were translated into practice. The difficulties that arise when trying to implement the regulations are already evident on the textual level and seem to be traceable in Lev 15 itself. In effect, the first prescription for the male discharge is the most detailed one, and the other cases appear to build on it. This suggests, therefore, that these prescriptions with the missing details are stereotyped to an extent and may not be mere transcripts of actual practice. Nonetheless, their rhetorical shape means that they facilitate the interpretation and performance of ritual practice.

As a matter of fact, the reception of the text has generated ritual activity that is not described in the text. For example, there is no command in Lev 15 that a woman should wash herself after menstruation (as in the Damascus Document 4QD272 1 ii7b–17);[30] nor is there mention of a *mikve*[31] as a place for postmenstrual purification. This various ways in which the purity rules were interpreted in later times is arguably due to the gaps in the text that confronted ancient audiences. As I have shown, Lev 15 itself misses relevant details necessary for its implementation. The final section will therefore turn to reconsider the relationship between text and ritual.

10.3. Reconsidering the Genre of Lev 11–15: Ritualized Bodies Between Ritual and Text

As explained at the outset, the laws in Lev 11–15 are characterized in different, and at times conflicting ways, in the scholarly debate. For instance, they are sometimes seen as programmatic on account of their integration within the overall structure of the pentateuchal narrative (among other observations). A sociohistorical contextualization in exilic times—that is, at a time when the cult was no longer operational—may account for this interpretation of Lev 11–15. By contrast, other scholars understand these laws as a reflection of actual cultic practice[32] and as a means to guide that practice. Still, one could argue that "even

---

30. I. C. Werrett, *Ritual Purity and the Dead Sea Scrolls*, STDJ 72 (Leiden: Brill, 2004), 54.
31. The controversies that surround the interpretation of finds of *mikvot* from the late Second Temple period make clear that these baths cannot be seen just as reflections of ritual observance. They do not reflect practices on a broad scale until the third century CE.
32. See B. Levine, *Leviticus*, JPS Torah Commentary (Philadelphia: Jewish Publication Society, 1989), xxxvii: "There is every reason to accept the cultic practice presented in Leviticus as essentially realistic." Literary and form-critical studies neglect to consider archaeological studies

if the prescriptive texts served as a priestly manual in the Second Temple period, these foundational ritual texts probably served primarily a theological and literary (rhetorical) purpose."[33] Hence, among those who regard Lev 11–15 as a manual, some view its *Sitz im Leben* "within the framework of an early Jewish (post-exilic) worship service centered either on reading or preaching."[34] In the latter interpretation, then, the practice of the texts and the practice of the rituals they describe are somehow made to coincide.

When speaking about ritual, one has therefore to consider, besides form-historical aspects, religious-historical and ethnological ones as well.[35] Christophe Nihan stresses that studies on purity often fail to investigate the sociological and historical background of these concepts, whereas his analysis of the purity concept in Leviticus is sketched against the historical context of the Persian period. According to him and others, the rhetorical strategies of Leviticus serve to validate the only institution in the Second Temple period: the (Aaronide) priesthood. The priests would have used the regulations to guarantee their grip on ritual practices. In turn, they elevated the authority of the text. The observance of the text (Torah) and the institution of the temple became intrinsically connected. "Through reading, hearing, copying or commenting upon Leviticus, the ancient audience was gradually educated in a distinctive model of society that, by construing the related oppositions between sacred and profane and between clean and unclean as central oppositions, subordinates social organization to the temple, and while conferring on members of Israel a degree of priestly competency on the domestic sphere, simultaneously establishes the authority of the priesthood over civil matters."[36] Hence, the chapters could have served as a manual in order to train the new (Second Temple) priestly class and to cement their claim to authority. This characterization stresses the text's literary *Sitz im Leben* in a context of study, and as a consequence it implies a socioreligious function of those who transmit the text: the priestly circle. However, it does not directly confirm the text's concrete application in ritual procedures. The actual

---

that underscore the changes that can be observed in the way rituals were practiced, as opposed to their immutability or continuity. See further W. Zwickel, *Der Tempelkult in Kanaan und Israel: Studien zur Kultgeschichte Palästinas von der Mittelbronzezeit bis zum Untergang Judas*, FAT 10 (Tübingen: Mohr Siebeck, 1994), 340–44.

33. Bibb, *Ritual Words*, 44.
34. E. Gerstenberger, *Leviticus: A Commentary*, trans. D. W. Stott, OTL (Louisville, KY: Westminster John Knox Press, 1996), 4.
35. Compare Knierim, *Text and Concept*, 98–106.
36. Nihan, "Forms and Functions of Purity," 362. Compare with Gorman, *Ideology of Ritual*, 229: "The rituals depicted in the texts, however, present a means by which the priests thought their world of meaning and significance could be enacted, actualized, and realized. The Priestly ritual texts, thus, embody the Priests' thinking 'theologically'; the rituals proper present ways of 'doing' theology."

practice of the texts would lie then foremost in education: "Ritual was not only a way of acting, it was also a way of thinking, speaking, and creating."[37]

In light of this I would like to come back to the distinction, referred to in the beginning of this essay, between text and ritual and the role that the body plays in the regulations in Leviticus. In an intriguing way, Watts asserts a double characterization of the priestly work: "P's rhetorical goals may include the validation of the ritual and its form on the basis of ostensibly ancient textual authority, and/or persuasion to motivate performance of rituals, and/or persuasion to accept the whole text's authority (torah) because of its authoritative instruction on ritual performance."[38] Using an "and/or" statement, he stresses the ritual function of the text but likewise the importance of the text for validating the ritual. Could this be a way to reconcile the twofold characterization of the *torot* as ritual and text?

Indeed, in my own interpretation, I have tried to show the interrelatedness of the textual and the ritual dimensions by referring to the body. In a similar way, my findings oscillate between an "and/or" statement concerning the role of the body: the body is framed by the textual and/or ritual performance. The ritualized body is characterized by its materiality and its textuality likewise. The regulations allow the body to come into being through its performativity. The priests have a grip on the body through their textual discourse.

I have sketched how gender and gender relations, concepts of body and purity, emerge from, and are standardized in, the priestly discourse. The text's communicative structure functions in times and situations beyond the priestly office. This is evident from the texts' discursive structure, as, for example, in the gaps, but also in the almost nonexistent intertextual reflections in narrative texts from the Hebrew Bible as well as in extratextual finds. Specific ritual facilities for washing are neither prescribed by Lev 15 nor mentioned in other biblical texts. The vast corpus of literature found in the vicinity of Qumran attests to interpretations of Lev 15 which enforced its purity regulations, placing the menstruating woman, and with it the female body and the absolute purity of the temple/community, at the center of interest. One can observe a tendency in these writings to prolong the periods of purification when compared to those that are prescribed in the Hebrew Bible. The Messianic Rule and the Temple Scroll require, for example, a "three-day purification for an impure person before entering into the sacred assembly of the holy city"[39] (with reference to 12QT 45:7–12). The multiplicity of interpretations and practices of these texts within Second Temple Judaism

---

37. Gorman, *Ideology of Ritual*, 234.
38. J. W. Watts, "Ritual Rhetoric in the Pentateuch: The Case of Leviticus 1–16," in *The Books of Leviticus and Numbers*, ed. T. Römer, BETL 215 (Leuven: Peeters, 2008), 307–18 at 309.
39. H. Harrington, "Interpreting Leviticus in the Second Temple Period: Struggling with Ambiguity," in *Reading Leviticus: A Conversation with Mary Douglas*, ed. J. Sawyer, JSOTSup 22 (Sheffield: Sheffield Academic Press, 1996), 214–29 at 218.

illustrates that it is only possible to reconstruct the ritual practice with the help of Leviticus when we fill in certain gaps.[40] Thus, the regulations in Lev 11–15, through this need to interpret the gaps, motivated the creation of new rituals. These processes in effect generated ritualized bodies through text and ritual alike.

It is in such mediated ways that the literary texts affect everyday life even up to the present day, as is shown by the revived discussion among the different streams of Judaism regarding their practice. In short, the regulations in Lev 12 and 15 do not support any conclusions about real-world cultic-ritual praxis. The praxis of the texts is realized first of all in the fact that the gendered body is produced through discourse.

On the textual level, a person or an object is declared by the priest to be pure or impure, regardless weather this status is traceable back to a specific physical condition; for example, objects within a house that is stricken with eczema become unclean only once the house is declared by a priest to be unclean (Lev 14:36). Hence, the designation of uncleanness does not adhere until the priest applies it. Furthermore, the woman's period of purification after the birth of a girl is twice as long as after the birth of a boy (Lev 12), although this has no basis in the actual duration of the postpartum bleeding. The cultic state of impurity that results from menstruation (*ndh*) lasts seven days regardless of how long the monthly bleeding endures (Lev 15). The purity regulations in Lev 12 and 15 are primarily not descriptions of physiological processes. Rather, with the aid of the body, they construct ritual purity/impurity. The praxis of the texts is realized first of all in producing the gendered body through discourse. The rituals proper present ways of what I would call "doing body." This can be described as "textualization of ritual"[41] and "scripturalization of cult."[42]

I have been hesitant in labeling Lev 11–15 "ritual text" in the sense of their being a ritual handbook. These chapters definitely refer to a priestly ideology of ritual while referring to rituals by which bodies emerge. Body and Torah (practices) are intertwined, or as Howard Eilberg-Schwartz has phrased it: the People of the Book are referred to as "People of the Body."[43] I have described this circular interdependence along the concept of "ritualized body" that seems to be a means of enacting the priestly theology: purity is realized in the textualized practice of the body.

---

40. Compare with D. Erbele-Küster, "Archaeological and Textual Evidence for Menstruation as Gendered Taboo in the Second Temple Period?," in *Gender and Social Norms in Ancient Israel, Early Judaism and Christianity: Texts and Material Culture*, ed. M. Bauks and K. Galor, Journal of Ancient Judaism Supplements 28 (Göttingen: Vandenhoeck & Ruprecht, 2019), 169–84.

41. Compare with C. Bell, *Ritual Perspectives and Dimensions* (Oxford: Oxford University Press, 1997), 202–5.

42. G. Anderson, "Sacrifice and Sacrificial Offerings: Old Testament," *ABD* 5:882–85 at 873.

43. H. Eilberg-Schwartz, ed., *The People of the Body: Jews and Judaism from an Embodied Perspective* (Albany: State University of New York Press, 1992).

BIBLIOGRAPHY

Anderson, G. "Sacrifice and Sacrificial Offerings: Old Testament." *ABD* 5:870–86.
Beil, C. *Ritual Perspectives and Dimensions*. Oxford: Oxford University Press, 1997.
Bergen, W. J. *Reading Ritual: Leviticus in Postmodern Culture*. JSOTSup 417. London: T&T Clark, 2010.
Bibb, B. D. *Ritual Words and Narrative Worlds in Leviticus*. New York: T&T Clark, 2009.
Butler, J. *Bodies That Matter: On the Discursive Limits of "Sex."* London: Routledge, 1993.
Cohen, S. *The Beginnings of Jewishness: Boundaries, Varieties, Uncertainties*. Berkeley: University of California Press, 1999.
Douglas, M. *Leviticus as Literature*. Oxford: Oxford University Press, 1999.
———. *Purity and Danger: An Analysis of the Concepts of Pollution and Taboo*. London: Routledge and Kegan Paul, 1966.
Eilberg-Schwartz, H., ed. *The People of the Body: Jews and Judaism from an Embodied Perspective*. Albany: State University of New York Press, 1992.
———. *The Savage in Judaism: An Anthropology of Israelite and Ancient Judaism*. Bloomington: Indiana University Press, 1990.
Ellens, D. *Women in the Sex Texts in Leviticus and Deuteronomy: A Comparative Conceptual Analysis*. LHBOTS 458. London: T&T Clark, 2008.
Erbele-Küster, D. "Archaeological and Textual Evidence for Menstruation as Gendered Taboo in the Second Temple Period?" Pages 169–84 in *Gender and Social Norms in Ancient Israel, Early Judaism and Christianity: Texts and Material Culture*. Edited by M. Bauks and K. Galor. Journal of Ancient Judaism Supplements 28. Göttingen: Vandenhoeck & Ruprecht, 2019.
———. *Body, Gender and Purity in Leviticus 12 and 15*. LHBOTS 539. London: T&T Clark, 2017.
———. "Die Körperbestimmungen in Lev 11–15." Pages 209–24 in *Menschenbilder und Körperkonzepte im Alten Israel, in Ägypten und im Alten Orient*. Edited by A. Berlejung, J. Dietrich, and J. F. Quack. ORA 9. Tübingen: Mohr Siebeck, 2012.
———. *Körper und Geschlecht: Studien zur Anthropologie von Lev 12 und 15*. WMANT 121. Neukirchen-Vluyn: Neukirchner Verlag, 2008.
———. "'She Shall Remain in (Accordance to) Her-Blood-of-Purification': Ritual Dynamics of Defilement and Purification in Leviticus 12." Pages 59–70 in *Sacrifice, Cult, and Atonement in Early Judaism and Christianity: Constituents and Critique*. Edited by H. L. Wiley and C. A. Eberhart. Atlanta: Society of Biblical Literature, 2017.
Frevel, C. "Purity Conceptions in the Book of Numbers in Context." Pages 369–411 in *Purity and the Forming of Religious Traditions in the Ancient Mediterranean World and Ancient Judaism*. Edited by C. Frevel and C. Nihan. Dynamics in the History of Religion 3. Leiden: Brill, 2013.
Gerstenberger, E. *Leviticus: A Commentary*. Translated by D. W. Stott. OTL. Louisville, KY: Westminster John Knox Press, 1996.
Gilders, W. K. *Blood Ritual in the Hebrew Bible: Meaning and Power*. Baltimore: Johns Hopkins University Press, 2004.
Gorman, F. H. *The Ideology of Ritual: Space, Time and Status in the Priestly Theology*. JSOTSup 91. Sheffield, 1990.

———. "Pagans and Priests: Critical Reflections on Method." Pages 96–110 in *Perspectives in Purity and Purification in the Bible*. Edited by B. Schwartz, D. P. Wright, J. Stackert, and N. S. Meshel. LHBOTS 474. London: T&T Clark, 2008.

Harrington, H. "Interpreting Leviticus in the Second Temple Period: Struggling with Ambiguity." Pages 214–29 in *Reading Leviticus: A Conversation with Mary Douglas*. Edited by J. Sawyer. JSOTSup 22. Sheffield: Sheffield Academic Press, 1996.

Knierim, R. *Text and Concept in Leviticus 1:1–9: A Case in Exegetical Method*. FAT 2/1. Tübingen: Mohr Siebeck, 1992.

Levine, B. A. *Leviticus*. The JPS Torah Commentary. Philadelphia: Jewish Publication Society, 1989.

Liss, H. "Ritual Purity and the Construction of Identity." Pages 329–54 in *The Books of Leviticus and Numbers*. Edited by T. Römer. BETL 215. Leuven: Peeters, 2008.

Marsman, H. *Women in Ugarit and Israel: Their Social and Religious Position in the Context of the Ancient Near East*. OtSt 49. Leiden: Brill, 2003.

Marx, A. *Les systèmes sacrificiels de l'Ancien Testament: Formes et fonctions du culte sacrificiel à Yhwh*. VTSup 105. Leiden: Brill, 2005.

Mauss, M. "Les techniques du corps." *Journal de Psychologie* 32 (1934): 271–93.

Milgrom, J. *Leviticus 1–16: A New Translation with Introduction and Commentary*. AB 3A. New York: Doubleday, 1991.

Nihan, C. "Forms and Functions of Purity in Leviticus." Pages 311–68 in *Purity and the Forming of Religious Traditions in the Ancient Mediterranean World and Ancient Judaism*. Edited by C. Frevel and C. Nihan. Dynamics in the History of Religion 3. Leiden: Brill, 2013.

———. *From Priestly Torah to Pentateuch: A Study in the Composition of the Book of Leviticus*. FAT 2/25. Tübingen: Mohr Siebeck, 2007.

Ruane, N. J. *Sacrifice and Gender in Biblical Law*. Cambridge: Cambridge University Press 2013.

Watts, J. W. *Ritual and Rhetoric in Leviticus: From Sacrifice to Scripture*. Cambridge: Cambridge University Press, 2007.

———. "Ritual Rhetoric in the Pentateuch: The Case of Leviticus 1–16." Pages 307–18 in *The Books of Leviticus and Numbers*. Edited by T. Römer. BETL 208. Leuven: Peeters, 2008.

Werrett, I. C. *Ritual Purity and the Dead Sea Scrolls*. STDJ 72. Leiden: Brill, 2004.

Whitekettle, R. "Leviticus 12 and the Israelite Women: Ritual Process, Liminality and the Womb." *ZAW* 107 (1995): 397–408.

Wright, D. *The Disposal of Impurity: Elimination Rites in the Bible and in Hittite and Mesopotamian Literature*. SBLDS 101. Atlanta: Scholars Press, 1987.

Zwickel, W. *Der Tempelkult in Kanaan und Israel: Studien zur Kultgeschichte Palästinas von der Mittelbronzezeit bis zum Untergang Judas*. FAT 10. Tübingen: Siebeck Mohr, 1994.

CHAPTER 11

The Reception of Ritual Laws in the Early Second Temple Period: Evidence from Ezra-Nehemiah and Chronicles

Julia Rhyder

AN IMPORTANT IDEA ADVANCED by ritual theorists and biblical scholars alike is that the writing of ritual texts "fosters the standardization of ritual."[1] It is axiomatic in ritual studies that written rituals appear stabilized and unified in ways that can rarely be achieved in actual ritual practice that, despite being characterized by repetition and fixity, is also subject to contestation and variation.[2] This understanding of "ritual textualization" can arguably be traced to the ritual theories of Catherine Bell.[3] Building on the work of Jack Goody, Bell argued that the fixing of specific ritual sequences in writing enables a particular version of a given ritual to define what is "orthodox" to the exclusion of other conceptions of the same ritual action.[4] Moreover, as ritual texts gain authority, she observed that ritual power becomes concentrated in the hands of those who have access to the text and the right to interpret it.[5] Although the discussion has taken various avenues following Bell's theoretical articulation over twenty years ago, the idea that ritual texts promote "an ideal of uniformity and the elimination or marginalization of alternatives"[6] continues to strongly influence subsequent studies of the textualization of ritual.

---

1. C. Bell, "Ritualization of Texts and Textualization of Ritual in the Codification of Taoist Liturgy," *HR* 27.4 (1988): 366–92 at 390.
2. See, e.g., C. Bell, *Ritual Theory, Ritual Practice* (Oxford: Oxford University Press, 1992); C. Bell, *Ritual: Perspectives and Dimensions* (Oxford: Oxford University Press, 1997); C. Humphrey and J. Laidlaw, *The Archetypal Actions of Ritual: A Theory of Ritual Illustrated by the Jain Rite of Worship*, Oxford Studies in Social and Cultural Anthropology (Oxford: Clarendon Press, 1994); C. De Pee, *The Writing of Weddings in Middle Period China: Text and Ritual Practice in the Eighth Through Fourteenth Centuries*, SUNY Series in Chinese Philosophy and Culture (Albany: State University of New York Press, 2007).
3. See esp. Bell, "Ritualization of Texts"; Bell, *Ritual Theory*; Bell, *Ritual*. "Textualization," as defined by Bell ("Ritualization of Texts," 390) is "the generation of textual objects that structure social interactions around their use and transmission." She considers ritual textualization specifically to be "the emergence of authoritative textual guidelines" (*Ritual*, 204).
4. Among Goody's works that influenced Bell, see esp. J. Goody, *The Logic of Writing and the Organization of Society* (Cambridge: Cambridge University Press, 1986).
5. See Bell, *Ritual*, 204.
6. Bell, *Ritual Theory*, 137.

In the case of ancient Israel, Sarianna Metso and Eugene Ulrich have argued that the ritual laws of Leviticus were intended to have just such a standardizing effect on ritual practice by providing "clear uniform instructions for correct procedures in the traditional sacred rituals."[7] This cultic function explains, in their view, the relative exactitude with which the text of Leviticus was transmitted in the late Second Temple period. Scholars generally agree that the text of Leviticus shows a greater degree of uniformity than other books of the Hebrew Bible.[8] Not only do the MT, LXX, and SP of Leviticus stem from closely related parent texts, but the seventeen Leviticus manuscripts found at the Dead Sea (fourteen Hebrew manuscripts, one Aramaic translation [4Q156] and two Greek manuscripts [4Q119–20]) evince very limited variation, both from one another and also from MT, LXX, and SP. Mesto argued, in greater detail, that Leviticus might have attained this high level of standardization because priestly scribes sought to give the appearance of fixed, stable ritual practice by preserving a more or less stable textual base for the Leviticus prescriptions. "Evidently," Metso has written, "their rationale was *not* careful preservation of a 'standard text' of the *scriptural* book—otherwise, why were Exodus and Numbers allowed textual development?—but preservation of instructions for standard praxis for the sacred rituals and orthodox priestly traditions to be practiced in the temple and beyond."[9]

This theory concerning the transmission of Leviticus complements the work of James W. Watts concerning the book's rhetorical impact. Framed as YHWH's direct

---

7. S. Metso and E. Ulrich, "The Old Greek Translation of Leviticus," in *The Book of Leviticus: Composition and Reception*, ed. R. Rendtorff and R. A. Kugler, VTSup 93, FIOTL 3 (Leiden: Brill, 2003), 247–68 at 267.

8. On the textual stability of Leviticus, see, e.g., K. A. Mathews, "The Leviticus Scrolls (11QpaleoLev) and the Text of the Hebrew Bible," *CBQ* 48.2 (1986): 171–207; E. Ulrich, "'4QLev-Num^a,' '4QLev^b,'" in *Qumran Cave 4: VII. Genesis to Numbers*, ed. E. Ulrich and F. M. Cross, DJD 12 (Oxford: Clarendon Press, 1994), 153–87; E. Eshel, "Book of Leviticus," in *Encyclopedia of the Dead Sea Scrolls*, ed. L. H. Schiffman and J. C. VanderKam (Oxford: Oxford University Press, 2000), 1:488–93; P. W. Flint, "The Book of Leviticus in the Dead Sea Scrolls," in *The Book of Leviticus: Composition and Reception*, ed. R. Rendtorff and R. A. Kugler, VTSup 93 (Leiden: Brill, 2003), 323–41; S. Metso, "Evidence from the Qumran Scrolls for the Scribal Transmission of Leviticus," in *Editing the Bible: Assessing the Task Past and Present*, ed. J. S. Kloppenborg and J. H. Newman, RBS 69 (Atlanta: Society of Biblical Literature, 2012), 67–79.

9. Metso, "Evidence from the Qumran Scrolls," 69; compare Metso and Ulrich, "Old Greek," 267. Russell Hobson has argued that a similar "level of standardization" to that which was observed in "the scrolls of the Pentateuchal texts from the late Second Temple period" can be observed in certain ritual materials in Mesopotamia (R. Hobson, *Transforming Literature into Scripture: Texts as Cult Objects at Nineveh and Qumran* [Sheffield: Sheffield Equinox Press, 2012], 153). From his survey of cuneiform texts preserved in multiple copies, Hobson observed that the eighteen tablets found at the library of Ninevah preserving the instructions of the *Mîs-Pî* "Opening of the Mouth" ritual displayed less variation than other materials, such as the Gilgamesh epic or the Laws of Hammurabi, which differed considerably from one copy to another. This may suggest that ancient ritual texts often exhibited a greater level of fixity and stability than nonritual compositions. See, however, the essay by Y. Feder in this volume, which suggests that Hittite ritual texts might not display such a trend toward stability.

The Reception of Ritual Laws in the Early Second Temple Period 257

speech to his chosen prophet Moses (and on occasion Aaron [e.g., Lev 10:8–11]), Leviticus repeatedly asserts its unique authority among the Israelite community and mandates that their ritual practice conform to its prescriptions.[10] As a result, ancient audiences would have been invited to consider Leviticus as the "standard, indeed, definitive instructions for Israel's most important cultic practices,"[11] marginalizing competing versions of Israel's rituals. Moreover, Watts has suggested that the elevation of Leviticus as a ritual standard went hand in hand with the promotion of the Aaronide priesthood, since this is the only institution that the book presents as administering Israel's cult and applying its ritual law.[12]

The work of Metso, Ulrich, and Watts offers important insights into the possible role that the writing of ritual law, and especially the laws of Leviticus, might have played in promoting particular ritual standards for the Israelite cult. However, so far this discussion of the effects of ritual textualization in ancient Israel has been largely based on the internal evidence within Leviticus, or from what can be reconstructed about its transmission from manuscript evidence. One question that remains is how the earliest reception of these ritual laws in the narratives of early Second Temple texts such as Ezra-Nehemiah and Chronicles might contribute to our understanding of their standardizing tendency. Of course, these narratives attest only to the imaginative responses of Israelite scribes to ritual laws, as opposed to how ritual texts were used in actual performance; they are "textual *representation[s]* of a ritual performance" that must not be confused with "ritual performance itself."[13] However, observing how scribes engaged with pentateuchal ritual laws provides valuable evidence of how these ritual materials were imagined to work in practice and what such imaginings might reveal about the extent to which ritual texts provided a ritual standard in Second Temple times.

The value of this evidence has been partly recognized by Watts, who has analyzed selected narratives, such as Ezra's reading of the law in Neh 8:1–12, in order to understand the elevation of the Torah to the status of scripture in the Persian period and the role of ritual law in this process.[14] Several other studies

---

10. See esp. the use of formulaic phrases such as *z't twrt* "this is the law of X," *ḥqt 'wlm ldrtykm* "an everlasting statute throughout your generations," *bkl mwšbtykm* "in all your settlements."

11. J. W. Watts, *Ritual and Rhetoric in Leviticus: From Sacrifice to Scripture* (Cambridge: Cambridge University Press, 2007), 65.

12. See, e.g., J. W. Watts, "Scripturalization and the Aaronide Dynasties," *JHebS* 13.6 (2013): 3–8, doi:10.55.08/jhs.2013.v13.a6. For further discussion, see J. Rhyder, *Centralizing the Cult: The Holiness Legislation in Leviticus 17–26*, FAT 134 (Tübingen: Mohr Siebeck, 2019), 136–52, 177–88.

13. W. K. Gilders's essay in the present volume is also interested in textual rituals in which earlier rituals texts are received and interpreted, although he is focused on rabbinic literature rather than Ezra-Nehemiah and Chronicles. The quotes are taken directly from pp. 312–13 of this volume.

14. J. W. Watts, "Ritual Legitimacy and Scriptural Authority," *JBL* 124.3 (2005): 401–17; J. W. Watts, "Using Ezra's Time as a Methodological Pivot for Understanding the Rhetoric and Functions of the Pentateuch," in *The Pentateuch: International Perspectives on Current Research*, ed. T. B. Dozeman, K. Schmid, and B. Schwartz, FAT 78 (Tübingen: Mohr Siebeck, 2011), 489–506.

have taken similar interest in the references to the Torah in the rituals described in Ezra-Nehemiah and Chronicles as evidence of the growing authority of the Pentateuch in the scribal circles of the Second Temple period.[15] However, one aspect of this discussion that remains underdeveloped is the seeming compatibility between citing the Torah as a ritual authority while at the same time describing ritual performances in which the ritual law is not strictly adhered to. While Ezra-Nehemiah and Chronicles narrate ritual celebrations in which the Torah functions as a respected source of ritual information, the imaginative ritual practice often diverges in significant ways from any legal norm.[16]

This essay examines three cases in which pentateuchal ritual law is employed in Ezra-Nehemiah and Chronicles and reveals the complex articulation between text and (imagined) ritual that characterizes the reception of ritual law in Second Temple traditions.[17] Ezra-Nehemiah and Chronicles provide an excellent starting point for studying the use of ritual law in the Second Temple period, since they present a set of texts that is fairly coherent in genre and dating; for all of their differences, scholars generally agree that these books constitute "histories" of ancient Israel (the reliability of which remains much debated) that were compiled during the late Persian or early Hellenistic period (fourth or third century BCE).[18] Furthermore, the Torah to which they refer, although unlikely

---

15. See esp. J. R. Shaver, *Torah and the Chronicler's History Work: An Inquiry into the Chronicler's References to Laws, Festivals, and Cultic Institutions in Relationship to Pentateuchal Legislation*, BJS 196 (Atlanta: Scholars Press, 1989); R. Rendtorff, "Chronicles and the Priestly Torah," in *Texts, Temples, and Traditions: A Tribute to Menahem Haran*, ed. M. V. Fox et al. (Winona Lake, IN: Eisenbrauns, 1996), 259–66; H.-S. Bae, *Vereinte Suche nach JHWH: Die Hiskianische und Josianische Reform in der Chronik*, BZAW 355 (Berlin: de Gruyter, 2005); W. M. Schniedewind, *How the Bible Became a Book: The Textualization of Ancient Israel* (Cambridge: Cambridge University Press, 2005), 175; H. K. Harrington, "The Use of Leviticus in Ezra-Nehemiah," *JHebS* 13 (2013), doi:10.55.08/jhs.2013.v13.a3; M. LeFebvre, *Collections, Codes, and Torah: The Re-characterization of Israel's Written Law*, LHBOTS 451 (New York: T&T Clark, 2006), 103–38.

16. As observed by M. Fishbane, "Revelation and Tradition: Aspects of Inner-Biblical Exegesis," *JBL* 99.3 (1980): 343–61; M. Fishbane, *Biblical Interpretation in Ancient Israel* (Oxford: Clarendon Press, 1985); H. Najman, "Torah of Moses: Pseudonymous Attributions in Second Temple Writings," in *The Interpretation of Scripture in Early Judaism and Christianity: Studies in Language and Tradition*, ed. C. A. Evans, Journal for the Study of the Pseudepigrapha Supplement Series 33 (Sheffield: Sheffield Academic Press, 2000), 202–16.

17. Compare with Nathaniel Levtow's essay "Text Production and Destruction in Ancient Israel: Ritual and Political Dimensions," in *Social Theory and the Study of Israelite Religion: Essays in Retrospect and Prospect*, ed. S. M. Olyan, RBS 71 (Atlanta: Society of Biblical Literature, 2012), 111–39; while it focuses on texts other than Ezra-Nehemiah and Chronicles, it also engages Bell's theories in arguing against static conceptions of Israelite scribal activity in which writing is assumed to be "an essentially conservative activity" (112).

18. On the dating of Ezra-Nehemiah, see, e.g., the summary in H. G. M. Williamson, *Ezra, Nehemiah*, Word Books 16 (Waco, TX: Word Biblical Commentary, 1985), xxxv–xxxvi; on Chronicles, see, e.g., G. N. Knoppers, *1 Chronicles 1–9: A New Translation with Introduction and Commentary*, AB 12 (New York: Doubleday, 2004), 101–17. This does not preclude the possibility that texts were added to these books beyond the third century BCE. However, it seems highly probable that at least

to be identical to the MT, probably corresponds to a fairly developed version of the Pentateuch.[19] Admittedly, the specific texts analyzed here inform us of only selected aspects of the possible influence of ritual texts of the Pentateuch in the scribal practices of the Second Temple period. Yet, the diverse ways in which these scribes imagined that the law might be ideally applied already suggests that the link between ritual texts and ritual standards might have been more complex than is usually acknowledged by scholars.

11.1. Ritual Law and Ritual Innovation in the Celebration of Sukkôt in Neh 8:13-18

Nehemiah 8:13-18 recount the celebration of Sukkôt by the people of Jerusalem following Ezra's public reading of the law. The account is missing from 1 Esdras, which strongly suggests that it is a late addition to Neh 8 that describes

---

a first version of each of these books was already in circulation by the early Hellenistic period. My decision to treat examples from Ezra-Nehemiah and Chronicles together does not stem from any conviction that these books were compiled by the same scribe ("the Chronicler"), as was traditionally assumed (L. Zunz, *Die gottesdienstlichen Vorträge der Juden historisch entwickelt: Ein Beitrag zur Altertumskunde und biblischen Kritik, zur Literatur- und Religionsgeschichte* [Berlin: A. Asher, 1832], 19–29; F. C. Movers, *Kritische Untersuchungen über die biblische Chronik: Ein Beitrag zur Einleitung in das Alte Testament* [Bonn: Habicht/Georgi, 1834]; S. Driver, *An Introduction to the Literature of the Old Testament*, 9th ed., International Theological Library [New York: Meridan Books, 1956], 535–40; E. L. Curtis and A. A. Madsen, *A Critical and Exegetical Commentary on the Books of Chronicles*, International Critical Commentary [Edinburgh: T&T Clark, 1910], 27–36). I instead follow S. Japhet, "The Supposed Common Authorship of Chronicles and Ezra-Nehemiah Investigated Anew," *VT* 18.3 (1968): 330–71; H. Williamson, *1 and 2 Chronicles* (Grand Rapids: Eerdmans; London: Marshall-Morgan & Scott, 1987), 5–11; and others who have argued that these books were most likely composed as independent works.

19. The authors of Ezra-Nehemiah and of Chronicles refer to the Torah under a large variety of titles: "the book of Moses" (e.g., Ezra 6:18; Neh 13:1; 2 Chr 35:12); "the law of Moses" (e.g., Ezra 3:2; 7:6; 2 Chr 23:18; 30:10); "the book of the law of Moses" (e.g., Neh 8:1); "the commandments of Moses" (e.g., 2 Chr 8:13); "the law of YHWH" (e.g., Ezra 7:10; 1 Chr 16:40; 2 Chr 31:3, 4; 35:26); "the law of your God" (e.g., Ezra 7:14, 26); "the book of the law of God" (e.g., Neh 8:18); "the book of the law of YHWH" (e.g., Neh 9:3; 2 Chr 17:9; 34:14); "the law of God" (e.g., Neh 8:8; 10:29, 30); "the book of the covenant" (e.g., 2 Chr 34:30); "the book of the law" (e.g., Neh 8:3; 2 Chr 34:15); "the book" (e.g., Neh 8:5, 8); "the law" (e.g., Ezra 10:3; Neh 8:2, 7, 9, 13, 14; 10:35, 37; 13:3; 2 Chr 34:19); "the word of YHWH by the authority of Moses" (e.g., 2 Chr 35:6); and perhaps also "the word of YHWH" (1 Chr 15:15). Despite this diversity, there is a clear and consistent connection between the law and the figure of Moses, which supports identifying the Torah in these books with the Pentateuch; see H. G. M. Williamson, "History," in *It Is Written: Scripture Citing Scripture; Essays in Honour of Barnabas Lindars*, ed. D. A. Carson and H. G. M. Williamson (Cambridge: Cambridge University Press, 1992), 25–38 at 25. However, the Pentateuch would have certainly remained in a fluid state at the time Ezra-Nehemiah and Chronicles were written and should not simply be equated with the MT.

an entirely invented occasion.[20] Verse 13 recounts how Ezra, the Levites, and the heads of families came together to study the Torah.

14 *wymṣ'w ktwb btwrh 'šr ṣwh yhwh byd mšh 'šr yšbw bny yśr'l bskwt bḥg bḥdš hšby'y* 15 *w'šr yšmy'w wy'byrw qwl bkl 'ryhm wbyrwšlm l'mr ṣ'w hhr whby'w 'ly zyt w'ly 'ṣ šmn w'ly hds w'ly tmrym w'ly 'ṣ 'bt l'št skt kktwb* 16 *wyṣ'w h'm wyby'w wy'św lhm skwt 'yš 'l ggw wbḥṣrtyhm wbḥṣrwt byt h'lhym wbrḥwb š'r hmym wbrḥwb š'r 'prym*

14 And they found written in the law that YHWH commanded by the authority of Moses that the sons of Israel shall dwell in booths during the festival of the seventh month, 15 and that they should announce and proclaim in all their towns and in Jerusalem as follows: "Go out to the mountain and bring branches of olive and of pine, of myrtle, palm and other trees to make booths, as it is written." 16 And the people went out and fetched them and made booths for themselves, each person on his own roof, and in their courts, and in the courts of the house of God, and in the square of the Water Gate, and in the square of the Gate of Ephraim.

The entire account is framed as a story of Torah observance: it is only when Ezra, the Levites and the heads of families find relevant instructions in the Mosaic Torah that they decide to instigate the celebration (v. 14), and the specific rites that must be proclaimed in verse 15 are all undertaken *kktwb* "as it is written" in the law.[21] The meaning of the *kktwb* formula is a matter of scholarly discussion. It occurs in several passages in Ezra-Nehemiah and Chronicles,

---

20. Some scholars argue that the celebration of Sukkôt was originally found at the end of 1 Esdras but has somehow been lost; see, e.g., W. R. Rudolph, *Esra und Nehemia samt 3 Esra*, Handbuch zum Alten Testament 20 (Tübingen: Mohr Siebeck, 1949), xiv–xv; L. L. Grabbe, "Chicken or Egg? Which Came First, 1 Esdras or Ezra-Nehemiah?," in *Was 1 Esdras First? An Investigation into the Priority and Nature of 1 Esdras*, ed. L. S. Fried, AIL 7 (Atlanta: Society of Biblical Literature, 2011), 31–44 at 38, 43. However, Arie van der Kooij and Zipora Talshir, among others, have defended 1 Esd 9:55 as a logical place at which to end the book, with Talshir in particular pointing out that the ending shares important parallels with that of Chronicles, with both books ending with a verb in midsentence. See A. van der Kooij, "On the Ending of the Book of 1 Esdras," in *VII Congress of the International Organization for Septuagint and Cognate Studies*, ed. C. E. Cox, Septuagint and Cognate Studies 31 (Atlanta: Scholars Press, 1991), 37–49; Z. Talshir, "Ancient Composition Patterns Mirrored in 1 Esdras and the Priority of the Canonical Composition Type," in *Was 1 Esdras First? An Investigation into the Priority and Nature of 1 Esdras*, ed. L. S. Fried, AIL 7 (Atlanta: Society of Biblical Literature, 2011), 109–30. While the ritual occasion described in Neh 8:13–18 is most likely a literary invention, Sukkôt would have almost certainly been a well-known festival among the first readers of this text. Likewise with regard to Hezekiah's Passover in 2 Chr 30 (discussed below): while this specific occasion probably never transpired, Passover would have been observed by the earliest readers of the account.

21. Compare the formula *ktwb btwrh* in v. 14.

as well as a single text of Joshua (8:31) and selected passages of 1–2 Kings (1 Kgs 2:3; 2 Kgs 14:6; 23:21). In each case, the law/book of Moses (or *spr hbryt* "book of the covenant" in 2 Kgs 23:21; *twrt yhwh* "law of YHWH" in 2 Chr 31:3; 35:26) is the authority that is cited as justifying a given course of action. The formula therefore supports the view that Second Temple scribes viewed the Mosaic Torah as providing a guide for behavior that should (ideally) be followed, since they praise actions that were done "as it is written" in the Torah and denounce those that were not.

However, scholars recognize that the *kktwb* formula should not always be taken literally. While it is sometimes used in contexts where a clear legal precedent for the described action can be found in the Pentateuch, in other cases no corresponding ruling can be found (at least in the versions of the Pentateuch that are known to us). For instance, in Ezra 6:18 the priests and Levites are said to have been divided into particular groupings (*plgwt* "courses") "in accordance with the writing of the book of Moses" (*kktb spr msh*), even though, as far as we can tell, there is no corresponding law preserved in the Pentateuch for such divisions.[22] In this case, the *kktwb* formula seems to be a mechanism of "pseudonymously"[23] attributing legal innovation to the Mosaic Torah to legitimate the founding of new divisions between priests and Levites. It is thus a way of authorizing new legal rulings by claiming Mosaic authority.

In the case of Neh 8:13–18, however, there is good reason to believe that the authors of these verses did indeed know a law in the Torah that contained similar instructions for the Festival of Sukkôt, and that it was for this reason that they claimed that the actions were performed *kktwb*. The description of the celebration in Neh 8:14–16 shares a number of striking similarities with Lev 23:39–43. This law commands that the celebration of Sukkôt take place in the seventh month of the year. The Israelites are also required to live in booths ("you shall live in booths seven days," Lev 23:42) and to collect foliage for the celebration ("you shall take the fruit of splendid trees, fronds of palms, branches of leafy trees, and willows of the stream," Lev 23:40). These requirements are not found in other pentateuchal instructions for the Festival of Sukkôt.[24] The strength of the correspondances between Neh 8:14–16 and Lev 23:39–43 therefore makes it probable that the person who wrote the former had the text of the Leviticus law

---

22. In 1 Chr 23–26 it is David who is said to have founded these divisions.
23. Najman, "Torah of Moses," 203.
24. In Exod 23:16 and 34:22 the festival, which is here termed *hg h'sp* "the Festival of the Ingathering," is dated simply to the "end of the year." Deuteronomy 16:13, for its part, commands that *hg hskwt* "the Festival of Sukkôt" be observed simply "when you have gathered in the produce from your threshing floor and from your wine press." While Num 28:12 shares the same idea as Lev 23:39–43 that a festival should be held on the fifteenth day of the seventh month, it never refers to this festival as *skwt*; cf. Ezek 45:25.

in mind when claiming that the celebration was held in accordance with written authority.

Yet, despite claiming that the festival adheres to the law, the ritual actions described in verses 15–16 differ in important respects from what the law of Lev 23:39–43 prescribes.[25] Not only is the foliage different in the two texts (with fruit entirely missing from Neh 8), but the function of the branches also differs: whereas Lev 23:40 commands the branches be used as instruments of "rejoicing" (śmḥ), in Neh 8:16 the branches are used as a material for constructing the booths, which are then placed on the roofs of the houses, in the public square, and within the temple grounds.[26]

To explain this difference, Juha Pakkala argues that the author of Neh 8 must have known an "early or middle form of the law" of Lev 23:39–43 that was later "heavily edited so that parts of the law that Neh 8:13–18 refers to are no longer present in the current versions of the Pentateuch."[27] While this is possible, it is unlikely given that no other Second Temple text besides Neh 8:13–18 attests to the use of the branches as building materials, let alone ascribes such a usage to the law.[28] Others have suggested that the differences between Neh 8:13–18 and Lev 23:39–43 are due to ambiguities in the wording of the Leviticus instruction. For example, Michael Fishbane suggests that, because Lev 23:39–43 do not prescribe with which material the Israelites should construct the booths, the author of Neh 8:13–18 was forced to engage in etymological speculation, taking "the fact that the noun *skwt* is derivable from the verbal stem *skk* 'to cover over [with branches]'"[29] as reason to assume that the branches were the intended material. However, this overlooks the fact that Lev 23:40 clearly ascribes an alternative usage to the branches—namely, as instruments of rejoicing—which the scribes

---

25. This has been widely noted by scholars. See, e.g., Shaver, *Torah*, 102; Williamson, "It Is Written," 29–30; H. Ulfgard, *The Story of "Sukkot": The Setting, Shaping, and Sequel of the Biblical Feast of Tabernacles*, Beiträge zur Geschichte der biblischen Exegese 34 (Tübingen: Mohr Siebeck, 1998), 132–34; G. J. Venema, *Reading Scripture in the Old Testament: Deuteronomy 9–10; 31—2 Kings 22–23—Jeremiah 36—Nehemiah 8*, trans. C. E. Smit, OtSt 48 (Leiden: Brill, 2004), 177–78; J. Pakkala, *Ezra the Scribe: The Development of Ezra 7–10 and Nehemiah 8*, BZAW 347 (Berlin: de Gruyter, 2004), 158–64; LeFebvre, *Collections, Codes, and Torah*, 108–9.

26. There is also no obvious precedent in Lev 23:39–43 for the command to "announce and proclaim" (yśmyʿw wyʿbyrw qwl) the collection of branches (Neh 8:15). This could, however, be a reference to Lev 23:4 and 37, which require the Israelites to proclaim (qrʾ) all the festivals listed in the main festal calendar; see further Williamson, "It Is Written," 30; J. Milgrom, *Leviticus 23–27: A New Translation with Introduction and Commentary*, AB 3C (New York: Doubleday, 2001), 2064.

27. Pakkala, *Ezra the Scribe*, 204; see further Shaver, *Torah*, 103.

28. Note that 2 Maccabees 10:7; Jubilees 16:29–31; Josephus, *Ant.* 3.245; and m. Sukkah 4:1–7 all follow Lev 23:39–43 in describing the branches as instruments of rejoicing.

29. Fishbane, *Biblical Interpretation*, 111. For similar ideas, see, e.g., J. Blenkinsopp, *Ezra-Nehemiah: A Commentary*, OTL (London: SCM Press, 1989), 291–92; Williamson, "It Is Written," 30–31; Milgrom, *Leviticus 23–27*, 2066–67; Harrington, "Use of Leviticus," 14–17; LeFebvre, *Collections, Codes, and Torah*, 110.

responsible for the account in Neh 8 have ignored.[30] It also cannot explain why the foliage specified in the two texts differs so widely.[31]

It seems more plausible to suppose that the description of Sukkôt in Neh 8, while modeled on the ritual text of Lev 23, includes ritual innovations for which there is no basis in the Torah.[32] The new use of the branches correlates the collective dimension of the feast—already emphasized in Lev 23 through the remembrance of the exodus (Lev 23:43)—more directly with the sphere of the household by requiring that the booths be constructed on the roofs of individual houses. It thereby presents a new conception of how the feast was to be applied to the urban context of Jerusalem.[33] When it came to specifying the branches to be collected, it seems that the scribes responsible for Neh 8 simply felt no need to follow Lev 23 with realistic accuracy. Yet, despite introducing various adaptations, the account of Neh 8 can still claim to be based on, and even aligned with, the instructions found in the Torah of Moses. Moreover, by depicting the communal officials as having found ($mṣ'$) these ritual specifics written in the law, the innovations are themselves "pseudonymously attributed"[34] to Mosaic Torah.

Doing rituals "by the book" in this case therefore was not a matter of slavishly applying the Torah's instructions to ensure ritual precision. It is instead a communal enterprise of interpreting and applying the law to the ritual occasion at hand. The communal deliberation described in verse 13 sees nonclerical authorities as well as cultic figures convening to study the law, and it is within this context of a communal deliberation that it is determined how the Torah should be used to inform ritual practice. The account of Neh 8 therefore reveals the application of ritual law as being dynamic as opposed to static: that is, while the law provides the standard, in practice it must be mediated. The subsequent success of the festival, as reported in verses 17–18, has the effect of not only validating the changes but also affirming the authority of those who interpreted the law in this way. Note that Neh 8 does not limit the interpretation of

---

30. Some scholars claim that Lev 23:40 does not explain what is to be done with the branches but only commands that the Israelites "take" ($lqḥ$) them; see, e.g., D. J. Clines, *Ezra, Nehemiah, Esther*, New Century Bible Commentary (Grand Rapids, MI: Eerdmans; London: Marshall Morgan & Scott, 1984), 187; Blenkinsopp, *Ezra-Nehemiah*, 291–92. However, the context of the verse makes clear that the purpose of collecting the foliage is to put it to use in rejoicing during the seven-day celebration.

31. While attempts have been made to harmonize the two lists of foliage (see, e.g., Milgrom, *Leviticus 23–27*, 2042), there remains the question of why not only the type but also the number of branches and/or fruit differ in Neh 8 and Lev 23.

32. As argued by Ulfgard, *Story of "Sukkot,"* 132–35.

33. See further J. Rhyder, "Space and Memory in the Book of Leviticus," in *Scripture as Social Discourse: Social-Scientific Perspectives on Early Jewish and Christian Writings*, ed. T. Klutz, C. A. Strine, and J. M. Keady (London: T&T Clark, 2018), 83–96 at 90.

34. Najman, "Torah of Moses," 203.

the law to priestly figures but includes customary leaders (namely, the heads of families) that are not specified in the Pentateuch as interpreting ritual law. Thus, the ritual hierarchies that are legitimated through successful interpretation of the law are arguably dynamic, as is the interpretation of the law they promulgate.

11.2. Supplementing Ritual Law: Hezekiah's Passover in 2 Chr 30

The role of communal leaders in supplementing and adapting ritual law is also attested in the account of Hezekiah's Passover in 2 Chr 30. Here, however, there is a new focus on royal authority in the interpretation of the Torah. This chapter has no parallel in Kings, forming part of the Chronicler's greatly expanded description of Hezekiah's reform (2 Chr 29:3–31:21).[35] Most commentators therefore conclude that the Passover account is a literary invention of the Chronicler.[36] Sara Japhet, by contrast, argues that the "unconventional and non-standard features of the story," such as its date in the second month (vv. 2–3) and the eating of the Passover sacrifice by unclean members of the community (vv. 18–20) suggest that the account must be historically accurate, because the Chronicler would never have invented a story that so openly flouts "accepted, legitimate principles."[37]

Yet, there is good reason to assume that the negotiation of new ritual contingencies by Hezekiah and his leadership is key to the story's overall logic. Hezekiah sends an invitation to all Israel and Judah to celebrate Passover at the temple in Jerusalem, "for they had not kept it in great numbers, as it is written (*kktwb*)" (v. 5; cf. v. 1). This reference to written instruction most likely refers to Deut 16:2–7, which decree that Passover is to be observed by the whole community at YHWH's chosen place.[38] But in attempting to celebrate a centralized

---

35. While I employ here the term "Chronicler" in this essay, this is merely a matter of convenience, and does not rule out the possibility that Chronicles was composed by a group of scribes as opposed to a single author.

36. See, e.g., Curtis and Madsen, *Critical and Exegetical Commentary*, 471; S. J. De Vries, "Festival Ideology in Chronicles," in *Problems in Biblical Theology: Essays in Honor of Rolf Knierim*, ed. H. T. C. Sun et al. (Grand Rapids, MI: Eerdmans, 1997), 104–24 at 114; R. W. Klein, *2 Chronicles: A Commentary* (Hermeneia; Minneapolis: Fortress, 2012), 429–30; S. Chavel, "The Second Passover, Pilgrimage, and the Centralized Cult," *HTR* 102 (2009): 1–24 at 5–6.

37. S. Japhet, *I and II Chronicles: A Commentary*, OTL (Louisville, KY: Westminster John Knox Press, 1993), 935.

38. As argued, for instance, in ibid., 941; H. Donner, *Aufsätze zum Alten Testament aus vier Jahrzehnten*, BZAW 224 (Berlin: de Gruyter, 1994), 229; T. Schaack, *Die Ungeduld des Papiers: Studien zum alttestamentlichen Verständnis des Schreibens anhand des Verbums katab im Kontext administrativer Vorgänge*, BZAW 262 (Berlin: de Gruyter, 1998), 107; K. L. Spawn, *"As It is Written" and Other Citation Formulae in the Old Testament: Their Use, Development, Syntax, and Significance*, BZAW 311 (Berlin: de Gruyter, 2002), 111–12; L. C. Jonker, *Reflections of King Josiah in Chronicles: Late Stages of the Josiah Reception in 2 Chr 34f.*, Textpragmatische Studien zur Hebräischen Bibel 2 (Gütersloh: Gütersloher Verlagshaus, 2003), 70.

Passover in accordance with the law, Hezekiah faces a problem—namely, "they were unable to observe it at its time (*lʾ yklw lʿśtw bʿt hhyʾ*)," which, according to the priestly traditions of the Pentateuch is the fourteenth day of the first month (see Exod 12:6; Lev 23:5; Num 9:3, 5; 28:16)—"because the priests had not been consecrated in sufficient number, nor had the people been gathered to Jerusalem" (v. 3).[39] Hezekiah consults "his chiefs and all the assembly in Jerusalem" (v. 2) and together they decide that the Passover is to be held in the second month. This date is already foreshadowed in Num 9:6–13 as a provision for individuals who are unclean or away on a journey and so "are unable to observe the Passover in its time (*wlʾ yklw lʿśt hpsh bywm hhwʾ*)" (Num 9:6). While 2 Chr 30:2–3 do not cite the law of Num 9 specifically—Hezekiah and the leaders reach their decision without consulting the law—most scholars agree that the ruling is "a collective application" ("*ein kollektive Anwendung*") of what was prescribed with reference to individuals in Num 9:6–13.[40]

This view, it must be said, is occasionally disputed. Simeon Chavel has argued that, since there is no citation formula or direct reference to the law in 2 Chr 30:2–4, there are no grounds to assume that Hezekiah's Passover is an expanded application of Num 9.[41] John Choi has also disputed that 2 Chr 30 is an exegetical development of Num 9.[42] He has argued that the narrative's focus on the concern for how factors of purity and distance might affect when to hold the Passover is "a derivative of the Chronicler's broader ideological concerns"[43] regarding the reinstatement of proper, centralized worship in the Jerusalem temple. There is no need, then, to assume that the Chronicler had a pentateuchal text in mind when exploring the challenges facing Hezekiah when holding a centralized Passover celebration.

---

39. In Deut 16:1–8, Passover / Unleavened Bread is said to be held in *hdš hʾbyb* "the month of Abib" (cf. Exod 23:15; 34:18 with reference to Unleavened Bread). However, this most likely refers to an agricultural event—"the time of ingathering"—rather than a month of the year, as Jan Wagenaar has convincingly demonstrated; see J. Wagenaar, *Origin and Transformation of the Ancient Israelite Festival Calendar*, BZABR 6 (Wiesbaden: Harrassowitz Verlag, 2005), 139–41. The solution of holding the Passover on "the fourteenth day of the second month" therefore reflects the influence of the priestly calendrical program, which, in addition to Exod 12:6; Lev 23:5; Num 9:3, 5; 28:16, is also attested in Ezek 45:21. It is curious that the Chronicler does not mention in v. 3 that the rededication of the temple by Hezekiah had lasted until at least the sixteenth day of the first month (2 Chr 29:17). This would have necessarily ruled out the possibility that Passover could be held on its usual date that year. The omission of this detail by the Chronicler supports reading the account as a response to Num 9 (see further below), since the Chronicler seems to stress only those issues that are listed in that text as relevant criteria for observing Passover in the second month (namely, defilement and distance).

40. Bae, *Vereinte Suche*, 129. See further Fishbane, "Revelation and Tradition," 154–57, 345; Williamson, *1 and 2 Chronicles*, 366; Shaver, *Torah*, 111–12; Schaack, *Die Ungeduld des Papiers*, 107–16; Jonker, *Reflections of King Josiah*, 64–68.

41. Chavel, "Second Passover," 1–24.

42. J. H. Choi, *Traditions at Odds: The Reception of the Pentateuch in Biblical and Second Temple Period Literature*, LHBOTS 518 (New York: T&T Clark, 2010), 60–65.

43. Ibid., 62.

It is indeed peculiar that the law is not explicitly mentioned in 2 Chr 30:2–4. However, while there is no reference to the law in verses 2–4, the Chronicler does refer to written authority in verse 18 when discussing who ate the Passover. In verses 17–19, the Chronicler addresses a new problem that arises after having moved the Passover to the second month.

17 *ky rbt bqhl 'šr l' htqdšw whlwym 'l šhyṭ hpshym lkl l' ṭhwr lhqdyš lyhwh* 18 *ky mrbyṭ h'm rbt m'prym wmnšh yšškr wzblwn l' hṭhrw ky 'klw 't hpsh bl' kktwb ky htpll yḥzqyhw 'lyhm l'mr yhwh hṭwb ykpr b'd* 19 *kl lbbw hkyn ldrwš h'lhym yhwh 'lhy 'bwtyw wl' kṭhrṭ hqdš* 20 *wyšm' yhwh 'l yḥzqyhw wyrp' 't h'm*

17 For there were many in the assembly who had not sanctified themselves, and so the Levites had to slaughter the Passover sacrifice for everyone who was not clean, to make it holy to YHWH. 18 For a multitude of the people, many from Ephraim, and Manasseh, Issachar, and Zebulun, had not purified themselves, yet they ate the Passover—not as it is written! Therefore Hezekiah had prayed for them, saying: "May YHWH who is good atone for everyone 19 who sets his heart to seek the God YHWH, God of his ancestors, although not according to the cleanness of the sanctuary." 20 And YHWH listened to Hezekiah, and healed the people.

It is noteworthy that verse 18 states that the Passover was eaten by unclean pilgrims "not as it is written (*bl' kktwb*)." The does not definitely prove that the Chronicler had a text of the Pentateuch in mind, but since Num 9 addresses (and forbids) the eating of the Passover by unclean members of the community, it is plausible to imagine that this law (or a version of it) was what the Chronicler had in mind. Of course, we cannot rule out the possibility that the Chronicler was here inventing a legal precedent for which there was none, or that the Chronicler knew a different law to which we no longer have access. However, the similarities in the wording of 2 Chr 30:3 (*l' yklw l'štw b't hhy'*) and Num 9:6 (*wl' yklw l'št hpsh bywm hhw'*) highlighted by Fishbane and Thomas Schaack among others, arguably adds weight to the idea that the Chronicler knew Num 9 specifically.[44]

Nevertheless, Hezekiah's Passover does not simply constitute an expanded application of the law of Num 9: it introduces a new issue in the implementation of the law. When trying to hold the Passover in Jerusalem, Hezekiah faces not only the problem that the priests were unable to consecrate themselves in time for Passover in the first month but also the problem that the nonpriestly celebrants who have traveled from afar ("from Ephraim, and Manasseh, Issachar,

---

44. Fishbane, "Revelation and Tradition," 156; Schaack, *Die Ungeduld des Papiers*, 108.

and Zebulun") have arrived in Jerusalem ritually unclean. This outcome is hardly surprising, since the "lack of time and facilities"[45] while traveling would have almost certainly left many of the pilgrims unable to properly prepare themselves for the sacrifice. However, there seems to be no legal precedent for what Hezekiah should do in such a situation: the ritual provision (in Num 9) that would have pertained in such a case of *individual* uncleanliness (namely, waiting until the second month) has already been applied by Hezekiah and his leaders to the case of *collective* defilement of the priests.

This account arguably touches on a more general issue of how to host a centralized Passover as per the law of Deut 16: specifically, how are the Israelites expected to pilgrimage to Jerusalem for Passover and yet simultaneously avoid becoming unclean and so disqualify themselves from partaking in the sacrifice? This applies whether the Passover is held in the first month (as per the standard procedure) or the second (as per the provision in the case of distance or defilement), since in both cases the Israelites would be required by Deut 16 to travel to the central sanctuary.[46]

In order to address this problem, the Chronicler devises a complex, two-part solution in which new ritual roles, and the ritual influence of Hezekiah himself, provide the necessary means to ensure the Passover's success. In both cases, the authority of the ritual Torah remains in the foreground but requires supplementation. First, in verse 17, the Chronicler instigates an emergency measure whereby the Levites perform the slaughter of the Passover sacrifice on behalf of those who were not clean.[47] This is an innovation when compared to Exod 12:6 and Deut 16:2; these laws state that the heads of families shall slaughter their own Passover lambs. Given the absence of a legal precedent, the Chronicler attempts to depict the measure as an extension of what the law prescribes with regard to the ritual roles of the Levites. However, in so doing he, in fact, engages in further invention. Immediately prior to verse 17 we read concerning the priests and the Levites

16 wyʿmdw ʿl ʿmdm kmšpṭm ktwrt mšh ʾyš hʾlhym hkhnym zrqym ʾt hdm myd hlwym

16 And they stood at their posts according to their custom, according to the Torah of Moses, the man of God. The priests dashed the blood from the hand of the Levites.

---

45. Japhet, *I and II Chronicles*, 952.
46. As noted by Chavel, "Second Passover," 21–23.
47. See, however, 2 Chr 35:6 (discussed below), where the role of slaughtering the Passover lamb is permanently assigned to the Levites, and in apparent fulfillment of the law.

There is no relevant Torah instruction either for the positioning of the Levites and the priests or for the role of the Levites in transporting the blood.[48] Nevertheless, the Chronicler justifies the elevation of the Levites in the Passover ritual—and a revised ritual hierarchy in which they occupy a more senior position—by casting their new ritual roles as being in conformity to the law. This further illustrates that it was "possible to describe as Torah of Moses some law or practice without an explicit pentateuchal basis, for the sake of authorization."[49]

A similar mix of concession to the Torah and ritual innovation can be seen in the Chronicler's solution to the eating of the Passover by unclean pilgrims. The Chronicler makes no attempt to pass this off as anything but a ritual error, done in flagrant disregard of legal precedent (see v. 18a). Yet, remarkably, this transgression has no negative impact on the festival. Hezekiah prays for the people (vv. 18b–19), asking YHWH to atone ($\underline{kpr}$) for their mistake, and successfully ensures that the people are healed (rp'). The ritual then continues with success, with all the people eating the sacrificial meal for the full seven days of the festival, and then a spontaneous seven days extra on account of their great joy. It is presumably Hezekiah's unique authority as the royal leader that makes such an outcome possible.

It is difficult to know whether this solution—the royal leader praying for the unclean participants—established a new norm or was simply a one-off response to a ritual emergency. The fact that there was probably no royal leader of the cult at the time that 2 Chr 30 was composed suggests that the measure was not intended to be literally applied every time the Passover was held and unclean pilgrims were present, or, if it was intended to be applied, it would have required resignification in order to incorporate a different sociocultic figure. Nevertheless, it illustrates the general principle that, in new contexts, the ritual law was open to being reconfigured and adapted. New roles could be attributed to ritual actors, such as the Levites, within the authority of the law, and the legitimacy of ritual leaders, such as Hezekiah, his chiefs, and the assembly is affirmed, because despite all the obstacles, they enable the Passover to be held as a centralized festival in accordance with Deut 16.

11.3. Ritual Roles and Ritual Authorities in Josiah's Passover (2 Chr 35:1–19)

One final example concerns the use of ritual law in Josiah's Passover in 2 Chr 35:1–19. This text constitutes a much-reworked version of the brief note in 2 Kgs

---

48. As noted by Japhet, *I and II Chronicles*, 950; Bae, *Vereinte Suche*, 131–33.
49. Najman, "Torah of Moses," 213.

23:21–23 stating that Josiah observed the Passover. The Chronicler here expands his source into an elaborate account of the Passover, which is positioned as the climax of Josiah's cultic reforms.[50] In this imaginative description of the Passover sacrifice, 2 Chr 35:10–13 state

> 10 wtkwn hʿbwdh wyʿmdw hkhnym ʿl ʿmdm whlwym ʿl mhlqwtm kmṣwt hmlk 11 wyšḥṭw hpsḥ wyzrqw hkhnym mydm whlwym mpšyṭym 12 wysyrw hʿlh lttm lmplgwt lbyt ʾbwt lbny hʿm lhqryb lyhwh kktwb bspr msh wkn lbqr 13 wybšlw hpsḥ bʾš kmšpṭ whqdšym bšlw bsyrwt wbdwdym wbṣlḥwt wyryṣw lkl bny hʿm

> 10 When the service had been prepared for, the priests stood in their place, and the Levites in their divisions according to the command of the king. 11 And they slaughtered the Passover sacrifice and the priests dashed [the blood] from their hands, and the Levites did the skinning. 12 They removed the burnt offering to give it, according to their divisions by ancestral houses, to the sons of the people, to offer to YHWH as it is written in the book of Moses. And they did the same with bulls. 13 And they boiled the Passover lamb in fire according to the custom, and they boiled the holy offerings, in the pots and in the caldrons and in the pans, and they hurriedly brought them to all the sons of the people.

Perhaps the best-known example of the use of ritual law in this pericope is the harmonization of competing Passover instructions for the preparation of the Passover lamb (v. 13). In seeking to conform his account to the Mosaic Torah, the Chronicler must navigate two contradictory pentateuchal instructions for how to prepare the Passover sacrifice: while in Deut 16:7 the Israelites are told to boil (bšl) the meat, Exod 12:9 explicitly commands the Israelites not to consume the meat raw or boiled (bšl) but instead to roast it in fire (ṣly ʾš). In an attempt to mediate between the two texts, 2 Chr 35:13 states that the Levites "boiled the Passover lamb in fire according to the custom (wybšlw hpsḥ bʾš kmšpṭ)."[51]

---

50. As argued, e.g., by R. B. Dillard, *2 Chronicles*, Word Bible Commentary 15 (Waco, TX: Word Books, 1987), 287; Jonker, *Reflections of King Josiah*, 24–25, 34–47; O. Dyma, *Die Wallfahrt zum Zweiten Tempel: Untersuchungen zur Entwicklung der Wallfahrtsfeste in vorhasmonäischer Zeit*, FAT 2/40 (Tübingen: Mohr Siebeck, 2009), 137; Choi, *Traditions at Odds*, 66–67.

51. As argued by Fishbane, "Revelation and Tradition," 134–36; Williamson, *1 and 2 Chronicles*, 407; R. Albertz, *A History of Israelite Religion in the Old Testament Period*, trans. J. Bowden, 2 vols. (London: SCM Press, 1994), 2:548; Japhet, *I and II Chronicles*, 1053; Z. Talshir, "Several Canon-Related Concepts Originating in Chronicles," *ZAW* 113.3 (2001): 386–403 at 389; Schniedewind, *How the Bible Became a Book*, 175; Jonker, *Reflections of King Josiah*, 68–69; Bae, *Vereinte Suche*, 147–48; I. Kalimi, *The Reshaping of Ancient Israelite History in Chronicles* (Winona Lake, IN: Eisenbrauns, 2005), 156–58; E. Ben Zvi, "Revisiting 'Boiling in Fire' in 2 Chronicles 35:13 and

While this solution borders on the absurd (how does one boil in fire?) the combination allows the two authoritative instructions to simultaneously inform the ritual, while also overcoming the exegetical problem of how two conflicting laws might simultaneously be considered normative.

This concern to reconcile divergent traditions forms part of a broader trend in the Passover account to depict Josiah as applying the entire range of earlier prescriptions and authorities available to him as he institutes a fully reformed cult.[52] This involves using the Pentateuch to authorize the permanent fixing of the Levites as key ritual specialists in the sacrifice. In 2 Chr 35:3–6, Josiah commissions the Levites to cease their service as bearers of the ark and to assume responsibility for virtually all relevant tasks for the Passover sacrifice that are not already reserved to the priests.

3 wy'mr llwym hmbwnym lkl yśr'l hqdwśym lyhwh tnw 't 'rwn hqdš bbyt 'šr bnh šlmh bn dwyd mlk yśr'l 'yn lkm mś' bktp 'th 'bdw 't yhwh 'lhykm w't 'mw yśr'l 4 whkwnw lbyt 'bwtykm kmḥlqwtykm bktb dwyd mlk yśr'l wbmktb šlmh bnw 5 w'mdw bqdš lplgwt byt h'bwt l'ḥykm bny h'm wḥlqt byt 'b llwym 6 wšḥṭw hpsḥ whtqdśw whkynw l'ḥykm l'śwt kdbr yhwh byd mśh

3 And he said to the Levites who taught all Israel and who were holy to YHWH: "Put the holy ark in the house that Solomon son of David the king of Israel built; you now have no burden upon your shoulders. Now, serve YHWH your God and his people Israel. 4 Prepare yourselves by your ancestral houses, according to your divisions in the written instruction of David, the king of Israel, and the writing of Solomon, his son. 5 Stand in the sanctuary according to the groupings of the ancestral houses of your brothers, the sons of the people, and by ancestral house divisions of the Levites. 6 Slaughter the Passover sacrifice, sanctify yourselves, and make preparations for your brothers, to act according to the word of YHWH by the authority of Moses.

Of particular interest is Josiah's command to the Levites in verse 6 that they should slaughter the Passover sacrifice. While in 2 Chr 30:16–17 the role of slaughtering the Passover lamb is treated as an emergency measure in response to the high number of impure pilgrims, Josiah now assigns it to the Levites on

---

Related Passover Questions: Text, Exegetical Needs and Concerns, and General Implications," in *Biblical Interpretation in Judaism and Christianity*, ed. I. Kalimi and P. J. Haas, LHBOTS 439 (London: T&T Clark, 2006), 238–50.

52. Japhet, *I and II Chronicles*, 1048; Jonker, *Reflections of King Josiah*, 46, 70; Bae, *Vereinte Suche*, 148–49.

a permanent basis and even claims that it is in accordance with Mosaic Torah.[53] Given that no law reserves this role to the Levites, Hugh Williamson argues that the phrase *kdbr yhwh byd mšh* in verse 6b is intended to qualify only the immediately preceding clause ("make preparations for your brothers").[54] However, it seems more likely that the phrase qualifies all three of the preceding imperatives ("slaughter" [*šḥṭ*], "sanctify" [*qdš* Hitpael] and "make preparations" [*kwn* Hiphil]), since they are all coordinated by *waw* conjunctions, with the infinitive construct "to act" *lʿśwṯ* serving as a summary of the three actions taken together. This is therefore a remarkable case in which a ritual role that was previously acknowledged as an innovation (2 Chr 30:17) is transformed without comment into a requirement mandated by law.

A similar phenomenon applies to the role of flaying (*pšṭ*) the sacrificial animal (v. 11). Second Chronicles 30:11–12 (cited above) state that the Levites flayed the animal (v. 11) and distributed it according to ancestral houses, so that it might be offered in accordance with "the book of Moses" (v. 12). Earlier in 2 Chronicles the skinning of the animal is assumed to be the prerogative of the priests (see 2 Chr 29:34). However, during the rededication of the temple by Hezekiah, we are told that "the priests were too few and could not flay all of the offerings" (29:34), which required the Levites to step in and perform this role. By the time we arrive at Josiah's Passover, this temporary role has morphed into a permanent one and is moreover authorized by its association with the Mosaic Torah.

Here the Chronicler's claim to fulfill the law could have been an attempt to contribute to broader debates in the Second Temple period concerning the roles of the offerer and of the priests in the sacrificial process—debates that are preserved in the various textual traditions of the book of Leviticus itself. According to the MT and SP of Lev 1, it is the offerer who slaughters and skins the sacrifice of the burnt offering (see specifically Lev 1:5–6). However, the LXX preserves a different reading in which plural verbs are used to describe both actions (slaughtering and flaying), thereby reserving these responsibilities to the priests themselves. A similar view is also preserved in the *Temple Scroll* (11Q19 34:7–14). It is therefore possible that the Chronicler knew a textual tradition of Leviticus in which the slaughter and flaying of the animal was not a lay prerogative. Nevertheless, the Chronicler's claim that this is the role of the Levites specifically would remain an innovation vis-à-vis the law.[55] By claiming that the Levites' role in the sacrifice is authorized by the Torah, the Chronicler

---

53. As seen by Fishbane, "Revelation and Tradition," 138, 154; Bae, *Vereinte Suche*, 142–45.

54. Williamson, *1 and 2 Chronicles*, 406.

55. Ezek 44:11 shares the same view as the Chronicler that the Levites are responsible for slaughtering the sacrifices. However, the two texts diverge in how they assess these responsibilities: Ezek 44 construes the role of slaughtering the sacrifice as a form of punishment for the Levites for

may have sought to affirm one conception of the sacrificial ritual—one in which the lay offerer performs a far less active role—over other competing versions.

Nevertheless, the role of the laity has not been removed entirely from the Chronicler's account of the Passover. Verse 12 states that the Levites distributed the burnt offering "according to their divisions by ancestral houses, to the sons of the people, to offer to YHWH as it is written in the book of Moses." This statement could be an attempt to accommodate the law of Exod 12:3–4, which situates the Passover ritual within a household setting.[56] While the result is far from a literal application of the domestic rite of Exod 12—according to P, both the slaughter and the distribution of the Passover lamb is performed by the heads of families—the new ritual authority of the Levites is nonetheless construed in 2 Chr 35 as being in broad agreement with earlier traditions in which lay leaders played a more dominant role.

Finally, the account of Josiah's Passover provides unique insights into the possible ways in which pentateuchal ritual law was used in combination with other written authorities in determining ritual actions. While Josiah directs the Levites to act according to the Torah of Moses (v. 6), he also commands them to "prepare yourselves by your ancestral houses, according to your divisions in the written instruction (*ktb*) of David, the king of Israel, and the writing (*mktb*) of Solomon, his son" (v. 4). The mention of alternative ritual instructions to the Mosaic Torah is as mysterious as it is significant. The *ktb* of David may refer to the *tbnyt* "plan" for the temple, which consists of written directions for the building of the temple and its furnishings, as well the assignments for the temple personnel set out in 1 Chr 23–26.[57] In the case of "the *mktb* of Solomon," this is more peculiar, since nowhere is this figure said to have authored an additional set of instructions to those of David. The Chronicler may perhaps be referring to Solomon's implementation of David's writings, said to have been accomplished in 2 Chr 8:12–15.[58]

Irrespective of whether these writings of David and Solomon ever existed or were simply invented by the Chronicler, their citation shows how the ritual laws of the Pentateuch could be used in combination with other written documents in defining ritual convention. In seeking to affirm new ritual roles or particular conceptions of ritual practice, the Chronicler felt free to select between the writings

---

their previous disobedience, while the Chronicler presents this responsibility in an entirely positive light. See further Bae, *Vereinte Suche*, 146.

56. As argued by Fishbane, *Biblical Interpretation*, 137; Albertz, *History of Israelite Religion*, 2:548; Bae, *Vereinte Suche*, 146–47.

57. As suggested by S. J. De Vries, "Moses and David as Cult Founders in Chronicles," *JBL* 107.4 (1988): 619–39 at 626.

58. For this idea, see ibid., 631; Williamson, *1 and 2 Chronicles*, 405; Bae, *Vereinte Suche*, 144; Klein, *2 Chronicles*, 520.

attributed to diverse figures associated with the establishment of YHWH's cult.[59] This illustrates well how the acknowledgment of the authority of Mosaic Torah did not necessarily result in the marginalization of alternative conceptions of ritual practice. Instead, determining how ritual law should influence ritual action required negotiation, not only between contradictory laws within the Pentateuch or alternative versions of the same ritual action but also between the Mosaic Torah and other authoritative traditions. Moreover, it is the skilled mediation of the royal leader that ensures that each source of authority is duly recognized.

11.4. Toward a New Understanding of the Textualization of Ritual

It should again be stressed that the evidence surveyed here says nothing about how ritual texts were used in actual ritual practice, especially given the imaginative nature of the specific texts discussed. Nevertheless, the study of early Second Temple traditions like Ezra-Nehemiah and Chronicles arguably provides important insights into how ritual laws shaped the way scribes imagined ritual practice. From the three examples analyzed above, it is evident that the scribes responsible for Ezra-Nehemiah and Chronicles considered the ritual texts of the Pentateuch to offer relevant guides for how ritual action should be ideally configured—a conclusion that broadly affirms the insights of Metso, Ulrich, and Watts about the role of pentateuchal texts in setting ritual standards. The ritual narratives from Ezra-Nehemiah and Chronicles reveal that ritual laws were considered to offer relevant precedents for determining appropriate ritual conduct; ritual practice that intentionally disregarded the law was considered inappropriate and thus something to avoid.

However, while the scribes responsible for these texts accepted the normative authority of the law, they did not view it in a rigidly prescriptive manner. Ritual laws seem rather to have been understood as providing exemplars of ritual action that were compatible with innovation and able to be negotiated with respect to other authorities, be they written or customary. Indeed, the Second Temple literature surveyed here describes processes of interpretation, adaptation, and supplementation of the ritual law, according to the context and the ruling of

---

59. David's authority to instigate new cultic norms even extends to explicitly revising the Mosaic Torah. In 1 Chr 23:24–27, David lowers the minimum age requirement for Levitical service from thirty (as per Num 4:3) to twenty (cf. 2 Chr 31:17; Ezra 3:8), demonstrating his ability not only to implement Mosaic ritual regulations but to actively regulate the cultic service in ways that the law did not anticipate. See further W. M. Schniedewind, "The Chronicler as an Interpreter of Scripture," in *The Chronicler as Author: Studies in Text and Texture*, ed. M. P. Graham and S. L. McKenzie, JSOTSup 263 (Sheffield: Sheffield Academic Press, 1999), 158–80 at 169–72; Bae, *Vereinte Suche*, 154.

communal officials. These officials differ across the books studied, with Neh 8 focusing more on the role of Ezra, the priests, and the Levites, as well as the customary leaders of households, while the Chronicler emphasizes the ritual role of the king, and also that of the Levites, the chiefs, and the assembly of Jerusalem in the Passover celebrations of 2 Chr 30 and 35. Yet, in both cases, the application of ritual law has elements of the dynamic rather than the rigidity implied in "orthodoxy." Indeed, the fact that some of these officials, and especially the king, are not previewed in the pentateuchal ritual traditions provides further evidence of the flexibility with which the ritual laws are later being interpreted.

In addition, the evidence in Ezra-Nehemiah and Chronicles suggests that ritual law serves functions that extend beyond that of providing a ritual standard. It is used to diverse effect, often as a means of conferring authority on key officials, such as the royal leader, as well as other communal figures. The Aaronide priests, who might have been expected to assume a more dominant role as the ritual Torah becomes consolidated, do not monopolize ritual roles in these books. Rather, referencing the Torah can be used as a mechanism for justifying new ritual roles, such as those of the Levites, thereby negotiating new ritual hierarchies. Moreover, these new roles are construed as being essential to the adherence to the ritual law, despite the fact that they are not mentioned within the pentateuchal text itself.

Paradoxically, then, the citing of ritual law can be used as a means of justifying departures from its prescriptions. Whether this is to pseudonymously attribute ritual innovation to Mosaic Torah (as in the building of the booths in Neh 8), to highlight the need for greater specificity in the ritual prescriptions (as in the case of Hezekiah's centralized Passover), or to weigh in on ritual debates (as in the appointment of the Levites to the role of slaughtering and flaying the sacrifice in 2 Chr 35), the law remains integral to legitimizing and validating the innovation.

Last, it might be argued that ritual law is also used in these narratives in a manner that can be primarily exegetical, as is particularly the case in the reconciling of conflicting instructions for the preparation of the Passover in 2 Chr 35:13. This may have been a purely intellectual exercise, in which scribes, as part of a "discourse about ritual authority"[60] debated the contradictions and inconsistencies within the law itself.

In sum, this essay has demonstrated that by developing the conversation between the pentateuchal text and other Second Temple writings, which provide evidence of first reception, scholars gain the opportunity to test our theories

---

60. R. Schmitt, "Leviticus 14.33–57 as Intellectual Ritual," in *Text, Time, and Temple: Literary, Historical, and Ritual Studies in Leviticus*, ed. F. Landy, L. M. Trevaskis, and B. D. Bibb, Hebrew Bible Monographs 64 (Sheffield: Sheffield Phoenix Press, 2014), 196–203 at 196.

about the probable usage of pentateucal ritual materials, at least in how scribes imagined these texts being used in the idealized ritual occasions of which they wrote. Beyond this, early Second Temple evidence has implications for our understanding of the more general effect of the textualization of ritual, as conceived by ritual theorists. To some degree it supports Bell's argument that the writing of ritual texts promotes "an ideal of uniformity," but it is also evident in these accounts of ritual performances that the acceptance of pentateuchal ritual law as a standard does not necessarily lead to the "elimination or marginalization of alternatives."[61] To be sure, Bell herself acknowledges that even written rituals undergo processes of negotiation and adaptation. She anticipates that ritual texts, as they gain authority, generate a "proliferation of texts amending the tradition and institutions legitimizing the emendations."[62] However, Bell does not explain how such "variation among texts,"[63] and the accompanying debates surrounding their application, might be congruent with the uniformity and standardization that she associates with the textualization of ritual.

The Second Temple evidence surveyed here suggests that the processes of amending written rituals, and the degree of innovation that this facilitates, are greater than Bell's theory might allow. The textualization of ritual serves diverse functions, to which Bell only alludes: these go beyond the setting of ritual standards. Hence, we can claim that early Second Temple descriptions of rituals not only reveal a previously unrecognized complexity in the usages to which ritual texts are put in the scribal practices of ancient Israel; they also illustrate the potential for biblical scholars to contribute to broader conceptualizations of the textualization of ritual.

BIBLIOGRAPHY

Albertz, R. *A History of Israelite Religion in the Old Testament Period*. Translated by J. Bowden. 2 vols. London: SCM Press, 1994.
Bae, H.-S. *Vereinte Suche nach JHWH: Die Hiskianische und Josianische Reform in der Chronik*. BZAW 355. Berlin: de Gruyter, 2005.
Bell, C. "Ritualization of Texts and Textualization of Ritual in the Codification of Taoist Liturgy." *HR* 27.4 (1988): 366–92.
———. *Ritual: Perspectives and Dimensions*. Oxford: Oxford University Press, 1997.
———. *Ritual Theory, Ritual Practice*. Oxford: Oxford University Press, 1992.
Ben Zvi, E. "Revisiting 'Boiling in Fire' in 2 Chronicles 35:13 and Related Passover Questions: Text, Exegetical Needs and Concerns, and General Implications." Pages

---

61. Bell, *Ritual Theory*, 137.
62. Ibid.
63. Bell, *Ritual*, 202.

238–50 in *Biblical Interpretation in Judaism and Christianity*. Edited by I. Kalimi and P. J. Haas. LHBOTS 439. London: T&T Clark, 2006.
Blenkinsopp, J. *Ezra-Nehemiah: A Commentary*. OTL. London: SCM Press, 1989.
Chavel, S. "The Second Passover, Pilgrimage, and the Centralized Cult." *HTR* 102 (2009): 1–24.
Choi, J. H. *Traditions at Odds: The Reception of the Pentateuch in Biblical and Second Temple Period Literature*. LHBOTS 518. New York: T&T Clark, 2010.
Clines, D. J. *Ezra, Nehemiah, Esther*. New Century Bible Commentary. Grand Rapids, MI: Eerdmans; London: Marshall Morgan & Scott, 1984.
Curtis, E. L., and A. A. Madsen. *A Critical and Exegetical Commentary on the Books of Chronicles*. International Critical Commentary. Edinburgh: T&T Clark, 1910.
De Pee, C. *The Writing of Weddings in Middle Period China: Text and Ritual Practice in the Eighth Through Fourteenth Centuries*. SUNY Series in Chinese Philosophy and Culture. Albany: State University of New York Press, 2007.
De Vries, S. J. "Festival Ideology in Chronicles." Pages 104–24 in *Problems in Biblical Theology: Essays in Honor of Rolf Knierim*. Edited by H. T. C. Sun, K. L. Eades, J. M. Robinson, and G. I. Moller. Grand Rapids, MI: Eerdmans, 1997.
———. "Moses and David as Cult Founders in Chronicles." *JBL* 107.4 (1988): 619–39.
Dillard, R. B. *2 Chronicles*. Word Bible Commentary 15. Waco, TX: Word Books, 1987.
Donner, H. *Aufsätze zum Alten Testament aus vier Jahrzehnten*. BZAW 224. Berlin: de Gruyter, 1994.
Driver, S. *An Introduction to the Literature of the Old Testament*. 9th ed. International Theological Library. New York: Meridan Books, 1956.
Dyma, O. *Die Wallfahrt zum Zweiten Tempel: Untersuchungen zur Entwicklung der Wallfahrtsfeste in vorhasmonäischer Zeit*. FAT 2/40. Tübingen: Mohr Siebeck, 2009.
Eshel, E. "Book of Leviticus." Pages 488–93 in vol. 1 of *Encyclopedia of the Dead Sea Scrolls*. Edited by L. H. Schiffman and J. C. VanderKam. 2 vols. Oxford: Oxford University Press, 2000.
Fishbane, M. *Biblical Interpretation in Ancient Israel*. Oxford: Clarendon Press, 1985.
———. "Revelation and Tradition: Aspects of Inner-Biblical Exegesis." *JBL* 99.3 (1980): 343–61.
Flint, P. W. "The Book of Leviticus in the Dead Sea Scrolls." Pages 323–41 in *The Book of Leviticus: Composition and Reception*. Edited by R. Rendtorff and R. A. Kugler. VTSup 93. Leiden: Brill, 2003.
Goody, J. *The Logic of Writing and the Organization of Society*. Cambridge: Cambridge University Press, 1986.
Grabbe, L. L. "Chicken or Egg? Which Came First, 1 Esdras or Ezra-Nehemiah?" Pages 31–44 in *Was 1 Esdras First? An Investigation into the Priority and Nature of 1 Esdras*. Edited by L. S. Fried. AIL 7. Atlanta: Society of Biblical Literature, 2011.
Harrington, H. K. "The Use of Leviticus in Ezra-Nehemiah." *JHebS* 13 (2013). doi:10.55.08/jhs.2013.v13.a3.
Hobson, R. *Transforming Literature into Scripture: Texts as Cult Objects at Nineveh and Qumran*. Sheffield: Sheffield Equinox Press, 2012.
Humphrey, C., and J. Laidlaw. *The Archetypal Actions of Ritual: A Theory of Ritual Illustrated by the Jain Rite of Worship*. Oxford Studies in Social and Cultural Anthropology. Oxford: Clarendon Press, 1994.

Japhet, S. *I and II Chronicles: A Commentary*. OTL. Louisville, KY: Westminster John Knox Press, 1993.

———. "The Supposed Common Authorship of Chronicles and Ezra-Nehemiah Investigated Anew." *VT* 18.3 (1968): 330–71.

Jonker, L. C. *Reflections of King Josiah in Chronicles: Late Stages of the Josiah Reception in 2 Chr 34f.* Textpragmatische Studien zur Hebräischen Bibel 2. Gütersloh: Gütersloher Verlagshaus, 2003.

Kalimi, I. *The Reshaping of Ancient Israelite History in Chronicles*. Winona Lake, IN: Eisenbrauns, 2005.

Klein, R. W. *2 Chronicles: A Commentary*. Hermeneia. Minneapolis: Fortress, 2012.

Knoppers, G. N. *1 Chronicles 1–9: A New Translation with Introduction and Commentary*. AB 12. New York: Doubleday, 2004.

Kooij, A. van der. "On the Ending of the Book of 1 Esdras." Pages 37–49 in *VII Congress of the International Organization for Septuagint and Cognate Studies*. Edited by C. E. Cox. Septuagint and Cognate Studies 31. Atlanta: Scholars Press, 1991.

LeFebvre, M. *Collections, Codes, and Torah: The Re-characterization of Israel's Written Law*. LHBOTS 451. New York: T&T Clark, 2006.

Levtow, N. B. "Text Production and Destruction in Ancient Israel: Ritual and Political Dimensions." Pages 111–39 in *Social Theory and the Study of Israelite Religion: Essays in Retrospect and Prospect*. Edited by S. M. Olyan. RBS 71. Altanta: Society of Biblical Literature, 2012.

Mathews, K. A. "The Leviticus Scrolls (11QpaleoLev) and the Text of the Hebrew Bible." *CBQ* 48.2 (1986): 171–207.

Metso, S. "Evidence from the Qumran Scrolls for the Scribal Transmission of Leviticus." Pages 67–79 in *Editing the Bible: Assessing the Task Past and Present*. Edited by J. S. Kloppenborg and J. H. Newman. RBS 69. Atlanta: Society of Biblical Literature, 2012.

Metso, S., and E. Ulrich. "The Old Greek Translation of Leviticus." Pages 247–68 in *The Book of Leviticus: Composition and Reception*. Edited by R. Rendtorff and R. A. Kugler. VTSup 93. FIOTL 3. Leiden: Brill, 2003.

Milgrom, J. *Leviticus 23–27: A New Translation with Introduction and Commentary*. AB 3C. New York: Doubleday, 2001.

Movers, F. C. *Kritische Untersuchungen über die biblische Chronik: Ein Beitrag zur Einleitung in das Alte Testament*. Bonn: Habicht/Georgi, 1834.

Najman, H. "Torah of Moses: Pseudonymous Attributions in Second Temple Writings." Pages 202–16 in *The Interpretation of Scripture in Early Judaism and Christianity: Studies in Language and Tradition*. Edited by C. A. Evans. Journal for the Study of the Pseudepigrapha Supplement Series 33. Sheffield: Sheffield Academic Press, 2000.

Pakkala, J. *Ezra the Scribe: The Development of Ezra 7–10 and Nehemia 8*. BZAW 347. Berlin: de Gruyter, 2004.

Rendtorff, R. "Chronicles and the Priestly Torah." Pages 259–66 in *Texts, Temples, and Traditions: A Tribute to Menahem Haran*. Edited by M. V. Fox et al. Winona Lake, IN: Eisenbrauns, 1996.

Rhyder, J. *Centralizing the Cult: The Holiness Legislation in Leviticus 17–26*. FAT 134. Tübingen: Mohr Siebeck, 2019.

———. "Space and Memory in the Book of Leviticus." Pages 83–96 in *Scripture as Social Discourse: Social-Scientific Perspectives on Early Jewish and Christian*

Writings. Edited by T. Klutz, C. A. Strine, and J. M. Keady. London: T&T Clark, 2018.

Rudolph, W. R. *Esra und Nehemia samt 3 Esra*. Handbuch zum Alten Testament 20. Tübingen: Mohr Siebeck, 1949.

Schaack, T. *Die Ungeduld des Papiers: Studien zum alttestamentlichen Verständnis des Schreibens anhand des Verbums katab im Kontext administrativer Vorgänge*. BZAW 262. Berlin: de Gruyter, 1998.

Schmitt, R. "Leviticus 14.33–57 as Intellectual Ritual." Pages 196–203 in *Text, Time, and Temple: Literary, Historical, and Ritual Studies in Leviticus*. Edited by F. Landy, L. M. Trevaskis, and B. D. Bibb. Hebrew Bible Monographs 64. Sheffield: Sheffield Phoenix Press, 2014.

Schniedewind, W. M. "The Chronicler as an Interpreter of Scripture." Pages 158–80 in *The Chronicler as Author: Studies in Text and Texture*. Edited by M. P. Graham and S. L. McKenzie. JSOTSup 263. Sheffield: Sheffield Academic Press, 1999.

———. *How the Bible Became a Book: The Textualization of Ancient Israel*. Cambridge: Cambridge University Press, 2005.

Shaver, J. R. *Torah and the Chronicler's History Work: An Inquiry into the Chronicler's References to Laws, Festivals, and Cultic Institutions in Relationship to Pentateuchal Legislation*. BJS 196. Atlanta: Scholars Press, 1989.

Spawn, K. L. *"As It is Written" and Other Citation Formulae in the Old Testament: Their Use, Development, Syntax, and Significance*. BZAW 311. Berlin: de Gruyter, 2002.

Talshir, Z. "Ancient Composition Patterns Mirrored in 1 Esdras and the Priority of the Canonical Composition Type." Pages 109–30 in *Was 1 Esdras First? An Investigation into the Priority and Nature of 1 Esdras*. Edited by L. S. Fried. AIL 7. Atlanta: Society of Biblical Literature, 2011.

———. "Several Canon-Related Concepts Originating in Chronicles." *ZAW* 113.3 (2001): 386–403.

Ulfgard, H. *The Story of "Sukkot": The Setting, Shaping, and Sequel of the Biblical Feast of Tabernacles*. Beiträge zur Geschichte der biblischen Exegese 34. Tübingen: Mohr Siebeck, 1998.

Ulrich, E. "'4QLev–Num^a,' '4QLev^b.'" Pages 153–87 in *Qumran Cave 4: VII. Genesis to Numbers*. Edited by E. Ulrich and F. M. Cross. DJD 12. Oxford: Clarendon Press, 1994.

Venema, G. J. *Reading Scripture in the Old Testament: Deuteronomy 9–10; 31–2 Kings 22–23—Jeremiah 36—Nehemiah 8*. Translated by C. E. Smit. OtSt 48. Leiden: Brill, 2004.

Wagenaar, J. *Origin and Transformation of the Ancient Israelite Festival Calendar*. BZABR 6. Wiesbaden: Harrassowitz Verlag, 2005.

Watts, J. W. *Ritual and Rhetoric in Leviticus: From Sacrifice to Scripture*. Cambridge: Cambridge University Press, 2007.

———. "Ritual Legitimacy and Scriptural Authority." *JBL* 124.3 (2005): 401–17.

———. "Scripturalization and the Aaronide Dynasties." *JHebS* 13.6 (2013). doi:10.55 .08/jhs.2013.v13.a6.

———. "Using Ezra's Time as a Methodological Pivot for Understanding the Rhetoric and Functions of the Pentateuch." Pages 489–506 in *The Pentateuch: International Perspectives on Current Research*. Edited by T. B. Dozeman, K. Schmid, and B. Schwartz. FAT 78. Tübingen: Mohr Siebeck, 2011.

Williamson, H. G. M. *1 and 2 Chronicles*. Grand Rapids, MI: Eerdmans; London: Marshall-Morgan & Scott, 1987.
———. *Ezra, Nehemiah*. Word Books 16. Waco, TX: Word Biblical Commentary, 1985.
———. "History." Pages 25–38 in *It Is Written: Scripture Citing Scripture; Essays in Honour of Barnabas Lindars*. Edited by D. A. Carson and H. G. M. Williamson. Cambridge: Cambridge University Press, 1992.
Zahn, M. M. *Rethinking Rewritten Scripture: Composition and Exegesis in the 4QReworked Pentateuch Manuscrips*. STDJ 103. Leiden: Brill, 2011.
Zunz, L. *Die gottesdienstlichen Vorträge der Juden historisch entwickelt: Ein Beitrag zur Altertumskunde und biblischen Kritik, zur Literatur- und Religionsgeschichte*. Berlin: A. Asher, 1832.

CHAPTER 12

Text and Ritual in the Dead Sea Scrolls

Daniel K. Falk

THERE ARE TWO MAIN AREAS in which the Dead Sea Scrolls can offer valuable opportunities for investigating the ritual texts in the Pentateuch. First, they preserve the earliest scriptural manuscripts—copied in the late Second Temple period—and provide direct witness to textual variation from the earliest period, multiple literary editions of some texts, a rich and diverse activity of rewriting pentateuchal texts, and both explicit and implicit interpretation. This allows a view of the development of pentateuchal texts about ritual and interpretations of them during the late Second Temple period that is impossible for the origins of Israelite rituals and the composition of the Pentateuch. Nevertheless, it is often difficult to know if we are dealing with elements of actual ritual practice as opposed to more theoretical exegesis or imaginary ideals.[1] Second, the Dead Sea Scrolls give witness to a Jewish movement with a particularly dense ritual life, including ritual examinations and loyalty vows, apotropaic rituals, purification rituals, cursing and expulsion rituals, ritualized assemblies, and more.[2] Moreover, they provide the richest body of early Jewish prayer texts that we can be confident were used in communal liturgy, and the only direct evidence of a comprehensive liturgical cycle from the Second Temple period. The distinctive advantage of this material is that we have not only descriptive and prescriptive texts of rituals and prayers but also multiple copies of liturgical scrolls for various specific ritual occasions and descriptions of religious life of the broader Jewish movement by contemporary writers, who refer to them as Essenes.[3] The present study will focus on the category of prayer texts, and four cases in particular: purification rituals, collections of liturgical prayers, the wearing of *tefillin*, and the covenant ceremony. Each of these examples involves rituals

---

1. An example of the latter would be the temple rituals described in the *Temple Scroll*: clearly much in the *Temple Scroll* describes imagined ideals, such as the extension of purity. It is uncertain whether the additional first fruits festivals represent extrapolation or some sort of actual practice.
2. R. A. Kugler, "Making All Experience Religious: The Hegemony of Ritual at Qumran," *JSJ* 33.2 (2002): 131–52.
3. Philo, *Good Person* 75–91; Philo, *Hypothetica* 11.1–8; Josephus, *J.W.* 2.119–61; *Ant.* 18.18–22.

that we can be confident were actually practiced, are attested by two or more different types of evidence, and go beyond pentateuchal precedents. I argue that they offer valuable insights by means of analogy concerning the incomplete nature of ritual information provided by textual sources, the complex relationship between textual description and ritual performance in a living community, and possible functions of written accounts of ritual.

In this essay, I am treating prayer as a ritual activity and, moreover, as one of the most prominent rituals attested in the Dead Sea Scrolls. This deserves a brief discussion, since prayer seldom receives specific treatment in books on ritual studies. It may be sufficient for the present purpose to refer to a standard definition of ritual as "the performance of more or less invariant sequences of formal acts and utterances not encoded by the performers," in which the words and acts are "invested with meaning" beyond their everyday significance.[4] Even if ad hoc, spontaneous and personal prayer would not qualify as a ritual act, prayer is at the very least an important verbal element in some rituals—for example, the purification ritual examined below. More to the point, however, are cases where the recitation of the prayer in a communal context is the central act and where the performance of this prayer is constrained in terms of time, space, form, manner, and so on—that is, what is often referred to as liturgical prayer.[5] The conception of prayer as a religious obligation of the community in Judaism is accompanied by regulations in terms of time, place, manner. This is clearly attested in the Mishnah (esp. m. Berakot) and is often thought to derive from correspondence with the ritual of the sacrificial cult.[6] In this conception of prayer, the mere words alone are not necessarily prayer. In a discussion of the obligation to recite the *Shema'*—one of the core prayers in the synagogue liturgy—the Mishnah notes that if one had been reading those passages at the time for recital, one has fulfilled the obligation of the prayer only if intending to pray (m. Berakot 2:1). That is, prayer here is treated as a performative. Although some have argued that such a conception of prayer as a religious obligation develops in Judaism only following the destruction of the temple in 70 CE, with prayer taking the place of the sacrificial cult,[7] the correspondence of prayer and sacrifice is attested in the Hebrew Bible. Gary A. Anderson argues that prayer is

---

4. R. A. Rappaport, *Ritual and Religion in the Making of Humanity*, Cambridge Studies in Social and Cultural Anthropology 110 (Cambridge: Cambridge University Press, 1999), 24.

5. The terms "liturgy" and "liturgical" are often used to refer to form (for example, invariant sequence), but they better refer to function: as "work of the people" liturgy refers to action as an obligation, whether a civic duty or service to a deity.

6. See S. C. Reif, *Judaism and Hebrew Prayer: New Perspectives on Jewish Liturgical History* (Cambridge: Cambridge University Press, 1993), 98–102.

7. For example, E. Fleischer, "On the Beginnings of Obligatory Jewish Prayer" (Hebrew), *Tarbiz* 58 (1990): 397–441. See discussion in D. K. Falk, *Daily, Sabbath, and Festival Prayers in the Dead Sea Scrolls*, STDJ 27 (Leiden: Brill, 1998), 3–7.

treated as a cultic act in the Hebrew Bible and that praise is an activity closely correlated with sacrifice and as a public fulfilment of vow.[8]

In any case, in the Dead Sea Scrolls—the corpus of concern in this study—there can be no question that prayer is highly regulated as an obligatory religious act. Not only is prayer a key element of various rituals, such as in the purification rituals and the covenant ceremony, but it is also a ritual act in and of itself. The *Community Rule* indicates a theory of prayer as divinely ordained speech that is a required religious service of the community to God and tantamount to sacrifice (e.g., 1QS 9:4–5; 10:6–9, 14). Moreover, it treats prayer as parallel to other ritualized activities in the sectarian community, including ritual meals, study, and judgment (e.g., 1QS 6:2–8). Numerous liturgical scrolls of prayers, such as the collection of *Daily Prayers*, prescribe prayers with fixed rubrics and wording for specific occasions and times. John J. Collins notes, "The very fact that written prayer texts are found at Qumran shows a tendency toward standardization and institutionalization. As Shemaryahu Talmon has observed, 'institutionalized prayer is a prayer in which the spontaneous, the individual, and the sporadic are replaced by the conventional, the universal and the periodic.' As such, institutionalized prayer must be seen as part of the ritual of the *yaḥad*."[9] The roughly three dozen *tefillin* may be regarded as ritual objects related to prayer. By all indications in the Dead Sea Scrolls, the practice of prayer is highly ritualized, regulated in terms of time, place, content, sequence, and posture—and possibly movement. Moreover, the broader context of the cycle of prayers comprises a ritual sequence, so that any one prayer does not stand alone but is in relation to the rest of the cycle.

In short, although the data in the sources are incomplete, the prayer practices attested in the Dead Sea Scrolls reflect most of the ritual elements identified by Ronald L. Grimes (ritual space, ritual objects, ritual time, ritual sound and language, ritual identity, ritual action).[10]

12.1. Text and Ritual

Little is to be found in the major theorists of ritual on the problem of the relationship with texts and textuality, because the major theories are primarily based on ethnographic data drawn from predominantly oral societies. In his excellent article on ritual in the Dead Sea Scrolls, Collins—after summarizing the salient

---

8. G. A. Anderson, "The Praise of God as a Cultic Event," in *Priesthood and Cult in Ancient Israel*, ed. S. M. Olyan and G. A. Anderson, JSOTSup 125 (Sheffield: JSOT Press, 1991), 15.

9. J. J. Collins, "Prayer and the Meaning of Ritual in the Dead Sea Scrolls," in *Prayer and Poetry in the Dead Sea Scrolls and Related Literature: Essays in Honor of Eileen Schuller on the Occasion of Her 65th Birthday*, ed. J. Penner, K. M. Penner, and C. Wassen, STDJ 98 (Leiden: Brill, 2012), 75.

10. R. L. Grimes, *Beginnings in Ritual Studies*, rev. ed., Studies in Comparative Religion (Columbia: University of South Carolina Press, 1995), 24–39, 65–69.

features of ritual theories that inform his study—warns that universal explanations in theories do not account for the variation of phenomena. Judaism is a practice-based religion, but also one focused on texts that convey meaning. "What is true of Brahmin rituals is not necessarily true of the Dead Sea Scrolls. The *yaḥad* was an unusually literate community, and it placed a high value on the intentions of its members ... regarded study ... of the Torah, as an act of piety, and ... psalms and traditional prayers as media of instruction."[11] Therefore, Collins seeks to balance a study of the action of prayer on its own for meaning not connected with words, with intention and meaning expressed in words. "Since many of these prayers are associated with rituals, they provide an opportunity to test the light that verbalized statements can shed on the meaning of rituals."[12]

Before we move to discuss some case studies from among the Dead Sea Scrolls, it will be useful to review a few efforts to classify relationships between text and rituals. In his book on the liminal theology of Paul, Christian Strecker gives the following initial taxonomy.[13]

1. A text contains instructions for executing a ritual.
2. A text reports or mentions the performance of a ritual.
3. A text concerns itself with the meaning, function, or proper performance of a ritual.
4. A text derives directly from ritual use.
5. A text itself has a direct ritual function.
6. A text is connected synecdochically with a ritual.

By the last point—which he regards as the "most complex and interesting relationship between ritual and text"—he means cases where a ritual inspired or shaped a literary text that is not otherwise "about" ritual, in the manner of a "pretext" in theories of intertextuality.[14]

---

11. Collins, "Prayer and the Meaning of Ritual," 72.
12. Ibid., 73.
13. C. Strecker, *Die liminale Theologie des Paulus: Zugänge zur paulinischen Theologie aus kulturanthropologischer Perspektive*, Forschungen zur Religion und Literatur des Alten und Neuen Testaments 185 (Göttingen: Vandenhoeck & Ruprecht, 1999), 78. "1. Ein Text enthält Anweisungen zur Ausführung eines Rituals. 2. Ein Text berichtet oder konstatiert den Vollzug eines Rituals. 3. Ein Text beschäftigt sich mit der Bedeutung, Funktion oder rechten Durchführung eines Rituals. 4. Ein Text entstammt direkt rituellem Gebrauch. 5. Ein Text besitzt unmittelbar selbst rituelle Funktion. 6. Ein Text ist mit einem Ritual synekdochisch vernetzt."
14. He cites F. H. Gorman Jr.: "Ritual structures and ritual processes may serve as the basis for story and narrative. Ritual may serve as the background for narrative construction and development. Indeed, ritual may generate narrative and story in such a way that ritual dynamics will be reflected within narrative" ("Ritual Studies and Biblical Studies: Assessment of the Past; Prospects for the Future," *Semeia* 67 [1994]: 23).

This classification is a useful starting point, especially for analysis of the Bible. As Richard E. DeMaris notes, it emphasizes that "the interface between text and rite is varied and complex: a given text may describe, prescribe, or interpret a rite; the verbal elements of a rite may appear directly in a text or a text may do no more than hint at or echo a rite."[15] But for the purpose of analyzing the dynamics of text and ritual in the Dead Sea Scrolls, it is still too limited because it does not address the materiality of texts in relation to ritual.[16]

A conference at Stanford in 2002 entitled Rituals in Ink was specifically devoted to the relationship between rituals and texts in ancient Roman religion.[17] The editors distinguish "several textual levels for ritual: rituals recorded on stone or paper; rituals incorporated or adapted within imaginative literature; and rituals identified and reconstructed by commentators on ancient religion. Ancient authors themselves often employed commonly known rituals as structural devices to enhance communication between the text and its recipients."[18]

Acknowledging that ritual should be viewed as a performance and not a mere repetition of a script, the essays do not view text as a reliable basis for reconstructing ritual. Rather the various essays—from different perspectives—engage in two different tasks: the process of analyzing a ritual through text, and seeking to understand how "the literary representation of ritual" is inseparable from what ritual does.[19]

Jörg Rüpke, for example, seeks an "integrative approach" to ritual and interpretation, as interrelated activities, where "writing, literature, might be part of the performance."[20] Emphasizing the singularity of performance, he nevertheless insists that texts "are not only part of the actual performance, but also part of its context, part of the performers' and audiences' knowledge.... The individual performance cannot be analyzed in isolation from previous communication

---

15. R. E. DeMaris, *The New Testament in Its Ritual World* (London: Routledge, 2008), 6.

16. Strecker's fifth category concerns the texts that may constitute a ritual act when read, such as the greeting or doxology in Paul's letters, not the embodied materiality of a manuscript itself as a ritual object (Strecker, *Liminale Theologie*, 78 n 31).

17. A. Barchiesi, J. Rüpke, and S. A. Stephens, eds., *Rituals in Ink: A Conference on Religion and Literary Production in Ancient Rome Held at Stanford University in February 2002*, Potsdamer Altertumswissenschaftliche Beiträge 10 (Stuttgart: Steiner, 2004).

18. Ibid., vii.

19. S. C. Stroup, "Rituals of Ink?," in *Rituals in Ink: A Conference on Religion and Literary Production in Ancient Rome Held at Stanford University in February 2002*, ed. A. Barchiesi, J. Rüpke, and S. A. Stephens, Potsdamer Altertumswissenschaftliche Beiträge 10 (Stuttgart: Steiner, 2004), 141–48 at 142.

20. J. Rüpke, "Acta aut Agenda: Relations of Script and Performance," in *Rituals in Ink: A Conference on Religion and Literary Production in Ancient Rome Held at Stanford University in February 2002*, ed. A. Barchiesi, J. Rüpke, and S. A. Stephens, Potsdamer Altertumswissenschaftliche Beiträge 10 (Stuttgart: Steiner, 2004), 23–43 at 25–26; see also in that volume M. Beard, "Writing Ritual: The Triumph of Ovid," 115–26; D. D. Leitao, "Ritual? What Ritual?," 149–53.

about previous performances or normative communication about the ritual 'as such': The existence of a written prescription for the performing of the ritual is but a particular case of this general mechanism."[21]

The essays in this volume do not offer much in the way of taxonomy, but they simultaneously clarify the distinction between ritual as performance and a literary representation of a ritual, on the one hand, and problematize that distinction by arguing that these are interconnected, on the other hand. This suggests that we should think in terms of continuums rather than binary alternatives.

In a recent article, Ristro Uro details a variety of complex interactions between ritual and writing in early Christianity. Drawing on theories of orality and literacy, and social memory (especially Harvey Whitehouse), Uro argues that ritual played a key role in the maintenance and transmission of Christian traditions, serving as a "site of memory."[22] Second, he argues that "ritual practices influenced sacred stories and vice versa."[23] Third, referring to William Graham's concept of "scriptural orality," he notes that "in a certain sense most, if not all, of the earliest Christian literary works surviving today functioned early on as 'liturgical' texts, since they were read aloud in the gatherings of early Christians."[24] Fourth, he states that "early Christian books do not merely contain 'ritual fragments'; they are themselves ritual instruments or even ritual objects."[25] These last two points should be distinguished, for they concern the (disembodied) text and the (embodied) textual artifact respectively.

> In addition to being used for the dissemination of information, scriptures can have numerous other ritual functions: they can be devoutly touched in the hope of luck and blessing, solemnly processed in ritual pageantry, chanted or sung in unthinking repetition; scriptural passages can be carried in amulets to protect their holders (cf. the Jewish *tefillim*), and so on.... In general terms: the magical use of literacy and books on the one hand, on the other their use for communicating explicit religious knowledge in the form for example of biblical narratives, creeds and interpretations, can be understood as opposite ends of the interface between ritual and writing—although magic can naturally support religious teaching as well (the authority of the scriptures, for example).[26]

21. Rüpke, "Acta aut Agenda," 26.
22. R. Uro, "The Interface of Ritual and Writing in the Transmission of Early Christian Traditions," in *Mind, Morality and Magic: Cognitive Science Approaches in Biblical Studies*, ed. I. Czachesz and R. Uro (Durham: Acumen, 2013), 67, 72.
23. Ibid., 69.
24. Ibid., 69–70.
25. Ibid., 69.
26. Ibid., 75.

All of these points are applicable in the Dead Sea Scrolls, and even more so demonstrable.

Two points in particular I would add to the preceding: first, it is important to distinguish performed rituals from fictional presentations in texts, and second, it is important to distinguish between a textual presentation of a ritual and a text that is itself a ritual artifact. I will discuss these further below, but for now, I emphasize in general that texts are not rituals and rituals are not texts, although the matter is a bit more complicated when we are dealing with texts as ritual objects. The literary analysis of a textual description of or prescription for a ritual does not qualify as an analysis of the ritual. Ritual is a performance and can only be analyzed as performance. Analyzing a text related to a ritual is analogous to analyzing a concert on the basis only of a musical score, or a performance of *Hamlet* on the basis of a script.

12.2. Studies on Ritual in the Dead Sea Scrolls

The first application of ritual theory to the Dead Sea Scrolls was an article by Steven Weitzman in 1997, in which he argued that "the Qumran liturgical material can help us to see how a contemporary liturgical genre influenced Pseudo-Philo's re-shaping of the Song of Deborah," specifically, "Pseudo-Philo fused into the song motifs drawn from the petitionary prayer genre and the ritual context in which it was used."[27] Key points emerging from this study include the inseparability of ritual and interpretation, and the literary use of ritual practice for different rhetorical purposes.

In 2002, Rob A. Kugler compiled a preliminary inventory of rituals attested in the Dead Sea Scrolls according to Catherine M. Bell's sixfold typology of rituals.[28] He noted, "The evidence of ritual density at Qumran appears overwhelming.... By promoting communal submission to priestly authority, standards for initiation and expulsion, patterns of feasting and fasting, carefully delineated constructions of time, and strict purity requirements, the rituals entangled community members inextricably with God's will for the cosmos and drew them away from the profane world of their Jewish and non-Jewish neighbors. As a result, ritual at Qumran was hegemonic, making every aspect of their experience religious in Durkheim's sense of the word."[29] Kugler also noted that interpretation of scripture was the "basis for the group's ritual practices."[30]

---

27. S. Weitzman, "Revisiting Myth and Ritual," *DSD* 4.1 (1997): 26.
28. Kugler, "Making All Experience Religious," 131–52; C. Bell, *Ritual: Perspectives and Dimensions* (Oxford: Oxford University Press, 1997), 91–137.
29. Kugler, "Making All Experience Religious," 149.
30. Ibid., 131.

Russell C. D. Arnold in his dissertation carried out a much more extensive classification of ritual attested in the Dead Sea Scrolls according to Bell's typology, published as a monograph in 2006.[31] In a 2011 article, Arnold summarized, "One of the first things that we notice about Qumran is the pervasiveness of ritual in the life of the community. As many as one-fourth of the nonbiblical texts discovered in the Qumran caves can be classified as ritual or liturgical."[32] He notes that a preponderance of the ritual evidence at Qumran is of the spoken parts, which he explains as "an outgrowth of the Qumran community's strong emphasis on the importance of proper speech."[33] In both his monograph and his article, Arnold focuses on describing the variety of ritual practice and meaning of it but does not grapple with the particular problem of the relationship of text to ritual practice or the meaning of this particular relationship. In the effort to get "behind the text," he gives little attention to one of the key bits of data offered in the scrolls: the scrolls themselves as ritual artifacts. The fact of texts and the nature of those texts to ritual performance are primary data for the holistic context of ritual performance. He does give some comments on the importance of being "sensitive" to the relationship between text and ritual but does not offer a more detailed taxonomy beyond "descriptive" and "prescriptive."[34]

Daniel Stökl Ben Ezra also attempted to "develop a typology of ritual activity" in a 2011 article, noting, "In recent years, much progress has been made in the study of Qumran religion by studies cataloguing and systematizing Qumran liturgical texts. Rituals, however, are larger than words. Ritual studies are particularly interesting for their attention to the non-verbal aspects of ritual and even for wholly non-verbal rituals."[35] Beyond the recognition that text and ritual are not the same, however, he also ignores the relationship of text to ritual, as part of context.

An article by Collins in 2012 uses as a foil Frits Staal's provocative article "The Meaninglessness of Ritual," in which Staal argued that the essence of ritual is the performance according to rules and that meanings attached to rituals are secondary and not essential.[36] Relevant to the relationship of text to ritual,

---

31. R. C. D. Arnold, *The Social Role of Liturgy in the Religion of the Qumran Community*, STDJ 60 (Leiden: Brill, 2006).

32. R. C. D. Arnold, "The Dead Sea Scrolls, Qumran, and Ritual Studies," in *The Dead Sea Scrolls in Context: Integrating the Dead Sea Scrolls in the Study of Ancient Texts, Languages, and Cultures*, ed. A. Lange, E. Tov, and M. Weigold, VTSup 140 (Leiden: Brill, 2011), 2:547–62 at 550.

33. Ibid., 2:548.

34. Ibid., 2:561.

35. D. Stökl Ben Ezra, "When the Bell Rings: The Qumran Rituals of Affliction in Context," in *The Dead Sea Scrolls in Context: Integrating the Dead Sea Scrolls in the Study of Ancient Texts, Languages, and Cultures*, ed. A. Lange, E. Tov, and M. Weigold, VTSup 140 (Leiden: Brill, 2011), 2:533–46 at 533.

36. Collins, "Prayer and the Meaning of Ritual," 69, 84; F. Staal, "The Meaninglessness of Ritual," *Numen* 26.1 (1979): 2–22.

he notes that what a prayer does as a performance is more important that what it says. "The daily recitation of prayers at fixed times constitutes a habitus, which itself implies a religious attitude regardless of the content of the prayers."[37] Second, building on Kugler's observation of ritual at Qumran as hegemonic, Collins emphasizes that it is rooted in the concepts of preordained speech and authoritative texts. "Prayer, 'in accordance with the decree recorded forever' was an integral part of that ritual.... The ritualized life, then, was essentially a life of obedience (to Torah)."[38] Thus, in this setting, text served as an authoritative basis for ritual practice. This is critical, and separates traditions focused on textual authority from the types of traditions that have been the focus of ritual theorists. Third, he acknowledges that there may be discrepancy between the words spoken and the "extraverbal" components, including the hierarchical order of the procession in the case of the covenant ceremony.[39]

Jutta Jokiranta draws on theories of repetition and tedium by cognitive scientists in a 2013 article on the "ritual system" of the Qumran movement.[40] She argues that elements of high emotional connection balanced the repetition of ritual and potential for frustration and boredom. For our purposes, this study is important for considering the role of ritual in the transmission of teaching, and the importance of frequency and repetition in this transmission.[41]

There are many good insights in all of these studies, but they offer little in the way of the central problem of this volume: the relationship between text and ritual. Qumran has unique data for the study of this problem in the ancient world because of the density of its ritual life and the abundance of texts dealing with ritual in various ways. Moreover, numerous manuscripts seem likely to be used directly in ritual. In what follows, I will focus on just a few case studies that illustrate aspects of the relationship between text and ritual.

12.3. Text and Ritual in the Dead Sea Scrolls: Case Studies

12.3.1. Purification Liturgies

Three manuscripts contain series of liturgies for various occasions of ritual purification (4Q512, 4Q414, 4Q284), ranging in date from the early first century

---

37. Collins, "Prayer and the Meaning of Ritual," 71.
38. Ibid., 76.
39. Ibid., 78.
40. J. Jokiranta, "Ritual System in the Qumran Movement: Frequency, Boredom, and Balance," in *Mind, Morality, and Magic: Cognitive Science Approaches in Biblical Studies*, ed. I. Czachesz and R. Uro (Durham: Acumen, 2013), 144–63.
41. See Uro, "Interface of Ritual and Writing," 62.

BCE (4Q512) to as late as the mid-first century CE (4Q414, 4Q284).[42] Although all three manuscripts are very fragmentary and it is difficult to determine the sequence, the liturgies are highly formulaic and are so similar in form, content, and function across the three scrolls that they must be closely related and refer to the same rituals. The manuscripts contain two types of material: ritual instructions and prayers. The ritual instructions refer to God and the person undergoing purification in the third person and indicate ritual actions (immersion, sprinkling, washing of clothes, and prayers), occasion and time, place, movement, and gestures. Each prayer is introduced with a rubric of the form "He shall bless, he shall recite and say," and each begins with the blessing formula, "Blessed are you, God of Israel."

The prayers in 4Q414 (*Ritual of Purification A*) and 4Q512 (*Ritual of Purification B*) are spoken in the first person singular by the individual undergoing purification. There are four passages with apparent close overlap between these two scrolls, and it is likely that they are similar but not identical versions of a liturgical collection of prayers.[43] Parts of twenty-one prayers survive in 4Q512 and eight in 4Q414. Allowing for the possibility that three of these could be overlapping between the two manuscripts, there are at least twenty-six different prayers for the person undergoing purification. That is, a unique prayer is uttered at each stage in the purification process—before immersion, after immersion while standing in the water, before sprinkling, and after sprinkling—as well as different times and occasions. Prayers before purification make mention of the requirement and include expressions of confession of sin and request for forgiveness. Prayers after purification contain praise and thanksgiving for cleansing. Unlike in biblical law, there are rituals for purification on the first, third, and seventh days of the purification process and these all include different prayers. For example, a fragment from 4Q414 preserves part of the end of a prayer before immersion that refers to purification on the first, third, and seventh days; ritual instruction concerning immersion; and the beginning of a prayer following immersion.

And you will purify us according to [your] holy laws [...] 2 for the first, the third, and the se[venth ...] 3 in the truth of your covenant[...] 4 to be purified from the impurity of [...] 5 And afterwards he will enter the

---

42. M. Baillet, "512. Rituel de Purification," in *Qumrân Grotte 4.3 (4Q482–4Q520)*, ed. M. Baillet, DJD 7 (Oxford: Clarendon, 1982), 262–86; E. Eshel, "414. 4QRitual of Purification A," in *Qumrân Cave 4.25: Halakhic Texts*, ed. J. M. Baumgarten et al., DJD 35 (Oxford: Clarendon, 1999), 135–56; J. M. Baumgarten, "284. 4QPurification Liturgy," in *Qumrân Cave 4.25: Halakhic Texts*, ed. J. M. Baumgarten et al., DJD 35 (Oxford: Clarendon, 1999), 123–29.

43. 4Q414 2 ii–4 cf. 4Q512 42–44 ii; 4Q414 7 8–9 cf. 4Q512 7–9, 2–3; 4Q414 11 1–3 cf. 4Q512 11 3–5; 4Q414 27–28, 1–3; cf. 4Q512 40–41, 3–6; Eshel, "414. 4QRitual of Purification A," 136–37.

water [and wash his body and bless.] 6 He will recite and say: Blessed are y[ou, God of Israel, . . .] 7 by what comes of your lips [the purification of all (people) has been required. (4Q414 2 ii–4 1–10 [cf. 4Q512 42–44])[44]

A fragment in 4Q512 gives ritual instructions related specifically to purification on the third day, a prayer before sprinkling, then ritual instructions concerning purification by sprinkling, and the beginning of a prayer after sprinkling.

On the third day [. . . And he shall ble]ss and recite and sa[y]: [Blessed are] 2 [yo]u, O God of Israel, [you commanded . . .] to cleanse themselves from [the impurity of] 3 [. . .] soul in the atonem[ent that you desire . . .] holy ash [. . .] 4 [. . .] in purify[ing] waters [. . .] in permanent streams,[45] 5 and waters of washing for cleansing appropriate for each time [. . .] his clothes. And then [they (?) shall sprinkle on him] 6 the waters for sp[rin]kling so as to cleanse him and all [. . .] 7 And aft[er] he has been [s]prinkled with water[s of sprinkling, he shall recite and say, Blessed are you,] 8 O Go[d of Israe]l, for you gave [us . . .] 9 and from the filth of uncleanness. And today [. . .] 10 impurity, to consecrate oneself for you and [. . . (4Q512 1–6)

Two fragments in 4Q512 give ritual instructions for purification on the seventh day for someone with a discharge, followed by the beginning of a prayer after immersion.

[. . .] his unclean flow [. . .] (4Q512 10)
[And when] he [has completed] the seven days of [his] puri[fication . . .] 3 [. . . then] he shall wash his clothes in w[ater and bathe his body . . .] 4 and he shall cover (his nakedness) with his clothes and bless wh[ere he stands[46] . . . And he shall recite and say, Blessed are You,] 5 O God of Isr[ae]l [. . .] (4Q512 11)

As Joseph M. Baumgarten has noted, a seven-day regimen with purification rituals on the first, third, and seventh days—including immersion, sprinkling, and prayers—seems to be applied to all forms of impurity.

---

44. Unless otherwise indicated, translations from the Dead Sea Scrolls are adapted from D. W. Parry and E. Tov, *The Dead Sea Scrolls Reader*, 2nd ed., 2 vols. (Leiden: Brill, 2014). Translations from 4Q512 are adapted from M. O. Wise, M. G. Abegg Jr., and E. M. Cook, eds., *The Dead Sea Scrolls: A New Translation* (rev. ed.; San Francisco: HarperSanFrancisco, 2005), 477–81.

45. For this reading of line 4, see J. M. Baumgarten, "The Purification Rituals in DJD 7," in *The Dead Sea Scrolls: Forty Years of Research; Papers Read at a Symposium Sponsored by Yad Izhak Ben-Zvi at the University of Haifa and at Tel Aviv University, March 20–24, 1988*, ed. D. Dimant and U. Rappaport, STDJ 10 (Leiden: Brill; New York: Magnes; Jerusalem: Yad Ben-Zvi, 1992), 207.

46. For this reconstruction, see ibid., 201–2.

Additionally, purification rituals with prayers are prescribed for consecration before calendrical occasions, specifically Sabbaths and festivals.

> [...] and for the appointed time of the Sabbath, for the Sabbaths of all the weeks of 2 [... and the] appoint[ed time of ... and] the four seasons of 3 [the year on the days of ... and] the season of the ha[rve]st, the end of see[d time] and of grass[47] 4 [...] 5 [...] in water [...] to consecrate oneself 6 [...] he will [bless] and recite [and say,] Blessed are You, 7 [O God of Israel ...] to have compassion [on us ...] (4Q512 33+35; cf. 4Q284 1 3–6)

Baumgarten argues on the basis of a parallel passage in 4Q284 (frg. 1 3–6), which refers to the "Rule of Thanksgivings" for Israel, that this is a ritual for the community in general.[48]

The prayers in 4Q284—at least in the three that are partly preserved—lack a first-person voice, speak of the people at large in the third person plural, and focus on waters of sprinkling and the completion of purification on the seventh day. It may be that this scroll contained a collection of liturgies for a priest administering sprinkling, although the fragmentary condition disallows certainty.

Despite the impossibility of reconstructing the rituals from the poorly preserved fragments, the entirety of these three scrolls is devoted to communicating ritual information related to the recital of prayers. In addition to specific wording and standardized formulas, they specify places and times for prayers: "[I am standing] before you at the appointed ti[me" (4Q512 29–32 6; cf. 4Q414 8 2); "[in] the midst of his people" (4Q512 34 14); "he sto]od at [his] station[" (4Q512 27 3); "and] bless there [the God of Israel" (4Q512 15 i–16 11–12); "t]o the sanctuary" (4Q512 56–58 3); "and after [the] sun [sets] on the [...] day [...]" (4Q512 48–50 5); "in]that [day" (4Q512 64); "on the third day" (4Q512 1–6 1); "after the setting of] the sun on the seventh day [" (4Q284 2 ii 3–4); "[...] its fixed times [...] when the sun sets on the [seventh] day [...]" (4Q284 3 1–2; cf. 6 2). The requirement of reciting a prayer immediately after immersion, while still standing in the water, is otherwise unattested in Jewish purification practices.[49] The instructions are concerned for strict ritual sequence, for example, "and] when [he] has completed[" (4Q512 21–22 1); "And aft[er] he has been [s]prinkled with water[s of sprinkling, he shall say" (4Q512 1–6 7). They specify posture (standing); gestures (spreading of hands in prayer [4Q512 42–44 ii 6]; extending

---

47. For this restoration of line 3, see Baumgarten, "284. 4QPurification Liturgy," 125.

48. See J. M. Baumgarten, "The Purification Liturgies," in *The Dead Sea Scrolls After Fifty Years: A Comprehensive Assessment*, ed. P. W. Flint and J. C. VanderKam (Leiden: Brill, 1999), 2:200–12 at 203–6.

49. Ibid., 202.

of hand [for inspection?; 4Q512 21–22 1]); dress ("and he shall cover (his nakedness) with his clothes" [4Q512 11 4]; "[...] his [garm]ents and wra[p" [4Q512 18 2]); and emotional display ("with joy" [4Q512 18 3, 24 3]).

What is the purpose of these scrolls and who are they for? In the first instance, these scrolls are significantly different from other texts among the Dead Sea Scrolls that address the topic of ritual purification. These include self-standing collections of laws, such as *4QTohorot A* (4Q274), *4QTohorot B^b* (4Q277), and *4QOrdinances^c* (4Q514); the *Temple Scroll*, which presents itself as a book of Torah spoken directly in God's voice; and composite works that combine laws and admonition (*Damascus Document*; *MMT*). In their treatments of purification, all of these focus on defining such matters as who and what needs purification under certain conditions, and when the purification is complete and a person is permitted to eat pure food.[50] In a theological section of the *Community Rule*, on the other hand, is an idealogical treatment of purification (1QS 3:4b–12a) that insists on the prerequisite of penitence and submission to the covenant. None of these treatments of purification, however, are concerned with describing the ritual actions, and none indicate that prayers are recited at various stages of the immersions and sprinklings. Josephus also gives no hint that Essenes offered prayers during purification rituals, although he highlights both their purifications and their prayers as extraordinary (*J.W.* 2.128–31, 150, 161; *Ant.* 18.19). There continues to be debate among scholars as to whether there is a unified purity system reflected among the scrolls found at Qumran.[51] What is important here, though, is that scrolls of different genre and purpose provide very different information. 4Q284, 4Q414, and 4Q512 are neither literary descriptions nor halakhic treatments of ritual purification, although they do assume halakhic positions that are consistent with other texts found at Qumran (defilement lasts until sundown; immersion is required before eating; immersion is required on the first day; purification has spiritual significance even though repetitive; purification is required for appointed times).[52] Rather, they are unique in representing ritual scripts for purification and are concerned with the sequence of ritual and the prayers. 4Q414 and 4Q512 are ritual scripts for the person undergoing purification, and 4Q284 seemingly for an officiating priest.

50. See 4Q274; 4Q277; 4Q514 1 i–iii; 4QD^a 6 i–iii; 11QT^a 45, 48–51; CD 10:10b–13; 4QMMT^c 1–2 iii 4b–iv 1.

51. For example, see the debate between I. C. Werrett, *Ritual Purity and the Dead Sea Scrolls*, STDJ 27 (Leiden: Brill, 2007), 2–3; and H. K. Harrington, *The Purity Texts*, Companion to the Qumran Scrolls (London: T&T Clark, 2004), 12. On the difficulties of weighing silence in the texts with regard to features of ritual practice, see M. A. Daise, "Ritual Density in Qumran Practice: Ablutions in the *Serekh Ha-Yaḥad*," in *New Perspectives on Old Texts: Proceedings of the Tenth International Symposium of the Orion Center for the Study of the Dead Sea Scrolls and Associated Literature, 9–11 January, 2005*, ed. E. Glickler-Chazon, B. Halpern-Amaru, and R. A. Clements, STDJ 88 (Leiden: Brill, 2010), 51–66.

52. Baumgarten, "Purification Liturgies."

Moreover, the material evidence strongly suggests that 4Q414 and 4Q512 were liturgical scrolls for the personal use of an individual: both of these are rare instances of opisthographs, both written secondarily on the verso of a scroll—an indication of a personal copy. Neither is the case of recycling a discarded scroll. Most strikingly, 4Q512 was inscribed on the reverse of a collection of prayers for each day of a month (4Q503 *Daily Prayers*) that have the same formal features of the prayers in 4Q512.[53] This strongly suggests an intentional collection of liturgical prayers. The small format of these scrolls—under 15 cm tall—would have made them easily portable. 4Q284 could have been smaller yet, with as few as eleven lines, but it is too fragmentary to be certain.[54] It is also notable that both 4Q414 and 4Q512 employ distinctive marginal signs to mark the beginning of each ritual. This practice is found in only a small group of manuscripts, and especially in liturgical scrolls.[55] Whether these scrolls were actually carried and used as a script during rituals or were for learning recitations at home is uncertain, they should be regarded as liturgical scrolls directly in connection with the performance of rituals.

In the case of these scrolls, prayer is a significant, scripted element in a complex ritual. In the following case, the communal recitation of prayer is the ritual act.

12.3.2. Collections of Liturgical Prayers

One of the most characteristic features of ritual attested in the Dead Sea Scrolls is a comprehensive cycle of communal, liturgical prayers or psalms for all occasions of the calendar: days of the month, days of the week, Sabbaths, and festivals. These represent the oldest extant Jewish prayer books, but unlike the prayer books of the later synagogue, the liturgical prayers at Qumran are grouped into collections for each occasion. There are also collections of prayers for purification rituals, apotropaic and exorcism prayers and songs, and some other unidentified rituals.[56] In all of these cases, there are rubrics identifying the occasion and giving brief instructions for recital, followed by the text of the prayers. For example, from the *Daily Prayers*: "On the fif[teenth of

---

53. D. K. Falk, "Material Aspects of Prayer Manuscripts at Qumran," in *Literature or Liturgy? Early Christian Hymns and Prayers in Their Literary and Liturgical Context in Antiquity*, ed. C. Leonhard and H. Löhr, Wissenschaftliche Untersuchungen zum Neuen Testament 2/363 (Tübingen: Mohr Siebeck, 2014), 52–56.

54. Ibid., 65–66.

55. D. K. Falk, "In the Margins of the Dead Sea Scrolls," in *Bible as Notepad: Tracing Annotations and Annotation Practices in Late Antique and Medieval Biblical Manuscripts*, ed. L. I. Lied and M. Maniaci, Manuscripta Biblica 3 (Berlin: de Gruyter, 2018), 10–38.

56. D. K. Falk, "Prayer in the Qumran Texts," in *The Early Roman Period*, vol. 3 of *The Cambridge History of Judaism*, ed. W. Horbury, W. D. Davies, and J. Sturdy (Cambridge: Cambridge University Press, 1999), 3:852–76.

the month in the ev[e]ning they shall bless. They shall recite, [say]ing: Blessed is the Go[d of Israel]" (4Q503 103 6–7). From the *Festival Prayers*: "Prayer for the Day of Atonement. Remem[ber O L]ord [...]" (1Q34 2+1 6). There is a completely different text for each occasion, unlike the later synagogue liturgy where the Amidah is used on all occasions with adaptations.

These appear to be scripts for the verbal part of ritualized prayers, with only a brief rubric about the occasion. We will return to the issue of ritual context in a moment, but for now I want to reinforce that these we can properly call ritual texts. Moreover, the scrolls themselves were likely used directly in relation to the ritual, either as a performative script or at least for learning the prayers. In a recent article I argued that several features suggest that most of these liturgical scrolls were personal copies: they tend to be small format scrolls and have the appearance of nonexpert "budget" copies.[57] Most significantly, there are several cases of what appear to be intentional collections of prayers, with the addition of another collection of prayers on the reverse. Two cases are especially compelling. On the recto of one papyrus is the only surviving copy of *Daily Prayers* (4Q503), a collection of morning and evening liturgical prayers for days of a month. On the verso, seemingly another scribe copied afterward a collection of instructions and prayers for purification rituals (4Q512). The two sets of prayers share the same formal features, which suggests that this is not the reuse of a defunct scroll but the creation of an intentional compilation of liturgical prayers. Another papyrus scroll is similar. The recto has a copy of *Festival Prayers* (4Q509, 4Q505), and on the verso a copy (or excerpt) of the *War Scroll* (4Q496) was copied a few years later (both dated paleographically around the second quarter of the first century BCE). About a century later, someone added to the verso a copy of prayers for days of the week known as *Words of the Luminaries* (4Q506). Once again, the prayers on both sides have the same formal features but are significantly different than the prayer type on the other example just mentioned. It is by no means accidental that these two collections of prayers with the same form for different occasions end up on front and back of the same scroll: they constitute an intentional collection in a personal scroll. Possibly this could suggest as well that the *War Scroll*—sandwiched between these two—was regarded as a liturgical text in some way.[58]

Thus, along with the purification liturgies discussed previously, it is appropriate to consider the liturgical prayer collections as ritual texts in the fullest sense. These represent scripts for the performance of ritual as opposed to descriptions

---

57. Falk, "Material Aspects," 74–75.
58. D. K. Falk, "Prayer, Liturgy, and War," in *The War Scroll, Violence, War and Peace in the Dead Sea Scrolls and Related Literature: Essays in Honour of Martin G. Abegg on the Occasion of His 65th Birthday*, ed. K. Davis et al., STDJ 115 (Leiden: Brill, 2015), 275–94 at 291–93.

of ritual in a narrative or prescriptions for ritual in a rule book. For the sake of comparison, I suggest a grid (grid 12.1) with a continuum of description-prescription-script as the horizontal axis, and for the vertical axis a continuum of index-outline-detail. The latter continuum distinguishes between mere reference to ritual, a skeleton description of ritual, and an account with specific details. On this grid, these liturgical scrolls would be in the top right quadrant.

In addition to these scrolls of prayers, there are various other references throughout the scrolls to communal prayers at set times, both descriptions and prescriptions. It may be tempting to try to use all of this material to reconstruct the ritual world of Qumran, but the materials are found in differing genres with various rhetorical purposes. For example, a famous prescription of times of prayer is part of a song of the Maskil—an instructor and liturgical master for the community—at the end of the *Community Rule* (1QS 9:26–10:16). This calendar of sacred times meshes well with the types and occasions for prayer we find throughout the scrolls.[59] To whatever degree it may reflect ritual practice in the Essene movement, it serves primarily a rhetorical function in the *Community Rule*. On the grid described above, it would be placed in the central column—as prescribing ritualized prayer—and slightly lower than the middle, since it gives only a vague, allusive outline.

All of the varying types of material belong to the larger context of prayer in the community: how prayer is described and portrayed and—as Carol A. Newsom has argued—how these seem intended to shape the experience of the community in and through prayer.[60] Another part of this larger context is the wider network of language associated with prayer. For example, there is a remarkable overlap of language among the liturgical prayers, astronomical language, and descriptions of both angels and humans at worship and war.[61] This suggests, that the community regarded worship as a means of spiritual warfare in the present, although caution is necessary. Each of these texts have their own rhetoric and agenda. The use of language about prayer does not necessarily map directly back onto what rituals of prayer "mean."

The ritual context of prayer is not merely the immediate actions and utterances of an individual performance or prayers in isolation but includes the entire system of prayers. This point is most dramatically illustrated by three

---

59. See D. K. Falk, "Qumran and the Synagogue Liturgy," in *The Ancient Synagogue from Its Origins Until 200 CE: Papers Presented at an International Conference at Lund University, October 14–17, 2001*, ed. B. Ollson and M. Zetterholm, Coniectanea Biblica: New Testament Series 39 (Stockholm: Almqvist & Wiksell, 2003), 404–34 at 426–27.

60. C. A. Newsom, *The Self as Symbolic Space: Constructing Identity and Community at Qumran*, STDJ 52 (Leiden: Brill, 2004), 182–87, 191, 202–8. For example, "By engaging in structured social practices and learning to speak the language of the figured world, the novice both receives a new identity and contributes to the construction of the community" (187).

61. Falk, "Prayer, Liturgy, and War," 285–86.

examples.[62] First, the *Words of the Luminaries* (4Q504, 4Q506) is a collection of lengthy prayers for days of the week that consist of historical remembrances followed by petition for mercy and/or spiritual strengthening. The most striking feature is that the historical remembrances recount a progressive narrative over the course of the week from creation, through exodus from Egypt, monarchy, and exile to the contemporary Second Temple period.[63] Second, the *Songs of the Sabbath Sacrifice* (4Q400–407, *11QShirShabb*) consists of a series of thirteen mystical songs (for the first quarter of the year, or to be repeated quarterly) that describe heavenly worship, progressing in a structured sequence throughout the thirteen weeks, culminating in a vision of the divine chariot throne and the heavenly priestly vestments. Third, the *Daily Prayers* (4Q503) consists of a sequence of morning and evening prayers over the course of the first month, apparently marking Sabbaths and Passover according to their dates on the 364-day solar calendar. Similarly, the festival prayers and purification prayers are different for each occasion and may have formed a liturgical sequence as well, although they are too fragmentary to determine. This feature of different prayers for each occasion, marking a liturgical progression over a sequence of prayers, is fundamentally different than the system of prayers of the later synagogue, where a prayer is modified for use on various occasions. Moreover, the sacred calendars found at Qumran detail a comprehensive system of appointed times for prayer.

The different types of material related to calendrical prayer may be highlighted by plotting on grid 12.1. Whereas the collections of prayers for calendrical occasions—providing detailed scripts—occupy the top right square, a poetic calendar of times of prayer at the end of some copies of the *Community Rule* (1QS 9:26–10:8; cf. 4QS^{b,d,f}) merely lists appointed times required for prayer and so belongs in the middle square (prescriptive in outline). A prose account of psalms and songs attributed to David for use at daily, Sabbath, and festival offerings in 11QPsalms^a (*David's Compositions*) is a mere indexical description and would belong to the lower left square.

Another consideration we should add is facticity. The petitionary prayers found at Qumran show analogous form and language to the classic petitionary prayers of the Second Temple period, epitomized in Dan 9; Ezra 9; Neh 9; and other examples.[64] We can have no certainty, however, that these latter prayers

---

62. See D. K. Falk, "Liturgical Progression and the Experience of Transformation in Prayers from Qumran," *DSD* 22 (2015): 267–84.

63. E. Glickler-Chazon, "'4QDibHam': Liturgy or Literature?," *Revue de Qumran* 15 (1992): 447–55.

64. See E. Glickler-Chazon, "The 'Words of the Luminaries' and Penitential Prayer in Second Temple Times," in *The Development of Penitential Prayer in Second Temple Judaism*, vol. 2 of *Seeking the Favor of God*, ed. M. J. Boda, D. K. Falk, and R. A. Werline (Leiden: Brill, 2007), 2:177–86.

were ever recited liturgically by the community. They could be idealized prayers composed as literary works, based on shared prayer themes. Nevertheless, there can be little question that models of prayer—even of fictive prayers, and especially prayers attributed to patriarchs—had a profound influence in shaping actual prayers of the community, and their experience of prayer, as Weitzman's study cited earlier emphasized.[65] Thus, I suggest a continuum from fictive to performed ritual. This might be combined in a grid with another continuum concerning the distance from ritual performance, whether distant or indirect at one end to near or direct at the other (grid 12.2). At the distant/indirect end of the spectrum would belong metaritual texts such as the various calendrical texts. These do not describe, prescribe, or provide a script for a ritual but describe or prescribe relevant contextual elements for ritual performance. These might relate to actual performance and so belong in the top left quadrant, where I would plot the poetical times of prayer in 1QS 9–10. On the other hand, these might be more idealized than real, as is probably the case with 11QPs[a] *David's Compositions*, with its improbably large collection (3600 psalms and 450 songs) or the liturgical calendar in 4Q334, which ascribes suspiciously high numbers of songs for morning and evening recital—for one evening is assigned eight songs and forty some words of praise. These might best be placed in the lower left quadrant. The liturgical collections of prayers would belong in the top right quadrant as directly related to performance, and the eschatological blessings of the *Rule of Blessing*, for the messianic age, might best be plotted in the lower right quadrant.

12.3.3. Tefillin and the Shema‘

Remains of over two dozen *tefillin* (or "phylacteries") were found at Qumran.[66] These are small, sealed leather pouches worn on the arm and forehead containing tiny leather strips inscribed with scriptural passages that mention God's laws as a "sign" and "emblem" on one's hand and forehead (Exod 13:1–10, 11–16; Deut 6:4–9; 11:13–21; although there is some minor variation in the contents of the passages found at Qumran).

> It shall serve for you as a sign on your hand and as a reminder on your forehead. (Exod 13:9)
> It shall serve as a sign on your hand and as an emblem on your forehead. (Exod 13:16)

---

65. Weitzman, "Revisiting Myth and Ritual," 43.
66. See Y. B. Cohn, *Tangled Up in Text: Tefillin and the Ancient World*, BJS 351 (Providence, RI: Brown Judaic Studies, 2008), 56–67, and the references cited there.

> Bind them as a sign on your hand, fix them as an emblem on your forehead, and write them on the doorposts of your house and on your gates. (Deut 6:8–9)
>
> You shall put these words of mine in your heart and soul, and you shall bind them as a sign on your hand, and fix them as an emblem on your forehead. (Deut 11:18)[67]

The *tefillin* found at Qumran are examples of ritual objects, but the exact nature of that connection to ritual at Qumran is unclear. According to traditional rabbinic practice, *tefillin* are worn during morning prayer in conjunction with recitation of the *Shemaʿ*, one of the two central prayers of the synagogue liturgy. Of course, these scriptural passages almost certainly do not envision or command the ritual of making pouches of bound texts and tying them on to one's body in relation to daily prayer—this is a later interpretation of the passage, based on the injunction in the Deuteronomy passages to recite these laws "when you lie down and when you rise" (Deut 6:7; 11:19), attested explicitly first in Josephus (*Ant.* 4.212–13). What is important for us, however, is that it illustrates the inseparable connection between interpretation and ritual.[68] We probably cannot solve the problem of which came first, the interpretation or the ritual, but the scriptural texts emphasize the intent as reminder. It would be natural, then, for a ritual based on these passages to have a reflexive significance: what the ritual "says" is to the actor. This seems to be how Josephus understands the wearing of *tefillin*. On the other hand, it could also serve as an index to others: this is a person devoted to Torah; this is a house devoted to Torah. Matthew's Gospel assumes this purpose in Jesus's critique of oversized *tefillin* mentioned in Matt 23:5. The *tefillin* found at Qumran, however, are surprisingly tiny (e.g., 13 × 20 mm) and not apparently designed for visibility. As a third option, a recent study by Yehudah B. Cohn persuasively argues that the practice of wearing *tefillin* originated in the late–Second Temple period as an amulet worn to ensure long-life, analogous to Greek magical practices.[69] He suggests that recital of the *Shemaʿ* may have originated as a protective magical practice as well, and its connection with *tefillin* as a recited consecration of the amulet, as is frequently attested for amulets in various cultures.[70]

In any case, no text from Qumran mentions the use of *tefillin*, nor clearly refers to recitation of the *Shemaʿ*, so we simply do not know if these artifacts were used in any particular way in connection with prayer. This fact itself is very

---

67. Unless otherwise indicated, biblical translations are from the New Revised Standard Version.
68. See Rüpke, "Acta aut agenda," 25, 40.
69. Cohn, *Tangled Up*, 93.
70. Ibid., 100–102.

enlightening: if it were not for the chance find of these artifacts, we would have no indication from any of the texts from Qumran or accounts of the Essenes that members of this movement wore *tefillin*.

Evidence suggests that the *tefillin* were prepared in a ritualized manner. There are particular standards in mind for the form, material, preparation of the pouches with compartments, the content and tying of the inscribed strips, and binding on the body. These are, on the one hand, surprisingly consonant with rabbinic norms for *tefillin*,[71] but, on the other hand, also resonant with magical amulets in the ancient world.[72]

In the unusual way that the strips were inscribed, there was no consideration for the content of the texts, but there were clearly some other concerns.[73] The strips may have odd shapes, but the front side is always inscribed along the long edge and is invariably filled completely. The writing on the reverse is chaotic, with only two consistent principles: first, it is always written perpendicular to the front—even where this means creating an absurdly narrow column, sometimes as narrow as a single word[74]—and second, the middle of the strip is always left blank. The verso usually starts not at the top but often in the lower half, even if it is directly following from the text on the front. There seems to be a desire to have the text on the verso end at the bottom of the slip, leaving any blank spaces in the middle of the sheet, even though this sometimes results in an awkward arrangement of the text, with the scribe running out of space, turning the sheet around to inscribe upside down on the other half, and so on. In breaking the text on the verso, there often seems to be no consideration for the content: sometimes the text may break in the middle of a sentence to continue on the verso of a different sheet. The purpose of the gap in the middle is probably so that no text will appear on the outside of the packet when folded and tied up. Moreover, the most obvious feature is that the leather strips are tied up and sealed, so the texts do not function as text at all after their ritualized preparation. The closest analogue is to amulets—for example, the Ketef Hinnom amulets inscribed with the Priestly Blessing.

In the case of Qumran, we simply do not know what rituals may have been associated with their use, since no text even mentions them. Were they donned

---

71. L. H. Schiffman, "Phylacteries and Mezuzot," in *Encyclopedia of the Dead Sea Scrolls*, ed. L. H. Schiffman and J. C. VanderKam (Oxford: Oxford University Press, 2000), 2:675–77.

72. Cohn, *Tangled Up*, 96–98.

73. Falk, "Material Aspects," 75–80.

74. G. J. Brooke has suggested that inscribing the verso perpendicular to the recto on a parchment may be inherited from the use of a papyrus. See G. J. Brooke, "Between Scroll and Codex? Reconsidering the Qumran Opisthographs," in *On Stone and Scroll: Essays in Honour of Graham Ivor Davies*, ed. J. K. Aitken, K. J. Dell, and B. A. Mastin, BZAW 420 (Berlin: de Gruyter, 2011), 123–38 at 131. This is possible, but if so, it is still difficult to explain the striking variance with regard to content and order of passages, and peculiar layouts of the text of the verso.

in a ritualized manner? From the manner of preparation, we might reasonably assume so. Was a recitation such as the *Shemaʿ* associated with wearing them? Were they worn all day? We simply do not know. It is plausible, though, that they served as protective amulets. Protection from evil was a major concern of their ritualized life.

Even if we cannot be certain of a ritual connection between the wearing of *tefillin* and the *Shemaʿ* at Qumran, there is reason to believe that the community recited the *Shemaʿ* in morning and evening. Here we have an entirely different kind of evidence. First, we have a possible allusion to recital of the *Shemaʿ* in a poetic calendar of times of prayer at the end of a copy of the *Community Rule*.

> With the arrival of day and night I will enter into the covenant of God. And with the departure of evening and morning I will recite his laws ... as soon as I stretch out my hand or my foot, I will bless his name; as soon as (I) go out or come in, to sit down or rise up, and while I recline on my couch, I will praise him. I will bless him with the lifting up of the utterance of my lips in the assembly of men. (1QS 10:10–14, my translation)[75]

If this is accepted as an allusion to recital of the *Shemaʿ*, could the reference to recitation in assembly (1QS 10:14) be taken as some indication of a communal, ritual context? It is dubious whether the poem allows any concrete clues to reconstruction of ritual practice: it is not a guide to the practice of specific rituals but a rhetorical presentation of a life totally immersed in prayer. What is intriguing is to imagine the purpose of such Maskil songs in the life of the community, with many similar ones among the *Thanksgiving Hymns*. It is possible they are for private meditation, but it is more likely that they were recited. Newsom has explored how such immersion in the idealized religious experience of the Maskil would serve to inculcate a sectarian subjectivity.[76] In a sense, we have a ritualized reflection on ritual.

The second type of evidence is an interpretation of the *Shemaʿ* embedded in the manifesto at the beginning of the *Community Rule*:

> 1QS 1:1 A text belonging to [the Maskil, who is to teach the ho]ly ones how to live according to the book of the community's rule. He is to teach them to seek 2 God with all their heart and with all their soul, to do that which is good and upright before him, just as 3 he commanded through Moses and all his servants the prophets ...

---

75. See Falk, "Qumran and the Synagogue Liturgy," 405–6.
76. Newsom, *Self as Symbolic Space*, 191–286.

11 ... All who volunteer for his truth are to bring the full measure of their knowledge, strength, and 12 wealth into the community of God. Thus will they purify their knowledge in the truth of God's laws, properly exercise their strength 13 according to the perfection of his ways, and likewise their wealth by the canon of his righteous counsel.[77]

The allusion to Deut 6:4–5 is clear:

Hear, O Israel: The LORD is our God, the LORD alone. 5 You shall love the LORD your God with all your heart, and with all your soul, and with all your might. 6 Keep these words that I am commanding you today in your heart.

On the surface, recitation of the *Shemaʿ* unites all Israel under loyalty to one God. But the *Community Rule* thoroughly inflects the *Shemaʿ* with sectarian meaning. It is interpreted as an obligation of utter loyalty to the sectarian community. Loving God with all one's heart, soul, and strength means committing one's knowledge, actions, and resources to the service of the sectarian community.

The sectarian meaning of the *Shemaʿ* to reinforce boundaries from other Jews is evident from the middle of that passage:

He is to teach them to love everything 4 he chose and to hate everything he rejected, to distance themselves from all evil 5 and to hold fast to all good deeds; to practice truth, justice, and righteousness 6 in the land, and to walk no longer in a guilty, willful heart and lustful desires, 7 wherein they did every evil thing. He is to induct all who volunteer to live by the laws of God 8 into the covenant of mercy, so as to be joined to God's society and walk faultless before him, according to all 9 that has been revealed for the times appointed them. He is to teach them both to love all the children of light—each 10 commensurate with his rightful place in the council of God—and to hate all the children of darkness, each commensurate with his guilt 11 and the vengeance due him from God. (1QS 1:3b–11a)

They are obligated to hate other Jews who think and practice differently and to pronounce them as damned by God. This text inflects a sectarian meaning for the *Shemaʿ* by means of allusion and interpretation. We would be wrong to think that this rhetorical text gives us the meaning of the ritual, but it is part of the context.

---

77. Translations from 1QS, unless otherwise indicated, are adapted from Wise, Abegg, and Cook, *Dead Sea Scrolls*, 117.

From this example, we see several completely different types of evidence: a ritual artifact that tells nothing about its use but does reflect ritualization in its production, a report of ritual practice in a poem that might be a ritualized recital itself, and an interpretation that gives sectarian meaning to a ritual. It is not clear that we could be justified in combining these various pieces of evidence in an attempt to reconstruct ritual practice, let alone meaning. More to the point, they problematize the relationship between text and ritual in different ways. With the *tefillin* as ritual artifacts, the materiality of text is in the fore. I would suggest an important addition to a taxonomy of text and ritual is a continuum between an instrumental and material use of text in ritual. On a grid with this as the horizontal axis, and the vertical axis a continuum of literary to ritual (grid 12.3), the *tefillin* would be in the top right quadrant, and the description of *Shema'* in the bottom left quadrant. The collections of liturgical prayers would belong in the top left quadrant: the text plays a functional role in the ritual recitation of prayer.

12.3.4. Covenant Ceremony

The sectarian annual covenant ceremony described in the *Community Rule* (lQS 1:18–2:18) presents a special problem. It reads as an outline script for the central rite of passage of the sectarian community, an annual ritual of initiation and reaffirmation, apparently at Pentecost. It consists of a mustering of the entire community with recitations in three movements by priests, Levites, and the congregation:

1. a. Praise of God (priests and Levites)
   b. Response by congregation: Amen Amen
2. a. Recitation of God's dealings with Israel (priests)
   b. Recitation of Israel's sins (Levites)
   c. Confession of sin (congregation)
3. a. Blessings on insiders (priests)
   b. Curses on outsiders (Levites)
   c. Curses on apostates (priests and Levites)
   d. Response by congregation: Amen Amen

Although the sequence of recitations as described in 1QS 1:16–2:18 is in part based on the form of postexilic communal confessions (e.g., Neh 9, Ezra 9, Dan 9, Bar 1:15–3:8), I have argued that it is uniquely adapted by replacing a petition for mercy and forgiveness with blessing on the covenanters and cursing on outsiders and apostates, so that the whole functions as a ritual of confirmation.[78] Arnold has extended this argument to claim that, although the ritual

---

78. Falk, *Daily, Sabbath, and Festival Prayers*, 219–26.

includes confession of sin, there is no actual penitence: these are merely preordained words.[79] This might overstate the case somewhat, but there is in any case a significant disjunction between words spoken and what a ritual does. It is an important reminder that rituals have syntax: sequence and context matter. Moreover, the words spoken are not necessarily the most important part of a ritual, and we should keep that in mind in cases where all we have are words preserved without information on ritual context.

With regard to the context of the covenant ceremony, it should be noted that it was not included in all versions of the *Community Rule*. It is preserved complete only in 1QS, where it is part of an extended ideological introduction (1QS 1–4), which is partly preserved in 4QS^a, 4QS^b, and 4QS^c. This section was probably absent from at least two manuscripts, 4QS^d and 4QS^e. It is clear that the *Community Rule* is a composite work attested in at least three very different recensions at Qumran, and the covenant ceremony is attested in manuscripts of two recensions. The complex relationship among the different recensions and their dates defies attempts at explanations of linear developments.[80] Thus it is necessary to take into account the appearance and rhetorical function of the covenant ceremony in different recensions of the *Community Rule*—probably synchronically—as part of its larger context.

It is also important to recognize that the covenant ceremony as presented in 1QS does not provide the entire ceremony. Most of it is mere outline, with the content of only certain recitations provided: the confession of sin and the blessings and curses. This reinforces that the purpose is not to provide a guide to the performance of the ritual. As Newsom has compellingly argued, features of the ceremony are summoned for rhetorical purposes having to do with formation of sectarian subjectivity.[81] The utterances supplied are those that most sharply reinforce boundaries and identity. It is also not clear how close the outline would correspond to actual performance. Here it is important to recall the principle that each instance of a performance is unique; no account of it can be regarded as a representation of the ritual.

Hence, on grid 12.1, the covenant ceremony in the *Community Rule* would fit in the row "outline." It is harder to determine whether it belongs in the column of "description" or "prescription": at one level the language is that of prescription, but in the context of the *Community Rule* it has a completely different function than prescribing: it recalls for rhetorical effect. On grid 12.2, the covenant ceremony would belong in the top left quadrant: related to a performed

---

79. Arnold, *Social Role of Liturgy*, 61–67.
80. See summary of debate and evidence in A. Schofield, *From Qumran to the Yahad: A New Paradigm of Textual Development for the "Community Rule,"* STDJ 77 (Leiden: Brill, 2009), 69–78, 84–88, 103–6, 125–30.
81. Newsom, *Self as Symbolic Space*, 117–27.

ritual, but indirectly. As a literary text descriptive of ritual, it would belong in the bottom left quadrant of grid 12.3.

But I wish to emphasize a different point, having to do, once again, with materiality. And for this, it will be helpful to compare with two other analogous accounts of a community ritual. First, the Iguvine Tables consist of seven bronze sheets from Umbria engraved on both sides with religious rituals of a priestly fraternity, dating from the early third to the mid-first century BCE.[82] They detail sacrifices and prayers at purification rituals and feasts, including rubrics specifying exact words (for example, "use this formula," "thus pray during the libation"). The rituals include a ceremonial mustering of the community with blessings, and ritual expulsion and cursing of traditional enemies. If this is an accurate summary—and there is significant uncertainty and debate—it is an intriguing analogue to the mustering of the congregation in the covenant ceremony in 1QS, with blessing and curse rituals and various prescribed declarations and prayers.[83]

The second example is the Carmen Arvale, a Latin chant of the Arval priests of ancient Rome.[84] This chant survives because it was inscribed on a marble slab that displayed the protocols of the priestly fraternity, including instructions for the annual festival of Ambarvalia held in a sacred grove near Rome involving sacrifice, a ritual dance, and chanted prayer for fertility of the plowed fields. It refers to communal recitation of the chant using books. Although the inscription dates to 218 CE, the archaic language of the chant indicates that it dates from before the fourth century BCE. Most importantly for our purposes, here we have reference to the use of sacred books of prayer used in ritual, although none have survived for us.

In both cases, these are constitutional rituals of communities with intriguing analogues to the covenant ceremony, but with a very important difference having to do with materiality: these are monumental texts. Who are they for? With regard to the protocols of the Arval Brethren, Rüpke notes, "The texts hardly could give coaching for new priests: rituals normally were represented in summary fashion.... Therefore the epigraphical texts were present in the ritual, but were not suitable as 'scripts,' as guidance for performing the ritual."[85] Rüpke disagrees with John Scheid's judgment that the texts are "documentation for the deity about the dutifully performed cult," and he argues that they are intended for the "members of the priesthood itself."[86] The text is read by the same people

---

82. J. W. Poultney, *The Bronze Tables of Iguvium*, Philological Monographs 18 (Oxford: Blackwell, 1959).

83. On the debate concerning the nature of the ritual, see J. B. Wilkins, "The Iguvine Tablets: Problems in the Interpretation of Ritual Text," in *Territory, Time, and State: The Archaeological Development of the Gubbio Basin*, ed. C. Malone and S. Stoddart (Cambridge: Cambridge University Press, 1994), 152–72.

84. F. Chapot and B. Laurot, *Corpus de prières grecques et romaines*, Recherches sur les Rhétoriques Religieuses 2 (Turnhout: Brepols, 2001), 233–34.

85. Rüpke, "Acta aut agenda," 35.

86. Ibid., 35–36.

who performed the rituals. In any case, my point is simply that this different material context matters and requires attention.

I suggest a fourth grid (grid 12.4), then, with the horizontal axis describing the availability of the material, ranging from display to concealed. The vertical axis describes the prominence of the text, ranging from exposed to covered. On this grid, the monumental ritual texts mentioned above would occupy the bottom left quadrant: they are exposed texts on display. Tomb inscriptions, on the other hand, are exposed texts, but in a concealed location, and would belong in the bottom right quadrant. The *tefillin*, discussed earlier, are both closed texts and concealed and would belong in the top right quadrant. A ceremonial book such as a processional gospel would belong in the top left quadrant. That is, in the top row, it is the object that is prominent: these have a ritual function without the text being visible. In the bottom row it is the text that is prominent. In the left column, visibility for people is important, whereas in the right column, visibility for god(s). In the context of the finds at Qumran, it is striking that—with the exception of the *tefillin*—no other text would fit in these categories: there are no display texts and no exposed texts. All the other texts from Qumran would fit between these categories, in the middle of the grid: scrolls that would be unrolled for reading—either for study or in the context of ritual performance—and put away afterward. That many scrolls were found with the beginning in the innermost layer attests active use, as does much evidence of repair and correction.[87] Little is known, however, about the realia of the handling and storage of the scrolls at Qumran, although some recent studies have sought to better understand the Qumran collection in the context of ancient libraries and book culture.[88]

12.4. Conclusions

This brief investigation does not do justice to the considerable wealth of ritual material among the Dead Sea Scrolls corpus. As Kugler put it, "Ritual at Qumran was hegemonic, making every aspect of their experience religious."[89] I have in the past made several attempts to inventory and classify the various types of liturgical material and to sketch out a synthesis of the religious life attested by these scrolls.[90] What happens when one does this, however, is that one combines

---

87. E. Tov, *Scribal Practices and Approaches Reflected in the Texts Found in the Judean Desert*, STDJ 54 (Leiden: Brill, 2004), 108–9, 122–25, 222–30.

88. For example, S. White Crawford and C. Wassen, *The Dead Sea Scrolls at Qumran and the Concept of a Library*, STDJ 116 (Leiden: Brill, 2015).

89. Kugler, "Making All Experience Religious," 152.

90. Falk, "Prayer in the Qumran Texts"; D. K. Falk, "Religious Life at Qumran," in *Celebrating the Dead Sea Scrolls: A Canadian Collection*, ed. P. W. Flint, J. Duhaime, and K. S. Baek, EJL 30 (Atlanta: Society of Biblical Literature; Leiden: Brill, 2011), 253–85.

all sorts of data of completely different kinds. This in itself is not the problem. In fact, it is one of the tremendous gifts of Qumran that we can draw on descriptive and prescriptive texts, archaeological evidence, and external reports about the Essenes. This is an almost unparalleled wealth for reconstruction of ritual in the ancient Mediterranean world. The problem is that one tends to fall into the trap of expecting similar information from the different types of sources.

The questions asked by this volume about defining the complicated relationships between text and ritual are vital. By focusing on just a few intriguing cases, I have tried to illustrate the range of issues involved with regard to the particular situation of the Dead Sea Scrolls, but by extension to some degree at least to other related corpora. I would like to reinforce two most important points. The first is that with the scrolls we have a unique situation in having a significant body of texts that are also ritual artifacts. Much more thought needs to be given to the opportunities this offers and its implications. The second point is that although we are reminded by the physical evidence from Qumran what is missing because of the fragmentary nature of the scrolls, a ritual theory approach equally reminds us what we are missing even when we have texts. Even with rich texts surviving, we are missing the most important aspects of a ritual performance: it is like missing a concert and only reading the program notes. At least being more disciplined in identifying the complex relationships between text and ritual, we can begin to be on surer footing.

12.5. Appendix

GRID 12.1. Ritual as Script

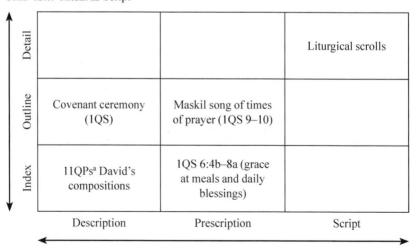

	Description	Prescription	Script
Detail			Liturgical scrolls
Outline	Covenant ceremony (1QS)	Maskil song of times of prayer (1QS 9–10)	
Index	11QPs^a David's compositions	1QS 6:4b–8a (grace at meals and daily blessings)	

GRID 12.2. Ritual as Performance

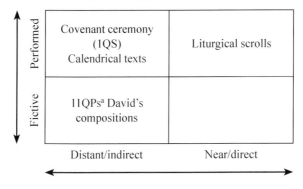

GRID 12.3. Ritual as Text

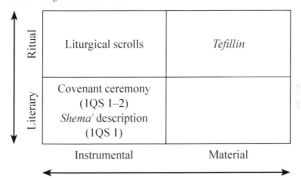

GRID 12.4. Material Context

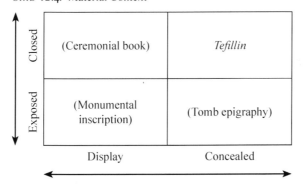

BIBLIOGRAPHY

Anderson, G. A. "The Praise of God as a Cultic Event." Pages 15–33 in *Priesthood and Cult in Ancient Israel*. Edited by S. M. Olyan and G. A. Anderson. JSOT 125. Sheffield: JSOT Press, 1991.

Arnold, R. C. D. "The Dead Sea Scrolls, Qumran, and Ritual Studies." Pages 547–62 in vol. 2 of *The Dead Sea Scrolls in Context: Integrating the Dead Sea Scrolls in the Study of Ancient Texts, Languages, and Cultures*. Edited by A. Lange, E. Tov, and M. Weigold. VTSup 140. Leiden: Brill, 2011.

———. *The Social Role of Liturgy in the Religion of the Qumran Community*. STDJ 60. Leiden: Brill, 2006.

Baillet, M. "512. Rituel de Purification." Pages 262–86 in *Qumrân Grotte 4.3 (4Q482–4Q520)*. Edited by M. Baillet. DJD 7. Oxford: Clarendon, 1982.

Barchiesi, A., J. Rüpke, and S. A. Stephens, eds. *Rituals in Ink: A Conference on Religion and Literary Production in Ancient Rome Held at Stanford University in February 2002*. Potsdamer Altertumswissenschaftliche Beiträge 10. Stuttgart: Steiner, 2004.

Baumgarten, J. M. "284. 4QPurification Liturgy." Pages 123–29 in *Qumrân Cave 4.25: Halakhic Texts*. Edited by J. M. Baumgarten, T. Elgvin, E. Eshel, E. Larson, M. R. Lehmann, S. Pfann, and L. H. Schiffman. DJD 35. Oxford: Clarendon, 1999.

———. "The Purification Liturgies." Pages 200–12 in vol. 2 of *The Dead Sea Scrolls After Fifty Years: A Comprehensive Assessment*. Edited by P. W. Flint and J. C. VanderKam. Leiden: Brill, 1999.

———. "The Purification Rituals in DJD 7." Pages 199–209 in *The Dead Sea Scrolls: Forty Years of Research; Papers Read at a Symposium Sponsored By Yad Izhak Ben-Zvi at the University of Haifa and at Tel Aviv University, March 20–24, 1988*. Edited by D. Dimant and U. Rappaport. STDJ 10. Leiden: Brill; New York: Magnes; Jerusalem: Yad Ben-Zvi, 1992.

Beard, M. "Writing Ritual: The Triumph of Ovid." Pages 115–26 in *Rituals in Ink: A Conference on Religion and Literary Production in Ancient Rome Held at Stanford University in February 2002*. Edited by A. Barchiesi, J. Rüpke, and S. A. Stephens. Potsdamer Altertumswissenschaftliche Beiträge 10. Stuttgart: Steiner, 2004.

Bell, C. *Ritual: Perspectives and Dimensions*. Oxford: Oxford University Press, 1997.

Brooke, G. J. "Between Scroll and Codex? Reconsidering the Qumran Opisthographs." Pages 123–38 in *On Stone and Scroll: Essays in Honour of Graham Ivor Davies*. Edited by J. K. Aitken, K. J. Dell, and B. A. Mastin. BZAW 420. Berlin: de Gruyter, 2011.

Chapot, F., and B. Laurot. *Corpus de prières grecques et romaines*. Recherches sur les Rhétoriques Religieuses 2. Turnhout: Brepols, 2001.

Cohn, Y. B. *Tangled Up in Text: Tefillin and the Ancient World*. BJS 351. Providence, RI: Brown Judaic Studies, 2008.

Collins, J. J. "Prayer and the Meaning of Ritual in the Dead Sea Scrolls." Pages 69–85 in *Prayer and Poetry in the Dead Sea Scrolls and Related Literature: Essays in Honor of Eileen Schuller on the Occasion of Her 65th Birthday*. Edited by J. Penner, K. M. Penner, and C. Wassen. STDJ 98. Leiden: Brill, 2012.

Daise, M. A. "Ritual Density in Qumran Practice: Ablutions in the *Serekh Ha-Yaḥad*." Pages 51–66 in *New Perspectives on Old Texts: Proceedings of the Tenth International Symposium of the Orion Center for the Study of the Dead Sea Scrolls and

Associated Literature, 9–11 January, 2005. Edited by E. Glickler-Chazon, B. Halpern-Amaru, and R. A. Clements. STDJ 88. Leiden: Brill, 2010.

DeMaris, R. E. *The New Testament in Its Ritual World*. London: Routledge, 2008.

Eshel, E. "414. 4QRitual of Purification A." Pages 135–56 in *Qumrân Cave 4.25: Halakhic Texts*. Edited by J. M. Baumgarten, T. Elgvin, E. Eshel, E. Larson, M. R. Lehmann, S. Pfann, and L. H. Schiffman. DJD 35. Oxford: Clarendon, 1999.

Falk, D. K. *Daily, Sabbath, and Festival Prayers in the Dead Sea Scrolls*. STDJ 27. Leiden: Brill, 1998.

———. "In the Margins of the Dead Sea Scrolls." Pages 10–38 in *Bible as Notepad: Tracing Annotations and Annotation Practices in Late Antique and Medieval Biblical Manuscripts*. Edited by L. I. Lied and M. Maniaci. Manuscripta Biblica 3. Berlin: de Gruyter, 2018.

———. "Liturgical Progression and the Experience of Transformation in Prayers from Qumran." *DSD* 22 (2015): 267–84.

———. "Material Aspects of Prayer Manuscripts at Qumran." Pages 33–87 in *Literature or Liturgy? Early Christian Hymns and Prayers in Their Literary and Liturgical Context in Antiquity*. Edited by C. Leonhard and H. Löhr. Wissenschaftliche Untersuchungen zum Neuen Testament 2/363. Tübingen: Mohr Siebeck, 2014.

———. "Prayer in the Qumran Texts." Pages 852–76 in *The Early Roman Period*, vol. 3 of *The Cambridge History of Judaism*. Edited by W. Horbury, W. D. Davies, and J. Sturdy. Cambridge: Cambridge University Press, 1999.

———. "Prayer, Liturgy, and War." Pages 275–94 in *The War Scroll, Violence, War and Peace in the Dead Sea Scrolls and Related Literature: Essays in Honour of Martin G. Abegg on the Occasion of His 65th Birthday*. Edited by K. Davis et al. STDJ 115. Leiden: Brill, 2015.

———. "Qumran and the Synagogue Liturgy." Pages 404–34 in *The Ancient Synagogue from Its Origins Until 200 CE: Papers Presented at an International Conference at Lund University, October 14–17, 2001*. Edited by B. Ollson and M. Zetterholm. Coniectanea Biblica: New Testament Series 39. Stockholm: Almqvist & Wiksell, 2003.

———. "Religious Life at Qumran." Pages 253–85 in *Celebrating the Dead Sea Scrolls: A Canadian Collection*. Edited by P. W. Flint, J. Duhaime, and K. S. Baek. EJL 30. Atlanta: Society of Biblical Literature; Leiden: Brill, 2011.

Fleischer, E. "On the Beginnings of Obligatory Jewish Prayer" (Hebrew). *Tarbiz* 58 (1990): 397–441.

Glickler-Chazon, E. "'4QDibHam': Liturgy or Literature?" *Revue de Qumran* 15 (1992): 447–55.

———. "The 'Words of the Luminaries' and Penitential Prayer in Second Temple Times." Pages 177–86 in *The Development of Penitential Prayer in Second Temple Judaism*. Vol. 2 of *Seeking the Favor of God*. Edited by M. J. Boda, D. K. Falk, and R. A. Werline. EJL 25. Leiden: Brill, 2007.

Gorman, F. H., Jr. "Ritual Studies and Biblical Studies: Assessment of the Past; Prospects for the Future." *Semeia* 67 (1994): 13–36.

Grimes, R. L. *Beginnings in Ritual Studies*. Rev. ed. Studies in Comparative Religion. Columbia: University of South Carolina Press, 1995.

Gruenwald, I. *Rituals and Ritual Theory in Ancient Israel*. Brill Reference Library of Judaism. Leiden: Brill, 2003.

Harrington, H. K. *The Purity Texts*. Companion to the Qumran Scrolls 5. London: T&T Clark, 2004.

Jassen, A. P. "Religion in the Dead Sea Scrolls." *Religion Compass* 1.1 (2007): 1–25.

Jokiranta, J. "Ritual System in the Qumran Movement: Frequency, Boredom, and Balance." Pages 144–63 in *Mind, Morality, and Magic: Cognitive Science Approaches in Biblical Studies*. Edited by I. Czachesz and R. Uro. Durham: Acumen, 2013.

Kugler, R. A. "Making All Experience Religious: The Hegemony of Ritual at Qumran." *JSJ* 33.2 (2002): 131–52.

Leitao, D. D. "Ritual? What Ritual?" Pages 149–53 in *Rituals in Ink: A Conference on Religion and Literary Production in Ancient Rome Held at Stanford University in February 2002*. Edited by A. Barchiesi, J. Rüpke, and S. A. Stephens. Potsdamer Altertumswissenschaftliche Beiträge 10. Stuttgart: Steiner, 2004.

Newsom, C. A. *The Self as Symbolic Space: Constructing Identity and Community at Qumran*. STDJ 52. Leiden: Brill, 2004.

Parry, D. W., and E. Tov. *The Dead Sea Scrolls Reader*. 2nd ed. 2 vols. Leiden: Brill, 2014.

Poultney, J. W. *The Bronze Tables of Iguvium*. Philological Monographs 18. Oxford: Blackwell, 1959.

Rappaport, R. A. *Ritual and Religion in the Making of Humanity*. Cambridge Studies in Social and Cultural Anthropology 110. Cambridge: Cambridge University Press, 1999.

Reif, S. C. *Judaism and Hebrew Prayer: New Perspectives on Jewish Liturgical History*. Cambridge: Cambridge University Press, 1993.

Rüpke, J. "Acta aut Agenda: Relations of Script and Performance." Pages 23–43 in *Rituals in Ink: A Conference on Religion and Literary Production in Ancient Rome Held at Stanford University in February 2002*. Edited by A. Barchiesi, J. Rüpke, and S. A. Stephens. Potsdamer Altertumswissenschaftliche Beiträge 10. Stuttgart: Steiner, 2004.

Schiffman, L. H. "Phylacteries and Mezuzot." Pages 675–77 in vol. 2 of *Encyclopedia of the Dead Sea Scrolls*. Edited by L. H. Schiffman and J. C. VanderKam. Oxford: Oxford University Press, 2000.

Schofield, A. *From Qumran to the Yaḥad: A New Paradigm of Textual Development for the "Community Rule."* STDJ 77. Leiden: Brill, 2009.

Staal, F. "The Meaninglessness of Ritual." *Numen* 26.1 (1979): 2–22.

Stökl Ben Ezra, D. "When the Bell Rings: The Qumran Rituals of Affliction in Context." Pages 533–46 in vol. 2 of *The Dead Sea Scrolls in Context: Integrating the Dead Sea Scrolls in the Study of Ancient Texts, Languages, and Cultures*. Edited by A. Lange, E. Tov, and M. Weigold. VTSup 140. Leiden: Brill, 2011.

Strecker, C. *Die liminale Theologie des Paulus: Zugänge zur paulinischen Theologie aus kulturanthropologischer Perspektive*. Forschungen zur Religion und Literatur des Alten und Neuen Testaments 185. Göttingen: Vandenhoeck & Ruprecht, 1999.

Stroup, S. C. "Rituals of Ink?" Pages 141–48 in *Rituals in Ink: A Conference on Religion and Literary Production in Ancient Rome Held at Stanford University in February 2002*. Edited by A. Barchiesi, J. Rüpke, and S. A. Stephens. Potsdamer Altertumswissenschaftliche Beiträge 10. Stuttgart: Steiner, 2004.

Tov, E., *Scribal Practices and Approaches Reflected in the Texts Found in the Judean Desert*. STDJ 54. Leiden: Brill, 2004.

Uro, R. "The Interface of Ritual and Writing in the Transmission of Early Christian Traditions." Pages 62–76 in *Mind, Morality, and Magic: Cognitive Science Approaches in Biblical Studies*. Edited by I. Czachesz and R. Uro. Durham: Acumen, 2013.

Weitzman, S. "Revisiting Myth and Ritual in Early Judaism." *DSD* 4.1 (1997): 21–54.

Werrett, I. C. *Ritual Purity and the Dead Sea Scrolls*. STDJ 27. Leiden: Brill, 2007.

White Crawford, S., and C. Wassen, *The Dead Sea Scrolls at Qumran and the Concept of a Library*. STDJ 116. Leiden: Brill, 2015.

Wilkins, J. B. "The Iguvine Tablets: Problems in the Interpretation of Ritual Text." Pages 152–72 in *Territory, Time, and State: The Archaeological Development of the Gubbio Basin*. Edited by C. Malone and S. Stoddart. Cambridge: Cambridge University Press, 1994.

Wise, M. O., M. G. Abegg Jr., and E. M. Cook, eds. *The Dead Sea Scrolls: A New Translation*. Rev. ed. San Francisco: HarperSanFrancisco, 2005.

CHAPTER 13

"And They Would Read Before Him the Order for the Day": The Textuality of Leviticus 16 in Mishnah Yoma, Tosefta Kippurim, and Sifra Aḥare Mot

William K. Gilders

IN ITS PRESENT LITERARY FORM and context, Lev 16 consists of instructions for a complex ritual performance, spoken to Moses by Yahweh to be conveyed to Aaron, who is to put the instructions into practice (vv. 1–2). Near the end of the chapter (vv. 32–33), Yahweh specifies that succeeding anointed priests are to continue the prescribed performance to achieve the designated results—indicated with the Hebrew verb *kpr* ("effect removal" or "clearing"[1])—and gives notice that the rite will be carried out once each year (vv. 29–30, 34a). The chapter concludes with a narrative declaration that the prescribed rites were in fact performed "as Yahweh had commanded Moses (*k'šr ṣwh yhwh 't-mšh*; v. 34b). Leviticus 16, therefore, appears as a prescriptive ritual text, a ritual manual, which was put into practice.

Readers of Lev 16 have before them a literary construction and presentation of a ritual performance. The literary character of Lev 16 as a performance manual raises questions about the text's relationship to living practice: what actions are to be performed on the basis of the text and how are they to be carried out? These questions are addressed in various ways—explicitly and implicitly—in later texts, such as those composed by the rabbinic Sages of the centuries after 70 CE. In this study of the reception of Lev 16, I will be dealing with three rabbinic documents: the Mishnah tractate Yoma (m. Yoma), the Tosefta tractate Kippurim (t. Kippurim), and the halakhic midrash Sipra on the Torah portion Aḥare Mot (Lev 16:1 and the following). The basic guiding question in dealing with these three works will be: how did they deal with Lev 16 as a ritual text?

An important theoretical starting point in dealing with all of these documents—Lev 16 and its rabbinic receptions—is to distinguish between the textual

---

1. On the translation "effect removal," see W. K. Gilders, *Blood Ritual in the Hebrew Bible: Meaning and Power* (Baltimore: Johns Hopkins University Press, 2004), 28–29; on "clearing," see M. B. Hundley, *Keeping Heaven on Earth: Safeguarding the Divine Presence in the Priestly Tabernacle*, FAT 2/50 (Tübingen: Mohr Siebeck, 2011), 188–89.

representation of a ritual performance (whether prescriptive or descriptive) and ritual performance itself; as the anthropologist Roy Rappaport put it, "Unless there is a performance there is no ritual. This is obvious in the case of fleeting greeting rituals which serve to order ongoing interaction, but it is no less true of elaborate liturgical rituals. Liturgical orders may be inscribed in books, but such records are not themselves rituals. They are merely descriptions of rituals or instructions for performing them.... Liturgical orders are realized—made into *res*—only by being performed."[2] From this starting point, I will explore several issues about the nature and function of ritual texts (or, to put it differently, textual rituals), particularly about how such texts connect with one another: specifically, I am concerned with how a textual ritual can embody interpretations of an earlier textual ritual.

Mishnah tractate Yoma—redacted in the early third century CE on the basis of apparently older traditions—is, in form, a descriptive ritual text, purporting to narrate how the rites of the Day of Atonement ("Day of Removal"; *ywm hkpwrym*) were performed in the Second Temple, prior to its destruction by the Romans in 70 CE. But there are several points at which this work ceases to be simply descriptive in form and moves into explicit debates about proper practice, departing from the impression that everything had been settled in the Second Temple period, indicating that the how and why of ritual performance remained open to dispute. Also, while m. Yoma appears to describe *past* performances, it has been characterized by scholars as implicitly functioning as a model for the future as well as a present substitute for living practice, so that the practice of talking about ritual substitutes for the ritual itself.[3] Tosefta Kippurim, as its name indicates, stands as a supplement to m. Yoma, frequently elaborating on the Mishnah and explaining opaque elements. The work must have reached its received form subsequent to the redaction of the Mishnah, probably in the fourth century CE.[4]

Whereas the Mishnah and Tosefta focus on describing what is supposed to have happened in the Second Temple, Sifra Aḥare Mot is an exegetical work that focuses on explicating the prescriptions in the biblical text. It blends textual

---

2. R. A. Rappaport, *Ritual and Religion in the Making of Humanity*, Cambridge Studies in Social and Cultural Anthropology 110 (Cambridge: Cambridge University Press, 1999), 37. This is a perspective forcefully advanced by J. W. Watts in his contribution to this volume.

3. For a brief summary and evaluation of views, along with his own thesis that rabbinic discourse about sacrificial rituals was a means by which the rabbis asserted their authority, see N. S. Cohn, *The Memory of the Temple and the Making of the Rabbis* (Philadelphia: University of Pennsylvania Press, 2012), 2–3.

4. For a useful survey of opinions about the composition and date of the Tosefta, see R. Zeidman, "An Introduction to the Genesis and Nature of Tosefta, the Chameleon of Rabbinic Literature," in *Introducing Tosefta: Textual, Intratextual and Intertextual Studies*, ed. H. Fox and T. Meacham (Hoboken, NJ: Ktav, 1999), 73–97.

elucidation with prescriptive statements and some descriptive material. However, since m. Yoma and t. Kippurim assume that the biblical prescriptions are the basis of the rituals of the Second Temple (see, for example, m. Yoma 1:3 and t. Kippurim 1:8), there is clearly a complex relationship between these three documents of rabbinic Judaism.

With these introductory points in mind, I will explore some concrete case examples, beginning with the status of Lev 16 as a textual manual in m. Yoma.[5]

13.1. Leviticus 16 as an Authoritative Text in Mishnah Yoma

Mishnah Yoma 1:3 refers to the authoritative status of Lev 16 as the textual *manual* (*sdr*; "order") for the rites performed on the Day; it is a text that is read to the high priest and that he himself is urged to read, precisely for instruction in the performance of the rites of the Day:

> Some members of the eldership of the Council were brought to him, and they would read before him the Order for the day (*wqwryn lpnyw bsdr hywm*). They would say to him: "High Priest, Sir, read it aloud yourself, in case you have forgotten anything or haven't already learned it!"

This "Order" (clearly a written text to be read), was presumably Lev 16.[6] Thus, the rites of the Day are presented as being performed on the basis of an established ritual text, which is treated as a practical manual for performance. This is noteworthy given the evident difficulties involved in treating Lev 16 as a straightforward performance manual—which I will address later in this essay. But the Mishnah treats Lev 16 as a text the high priest must hear read and must read himself if he is to carry out his duties correctly. The Mishnah resists, therefore, the idea that cultic practice is mainly a function of oral tradition or practical experience. Written and read *text* is the guarantor of correct practice. In this text's ritual performance, textuality is crucial. Mishnah Yoma 5:7 reinforces this theme with a strong affirmation of the authority of Lev 16 for the Day's ritual complex, particularly for the *sequence* of ritual performances: "Every performance of the Day of Atonement which is reported was according

---

5. For the Hebrew text of m. Yoma, I have followed the edition of Chanoch Albeck (*Shisha Sidrei Mishnah*, 6 vols. [Jerusalem: Mosad Bialik, 1952–59], 2:223–47). All translations in this paper are my own, prepared with reference to the translations by Herbert Danby (*The Mishnah* [Oxford: Oxford University Press, 1933]) and Jacob Neusner (*The Mishnah: A New Translation* [New Haven: Yale University Press, 1988]), both of which must be used with some caution.

6. Albeck, *Shisha Sidrei Mishnah*, 2:223.

to the Order (*kl m'śh ywm hkpwrym h'mwr 'l hsdr*)." The Mishnah presents what it reports being performed as based on a textual manual.

But, as the second part of m. Yoma 1:3 indicates, this written manual was clearly not sufficient for all purposes:

> On the day before the Day of Atonement, in the morning, they stationed the high priest at the eastern gate of the Temple courtyard and they led past him bullocks, and rams, and sheep, so that he would be fully versed and confident in the ritual procedure (*kdy šyh' mkyr wrgyl b'bwdh*).

While of fundamental significance, the scriptural text is not the only source of relevant information. According to the Mishnah, the high priest is also given practical instruction. He must see the various animals—presumably so that he will not mix them up during the ritual performance![7] Thus, we find an implicit question raised about the sufficiency of the ritual manual. Another crucial issue concerns the interpretation of prescriptive details in the text itself.

13.2. The Incense Controversy in m. Yoma and t. Kippurim[8]

According to m. Yoma 1:5, when the high priest was passed from the custody of the Council (*bt dyn*) to the custody of the priesthood, he was made to swear an oath not to depart in any way from the instructions he had been given by the Council elders, and at this adjuration, both the high priest and the elders would weep:

> The eldership of the Council transferred the high priest to the eldership of the priesthood, and they brought him up to the upper level of the House of Abtinus where they made him swear an oath, after which they took their leave and departed. This is what they said to him: "High Priest, Sir, we are representatives of the Council, and you are our representative and the representative of the Council. We make you swear an oath, by Him Who caused His Name to dwell in this House, that you will not deviate in

---

7. As J. Neusner commented, "The high priest . . . cannot even be relied upon to know the difference between a bullock and a ram" (*A History of the Mishnaic Law of Appointed Times, Part Three*, Studies in Judaism in Late Antiquity 34 [Leiden: Brill, 1982], 71).

8. For the Hebrew text of t. Kippurim, I have followed the edition of S. Lieberman, *The Tosefta*, 4 vols., 2nd ed. (Jerusalem: Jewish Theological Seminary of America, 1992). All translations of the text are my own. There is, unfortunately, only one English translation of the complete work, prepared by Neusner (*The Tosefta*, 6 vols. [New York: Ktav, 1977–81]), which must be used with great caution.

a single thing from what we have told you!" The high priest then would turn away and weep, and the eldership of the Council would turn away and weep.

The Tosefta (t. Kippurim 1:8) explicitly addresses the question raised by the ambiguous Mishnah: Why did the high priest and the Council elders "turn away and weep"? The answer: Because of the necessity of the oath. That is, there was collective grief at the fact that the Council could not trust the high priest to perform the rites in the correct manner and so had to bind him with an oath.

Why was the high priest's reliability so in question? In answer to this question, the Tosefta proceeds to explain that the oath was necessitated by a halakhic dispute centered on the sectarian Boethusian interpretation of Lev 16:12–13, which sets out how Aaron is to enter the adytum of the shrine and burn incense: "Then [Aaron] must take a censer full of burning coals from off of the altar before Yahweh and handfuls of fine-ground spice incense and convey them inside the curtain. He must place the incense upon the fire before Yahweh and the incense cloud will cover the footrest ($\underline{kprt}$) that is atop the Pact and he will not die."

The Boethusian interpretation (as presented by the Tosefta) focuses on the second half of verse 13 and its explanation of the purpose of the incense cloud; if it is to cover the footrest over the Pact, so that the high priest will be protected from death—apparently resulting from seeing the manifest Presence of God—it follows that the incense should be placed on the coals before entering the adytum, so that that the cloud of incense will shield the place of the Pact from the priest's sight. In this interpretation, verses 12 and 13 are not presenting a simple sequence of ritual instructions, according to which everything would be conveyed inside the curtain before the incense is placed on the coals. Rather, the incense is to be placed on the coals *before* everything is taken inside.

The rabbinic Sages, however, insist that the text *does* present straightforward ritual instructions, and to support their argument they focus on the first half of verse 13, particularly the instruction that the incense be placed on the coals "before Yahweh" ($\underline{lpny\ yhwh}$), which they clearly understand to mean inside the adytum, "inside the curtain" (Lev 16:12):

> The Sages said to them: "But has it not already been said immediately before this in Scripture: *'He must place the incense upon the fire before the LORD'*? [Lev 16:13a] So, all who burn incense only burn incense inside the adytum!"

According to the Tosefta, the correctness of the rabbinic interpretation was confirmed by the historical incident ($m'\acute{s}h$) that had made it necessary to place the high priest under an oath: a Boethusian high priest followed Boethusian halakhah and suffered death as a result—a clear sign that it is *not* the Boethusian form of the incense performance that wards off death!

Finally, another aspect of the Tosefta's presentation is worth noting. While the Boethusians are portrayed as insisting on a fairly literal understanding of the relationship between the cloud of incense and the preservation of the life of the high priest, the Sages argue that there is no real danger in an unclouded view of the interior of the adytum; instead, they insist that the statement in Lev 16:13 refers simply to the risk of producing incense that smokes insufficiently:

> The Sages said to them: "But has it not already been said immediately before this in Scripture: *'He must place the incense upon the fire before the LORD'*? [Lev 16:13a] So, all who burn incense only burn incense inside the adytum!" To which the Boethusians replied: "If so, why is it said in Scripture: *'The incense cloud will cover'*?" To which the Sages replied: "It teaches that he would place into it something causing smoke to rise. So, if he did not place into it something causing smoke to rise, he would be liable to the death penalty."

The issue, argue the Sages, is failure of proper ritual performance, failure to carry out the prescribed norms. The rabbinic interpretation combines concern with ritual precision with theological assumptions that influence the interpretation of practice. This rabbinic insistence on reading Lev 16 as a precise manual, in tandem with theological assumptions about practice, is particularly evident in the next example I will discuss.

13.2.1. The Confessions in m. Yoma, t. Kippurim, and Sifra Aḥare Mot[9]

According to Lev 16:6, "Aaron must present the sin-purification offering (*ḥṭ't*) bullock that is for himself and he must effect removal (*wkpr*) on his own behalf

---

9. For the Hebrew text of Sifra there is, regrettably, no critical edition for Aḥare Mot. I have used the version of the text in the edition by S. Koleditzky, *Sifra with the Commentary of Rabbenu Hillel* (Jerusalem: n.p., 1962), which includes his own commentary, and that of Hillel ben Eliakim (Rabbenu Hillel). I have also consulted the edition of H. Weiss, *Sifra: Commentar zu Leviticus* (Vienna: Schlossberg, 1862), and the facsimile edition of the best extant manuscript of Sifra, Assemani 66 (also known as Vatican 66), published by L. Finkelstein, *Sifra or Torat Kohanim* (New York: Jewish Theological Seminary of America, 1956), which fortunately includes all of the material treated in this study. The only complete English translation of the material treated here is J. Neusner, *Sifra: An Analytical Translation*, 4 vols. (Atlanta: Scholars Press, 1987). As A. Yadin-Israel notes, "The problems with Neusner's translation are legion" (*Scripture and Tradition: Rabbi Akiva and the Triumph of Midrash* [Philadelphia: University of Pennsylvania Press, 2015], 232 n. 21). Several of these problems will be highlighted in my discussion.

and on behalf of his household." This is apparently an anticipatory summary of the ritual Aaron will perform with his bull, placed here to emphasize the significance of the performance. Thus, the words *wkpr* refer to the whole ritual performance prescribed in detail in 16:11b–14. Following this anticipatory summary, Lev 16:7–10 sets out the procedures for selecting the so-called scapegoat and the goat that will be offered as the people's "sin-purification offering" (*ḥṭ't*). Then, in Lev 16:11a, the text presents a *Wideraufnahme* of Lev 16:6, returning to the prescriptions for the offering of Aaron's "sin-purification offering" bull. Thus, both Lev 16:6 and 16:11a are anticipatory summaries of the ritual Aaron will perform with his bull, which frame the instructions for the procedure for selecting the "scapegoat" and the people's *ḥṭ't* goat.

The rabbis, however, understood *wkpr* in *both* occurrences (v. 6 and v. 11a) as referring not to the subsequent blood-focused performance of Lev 16:11b–14 but to a distinct performance of a verbal confession. Moreover, rather than understanding Lev 16:11a as a *Wiederaufnahme*, the rabbis took it as an independent ritual prescription. Thus, in their view, the confession was made *twice*, once before the lots performance with the two goats for the people, and once afterward, immediately prior to the slaughter of the "sin-purification offering" bull.

Mishnah Yoma's presentation of the ritual performance simply assumes this interpretation, without explanation or argument, as if it were the obvious sense of the original textual prescription (m. Yoma 3:8 and 4:2).

Sifra, however, clearly recognizes that there is room for dispute and advances a brief but cogent exegetical argument (Aḥarei Mot parashah 2:2–3):

> Scripture refers to removal (*kprh*) in the case of the bullock [in 16:6] and it refers to removal in the case of the goat [in 16:10, 21–22]. Just as removal referred to in the case of the goat is verbal confession, so is removal referred to in the case of the bullock verbal confession—without blood. If you desire further scriptural proof, it says: "Aaron must present the sin-purification offering bullock that is for himself and he must effect removal on his own behalf and on behalf of his household" [Lev 16:6, 11]. This is *before* it is slaughtered!

Here, the Sages make use of the exegetical technique of *gezerah shavah*, linking texts through shared vocabulary. Just as *lkpr* in Lev 16:10—understood to point ahead to the ritual of verses 21–22—refers to the act of confession, likewise the verb refers to confession in verses 6 and 11. The argument also emphasizes the sequence of the text, noting that the verb *kpr* appears prior to the slaughter of the bull, this point depending upon the assumption that the text is setting out a clear and simple sequence of ritual prescriptions.

Having made the case in its treatment of Lev 16:6 that w__k__pr ("he must effect removal") refers to a verbal confession, when Sifra arrives at Lev 16:11a, it simply states again the conclusion that w__k__pr indicates the performance of a confession and sets out, again, the wording of the confession (Aḥare Mot pereq 2:9).

The hermeneutical assumption apparently at work here is common and foundational in the rabbinic approach to Scripture: resistance to the idea that any detail of the text is redundant or superfluous. As applied to a ritual text, it has the effect of negating any literary "artistry" or nonlinear aspects in the setting out of the prescriptions. The text is read *very* literally, as setting out a clear, coherent set of ritual prescriptions, with every word of the text serving this purpose. For the rabbis of Sifra (as well as those of m. Yoma), Lev 16 was very much a ritual manual, its every detail serving the purpose of giving instruction in correct performance. Indeed, the terminology is taken as essentially and specifically performative, rather than general or abstract. Thus, w__k__pr is understood to refer to a specific performance and not simply to summarize a whole ritual complex.

The result is that the rabbinic rite of the Day of Atonement differs significantly from what Lev 16 actually appears to prescribe. While the biblical text indicates that Aaron is to perform the procedure for identifying the two goats for the people, one as a "sin-purification offering" for the altar and the other as the scapegoat, and then proceed to the offering of his own "sin-purification offering" bull,[10] the rabbinic ritual bookends the identification of the two goats with the two verbal confessions over the bull, framing this performance.

As the argument in Sifra indicates, a driving motivation for the inclusion of a confession over the bull was the existence of such a confession performed on the scapegoat (Lev 16:21). Since the scapegoat apparently dealt with the sins of the people—and not, presumably, those of the high priest—a perceived lack was felt to exist in the absence of a corresponding rite of confession for the high priest's sins. The somewhat awkward formulation and location of Lev 16:6 and 11a provided the basis for filling this perceived lack. The repetition of the formula could have been problematic. But it in fact served the creation of an elegant ritual structure, which has an indexical thrust. By placing the high priest's two confessions as a frame around the procedure for identifying the two goats for the people, his significance for that procedure is reinforced. The two confessions both draw attention to the high priest and emphasize his own need for divine forgiveness. Thus, while his special status as a ritual actor is marked, at the very same time his human frailty is also highlighted. While the people need the high priest to act for them, what they need, he also needs, and his ability to serve the people depends on his own quest for forgiveness: to perform the identification of the

---

10. For this reading of Lev 16:6–11, see, e.g., J. Milgrom, *Leviticus 1–16: A New Translation with Introduction and Commentary*, AB 3A (New York: Doubleday, 1991), 1018–24.

people's goats, he must enter through a ritual doorway of confession and petition for forgiveness, and he must exit that process through that same portal in order to continue with his own atoning rites. Whether it was a creation of the rabbis (which I believe to be the case), or the product of older, Second Temple–period textual interpretation (for which we have no evidence), this particular reading of Lev 16:6 and 11a allowed for the creation of a conceptually rich ritual structure.

On a more general note, this illustrates the fact that ritual texts cannot be assumed to provide unambiguous access to the performances that are ostensibly based upon them. Such texts always require interpretation, and it is frequently impossible to anticipate what interested readers will do with documents they regard as ritual manuals. Could we arrive at the ritual complex the rabbis envisaged with only Lev 16 itself, absent the rabbis' exegetical and prescriptive texts? Could we anticipate their exegetical moves? The lesson to be drawn here is that considerable caution should be exercised in assuming that what a modern reader takes as the straightforward sense of a ritual text provides an unobstructed view of lived performance based on that text.

Of course, for many modern scholars, the rabbinic interpretation of Lev 16:6 and 11a is a "misinterpretation." The rite performed by the rabbinic high priest is not, in fact, what Lev 16 prescribes. From a historical-critical perspective, the original authors or tradents of the biblical text did not intend for the high priest to lay both of his hands on the head of the "sin-purification offering" bull and recite, two times, a verbal confession. But, clearly, "misinterpretation" of ritual texts can lead to specific types of ritual performance as much as "correct" interpretation.

13.2.2. The Wording of the Confessions

The Mishnah and Sifra agree that *wkpr* in Lev 16:6 and 11a indicate performance of a verbal confession and not the blood-focused rites performed inside the Shrine, which are set out in Lev 16:11b–14. Both works give a text of this confession. However, notably, they disagree about the precise wording of the confession. The Mishnah gives, without specific attribution, and without any indication of dispute, a confession that begins, "O LORD, I have committed iniquity, and transgressed, and sinned before you" (*'n' hšm 'wyty pš'ty ht'ty lpnyk*; m. Yoma 3:8 and 4:2). The Mishnah gives the impression of setting out an unproblematic presentation of a well-known recitation, a received tradition of what was said in the Second Temple.

For its part, Sifra first reproduces the words of the confession given in the Mishnah. But it attributes this formulation specifically to Rabbi Meir. Thus, what the Mishnah presents as an anonymous given, Sifra treats as the opinion advanced by a single rabbinic voice. Sifra then further problematizes the

Mishnah's confession by having Rabbi Meir defend it against implied criticism. He explains the sequence of confessing first iniquity, then transgression, and finally sin by quoting Lev 16:21, which lists the offenses of the people that Aaron confesses over the scapegoat as "iniquities" (*'wnt*), "transgressions" (*pš'ym*), and "sins" (*ḥṭ't*).[11] Rabbi Meir's defense of his version of the confession (which the Mishnah endorses) appears solid, for it depends on taking Lev 16:21 as providing unproblematic ritual instruction—in line with the approach that lies behind the understanding that the high priest recited two confessions over his bull.

Sifra, however, rejects this approach in this instance by offering the response of "the Sages" (*wḥkmym 'wmrym*), the majority counterview. The Sages first identify the three types of wrongs, explaining that "iniquities" (*'wnt*) are deliberate wrongs (*zdwnwt*), "transgressions" (*pš'ym*) are rebellious acts (*mrdym*), and "sins" (*ḥṭ't*) are inadvertent offenses (*šggwt*). The crucial point is their identification of "sins" (*ḥṭ't*) as *inadvertent* offenses, the least serious type. Having so identified "sins," they question the appropriateness of mentioning these last, as in Rabbi Meir's (and the Mishnah's) version of the confession: "After he makes confession for the deliberate wrongs and for the rebellious acts, does he turn about and make confession for the inadvertent offenses (*m'ḥr šhw' mtwdh 'l hzdwnwt w'l hmrdym ḥwzr wmtwdh 'l hšggwt*)?" For the Sages, ritual words matter, since they carry theological weight. On this basis, they offer a different version of the confession, which places "sins" first, followed by "iniquities" and "transgressions."[12] In this form of confession, the high priest moves—appropriately, according to the theological perspective asserted by the Sages—from the least serious to the most serious offenses. The Sages then reinforce the argument for their version of the confession by citing biblical prooftexts of confessions that begin with "sins" (Ps 106:6; 1 Kgs 8:47; Dan 9:5) (Aḥare Mot parashah 2:5). Then, clearly for emphasis, the Sages repeat the main point of their argument, citing again the opening words of the confession in their alternative version.

---

11. *w'wmr whtwdh 'lyw 't kl 'wnwt bny yśr'l w't kl pš'yhm lkl ḥṭ'wtm*. Neusner seems to have misconstrued *w'wmr* in Rabbi Meir's statement in parashah 2:4 as referring to something the high priest said as part of the confession, rendering it as, "And the high priest further says," followed by the words of Lev 16:21 (*Sifra*, 3:13). However, it makes better sense of the text to take *w'wmr* as the introduction of a biblical prooftext given by Rabbi Meir to support his (and the Mishnah's) version of the confession, since the words of Lev 16:21 are not otherwise presented as part of the confession (compare m. Yoma 3:8; 4:2). Thus, it means, "And [Scripture] says . . ."

12. Neusner simply reproduced the Mishnah's version of the confession, with "sins" still in the last place, thus completely negating the thrust of the Sages' argument (*Sifra*, 3:13). Sifra, however, clearly gives a different version of the confession than the one that appears in the Mishnah, which is required by the Sages' argument. It is not clear if Neusner was here dependent on a poor version of Sifra, in which a sloppy copyist or editor simply reproduced the Mishnah's confession, or if Neusner himself was sloppy in simply copying and pasting from one part of his English translation into another. I suspect it is the latter, as every edition of Sifra in Hebrew I have consulted shows the necessary distinction. Most notably, this is the reading in Assemani 66.

Tosefta Kippurim 2:1 seems to have the same material as Sifra. We may wonder if Tosefta is quoting Sifra, or if Sifra is quoting Tosefta, or if they are both drawing on a third independent source. In any event, the two works apparently agree in offering a critique of what m. Yoma takes for granted. Ultimately, it was the version of the confession found in Sifra and the Tosefta that became normative in rabbinic Judaism, not the one that appears in the Mishnah.[13]

Returning now to Sifra—the Sages then finally address Rabbi Meir's appeal to Lev 16:21, citing along with it Exod 34:7, which also refers to "sins" after other types of offenses. Their response is that these texts do not have significance as ritual instruction. Rather, they spell out the *theology* of the ritual act: "But, when he has confessed the deliberate and defiant acts it is as if they are inadvertent acts before [God] (*'l ḵywn šhyh mṯwḏh 'l hzḏwnwṯ w'l hmrḏym ḵylw hm šggwṯ lpnyw*) (par. 2:6). Thus, for Sifra, Lev 16:21 does not indicate the order in which wrongs are to be mentioned, and it implicitly criticizes the Mishnah's implicit interpretation of that text as providing unambiguous ritual information.

Thus, in interpreting a ritual text, the rabbis of Sifra seem to regard foundational theological commitments as important for correct elucidation of formal prescriptions. Lev 16:21 cannot be taken as a straightforward prescription, unlike Lev 16:6 and 11a, which are taken "literally" as formal procedural prescriptions, because to do so would lead to a theologically problematic ritual performance. Of course, one must begin with their assumption that confessing inadvertent sins after deliberate and willful misdeeds is incorrect, which Rabbi Meir and the Mishnah clearly do not. But this is a common issue in disputes over ritual performance—as I have indicated in my treatment of the incense controversy. Much inevitably turns on assumptions brought to ritual performances and their textual presentations.

Again, we have an example of the rabbis debating the details of ritual performance in terms of scriptural exegesis as if the matter were not already settled. While m. Yoma gives the impression that the wording of the confession was a settled matter, Sifra challenges this impression, asserting either that the confession should be revised or that in fact the Mishnah was reporting incorrectly what had been said in the Second Temple.

It should be noted that, having made the case for its distinctive version of the confession, when Sifra comes to the second recitation, which it takes to be prescribed by Lev 16:11a, it simply gives this distinctive version, which begins,

---

13. See, e.g., Maimonides, *Mishneh Torah, Sefer Avodah, Hilchot Avodat Yom HaKippurim* 2:6 (English translation: M. Lewittes, *The Code of Maimonides, Book Eight: The Book of Temple Service*, Yale Judaica Series 12 [New Haven: Yale University Press, 1957], 393); see also the liturgy for the Day of Atonement in the traditional *Maḥzor*.

"I have sinned, I have committed iniquities, I have transgressed," with no further explanation or defense (per. 2:9).[14]

To bring this discussion of Sifra's treatment of Lev 16 to a conclusion, I must briefly address the important recent contribution of Azan Yadin-Israel to the understanding of this document, in which he argues persuasively that Sifra "is not a fundamentally interpretive text."[15] Rather, in its two distinct "constituent components"—teachings attributed to named tannaim and anonymous material—midrashic interpretation is used in distinctive ways to buttress "oral-tradition halakhot"; in the case of material assigned to named tannaitic figures, there is explicit recognition of "the authority of extra-scriptural traditions," while in the anonymous material, midrashic explanation functions to "camouflage" a process whereby extrascriptural halakhah is portrayed as, in fact, fully rooted in Scripture.[16] My treatment of Sifra is in no way intended as a challenge to the overall argument of Yadin-Israel's masterful study, which I find quite compelling. Rather, I wish simply to highlight a few striking instances where the midrashic content of Sifra does appear to be authentically exegetical—that is, it is motivated by and directly addresses features of the source text that require elucidation. As I have emphasized, the cases I have examined all involve the rabbis treating Lev 16 as a ritual manual. More extensive engagement with Sifra's treatment of ritual instructions would be required to test whether there is any consistent pattern at work in the document when its midrashim engage biblical texts as performance manuals. That project, however, is beyond the scope of this present study.

13.3. Conclusion

To conclude this essay, I return to m. Yoma and its account of how the high priest wrapped up the public ceremony of the Day of Atonement. According to m. Yoma 7:1, the high priest received a Torah scroll, which was formally passed to him from the hands of three officials, a performance that clearly draws attention to itself and to the object at its center. He then read out Lev 16, followed by Lev 23:26–32. Having rolled up the scroll, he then recited Num 29:7–11 from

---

14. Neusner (*Sifra*, 3:16–17) incorrectly reproduced the version of the confession as it appears in m. Yoma 3:8. He also commented that the confession "is familiar from the preceding chapter; I cannot account for the duplication" (ibid., 3:17), apparently unaware that the source of the repetition is the rabbis' distinctive understanding of the repetition of w$\underline{k}$pr in Lev 16:6 and 11a, which is also reflected in the Mishnah. This was a remarkable mistake on the part of this influential expositor of rabbinic literature!

15. Yadin-Israel, *Scripture and Tradition*, 100.

16. Ibid., 5.

memory. The readings and the recitation clearly set out for the congregation the textual basis for the rites that had just been completed. This element of the Day's ceremony, not itself prescribed in any of the biblical texts, reinforces the Mishnah's insistence that the Day's rituals were conducted according to a textual manual.

This textual manual, of course, had to be interpreted so that it could be applied. As I have made clear with the several examples I have discussed, this was a fraught process, because there are a number of ambiguities in that manual, which challenge applying it as a simple set of ritual instructions. Nevertheless, the rabbinic approach generally involved treating Lev 16 as embodying a clear set of simple and sequential ritual prescriptions. This interpretation of a ritual document, treated as a ritual manual, came to be embodied in the rabbinic texts (Mishnah, Tosefta, and Sifra), which themselves became ritual manuals—also requiring interpretation in new contexts.

BIBLIOGRAPHY

Albeck, C. *Shisha Sidrei Mishnah*. 6 vols. Jerusalem: Mosad Bialik, 1952–59.
Cohn, N. S. *The Memory of the Temple and the Making of the Rabbis*. Philadelphia: University of Pennsylvania Press, 2012.
Danby, H. *The Mishnah*. Oxford: Oxford University Press, 1933.
Finkelstein, L., ed. *Sifra or Torat Kohanim*. New York: Jewish Theological Seminary of America, 1956.
Gilders, W. K. *Blood Ritual in the Hebrew Bible: Meaning and Power*. Baltimore: Johns Hopkins University Press, 2004.
Hundley, M. B. *Keeping Heaven on Earth: Safeguarding the Divine Presence in the Priestly Tabernacle*. FAT 2/50. Tübingen: Mohr Siebeck, 2011.
Koleditzky, S., ed. *Sifra with the Commentary of Rabbenu Hillel*. Jerusalem: n.p., 1961.
Lewitess, S. *The Code of Maimonides, Book Eight: The Book of Temple Service*. Yale Judaica Series 12. New Haven: Yale University Press, 1957.
Lieberman, S., ed. *The Tosefta*. 4 vols. 2nd ed. Jerusalem: Jewish Theological Seminary of America, 1992.
Milgrom, J. *Leviticus 1–16: A New Translation with Introduction and Commentary*. AB 3A. New York: Doubleday, 1991.
Neusner, J. *A History of the Mishnaic Law of Appointed Times, Part Three*. Studies in Judaism in Late Antiquity 34. Leiden: Brill, 1982.
———. *The Mishnah: A New Translation*. New Haven: Yale University Press, 1988.
———. *Sifra: An Analytical Translation*. 4 vols. Atlanta: Scholars Press, 1988.
———. *The Tosefta*. 6 vols. New York: Ktav, 1977–81.
Rappaport, R. A. *Ritual and Religion in the Making of Humanity*. Cambridge Studies in Social and Cultural Anthropology 110. Cambridge: Cambridge University Press, 1999.
Weiss, H., ed. *Sifra: Commentar zu Leviticus*. Vienna: Schlossberg, 1862.

Yadin-Israel, A. *Scripture and Tradition: Rabbi Akiva and the Triumph of Midrash.* Philadelphia: University of Pennsylvania Press, 2015.

Zeidman, R. "An Introduction to the Genesis and Nature of Tosefta, the Chameleon of Rabbinic Literature." Pages 73–97 in *Introducing Tosefta: Textual, Intratextual and Intertextual Studies.* Edited by H. Fox and T. Meacham. Hoboken, NJ: Ktav, 1999.

CONTRIBUTORS

Dorothea Erbele-Küster is Senior Lecturer of Gender, Diversity, and Biblical Literature at Johannes Gutenberg University Mainz. Among her several works on Leviticus and cultural anthropology is her recent book *Body, Gender and Purity in Leviticus 12 and 15*.

Daniel K. Falk is Chaiken Family Chair in Jewish Studies and Professor of Classics and Ancient Mediterranean Studies at the Pennsylvania State University. He is the author of *Daily, Sabbath, and Festival Prayers in the Dead Sea Scrolls* and *Parabiblical Texts: Strategies for Extending the Scriptures Among the Dead Sea Scrolls*.

Yitzhaq Feder is Lecturer in the Department of Biblical Studies at the University of Haifa. His most recent book is *Purity and Pollution in the Hebrew Bible: From Embodied Experience to Moral Metaphor*.

Christian Frevel is Professor of Old Testament Studies in the Department of Catholic Theology at Ruhr University Bochum and Extraordinary Professor at the Department of Old Testament and Hebrew Scriptures of the University of Pretoria, South Africa. He has authored and edited numerous works on the Pentateuch, with a particular focus on the book of Numbers. His most recent monograph is *Desert Transformations: Studies in the Book of Numbers*.

William K. Gilders is Associate Professor in the Department of Religion and Tam Institute for Jewish Studies at Emory University. He is the author of *Blood Ritual in the Hebrew Bible: Meaning and Power* as well as several articles on ancient Israelite religious practice interpreted from the perspective of anthropology and ritual theory.

Dominique Jaillard is Professor of the History of Religion at the Faculty of Arts at the University of Geneva. A specialist in ancient Greek religion, Jaillard is the author of *Configurations d'Hermès: Une théogonie hermaïque*.

Giuseppina Lenzo is Senior Lecturer of History and Religion of Ancient Egypt at the Institute of Archaeology and Classical Studies at the University of Lausanne. She is the author of *Les stèles de Taharqa à Kawa*.

Lionel Marti is a Research Fellow of the Centre National de la Recherche Scientifique, with a research focus on ancient Syria and Assyria. He is the author of *Nomades et sédentaires à Mari: La perception de la taxe-sugâgûtum*.

Patrick Michel is Senior Lecturer of Ancient History at the Institute of Archaeology and Classical Studies at the University of Lausanne. He works on the religion of Late Bronze Age Syria and Anatolia and religious contacts between Hittite Anatolia and North Syrie (Emar). He is the author of *Le culte des pierres à Emar à l'époque Hittite*.

Christophe Nihan is Professor of Old Testament/Hebrew Bible at the University of Münster, as well as a member of the UMR 7192 in Paris. He is the author of *From Priestly Torah to Pentateuch: A Study in the Composition of the Book of Leviticus* as well as several articles and essays on Israelite rituals and priestly traditions.

Julia Rhyder is Assistant Professor of Near Eastern Languages and Civilizations at Harvard University. She is the author of *Centralizing the Cult: The Holiness Legislation in Leviticus 17–26*.

Rüdiger Schmitt is Associate Professor at the Cluster of Excellence "Religion and Politics" at the University of Münster. He is the author of several books on ancient Israelite religion and material culture, most recently *Die Religionen Israels/Palästinas in der Eisenzeit: 12.–6. Jahrhundert v. Chr.*

Jeremy D. Smoak is Senior Lecturer in the Department of Near Eastern Languages and Cultures at the University of California, Los Angeles. He is the author of *The Priestly Blessing in Inscription and Scripture: The Early History of Numbers 6:24–26*.

James W. Watts is Professor of Hebrew Bible in the Department of Religion at Syracuse University. He is the author of *Ritual and Rhetoric in Leviticus: From Sacrifice to Scripture* and co-author with Yohan Yoo of *Cosmologies of Pure Realms and the Rhetoric of Pollution*.

INDEX OF ANCIENT SOURCES

Biblical Sources
Leviticus
  1–7 143
  1:14–17 144
  5 199
  5:7–13 144
  5:20–26 199
  8:10–12 144
  11–15 180, 241–43, 249–52
  12 179–83, 243–46
  12:3 243–45
  12:8 144
  15 247–49
  16 312–24
  16:6, 11a 317–18
  16:12–13 316–17
  16:29–34 144–45
  23:39–43 261–63

Numbers
  5–6 198–99
  6:22–27 199–206, 215–32
  9 265–67

Deuteronomy
  16 267–68
  29:24 230
  29:29 230

Nehemiah
  8:3–13 231
  8:13–18 259–64

2 Chronicles
  30 264–68
  35:1–19 268–73

Akkadian Sources
Royal inscriptions
  Ambos, *Mesopotamische Baurituale*,
    II.A.3 88, 92
  Grayson, RIMA 1, text A. 0.77.7 95
  Grayson, RIMA 1, text A. 0.78.11 84
  Grayson, RIMA 1, text A. 0.78.17 95
  Grayson, RIMA 1, text A. 0.102.10 92
  Grayson, RIMA 2, text A.
    0.101.133 83–84
  Grayson, RIMA 2, text A.
    0.87.1 93–94, 95
  Grayson, RIMA 2, text A. 0.101.50 90
  Leichty, Royal Inscriptions, text
    114 96–100
  Luckenbill, OIP 2, 137 84–85
  Luckenbill, OIP 2, 138–39 93
  Luckenbill, OIP 2, 144–45 86
  Parpola, SAA 10, text 14 85–86

Ancient Israelite Inscriptions
  Arad 16 227
  Arad 21 227
  KAjr 18:1 225
  KAjr 19:1 225
  KH 1–2 201–4, 219
  Lachish 3:20 226
  Lachish 6:4 226
  TAD C3:15: 126–28 164–65

Index of Ancient Sources

Dead Sea Scrolls
1QS 1:1–13   300–301
1QS 1:16–2:18   302–3
1QS 9:26–10:8   296–97
1QS 10:10–14   300
4Q284   288–93
4Q400–407   296
4Q414   288–93
4Q503   294, 296
4Q504   296
4Q506   296
4Q512   288–93

Egyptian Sources
P. BM EA 9901 (Hunefer)   39
P. BM EA 10010   43
P. BM EA 10470 (Ani)   37, 38, 39, 46
P. BM EA 10473   47
P. BM EA 10477 (Nu)   37, 46
P. BM EA 10490 (Nedjmet)   49–50
P. Cairo JE 95838 (Gatseshen)   51
P. Cairo S.R. VII 10653   45
P. Greenfield (P. BM EA 10554)   38–39, 50–51
P. New York MMA 25.3.31   42
P. New York MMA 25.3.32   42
P. Turin 1791   35
P. Turin inv. suppl. 8438 (Kha)   44

Bricks BM EA 41544-41545-41546-41547   44

Mummy BM EA 22939   48

Statue Louvre A 66   49

Greek Sources
CGRN 86 D. 10–24   64–65
SEG 32.147   62

Deipnosophistae 473b–c   66–67

Euripides, *Hippolytos* 952–54   68
Hesiod, frag. 357   73
Philodemus of Gadara, *De musica* 4, col. 21.6–13   74
Pindar, *Hymns* 6.127–28   74
Pindar, *Nemean* 4.44–46   73
Plato, *Politicus* 277d   73
Plato, *Phaedrus* 228e   73
Plato, *Sophista* 259e, 262b–e   73

Texts from Emar
Emar 369   113, 114
Emar 370   113, 117–18
Emar 373   111–13, 114, 115–16
Emar 471   116
Emar 472   117

Hittite Sources
KBo 17.65+   127–28
KBo 39.8++   125–26
KUB 32.133   138–39
Ritual of Maštigga MS II.B   130–31

Josephus
Ant. 13.65–71   165
Jewish War 7.421–436   165

Rabbinic Sources
m. Yoma   312–24
m. Yoma 1:3   314–15
m. Yoma 1:5   315–16
m. Yoma 5:7   314–15
m. Yoma 7:1   323–24
t. Kippurim 1:8   316–17
t. Kippurim 2:1   322
Sifra Aḥare Mot   318–20, 320–23

Ugaritic Sources
RS 24.264+   135
RS 24.643   135

SUBJECT INDEX

Aaron. *See* high priest; priests: Aaronides
afterlife, 7, 12, 31–32, 35–39, 49–51, 201, 202
altars, 16, 72, 154, 157, 158, 160, 161, 163
amulets, 7, 12, 43–48, 53, 152, 160, 162, 285. *See also* Ketef Hinnom silver plates; *tefillin*
anointing, 15, 113–15, 144
Arad, 157, 159, 163, 166
archaeology. *See* material culture
Assarhaddon (king), 14, 96–100
Athens, 61–62, 64, 66

Babylon, rebuilding of, 96–97
bamot, 158, 159
Beersheba, 157–58, 159, 166
Bell, Catherine, 3–5, 18, 196, 197–98, 207–10, 255, 275, 286
binding, 72–73
birth, 17, 90, 127–28, 179–83, 242, 243, 245–56
blessing, priestly. *See under* Priestly Blessing
blood, 20, 179–80, 183n48, 244, 245, 268
bodies, 19–20, 240–48, 251–52
bricks, 12, 43–45, 53, 87, 89–90
building construction, 14, 82–96, 101–2, 262–63. *See also* foundation deposits; foundation rituals
burial, 7, 37–39, 44, 160–61, 166, 201

calendars, 5, 13, 61–65, 179, 181, 265n39, 291, 293, 296, 307

Carmen Arvale, 304
centralization, 17, 23, 151, 158, 163–67, 208–9, 264–65, 267
Chaldeans, 83–84, 90, 95–96
checklists, 4–6, 7, 9, 135
Christianity, 12n34, 175, 207
circumcision, 19, 179–80, 181n45, 243–45
codification, 3, 9, 13, 18, 191, 217–19
comparatism, 1, 7–8, 22–23
confession, 22, 199, 289, 302–3, 317–22
contamination. *See* purity and impurity
covenant ceremonies, 21, 280, 288, 302–4, 306–7
Crete, 70
cult places. *See under* places, cultic

David (king), 20, 261n22, 272, 273n59
Dead Sea Scrolls. *See* Qumran: ritual texts from
death. *See* afterlife; burial; funerary texts
divination, 82–83, 137. *See also* omens; oracles
diviners, 84–85, 87, 113, 115, 118–19, 140
divine speech, 11, 19, 143, 221–25, 228
Douglas, Mary, 177, 197

economics, 17, 25, 63, 118, 145, 181–82
education, 250–51
elders, 163, 314, 315–16
Elephantine, 16, 152, 163–65, 167, 192, 206, 208
Emar, 14–15, 107–9, 118–19, 140
temple of the diviner, 110

331

Subject Index

'En Ḥaṣeva, 158–59, 166
epigraphy. *See* inscriptions
Essenes, 280, 292, 295, 299, 306
ethics, 177, 192
ethnography, 2, 172, 184, 282
Eucharist, 207
exegesis, 270, 274, 280, 318, 322, 323
exorcists, 87
Ezra (figure), 231, 259–60

family cult, 153, 159–60, 162, 165–66, 204. *See also* places, cultic: domestic
festivals, 122–23, 137, 141
   Day of Atonement (Yôm Kippur), 21–22, 144, 195, 223–24, 294, 312–24
   Dipóleia, 62, 63
   ḫišuwa, 136
   of Nerik, 136
   Passover, 183n50, 195, 265n39: Hezekiah's, 20, 260n20, 264–67; Josiah's, 20, 268–72
   Sabbath, 291
   Sukkôt, 20, 259–63
   wag-feast, 49, 53
   zukrum, 15, 111–15, 118
figurines, 16, 44, 90–91, 152, 154, 156, 158, 160–63
firstborns, 10n30, 17, 182
food prohibitions, 10
fortresses, 157, 158, 159
foundation deposits, 7, 14, 78, 88–96, 101
foundation rituals, 84–90, 92, 100, 101
funerary texts, 35, 52–53, 123
   Book of the Dead, 12–13, 30, 32–54. *See also* standardization: of the *Book of the Dead*
   Coffin Texts, 33–34
   Pyramid Texts, 31, 33–34

gaps, 19, 26, 27, 241, 243, 248–49, 251–52
gender, 19–20, 179–82, 240–48, 251
genital discharges, 180, 242, 247, 290
Gerizim, 17, 163, 165–66, 167, 192

Hattuša archives, 122, 127–29, 132–41
hemerologies, 85–86
Hezekiah (king), 151, 264–68

hierarchies, 19, 21, 138–39, 174, 194, 198, 223, 231–32, 264, 268, 274
high priest, 22, 142, 165, 205, 215–17, 219–20, 314–21, 324
Hittite empire, 107–9, 122
holiness, 180
Ḥorvat Qitmit, 158–59, 166
hymns, 13, 58, 71–72

Idumea, 16
Iguvine Tables, 304
immersion, 289, 290, 291, 292
incantations, 81, 100–101, 137
incense, 22, 151, 154, 157, 158, 163, 316–17
indexical approaches to ritual, 17, 174, 175, 319
innovation. *See* ritual: innovation
inscriptions, 25, 58, 165. *See also* letters
   on bricks, 90
   commemorative, 5, 14–15, 78–79, 81, 90–92, 101
   foundation, 90–96, 97, 100–101
   as means of divine communication, 91, 93
   royal, 78–79, 82–86, 89, 90–96
Islam, 12n34
Israel, as ethnic group, 8, 210, 232. *See also* Pentateuch: as identity reservoir

Jerusalem
   caves, 156, 161, 166
   priesthood, 146–47, 190, 219
   temple, 16, 27, 164, 165, 167, 174, 182n46, 192, 196, 208, 219
Josiah (king), 151, 158, 269, 270, 272
Judah
   Iron Age, 16, 151, 154–59, 166–67
   postexilic, 16, 151, 159–67, 189, 209–11
Judaism, 11–12, 17, 26–27, 189–90, 206–7, 209–11, 252, 281, 283

Ketef Hinnom silver plates, 9, 18, 142, 201–3, 204–5, 219, 299
kings. *See also* textualization: and royal authority *and names of individual kings*
   as builders, 14, 81, 96–100

Subject Index

as library founders, 79–80
as ritual agents, 5, 20, 101, 128–29, 267–68, 272–73, 274
Kizzuwatna, 138–39
archives, 125–28, 130–36
Kos, 64–65
Kuntillet 'Ajrud, 158, 225–26

Lachish, 16, 154–56, 157, 160, 162–63, 167
law. *See also* Pentateuch; textualization
adaptation of, 20, 128–29, 144–45, 268
application of, 249, 251, 258–59, 263–66, 270–71, 273–74
legitimation of, 261
oral, 61, 63
sacred, 61, 63–64, 71
Leontopolis, 17, 165, 167
letters, 116–17
epistolary discourse, 19, 215, 222–31, 232
to gods, 78, 79–80
Levites. *See under* priests
libraries, 79–80, 305
linguistic approaches to ritual, 17, 177–78
liturgies, 32–33, 48, 50, 52–53, 280–81, 286, 288–97, 306–7, 313

magic, 32, 33–34, 52–53, 54, 72, 285. *See also* divination; omens
Makkedah, 163, 167, 206
manuals, 4, 22, 87, 191, 192, 250, 312, 314–15, 317, 319, 323–24
maṣṣebot, 157, 158–59
material culture
and the study of ritual, 2, 10, 24–26, 39, 53, 151–52, 154n11, 249–50
of Judah, 16, 151–66
meat, 13, 20, 63, 269
medicine, 7, 138
memorialization, 14, 92–96, 101–2
memory aids, 15, 117, 135–36, 141, 293–94
memory variants, 126–27, 132
mikvot, 249
Moses, 8, 210, 223–24, 259n19
motherhood, 17, 19, 179–81, 245–46
mummies, 38, 39, 43–48, 49, 53
Muršili II (king), 107

music, 51, 70–71, 73, 87
Mykonos, 64, 65
myths, 8n22, 60, 63, 67, 190

necromancy, 156, 161
Nineveh archives, 79–81, 256n9

offerings. *See also* sacrifice
burnt (or "rising"), 115–16, 164, 179, 181, 182, 271–72
cereal, 164
funerary, 39
kubadu, 15, 115–16
sin (or "sin-purification"), 142, 179, 181, 182n46, 318, 319
texts deposited in Greek sanctuaries, 68–71
well-being, 116, 175
wood, 11n33
omens, 81, 82n19, 96, 98, 99, 113, 138
oracles, 11, 58, 60, 66, 99–100, 132–33, 138
orality, 19, 67, 74, 192, 215, 229, 231, 232
orthodoxy, 189, 198, 206–7, 209, 255, 274
orthopraxy, 207

palaces, Mesopotamian, 80–81, 91, 94
Passover. *See under* festivals
Pentateuch. *See also* Priestly traditions
definition of, 8
as identity reservoir, 18, 190, 209–11
reception history, 11–12, 257–73
ritualized reading of, 228, 230
transmission history, 11, 16, 206–7, 259n19, 262, 280
places, cultic, 153, 166–67. *See also names of individual sanctuaries*
caves, 156, 160
domestic, 16, 154–55, 160
local, 156–57, 162–63
open-air, 158–59
regional shrines, 16, 157–58, 162–63, 165, 204
pollution. *See* purity and impurity
polytheism, 58, 60–61, 74
pottery, 156, 158, 201
prayer, 21, 117–18, 267, 268, 280–82, 288–306

Subject Index

priestesses, 15, 51, 110–11, 113
Priestly Blessing, 9, 18–19, 199–206, 215–25, 227–32
Priestly traditions, 9, 15–16, 25, 141, 194, 204, 251. *See also* Priestly Blessing
   dating of, 146, 217–18
   Holiness legislation, 145
   narrativization, 9n25, 16, 142
   redaction of, 144–45, 182n48
   transmission history, 11, 121, 142–43, 256, 271
priests. *See also* high priest
   Aaronides, 8, 19, 200, 204, 205–6, 210, 223–24, 228–30, 232, 250, 257, 274
   consecration of, 112–15, 265–66
   lector, 38
   Levites, 205, 231, 261, 267–68, 270–72, 273n59, 274
   processions, 111–13
prophecy, 83
pseudonymous attributions, 260–61, 263, 274
purification, 21, 179–83, 195, 244–49, 280, 288–93
purity and impurity, 19–20, 176, 177, 179–80, 197–98, 240–52, 266–67, 292

quarrels, domestic, 125, 130
Qumran. *See also* standardization: at Qumran
   community, 280, 295, 300–301, 302, 303, 305
   rituals at, 21, 208, 282, 287–88, 295, 300, 302
   ritual texts from, 21, 24, 251, 280–82, 288–307

rabbinic interpretation, 21–22, 26, 312–24
Ras Shamra, 1–2
reading, 4, 19, 67, 71, 73, 174, 202, 220, 226–27, 230–31, 250, 281, 305. *See also* Pentateuch: ritualized reading of
rewriting, 280
ritual. *See also* foundation rituals; Qumran: rituals at
   definition of, 195, 281
   density, 18, 21, 195–98, 211, 280, 286

   efficacy, 39, 53, 72–73, 137–38, 268
   function of, 207
   grammar, 178
   innovation, 7, 20, 182, 198–99, 208, 252, 259–64, 267–68, 273–74
   interpretation, 3, 11, 12, 22, 27, 173, 183, 189, 247, 249, 263–64, 273, 284, 320
   performance, 2–4, 13, 172, 183, 193, 229–32, 284–85, 303, 314–15, 319–20
   as site of memory, 285
   variation, 18, 60, 193, 195, 197, 207–11, 244–45, 255, 258, 303
ritual agents, 3, 66–67, 108, 113, 131–34, 243. *See also* divination: diviners; kings: as ritual agents; priests; priestesses
ritual authority, 215–16, 220–25, 228, 231–32. *See also* textualization: and ritual authority
ritual-household, 189–90, 192
ritual objects. *See* text: as ritual objects *and names of individual objects*
ritual theory, 1–3, 17, 20, 173, 175–76, 240, 255, 306. *See also* indexical approaches to ritual; linguistic approaches to ritual; rhetorical approaches to ritual; symbolic approaches to ritual
ritualization, 173, 175–76, 198, 202–3, 241, 302, 312
rhetorical approaches to ritual, 10–11, 17, 18–19, 172, 173, 175, 176, 181, 220–21, 243, 256–57
Rome, 68, 304
royalty. *See* king

Sabbath. *See under* festivals
sacrifice, 22, 30–31, 93, 163–64, 178, 181–83, 218, 269–72, 281–82, 316–18
sages, 316–17, 318, 321–22
Samaria, 10, 151, 156, 165–67, 189, 206, 208
sanctuaries. *See names of individual sanctuaries*
Sargonids, 78–79, 97–98
scribes, 124–34, 138–39, 228, 229n49
scripturalization, 184, 191, 194, 195, 208–9, 220, 252, 257

Sennacherib (king), 97
sexual intercourse, 180, 248
Sinai, 19, 196, 204, 215, 216, 221, 222–25, 232
Solomon (king), 20, 272
spells, 7, 12–13, 34–39, 43–50, 52–54
standardization
  of the body, 251
  of the *Book of the Dead*, 51–52
  of Leviticus, 255–57
  at Qumran, 282
  of ritual practice, 10, 20–21, 118, 208, 256, 273–75
standing stones, 111–12, 114. See also *maṣṣebot*
statues, 15, 111–13, 115n32, 118. See also figurines
Sukkôt. *See under* festivals
Šuppiluliuma I (king), 107n2
symbolic approaches to ritual, 17, 18, 173–74, 176–78, 192

tabernacle, 8, 142, 143, 206, 222
tablets. *See* inscriptions
teffilin, 7, 21, 280, 282, 297–302, 305
temples. *See names of individual temples*
text, 140, 172–73, 283. *See also* checklists; exegesis; funerary texts; gaps; letters; manuals; offerings: texts deposited in Greek sanctuaries; Qumran: ritual texts from; Ugarit, ritual texts from
  definition of, 58–59, 68–69, 73–74
  development of, 11, 36, 40–41, 52, 256, 294
  duplicates, 126–27, 137, 142, 146
  iconic, 12, 175
  as ritual object, 4, 21, 58, 68–70, 72, 101, 284–86, 287

  as ritual script, 13, 72, 135–36, 202, 208, 250, 294
  textualization, 24, 110, 174–76, 183–84, 193, 198–99, 252, 257, 273–75, 312–13
  definition of, 3, 255n3
  and ritual authority, 71, 137–40, 142–43, 146–47, 200, 205–6
  ritual effects of, 6–7, 60, 134–41, 194, 206–8
  and royal power, 138–40
tombs, 30, 34, 36, 39, 44–45, 305, 307
  cachettes, 40, 45
Torah. *See* Pentateuch
Tutankhamun (king), 45, 47

Ugarit, ritual texts from, 1–2, 5n10, 16, 62–63, 129, 135–36

variance. *See* ritual: variation
vassals, 107–9
veiling, 15, 111–13
vignettes, 38, 40, 41, 46–47, 52
votives, 14, 69–71, 72–73, 100, 101, 161, 163

weddings, 3–4
wilderness, 8, 197
writing, 13, 14, 20, 32, 39, 58, 68, 69, 78, 202, 285. *See also* memorialization; rewriting

Yahwism, 16–17, 151–67, 190, 210n73
Yehud. *See* Judah: postexilic
Yôm Kippur. *See under* festivals

Zephaniah (priest), 230–31

Printed in the United States
by Baker & Taylor Publisher Services